The Varieties of History

THE
VARIETIES
OF
HISTORY

From Voltaire to the Present

Edited, Selected, and Introduced
by FRITZ STERN

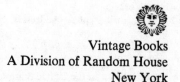

Vintage Books
A Division of Random House
New York

To

HENRY L. ROBERTS

in friendship

VINTAGE BOOKS EDITION, September 1973

Copyright © 1956, 1972 by Fritz Stern

All rights reserved under International and Pan-American Copyright Conventions. Published in the United States by Random House, Inc., New York, and simultaneously in Canada by Random House of Canada Limited, Toronto. Originally published by The World Publishing Company in 1956 and, in a revised edition, in 1972.

Library of Congress Cataloging in Publication Data

Stern, Fritz Richard, 1926–   ed.
    The varieties of history.
    Reprint of the ed. published by Meridian Books, New York.
    1. Historiography—Addresses, essays, lectures.
I. Title.
D13.S82   1973   907′.2   73–6547
ISBN 0–394–71962–X

Manufactured in the United States of America
78

CONTENTS

A NOTE TO
THE SECOND EDITION

Times have changed since *The Varieties of History* was first published, and so has the place of history in our intellectual world. The study of the past as a uniquely important humanistic inquiry no longer commands the kind of automatic acceptance it once did. Other disciplines have come to the fore and other interests prevail. Though their recent achievements have been extraordinary, historians in the last few years have become uncertain about the premises and functions of their work. This anthology was intended principally as an introduction to the study of history. By illustrating the different visions of history that inspired its practitioners, by demonstrating that history is an ever-changing, self-renewing discipline, this book may help to formulate new answers to the old question, "What is History?" It also suggests the recurrent need to redefine history in a broader context, responsive to the intellectual currents and political concerns of a particular age.

Is history in crisis again? The answer seems to be yes, and the crisis comes from within and without the historical discipline. To some extent, the sense of crisis within the profession indicates concerns that have often assailed the modern historian: the fragmentation of the field, the disparateness of the new knowledge, the fading of the great syntheses, the identity of history in relation to the social sciences. Historians are aware as well of a growing public indifference to history, born perhaps of a sense that the present is so radically different from the past that the reconstruction of that past seems only of antiquarian interest. It may be part of our professional and social predicament that at the very time when historical knowledge is of critical importance it is in fact neglected.

9

For this new edition I have selected essays by Fernand Braudel, Harold Perkin, Robert Fogel, and C. Vann Woodward. These essays, I think, properly exemplify the remarkable vitality and range of recent historiography; for it is paradoxical that the present discontent with history coincides with a remarkable surge of historical work, measured both in quantity and quality.

I chose Braudel and Perkin because both have been close to schools in France and England that have promoted new and important types of historical study. Each in his own way defines his vision of a new broad history, and each in his own work embodies this ideal. In selecting recent American essays I sought for statements that would illuminate both the promise and the predicament of history today. Robert Fogel demonstrates the extraordinary impact of other disciplines on history and acknowledges that the related changes in method pose new difficulties for the discipline. C. Vann Woodward's essay analyzes how a particular crisis in the society at large—the racial conflict in contemporary America—impinges on historians.

Historians respond to the several crises in their profession and their society in different fashions. Some reaffirm and redefine the old faith, as did Marc Bloch before being shot by the Germans in the Second World War. Others bear out the truth of C. Vann Woodward's contention that "The demagoguery, the cant, and the charlatanry of historians in the service of a fashionable cause can at times rival that of politicians." To know the persistent problems that historians have confronted in the past may help to put the present in a different perspective.

For the rest, I have left the text unchanged. If I were to write the Introduction today, it would probably turn out differently. But it would still affirm Maitland's contention that "orthodox history seems to me a contradiction in terms," that the study of the past needs to be free and objective, and that this study is likely to prove instructive, pleasurable, sobering, and liberating, and is more needed than ever in an age that takes none of the virtues of historical study for granted.

INTRODUCTION

> "An orthodox history seems to me a contradiction in terms."—
> F. W. MAITLAND

This is a book by historians about history, personal reflections on an ancient but ever varying discipline. In writing about their task, which is to reconstruct a past that they have never known, and that they can neither deduce from first principles nor create by an act of the imagination, they reveal their diverse presuppositions, concerns, and ambitions. And they also reveal that their work is difficult yet pleasurable, constantly changing yet in some respects uniform, sometimes drudgery and sometimes inspiration. It is, in short, a human task, akin in its pleasures and conflicts to all other human activity.

As the present work will show, modern historians have written in a variety of genres, but the multiplicity of style cannot obscure the two basic tendencies which have affected all modern historians. First, the transformation of history into an academic discipline—indeed, according to some into a science—with all the arduous consequences this entailed. Second, society's growing demand for history, the indisputable fact that in the short time since the American and French Revolutions the Western world has become intensely historical-minded. These two developments are both manifestations of the cultural revolution which has shaped modern times: the secularization of thought, the growth of science and the questioning of all systems embodying eternal truths.

Related in origin though they may be, the two tendencies are nevertheless at odds with one another. The scientific historian, or simply the contemporary professional historian, has become a specialist, ill-equipped to meet the heightened demands of society. The historian may know that Western man has come to think that the knowledge of the past may help reveal the meaning of human experience and that the recollection of the past may harden our resolution and inform our vision in the struggles of the present. He may even sense the truth of Wilhelm Dilthey's contention that man can know himself only in history and not through introspection alone. But the practicing historian, as a rule, is wary of assuming such creative burdens. In short, just as the historian was getting ready to become an academic monk, shut up in his study with his sources, the world about him sought him as a preacher. And often the historian, whether he succumbed to or resisted the outside pressure, felt that he was in danger of betraying his responsibilities.

Nothing is more characteristic of the history of the last two hundred years than the demand from within the profession that history must once again become broader, more inclusive, more concerned with the deeper aspects of human experience. There are abundant signs at the end of this postwar decade that we are on the threshold of another period of reconsidering the purposes and methods of history.

Whatever the outcome of this next stage of historical self-criticism, it is unlikely that the historian's role in society will diminish, even though some historians may find their contemporary status uncomfortable and would, I suspect, cheerfully trade their present role and renown for the sheltered life of their predecessors. But as long as society seeks knowledge of the past, the historian must accept his responsibility to society, without violating his responsibility to the past.

How does the historian fulfill his task? Some of the characteristic answers will be found in this book, and it will be seen that no general agreement prevails among historians, that no single doctrine has ever captured Clio completely. One reason for this continuing variety, as Mommsen noted in his Rectorial Address, is that history is too difficult; it cannot be learned. The techniques of historical scholarship can be acquired, like the techniques of any other craft. But the art of history, the manner of combining individual facts into a truthful and persuasive whole, involves so much that is individual as well as timebound that the writing of history must always be changing and varying. And yet I am confident that the following essays will convey to the reader a sense of what historians at their best should strive to do.

The nature of the historian's task cannot but be illuminated by this quick direct glimpse into the history of history writing and the shifting conditions under which it has been carried on during the last two centuries. History, as we shall see, varies as the life and spirit of different ages vary, and that is why at different times and in different countries diverse types of history have prevailed. No one could expect Macaulay and Treitschke to hold identical views on history. Indeed at any one time different, often antithetical, histories are written. Burckhardt and Marx were contemporaries, as were Bury and Trevelyan, as are Geyl and Toynbee today.

To the cultural differences must be added the human factor, the obvious individual differences among historians. These differences are decisive in determining the writing of history, even after the discipline of history has been firmly established and even after it has made its uniform demands on historians. In the last analysis what will shape a particular history is the historian's conception of the past, whether or not he has formulated it, whether or not he is fully conscious of it. These conceptions, compounded of tradition and temperament, govern the writing of history. It is the purpose of this anthology to suggest the variety of modern history by recalling the diversity of historians' thoughts on their discipline.

2.

In selecting these particular essays I have kept two aims in view: to present the reflections of practicing historians on the persistent problems and pleasures of history, and to exemplify, as far as possible, the major movements within historiography since 1750. Programmatic appeals will therefore be found here, side by side with essays chosen for their intrinsic, timeless excellence; it was my hope, not always realizable, to find these two qualities combined in every essay. Finally, these pieces have been chosen as representative—in one or two instances even the deficiencies themselves are representative—as they evoke the characteristic moods and intellectual presuppositions of modern historians. If the present work had sought to present only the masterpieces of recent historians then the dreary selections from a Nazi or Soviet historian would have found no place; in a work that seeks to show the various modes of modern historiography, these selections do belong.

In the hope that even if history does not teach us, historians may, my emphasis throughout has been on the practicing historian, a test which ruled out admittedly significant and influential reflections on history by philosophers and theologians. Nor have I included historians' writings which were technical inquiries into the philosophy of history. The reader will not find here any analysis of the significance and patterns of history, any excursion into the logic or epistemology of historical inquiry. To treat these problems adequately requires a different volume. Even so, many of the present essays touch on that region where philosophy and history meet; yet they do so in a non-technical manner, indeed in a manner which I think is characteristic of most practicing historians. The reader will note that history is deeply imbedded in philosophy and that the historian senses this, even when he refuses to deal with it explicitly. Speaking to the British Academy, a few years ago, on "The Present State of Historical Studies," E. L. Woodward explained that he would not approach "the fundamental problem of the nature of historical knowledge. I am in good company if I evade a master problem of this kind, since nearly all English historians have evaded it."

I have limited this book to historians after Voltaire, for it would have been impossible within the given space to be sufficiently representative of earlier times as well. Yet the choice of Voltaire as a starting point is by no means capricious; he himself was a very self-conscious pioneer of a new type of philosophical and cultural historian, dedicated to truth, though intensely partisan, and a thoroughly modern man in his emphasis on history as promoting the enlightenment of men in a secular world. Voltaire excepted, the book deals with the period after 1800, when history was established as an independent and critical discipline with its own continuity and when the explanation of historical events by their origins was for the first time widely accepted among historians. That I have limited this collection to Western historians needs no apology. In the few cases, where I could choose among essays of equal merit, I have preferred those not otherwise easily accessible to English-speaking readers. As far as possible I have selected self-contained essays that could be reproduced in their original form, without having to be cut or wrenched from their context.

While searching for appropriate essays I made the discovery, disheartening to an editor, that most historians seem reluctant to articulate their views about history. They hold their views and make their choices, but shy away from expounding their presuppositions. This meant that, regrettably, some of the greatest historians could not be represented here, among them Tocqueville, Maitland, and Halévy. Others—Burckhardt, Croce, Dilthey, and Pieter Geyl for example—had to be omitted because none of their shorter writings embodied the essence of their thought sufficiently to be truly representative.

To many historians, especially in the nineteenth century, the thought of an explicit definition of their task may well have been repugnant, for it would necessarily have involved so much of the very thing they sought to extinguish, their own selves. The one time when historians seem to be willing to overcome their reluctance is when they are being attacked or are themselves attacking prevailing forms of historiography. Mostly, however, they prefer to let their finished work testify for them, and as to theory content themselves with occasional asides, usually in letters. Thus in Tocqueville, surely one of the most perceptive and self-critical of men, I could find no systematic discussion of history; but in a letter in which he mentioned that he was casting about for a subject —eventually to be the Old Regime—he wrote: "It must be recent and must enable me to relate facts to ideas and the philosophy of history to history itself."

In England the custom of requiring an inaugural lecture of professors has often furnished the occasion for memorable credos by historians. Perhaps every historian ought at one time or another to prepare such an inaugural lecture, even if he never delivers it. Such critical self-awareness would reveal to the historian the truth that Buckle long ago noted in the unjustly neglected pages of his *History of Civilization in England:* "There must always be a connexion between the way in which men contemplate the past, and the way in which they contemplate the present; both views being in fact different forms of the same habits of thought, and therefore presenting in each age, a certain sympathy and correspondence with each other." The historian has always been close to his particular age and even the most detached researcher holds to presuppositions which are deeply intertwined with the basic assumptions of his age. Certainly the ascendency of the scientific ideal over history reflected the dominant spirit of the nineteenth century, and yet at the same time the individual historian continued to respond creatively to particular political crises, to new social questions agitating his society. In the following pages I shall examine briefly this interaction between the development of historical writing and the political and intellectual vicissitudes of Western society.

In the nineteenth century—in the years, say, from Niebuhr's work in 1811 to Bury's Lecture in 1903—history came into its own as an independent field of inquiry. It severed, or tried to sever, its ties with philosophy and literature, seeking to reconstruct the past *wie es eigentlich gewesen,* "as it actually was." Ranke meant this now famous phrase as a modest self-denial, feeling that history ought no longer to play the role of philosopher or judge; only later was it taken as a boast, as if history could in fact achieve this kind of exactitude. Through the application of the critical method to the newly discovered and collected sources the historians were in fact able to reconstruct vast segments of the past and their crowning achievement was the historical reconstruction of the Middle Ages. By the middle of the last century historians began to consider their craft a science, and for some zealots it possessed the same objectivity and yielded, or was about to yield, the universal laws of human development comparable to those of the natural sciences. It became an academic discipline, first in Germany and gradually elsewhere; professional journals and associations were founded, and the free field of the eighteenth century where amateurs had been almost sole masters became fenced in; it was divided into ever smaller fields, reserved for the deeper plowing of the specialist. Historical thought grew narrower even as research and interpretation became more rigorous. At the same time, the close ties which earlier had linked historians with public and political life were loosened; Niebuhr, Macaulay, and Tocqueville had been steeped in the politics of their countries and their historical sense had been sharpened accordingly. Not until the two world wars in our own century did historians again obtain the same practical insight into political affairs, with the same benefit to their work.

But in spite of the temporary estrangement between historians and public life and in spite of their increasing attachment to the University, the deeper contact between historians and their culture remained constant, as it must. At the very beginning of modern historiography, in those upper reaches of history where it touches philosophy and religion, the influence of the entire pre-Romantic and Romantic movement was decisive. It guided the transformation, as Thierry put it, from the century of ideas to the century of facts. This remains true even if neither the break nor the distinction was so complete as was once believed and even if the historical ideas of the eighteenth century inspired and guided the nineteenth century search after facts. A study of the period between Voltaire and Ranke, such as Friedrich Meinecke inaugurated in his several works on *Historismus,* would reveal the many ways in which this change occurred and would show, in a particular instance, the diversity of elements that shape the course of historiography. In such a study it is not only the thought of Rousseau, Herder, Burke, Kant, and Hegel, that one would have to consider, but the obscurer beginnings of the first academic historical school in Göttingen, overshadowed though it was by the more spectacular achievements of other men in other places. Likewise one would have to study the adaptation of philology to history, and the permeation of both by the newly won sense that every people has its unique character and development, rooted in its speech and revealed in its myths. And one would have to give Sir Walter Scott his due, for every historian of the early nineteenth century was stirred and inspired by Scott's bold reconstructions of the past, and admitted the deep effect of these fictions upon his own historical sense.

To the great interest in the unique, the particular, and the local—characteristic of Scott and the Romantics—was added an overwhelming passion for truth, embodied in the critical method. This last, to be sure, was taken over from the philologists of the late eighteenth century. In those years, especially in Germany, philology and history were almost identical, and many historians began their academic training and careers as philologists. In the famous Appendix to his first work, Ranke riddled the hitherto unchallenged credibility of Renaissance historians, and soon his colleagues, learning to shun all commentaries that were not contemporaneous with the event described, resolved to search for original sources, authenticate them, and reconstruct the past from them alone.

Nor should one forget that that first generation of historians lived through shattering political experiences. The upheavals caused by the French Revolution and Napoleon's arrogant career, the destruction of ancient institutions and beliefs, and the politicizing of men's minds had a profound, lasting impact on historians. To have lived through all this could not but affect their historical imagination. As Niebuhr recognized, "When a historian is reviving former times, his interest in them and sympathy with them will be the deeper, the greater the events he has witnessed with a bleeding or rejoicing heart."

The revolution of that quarter-century had lifted history out of its previous confines. This apparent break with the past dramatized the very stuff of history: men's ambitions, passions, hatreds battling against society and established order, the unpredictability of war, and the conflict between change and continuity. Beneath the abstractions of Hegel's *Philosophy of History* runs the course of violent life, of "world-historical" characters destroying the happiness of peoples while fulfilling the destiny of an age; the Revolution was as real in Hegel as was the sack of Rome in St. Augustine's *City of God*. After such upheavals, the historian always must explain as best he can; and the secularized public mind was no longer satisfied with theological reasons such as De Maistre's. More than partisanship, it was the presence of the Revolution as a historical riddle that drove generation after generation of the best historians to study it and to continue the debate concerning it.

It has often been remarked that the nineteenth century was the political age par excellence: the great issues from the French Revolution to the Reform Bills in England and the successful unifications of Italy and Germany—all were political in essence and the political agitation was charged with the memory of past triumphs or past dangers. The role that ideology plays in our century, history tended to play in the last century, and both conservatives and liberals used historical slogans to shape and sustain their ambitions. Many of the nineteenth century historians became partisans of these struggles, indeed were drawn to history in order to become better partisans. Thierry admits, as will be seen in the essay below, that he turned to history to serve the liberal cause, and the same was true of Thiers, Guizot, Michelet, and Lamartine. Macaulay and Carlyle in England, Droysen, Sybel and Treitschke in Germany, all mixed history with politics, and while their work was scholarly and original, the political bias was unmistakable. Of Bancroft's *History of the United States* it was said that "every volume voted for Jackson."

The Revolution had quickened nationalism as well, and historians often became the high priests of that faith, revealing to their people its past glories. For the middle class audience that responded so enthusiastically to the historians, national history served as a kind of collective and flattering genealogy. But even in that age of nationalism historians like Guizot remembered the abiding unity of European civilization, and Ranke, always true to his ideal of universal history, had so deep a sense of that unity that in October 1870, at the height of Prussia's triumph, he warned his countrymen not to inflict permanent injury on the French.

These mid-nineteenth century historians were political historians in a double sense, and their impact upon their society was of incalculable importance. In his thoughtful and incisive works on English historiography, Herbert Butterfield has examined the Whig view of history and has aptly remarked: "Whatever it may have done to our history, it had a wonderful effect on English politics." Other countries have been less fortunate in the images that historians have created and popularized. Consider, for example, the growing alienation of the Germans from the West, culminating tragically in the collapse of German democracy in the 1930's; in some measure at least, this collapse must be ascribed to the misunderstanding of Western liberal thought which German historians perpetuated and to their inadequate representation of Germany's own history and society.

Throughout the last century, the national state welcomed and promoted the work of historians. In the 1820's and 1830's the great historical collections, such as the *Monumenta Germaniae Historica,* were undertaken, often with government subsidies. In 1834 in France, where Guizot was Minister of Education, the Government appropriated a large annual credit for archival studies; five years later the famous École des Chartes was established. Gradually historians gained access to government papers, and in 1880 the Vatican, too, opened sections of its archives. These archival sources were eagerly exploited by historians, who concentrated on political history, regarding the state as the chief agent of historical change. But they did so to excess, and J. R. Green, whose immensely popular *Short History of England* broke with this narrow conception of history, frequently protested against "the absolute madness to try and dissociate the 'social and aesthetic' from the political."

These favors accorded by the state had their debilitating effects as well: even before 1914 some historians had become uncritical, irresponsible propagandists. During the First World War the standards of historical truth were almost everywhere debased, and historians often led the chorus of national hatreds. Service of the state turned into subservience, and this voluntary abdication of critical detachment was followed in the 1930's by the enforced submission to authority in countries where political liberty had been extinguished.

Quite apart from these political developments, but very much in tune with the philosophical revival of the period, the years from 1890 to 1914 witnessed a critical and highly fruitful reexamination of the theory of history, which in the decades since 1920 has come to permeate the presuppositions of most practicing historians. The prewar psychological discoveries of William James, Freud, and Dilthey, the "new" realism in the interpretation of man and society as exemplified in the works of Zola, of Shaw and Ibsen, the culmination of European imperialism and the emergence of world politics, necessarily had a deep impact on historical thought as well.

In one sense this reappraisal consisted of a reaction against the presumed identity of history and the natural sciences which had marked nineteenth century thought, and also against mere historical empiricism. J. B. Bury's lecture of 1903 may be taken as the culmination of that earlier mood of certainty. According to this view, the historian's task was to reconstruct the past from the available sources, to establish cause and effect in history, just as the natural scientists did in investigating natural processes. This ideal had never been universally accepted and certainly had not been substantiated in historical works; it had helped, however, to rear a generation of academic scholars and specialists. It had taught them to be severely detached from their work, to be "neutral in thought and action," and this had often enfeebled their work.

In 1874, in his essay on the "Use and Disadvantage of History," Nietzsche had already contended that historical thinking had overpowered the creative, spontaneous forces of life, and that historians had succumbed to a lifeless scientism. Anyone familiar with the more arid practices of the academic historian will understand Nietzsche's attack and welcome his passionate demand that the historian needs moral courage and intellectual involvement as well as erudition. But the goal of objectivity, the demand that history must not be the handmaiden of politics or theology, nor yet the effervescence of passion, had its indispensable merit, as well; two years before Nietzsche's essay, Fustel de Coulanges, anxious to import into France the scientific study of history, complained that for the preceding fifty years, historiography in France had been "a kind of permanent civil war."

Nietzsche's attack went unnoticed, though it anticipated by only twenty years the more general critique of the positivism and historical empiricism upon which the ordinary historian had come to rely. When the German historian Karl Lamprecht called for a new, scientific type of *Kulturgeschichte*, which would search for the socio-psychic elements affecting the various collective units of history—societies or classes—the scientific temper was already in decline. The philosophical presuppositions of the scientific historian, as seen in Fustel de Coulanges and Bury, were undermined by Rickert's critical analysis of the logical and methodological difference of history and the natural sciences and by Dilthey's insistence on the necessary psychological involvement of the historian in any understanding of the past. It is only in the last decade or so that the implications of Dilthey's historical thought have been elaborated and, to some extent, popularized. His goal had been to find an epistemological basis for the historian's highly individual, psychologically complex, task of reinterpreting the past—a task that in Dilthey's view was far more exacting of all the historian's faculties than the earlier practice of the historical empiricist.

At a different level the presuppositions of the scientific historians were challenged by Croce's essay on history as an art (1893), by Trevelyan's plea in defense of Clio as a Muse (1903), and, during the same year, by Eduard Meyer's critique of scientific history. As this retreat from scientism was taking place, particularly in Germany and England, the French sought to push the limits of historical science even further; the school which Henri Berr founded around 1900 aspired to deepen history by making it the synthesizing science among the emergent social sciences. In America meanwhile, a New History was launched by James Harvey Robinson, at once skeptical of the earlier ideals of objectivity and passionately devoted to the immediate social usefulness of all science, including history.

Together with a critique of the scientific tradition in history went a growing concern about the dangers of excessive specialization. By the end of the last century new sub-divisions of history had sprung up: economic, social, and legal history appeared as recognized branches on the main trunk of history which continued to be political and diplomatic. In the first decades of the twentieth century, the history of ideas, culture, and art began to flourish. At the same time, the other cultural sciences, as Dilthey called them, developed new insights, and historians felt that their traditional modes of analysis could be deepened by the contributions of Durkheim, Weber, and Freud.

Historians themselves realized that their excessive specialization had jeopardized their achievements and, by tearing them from the other humanities, especially from literature, had alienated them from the great reading audience. Mommsen had gracefully yielded to his publisher's entreaties for a popular *History of Rome,* but after he produced this model, historians emulated his fifteen hundred shorter and more "learned" works, not his literary masterpiece.

The public could hardly be expected to read these recondite monographs on minute topics, with which historians began and often ended their careers. Nor could students acquire from them an adequate idea of the way modern scholarship had reconstructed the past. Hence the simultaneous drive towards great collaborative efforts—the several series edited by Lavisse in France, the *Cambridge Modern History,* Justin Winsor's *Narrative and Critical History of America,* and Albert Bushnell Hart's *American Nation Series* —in the hope that a team of specialists could do what a single historian could no longer accomplish.

Specialization, partly a necessity caused by the success of history and the abundance of its sources, survived the retreat from science and positivism; and for every narrative historian like G. M. Trevelyan there were a hundred historians who stuck to the narrow limits of their specialty. This reinforced their reluctance to break with the older type of political and national history, and the attempts at supranational or comparative history have remained few, even though the historical changes of the last twenty years have demonstrated the inadequacy of the national approach. Our universities, even today, maintain an academic Monroe Doctrine, severely separating American and European history, whereas for some periods at least they should properly be studied together. By being narrow, even parochial, historians often avoid the basic problems of the meaning of history. No wonder that after both World Wars vast synthetic works, notably Spengler's and Toynbee's, sketching, explaining, and even predicting the pattern of historical development in a "morphology" of civilizations, should have won large audiences.

Toynbee's success epitomizes in some ways the difficulties which historiography encounters today. His work has been severely critized by historical scholars, by none more incisively than by Pieter Geyl, but the public response, especially to the one-volume abridgment of his massive work, was overwhelmingly favorable. In a grandiose manner Toynbee triumphed over the limits of the conventional historian and by his rather simple explanation of the growth and decline of civilizations captured, at least for a time, the public's imagination. The scholar boggles at it and sees the unsoundness of it, but he must also reckon with the reasons for Toynbee's success, and in passing he might be grateful that it was Toynbee, rather than another philosopher-prophet with less gentle commitments, who erected the most popular postwar system.

The historian himself cannot escape this pressure for synthesis and meaning; it is heard within the profession as well as outside. On the one hand, there is a demand for definite principles of historical judgment. Relativism, often incorrectly equated with what the Germans call historicism, has become suspect. There is general impatience with historians who simply tell a story, and the British historian, Barraclough, has recently insisted that history "must have some constructive purpose, some criterion of judgment. What that criterion will be is of secondary importance, so long as we no longer regard preoccupation with the past as an end in itself." On the other hand, the impact of the social sciences has sometimes gone beyond the beneficial point of stimulation and suggestiveness, and led some historians to join the social scientist's search for laws and generalities together with new, seemingly scientific terminology. The historian cannot escape these challenges; he broods, alone or in groups, over the presuppositions of his discipline, the logic and the method of his work, the place it should occupy among other, newer pursuits.

Nor is the present introspection simply the result of history's own development. History grew and flourished in its distinctive modern form in a century dedicated to science, rationality, and human freedom. The historian's work sustained and was in turn sustained by these ideas. Today the moral climate is different, and in the future the historian may well have to struggle to preserve for himself and for society a sense of the freedom of man, even as he recognizes more pervasive uniformities, even as he sees man clutching at new faiths and systems which deny or infringe the reality of freedom, and even as the organized body politic may seek to overwhelm it.

The tragic experiences of the 1930's and 1940's have had a profoundly unsettling effect on historiography, and some of the basic presuppositions and categories of explanation of an earlier period no longer seem adequate today. The generous faith in rationality and the possibilities of human progress which underlay much of earlier historical thought seems discredited today, and yet the deepening of our historical experiences need not lead to its abandonment, but perhaps to a stronger sense of the precariousness of human freedom and to a still greater dedication to it.

3.

If we turn from the external development of historiography to the task of the individual historian, we shall come to understand the permanent, internal reasons for the constant variety of history. That history is both an art and a science, that at his best the historian must be artist, philosopher, and scientist, has been said many times before. Only a few great historians—Tocqueville or Mommsen or Thucydides—have come close to achieving this kind of creative harmony. But the writing of history inflicts on every historian choices for which neither his method nor his material provides a ready answer. Some answers only the historian himself can give, and this has kept history a live, changing pursuit.

Even after it became a discipline, history preserved its immediacy to life, and of all the intellectual concerns of man, save art, it remains closest to a sense of life. History is the cognitive expression of the deep-rooted human desire to know the past which, in a spontaneous untutored way, is born afresh with every child that searches the mystery of its being. History springs from a live concern, deals with life, serves life. A discipline so close to life cannot remain fixed; it changes with time, with the impact of new hopes, thoughts, and fears. The history of historiography records the interaction between the fixed elements in history—the critical, systematic method and the sources—and the time-bound elements embodied in the historian.

If the historian's method allowed him to recapture the

History change because it evaluated a changing life

whole past, then the connection between history and life would be much looser, and he would become a superior technician. But the past is dead and neither it nor the men who made it can be resuscitated. Time, devotion, and imaginative research cannot recover nor, in any strict sense, restore the past; the archaeologist may resurrect the physical aspect of a town, but the historian, even if all possible records had been preserved, could not claim to have resurrected its life or spirit. He none the less strives to do so, and the great historian will try to penetrate beyond the descriptive fact to the causes, the material conditions, the mood, the human motives and ambitions of a particular epoch. But he succeeds only partially, and he comes to realize that the bolder the reconstruction the more individual it will be, the more of his own self will be engaged. Hajo Holborn has put this very succinctly: "The central problems of a historical methodology or epistemology hinge upon the fact that an objective knowledge of the past can only be attained through the subjective experience of the scholar."

This personal, affective element is, of course, an essential condition of the historian's work. He cannot "extinguish the self," as Ranke once wished (though the selection from Ranke will show that he recognized and esteemed the human qualities which a historian required), any more than he can accept the claim of Fustel de Coulanges that it is "not I who speak, but history which speaks through me." To accept the inextinguishable role of the self and to reject the scientist's notion that historians can be passive recorders of the past does not in the least ease the historian's responsibility. It only enhances it.

When Mazzini said that he would "undertake to declare the personal feelings of any historian, after reading twenty pages of his history," he thought of more than bias. Tell a historian "as you are, so shall you write," tell him that his personal imprint is as evident in a monograph as it is in a literary masterpiece, and he will understand that the qualities which he needs as a historian are those he requires in life. Can one really analyze the greatness of Mommsen's or Tocqueville's work without remembering the nobility and generosity of their minds? And is it irrelevant that the great historians of the last century were men of passion, men of great moral energy? Does it make any sense to ask whether it was Tocqueville the historian or the man who wrote: "Life is neither pleasure nor pain, but a serious matter with which we are charged and which we must lead and terminate with honor?"

The historian's fundamental commitment is to truth, as it has been for centuries. On one level this involves only technical problems: the collecting and rigorous weighing of evidence, the scrupulous application of the critical method. Thus the science of history can establish the facts of Napoleon's career, but, as Pieter Geyl in his *Napoleon: For and Against* has shown, the meaning of these facts will be endlessly debated, and "the argument goes on." At the higher level of interpretation and reconstruction, certainty is not only harder to attain, but the very existence of truth in history is an unresolved problem of epistemology and involves profound questions about the nature of historical judgment.

But as I have said before, the impossibility of attaining absolute truth heightens the historian's responsibility. His judgment permeates his work, and with his judgment enter his bias, his aspirations, and threaten to distort the work of reconstruction. How indeed can bias and temperamental predeliction be shut out when the historian is dealing with precisely that subject—men and affairs—that most intensely engages our sympathy? The historian should neither completely repress nor cheerfully unleash his bias; he should, above all, become aware of it, and judge whether it is compatible with historical work. For the rest he will have to rely on his sense of truth and must remember that even if the existence of Truth be problematical, truthfulness remains the measure of his intellectual and moral achievement. Amidst frequent temptations he will remember William James' proud complaint: "I have to forge every sentence in the teeth of irreducible and stubborn facts."

From beginning to end the historian's person is involved in his work, and the more he is conscious of this the more wisely he may choose. At the very outset the selection of a topic, whether for a monograph or a general history, involves his whole self, his capabilities, his judgment. He must choose the specialty as well, ranging from traditional political history ("drum and trumpet histories," as J. R. Green derisively called it) to the history of ideas, wars, and sanitation. This selection is no easy task, and the punishment for an unharmonious choice can be years of anguished drudgery, years poisoned by the growing uncongeniality of the subject. Happy the historian who, like Macaulay, can exclaim in the middle of his work: "I am more and more in love with the subject." The responsibility for this choice is the historian's. Huizinga tells the story of a colleague who refused students' requests for a topic with the curt: "You might as well ask me to pick a wife for you."

In composing his work, the historian will find that his material usually suggests a particular form, but he may still find that one historical genre or another offers better clues or insights. Shall he write a narrative or an analytical history, shall he evoke the national past as Michelet tried to do, or the spirit of a culture, as Burckhardt and Huizinga did? Or shall he write an institutional study like Tocqueville? The historian is not able to decide in any rigid way; he cannot vote for Burckhardt and be done with it. The masters of the past cannot be copied; they can only make us see our situation more clearly and, perhaps, ourselves more humbly.

As he proceeds with his work, the historian may often find that he is repeating in his own person the various controversies over historical methods and purposes that have agitated the profession for so long. More often than not, he will find that he will not be able to resolve these conflicts, but will intuitively strike a balance between various possibilities. But if he were not even aware of the existence of these questions, his material would be left to speak for itself—dumbly. Should he, for example, become a mere observer of the past, striving for what F.J.E. Woodbridge once called past contemporaneity? Or should he search the past with the preoccupations of the present? How can he capture the uniqueness of the past and look for the uniformities and continuities of history as well? Will he be able to see "the familiar within the strange without losing the sense of either," as Jacques Barzun once defined the historian's diagnostic power? Shall he judge or merely record and explain? Shall he write a moralistic history, praising, according to his own traditions, the virtuous, and condemning the wicked, or should he identify himself with all antagonists, trying to understand the ways of men and the reasons for their responses to historical situations? These questions are not the historian's alone. They are inescapable in any analysis of human experience.

Whether the historian will incline towards one form rather than another will depend on his conception of the uses, the purposes of history. The earlier centuries held with Bolingbroke that history was "philosophy teaching by example," that history should teach moral principles and political wisdom.

This view reappeared in J. R. Seeley's inaugural lecture of 1869 when he demanded that history must be "a school for statesmanship." Fifty years later Harry Elmer Barnes still urged that the science of history become an instrument of social reform. In our own day there is a characteristic difference between a leading economic historian's demand that "a good causal analysis of a past event should consider not only what the contemporaries thought was causally relevant but also causes which contemporaries knew nothing of but which are suggested by the modern body of knowledge about human affairs," and G. M. Young's injunction "to go on reading till you hear the people speaking. The essential matter of history is not what happened, but what people thought, and said about it. . . ." Over the past decade there has been a vigorous struggle between the proponents of present-mindedness and historical-mindedness, between those who considered the past subservient to the needs of the present and those who wanted to pursue it for its own sake.

The freedom of the historian, the indeterminacy of his work, entails dangers as well. In the early nineteenth century, as we have seen, the tie between history and philosophy was loosened; to see the past as it had happened, and not through any preconceived system, was the essence of historicism. But once this was done, it left the historian, at least the secular historian, without definite categories of judgment or criticism. Meinecke's essay deals with precisely this problem. Having rid itself of Hegelians, Idealists, and theologians, history was left vulnerable to other, non-historical interpretations. It has remained a steady temptation to philosophers, scientists, and pseudo-scientists, and political ideologues, to demonstrate that the past follows a particular pattern, that it proves their *a priori* principles or political contentions.

The historian, too, can succumb to the same kind of temptation, either consciously or unconsciously. Herbert Butterfield has analyzed the often unconscious presuppositions of the Whig interpreters of history and Lionel Trilling has done the same for the liberal American historian, V. L. Parrington. The conscious attempts to force a pattern on history are more easily recognized, and from Bossuet to Toynbee—to take examples only from the modern period—there have been recurrent instances of historians who thought they had at last discovered *the* determining factor in history: Marx's economic determinism, Buckle's laws of intellectual progress, Taine's milieu and race, or Lamprecht's socio-psychic factors. Sometimes historians have borrowed laws and concepts from other fields—Darwinism or Spencer's organismic theories, or, more recently, Freudian categories—at first as illuminating metaphors, later as valid historical categories. Even today, when our pluralistic outlook leads us to reject deterministic or monistic explanations, such concepts are often smuggled in under a different name, as "the main factor" or "primary emphasis." There is an enormous difference between a historical sense for detail, which can see a whole world in a single incident, and the non-historical view which will reduce the world to a single force or factor. The former is illuminated by an ingenious remark that F. W. Maitland once made: "But if some fairy gave me the power of seeing a scene of one and the same kind in every age of history of every race, the kind of scene that I would choose would be a trial for murder, because I think that it would give me so many hints as to a multitude of matters of the first importance."

Actually, the thoughtful historian must always proceed from the how to the why, from the external course to the internal cause, and his most intricate task is to explain without explaining too much. The how and the why, of course, are inseparable, and here as everywhere the historian must have both a sense of the complexity of human life and the belief that this complexity is comprehensible. While explaining the course of Roman history he must make allowances for contingency, for Pascal's mischievous observation that if "Cleopatra's nose had been shorter, the whole aspect of the world would have been different."

This need for a balance is exemplified in the historian's treatment of human motivation. There is a significant distinction between pondering the various psychological insights of literature and psychiatry and reducing a complex range of questions to a particular psychological mechanism. Freud's work can be, and increasingly will be, of great value for the historian, but primarily in deepening our view of the complexity of human action and not in offering any general theory of historical events or processes. In the end, the historian's judgment about human character will depend on his view of man, and that is why neither a complete misanthrope nor Shaw's Androcles, who could see no evil, would make a good historian. Finally the historian must avoid the tendency which Tocqueville found common among historians in democratic times, that in their writings "the au-

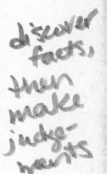

discover facts, then make judgements

thor often appears great, but humanity is always diminutive."

It is unnecessary to list all the ways of systematically simplifying history. In our time, when the demand for explanation and analysis is insistent and pervasive, this reduction of complexity to simplicity is perhaps the chief danger to the historical sense. A historian's reductionism is usually quite apparent and easily distinguishable from a valid attempt to explain. Luther did not break the unity of the Roman Church in order to marry a nun; National Socialism was not the result of monopoly capitalism or of the authoritarian character of the German family. These can be spotted easily, for our historical sense, as Namier defined it, is "an intuitive understanding of how things do not happen." In explaining the past there are no hard and fast rules. It is a matter of degree, of historical tact. Often the great historian, at least in our age, will be content with a suggestive tentativeness, knowing that the complexity of history is in itself an expression of the great and unpredictable variety of man.

I have tried to suggest some of the characteristic problems which the historian encounters. How he resolves them depends in part on which of many simultaneous styles of historical writing he tries to emulate. More importantly, it depends on the historian's own mind and temperament. It is the deeper, less conscious inclinations and faculties of the historian that mould his work: the nature of his sensibility and mind, his awareness of himself and others. It will indeed have a great deal to do with his original motives in becoming an historian.

4.

What does impel a man to become a historian? Historians have given a great many answers, and some will be found in the following essays, often as asides. One answer that most historians might be loath to give, at least publicly, is perhaps the most common and certainly the most powerful impulse: pleasure. The story is told of earnest graduate students at an Eastern university who invited a formidable historian to talk on why she became a historian, and the shattering effect of her first sentence: "It is such fun!"

To be sure, the pleasures of history are themselves diverse, and every historian will have his particular passion. A great many historians have been drawn to their work by the aesthetic pleasure they experience in reliving the past, in seeing the variety, charm and strangeness of a remote age, listening to it and discovering the traces of its genius. Ranke, Burckhardt, J. R. Green, Croce, and Huizinga,—to mention but a few—have expressed the spontaneous love and sympathy which they felt for an earlier time and which had led them to history. I doubt that any of the great historians has ever been entirely without this love.

For some it may be a more intellectual pleasure, though it is obviously impossible to draw up a historian's calculus of pain and pleasure. Some find delight in tracking down an elusive source, in finding, often accidentally, a clue to some obscure problem, others in trying to infer the meaning of an event, the spirit of an age, the causes of a crisis. Whatever the source of pleasure, it is always tempered by a sense of intellectual obligation; that is why historians' letters often express, in alternation, delight and despair, certainty and ambiguity about their work.

Many of these pleasures the historian communicates, or should communicate, to his reader. For both of them the study of the past should be a liberating experience, one which tears them away from the parochialism of time and place and enlivens the imagination. Macaulay was right in comparing history to foreign travel, Trevelyan that "it should breed enthusiasm." History records the vast possibilities of the past and suggests to the observer that the same range of possibilities must still prevail, that in some sense history must truly be the story of liberty. Is it not because history can arouse this impulse to liberty and dissent that, as Orwell noted, totalitarian regimes must extinguish it?

To some historians this emphasis on pleasure would seem frivolous. Contrast, say, Michelet and Fustel de Coulanges—less than a generation apart—and note the difference between the magnificent enthusiast, inspired by his superb sense of history and his love for the people to resurrect its past, and the self-conscious scientist, who in true Cartesian fashion doubted all received opinions, and in good positivistic style sought to build on authenticated facts alone. And yet even beneath Fustel's austerity one senses the pleasure with which he studied and contemplated the past, recognizing its uniqueness as well as its uniformities.

Few historians, then, would admit to having been drawn to history by mere pleasure or intellectual dedication; they may concede, as did Thierry, that they began with a severely practical motive, and that only gradually were they won over to enjoying history for its own sake. But even for them the discipline of history usually proved stronger than their partisan or personal motive, and the nineteenth century exacted a rigorous standard from historians which few violated. For other historians, such as Macaulay, it may have been the desire for immortal renown, which for him began with the confident expectation that his book would "for a few days supersede the last fashionable novel on the tables of young ladies," but would, he hoped, ultimately place him next to Thucydides, whom he thought the greatest of historians. Today historians may hope for some more tangible rewards; or they may write out of purely academic ambition for rank. The quality of the work is not unrelated to the quality of the impelling motive. Even the rigorous scholar should remember, however, that strict method and genuine pleasure are not incompatible, that in fact they were nearly always combined in the great historians of the past.

As I said at the beginning, the historian must serve two masters, the past and the present. And while his obligation to the past, his complete, unassailable fidelity to it, must always claim his first loyalty, he must accept the fact that the choices he makes as a historian are not of consequence to him alone, but will affect the moral sense, perhaps the wisdom, of his generation. And since he knows that his own being, his intellectual capabilities and his critical faculties as well as his deeper sense of righteousness and love, are engaged in the writing of history, he knows that his work, too, is a moral act.

Some seventy years ago, F. W. Maitland repeated what a historian had said long before: "In truth, writing this history is in some sense a religious act." The deeper sense of the image remains with us, and Miss Wedgwood is right that "it is as important for the historian today to be a good, and if possible a great, man as it was for the high dignitaries of the Mediæval Church." From these admonitions the historian can derive pride and abiding humility: his is a serious task, for which great predecessors have prepared him. As he deals with men and their lives in society, both past and present, he touches on the ultimate questions of human existence, as does religion itself. And as he deals with men and their creations, he will alternately feel pride and exultation, awe and sorrow, at how varied, complex, unpredictable, wretched and glorious is human life.

PART I

THE NEW PHILOSOPHICAL HISTORY: *Voltaire*

[Voltaire (1694-1778) rightly thought himself a pioneer of a new type of history. Rebelling against the prevailing ideals and forms of historiography—against supernatural history, narrow political or biographical chronicles, and the uncritical acceptance of ancient historians—he proposed and produced a secular and naturalistic history which would depict the life and spirit of peoples, their art, science and politics. His two masterpieces, *The Age of Louis XIV* (1752)[1] and the *Essay on the Manners and Customs of Nations* (1757), deal in a philosophical, interpretative manner with universal history, including not only some of the previously neglected aspects of western society but the progress of non-European peoples as well.

Although a violent partisan in his writings, Voltaire adhered to his own command that historians must sift fact from fable and must test the credibility of all historical evidence. He was critical, even contemptuous of older historians, and in his *Le Pyrrhonisme de L'Histoire* (1768), he excoriated their gullibility or deliberate falsifications. Of his own *Essay on the Manners and Customs of Nations* he wrote: "Mankind dictated it and truth acted as the scribe." Believing that history could play a powerful role in the enlightenment of men and in the creation of a rational, humane society, he sought to promote the writing and study of history, particularly modern history.

The following selections were translated for this volume
by Jacques Barzun.]

ON HISTORY: ADVICE TO A JOURNALIST

What our journalists like best to go in for, perhaps, is narrative history. For history, being most nearly accessible to
every man, is most to their taste. Not because one isn't really
as much interested in finding out the facts of Nature as the
doings of Sesostris or Bacchus, but because it always takes
more pains and application to look into, let us say, the kind
of machine that could provide Paris with plenty of water—
which we surely need; whereas all one has to do in order to
learn the old wives' tales handed down to us under the name
of history is to open one's eyes and read. These tales are told
over and over again, even though they do not much matter
to us.

If you are going to give an account of ancient history, I
entreat you to exclude all the usual tirades against certain
conquerors. Let the satirists Juvenal and Boileau pour ridicule
on Alexander from the safety of their study, though they
would have bored him with their praises had they lived under
his reign. Let them call Alexander mad. You who are an
impartial philosopher should look upon Alexander, the gener-
alissimo of Greece, as rather like Scanderbeg or Huniady;
like them he was bound to avenge his country, but he was
more fortunate than they, of greater stature, more civilized,
and more majestic. Don't depict him merely as one who
overcame the power of all the foes of Greece and extended
his conquests as far as India, wherever Darius ruled. Show
him rather as a lawgiver in the midst of war, as one establishing colonies and trade routes, founding Alexandria and
Scandaron which to this day are the center of near Eastern
commerce. That is the way to judge a King and that is what
is generally forgotten. What good citizen would not rather
hear about the towns and harbors Caesar built and the calen-
dar he reformed than about the men he slaughtered?

Above all, inculcate in the young a greater liking for the
history of recent times, which is essential for us to know, than
for ancient history, which only serves to satisfy our curiosity.
Let them reflect that modern history has the advantage of
being more certain, from the very fact that it is modern.

I should especially have you recommend that the study of

history begin with the century just before Charles Fifth, Leo Tenth and Francis First. That is the time when there occurred in the human mind as in the world itself, a revolution which changed everything.

The splendid century of Louis XIV completes what Leo X, all the Medicis, Charles Fifth and Francis First had initiated. I have long been at work on a history of the past century, a century which ought to serve as a model for the centuries to come. In it I try to show the progress of the human mind and of all the arts under Louis XIV. May I before I die leave this monument to the glory of my country! I have ample materials to erect this edifice. There is no lack of memoirs upon the benefits that the great Colbert secured and meant to secure for this nation and for the world; upon the tireless vigilance and foresight of a war minister [Louvois] who was born to be minister to a conqueror; upon the upheavals that occurred in Europe; upon the private life of Louis XIV, who was a model in his domestic behavior as he sometimes was in his conduct as King. I have memoirs upon the faults in him that are inseparable from his being human and that I want to talk about only as a set off to his virtues. I have already thought of applying to Louis XIV the fine saying of Henry IV to the ambassador of Don Pedro: "Do you mean to say your master hasn't enough virtues to afford some faults?" But I am afraid that I will have neither the time nor the strength to bring this grand design to completion.

I would have you make clear that although our modern histories, as written by contemporaries, are generally sounder than all the ancient histories, they are sometimes more doubtful as to details. This is what I mean: men differ among themselves in rank, party, religion. The soldier, the judge, the Jansenist, the Molinist, do not see eye to eye about the same facts. A Carthaginian would not have written about the Punic Wars in the same tone as a Roman, and he would have charged Rome with the same bad faith that Rome imputed to Carthage. We have hardly any ancient historians who wrote against one another upon the same event. If we had, this would raise doubts about things that we take today as unquestionable. But however improbable, they have our respect, and for two reasons: because they are old and because no one has contradicted them.

But we contemporary historians work under different conditions. We go through the same thing that happens among the great powers when they are at war: in Vienna, London, or Versailles bonfires are lit for battles nobody won. Each side claims the victory, each is right on his side of the line. Just look at the conflicts of opinion about Mary Stuart, the English Civil Wars, the troubles in Hungary, the Council of Trent. Talk about the Revocation of the Edict of Nantes to a Dutch burgomaster, you will find it a piece of ill-considered tyranny. Consult a minister of the French court and it is a wise policy. Indeed, the same nation at twenty years' distance does not think the same about the same event or the same man. I have seen this myself with regard to Louis XIV.

But what opposition am I going to run into about Charles XII? I have written up his strange career with the aid of the memoirs of M. de Fabrice who was his favorite for eight years; of the letters of M. de Fierville who was a French envoy at his court; of those of M. de Villelongue, who served him for many years as colonel; and of those of M. de Poniatowski. I consulted M. de Croissi, the French ambassador at Charles's court, and so on. I now learn that M. Nordberg, the King's chaplain, is writing a history of his reign. I am sure the chaplain will often have seen the same things with very different eyes from those of the favorite and the ambassador. What should one do in such a case? Revise my text at once about all matters in which this new historian is patently right and leave the rest to the judgment of the disinterested reader. What is my role in all this? Only that of a painter who tries, with a weak but truthful brush, to show men as they were. Everything about Charles XII and Peter the Great is a matter of indifference to me except the good the latter may have done mankind. I have no reason to flatter or abuse them. I shall treat them like Louis XIV, with the respect due to crowned heads that have just died, and with the respect due to truth, which will never die.

LETTER TO ABBÉ JEAN BAPTISTE DUBOS:
ON *The Age of Louis XIV*

October 30 [1738]
. . . . For a long time now I have been collecting materials for writing the history of the age of Louis XIV. It is not the life of the king I mean to write, nor is it the annals of his reign; it is rather the history of the human mind, examined in the century that sheds the most glory.

The work is divided into chapters. About twenty are devoted to general history: they are twenty frescoes of the great events of the time. The principal figures are in the foreground; the crowd is in the background. Woe to details! Posterity neglects them all; they are a kind of vermin that undermines large works. Whatever characterizes the century, what caused its overturns, what will matter a hundred years hence—that is what I want to set down today.

There is one chapter for Louis XIV's private life; two for the great changes in the administration of the commerce and finances of the kingdom; two for church affairs, among which are included the Revocation of the Edict of Nantes and the business of the *régale;* and five or six for the history of the arts, beginning with Descartes and ending with Rameau.

All I have by way of sources for the general history is some two hundred volumes of printed memoirs that everybody knows. The difficulty is to form a well-proportioned body out of these dispersed members and to depict in true colors, though with one stroke, everything that Larrey, Lamberti, Roussel, etc. etc. distort and dilute in their tomes.

For Louis XIV's private life I have the memoirs of M. Dangeau in forty volumes from which I have extracted forty pages. I have also what I have heard from old courtiers, servants, great lords and others. I report those facts about which they agree. The rest I leave to the talkers in salons and tellers of anecdotes. I have an extract from the famous letter of the King about M. de Barbesieux, whose faults he notes while forgiving him on his father's account. This gives Louis XIV's character far better than the flattery of Pellisson.

I know a good deal about the adventure of the Man in the Iron Mask, who died in the Bastille. I have talked with people who waited on him.

There is a kind of memorial, written in Louis XIV's hand, which must be in Louis XV's files. M. Hardion knows of it, undoubtedly, but I do not dare ask to see it.

On church affairs I have the mass of stuff born of party invective. I shall try to squeeze an ounce of honey from the bitter absinth of the Jurieus, Quesnels, Doucins and the rest.

For internal affairs, I am going through the memoirs of the intendants and the good books that exist on the subject. M. l'Abbé de St. Pierre has written a political diary of Louis XIV which I wish he would let me consult. I do not know whether he will perform this act of benevolence and win a place in paradise.

With regard to the arts and sciences, I think all that is

needed is to trace the onward march of the human mind in philosophy, oratory, poetry, and criticism; to show the progress of painting, sculpture, and music; of jewelry, tapestry making, glassblowing, gold-cloth weaving, and watchmaking. As I do this I want to depict only the geniuses that have excelled in these undertakings. God preserve me from devoting 300 pages to the story of Gassendi! Life is too short, time too valuable, to spend it in telling what is useless.

In short, sir, you can make out what my plan is even better than I can describe it. I am in no hurry to rear my edifice. *Pendent opera interrupta, minaeque murorum ingentes.* If you consent to guide me, I shall be able to say: *aequataque machina coelo.* Please see what you can do for me, for truth, and for a century that numbers you among its ornaments.

To whom shall you communicate your light and leading unless it be to a man who loves his country as much as truth and who is trying to write history neither as a flatterer, nor as eulogist nor again as a newspaperman, but as a philosopher? He who disentangled so ably the chaos of the origins of the French will no doubt help to throw light upon France's greatest days. Consider, sir, that you will be helping your disciple and admirer.

I shall be, my whole life long, with deep esteem

Gratefully yours,

VOLTAIRE

P.S. Please tell me if Lahode's book is worth buying, and what Lahode may be.

INTRODUCTION: *The Age of Louis XIV*

It is not solely the life of Louis XIV that is here to be depicted. A greater object is in view, which is to depict for posterity, not the actions of a single man, but the minds of men in the most enlightened century that ever was.

All periods have produced heroes and political leaders; all peoples have undergone revolutions; all histories are virtually equal in the eyes of any one who only wants to stuff his memory with facts. But whoever thinks, or what is still rarer, whoever has taste, will consider only four ages in the whole history of the world. Those four blessed ages are those in which the arts were perfected and which, by marking an epoch in the greatness of the human mind, stand as examples to posterity.

The first of those centuries that deserve true glory is that of Philip and Alexander, that of Pericles, Demosthenes, Aristotle, Plato, Apelles, Phidias and Praxiteles; this glory was confined within the limits of Greece; the rest of the earth as then known was barbaric.

The second age is that of Caesar and Augustus, known also through the names of Lucretius, Cicero, Livy, Virgil, Horace, Ovid, Varro and Vitruvius.

The third is that which followed the taking of Constantinople by Mohammed II. The reader may remember that at that time a family of ordinary citizens in Italy did what the kings of Europe should have done: the Medici called to Florence the scholars whom the Turks harried out of Greece. It was the time of Italy's glory. The fine arts had already taken a new lease on life; the Italians paid them the honor of calling them by the name of virtue—*virtú,* just as the early Greeks had given them the name of wisdom. Everything was tending toward perfection.

The arts, once again transplanted from Greece into Italy, found themselves in a favoring soil where they suddenly bore fruits. France, England, Germany, and Spain all wished in turn to enjoy such harvests, but either the arts failed to take root in those climates or, once there, degenerated very fast.

Francis I encouraged scholars who were nothing but scholars. He had architects, but they were neither Michelangelos nor Palladios: he wished in vain to found schools of painting. The Italian painters he summoned produced no French pupils. A few epigrams and racy tales constituted all that we could call our poetry. Rabelais' book was our only fashionable prose work in the time of Henry II.

In a word, the Italians had everything—if you except music, which had not yet been perfected, and experimental philosophy [physical science], which was unknown everywhere and which Galileo at last brought into being.

The fourth age is that of Louis XIV, and it is perhaps that one which, of the four, most nearly approaches perfection. Enriched by the discoveries of the other three, it has done more in certain genres than the other three put together. Not all the arts, it is true, have been carried farther than in the age of the Medici, of Augustus and of Alexander, but human reason in general has improved. A sane philosophy dates only from this most recent time, and one can truly say that from the last years of Cardinal Richelieu to those following the death of Louis XIV, a revolution took place in our arts, our minds, our manners and our government, that will forever mark the true glory of our country. This happy influence did not even stop within France; it spread to England, where it aroused the emulation which that daring and lively nation then needed. Our influence also carried taste to Germany and science to Russia; it revived Italy which was in apathy; and all of Europe was indebted for its polite behavior and play of mind to the court of Louis XIV.

One must not believe that these four great ages were free from misfortunes and crimes. The perfection of such arts as are carried on by peaceful citizens does not prevent princes from being ambitious, peoples seditious, priests and monks occasionally restless and treacherous. All centuries are alike in the wickedness of men, but I know only these four that are distinguished by high talents.

Before the age which I have named after Louis XIV and which begins about the time the French Academy was established, the Italians called all those who lived beyond their mountains Barbarians, and one must admit that the French to a certain extent deserved this insult. Their ancestors combined with the courtly gallantry of the Moors the uncouthness of the Goths. They lacked almost every one of the agreeable arts, which proves that the useful ones were neglected, for when the necessary has been brought to perfection, the agreeable and beautiful is soon cultivated. It is not surprising that painting, sculpture, poetry, oratory and philosophy should be almost unknown to a nation which had harbors on the Ocean and the Mediterranean, yet had no fleet; and which loved luxury to excess, yet possessed but a few crude manufactures.

The Jews, the Genoese, the Venetians, the Portuguese, the Flemings, the Dutch, and the English acted by turns as traders for the French, who lacked the principles of commerce. On his accession, Louis XIII did not own a single ship; Paris did not number 400,000 men and could not boast four handsome buildings. The other towns of the kingdom resembled the overgrown villages one can still see beyond the Loire. The entire nobility camped in the country in castles surrounded by moats, and oppressed those who tilled the soil. The main roads were almost impassable. The towns had no police, the state was penniless and the government without credit among foreign nations.

It cannot be denied that since the decline of Charlemagne's descendants, France had always more or less languished in this condition of weakness, for lack of good government.

For a state to be powerful, the people must either enjoy a freedom based on law or be ruled by a strong and unchallenged government. In France, the people were slaves almost till the reign of Philip Augustus; the lords were tyrants until that of Louis XI. The kings were always busy maintaining their authority against their vassals, and never had the time to think of the well-being of their subjects, much less the power to establish it.

Louis XI did much for the royal prerogative but nothing for the happiness and glory of the nation. To Francis I is due the birth of trade, navigation, literature, and the arts. But he proved too unlucky to make them take root in France and everything perished with him. Henry the Great was on the point of extricating the kingdom from the disasters and barbarism into which thirty years of strife had once again plunged her when he was assassinated, in his own capital, in the midst of the people whose welfare he was beginning to insure. Cardinal Richelieu, whose concerns were to keep down the house of Austria, the Calvinists, and the nobles, never enjoyed enough peace and power to reform the nation. But at least he resumed that noble enterprise.

Thus, for nine hundred years, the genius of the French was almost always constricted under a Gothic government, amid dissension and civil war, lacking fixed laws and customs, and changing every two centuries its perennially uncouth tongue. The undisciplined French nobles knew nothing but war and idleness; the clergy lived in disorder and ignorance; and the people, devoid of industry, stagnated in poverty.

The French took no part in the great discoveries and wonderful inventions of other nations: printing, powder-making, glass-making, the telescope, the slide rule, the pneumatic machine, and the true system of nature, were not their inventions. They jousted at tournaments while the Portuguese and Spanish discovered and conquered new worlds to the east and west of Europe. Charles V was already squandering the treasures of Mexico in Europe when a few subjects of Francis I discovered the untilled regions of Canada. But from this very slight achievement of the French at the beginning of the sixteenth century, one can see what they are capable of when led.

The object of the present work is to show what they did under Louis XIV.

The reader must not expect to find here, any more than in the survey of earlier centuries, the exhaustive detail of wars, of towns besieged, taken and retaken by force of arms, given and regained by treaty. A thousand incidents of interest to contemporaries are lost in the eyes of posterity. They disappear, and disclose only the very great events that settle the destinies of empires. Not everything that is done deserves recording. In this history, only that which merits the attention of the ages will be dealt with—that which depicts the genius and manners of men, or which serves to instruct and inculcate the love of country, of virtue, and of art.

The condition of France and the other European states before the birth of Louis XIV has already been indicated. Now we shall see the great political and military events of his reign. The management of home affairs, which is more important to the people, will be taken up separately. Louis XIV's private life, the details of his court and his reign, will occupy a large place. Other sections will deal with art and science and the progress of the human mind in his century. Lastly, I shall speak of the Church, which has for so long been allied with the state, acting sometimes as a prop, sometimes as a threat, and which, though established to teach morality, has often given itself over to politics and other human passions.

ON THE USEFULNESS OF HISTORY

The advantage consists chiefly in the comparison which a statesman or a citizen can draw between foreign laws and customs and those of his own country. This is what spurs modern peoples to emulation in the arts, in agriculture, and in trade.

The great errors of the past are also very useful in many ways. One cannot remind oneself too often of crimes and disasters. These, no matter what people say, can be forestalled. The history of the tyrant Christiern can prevent a nation from giving absolute power to a tyrant; and the undoing of Charles XII at Pultawa will warn a general not to plunge deep into the Ukraine without supplies.

It is because the celebrated Marshal de Saxe had read the details of the battles of Crécy, Poitiers, Agincourt, Saint-Quentin, Gravelines, etc. that he was bent upon waging, as far as possible, only wars of position.

Examples will exert a great influence upon the mind of a king who reads carefully. He will see that Henry IV did not undertake his great war, which was meant to change the European system, until he had assured himself of the sinews of war, so that he might be able to carry it on for several years without fresh financial aid.

. He will see that Queen Elizabeth resisted the powerful Philip II by the sole means of trade and wise economy, and that of the hundred ships she put to sea against the invincible armada, three-quarters were furnished by the trading centers of England.

France, uninvaded under Louis XIV despite nine years of most unlucky warfare, demonstrates the evident utility of the border fortresses he had built. It is in vain that the writer on the causes of the Fall of Rome [Montesquieu] blames Justinian for the same policy; he should have blamed only the emperors who neglected these frontier places and left the gates open to the barbarians.

One advantage that modern history has over ancient is to teach all the princes that ever since the fifteenth century, coalitions have always been formed against a too powerful state. The system of the balance of power was unknown to the ancients. This explains the triumph of the Romans who, possessing a militia superior to other peoples', were able to overcome them one by one, from the Tiber to the Euphrates.

It is necessary to bring to mind repeatedly the usurpations of the Popes, the scandalous strife of their schisms, the madness of theological quarrels, the wars engendered by these quarrels, and the horrors that resulted. If this knowledge were not made familiar, if only a small number of learned men knew these facts, the public could be as stupidly blind as in the time of Gregory VII. The disasters of those times of ignorance would infallibly rearise, because no one would take pains to prevent them. Everybody in Marseille knows through what oversight plague was brought in from the Levant—and takes precautions in consequence. Abolish the study of history, and you will probably see a new Saint Bartholomew in France and a new Cromwell in England.

THE CRITICAL METHOD: *Niebuhr*

[Statesman and scholar, Barthold Georg Niebuhr (1776-1831) had an influence second to none on the rise of historical scholarship. Inspired by his father, the famous traveller, Carsten Niebuhr, and by the Romantic writers of his day, Niebuhr turned early to a study of antiquity and had mastered twenty languages before he reached his thirtieth year. He began his career in the civil service of his native Denmark, entering the Prussian service just before the disaster of 1806. He became an important member of the Prussian reform movement, and in 1810 was appointed a lecturer at the newly founded University of Berlin. From 1816 to 1823 Prussian ambassador to the Vatican, he spent his last years at the University of Bonn. He was an exceptional man, of whom Dilthey said: "No young man should enter a university without having morally elevated himself by contemplating the figure of this great scholar."

Niebuhr's *History of Rome* (in 2 vols. 1811-1812; completely revised edition in 3 vols. 1827-1832) was the first attempt to reconstruct the historical origins of the Roman state; previous historians had dealt mostly with the triumph of Rome under the Empire. As the following selections show, Niebuhr sought to apply the critical method of the philologist to the study of ancient history and his work further discredited the authority of Livy. His own inferences about the early history of Rome, drawn from the few surviving sources, were not uniformly successful. Great as his divinatory power was, it sometimes misled him; his assumption, for example, that old songs and ballads had been the main sources of ancient historians was rejected by his successors. As a statesman, however, he had observed the basic institutions of a state at close hand, and his *History* focussed on these political institutions, and on Roman law and property relations. It became a model for historians, among them Ranke, Michelet, and Mommsen, despite the fact that it has been rightly called the "most unreadable of historical classics."

The following selections are taken from the Preface to the first and second edition of the *History of Rome* and have been translated by the Editor.]

PREFACE TO THE FIRST EDITION:
History of Rome

This portion of a Roman history, and a second which will follow soon, originated in lectures which I gave last winter at this University. They were begun with no thought of the general public beyond that of the lecture hall: when I decided upon publication, I had at first planned on a title taken from the original lectures, and thus it was provisionally announced. It became evident, however, that the change and enlargement of the audience necessitated a thorough revision; thus the original title, though preferable because of its unpretentiousness, had to be replaced by one that imposes on the work the burden of justifying a high-sounding name. Therefore I have left at the beginning of the book an indication of the original scope of this history of Rome which, however, applies only to the lectures. Indeed, I intend to carry these lectures to the point where the Middle Ages completely overwhelmed Rome and extinguished the last glimmering sparks of antiquity. The book, if fate allows me to complete it, will terminate where Gibbon's history commenced. His work surely renders a new treatment superfluous and foolhardy; and as for the more remote period, where Gibbon's work was and could afford to be deficient, the gaps can be filled without presuming to compete, by monographs on the constitution and administration of Rome, and similar subjects. . . .

The history of the first four centuries of Rome is admittedly uncertain and falsified. Yet it would be foolish to blame Livy for nevertheless having depicted them, with but a few reservations, as strictly historical. The excellence of his narrative is his justification, and in this respect as in others it is most fitting to compare him to Herodotus. We, however, have a different view of history and different requirements. Either we must give up writing the early history of Rome or we must do it differently, and not attempt a task which is doomed from the start, that of retelling what Livy had elevated to the level of historical credibility. We must try to eliminate fiction and forgery and to strain our vision in order to recognize the features of truth beneath all these incrustations.

The critic might be content with the excision of fiction, the destruction of fraud: he only seeks to expose a specious history and he is content to advance a few conjectures, leaving the greater part of the whole in ruins. But the historian demands something positive: he must discover at least with some probability the general connectedness of events, and by a more credible story replace that which he has sacrificed to his better judgment. If he omits from his work those investigations which he thought had led him to evoke the spirits of times past, then he must either renounce the use of these results or run the risk of appearing as if he wanted to give out, arrogantly and insolently, as historic truth a mere hypothesis or a questionable possibility—a heavy price to pay for greater elegance in composition.

The events of history presuppose the constitution and the fundamental laws as embodying the ethos of the nation; but the knowledge of these for the ancient period is all the more obscure and muddled because the events themselves have been falsified. One can perhaps attain the truth of these fundamental laws and of the constitution with greater clarity than is usually possible for history in the stricter sense. But that truth which is reached only through inferences—even though proven—can, without further detailed evidence, only be accepted as historical if it already had once before been generally accepted and confirmed by the common persuasion of many scholars. This, as a matter of fact, furnishes the same reinforced verification as would new sources of evidence.

These new sources, too, will be treated differently by different people—in the same way as people differ in judging another's work and method. Some restrict themselves to the collection of truncated fragments of reports from antiquity without attempting to solve their underlying riddles; they resist the impulse to strain their view in order to see the form of the whole to which the pieces belonged. Such a lifeless compilation of fragments is of no use; yet only a person who is completely satisfied with such a compilation has a right to criticize the attempt to discover meaning and structure where assuredly these once existed and where they could be discovered through some traces—even if the success of these efforts appears doubtful. No one else can demand that the limitations which he draws or accepts for himself should be generally binding.

Neither in my earlier studies nor during the course of my lectures did I use the more recent works on Roman history. Thus I was not tempted to engage in controversies which would have been inappropriate to this work and which in any case are of little benefit to science; they should be replaced by as complete an analysis as possible. If the hypothesis advanced is proven to be correct or most probable, then it does not require the explicit refutation of opposite opinions. Wherever, as indeed was the case in Beaufort's critical study,[1] identical investigations yielded identical results, the specific mention of the other author was sometimes impossible, and sometimes superfluous. For I read Beaufort's study only when a part of this volume had already gone to press; and for the rest, as well as for the next volume, the identity of views arose quite independently for I made no direct or indirect use of Beaufort, so that he was more a corroborator than a precursor. . . .

A book which claims to be a work of science rather than a work of art can plead for a gentle judgment of its diction and presentation. Even a master might have found it difficult to lessen the clumsiness inherent in such diffuse inquiries and to give a fluent expression to this collection of isolated parts. Irregularities of spelling and punctuation, which are certainly present in this volume, are in themselves trifles which offend only those eyes accustomed to the regularity of printed works but which to an older generation appear quite insignificant. An author, conscious of having sought the truth, of having written without partisanship or polemical intention, can demand attentive and disinterested examination and judgment of his work.

There is an enthusiasm which is engendered by the presence and the association of beloved friends; an immediate influence, whereby the muses appear to us, awakening joy and strength in us, and brightening our vision: to this I have all my life owed whatever was best in me. Thus it is to the friends in whose midst I returned to studies long abandoned or feebly pursued, that I owe thanks if the work is successful. Therefore I bless the beloved memory of my departed Spalding: therefore, too, allow me openly to express my thanks to you, Savigny, Buttmann, and Heindorf, without whom, and without our late friend [Spalding],[2] I should certainly never have had the courage to undertake this work, without whose affectionate sympathy and enlivening presence it would hardly have been accomplished.

PREFACE TO THE SECOND EDITION:
History of Rome

Like all other disciplines during the two centuries after the Renaissance, Roman History surrendered critical judgment to the written word and showed the same reluctance to go beyond it. The mere thought that the credibility and worth of ancient writers might be questioned would have been condemned as outrageous and impious. The task was to combine ancient testimony into an entity, evidence to the contrary notwithstanding. In an isolated instance they might venture to give one authority precedence over another, but without calling attention to the reasons for their preference or pursuing its consequences. Here and there a free spirit like Glareanus crashed through these barriers, but inevitably he would be condemned by his peers. And it was not the most learned who made these attempts nor were their ventures emulated. Brilliant and erudite scholars stayed within the established barriers. Out of countless scattered fragments they constructed the story of Roman antiquities, such as did not exist in any single work surviving from antiquity. Their achievement is admirable and must suffice for their imperishable fame. To reproach them for not transcending the limitations of their age is to be blind to the common lot of humanity, for only the favorites of the gods are free and they pay for their privilege by persecution. For history in the strict sense little was achieved: lifeless collections of fragments on periods for which the books of Livy are lost—mere isolated, unexploited notes.

About the middle of the seventeenth century philology entered upon a transition between the period of its earlier, uncontested greatness when it had realized the limits of its potentialities and therefore declined, and a new, richer, and more comprehensive greatness which it owed to the development of other disciplines. In the interval these other disciplines eclipsed it. Like all transitional periods, this one was uneasy and depressed. Bentley and a few others who partly created the new age and partly preserved the knowledge amassed by the old, towered as heroes over a generation of pygmies.[3] In general the seventeenth century witnessed the emancipation of intellect and science from their previous nonage. Great men taught their contemporaries to look upon the world with open eyes, to examine with untrammeled heart, to consider books—hitherto the scholar's entire world —merely as pictures of a life that was not immediately accessible, to use their intelligence and reason and judgment in all things. In Roman history, too, this spirit of youthful freedom manifested itself. . . .

At the end of the last century our country saw once more the dawn of a new age. Everywhere men became dissatisfied with superficialities, with vague, meaningless words. But the work of destructive criticism which had pleased the preceding age was no longer adequate. Like our forefathers we sought certain, positive knowledge; but we wanted true knowledge, not the illusory knowledge which had been overthrown. We now had a literature worthy of our nation and language —we had Lessing and Goethe—and for the first time this literature included a great part of Greek and Roman literature, not simply copied but in a sense created anew. This gain Germany owed to Voss,[4] whom our children's children will still have to praise as their benefactor. By being able to discover in the classical writers what they themselves had taken for granted, their conception of the earth and the gods, their household habits and their way of life, Voss began a new epoch in our knowledge of antiquity. He understood and interpreted Homer and Virgil as if they were his contemporaries, separated from him only by an interval of space. His example has been an inspiration to many, and has been further enhanced for me by the personal encouragement this old friend of my father has given me since childhood.

Just as some people take maps and landscapes for reality itself, so previous ages had looked upon the writings of ancient historians, without trying to use these sole surviving means to recall the objects they represented. This type of history had now become unsatisfactory unless it possessed the same clarity and distinction as the history of the present day.

It was a time when we were experiencing the most incredible and exceptional events, when we were reminded of many forgotten and decayed institutions by the sound of their downfall. And our hearts grew stronger in the face of exceptional danger, as we became more passionately attached to our princes and our country.

By that time philology had already reached that flourishing

state of which our people can now be proud. It had recognized its calling, to be the transmitter of eternity, thus affording us the enjoyment of unbroken identity, across thousands of years, with the noblest and greatest peoples of antiquity; to make us as familiar with their spiritual creations and their history as if no gulf separated us.

While Greek literature had enjoyed almost exclusive favor for a long time, the critical treatment of Roman history, the discovery of the forms of political life hitherto misunderstood was another fruit of that earlier period of philological activity. A multitude of fortunate circumstances combined to foster its growth. It was a joyous time when the University of Berlin was founded. To have enjoyed the enthusiasm and bliss of those months—while the material of the first volumes of this history was being prepared, first as lectures and then for publication—and to have been alive in 1813, this alone suffices to make a man's life happy despite his share of sadness.

In this state of delight the meaning of many an old mystery revealed itself to me, but many more were overlooked. In much I erred; much else remained disjointed and inadequately proven. For I had only the insufficient knowledge of a self-educated man who until then had been able to steal only occasional hours from his other duties, and I had reached my destination like a man walking in his sleep along a battlement. Despite these defects, the over-hasty composition of the first part which compelled me to introduce sundry corrections in the sequel of the work, the book received a largely favorable reception, which shows that the revival of Roman history was in harmony with the age. Indeed it seems evident to me that our age can recognize its providential calling to this inquiry; for were not within eleven years from the beginning of this work three new and rich sources opened to us by the publication of Lydus, Gaius, and Cicero's "Republic," while in the previous centuries nothing had been added?

I was perfectly aware of these defects of my work, though the critics often attacked not the weak spots but what was right. Because I recognized these defects and wanted to use the new discoveries, the continuation of my *History* came to a standstill. Before I proceeded to the rest, the first volume had to be rewritten. Meanwhile I was living in Italy, in Rome itself, and I was too busy seeing and appreciating to find much pleasure in working at books. . . .

Upon my return to Germany I planned the third volume, preparing for it by revising the first and correcting the second. In the new edition I was aiming at the greatest possible completeness of proofs and solutions, and this required extensive work. But, as all labor is lightened by the intensification of life, so my work drew its greatest inspiration from my lectures last winter on Roman antiquities. What Pyrrhus said to his Epirots—ye are my wings—expresses the feelings of the zealous teacher towards his listeners, whom he loves and who take part in his lectures with all their hearts. His own work is promoted not only by the desire to be clear, to present nothing as a truth which might admit of a doubt, but the sight of his audience and his immediate relation to it awaken a thousand thoughts while he is speaking. . . .

The reader will notice at once that this second edition is completely new, with but a few fragments of the old one preserved. It would have been much easier to retain the form of the first edition, but I resolved upon the more difficult work because it imparted unity and harmony to the whole. That whole, comprising this volume and the next two, is the work of a man in his maturity; his powers may have declined, but his beliefs are settled, and his views unalterable. The former edition should therefore be regarded as a youthful work. Our friends are often more tender-hearted towards us than we are ourselves, and a few may regret that some parts have disappeared. More than once I hesitated before overthrowing the old structure, but what had been built on suppositions since proven wrong could not remain nor could it be preserved by mere verbal changes which would simply disguise the original foundations. . . .

When a historian is reviving former times, his interest in them and sympathy with them will be the deeper, the greater the events he has witnessed with a bleeding or a rejoicing heart. His feelings are moved by justice and injustice, by wisdom or folly, by coming or departing greatness, as if all were going on before his eyes; and when he is thus moved, his lips speak, although Hecuba is nothing to the player. The perfect distinctness of such a vision breaks the power of obscure ideas and ambiguous words, prevents the infatuated desire to transfer from earlier, different times something which now would be entirely inapplicable. It prevents, to retain the poet's simile, fools from emerging as knight-errants to avenge Hecuba's sorrows. After this reminder, only a dishonest or very simple-minded reader could mistake my meaning.—All my political opinions are based on principles which can be found in Montesquieu and Burke, and the proverb *quien hace aplicaciones, con su pan se lo coma* suffices.

THE IDEAL OF UNIVERSAL HISTORY: *Ranke*

[Leopold von Ranke (1795-1886) is the father as well as the master of modern historical scholarship. Called the "Nestor of Historians," his fame rested not only on his massive output of scholarship—over sixty volumes—but on his formulation of the historical method, his conception of the unity of European history, and his mastery of nearly the whole of modern European history. Trained originally in philology, which he taught for several years, Ranke turned to history in the 1820's and was called to the University of Berlin in 1824. There he originated the historical seminar, which instructed advanced students in *Quellenkritik,* the critical study of the sources. Travelling widely in Europe, he discovered many of the archival sources for the history of modern states. History, he taught, should be written only from eyewitness reports and from the "purest, most immediate documents." While training two generations of historians at Berlin, he published his best known works, among them, *The History of the Popes* (1834-1836) and *German History in the Time of the Reformation* (1839-1843).

Inspiring these tangible achievements was Ranke's conception of history, which a later generation called historicism, and which has remained the dominant force in historiography. In his formative years a Romantic, with religious and strong philosophical leanings, he nevertheless sought to establish the study of history as an autonomous discipline, separate from philosophy and religion. Each event was unique and had to be understood as a discrete phenomenon, each period "was immediate to God," who had fashioned it. The historian must treat each period with unswerving impartiality. But the particular had to be grasped as a part of universal history; in his 86th year he set out on his life-long ambition to write a world history.

After the turn of the century, Ranke's reputation suffered somewhat, especially at the hands of Anglo-American historians who mistook his affectionate attachment to the particular and his hope to write history "as it actually happened" for a kind of pretentious positivism. Forgetting his own insistence on a universal history, on a supra-political history, these critics often reproached him for the narrow-mindedness of his successors.

These selections, the Preface to his first work and two fragments from his literary remains, translated by the Editor, suggest the inadequacy of such criticism, at least as applied to Ranke's conception of history.]

PREFACE: *Histories of the Latin and Germanic Nations from 1494-1514*

I must confess that the present book appeared to me more perfect before it was printed than now that it is. Still I am counting on kind readers who will be less mindful of its deficiencies than of its possible virtues. So as not to entrust it entirely to its own powers I shall begin with a brief exposition of its purpose, its subject and its form.

The purpose of a historian depends on his point of view and of the latter two things must be said. First, that it regards the Latin and Germanic nations as a unity. This differs from three analogous concepts: the concept of a universal Christendom, which would comprehend even the Armenians. The concept of the unity of Europe: for since the Turks are Asiatic and since the Russian Empire includes the whole of northern Asia one could not fully understand their history without investigating and penetrating the entire range of Asiatic affairs. Finally it differs from the most analogous concept, that of a Latin Christianity: Slavic, Lettic, and Magyar tribes which are part of the latter have a peculiar and particular nature which will not be treated here. By touching on what is foreign to this unity only where necessary, in passing and as something peripheral, the author will keep close to the racially kindred nations either of Germanic or Germanic-Latin descent, whose history is the core of all modern history.

In the introduction I shall try to show—primarily in the narrative of foreign undertakings—how these nations developed in unity and in common enterprise. This is one aspect of the point of view on which this book is based; the other emerges directly from the contents themselves. The book deals with only a small part of the history of these nations, a part which might well be considered as the beginning of modern history. But it is only histories, not history. On the one hand, the book comprises the founding of the Spanish monarchy and the destruction of Italian liberty; on the other hand, it comprises the formation of a double antagonism: a political antagonism originating in France and an ecclesiastical antagonism through the Reformation, in short the division of our nations into two hostile camps upon which all modern history is based.

Beginning with the period in which Italy, still at harmony with itself, enjoyed at least external freedom and, since the pope was there, might perhaps even be called predominant, the book further presents the division of Italy, its invasion by the French and the Spaniards, the destruction of all freedom in some states and of self-determination in others, and finally the victory of the Spaniards and the beginning of their domination. From the political insignificance of the Spanish kingdoms, it proceeds to their unification and the drive of the united kingdoms against the infidels and towards the deepening of the Christian faith. It seeks to show how the drive against the infidels led to the discovery of America and the conquest of the great empires there, and how, most important, the fight for Christianity led to the Spanish hegemony in Italy, Germany, and the Low Countries. Thirdly, the book will describe the fortunes and misfortunes of the French from the time when Charles VIII, as a champion of Christianity set out against the Turks, until Francis I, forty-one years later, called on the same Turks for help against the emperor. Finally, by investigating the origins of a political opposition against the Emperor within Germany, and the origins of an ecclesiastical opposition against the Pope within Europe, this book tries to pave the way for a more comprehensive historical view of the great schism brought about by the Reformation. The schism itself will be considered in its first phase. This book attempts to see these histories and the other, related histories of the Latin and Germanic nations in their unity. To history has been assigned the office of judging the past, of instructing the present for the benefit of future ages. To such high offices this work does not aspire: It wants only to show what actually happened (*wie es eigentlich gewesen*).

But whence the sources for such a new investigation? The basis of the present work, the sources of its material, are memoirs, diaries, letters, diplomatic reports, and original narratives of eyewitnesses; other writings were used only if they were immediately derived from the above mentioned or seemed to equal them because of some original information. These sources will be identified on every page; a second volume, to be published concurrently, will present the method of investigation and the critical conclusions.

Aim and subject mould the form of a book. The writing of history cannot be expected to possess the same free development of its subject which, in theory at least, is expected in a work of literature; I am not sure it was correct to ascribe this quality to the works of the great Greek and Roman masters.

The strict presentation of the facts, contingent and unattractive though they may be, is undoubtedly the supreme law. After this, it seems to me, comes the exposition of the unity and progress of events. Therefore, instead of starting as might have been expected with a general description of the political institutions of Europe—this would certainly have distracted, if not disrupted, our attention—I have preferred to discuss in detail each nation, each power, and each individual only when they assumed a preeminently active or dominant role. I have not been troubled by the fact that here and there they had to be mentioned beforehand, when their existence could not be ignored. In this way, we are better able to grasp the general line of their development, the direction they took, and the ideas by which they were motivated.

Finally what will be said of my treatment of particulars, which is such an essential part of the writing of history? Will it not often seem harsh, disconnected, colorless, and tiring? There are, of course, noble models both ancient and—be it remembered—modern; I have not dared to emulate them: theirs was a different world. A sublime ideal does exist: the event in its human intelligibility, its unity, and its diversity; this should be within one's reach. I know to what extent I have fallen short of my aim. One tries, one strives, but in the end it is not attained. Let none be disheartened by this! The most important thing is always what we deal with, as Jakobi says, humanity as it is, explicable or inexplicable: the life of the individual, of generations, and of nations, and at times the hand of God above them.

A FRAGMENT FROM THE 1830's

It has often been noted that a certain kind of antagonism exists between an immature philosophy and history. From *a priori* ideas one used to infer what must be. Without realizing that these ideas are exposed to many doubts, men set out to find them reflected in the history of the world. From the infinitude of facts, one then selected those which seemed to confirm these ideas. And this has been called the philosophy of history. One of these ideas which the philosophy of history presses time and again, as an irrefutable claim, is that the human race moves along a course of uninterrupted progress, in a steady development towards perfection. Fichte, one of the foremost philosophers in this field, assumes the existence of five epochs, a world plan, as he puts it: the dominion of reason as instinct; the dominion of reason as [external] authority; emancipation from the [external] authority of reason; reason as science; reason as art; or as stages which could occur in the life of an individual as well: innocence; the beginning of sin; the consummation of sinfulness; the beginning of justification; and the consummation of justification. If this or a similar pattern were to some extent true, then general history would have to investigate the progress which mankind makes in the indicated direction from century to century; in that case the scope of history would consist in tracing the development of these concepts in their appearance, their manifestation in the world. But this is by no means true. First of all, the philosophers themselves entertain entirely diverse opinions about the nature and selection of these, supposedly dominant, ideas. Furthermore they very wisely restrict their views to only a few nations in the history of the world, while regarding the life of all the others as naught, as a mere supplement. Otherwise it could not be overlooked for a moment that from the beginning to the present day the nations of the world have developed in the most diverse manner.

There are really only two ways of acquiring knowledge about human affairs: through the perception of the particular, or through abstraction; the latter is the method of philosophy, the former of history. There is no other way, and even revelation comprehends both abstract doctrines and history. One must distinguish clearly between these two sources of knowledge. Nevertheless those historians are also mistaken who consider history simply an immense aggregate of particular facts, which it behooves one to commit to memory. Whence follows the practice of heaping particulars upon particulars, held together only by some general moral principle. I believe rather that the discipline of history—at its highest—is itself called upon, and is able, to lift itself in its own fashion from the investigation and observation of particulars to a universal view of events, to a knowledge of the objectively existing relatedness.

Two qualities, I think, are required for the making of the true historian: first he must feel a participation and pleasure in the particular for itself. If he has a real affection for this human race in all its manifold variety to which we ourselves belong, an affection for this creature that is always the same yet forever different, so good and so evil, so noble and so bestial, so cultured and so brutal, striving for eternity yet enslaved by the moment, so happy and so wretched, content with so little and yet craving so much! If he feels this affection for the living being as such, then he will—without considering the progress of events—enjoy seeing how man has perennially contrived to live. He will readily follow the virtues which man sought, the faults which could be detected in him, his fortune and misfortune, the development of his nature under such diverse conditions, his institutions and his morals, and—so as to encompass everything—also the kings under whom men have lived, the sequence of events, and the development of major enterprises—and all this he will try to follow without any purpose beyond the pleasure in individual life itself. Just as one takes delight in flowers without thinking to what genus of Linnaeus or to what order and family of Oken[1] they belong; in short, without thinking how the whole manifests itself in the particular.

Still, this does not suffice; the historian must keep his eye on the universal aspect of things. He will have no preconceived ideas as does the philosopher; rather, while he reflects on the particular, the development of the world in general will become apparent to him. This development, however, is not related to universal concepts which might have prevailed at one time or another, but to completely different factors. There is no nation on earth that has not had some contact with other nations. It is through this external relationship, which in turn depends on a nation's peculiar character, that the nation enters on the stage of world history, and universal history must therefore focus on it. Some nations on earth were armed with this power before others and these came to exert a preeminent influence on the rest. The transformations which, for better or for worse, the world has experienced, will be seen to have originated chiefly in these nations. Hence we ought not to focus our attention on those general concepts which to some men appear as the dominant forces, but on those nations themselves that have played a preeminent, active role in history. We should concern ourselves with the influence which these nations have had on one another, with the struggles they have waged with one another, with their development in peace and war. For it would be completely wrong to see in the struggles of historic powers solely the operation of brute force and thus to seize only upon the ephemeral element of the phenomenon; for no state has ever subsisted without a spiritual base and a spiritual substance. In power itself there appears a spiritual substance, an original genius, which has a life of its own, fulfills conditions more or less peculiar to itself, and creates for itself its own domain. The task of history is the observation of this life which cannot be characterized through One thought or One word; the spirit which manifests itself in the world is not to be so confined; its presence suffuses the bounds of its existence; nothing is accidental in it, its appearance has its grounds in everything.

A FRAGMENT FROM THE 1860's

We must concede that history can never possess the unity of a philosophical system, but it does have an inner connection of its own. We see before us a series of events which follow one another and are conditioned by one another. If I say "conditioned," I certainly do not mean conditioned through absolute necessity. The important point is rather that human freedom makes its appearance everywhere, and the greatest attraction of history lies in the fact that it deals with the scenes of this freedom.

This freedom, however, is accompanied by force, by primal force. Without this force, freedom could exist neither in the course of events nor in the realm of ideas. At any moment, something new may spring up again, which can only be traced back to the original, common source of human behavior. Nothing exists entirely for the sake of something else; nothing is contained entirely in the reality of another. Still there prevails a deep, pervasive connection as well, of which no one is entirely independent and which penetrates everywhere. Freedom and necessity exist side by side. Necessity inheres in all that has already been formed and that cannot be undone, which is the basis of all new, emerging activity. What developed in the past constitutes the connection with what is emerging in the present. But this connection is not something arbitrarily assumed: it existed in a particular way and could be no other. It, too, is a proper object of knowledge. A longer series of concurrent and successive events linked together in such a relationship forms a century, an epoch. The disparity of epochs is due to the fact that the clash of the two antagonistic principles of freedom and necessity gives rise to new ages and new conditions. If we picture this sequence of centuries, each with its unique essence, all linked together, then we shall have attained universal history, from the very beginning to the present day. Universal history comprehends the past life of mankind, not in its particular relations and trends, but in its fullness and totality.

The discipline of universal history differs from specialized research in that universal history, while investigating the particular never loses sight of the complete whole, on which it is working.

The study of particulars, even of a single detail, has its value, if it is done well. Concerned with human affairs, it will always reveal something of immediate interest; even when dealing with minutiae, it is instructive, since everything human is worth knowing. But this specialized study, too, will always be related to a larger context; even local history will be related to the history of the whole country, a biography to the history of a major event in church and state, to an epoch of national or universal history. But all of these epochs themselves, as we have noted, belong in turn to the entire whole which we call universal history. The study of these epochs in a wider context is of a correspondingly greater value. The final goal—not yet attained—always remains the conception and composition of a history of mankind. Given the course which historical studies have taken in recent times and which must be continued insofar as history is to produce studies embodying thorough research and precise knowledge, there does exist the danger of losing sight of the universal, of the type of knowledge everyone desires. For history is not simply an academic subject: the knowledge of the history of mankind should be a common property of humanity and should above all benefit our own nation, without which our work could not have been accomplished.

There is no need to fear that we may end up in the vague generalities with which former generations were satisfied. After the success and effectiveness of the diligently and effectively pursued studies which have everywhere been undertaken, these generalities could now no longer be advanced. Nor can we return to those abstract categories which people used to entertain at various times. An accumulation of historical notes, with a superficial judgment of human character and morality, is just as unlikely to lead to thorough and satisfactory knowledge. In my opinion, we must work in two directions: the investigation of the effective factors in historical events and the understanding of their universal relationship.

To comprehend the whole while obeying the dictates of exact research will of course always remain an ideal goal, for it would comprise a solidly rooted understanding of the entire history of man. The investigation of a single detail already requires profound and very penetrating study. At the present time, however, we are all agreed that the critical method, objective research, and synthetic construction can and must go together. Historical research will not suffer from its connection with the universal; without this link, research would become enfeebled, and without exact research the conception of the universal would degenerate into a phantasm.

NATIONAL HISTORY AND
LIBERALISM: *Thierry*

[Augustin Thierry (1795-1856) epitomized the romantic historiography of the first half of the nineteenth century. After brief periods as secretary to Saint-Simon and as free-lance journalist, Thierry turned to history, publishing his first historical writings as letters in a newspaper. Drawn to his subject by a passion for liberty and guided by a fine sense of detail and development, he became, next to Guizot, the leading French historian of the time. His narrative style reflected the influence of his two masters, Chateaubriand and Sir Walter Scott. In 1826 he published the *History of the Norman Conquest of England* and in 1840 the *Récits des Temps Mérovingiens*. In these works he introduced his major historical interests: the racial antagonisms between conqueror and conquered, the rise of the communes in France, and the growth of the Third Estate. Although he had become blind in 1826, he was appointed by Guizot to direct the projected *Récueil des Monuments Inédits de L'Histoire du Tiers Etat,* and before his death he completed his own work on the history of the Third Estate in France.

The Preface to the Letters on the History of France (1820) and a part of the first letter were translated for this volume by J. Christopher Herold. Some of Thierry's foot-notes were omitted.]

PREFACE: *Letters on the History of France*

Of the twenty-five letters that make up this collection, ten were published in the *Courrier Français* toward the end of 1820; the others now appear in print for the first time. The many historical questions dealt with in the latter all bear directly on two main topics—the formation of the French nation and the communal revolution. I have tried to determine the exact point at which the history of the Frankish kings turns into the history of France, and to present in its true character the greatest social change to have taken place from the establishment of Christianity to the French Revolution.

As for the ten letters published earlier, their general intent was to subject to a rigorous examination several works on the history of France then regarded as classics. A few words of explanation are needed to show the motives that made me decide to reproduce almost textually these critical essays although the judgments they pronounce on our manner of writing and looking at history have become somewhat outdated after seven years.

In 1817 my predominant concern was to contribute my share to the triumph of constitutionalism. As a result I turned to historical works to find corroboration of my political beliefs. Giving myself over to these labors with all the ardor of youth, I soon noticed that history attracted me for its own sake, as a picture of past times, quite independently of the lessons I drew from it for the present. Though still subordinating the facts to the uses I expected to derive from them, I observed them with curiosity even when they proved nothing in favor of the cause I hoped to serve, and whenever a personality or an event of the Middle Ages appeared to me endowed with a little life or local color, I felt an involuntary emotion. This often-repeated experience soon upset all my notions of literature. By imperceptible degrees, I abandoned modern books for ancient ones, histories for chronicles, and then I thought I could catch a glimpse of the truth which our writers had stifled under their conventional formulas and pompous style. I endeavored to erase from my mind everything they had taught me; I rebelled, as it were, against my masters. The more renowned and trusted the author, the more I grew indignant at having believed him on his simple say-so and at seeing a crowd of people as credulous and as deceived _learned to question theories_

as I had been. Such was my frame of mind when, during the latter part of 1820, I addressed the ten letters mentioned above to the editor of the *Courrier Français*.

In those days, the histories by Velly and Anquetil were considered very instructive, and if somebody wanted to mention a solid work, he would cite Mably's *Observations* or Touret's *Abrégé*. M. de Sismondi's *History of the French,* M. Guizot's *Essays on the History of France,* and M. de Barante's *History of the Dukes of Burgundy,* had not yet appeared in print. I was justified, then, in saying that our modern historians described the events of the Middle Ages in a wholly false light. This I did with a zeal that earned me the gratitude of some people and saved my critical and historical essays from being utterly forgotten in the columns of the journal in which they were more or less buried. I had to go into these details in order to explain my silence on works that mark a genuine revolution in French historiography. A new road has been opened—by M. de Sismondi, to the science of facts; by M. Guizot, to breadth of view and subtlety of insight; by M. de Barante, to narrative truth.[1] The best one can do is follow in their footsteps. However, new ideas in order to prevail must overcome the tenacity of old habits, and in the book trade as in all other trades articles of long-established manufacture are assured of a market for a long time; therefore, a frontal attack on the false science may still be useful, even though the true science is already on the rise and the best thinking minds are beginning to rally around it.

There is no escaping the fact that, as concerns the history of France prior to the seventeenth century, public conviction, if I may use the expression, must be remolded from the bottom up. The various elements that constitute this conviction are either radically wrong or, at least, vitiated by some falsehoods. For instance, it would be difficult to think of two axioms of geometry more universally accepted than these two propositions: "Clovis was the founder of the French monarchy" and "Louis the Fat enfranchised the communes." Yet neither proposition stands up in the light of the facts such as they appear in the testimony of the time. But what is printed in so many books, taught by so many professors, and repeated by so many students must needs take on the authority of law and prevail over the facts themselves. Remembering the painful labors that were the price I had to pay for achieving my historical re-education alone and unguided, I wish to make this work easier for others who would undertake it and to substitute a little truth for the inanities of the schoolmasters,[2] and the prejudices of the public. To these prejudices, born of a lack of solid and conscientious study, I oppose the original documents of the past as well as that experience of political life which is among the privileges we enjoy in our own eventful era. No man of sense need accept the empty monarchic or republican abstractions offered by the writers of the old régime when all he has to do is call upon his own recollections and use them as a check on what he has read or heard about events long past: before long he will sense something alive stirring in the dust of vanished times. For there is not one among us children of the nineteenth century who does not know more on the score of rebellions and conquests, of the dismemberment of empires, of the fall and restoration of monarchies, of popular revolutions and the consequent reactions, than did Velly or Mably, or even Voltaire himself.

Something remains to be said of the method I followed in writing these letters. The majority are dissertations mingled with narratives and fragments from the original historians. There are certain specific events whose character has been long misunderstood and which, seen in their true perspective, can shed new light on the history of several centuries. In fact, I favored this kind of demonstration over any other wherever it was possible to make use of it. In matters historical, simple exposition is the safest method, and to introduce the subtleties of logical argumentation is not without danger to the truth. If I lavished so much detail on the political history of certain French towns, it was in order to conform to this principle. I wished to emphasize the democratic character of the process that led to the establishment of the communes, and I thought that I could do this more successfully by abandoning argumentation in favor of narration, putting myself in the background and letting the events speak. A naïve account of the insurrection of Laon and of the civil disturbances in Rheims will teach us more than would a learned theory on the origin of the Third Estate, which many people think suddenly sprang up from beneath the earth in 1789. It is true that this Third Estate, preferring peace to all other goods, feigned sleep during two centuries and thus caused itself to be forgotten; but its first appearance on the stage of political events foreshadowed those displays of energy, patriotism, and violence by which it was to distinguish itself in our times. Perhaps history has no place in the struggles and clashes of ideas of our days—but since it is persistently drawn into these debates, as happens every day, an important lesson may be drawn from it: that no one in France is anyone's freedman; that none of our rights is of recent origin; and that the present generation owes all its liberties to the courage of the generations that preceded it.

FIRST LETTER: *On the Need for a True History of France and on the Chief Defect of the Existing Histories*

In this era of political passions, at a time when an active mind can scarcely avoid taking part in the general ferment, I believe that I have found a way to peace in the serious study of history. By this I do not mean that the contemplation of the past and the experience of the ages have led me to write off as a youthful illusion the love of liberty with which I had set out: quite the contrary, I am becoming more and more attached to it. I still cherish liberty, but with a less impatient love. I remind myself that at all times, in all places, many men could be found who felt the same aspirations that I feel, even though their situations and opinions were different from mine, but that most of them died before they could witness the fulfillment of what they had anticipated in thought. The labors of this world are accomplished slowly, and each successive generation merely adds one more stone to the construction of the edifice dreamt of by ardent minds. This conviction of mine, which is sober rather than sad, does not free the individual from his obligation to keep within a straight path and to ignore the temptations of self-interest and vanity; nor does it release a people from its duty to maintain its national dignity. Indeed, if it is merely a misfortune to suffer oppression imposed by the force of circumstances, it is shameful to display servility.

I may be mistaken, but I believe that our patriotism would gain a great deal both in selflessness and in steadfastness if the knowledge of history, and particularly of French history, were more widely diffused among us and were to become in a certain sense more popular. If our eyes could sweep over that long-traveled road along which we are following our fathers, we would detach ourselves from the quarrels of the day, from the resentments of personal ambition and of partisanship, from petty fears and petty hopes. Our sense of security, our confidence in the future would be strengthened if we all realized that even in the most difficult times this country never lacked champions of justice and liberty. The spirit of independence is as firmly stamped on our history as on that of any other nation, ancient or modern. Our forefathers understood the meaning of liberty, they desired it as strongly as we do, and if they have failed to hand it down to us in its fullness and entirety, the fault was not theirs but that of human imperfection, for they overcame more obstacles than we shall ever encounter.

But is there a history of France which faithfully reproduces the ideas, the emotions, the social life of the men whose names we bear and whose destinies shaped ours? I think not. The study of our antiquities has convinced me of the exact opposite, and this want of a national history may have helped to prolong the instability of our opinions and the irritability of our minds. The true history of our nation, the history which would deserve to become popular, still lies buried in the dust of contemporary chronicles. No one has had the thought of rescuing it from there, and the inexact, falsified, and colorless compilations which, for lack of a better word, we honor by the name of "histories of France" continue to be reprinted. In those vague and pompous narratives, in which a few privileged personages monopolize the historic stage while the mass of the whole nation is hidden behind the mantles of the courtiers, we find neither serious instruction, nor any lessons applicable to ourselves, nor that sympathy which in general interests men in the fate of those who resemble them. Our provinces, our towns, all the things which each of us subsumes in his affections under the name of fatherland, should be shown such as they were in each century of the fatherland's existence; instead, we get nothing but the domestic annals of the ruling dynasty, births, marriages, deaths, palace intrigues, and wars that are indistinguishable from one another and whose episodes, invariably told with inadequate detail, lack life and color.

I have no doubt that many readers are beginning to become aware of the faults inherent in the methods of our modern historians. Under the delusion that history is something that comes all ready-made, these writers are content to accept their material such as they find it in the works of their immediate predecessors, whom they try to surpass only as literary craftsmen, by the splendor and purity of their style. I believe that the first historians courageous enough to set a new course and to go back to the very sources of history will find the public disposed to encourage and to follow them. But the labor of assembling into a single narrative body all the scattered or unknown details of our real history will be a long and arduous one; it will require great gifts and rare sagacity, and I hasten to say that I am not so presumptuous as to undertake it. Though drawn toward the study of history by an irresistible attraction, I am careful not to mistake the fire of my enthusiasm for a sign of talent. Deep inside, I bear the firm conviction that we do not yet possess a history of France, and my sole ambition is to share my conviction with the public; for I am certain that out of so vast a concourse of perceptive and active minds someone will soon emerge who will be worthy of fulfilling this sublime task—to be the historian of our country. Yet whoever would wish to attain this goal will have to test his powers thoroughly before he begins. A mere capacity for admiring so-called heroes is not enough: a broader basis of feeling and judgment is needed—love of people as people, regardless of fame or social rank, and a lively enough sensibility to enable him to attach himself to the destiny of a whole nation and to follow it through the centuries as one follows a friend in a perilous voyage.

This sensibility, which is the soul of history, was lacking in the writers who, up to this day, have written ours. They lacked the quickening sympathy which goes out to the mass of humanity and which embraces, as it were, entire nations. Their marked preference for certain historic figures, certain ways of life, certain classes, deprives their accounts of the true individuality of the nation. We vainly look to their writings if we want to discover our ancestors without distinction of rank or birth. Now, Heaven forbid that I should expect the history of France to trace the genealogy of each family. What I expect is that it should seek out the root of the interests, the passions, the ideas that are agitating us, uniting us, or dividing us; that it should uncover and trace to their origin the tracks of those irresistible emotions which pull each of us into one or the other of the several political parties and which exalt or lead astray our minds. There is nothing entirely new in anything we have witnessed in the past fifty years; and just as our names and descent enable us to trace our links with the Frenchmen who lived before the eighteenth century, just so our ideas and hopes and desires would link us to them, if only their thoughts and actions were faithfully reproduced for us.

Our distant predecessors in our quest for political freedom were the medieval townsmen [*bourgeois*] who six hundred years ago restored the walls and the civilization of the ancient municipalities. Let there be no mistake: these were worthy men, and the most numerous and most forgotten class of our nation deserves a new life in our history. It should not be imagined that the middle class or the common people awakened but yesterday to patriotism and action. If one lacks the courage to recognize the grandeur and generosity that animated the insurrections which from the eleventh to the thirteenth century resulted in the rise of communes throughout France, the revolts of the burgher class, and even the Jacqueries of the fourteenth century—even then he need but choose some other period, not of civil strife but of foreign invasion, and he will see that on the score of self-sacrifice and enthusiasm the Third Estate [*le dernier ordre de l'état*] never lagged behind the others. Whence came the succor which chased the English out of France and restored Charles VII to his throne when everything seemed lost and when all the military talent of the Dunois and Lahires could accomplish was to organize orderly retreats and avoid disaster? Was it not from an upsurge of patriotic fanaticism in the ranks of the poor hirelings and of the town and village militias? The religious aspect which this glorious revolution assumed was merely its form—the most vigorous symbol of popular inspiration. It is not to our historical classics but to the memoirs of the period that we must go in order to read about the naïve though bizarre aspects assumed by that inspiration of the mass—the mass which always acts impulsively, rarely gives the appearance of wisdom, and yet sweeps everything before it.

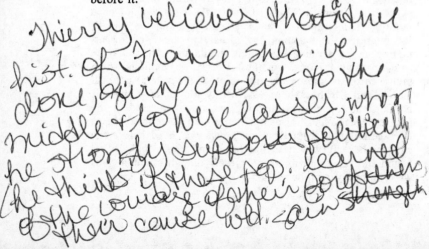

HISTORY AND LITERATURE:
Macaulay

[Thomas Babington Macaulay's (1800-1859) gifts were perfectly attuned to the possibilities of his age. Ambitious, self-confident, and deeply patriotic, Macaulay moved with ease from the House of Commons, to the Supreme Council of India, and finally to the Cabinet. His *History of England from the Accession of James II* (5 vols. 1849-1861) brought him uncommon fame and rewards throughout the English-speaking world. For this history of the Glorious Revolution and the years immediately following he was admirably prepared by his extensive research, his remarkable memory, and his wide general reading. The enthusiastic reception of the *History* can be attributed to its tone of untroubled certainty about the merits of the age—the triumph of liberty and wealth in England and the triumph of England in the world—and to the utterly lucid style which Macaulay had wrought with great pains so that the pages would "read as if they had been spoken off, and may seem to flow as easily as table talk." Later critics boggled at the shallow assurance of his judicial pronouncements on men and events, but only after the success of the novel "Whig interpretation" had become firmly established, a historical force itself. Though largely a political history, the celebrated third chapter belongs to the best that has been written in social history and fulfilled Macaulay's promise "to trace the progress of useful and ornamental arts, to describe the rise of religious sects and the changes of literary

taste, to portray the manners of successive generations, and
not to pass by with neglect even the revolutions which have
taken place in dress, furniture, repasts, and public amusements." Macaulay's essay "History," reprinted below, with
some passages omitted, appeared in the *Edinburgh Review*
in 1828, when he was 28. This essay, with a still earlier one
on Milton, established him as one of the leading young literary
men of England.]

HISTORY[1]

To write history respectably—that is, to abbreviate des-
patches, and make extracts from speeches, to intersperse in
due proportion epithets of praise and abhorrence, to draw up
antithetical characters of great men, setting forth how many
contradictory virtues and vices they united, and abounding
in *withs* and *withouts*—all this is very easy. But to be a
really great historian is perhaps the rarest of intellectual distinctions. Many scientific works are, in their kind, absolutely
perfect. There are poems which we should be inclined to
designate as faultless, or as disfigured only by blemishes
which pass unnoticed in the general blaze of excellence.
There are speeches, some speeches of Demosthenes particularly, in which it would be impossible to alter a word without
altering it for the worse. But we are acquainted with no
history which approaches to our notion of what a history
ought to be—with no history which does not widely depart,
either on the right hand or on the left, from the exact line.

The cause may easily be assigned. This province of literature is a debatable land. It lies on the confines of two distinct
territories. It is under the jurisdiction of two hostile powers;
and, like other districts similarly situated, it is ill defined, ill
cultivated, and ill regulated. Instead of being equally shared
between its two rulers, the Reason and the Imagination, it
falls alternately under the sole and absolute dominion of
each. It is sometimes fiction; it is sometimes theory.

History, it has been said, is philosophy teaching by examples. Unhappily, what the philosophy gains in soundness
and depth the examples generally lose in vividness. A perfect
historian must possess an imagination sufficiently powerful
to make his narrative affecting and picturesque. Yet he must
control it so absolutely as to content himself with the materials which he finds, and to refrain from supplying de-

ficiencies by additions of his own. He must be a profound
and ingenious reasoner. Yet he must possess sufficient self-
command to abstain from casting his facts in the mould of
his hypothesis. Those who can justly estimate these almost
insuperable difficulties will not think it strange that every
writer should have failed, either in the narrative or in the
speculative department of history.

It may be laid down as a general rule, though subject to
considerable qualifications and exceptions, that history begins
in novel and ends in essay. Of the romantic historians Herodotus is the earliest and the best. His animation, his simple-
hearted tenderness, his wonderful talent for description and
dialogue, and the pure sweet flow of his language, place him
at the head of narrators. He reminds us of a delightful child.
There is a grace beyond the reach of affectation in his awkwardness, a malice in his innocence, an intelligence in his
nonsense, an insinuating eloquence in his lisp. We know of
no writer who makes such interest for himself and his book
in the heart of the reader. At the distance of three-and-
twenty centuries, we feel for him the same sort of pitying
fondness which Fontaine and Gay are said to have inspired
in society. He has written an incomparable book. He has
written something better, perhaps, than the best history; but
he has not written a good history; he is, from the first to the
last chapter, an inventor. We do not here refer merely to
those gross fictions with which he has been reproached by
the critics of later times. We speak of that colouring which is
equally diffused over his whole narrative, and which perpetually leaves the most sagacious reader in doubt what to
reject and what to receive. The most authentic parts of his
work bear the same relation to his wildest legends which
Henry the Fifth bears to the *Tempest*. There was an expedi-
tion undertaken by Xerxes against Greece, and there was an
invasion of France. There was a battle at Platæa, and there
was a battle at Agincourt. Cambridge and Exeter, the Con-
stable and the Dauphin, were persons as real as Demaratus
and Pausanias. The harangue of the Archbishop on the Salic
Law and the Book of Numbers differs much less from the
orations which have in all ages proceeded from the right
reverend bench than the speeches of Mardonius and
Artabanus from those which were delivered at the council-
board of Susa. Shakspeare gives us enumerations of armies,
and returns of killed and wounded, which are not, we suspect,
much less accurate than those of Herodotus. There are pas-

sages in Herodotus nearly as long as acts of Shakspeare, in which everything is told dramatically, and in which the narrative serves only the purpose of stage-directions. It is possible, no doubt, that the substance of some real conversations may have been reported to the historian. But events which, if they ever happened, happened in ages and nations so remote that the particulars could never have been known to him, are related with the greatest minuteness of detail. We have all that Candaules said to Gyges, and all that passed between Astyages and Harpagus. We are, therefore, unable to judge whether, in the account which he gives of transactions respecting which he might possibly have been well informed, we can trust to anything beyond the naked outline; whether, for example, the answer of Gelon to the ambassadors of the Grecian confederacy, or the expressions which passed between Aristides and Themistocles at their famous interview, have been correctly transmitted to us. The great events are, no doubt, faithfully related. So, probably, are many of the slighter circumstances; but which of them it is impossible to ascertain. The fictions are so much like the facts, and the facts so much like the fictions, that, with respect to many most interesting particulars, our belief is neither given nor withheld, but remains in an uneasy and interminable state of abeyance. We know that there is truth, but we cannot exactly decide where it lies.

The faults of Herodotus are the faults of a simple and imaginative mind. Children and servants are remarkably Herodotean in their style of narration. They tell everything dramatically. Their *says hes* and *says shes* are proverbial. Every person who has had to settle their disputes knows that, even when they have no intention to deceive, their reports of conversation always require to be carefully sifted. If an educated man were giving an account of the late change of administration, he would say—"Lord Goderich resigned; and the King, in consequence, sent for the Duke of Wellington." A porter tells the story as if he had been hid behind the curtains of the royal bed at Windsor: "So Lord Goderich says, 'I cannot manage this business; I must go out.' So the King says—says he, 'Well, then, I must send for the Duke of Wellington—that's all.' " This is in the very manner of the father of history. . . .

The history of Thucydides differs from that of Herodotus as a portrait differs from the representation of an imaginary scene; as the Burke or Fox of Reynolds differs from his Ugolino or his Beaufort. In the former case the archetype is given, in the latter it is created. The faculties which are required for the latter purpose are of a higher and rarer order than those which suffice for the former, and, indeed, necessarily comprise them. He who is able to paint what he sees with the eye of the mind will surely be able to paint what he sees with the eye of the body. He who can invent a story, and tell it well, will also be able to tell, in an interesting manner, a story which he has not invented. If, in practice, some of the best writers of fiction have been among the worst writers of history, it has been because one of their talents had merged in another so completely that it could not be severed; because, having long been habituated to invent and narrate at the same time, they found it impossible to narrate without inventing.

Some capricious and discontented artists have affected to consider portrait-painting as unworthy of a man of genius. Some critics have spoken in the same contemptuous manner of history. Johnson puts the case thus: The historian tells either what is false or what is true: in the former case he is no historian; in the latter he has no opportunity for displaying his abilities: for truth is one; and all who tell the truth must tell it alike.

It is not difficult to elude both the horns of this dilemma. We will recur to the analogous art of portrait-painting. Any man with eyes and hands may be taught to take a likeness. The process, up to a certain point, is merely mechanical. If this were all, a man of talents might justly despise the occupation. But we could mention portraits which are resemblances—but not mere resemblances; faithful—but much more than faithful; portraits which condense into one point of time, and exhibit at a single glance the whole history of turbid and eventful lives—in which the eye seems to scrutinise us, and the mouth to command us—in which the brow menaces, and the lip almost quivers with scorn—in which every wrinkle is a comment on some important transaction. The account which Thucydides has given of the retreat from Syracuse is, among narratives, what Vandyck's Lord Strafford is among paintings.

Diversity, it is said, implies error: truth is one, and admits of no degrees. We answer that this principle holds good only in abstract reasonings. When we talk of the truth of imitation in the fine arts, we mean an imperfect and a graduated truth. No picture is exactly like the original; nor is a picture good in proportion as it is like the original. When Sir Thomas Lawrence paints a handsome peeress, he does not contemplate her through a powerful microscope, and transfer to the canvas the pores of the skin, the blood-vessels of the eye, and all the other beauties which Gulliver discovered in the Brobdingnagian maids of honour. If he were to do this, the effect would not merely be unpleasant, but, unless the scale of the picture were proportionably enlarged, would be absolutely *false*. And, after all, a microscope of greater power than that which he had employed would convict him of innumerable omissions. The same may be said of history. Perfectly and absolutely true it cannot be; for, to be perfectly and absolutely true, it ought to record *all* the slightest particulars of the slightest transactions—all the things done and all the words uttered during the time of which it treats. The omission of any circumstance, however insignificant, would be a defect. If history were written thus, the Bodleian library would not contain the occurrences of a week. What is told in the fullest and most accurate annals bears an infinitely small proportion to what is suppressed. The difference between the copious work of Clarendon and the account of the civil wars in the abridgment of Goldsmith vanishes when compared with the immense mass of facts respecting which both are equally silent.

No picture, then, and no history, can present us with the whole truth: but those are the best pictures and the best histories which exhibit such parts of the truth as most nearly produce the effect of the whole. He who is deficient in the art of selection may, by showing nothing but the truth, produce all the effect of the grossest falsehood. It perpetually happens that one writer tells less truth than another, merely because he tells more truths. In the imitative arts we constantly see this. There are lines in the human face, and objects in landscape, which stand in such relations to each other that they ought either to be all introduced into a painting together or all omitted together. A sketch into which none of them enters may be excellent; but, if some are given and others left out, though there are more points of likeness, there is less likeness. An outline scrawled with a pen, which seizes the marked features of a countenance, will give a much stronger idea of it than a bad painting in oils. Yet the worst painting in oils that ever hung at Somerset House resembles the original in many more particulars. A bust of white marble may give an excellent idea of a blooming face. Colour the lips and cheeks of the bust, leaving the hair and eyes unaltered, and the similarity, instead of being more striking, will be less so.

History has its foreground and its background; and it is principally in the management of its perspective that one artist differs from another. Some events must be represented on a large scale, others diminished; the great majority will be lost in the dimness of the horizon; and a general idea of their joint effect will be given by a few slight touches.

In this respect no writer has ever equalled Thucydides. He was a perfect master of the art of gradual diminution. His history is sometimes as concise as a chronological chart; yet it is always perspicuous. It is sometimes as minute as one of Lovelace's letters; yet it is never prolix. He never fails to contract and to expand it in the right place.

Thucydides borrowed from Herodotus the practice of putting speeches of his own into the mouths of his characters. In Herodotus this usage is scarcely censurable. It is of a piece with his whole manner. But it is altogether incongruous in the work of his successor, and violates, not only the accuracy of history, but the decencies of fiction. When once we enter into the spirit of Herodotus, we find no inconsistency. The conventional probability of his drama is preserved from the beginning to the end. The deliberate orations and the familiar dialogues are in strict keeping with each other. But the speeches of Thucydides are neither preceded nor followed by anything with which they harmonise. They give to the whole book something of the grotesque character of those Chinese pleasure-grounds in which perpendicular rocks of granite start up in the midst of a soft green plain. Invention is shocking where truth is in such close juxtaposition with it.

Thucydides honestly tells us that some of these discourses are purely fictitious. He may have reported the substance of others correctly. But it is clear from the internal evidence that he has preserved no more than the substance. His own peculiar habits of thought and expression are everywhere discernible. Individual and national peculiarities are seldom to be traced in the sentiments, and never in the diction. The oratory of the Corinthians and Thebans is not less Attic, either in matter or in manner, than that of the Athenians. The style of Cleon is as pure, as austere, as terse, and as significant as that of Pericles.

In spite of this great fault, it must be allowed that Thu-

cydides has surpassed all his rivals in the art of historical
narration, in the art of producing an effect on the imagination, by skilful selection and disposition, without indulging
in the licence of invention. But narration, though an important part of the business of a historian, is not the whole.
To append a moral to a work of fiction is either useless or
superfluous. A fiction may give a more impressive effect to
what is already known, but it can teach nothing new. If it
presents to us characters and trains of events to which our
experience furnishes us with nothing similar, instead of de-
riving instruction from it, we pronounce it unnatural. We do
not form our opinions from it, but we try it by our preconceived opinions. Fiction, therefore, is essentially imitative.
Its merit consists in its resemblance to a model with which
we are already familiar, or to which at least we can instantly
refer. Hence it is that the anecdotes which interest us most
strongly in authentic narrative are offensive when introduced
into novels; that what is called the romantic part of history
is in fact the least romantic. It is delightful as history, because
it contradicts our previous notions of human nature, and of
the connection of causes and effects. It is, on that very account, shocking and incongruous in fiction. In fiction, the
principles are given, to find the facts: in history, the facts
are given, to find the principles; and the writer who does not
explain the phenomena as well as state them performs only
one half of his office. Facts are the mere dross of history. It is
from the abstract truth which interpenetrates them, and lies
latent among them like gold in the ore, that the mass derives
its whole value: and the precious particles are generally combined with the baser in such a manner that the separation is
a task of the utmost difficulty. . . .

We begin, like the priest in Don Quixote's library, to
be tired with taking down books one after another for separate judgment, and feel inclined to pass sentence on them in
masses. We shall, therefore, instead of pointing out the defects and merits of the different modern historians, state
generally in what particulars they have surpassed their predecessors, and in what we conceive them to have failed.

They have certainly been, in one sense, far more strict in
their adherence to truth than most of the Greek and Roman
writers. They do not think themselves entitled to render their
narrative interesting by introducing descriptions, conversations, and harangues which have no existence but in their

own imagination. This improvement was gradually introduced. History commenced among the modern nations of
Europe, as it had commenced among the Greeks, in romance.
Froissart was our Herodotus. Italy was to Europe what Athens
was to Greece. In Italy, therefore, a more accurate and manly
mode of narration was early introduced. Machiavelli and
Guicciardini, in imitation of Livy and Thucydides, composed
speeches for their historical personages. But, as the classical
enthusiasm which distinguished the age of Lorenzo and Leo
gradually subsided, this absurd practice was abandoned. In
France, we fear, it still, in some degree, keeps its ground. In
our own country, a writer who should venture on it would be
laughed to scorn. Whether the historians of the last two
centuries tell more truth than those of antiquity, may perhaps
be doubted. But it is quite certain that they tell fewer falsehoods.

In the philosophy of history the moderns have very far
surpassed the ancients. It is not, indeed, strange that the
Greeks and Romans should not have carried the science of
government, or any other experimental science, so far as it
has been carried in our time; for the experimental sciences
are generally in a state of progression. They were better
understood in the seventeenth century than in the sixteenth,
and in the eighteenth century than in the seventeenth. But
this constant improvement, this natural growth of knowledge,
will not altogether account for the immense superiority of
the modern writers. The difference is a difference not in
degree but of kind. It is not merely that new principles have
been discovered, but that new faculties seem to be exerted.
It is not that at one time the human intellect should have
made but small progress, and at another time have advanced
far, but that at one time it should have been stationary, and
at another time constantly proceeding. In taste and imagination, in the graces of style, in the arts of persuasion, in the
magnificence of public works, the ancients were at least our
equals. They reasoned as justly as ourselves on subjects which
required pure demonstration. But in the moral sciences they
made scarcely any advance. During the long period which
elapsed between the fifth century before the Christian era
and the fifth century after it, little perceptible progress was
made. All the metaphysical discoveries of all the philosophers,
from the time of Socrates to the northern invasion, are not to
be compared in importance with those which have been made
in England every fifty years since the time of Elizabeth.

There is not the least reason to believe that the principles of government, legislation, and political economy were better understood in the time of Augustus Caesar than in the time of Pericles. In our own country the sound doctrines of trade and jurisprudence have been, within the lifetime of a single generation, dimly hinted, boldly propounded, defended, systematised, adopted by all reflecting men of all parties, quoted in legislative assemblies, incorporated into laws and treaties. . . .

Hence it is that in generalisation the writers of modern times have far surpassed those of antiquity. The historians of our own country are unequalled in depth and precision of reason; and even in the works of our mere compilers we often meet with speculations beyond the reach of Thucydides or Tacitus.

But it must at the same time be admitted that they have characteristic faults, so closely connected with their characteristic merits, and of such magnitude, that it may well be doubted whether, on the whole, this department of literature has gained or lost during the last two-and-twenty centuries.

The best historians of later times have been seduced from truth, not by their imagination but by their reason. They far excel their predecessors in the art of deducing general principles from facts. But unhappily they have fallen into the error of distorting facts to suit general principles. They arrive at a theory from looking at some of the phenomena; and the remaining phenomena they strain or curtail to suit the theory. For this purpose it is not necessary that they should assert what is absolutely false; for all questions in morals and politics are questions of comparison and degree. Any proposition which does not involve a contradiction in terms may by possibility be true; and if all the circumstances which raise a probability in its favour be stated and enforced, and those which lead to an opposite conclusion be omitted or lightly passed over, it may appear to be demonstrated. In every human character and transaction there is a mixture of good and evil: a little exaggeration, a little suppression, a judicious use of epithets, a watchful and searching scepticism with respect to the evidence on one side, a convenient credulity with respect to every report or tradition on the other, may easily make a saint of Laud, or a tyrant of Henry the Fourth.

This species of misrepresentation abounds in the most valuable works of modern historians. Herodotus tells his like a slovenly witness, who, heated by partialities and prejudices, unacquainted with the established rules of evidence, and uninstructed as to the obligations of his oath, confounds what he imagines with what he has seen and heard, and brings out facts, reports, conjectures, and fancies in one mass. Hume is an accomplished advocate. Without positively asserting much more than he can prove, he gives prominence to all the circumstances which support his case; he glides lightly over those which are unfavourable to it; his own witnesses are applauded and encouraged; the statements which seem to throw discredit on them are controverted; the contradictions into which they fall are explained away; a clear and connected abstract of their evidence is given. Everything that is offered on the other side is scrutinised with the utmost severity; every suspicious circumstance is a ground for comment and invective; what cannot be denied is extenuated or passed by without notice; concessions even are sometimes made; but this insidious candour only increases the effect of the vast mass of sophistry.

We have mentioned Hume as the ablest and most popular writer of his class; but the charge which we have brought against him is one to which all our most distinguished historians are in some degree obnoxious. Gibbon, in particular, deserves very severe censure. Of all the numerous culprits, however, none is more deeply guilty than Mr. Mitford. We willingly acknowledge the obligations which are due to his talents and industry. The modern historians of Greece had been in the habit of writing as if the world had learned nothing new during the last sixteen hundred years. Instead of illustrating the events which they narrated by the philosophy of a more enlightened age, they judged of antiquity by itself alone. They seemed to think that notions, long driven from every other corner of literature, had a prescriptive right to occupy this last fastness. They considered all the ancient historians as equally authentic. They scarcely made any distinction between him who related events at which he had himself been present, and him who, five hundred years after, composed a philosophic romance for a society which had in the interval undergone a complete change. It was all Greek, and all true! The centuries which separated Plutarch from Thucydides seemed as nothing to men who lived in an age so remote. The distance of time produced an error similar to that which is sometimes produced by distance of place. There are many good ladies who think that all the people in India

live together, and who charge a friend setting out for Cal-
cutta with kind messages to Bombay. To Rollin and
Barthelemi, in the same manner, all the classics were contemporaries.

Mr. Mitford certainly introduced great improvements; he
showed us that men who wrote in Greek and Latin sometimes told lies; he showed us that ancient history might be
related in such a manner as to furnish not only allusions to
schoolboys, but important lessons to statesmen. From that
love of theatrical effect and high-flown sentiment which had
poisoned almost every other work on the same subject his
book is perfectly free. But his passion for a theory as false,
and far more ungenerous, led him substantially to violate
truth in every page. Statements unfavourable to democracy are
made with unhesitating confidence, and with the utmost bitterness of language. Every charge brought against a monarch
or an aristocracy is sifted with the utmost care. If it cannot
be denied, some palliating supposition is suggested; or we
are at least reminded that some circumstances now unknown
may have justified what at present appears unjustifiable. Two
events are reported by the same author in the same sentence;
their truth rests on the same testimony; but the one supports
the darling hypothesis, and the other seems inconsistent with
it. The one is taken and the other is left.

The practice of distorting narrative into a conformity with
theory is a vice not so unfavourable as at first sight it may
appear to the interests of political science. We have compared the writers who indulge in it to advocates; and we may
add, that their conflicting fallacies, like those of advocates,
correct each other. It has always been held, in the most enlightened nations, that a tribunal will decide a judicial question most fairly when it has heard two able men argue, as
unfairly as possible, on the two opposite sides of it; and we
are inclined to think that this opinion is just. Sometimes, it
is true, superior eloquence and dexterity will make the
worse appear the better reason; but it is at least certain that
the judge will be compelled to contemplate the case under
two different aspects. It is certain that no important consideration will altogether escape notice.

This is at present the state of history. The poet laureate
appears for the Church of England, Lingard for the Church of
Rome. Brodie has moved to set aside the verdicts obtained by
Hume; and the cause in which Mitford succeeded is, we
understand, about to be reheard. In the midst of these dis-

putes, however, history proper, if we may use the term, is disappearing. The high, grave, impartial summing up of Thucydides is nowhere to be found.

While our historians are practising all the arts of controversy, they miserably neglect the art of narration, the art of interesting the affections and presenting pictures to the imagination. That a writer may produce these effects without violating truth is sufficiently proved by many excellent biographical works. The immense popularity which well-written books of this kind have acquired deserves the serious consideration of historians. Voltaire's *Charles the Twelfth*, Marmontel's *Memoirs*, Boswell's *Life of Johnson*, Southey's account of Nelson, are perused with delight by the most frivolous and indolent. Whenever any tolerable book of the same description makes its appearance the circulating libraries are mobbed; the book societies are in commotion; the new novel lies uncut; the magazines and newspapers fill their columns with extracts. In the meantime, histories of great empires, written by men of eminent ability, lie unread on the shelves of ostentatious libraries.

The writers of history seem to entertain an aristocratical contempt for the writers of memoirs. They think it beneath the dignity of men who describe the revolutions of nations to dwell on the details which constitute the charm of biography. They have imposed on themselves a code of conventional decencies as absurd as that which has been the bane of the French drama. The most characteristic and interesting circumstances are omitted or softened down, because, as we are told, they are too trivial for the majesty of history. The majesty of history seems to resemble the majesty of the poor King of Spain, who died a martyr to ceremony because the proper dignitaries were not at hand to render him assistance.

That history would be more amusing if this etiquette were relaxed, will, we suppose, be acknowledged. But would it be less dignified or less useful? What do we mean when we say that one past event is important and another insignificant? No past event has any intrinsic importance. The knowledge of it is valuable only as it leads us to form just calculations with respect to the future. A history which does not serve this purpose, though it may be filled with battles, treaties, and commotions, is as useless as the series of turnpike tickets collected by Sir Matthew Mite.

Let us suppose that Lord Clarendon, instead of filling

hundreds of folio pages with copies of state papers, in which the same assertions and contradictions are repeated till the reader is overpowered with weariness, had condescended to be the Boswell of the Long Parliament. Let us suppose that he had exhibited to us the wise and lofty self-government of Hampden, leading while he seemed to follow, and propounding unanswerable arguments in the strongest forms with the modest air of an inquirer anxious for information: the delusions which misled the noble spirit of Vane; the coarse fanaticism which concealed the yet loftier genius of Cromwell, destined to control a mutinous army and a factious people, to abase the flag of Holland, to arrest the victorious arms of Sweden, and to hold the balance firm between the rival monarchies of France and Spain. Let us suppose that he had made his Cavaliers and Roundheads talk in their own style; that he had reported some of the ribaldry of Rupert's pages, and some of the cant of Harrison and Fleetwood. Would not his work in that case have been more interesting? Would it not have been more accurate?

A history in which every particular incident may be true, may, on the whole, be false. The circumstances which have most influence on the happiness of mankind, the changes of manners and morals, the transition of communities from poverty to wealth, from knowledge to ignorance, from ferocity to humanity—these are, for the most part, noiseless revolutions. Their progress is rarely indicated by what historians are pleased to call important events. They are not achieved by armies, or enacted by senates. They are sanctioned by no treaties, and recorded in no archives. They are carried on in every school, in every church, behind ten thousand counters, at ten thousand firesides. The upper current of society presents no certain criterion by which we can judge of the direction in which the under current flows. We read of defeats and victories. But we know that nations may be miserable amidst victories and prosperous amidst defeats. We read of the fall of wise ministers and of the rise of profligate favourites. But we must remember how small a proportion the good or evil effected by a single statesman can bear to the good or evil of a great social system.

Bishop Watson compares a geologist to a gnat mounted on an elephant and laying down theories as to the whole internal structure of the vast animal, from the phenomena of the hide. The comparison is unjust to the geologists; but it is very applicable to those historians who write as if the

body politic were homogeneous, who look only on the surface of affairs and never think of the mighty and various
organisation which lies deep below. *fail in their task*

In the works of such writers as these, England, at the
close of the Seven Years' War, is in the highest state of
prosperity; at the close of the American war she is in a
miserable and degraded condition; as if the people were
not on the whole as rich, as well governed, and as well
educated at the latter period as at the former. We have read
books called Histories of England, under the reign of George
the Second, in which the rise of Methodism is not even
mentioned. A hundred years hence this breed of authors
will, we hope, be extinct. If it should still exist, the late
ministerial interregnum will be described in terms which
will seem to imply that all government was at an end; that
the social contract was annulled; and that the hand of every
man was against his neighbour, until the wisdom and virtue
of the new cabinet educed order out of the chaos of anarchy.
We are quite certain that misconceptions as gross prevail at
this moment respecting many important parts of our annals.

The effect of historical reading is analogous, in many respects, to that produced by foreign travel. The student, like
the tourist, is transported into a new state of society. He sees
new fashions. He hears new modes of expression. His mind
is enlarged by contemplating the wide diversities of laws,
of morals, and of manners. But men may travel far, and
return with minds as contracted as if they had never stirred
from their own market-town. In the same manner, men may
know the dates of many battles and the genealogies of
many royal houses, and yet be no wiser. Most people look at
past times as princes look at foreign countries. More than
one illustrious stranger has landed on our island amidst the
shouts of a mob, has dined with the King, has hunted with
the master of the stag-hounds, has seen the guards reviewed,
and a knight of the garter installed; has cantered along
Regent Street, has visited St. Paul's, and noted down its
dimensions; and has then departed, thinking that he has
seen England. He has, in fact, seen a few public buildings,
public men, and public ceremonies. But of the vast and complex system of society, of the fine shades of national character, of the practical operation of government and laws, he
knows nothing. He who would understand these things
rightly must not confine his observations to palaces and
solemn days. He must see ordinary men as they appear in

their ordinary business and in their ordinary pleasures. He must mingle in the crowds of the exchange and the coffee-house. He must obtain admittance to the convivial table and the domestic hearth. He must bear with vulgar expressions. He must not shrink from exploring even the retreats of misery. He who wishes to understand the condition of mankind in former ages must proceed on the same principle. If he attends only to public transactions, to wars, congresses, and debates, his studies will be as unprofitable as the travels of those imperial, royal, and serene sovereigns who form their judgment of our island from having gone in state to a few fine sights, and from having held formal conference with a few great officers.

The perfect historian is he in whose work the character and spirit of an age is exhibited in miniature. He relates no fact, he attributes no expression to his characters, which is not authenticated by sufficient testimony. But, by judicious selection, rejection, and arrangement, he gives to truth those attractions which have been usurped by fiction. In his narrative a due subordination is observed: some transactions are prominent; others retire. But the scale on which he represents them is increased or diminished, not according to the dignity of the persons concerned in them, but according to the degree in which they elucidate the condition of society and the nature of man. He shows us the court, the camp, and the senate. But he shows us also the nation. He considers no anecdote, no peculiarity of manner, no familiar saying, as too insignificant to illustrate the operation of laws, of religion, and of education, and to mark the progress of the human mind. Men will not merely be described, but will be made intimately known to us. The changes of manners will be indicated, not merely by a few general phrases or a few extracts from statistical documents, but by appropriate images presented in every line.

If a man, such as we are supposing, should write the history of England, he would assuredly not omit the battles, the sieges, the negotiations, the seditions, the ministerial changes. But with these he would intersperse the details which are the charm of historical romances. At Lincoln Cathedral there is a beautiful painted window, which was made by an apprentice out of the pieces of glass which had been rejected by his master. It is so far superior to every other in the church, that, according to the tradition, the vanquished artist killed himself from mortification. Sir Walter Scott, in the same manner, has used those fragments of truth which historians have scornfully thrown behind them in a manner which may well excite their envy. He has constructed out of their gleanings works which, even considered as histories, are scarcely less valuable than theirs. But a truly great historian would reclaim those materials which the novelist has appropriated. The history of the government, and the history of the people, would be exhibited in that mode in which alone they can be exhibited justly, in inseparable conjunction and intermixture. We should not then have to look for the wars and votes of the Puritans in Clarendon, and for their phraseology in Old Mortality; for one half of King James in Hume and for the other half in the Fortunes of Nigel.

The early part of our imaginary history would be rich with colouring from romance, ballad, and chronicle. We should find ourselves in the company of knights such as those of Froissart, and of pilgrims such as those who rode with Chaucer from the Tabard. Society would be shown from the highest to the lowest—from the royal cloth of state to the den of the outlaw; from the throne of the legate to the chimney-corner where the begging friar regaled himself. Palmers, minstrels, crusaders—the stately monastery, with the good cheer in its refectory and the high-mass in its chapel—the manor-house, with its hunting and hawking—the tournament, with the heralds and ladies, the trumpets and the cloth of gold—would give truth and life to the representation. We should perceive, in a thousand slight touches, the importance of the privileged burgher, and the fierce and haughty spirit which swelled under the collar of the degraded villain. The revival of letters would not merely be described in a few magnificent periods. We should discern, in innumerable particulars, the fermentation of mind, the eager appetite for knowledge, which distinguished the sixteenth from the fifteenth century. In the Reformation we should see not merely a schism which changed the ecclesiastical constitution of England and the mutual relations of the European powers, but a moral war which raged in every family, which set the father against the son and the son against the father, the mother against the daughter and the daughter against the mother. Henry would be painted with the skill of Tacitus. We should have the change of his character from his profuse and joyous youth to his savage and imperious old age. We should perceive the gradual progress of selfish and tyrannical passions in a mind not naturally insensible or ungenerous; and to the last we should detect some remains of that open and noble temper which endeared him to a people whom he oppressed, struggling with the hardness of despotism and the irritability of disease. We should see Elizabeth, in all her weakness and in all her strength, surrounded by the handsome favourites whom she never trusted, and the wise old statesmen whom she never dismissed, uniting in herself the most contradictory qualities of both her parents—the coquetry, the caprice, the petty malice of Anne—the haughty and resolute spirit of Henry. We have no hesitation in saying that a great artist might produce a portrait of this remarkable woman at least as striking as that in the novel of *Kenilworth,* without employing a single trait not authenticated by ample testimony. In the meantime, we should see arts cultivated, wealth accumulated, the conveniences of life improved. We should see the keeps where nobles, insecure themselves, spread insecurity around them, gradually giving place to the halls of peaceful opulence, to the oriels of Longleat, and the stately pinnacles of Burleigh. We should see towns extended, deserts cultivated, the hamlets of fishermen turned into wealthy havens, the meal of the peasant improved, and his hut more commodiously furnished. We should see those opinions and feelings which produced the great struggle against the House of Stuart slowly growing up in the bosom of private families, before they manifested themselves in parliamentary debates. Then would come the civil war. Those skirmishes on which Clarendon dwells so minutely would be told, as Thucydides would have told them, with perspicuous conciseness. They are merely connecting links. But the great characteristics of the age, the loyal enthusiasm of the brave English gentry, the fierce licentiousness of the swearing, dicing, drunken reprobates, whose excesses disgraced the royal cause—the austerity of the Presbyterian Sabbaths in the city, the extravagance of the independent preachers in the camp, the precise garb, the severe countenance, the petty scruples, the affected accent, the absurd names and phrases which marked the Puritans—the valour, the policy, the public spirit which lurked beneath these ungraceful disguises—the dreams of the raving Fifth-monarchy man; the dreams, scarcely less wild, of the philosophic republican—all these would enter into the representation, and render it at once more exact and more striking.

The instruction derived from history thus written would be of a vivid and practical character. It would be received by the imagination as well as by the reason. It would be not merely traced on the mind, but branded into it. Many truths, too, would be learned, which can be learned in no other manner. As the history of states is generally written, the greatest and most momentous revolutions seem to come upon them like supernatural inflictions, without warning or cause. But the fact is, that such revolutions are almost always the consequences of moral changes, which have gradually passed on the mass of the community, and which ordinarily proceed far before their progress is indicated by any public measure. An intimate knowledge of the domestic history of nations is, therefore, absolutely necessary to the prognosis of political events. A narrative defective in this respect is as useless as a medical treatise which should pass by all the symptoms attendant on the early stage of a disease, and mention only what occurs when the patient is beyond the reach of remedies.

A historian, such as we have been attempting to describe, would indeed be an intellectual prodigy. In his mind powers scarcely compatible with each other must be tempered into an exquisite harmony. We shall sooner see another Shakspeare or another Homer. The highest excellence to which any single faculty can be brought would be less surprising than such a happy and delicate combination of qualities. Yet the contemplation of imaginary models is not an unpleasant or useless employment of the mind. It cannot, indeed, produce perfection; but it produces improvement, and nourishes that generous and liberal fastidiousness which is not inconsistent with the strongest sensibility to merit, and which, while it exalts our conceptions of the art, does not render us unjust to the artist.

6

HISTORY AS BIOGRAPHY: *Carlyle*

[Thomas Carlyle (1795-1881) ranks among the most popular of nineteenth century literary historians. Learning from Sir Walter Scott to look upon the past as peopled by living men—"not abstractions . . . not diagrams and theorems; but men in buff coats and breeches, with color in their cheeks, with passions in their stomach and the idioms, features and vitalities of very men"—Carlyle sought to recapture the drama of the past. A stern moralist, his best known works, *The French Revolution* (1837), *Oliver Cromwell's Letters and Speeches: With Elucidations* (1845) and the *History of Frederick II of Prussia* (1858-1865) attested his originality of view as well as his political passion. In spite of his dictum that history is biography, Carlyle's first history, subtitled a "History of Sansculottism," was in effect an essay in social history, and his abiding concern with universal history transcended the strictly biographical, searching instead for the spiritual unity of an age. A vilifier of specialized "dry-as-dust" historians, he was in turn repudiated by them, and few historians, excepting his avowed disciple and later biographer J. A. Froude, acknowledged Carlyle as a member, much less a master of their craft.

Carlyle's essay "On History" (1830) is reprinted in its entirety, followed by selections from Lectures I and VI—*On Heroes, Hero-Worship, and the Heroic in History* (1840).]

ON HISTORY

Clio was figured by the ancients as the eldest daughter of
Memory, and chief of the Muses; which dignity, whether we
regard the essential qualities of her art, or its practice and
acceptance among men, we shall still find to have been fitly
bestowed. History, as it lies at the root of all science, is also
the first distinct product of man's spiritual nature; his earliest
expression of what can be called Thought. It is a looking both
before and after; as, indeed, the coming Time already waits,
unseen, yet definitely shaped, predetermined and inevitable,
in the Time come; and only by the combination of both is
the meaning of either completed. The Sibylline Books, though
old, are not the oldest. Some nations have prophecy, some
have not: but of all mankind, there is no tribe so rude that
it has not attempted History, though several have not arithmetic enough to count Five. History has been written with
quipo-threads, with feather-pictures, with wampum-belts; still
oftener with earth-mounds and monumental stone-heaps,
whether as pyramid or cairn; for the Celt and the Copt, the
Red man as well as the White, lives between two eternities,
and warring against Oblivion, he would fain unite himself in
clear conscious relation, as in dim unconscious relation he is
already united, with the whole Future, and the whole Past.

A talent for History may be said to be born with us, as
our chief inheritance. In a certain sense all men are historians.
Is not every memory written quite full with Annals, wherein
joy and mourning, conquest and loss manifoldly alternate;
and, with or without philosophy, the whole fortunes of one
little inward Kingdom, and all its politics, foreign and domestic, stand ineffaceably recorded? Our very speech is curiously historical. Most men, you may observe, speak only to
narrate; not in imparting what they have thought, which indeed were often a very small matter, but in exhibiting what
they have undergone or seen, which is a quite unlimited one,
do talkers dilate. Cut us off from Narrative, how would the
stream of conversation, even among the wisest, languish into
detached handfuls, and among the foolish utterly evaporate!
Thus, as we do nothing but enact History, we say little but
recite it, nay, rather, in that widest sense, our whole spiritual
life is built thereon. For, strictly considered, what is all
Knowledge too but recorded Experience, and a product of

History; of which, therefore, Reasoning and Belief, no less than Action and Passion, are essential materials?

Under a limited, and the only practicable shape, History proper, that part of History which treats of remarkable action, has, in all modern as well as ancient times, ranked among the highest arts, and perhaps never stood higher than in these times of ours. For whereas, of old, the charm of History lay chiefly in gratifying our common appetite for the wonderful, for the unknown; and her office was but as that of a Minstrel and Story-teller, she has now farther become a School-mistress, and professes to instruct in gratifying. Whether, with the stateliness of that venerable character, she may not have taken up something of its austerity and frigidity; whether in the logical terseness of a Hume or Robertson, the graceful ease and gay pictorial heartiness of a Herodotus or Froissart may not be wanting, is not the question for us here. Enough that all learners, all inquiring minds of every order, are gathered round her footstool, and reverently pondering her lessons, as the true basis of Wisdom. Poetry, Divinity, Politics, Physics, have each their adherents and adversaries; each little guild supporting a defensive and offensive war for its own special domain; while the domain of History is as a Free Emporium, where all these belligerents peaceably meet and furnish themselves; and Sentimentalist and Utilitarian, Sceptic and Theologian, with one voice advise us: Examine History, for it is 'Philosophy teaching by Experience.'

Far be it from us to disparage such teaching, the very attempt at which must be precious. Neither shall we too rigidly inquire: How much it has hitherto profited? Whether most of what little practical wisdom men have, has come from study of professed History, or from other less boasted sources, whereby, as matters now stand, a Marlborough may become great in the world's business, with no History save what he derives from Shakspeare's Plays? Nay, whether in that same teaching by Experience, historical Philosophy has yet properly deciphered the first element of all science in this kind: What the aim and significance of that wondrous changeful Life it investigates and paints may be? Whence the course of man's destinies in this Earth originated, and whither they are tending? Or, indeed, if they have any course and tendency, are really guided forward by an unseen mysterious Wisdom, or only circle in blind mazes without recognisable guidance? Which questions, altogether fundamental, one might think, in any Philosophy of History, have, since the era when Monkish Annalists were wont to answer them by the long-ago extinguished light of their Missal and Breviary, been by most philosophical Historians only glanced at dubiously and from afar; by many, not so much as glanced at.

The Truth is, two difficulties, never wholly surmountable, lie in the way. Before Philosophy can teach by Experience, the Philosophy has to be in readiness, the Experience must be gathered and intelligibly recorded. Now, overlooking the former consideration, and with regard only to the latter, let any one who has examined the current of human affairs, and how intricate, perplexed, unfathomable, even when seen into with our own eyes, are their thousandfold blending movements, say whether the true representing of it is easy or impossible. Social Life is the aggregate of all the individual men's Lives who constitute society; History is the essence of innumerable Biographies. But if one Biography, nay, our own Biography, study and recapitulate it as we may, remains in so many points unintelligible to us; how much more must these million, the very facts of which, to say nothing of the purport of them, we know not, and cannot know!

Neither will it adequately avail us to assert that the general inward condition of Life is the same in all ages; and that only the remarkable deviations from the common endowment and common lot, and the more important variations which the outward figure of Life has from time to time undergone, deserve memory and record. The inward condition of Life, it may rather be affirmed, the conscious or half-conscious aim of mankind, so far as men are not mere digesting-machines, is the same in no two ages; neither are the more important outward variations easy to fix on, or always well capable of representation. Which was the greatest innovator, which was the more important personage in man's history, he who first led armies over the Alps, and gained the victories of Cannæ and Thrasymene; or the nameless boor who first hammered out for himself an iron spade? When the oak-tree is felled, the whole forest echoes with it; but a hundred acorns are planted silently by some unnoticed breeze. Battles and war-tumults, which for the time din every ear, and with joy or terror intoxicate every heart, pass away like tavern-brawls; and, except some few Marathons and Morgartens, are remembered by accident, not by desert. Laws themselves, political Constitutions, are not our Life, but only the house wherein our Life is led; nay, they are but the bare walls of the house: all whose essential furniture, the inventions and traditions, and daily habits that regulate and support our existence, are the work not of Dracos and Hampdens, but of Phœnician mariners, of Italian masons and Saxon metallurgists, of philosophers, alchymists, prophets, and all the long-forgotten train of artists and artisans; who from the first have been jointly teaching us how to think and how to act, how to rule over spiritual and over physical Nature. Well may we say that of our History the more important part is lost without recovery; and, —as thanksgivings were once wont to be offered 'for unrecognised mercies,'—look with reverence into the dark untenanted places of the Past, where, in formless oblivion, our chief benefactors, with all their sedulous endeavours, but not with the fruit of these, lie entombed.

So imperfect is that same Experience, by which Philosophy is to teach. Nay, even with regard to those occurrences which do stand recorded, which, at their origin have seemed worthy of record, and the summary of which constitutes what we now call History, is not our understanding of them altogether incomplete; is it even possible to represent them as they were? The old story of Sir Walter Raleigh's looking from his prison-window, on some street tumult, which afterwards three witnesses reported in three different ways, himself differing from them all, is still a true lesson for us. Consider how it is that historical documents and records originate; even honest records, where the reporters were unbiased by personal regard; a case which, were nothing more wanted, must ever be among the rarest. The real leading features of a historical Transaction, those movements that essentially characterise it, and alone deserve to be recorded, are nowise the foremost to be noted. At first, among the various witnesses, who are also parties interested, there is only vague wonder, and fear or hope, and the noise of Rumour's thousand tongues; till, after a season, the conflict of testimonies has subsided into some general issue; and then it is settled, by majority of votes, that such and such a 'Crossing of the Rubicon,' an 'Impeachment of Strafford,' a 'Convocation of the Notables,' are epochs in the world's history, cardinal points on which grand world-revolutions have hinged. Suppose, however, that the majority of votes was all wrong; that the real cardinal points lay far deeper: and had been passed over unnoticed, because no Seer, but only mere Onlookers, chanced to be there! Our clock strikes when there is a change from hour to hour; but no hammer in the Horologe of Time peals through the universe when there is a change from Era to Era. Men understand not what is among their hands: as calmness is the characteristic of strength, so the weightiest causes may be most silent. It is, in no case, the real historical Transaction, but only some more or less plausible scheme and theory of the Transaction, or the harmonised result of many such schemes, each varying from the other and all varying from truth, that we can ever hope to behold.

Nay, were our faculty of insight into passing things never so complete, there is still a fatal discrepancy between our manner of observing these, and their manner of occurring. The most gifted man can observe, still more can record, only the *series* of his own impressions; his observation, therefore, to say nothing of its other imperfections, must be *successive*, while the things done were often *simultaneous*; the things done were not a series, but a group. It is not in acted, as it is in written History: actual events are nowise so simply related to each other as parent and offspring are; every single event is the offspring not of one, but of all other events, prior or contemporaneous, and will in its turn combine with all others to give birth to new: it is an ever-living, ever-working Chaos of Being, wherein shape after shape bodies itself forth from innumerable elements. And this Chaos, boundless as the habitation and duration of man, unfathomable as the soul and destiny of man, is what the historian will depict, and scientifically gauge, we may say, by threading it with single lines of a few ells in length! For as all Action is, by its nature, to be figured as extended in breadth and in depth, as well as in length; that is to say, is based on Passion and Mystery, if we investigate its origin; and spreads abroad on all hands, modifying and modified; as well as advances towards completion,—so all Narrative is, by its nature, of only one dimension; only travels forward towards one, or towards successive points: Narrative is *linear,* Action is *solid.* Alas for our 'chains,' or chainlets, of 'causes and effects,' which we so assiduously track through certain hand-breadths of years and square miles, when the whole is a broad, deep Immensity, and each atom is 'chained' and complected with all! Truly, if History is Philosophy teaching by Experience, the writer fitted to compose History is hitherto an unknown man. The Experience itself would require All-knowledge to record it,—were the All-wisdom needful for such Philosophy as would interpret it, to be had for asking. Better were it that mere earthly Historians should lower such pretensions, more suitable for Omniscience than for human science; and aiming only at some picture of the things acted, which picture itself will at best be a poor approximation, leave the inscrutable purport of them an acknowledged secret; or at most, in reverent Faith, far different from that teaching of Philosophy, pause over the mysterious vestiges of Him, whose path is in the great deep of Time, whom History indeed reveals, but only all History, and in Eternity, will clearly reveal.

Such considerations truly were of small profit, did they, instead of teaching us vigilance and reverent humility in our inquiries into History, abate our esteem for them, or discourage us from unweariedly prosecuting them. Let us search more and more into the Past; let all men explore it, as the true fountain of knowledge; by whose light alone, consciously or unconsciously employed, can the Present and the Future be interpreted or guessed at. For though the whole meaning lies far beyond our ken; yet in that complex Manuscript, covered over with formless inextricably-entangled unknown characters,—nay, which is a *Palimpsest,* and had once prophetic writing, still dimly legible there,—some letters, some words, may be deciphered; and if no complete Philosophy, here and there an intelligible precept, available in practice, be gathered; well understanding, in the mean while, that it is only a little portion we have deciphered; that much still remains to be interpreted; that History is a real Prophetic Manuscript, and can be fully interpreted by no man.

But the Artist in History may be distinguished from the Artisan in History; for here, as in all other provinces, there are Artists and Artisans; men who labour mechanically in a department, without eye for the Whole, not feeling that there is a Whole; and men who inform and ennoble the humblest department with an Idea of the Whole, and habitually know that only in the Whole is the Partial to be truly discerned. The proceedings and the duties of these two, in regard to History, must be altogether different. Not, indeed, that each has not a real worth, in his several degree. The simple husbandman can till his field, and by knowledge he has gained of its soil, sow it with the fit grain, though the deep rocks and central fires are unknown to him: his little crop hangs under and over the firmament of stars, and sails through whole untracked celestial spaces, between Aries and Libra; nevertheless it ripens for him in due season, and he gathers it safe into his barn. As a husbandman he is blameless in disregarding those higher wonders; but as a thinker, and faithful inquirer into Nature, he were wrong. So likewise is it with the Historian, who examines some special aspect of History; and from this or that combination of circumstances, political, moral, economical, and the issues it has led to, infers that such and such properties belong to human society, and that the like circumstances will produce the like issue; which inference, if other trials confirm it, must be held true and practically valuable. He is wrong only, and an artisan, when he fancies that these properties, discovered or discoverable, exhaust the matter: and sees not, at every step, that it is inexhaustible.

However, that class of cause-and-effect speculators, with whom no wonder would remain wonderful, but all things in Heaven and Earth must be computed and 'accounted for'; and even the Unknown, the Infinite in man's Life, had under the words *enthusiasm, superstition, spirit of the age* and so forth, obtained, as it were, an algebraical symbol and given value,—have now wellnigh played their part in European culture; and may be considered, as in most countries, even in England itself where they linger the latest, verging towards extinction. He who reads the inscrutable Book of Nature as if it were a Merchant's Ledger, is justly suspected of having never seen that Book, but only some school Synopsis thereof; from which, if taken for the real Book, more error than insight is to be derived.

Doubtless also, it is with a growing feeling of the infinite nature of History, that in these times, the old principle, division of labour, has been so widely applied to it. The Political Historian, once almost the sole cultivator of History, has now found various associates, who strive to elucidate other phases of human Life; of which, as hinted above, the political conditions it is passed under are but one, and though the primary, perhaps not the most important, of the many outward arrangements. Of this Historian himself, moreover, in his own special department, new and higher things are beginning to be expected. From of old, it was too often to be reproachfully observed of him, that he dwelt with disproportionate fondness in Senate-houses, in Battle-fields, nay, even in Kings' Antechambers; forgetting, that far away from such scenes, the mighty tide of Thought and Action was still rolling on its wondrous course, in gloom and brightness; and in its thousand remote valleys, a whole world of Existence, with or without an earthly sun of Happiness to warm it, with or without a heavenly sun of Holiness to purify and sanctify it, was blossoming and fading, whether the 'famous victory' were won or lost. The time seems coming when much of this must be amended; and he who sees no world but that of courts and camps; and writes only how soldiers were drilled and shot, and how this ministerial conjuror outconjured that other, and then guided, or at least held, something which he called the rudder of Government, but which was rather the spigot of Taxation, wherewith, in place of steering, he could tap, and the more cunningly the nearer the lees,—will pass for a more or less instructive Gazetteer, but will no longer be called a Historian.

However, the Political Historian, were his work performed with all conceivable perfection, can accomplish but a part, and still leaves room for numerous fellow-labourers. Foremost among these comes the Ecclesiastical Historian; endeavouring, with catholic or sectarian view, to trace the progress of the Church; of that portion of the social establishments, which respects our religious condition; as the other portion does our civil, or rather, in the long-run, our economical condition. Rightly conducted, this department were undoubtedly the more important of the two; inasmuch as it concerns us more to understand how man's moral well-being had been and might be promoted, than to understand in the like sort his physical well-being; which latter is ultimately the aim of all Political arrangements. For the physically happiest is simply the safest, the strongest; and, in all conditions of Government, Power (whether of wealth as in these days, or of arms and adherents as in old days) is the only outward emblem and purchase-money of Good. True Good, however, unless we reckon Pleasure synonymous with it, is said to be rarely, or rather never, offered for sale in the market where that coin passes current. So that, for man's true advantage, not the outward condition of his life, but the inward and spiritual, is of prime influence; not the form of Government he lives under, and the power he can accumulate there, but the Church he is a member of, and the degree of moral elevation he can acquire by means of its instruction. Church History, then, did it speak wisely, would have momentous secrets to teach us: nay, in its highest degree, it were a sort of continued Holy Writ; our Sacred Books being, indeed only a History of the primeval Church, as it first arose in man's soul, and symbolically embodied itself in his external life. How far our actual Church Historians fall below such unattainable standards, nay, below quite attainable approximations thereto, we need not point out. Of the Ecclesiastical Historian we have to complain, as we did of his Political fellow-craftsman, that his inquiries turn rather on the outward mechanism, the mere hulls and superficial accidents of the object, than on the object itself: as if the Church lay in Bishops' Chapter-houses, and Ecumenic Council-halls, and Cardinals' Conclaves, and not far more in the hearts of Believing Men; in whose walk and conversation, as influenced thereby, its chief manifestations were to be looked for, and its progress or decline ascertained. The History of the Church is a History of the Invisible as well as of the Visible Church; which latter, if disjoined from the former, is but a vacant edifice; gilded, it may be, and overhung with old votive gifts, yet useless, nay, pestilentially unclean; to write whose history is less important than to forward its downfall.

Of a less ambitious character are the Histories that relate to special separate provinces of human Action; to Sciences, Practical Arts, Institutions and the like; matters which do not imply an epitome of man's whole interest and form of life; but wherein, though each is still connected with all, the spirit of each, at least its material results, may be in some degree evolved without so strict a reference to that of the others. Highest in dignity and difficulty, under this head, would be our histories of Philosophy, of man's opinions and theories respecting the nature of his Being, and relations to the Universe Visible and Invisible: which History, indeed, were it fitly treated, or fit for right treatment, would be a province of Church History; the logical or dogmatical province thereof; for Philosophy, in its true sense, is or should be the soul, of which Religion, Worship is the body; in the healthy state of things the Philosopher and Priest were one and the same. But Philosophy itself is far enough from wearing this character; neither have its Historians been men, generally speaking, that could in the smallest degree approximate it thereto. Scarcely since the rude era of the Magi and Druids has that same healthy identification of Priest and Philosopher had place in any country: but rather the worship of divine things, and the scientific investigation of divine things, have been in quite different hands, their relations not friendly but hostile. Neither have the Brückers and Bühles, to say nothing of the many unhappy Enfields who have treated of that latter department, been more than barren reporters, often unintelligent and unintelligible reporters, of the doctrine uttered;

without force to discover how the doctrine originated, or what reference it bore to its time and country, to the spiritual position of mankind there and then. Nay, such a task did not perhaps lie before them, as a thing to be attempted.

Art also and Literature are intimately blended with Religion; as it were, outworks and abutments, by which that highest pinnacle in our inward world gradually connects itself with the general level, and becomes accessible therefrom. He who should write a proper History of Poetry, would depict for us the successive Revelations which man had obtained of the Spirit of Nature; under what aspects he had caught and endeavoured to body forth some glimpse of that unspeakable Beauty, which in its highest clearness is Religion, is the inspiration of a Prophet, yet in one or the other degree must inspire every true Singer, were his theme never so humble. We should see by what steps men had ascended to the Temple; how near they had approached; by what ill hap they had, for long periods, turned away from it, and grovelled on the plain with no music in the air, or blindly struggled towards other heights. That among all our Eichhorns and Wartons there is no such Historian, must be too clear to every one. Nevertheless let us not despair of far nearer approaches to that excellence. Above all, let us keep the Ideal of it ever in our eye; for thereby alone have we even a chance to reach it.

Our histories of Laws and Constitutions, wherein many a Montesquieu and Hallam has laboured with acceptance, are of a much simpler nature; yet deep enough if thoroughly investigated; and useful, when authentic, even with little depth. Then we have Histories of Medicine, of Mathematics, of Astronomy, Commerce, Chivalry, Monkery; and Goguets and Beckmanns have come forward with what might be the most bountiful contribution of all, a History of Inventions. Of all which sorts, and many more not here enumerated, not yet devised and put in practice, the merit and the proper scheme may, in our present limits, require no exposition.

In this manner, though, as above remarked, all Action is extended three ways, and the general sum of human Action is a whole Universe, with all limits of it unknown, does History strive by running path after path, through the Impassable, in manifold directions and intersections, to secure for us some oversight of the Whole; in which endeavour, if each Historian look well around him from his path, tracking it out with the *eye*, not, as is more common, with the *nose*, she may at last prove not altogether unsuccessful. Praying only that increased division of labour do not here, as elsewhere, aggravate our already strong Mechanical tendencies, so that in the manual dexterity for parts we lose all command over the whole, and the hope of any Philosophy of History be farther off than ever, —let us all wish her great and greater success.

FROM LECTURES ONE AND SIX:
On Heroes, Hero-Worship, and
The Heroic in History

Lecture One

We have undertaken to discourse here for a little on Great Men, their manner of appearance in our world's business, how they have shaped themselves in the world's history, what ideas men formed of them, what work they did;—on Heroes, namely, and on their reception and performance; what I call Hero-worship and the Heroic in human affairs. Too evidently this is a large topic; deserving quite other treatment than we can expect to give it at present. A large topic; indeed, an illimitable one; wide as Universal History itself. For, as I take it, Universal History, the history of what man has accomplished in this world, is at bottom the History of the Great Men who have worked here. They were the leaders of men, these great ones; the modelers, patterns, and in a wide sense creators, of whatsoever the general mass of men contrived to do or to attain; all things that we see standing accomplished in the world are properly the outer material result, the practical realisation and embodiment, of Thoughts that dwelt in the Great Men sent into the world: the soul of the whole world's history, it may justly be considered, were the history of these. Too clearly it is a topic we shall do no justice to in this place!

One comfort is, that Great Men, taken up in any way, are profitable company. We cannot look, however imperfectly, upon a great man, without gaining something by him. He is the living light-fountain, which it is good and pleasant to be near. The light which enlightens, which has enlightened the darkness of the world; and this not as a kindled lamp only, but rather as a natural luminary shining by the gift of Heaven; a flowing light-fountain, as I say, of native original insight, of manhood and heroic nobleness;—in whose radiance all souls feel that it is well with them. On any terms whatsoever, you will not grudge to wander in such neighbourhood for a while. These Six classes of Heroes, chosen out of widely-distant countries and epochs, and in mere external figure differing altogether, ought, if we look faithfully at them, to illustrate several things for us. Could we see *them* well, we should get some glimpses into the very marrow of the world's history. How happy, could I but, in any measure, in such times as these, make manifest to you the meanings of Heroism; the divine relation (for I may well call it such) which in all times unites a great man to other men; and thus, as it were, not exhaust my subject, but so much as break ground on it! At all events, I must make the attempt.

I am well aware that in these days Hero-worship, the thing I call Hero-worship, professes to have gone out, and finally ceased. This, for reasons which it will be worth while some time to inquire into, is an age that as it were denies the existence of great men; denies the desirableness of great men. Show our critics a great man, a Luther for example, they begin to what they call 'account' for him; not to worship him, but take the dimensions of him,—and bring him out to be a little kind of man! He was the 'creature of the Time,' they say; the Time called him forth, the Time did everything, he nothing—but what we the little critic could have done too! This seems to me but melancholy work. The Time call forth? Alas, we have known Times *call* loudly enough for their great man; but not find him when they called! He was not there; Providence had not sent him; the Time, *calling* its loudest, had to go down to confusion and wreck because he would not come when called.

For, if we will think of it, no Time need have gone to ruin, could it have *found* a man great enough, a man wise and good enough; wisdom to discern truly what the Time wanted, valour to lead it on the right road thither; these are the salvation of any Time. But I liken common languid Times, with their unbelief, distress, perplexity, with their languid doubting characters and embarrassed circumstances, impotently crumbling-down into ever worse distress towards final ruin;—all this I liken to dry dead fuel, waiting for the lightning out of Heaven that shall kindle it. The great man, with his free force direct out of God's own hand, is the lightning. His word is the wise healing word which all can believe in. All blazes round him now, when he has once struck on it, into fire like his own. The dry mouldering sticks are thought to have called him forth. They did want him greatly; but as to calling him forth—!—Those are critics of small vision, I think, who cry: "See, is it not the sticks that made the fire?" No sadder proof can be given by a man of his own littleness than disbelief in great men. There is no sadder symptom of a generation than such general blindness to the spiritual lightning, with faith only in the heap of barren dead fuel. It is the last consummation of unbelief. In all epochs of the world's history, we shall find the Great Man to have been the indispensable saviour of his epoch;—the lightning, without which the fuel never would have burnt. The History of the World, I said already, was the Biography of Great Men.

Such small critics do what they can to promote unbelief and universal spiritual paralysis; but happily they cannot always completely succeed. In all times it is possible for a man to arise great enough to feel that they and their doctrines are chimeras and cobwebs. And what is notable, in no time whatever can they entirely eradicate out of living men's hearts a certain altogether peculiar reverence for Great Men; genuine admiration, loyalty, adoration, however dim and perverted it may be. Hero-worship endures for ever while man endures. Boswell venerates his Johnson, right truly even in the Eighteenth century. The unbelieving French believe in their Voltaire; and burst-out round him into very curious Hero-worship, in that last act of his life when they 'stifle him under roses.' It has always seemed to me extremely curious this of Voltaire. Truly, if Christianity be the highest instance of Hero-worship, then we may find here in Voltaireism one of the lowest! He whose life was that of a kind of Antichrist, does again on this side exhibit a curious contrast. No people ever were so little prone to admire at all as those French of Voltaire. *Persiflage* was the character of their whole mind; adoration had nowhere a place in it. Yet see! The old man of Ferney comes up to Paris; an old, tottering, infirm man of eighty-four years. They feel that he too is a kind of Hero; that he has spent his life in opposing error and injustice, delivering Calases, unmasking hypocrites in high places;—in short that *he* too, though in a strange way, has fought like a valiant man. They feel withal that, if *persiflage* be the great thing, there never was such a *persifleur*. He is the realised ideal of every one of them; the thing they are all wanting to be; of all Frenchmen the most French. *He* is properly their god,—such god as they are fit for. Accordingly all persons, from the Queen

Antoinette to the Douanier at the Porte St. Denis, do they not worship him? People of quality disguise themselves as tavern-waiters. The Maître de Poste, with a broad oath, orders his Postillion, *"Va bon train;* thou art driving M. de Voltaire." At Paris his carriage is 'the nucleus of a comet, whose train fills whole streets.' The ladies pluck a hair or two from his fur, to keep it as a sacred relic. There was nothing highest, beautifulest, noblest in all France, that did not feel this man to be higher, beautifuler, nobler.

Yes, from Norse Odin to English Samuel Johnson, from the divine Founder of Christianity to the withered Pontiff of Encyclopedism, in all times and places, the Hero has been worshipped. It will ever be so. We all love great men; love, venerate, and bow down submissive before great men: nay can we honestly bow down to anything else? Ah, does not every true man feel that he is himself made higher by doing reverence to what is really above him? No nobler or more blessed feeling dwells in man's heart. And to me it is very cheering to consider that no sceptical logic, or general triviality, insincerity and aridity of any Time and its influences can destroy this noble inborn loyalty and worship that is in man. In times of unbelief, which soon have to become times of revolution, much down-rushing, sorrowful decay and ruin is visible to everybody. For myself in these days, I seem to see in this indestructibility of Hero-worship the everlasting adamant lower than which the confused wreck of revolutionary things cannot fall. The confused wreck of things crumbling and even crashing and tumbling all round us in these revolutionary ages, will get down so far; *no* farther. It is an eternal corner-stone, from which they can begin to build themselves up again. That man, in some sense or other, worships Heroes; that we all of us reverence and must ever reverence Great Men: this is, to me, the living rock amid all rushings-down whatsoever;—the one fixed point in modern revolutionary history, otherwise as if bottomless and shoreless.

Lecture Six

Neither, on the whole, does this constitutional tolerance of the Eighteenth century for the other happier Puritans seem to be a very great matter. One might say, it is but a piece of Formulism and Scepticism, like the rest. They tell us, It was a sorrowful thing to consider that the foundation of our English Liberties should have been laid by 'Superstition.' These

Puritans came forward with Calvinistic incredible Creeds,
Anti-Laudisms, Westminster Confessions; demanding, chiefly
of all, that they should have liberty to *worship* in their own
way. Liberty to *tax* themselves: that was the thing they should
have demanded! It was Superstition, Fanaticism, disgraceful
Ignorance of Constitutional Philosophy to insist on the other
thing!—Liberty to *tax oneself?* Not to pay-out money from
your pocket except on reason shown? No century, I think, but
a rather barren one would have fixed on that as the first right
of man! I should say, on the contrary, A just man will generally
have better cause than *money* in what shape soever, before de-
ciding to revolt against his Government. Ours is a most confused world; in which a good man will be thankful to see any
kind of Government maintain itself in a not insupportable
manner; and here in England, to this hour, if he is not ready to
pay a great many taxes which *he* can see very small reason in, it
will not go well with him, I think! He must try some other
climate than this. Taxgatherer? Money? He will say: "Take my
money, since you *can,* and it is so desirable to you; take it,—
and take yourself away with it; and leave me alone to my work
here. *I* am still here; can still work, after all the money you
have taken from me!" But if they come to him, and say,
"Acknowledge a Lie; pretend to say you are worshipping
God, when you are not doing it: believe not the thing that
you find true, but the thing that I find, or pretend to find true!"
He will answer: "No; by God's help, no! You may take my
purse; but I cannot have my moral Self annihilated. The purse
is any Highwayman's who might meet me with a loaded pistol:
but the Self is mine and God my Maker's; it is not yours; and
I will resist you to the death, and revolt against you, and, on
the whole, front all manner of extremities, accusations and
confusions, in defence of that!"—

Really, it seems to me the one reason which could justify
revolting, this of the Puritans. It has been the soul of all just
revolts among men. Not *Hunger* alone produced even the
French Revolution: no, but the feeling of the insupportable
all-pervading *Falsehood* which had now embodied itself in
Hunger, in universal material Scarcity and Nonentity, and
thereby become *indisputably* false in the eyes of all! We will
leave the Eighteenth century with its 'liberty to tax itself.' We
will not astonish ourselves that the meaning of such men as the
Puritans remained dim to it. To men who believe in no reality
at all, how shall a *real* human soul, the intensest of all realities,
as it were the Voice of this world's Maker still speaking to *us,*

—be intelligible? What it cannot reduce into constitutional doctrines relative to 'taxing,' or other the like material interest, gross, palpable to the sense, such a century will needs reject as an amorphous heap of rubbish. Hampdens, Pyms, and Ship-money will be the theme of much constitutional eloquence, striving to be fervid;—which will glitter, if not as fire does, then as *ice* does: and the irreducible Cromwell will remain a chaotic mass of 'madness,' 'hypocrisy,' and much else.

From of old, I will confess, this theory of Cromwell's falsity has been incredible to me. Nay I cannot believe the like, of any Great Man whatever. Multitudes of Great Men figure in History as false selfish men; but if we will consider it, they are but *figures* for us, unintelligible shadows; we do not see into them as men that could have existed at all. A superficial unbelieving generation only, with no eye but for the surfaces and semblances of things, could form such notions of Great Men. Can a great soul be possible without a *conscience* in it, the essence of all *real* souls, great or small? —No, we cannot figure Cromwell as a Falsity and Fatuity; the longer I study him and his career, I believe this the less. Why should we? There is no evidence of it. Is it not strange that, after all the mountains of calumny this man has been subject to, after being represented as the very prince of liars, who never, or hardly ever, spoke truth, but always some cunning counterfeit of truth, there should not yet have been one falsehood brought clearly home to him? A prince of liars, and no lie spoken by him. Not one that I could yet get sight of. It is like Pococke asking Grotius, Where is your *proof* of Mahomet's Pigeon? No proof!—Let us leave all these calumnious chimeras, as chimeras ought to be left. They are not portraits of the man; they are distracted phantasms of him, the joint product of hatred and darkness. . . .

Truly it is a sad thing for a people, as for a man, to fall into Scepticism, into dilettantism, insincerity; not to know a Sincerity when they see it. For this world, and for all worlds, what curse is so fatal? The heart lying dead, the eye cannot see. What intellect remains is merely the *vulpine* intellect. That a true *King* be sent them is of small use; they do not know him when sent. They say scornfully, Is this your King? The Hero wastes his heroic faculty in bootless contradiction from the unworthy; and can accomplish little. For himself he does accomplish a heroic life, which is much, which is all; but for the world he accomplishes comparatively nothing. The wild rude Sincerity, direct from Nature, is not glib in answering from the witness-box; in your small-debt *pie-powder* court, he is scouted as a counterfeit. The vulpine intellect 'detects' him. For being a man worth any thousand men, the response, your Knox, your Cromwell gets, is an argument for two centuries, whether he was a man at all. God's greatest gift to this Earth is sneeringly flung away. The miraculous talisman is a paltry plated coin, not fit to pass in the shops as a common guinea.

Lamentable this! I say, this must be remedied. Till this be remedied in some measure, there is nothing remedied. 'Detect quacks'? Yes do, for Heaven's sake; but know withal the men that are to be trusted! Till we know that, what is all our knowledge; how shall we even so much as 'detect'? For the vulpine sharpness, which considers itself to be knowledge, and 'detects' in that fashion, is far mistaken. Dupes indeed are many: but, of all *dupes,* there is none so fatally situated as he who lives in undue terror of being duped. The world does exist; the world has truth in it or it would not exist! First recognise what is true, we shall *then* discern what is false; and properly never till then.

7

HISTORY AS A NATIONAL EPIC: *Michelet*

[The only son of an impoverished printer whom Napoleon had persecuted, Jules Michelet (1798-1874) became the foremost historian of the French people. His historical works were highly personal creations, combining an immediate sympathy with the past—aroused first by his childhood visits to the Lenoir National Museum—a broad philosophical interest, a scrupulous attention to neglected primary sources, a rich, poetic style, and an ardent patriotism which led him to personify the object of his love, France, and to glorify equally, in his first works at least, each period of its history. In 1824 Michelet discovered by chance and immediately translated Vico's *Scienza Nuova* which gave philosophic sanction to his spontaneous belief that the people, and not only its leaders or its institutions, shaped history. An enthusiastic teacher, he published in 1827 a *Précis d'histoire moderne*, a brief, but highly original, essay on the unity of modern history, which until 1850 guided historical instruction in French schools. After a *History of Rome*, Michelet wrote the first six volumes of his *History of France* (1833-1843; eleven other, less judicious volumes, 1855-1867); these early volumes depicted in a series of tableaux the unfolding life of the French people, its physical environment, its spirit and its heroes, and ended with the poignant portrait of Saint Joan. Disappointed by the drab, inegalitarian character of the July Monarchy he interrupted his *History of France* in order to write a passionately partisan, anticlerical *History of the French Revolution* (7 vols. 1847-1853), which he had come to regard as France's liberation from the tyranny of priests and kings. "Not one of the great actors of the Revolution left me cold. I was one of them," he wrote. The chief actor remained the people itself—a theme which Michelet had already formulated in *The People* (1846), from which the following selection was taken.]

FROM THE INTRODUCTION: *The People*
To M. Edgar Quinet

This book is more than a book;—it is myself. That is the reason it belongs to you.

Yes, it is myself; and, I may venture to affirm, it is you also. As you have justly remarked, our thoughts, whether communicated or not, are ever in unison. We live with the same heart. A delightful harmony! It may surprise, but is it not natural? All our various works have sprung from the same living root:—"The sentiment of France, and the idea of our country."

Accept, then, this book of *The People*, because it is you, because it is myself! We represent, as much as any, perhaps— you by your military, I by my industrial, origin—the two modern conditions of the People, and their new advent.

I have made this book of *myself*, of my life, and of my heart. It is the fruit of my experience, rather than of my research. I have derived it from my observation, and my intercourse with friends and neighbours; I have gleaned it from the highway: fortune loves to favour him who ever follows the self-same thought. Lastly, I have found it, above all, in the reminiscences of my youth. To know the life of the people, their toils and sufferings, I had but to interrogate my memory.

For I, too, my friend, have worked with my hands. The true name of modern man, that of *workman*, I am entitled to, in more than one sense. Before I made books, I *composed* them literally; I arranged letters before I grouped ideas; and I am not ignorant of the sadness of the workshop, and the wearisomeness of long hours.

Sad times! It was the latter years of the Empire; all seemed to be lost at once to me—my family, my fortune, and my country. It is to those trials, doubtless, that I owe the best part of my nature; to them must be ascribed the little value I possess as a man and an historian. From these I have especially retained a profound sentiment of the people, the perfect knowledge of the treasure that is in them, *the virtue of sacrifice,* the tender remembrance of precious souls that I have known in the most humble conditions.

Nobody must be surprised, if, knowing as well as anybody the past condition of that people, and having shared their life myself, I feel a burning desire for truth when I am spoken to about them. When the progress of my history led me to study the questions of the day, and I cast my eyes upon the books in which they are discussed, I confess I was surprised to find them almost all in contradiction to my memory. I then shut the books, and placed myself among the people to the best of my power; the lonely writer plunged again into the crowd, listened to their noise, noted their words. They were perfectly the same people, changed only in outward appearance; my memory did not deceive me. I went about, therefore, consulting men, listening to their account of their own condition, and gathering from their lips, what is not always to be found in the most brilliant writers, the words of common sense.

This inquiry, begun at Lyons about ten years ago, I have prosecuted in other towns, studying, at the same time, with practical men of the most positive minds, the true situation of the rural districts so much neglected by our economists. The mass of new information I have thus acquired, and which is not in any book, would scarcely be credited. Next to the conversation of men of genius and profound erudition, that of the people is certainly the most instructive. If one be not able to converse with Beranger, Lamennais, or Lamartine, we must go into the fields and chat with a peasant. What is to be learned from the middle class? As to the *salons,* I never left them without finding my heart shrunk and chilled.

My varied studies of history had revealed to me facts of the greatest interest, unnoticed by historians:—the phases, for instance, and the vicissitudes of small properties before the Revolution.

My inquiry among *living* documents taught me likewise many things that are not in our statistics. I will mention one, which some will, perhaps, find trivial, but which I consider important and worthy of all attention. It is the immense increase of linen articles acquired by poor families about 1842, though wages have lowered, or, at least, diminished in value, by the natural diminution in the value of money. This fact, important in itself as an advance in cleanliness, which is connected with so many other virtues, is still more so, inasmuch as it proves an increasing stability in households and families,—above all, the influence of woman, who, gaining little by her own means, can only make this outlay by appropriating part of the wages of the husband. Woman, in these households, is economy, order, and providence. Every influence she gains, is an advancement in morality.

This instance was not altogether useless, to show the insufficiency of the documents gathered from statistics and other works of political economy, to make us comprehend the people; they give partial, artificial results, taken at a sharp angle, and which may be wrongly interpreted.

Writers, literally artists, whose course is directly the opposite of these abstract methods, would seem likely to bring the sentiment of life to the study of the people. Some of the most eminent among them have attempted this grand subject, and talent did not fail them; their success has been immense. Europe, long little inventive, receives with avidity the produce of our literature. The English scarcely write any thing now-a-days but articles in reviews: as for German books, who reads them but the Germans?

It would be worth while to examine whether these French books, which have so much popularity, so much authority, in Europe, represent France truly,—whether they have not exhibited certain exceptional, very unfavourable, shades of character,—whether these pictures, in which people see scarcely any thing but our vices and our defects, have not done our country immense harm among foreign nations. The talent, the honesty of the authors, and the well-known liberality of their principles, lent an overwhelming weight to their words. The world has received their books as a terrible judgment of France upon herself.

France has this serious point against herself,—that she shows herself naked to the nations. All others, in a manner, remain clothed and dressed. Germany,—nay even England, with all her inquiries, all her publicity, are, in comparison, little known. They cannot see themselves, not being centralised.

That which is first remarked on a naked figure, is its defects. These strike the eye at once. What would be the result, if an obliging hand placed over these very defects a magnifying glass that would make them appear colossal, and reflect upon them such a pitiless light that the most natural accidents of the skin should burst forth on the horror-struck eye?

That is precisely what has happened to France. Her undoubted defects, which are amply accounted for by her unbounded activity and the shock of interests and ideas, have expanded, under the hand of her powerful writers, into monstrous forms. And behold, Europe, even now, looks upon her as a monster herself. . . .

Let it suffice nations to be well assured, that this nation is by no means like its pretended portraits. It is not that our great painters have always been incorrect; but they have generally painted exceptional details, accidents at most, in each species:—the minority: the worst side of things. Grand views appeared to them too well known, trivial, and vulgar. They wanted effect; and they have often sought it in whatever deviated from the general rule. Sprung from agitation, from commotion, so to speak, they have been gifted with passion, with a tempestuous strength, with a touch occasionally true as well as fine and strong; but, generally, they have lacked the sense of majestic harmony.

Romantic writers had fancied that art lay especially in the horrible. These thought that the most infallible effects of art were in moral ugliness.

Vagabond love has seemed to them more poetical than domestic, theft than labour, the galleys than the workshop. If they had themselves descended, by their own personal sufferings, into the profound realities of present life, they would have seen that the family circle, toil, the humblest life of the people, have in themselves a sacred poetry. To feel and represent this, is not the business of the machinist; it is not necessary to accumulate here theatrical accidents. It is only necessary that we should have eyes formed for that gentle light, eyes to look into the dark, the petty, and the lowly; and the heart too helps us to see into those corners of the hearth, those shadows of Rembrandt.

Whenever our great writers have looked there, they have been admirable. But, generally, they have turned their eyes towards the fantastic, the violent, the whimsical, the exceptional. They have not deigned to warn us that they were sketching the exception. All readers, but especially foreigners, thought they were describing the rule. They said, "The people are so."

And I, who have sprung from them,—I, who have lived, toiled, and suffered with them—who, more than any other have purchased the right to say that I know them,—I come to establish against all mankind the personality of the people.

This personality I have not taken from the surface, in its picturesque or dramatic aspects. I have not seen it from without, but experienced it within; and, in this very experience, more than one deep quality of the people, which they possess within themselves without comprehending it, I have comprehended. Why? Because I was able to trace it to its historical origin, and see it issue from the depths of time. Whoever will confine himself to the present, the actual, will not understand them. He who is satisfied with seeing the exterior, and painting the form, will not even be able to see it. To see it accurately, and translate it faithfully, he must know what it covers: there is no painting without anatomy.

It is not in this little book that I can teach such a science. It is sufficient for me to give—suppressing every detail, methodical, learned, and initiatory—a few observations essential in the state of our manners,—some general results.

One word only here. The chief and most prominent feature which has always struck me the most, in my long study of the people, is, that among the disorders of destitution, and the vices of misery, I have found a richness of sentiment and a goodness of heart, very rare among the wealthy classes. Everybody, moreover, may have observed this. At the time of the cholera, who adopted the orphan children? The poor.

The faculty of devotedness, the power of sacrifice, is, I confess, my standard for classing mankind. He who possesses this quality in the highest degree, is the nearest to heroism. Intellectual superiority, which proceeds partly from education, can never be put in the balance against this sovereign faculty.

To this it is generally replied: "The lower class of people have generally but little foresight; they follow an instinct of goodness, the blind impulse of a good heart, because they do not foresee all that it may cost them." Even if this observation were just, it by no means does away with the unremitting devotedness, the indefatigable sacrifices, which one may see so often exemplified in hard-working families,—a devotedness which is not even exhausted in the immolation of one life, but which is often continued from one to another for several generations.

I have here many excellent stories which I might relate. I cannot do so; but I am strongly tempted, my dear friend, to tell you one story, viz., that of my own family. You are not yet acquainted with it; we converse more frequently about philosophical or political, than about personal matters. I yield to this temptation. I have a rare opportunity of acknowledging the persevering heroic sacrifices that my family have made for me, and of thanking my relations, lowly retired people, some of whom have hid in obscurity their superior gifts, desirous to live only in me. . . .

My greatest delight, which restored my heart, was, on Sunday or Thursday, to read two or three times over a canto of Virgil or a book of Horace. Gradually I retained them, in other respects I have never been able to learn a single lesson by heart. I well remember that in the midst of that thorough misery, privations of the present, fears for the future, the public enemy being at the gates (1814!), and my own enemies daily deriding me, one day, one Thursday morning, I sat ruminating about myself, without fire (the snow lay deep), not well knowing whether I should find bread at night, fancying it was all over with me. I had within me, but without any mixture of religious hope, a pure stoic sentiment. With my frost-bitten hand I struck my oaken table (which I have always preserved), and felt a powerfully joyous impulse of youth and future prospects. Tell me, friend, what should I fear now? I, who have suffered death so many times in myself and in my reading? And what should I desire? God has given me in History the means of participating in every thing. Life has but one hold on me, that which I felt on the 12th of February last, about thirty years after. I found myself, on a similar day, equally covered with snow, opposite the same table. One thing smote my heart: "Thou art warm—others are cold; that is not right. Oh! who will relieve me from this cruel inequality?" Then, looking at my hand, the one which, from 1814, still shows the traces of the cold, I said to myself for consolation, "If you were working with the people, you would not be working for them. Come, then, if you give its history to your country, I will pardon you for being happy."

To return. My faith was not absurd; it was founded upon will. I believed in the future, because I was making it my-

self. My studies ended soon and well.[1] I had the good
fortune to escape two influences which ruined young men,
—that of the majestic but sterile school of the Doctrinaires,
and of the manufactory of literature (*littérature industrielle*),
whose most miserable essays were then easily accepted by
the just-reviving book-trade.

I would not live by my pen. I wanted a real occupation.
I took the one my studies had prepared me for—teaching.
I thought even then, with Rousseau, that literature ought to
be the thing reserved, the grand luxury of life, the inward
blossom of the soul. It was a great happiness for me when,
in the morning, I had given my lessons, to return to my
faubourg near *Père-la-chaise*, and there to read at my leisure
all day long such poets as Homer, Sophocles, or Theocritus,
and occasionally the historians. One of my old companions
and dearest friends, M. Poret, was reading the same, about
which we used to converse together in our long walks to the
wood of Vincennes.

This life of ease lasted scarcely less than ten years, during
which time I never imagined that I should ever write. I
taught at once the languages, philosophy, and history. In
1821, I procured by competition the professorship in a
college. In 1827, two works, which appeared at the same
time, my *Vico* and *Précis d'Histoire Moderne,* gained me a
professorship in the École Normale.[2]

Teaching did me good service. The fierce trial at college
had altered my character—had made me reserved and close,
shy and distrustful. Marrying young, and living in great
retirement, I desired less and less the society of men. That
which I found in my pupils at the École Normale, and elsewhere, once more opened and expanded my heart. Those
young people, amiable and confiding, who believed in me,
reconciled me to mankind. I was touched, and often sad, to
see them succeed each other so rapidly before me. Hardly
had I become attached to them than they departed. They are
all dispersed, and several (so young!) are dead. Few have
forgotten me; for my part, whether they be living or dead,
I shall never forget them.

They had done me, without knowing it, an immense
service. If I had, as an historian, any special merit to sustain
me on a level with my illustrious predecessors, I should owe
it to teaching, which for me was friendship. Those great
historians have been brilliant, judicious, and profound; as
for me, I have loved more.

I have also suffered more. The trials of my boyhood are always before me; I have retained the impression of toil, of a hard laborious life; I have remained one of the people.

I said, just now, I grew up like grass between two paving-stones; but this grass has retained its sap as much as that of the Alps. My very solitude in Paris, my free study and my free teaching (ever free and every where the same), have raised, without altering me. They who rise, almost always lose by it; because they become changed, they become mongrels, bastards; they lose the originality of their own class, without gaining that of another. The difficulty is not to rise, but in rising to remain one's self.

Often, in these days, the rise and progress of the people are compared to the invasion of the *Barbarians*. The expression pleases me; I accept it. *Barbarians!* Yes, that is to say, full of new, living, regenerating sap. *Barbarians*, that is, travellers marching toward the Rome of the future, going on slowly, doubtless; each generation advancing a little, halting in death; but others march forward all the same.

We other Barbarians have a natural advantage; if the upper classes have culture, we have much more vital heat. They cannot work hard, neither have they intensity, eagerness, or conscience in work. Their elegant writers, true spoiled children of the world, seem to slide upon the clouds; or, proudly eccentric, deign not to regard the earth: how should they fertilise it? That earth must imbibe the sweat of man, and be impressed with his heat and living virtue. Our Barbarians lavish all that upon her, and she loves them. On the other hand, their love is boundless and too great; devoting themselves sometimes to details, with the delightful awkwardness of Albert Durer, or the excessive polish of Jean Jacques Rousseau, who does not sufficiently conceal his art: by this minute detail they compromise the whole. We must not blame them too much; it is the excess of the will, the superabundance of love, occasionally the luxuriancy of the sap; this sap, ill-directed or perplexed, wrongs itself: it wants to give every thing at once—leaves, fruit, and flowers; it bends and twists the branches.

These defects of great workmen are often found in my books, without their good qualities. No matter! They who come thus, with the sap of the people, do not the less bring into art a new degree of life and *rejuvenescence,* at the very least a grand effort. They generally fix their aim higher, farther than others, scarcely consulting their strength, but rather their heart. Let it be my part in the future to have not attained, but marked, the aim of history, to have called it by a name that nobody had given it. Thierry called it *narration*, and M. Guizot *analysis*. I have named it resurrection, and this name will remain.

Who would be more severe than I, if I were to criticise my own works? The public has treated me too well. Do you fancy that I do not see how very imperfect this present volume is? "Why, then, do you publish it? You must have surely some very great interest at stake?" An interest? Several, as you shall see. First, I lose by it many ties of friendship. Next, I emerge from a tranquil position, entirely in unison with my tastes. I postpone my great book, the monument of my life.

"To enter public life apparently?" Never. I have estimated myself. I have neither health, nor talent for the government of men.

"Why then do you publish it?" If you really insist on knowing, I will tell you.

I speak, because nobody would speak in my stead. Not that there is not a crowd of men more capable of doing so, but all are soured, all hate. As for me, I still loved. Perhaps, also, I knew better the antecedents of France; I lived in her grand eternal life, and not in her present condition. I was more alive in sympathies, more dead in interests; I came to the questions with the disinterestedness of the dead.

I was suffering, moreover, far more than any other from the deplorable divorce that some are endeavouring to produce among men, between different classes, I who combine them all within me.

The situation of France is so serious, that there was no room for hesitation. I do not exaggerate to myself the power of a book; but the question is one of duty, by no means of ability.

Well! I see France hourly declining, engulfed like an Atlantis. Whilst we were here quarrelling, this country is swallowed up.

Who does not see, that from east to west, a shadow of death is pressing upon Europe, and that every day there is less sun; that Italy has perished, that Ireland has perished, that Poland has perished, and that Germany is bent on destruction? O Germany! Germany!

If France were dying a natural death, if her hour had come, I should perhaps be resigned; and, like a passenger on board a sinking ship, cover up my head, and commend myself to God. But her situation is nothing like that; and hence I am indignant; the idea of our ruin is absurd, ridiculous; it proceeds only from ourselves. Who has a literature? Who still sways the mind of Europe? We, weak as we are. Who has an army? We alone.

England and Russia, two feeble bloated giants, impose an illusion on Europe. Great empires, weak people! Let France be united, for an instant; she is strong as the world.

The first thing is, that before the crisis we should re-connoitre ourselves well; and have not, as in 1792 and in 1815, to alter our line, manoeuvres, and system, in presence of the enemy.

The second is, that we should trust in France, and not at all in Europe.

Here, every one goes to seek friends elsewhere[3]:—the politician hies to London, the philosopher to Berlin, the Communist says, "Our brother Chartists!" The peasant alone has preserved the tradition of salvation; to him a Prussian is still a Prussian, an Englishman an Englishman. His common sense has been right against all of you, refined gentlemen though you are! Your friend Prussia and your friend England drank the other day to France, the health of Waterloo!"

Children, children, I say unto you,—Climb up a mountain, provided it be high enough: look to the four winds, you will see nothing but enemies.

Try, then, to understand one another. That perpetual peace which some promise you whilst the arsenals are smok-ing! (see that black smoke over Cronstadt and Portsmouth!) —let us try to begin that peace among ourselves. Doubt-less we are divided; but Europe believes us to be more divided than we are. That is what emboldens her. The harsh things we have to say, let us say them,—pour out our hearts, hide none of the evils, and seek well the remedies.

One people! one country! one France! Let us never be-come two nations, I entreat you. Without unity, we perish. How is it that you do not perceive this?

Frenchmen, of every condition, every class, every party, remember well one thing!—You have on earth but one sure friend, France! Before the ever-enduring coalition of aris-tocracies, you will always be guilty of one crime,—to have wished, fifty years ago, to deliver the world. They have not forgiven it, nor will they ever forget it. You are always their dread. Among yourselves, you may be distinguished by different party names; but you are, as Frenchmen, condemned together. In the face of Europe, know that France will never have but one inexpiable name, which is her true, eternal designation,—The Revolution!

January 24th, 1846

8

POSITIVISTIC HISTORY AND ITS CRITICS: *Buckle and Droysen*

[Although most historians of the mid-nineteenth century considered history a science if it attempted to reconstruct the past according to verified, original sources, some historians, especially those that had come under the sway of Positivist philosophy, thought history had to discover the general laws of human development. Among the latter historians none was more popular or perceptive than Henry Thomas Buckle (1821-1862), a self-educated historian who had neither studied nor taught at a University.

A sickly child and a slow learner, Buckle did not develop any marked intellectual interests until his extensive travels in 1840. During the next fifteen years he set himself a rigorous program of reading; by 1850 he had taught himself the use of nineteen languages. His boldly analytical *History of Civilization in England* (2 vols. 1856-1861) enjoyed an immediate success, not least because of his timely plea that if historians would only search for and discover the hidden regularities of human actions then history would become a true science. He hoped to accomplish for history what other inquirers had done for the natural sciences: collect a multitude of facts and derive from them general laws about historical development. Buckle readily asserted that his own work represented a mere beginning; his two-volume *History* was meant to be an introduction to a fifteen-volume work on the comparative history of the European civilizations. His general laws and his emphasis on the usefulness of statistics for the induction of such laws were attacked by professional historians, and the *History* has become a neglected classic. Yet Buckle's highly original studies of the intellectual development of England, France, Scotland, and Spain have lost none of their force or relevancy, and his belief that "The real history of the human race is the history of tendencies which are perceived by the mind, and not of events which are discerned by the senses" has come to be shared by many contemporary historians. The following selection from Volume I is shorn, for reasons of space, of Buckle's magnificently erudite footnotes.

A philologist and historian, a patriot and philosopher, Johann Gustav Droysen (1808-1884) was a leading member of the so-called Prussian school of historians and also one of the first critics of Buckle's *History*. His devotion to the political ideal of German unity, preferably under Prussian leadership, went together with a strong Hegelian sense of the ethical character of the state and found historical expression in his fourteen-volume history of Prussian policy from the Middle Ages to the Seven Years' War. His first work, a history of Alexander the Great (1833) already contained unmistakable allusions to contemporary German politics. A critic of the dominant school of Ranke and of the rigidly scientific direction in history, Droysen developed his own principles of historical theory which in their emphasis on understanding rather than on causal explanation and on the personal involvement of the historian with his work anticipated some characteristic twentieth century views. From 1857 until 1883, first at the University of Jena and then at Berlin, Droysen gave a course on the theory and methodology of history; in 1858 an outline of the course, *Principles of History*, was first distributed in manuscript form to his students. The following essay on Art and Method was published as an appendix to the first regular edition of the *Outline of the Principles of History* (1868), from which §86 is reprinted as well.]

BUCKLE: GENERAL INTRODUCTION TO THE *History of Civilization in England*
Chapter 1. *Statement of the resources for investigating history, and proofs of the regularity of human actions. These actions are governed by mental and*

physical laws: therefore both sets of laws must be studied, and there can be no history without the natural sciences.

Of all the great branches of human knowledge, history is that upon which most has been written, and which has always been most popular. And it seems to be the general opinion that the success of historians has, on the whole, been equal to their industry; and that if on this subject much has been studied, much also is understood.

This confidence in the value of history is very widely diffused, as we see in the extent to which it is read, and in the share it occupies in all plans of education. Nor can it be denied that, in a certain point of view, such confidence is perfectly justifiable. It cannot be denied that materials have been collected which, when looked at in the aggregate, have a rich and imposing appearance. The political and military annals of all the great countries in Europe, and of most of those out of Europe, have been carefully compiled, put together in a convenient form, and the evidence on which they rest has been tolerably well sifted. Great attention has been paid to the history of legislation, also to that of religion: while considerable, though inferior, labour has been employed in tracing the progress of science, of literature, of the fine arts, of useful inventions, and, latterly, of the manners and comforts of the people. In order to increase our knowledge of the past, antiquities of every kind have been examined; the sites of ancient cities have been laid bare, coins dug up and deciphered, inscriptions copied, alphabets restored, hieroglyphics interpreted, and, in some instances, long-forgotten languages reconstructed and rearranged. Several of the laws which regulate the changes of human speech have been discovered, and, in the hands of philologists, have been made to elucidate even the most obscure periods in the early migration of nations. Political economy has been raised to a science, and by it much light has been thrown on the causes of that unequal distribution of wealth which is the most fertile source of social disturbance. Statistics have been so sedulously cultivated, that we have the most extensive information, not only respecting the material interests of men, but also respecting their moral peculiarities; such as, the amount of different crimes, the proportion they bear to each other, and the influence exercised over them by age, sex, education, and the like. With this great movement physical geography has kept pace; the phenomena of climate have been registered, mountains measured, rivers surveyed and tracked to their source, natural productions of all kinds carefully studied, and their hidden properties unfolded: while every food which sustains life has been chemically analyzed, its constituents numbered and weighed, and the nature of the connexion between them and the human frame has, in many cases, been satisfactorily ascertained. At the same time, and that nothing should be left undone which might enlarge our knowledge of the events by which man is affected, there have been instituted circumstantial researches in many other departments; so that in regard to the most civilized people, we are now acquainted with the rate of their mortality, of their marriages, the proportion of their births, the character of their employments, and the fluctuations both in their wages and in the prices of the commodities necessary to their existence. These and similar facts have been collected, methodized, and are ripe for use. Such results, which form, as it were, the anatomy of a nation, are remarkable for their minuteness; and to them there have been joined other results less minute, but more extensive. Not only have the actions and characteristics of the great nations been recorded, but a prodigious number of different tribes in all parts of the known world have been visited and described by travellers, thus enabling us to compare the condition of mankind in every stage of civilization, and under every variety of circumstance. When we moreover add, that this curiosity respecting our fellow-creatures is apparently insatiable; that it is constantly increasing; that the means of gratifying it are also increasing, and that most of the observations which have been made are still preserved;—when we put all these things together, we may form a faint idea of the immense value of that vast body of facts which we now possess, and by the aid of which the progress of mankind is to be investigated.

But if, on the other hand, we are to describe the use that has been made of these materials, we must draw a very different picture. The unfortunate peculiarity of the history of man is, that although its separate parts have been examined with considerable ability, hardly any one has attempted to combine them into a whole, and ascertain the way in which they are connected with each other. In all the other great fields of inquiry, the necessity of generalization is universally admitted, and noble efforts are being made to rise from particular facts in order to discover the laws by which those facts are governed. So far, however, is this from being the usual course of historians, that among them a strange idea prevails, that their business is merely to relate events, which they may occasionally enliven by such moral and political reflections as seem likely to be useful. According to this scheme, any author who from indolence of thought, or from natural incapacity, is unfit to deal with the highest branches of knowledge, has only to pass some years in reading a certain number of books, and then he is qualified to be an historian; he is able to write the history of a great people, and his work becomes an authority on the subject which it professes to treat.

The establishment of this narrow standard has led to results very prejudicial to the progress of our knowledge. Owing to it, historians, taken as a body, have never recognized the necessity of such a wide and preliminary study as would enable them to grasp their subject in the whole of its natural relations. Hence the singular spectacle of one historian being ignorant of political economy; another knowing nothing of law; another nothing of ecclesiastical affairs and changes of opinion; another neglecting the philosophy of statistics, and another physical science; although these topics are the most essential of all, inasmuch as they comprise the principal circumstances by which the temper and character of mankind have been affected, and in which they are displayed. These important pursuits being, however, cultivated, some by one man, and some by another, have been isolated rather than united: the aid which might be derived from analogy and from mutual illustration has been lost; and no disposition has been shown to concentrate them upon history, of which they are, properly speaking, the necessary components. . . .

Our acquaintance with history being so imperfect, while our materials are so numerous, it seems desirable that something should be done on a scale far larger than has hitherto been attempted, and that a strenuous effort should be made to bring up this great department of inquiry to a level with other departments, in order that we may maintain the balance and harmony of our knowledge. It is in this spirit that the present work has been conceived. To make the execution of it fully equal to the conception is impossible: still I hope to accomplish for the history of man something equivalent, or at all events analogous, to what has been effected by other inquirers for the different branches of natural science. In regard to nature, events apparently the most irregular and capricious have been explained, and have been shown to be in accordance with certain fixed and universal laws. This has been done because men of ability, and, above all, men of patient, untiring thought, have studied natural events with the view of discovering their regularity: and if human events were subjected to a similar treatment, we have every right to expect similar results. For it is clear that they who affirm that the facts of history are incapable of being generalized, take for granted the very question at issue. Indeed they do more than this. They not only assume what they cannot prove, but they assume what in the present state of knowledge is highly improbable. Whoever is at all acquainted with what has been done during the last two centuries, must be aware that every generation demonstrates some events to be regular and predictable, which the preceding generation had declared to be irregular and unpredictable: so that the marked tendency of advancing civilization is to strengthen our belief in the universality of order, of method, and of law. This being the case, it follows that if any facts, or class of facts, have not yet been reduced to order, we, so far from pronouncing them to be irreducible, should rather be guided by our experience of the past, and should admit the probability that what we now call inexplicable will at some future time be explained. This expectation of discovering regularity in the midst of confusion is so familiar to scientific men, that among the most eminent of them it becomes an article of faith; and if the same expectation is not generally found among historians, it must be ascribed partly to their being of inferior ability to the investigators of nature, and partly to the greater complexity of those social phenomena with which their studies are concerned.

Both these causes have retarded the creation of the science of history. The most celebrated historians are manifestly inferior to the most successful cultivators of physical science: no one having devoted himself to history who in point of intellect is at all to be compared with Kepler, Newton, or many others that might be named. And as to the greater complexity of the phenomena, the philosophic historian is opposed by difficulties far more formidable than is the student of nature; since, while on the one hand, his observations are more liable to those causes of error which arise from prejudice and passion, he, on the other hand, is unable to employ the great physical resource of experiment, by which we can often simplify even the most intricate problems in the external world.

It is not, therefore, surprising that the study of the movements of Man should be still in its infancy, as compared with the advanced state of the study of the movements of Nature. Indeed the difference between the progress of the two pursuits is so great, that while in physics the regularity of events, and the power of predicting them, are often taken for granted even in cases still unproved, a similar regularity is in history not only not taken for granted, but is actually denied. Hence it is that whoever wishes to raise history to a level with other branches of knowledge, is met by a preliminary obstacle; since he is told that in the affairs of men there is something mysterious and providential, which makes them impervious to our investigations, and which will always hide from us their future course. To this it might be sufficient to reply, that such an assertion is gratuitous; that it is by its nature incapable of proof; and that it is moreover opposed by the notorious fact that everywhere else increasing knowledge is accompanied by an increasing confidence in the uniformity with which, under the same circumstances, the same events must succeed each other. It will, however, be more satisfactory to probe the difficulty deeper, and inquire at once into the foundation of the common opinion that history must always remain in its present empirical state, and can never be raised to the rank of a science. We shall thus be led to one vast question, which indeed lies at the root of the whole subject, and is simply this: Are the actions of men, and therefore of societies, governed by fixed laws, or are they the result either of chance or of supernatural interference? The discussion of these alternatives will suggest some speculations of considerable interest. . . .

Nor is it merely the crimes of men which are marked by this uniformity of sequence. Even the number of marriages annually contracted, is determined, not by the temper and wishes of individuals, but by large general facts, over which individuals can exercise no authority. It is now known that marriages bear a fixed and definite relation to the price of corn; and in England the experience of a century has proved that, instead of having any connexion with personal feelings, they are simply regulated by the average earnings of the great mass of the people: so that this immense social and religious institution is not only swayed, but is completely controlled, by the price of food and by the rate of wages. In other cases, uniformity has been detected, though the causes of the uniformity are still unknown. Thus, to give a curious instance, we are now able to prove that the aberrations of memory are marked by this general character of necessary and invariable order. The post-offices of London and of Paris have latterly published returns of the number of letters which the writers, through forgetfulness, omitted to direct; and, making allowance for the difference of circumstances, the returns are year after year copies of each other. Year after year the same proportion of letter-writers forget this simple act; so that for each successive period we can actually foretell the number of persons whose memory will fail them in regard to this trifling and, as it might appear, accidental occurrence.

To those who have a steady conception of the regularity of events, and have firmly seized the great truth that the actions of men, being guided by their antecedents, are in reality never inconsistent, but, however capricious they may appear, only form part of one vast scheme of universal order, of which we in the present state of knowledge can barely see the outline,—to those who understand this, which is at once the key and the basis of history, the facts just adduced, so far from being strange, will be precisely what would have been expected, and ought long since to have been known. Indeed, the progress of inquiry is becoming so rapid and so earnest, that I entertain little doubt that before another century has elapsed, the chain of evidence will be complete, and it will be as rare to find an historian who denies the undeviating regularity of the moral world, as it now is to find a philosopher who denies the regularity of the material world.

It will be observed, that the preceding proofs of our actions being regulated by law, have been derived from statistics; a branch of knowledge which, though still in its infancy, has already thrown more light on the study of human nature than all the sciences put together. But although the statisticians have been the first to investigate this great subject by treating it according to those methods of reasoning which in other fields have been found successful; and although they have, by the application of numbers, brought to bear upon it a very powerful engine for eliciting truth,—we must not, on that account, suppose that there are no other resources remaining by which it may likewise be cultivated; nor should we infer that because the physical sciences have not yet been applied to history, they are therefore inapplicable to it. Indeed, when we consider the incessant contact between man and the external world, it is certain that there must be an intimate connexion between human actions and physical laws; so that if physical science has not hitherto been brought to bear upon history, the reason is, either that historians have not perceived the connexion, or else that, having perceived it, they have been destitute of the knowledge by which its workings can be traced. Hence there has arisen an unnatural separation of the two great departments of inquiry, the study of the internal, and that of the external: and although, in the present state of European literature, there are some unmistakable symptoms of a desire to break down this artificial barrier, still it must be admitted that as yet nothing has been actually accomplished towards effecting so great an end. The moralists, the theologians, and the metaphysicians, continue to prosecute their studies without much respect for what they deem the inferior labors of scientific men; whose inquiries, indeed, they frequently attack, as dangerous to the interests of religion, and as inspiring us with an undue confidence in the resources of the human understanding. On the other hand, the cultivators of physical science, conscious that they are an advancing body, are naturally proud of their own success; and, contrasting their discoveries with the more stationary position of their opponents, are led to despise pursuits the barrenness of which has now become notorious.

It is the business of the historian to mediate between these two parties, and reconcile their hostile pretensions by showing the point at which their respective studies ought to coalesce. To settle the terms of this coalition, will be to fix the basis of all history. For since history deals with the actions of men, and since their actions are merely the product of a collision between internal and external phenomena, it becomes necessary to examine the relative importance of those phenomena; to inquire into the extent to which their laws are known; and to ascertain the resources for future discovery possessed by these two great classes, the students of the mind and the students of nature. This task I shall endeavor to accomplish in the next two chapters; and if I do so with anything approaching to success, the present work will at least have the merit of contributing something towards filling up that wide and dreary chasm, which, to the hindrance of our knowledge, separates subjects that are intimately related, and should never be disunited. . . .

Chapter 2. *Influence exercised by physical laws
over the organization of society and
over the character of individuals.*

If we inquire what those physical agents are by which the
human race is most powerfully influenced, we shall find that
they may be classed under four heads: namely, Climate, Food,
Soil, and the General Aspect of Nature; by which last, I
mean those appearances which, though presented chiefly to
the sight, have, through the medium of that or other senses,
directed the association of ideas, and hence in different
countries have given rise to different habits of national
thought. To one of these four classes may be referred all the
external phenomena by which Man has been permanently
affected. The last of these classes, or what I call the General
Aspect of Nature, produces its principal results by exciting
the imagination, and by suggesting those innumerable superstitions which are the great obstacles to advancing knowledge.
And as, in the infancy of a people, the power of such superstitions is supreme, it has happened that the various Aspects
of Nature have caused corresponding varieties in the popular
character, and have imparted to the national religion peculiarities which, under certain circumstances, it is impossible to
efface. The other three agents, namely, Climate, Food, and
Soil, have, so far as we are aware, had no direct influence of
this sort; but they have, as I am about to prove, originated the
most important consequences in regard to the general organization of society, and from them there have followed many
of those large and conspicuous differences between nations,
which are often ascribed to some fundamental difference in
the various races into which mankind is divided. But while
such original distinctions of race are altogether hypothetical,
the discrepancies which are caused by difference of climate,
food, and soil, are capable of a satisfactory explanation, and,
when understood, will be found to clear up many of the
difficulties which still obscure the study of history. I purpose,
therefore, in the first place, to examine the laws of these
three vast agents in so far as they are connected with Man
in his social condition; and having traced the working of
those laws with as much precision as the present state of
physical knowledge will allow, I shall then examine the remaining agent, namely, the General Aspect of Nature, and
shall endeavor to point out the most important divergencies
to which its variations have, in different countries, naturally
given rise.

Beginning, then, with climate, food, and soil, it is evident that these three physical powers are in no small degree dependent on each other; that is to say, there is a very close connexion between the climate of a country and the food which will ordinarily be grown in that country; while at the same time the food is itself influenced by the soil which produces it, as also by the elevation or depression of the land, by the state of the atmosphere, and, in a word, by all those conditions to the assemblage of which the name of physical Geography is, in its largest sense, commonly given.

The union between these physical agents being thus intimate, it seems advisable to consider them not under their own separate heads, but rather under the separate heads of the effects produced by their united action. In this way we shall rise at once to a more comprehensive view of the whole question; we shall avoid the confusion that would be caused by artificially separating phenomena which are in themselves inseparable; and we shall be able to see more clearly the extent of that remarkable influence which, in an early stage of society, the powers of Nature exercise over the fortunes of Man.

Of all the results which are produced among a people by their climate, food, and soil, the accumulation of wealth is the earliest, and in many respects the most important. For although the progress of knowledge eventually accelerates the increase of wealth, it is nevertheless certain that, in the first formation of society, the wealth must accumulate before the knowledge can begin. As long as every man is engaged in collecting the materials necessary for his own subsistence, there will be neither leisure nor taste for higher pursuits; no science can possibly be created, and the utmost that can be effected will be an attempt to economize labor by the contrivance of such rude and imperfect instruments as even the most barbarous people are able to invent.

In a state of society like this, the accumulation of wealth is the first great step that can be taken, because without wealth there can be no leisure, and without leisure there can be no knowledge. If what a people consume is always exactly equal to what they possess, there will be no residue, and therefore, no capital being accumulated, there will be no means by which the unemployed classes may be maintained. But if the produce is greater than the consumption, an overplus arises, which, according to well-known principles, increases itself, and eventually becomes a fund out of which, immediately or remotely, every one is supported who does not create the wealth upon which he lives. And now it is that the existence of an intellectual class first becomes possible, because for the first time there exists a previous accumulation, by means of which men can use what they did not produce, and are thus enabled to devote themselves to subjects for which at an earlier period the pressure of their daily wants would have left them no time. . . . .

Chapter 3. *Examination of the method by metaphysicians for discovering mental laws.*

It is hardly necessary to notice how, in numerous other instances, the progress of European civilization has been marked by the diminished influence of the external world: I mean, of course, those peculiarities of the external world which have an existence independent of the wishes of man, and were not created by him. The most advanced nations do, in their present state, owe comparatively little to those original features of nature which, in every civilization out of Europe, exercised unlimited power. Thus, in Asia and elsewhere, the course of trade, the extent of commerce, and many similar circumstances, were determined by the existence of rivers, by the facility with which they could be navigated, and by the number and goodness of the adjoining harbours. But in Europe, the determining cause is, not so much these physical peculiarities, as the skill and energy of man. Formerly the richest countries were those in which nature was most bountiful; now the richest countries are those in which man is most active. For in our age of the world, if nature is parsimonious, we know how to compensate her deficiencies. If a river is difficult to navigate, or a country difficult to traverse, our engineers can correct the error, and remedy the evil. If we have no rivers, we make canals; if we have no natural harbours, we make artificial ones. And so marked is this tendency to impair the authority of natural phenomena, that it is seen even in the distribution of the people, since, in the most civilized parts of Europe, the population of the towns is every where outstripping that of the country; and it is evident that the more men congregate in great cities, the more they will become accustomed to draw their materials of thought from the business of human life, and the less attention they will pay to those peculiarities of nature which are the fertile source of superstition, and by which, in every civilization out of Europe, the progress of man was arrested.

From these facts it may be fairly inferred, that the advance of European civilization is characterized by a diminishing influence of physical laws, and an increasing influence of mental laws. The complete proof of this generalization can be collected only from history; and therefore I must reserve a large share of the evidence on which it is founded, for the future volumes of this work. But that the proposition is fundamentally true, must be admitted by whoever, in addition to the arguments just adduced, will concede two premises, neither of which seem susceptible of much dispute. The first premiss is, that we are in possession of no evidence that the powers of nature have ever been permanently increased; and that we have no reason to expect that any such increase can take place. The other premiss is, that we have abundant evidence that the resources of the human mind have become more powerful, more numerous, and more able to grapple with the difficulties of the external world; because every fresh accession to our knowledge supplies fresh means, with which we can either control the operations of nature, or, failing in that, can foresee the consequences, and thus avoid what is impossible to prevent; in both instances, diminishing the pressure exercised on us by external agents.

If these premises are admitted, we are led to a conclusion which is of great value for the purpose of this Introduction. For if the measure of civilization is the triumph of the mind over external agents, it becomes clear, that of the two classes of laws which regulate the progress of mankind, the mental class is more important than the physical. This, indeed, is assumed by one school of thinkers as a matter of course, though I am not aware that its demonstration has been hitherto attempted by any thing even approaching an exhaustive analysis. The question, however, as to the originality of my arguments, is one of very trifling moment; but what we have to notice is, that in the present stage of our inquiry, the problem with which we started has become simplified, and a discovery of the laws of European history is resolved, in the first instance, into a discovery of the laws of the human mind. These mental laws, when ascertained, will be the ultimate basis of the history of Europe; the physical laws will be treated as of minor importance, and as merely giving rise to disturbances, the force and the frequency of which have, during several centuries, perceptibly diminished. . . .

Chapter 5. *Inquiry into the influence exercised by religion, literature, and government.*

The totality of human actions being thus, from the highest point of view, governed by the totality of human knowledge, it might seem a simple matter to collect the evidence of the knowledge, and, by subjecting it to successive generalizations, ascertain the whole of the laws which regulate the progress of civilization. And that this will be eventually done, I do not entertain the slightest doubt. But, unfortunately, history has been written by men so inadequate to the great task they have undertaken, that few of the necessary materials have yet been brought together. Instead of telling us those things which alone have any value,—instead of giving us information respecting the progress of knowledge, and the way in which mankind has been affected by the diffusion of that knowledge,—instead of these things, the vast majority of historians fill their works with the most trifling and miserable details: personal anecdotes of kings and courts; interminable relations of what was said by one minister, and what was thought by another; and, what is worse than all, long accounts of campaigns, battles, and sieges, very interesting to those engaged in them, but to us utterly useless, because they neither furnish new truths, nor do they supply the means by which new truths may be discovered. This is the real impediment which now stops our advance. It is this want of judgment, and this ignorance of what is most worthy of selection, which deprives us of materials that ought long since to have been accumulated, arranged, and stored-up for future use. In other great branches of knowledge, observation has preceded discovery; first the facts have been registered, and then their laws have been found. But in the study of the history of Man, the important facts have been neglected, and the unimportant ones preserved. The consequence is, that whoever now attempts to generalize historical phenomena, must collect the facts, as well as conduct the generalization. He finds nothing ready to his hand. He must be the mason as well as the architect; he must not only scheme the edifice, but likewise excavate the quarry. The necessity of performing this double labour entails upon the philosopher such enormous drudgery, that the limits of an entire life are unequal to the task; and history, instead of being ripe, as it ought to be, for complete and exhaustive generalizations, is still in so crude and informal a state, that not the most determined and protracted industry will enable any one to comprehend the really important actions of mankind, during even so short a period as two successive centuries.

On account of these things, I have long since abandoned my original scheme; and I have reluctantly determined to write the history, not of general civilization, but of the civilization of a single people. While, however, by this means, we curtail the field of inquiry, we unfortunately diminish the resources of which the inquiry is possessed. For although it is perfectly true, that the totality of human actions, if considered in long periods, depends on the totality of human knowledge, it must be allowed that this great principle, when applied only to one country, loses something of its original value. The more we diminish our observations, the greater becomes the uncertainty of the average; in other words, the greater the chance of the operation of the larger laws being troubled by the operation of the smaller. The interference of foreign governments; the influence exercised by the opinions, literature, and customs of a foreign people; their invasions, perhaps even their conquests; the forcible introduction by them of new religions, new laws, and new manners,—all these things are perturbations, which, in a view of universal history, equalize each other, but which, in any one country, are apt to disturb the natural march, and thus render the movements of civilization more difficult to calculate. The manner in which I have endeavoured to meet this difficulty will be presently stated; but what I first wish to point out, are the reasons which have induced me to select the history of England as more important than any other, and therefore as the most worthy of being subjected to a complete and philosophic investigation.

Now, it is evident that, inasmuch as the great advantage of studying past events consists in the possibility of ascertaining the laws by which they were governed, the history of any people will become more valuable in proportion as their movements have been least disturbed by agencies not arising from themselves. Every foreign or external influence which is brought to bear upon a nation is an interference with its natural development, and therefore complicates the circumstances we seek to investigate. To simplify complications is, in all branches of knowledge, the first essential of success. This is very familiar to the cultivators of physical science, who are often able, by a single experiment, to discover a truth which innumerable observations had vainly searched;

the reason being, that by experimenting on phenomena, we can disentangle them from their complications; and thus isolating them from the interference of unknown agencies, we leave them, as it were, to run their own course, and disclose the operation of their own law.

This, then, is the true standard by which we must measure the value of the history of any nation. The importance of the history of a country depends, not upon the splendour of its exploits, but upon the degree to which its actions are due to causes springing out of itself. If, therefore, we could find some civilized people who had worked out their civilization entirely by themselves; who had escaped all foreign influence, and who had been neither benefited nor retarded by the personal peculiarities of their rulers,—the history of such a people would be of paramount importance; because it would present a condition of normal and inherent development; it would show the laws of progress acting in a state of isolation; it would be, in fact, an experiment ready-made, and would possess all the value of that artificial contrivance to which natural science is so much indebted.

To find such a people as this is obviously impossible; but the duty of the philosophic historian is, to select for his especial study the country in which the conditions have been most closely followed. Now, it will be readily admitted, not only by ourselves, but by intelligent foreigners, that in England, during, at all events, the last three centuries, this has been done more constantly and more successfully than in any other country. I say nothing of the number of our discoveries, the brilliancy of our literature, or the success of our arms. These are invidious topics; and other nations may perhaps deny to us those superior merits which we are apt to exaggerate. But I take up this single position, that of all European countries, England is the one where, during the longest period, the government has been most quiescent, and the people most active; where popular freedom has been settled on the widest basis; where each man is most able to say what he thinks, and do what he likes; where every one can follow his own bent, and propagate his own opinions; where, religious persecution being little known, the play and flow of the human mind may be clearly seen, unchecked by those restraints to which it is elsewhere subjected; where the profession of heresy is least dangerous, and the practice of dissent most common; where hostile creeds flourish side by side, and rise and decay without disturbance, according to the wants of the people, unaffected by the wishes of the church, and uncontrolled by the authority of the state; where all interests, and all classes, both spiritual and temporal, are most left to take care of themselves; where that meddlesome doctrine called Protection was first attacked, and where alone it has been destroyed; and where, in a word, those dangerous extremes to which interference gives rise having been avoided, despotism and rebellion are equally rare, and concession being recognized as the groundwork of policy, the national progress has been least disturbed by the power of privileged classes, by the influence of particular sects, or by the violence of arbitrary rulers. . . .

Chapter 14. *Proximate causes of the French Revolution after the middle of the eighteenth century.*

That to which attention is usually drawn by the compilers of history is, not the change, but is merely the external result which follows the change. The real history of the human race is the history of tendencies which are perceived by the mind, and not of events which are discerned by the senses. It is on this account that no historical epoch will ever admit of that chronological precision familiar to antiquaries and genealogists. The death of a prince, the loss of a battle, and the change of a dynasty, are matters which fall entirely within the province of the senses; and the moment in which they happen can be recorded by the most ordinary observers. But those great intellectual revolutions upon which all other revolutions are based, cannot be measured by so simple a standard. To trace the movements of the human mind, it is necessary to contemplate it under several aspects, and then co-ordinate the results of what we have separately studied. By this means we arrive at certain general conclusions, which, like the ordinary estimate of averages, increase in value in proportion as we increase the number of instances from which they are collected. That this is a safe and available method, appears not only from the history of physical knowledge, but also from the fact, that it is the basis of the empirical maxims by which all men of sound understanding are guided in those ordinary transactions of life to which the generalizations of science have not yet been applied. Indeed, such maxims, which are highly valuable, and which in their aggregate form what is called common sense, are never collected with any thing like the precautions that the philosophic historian ought to feel himself bound to employ.

The real objection, therefore, to generalizations respecting the development of the intellect of a nation is, not that they want certainty, but that they lack precision. This is just the point at which the historian diverges from the annalist. That the English intellect, for example, is gradually becoming more democratic, or, as it is termed, more liberal, is as certain as that the crown of this country is worn by Queen Victoria. But though both these statements are equally certain, the latter statement is more precise. . . .

DROYSEN: ART AND METHOD

Poetry was composed before poetics arose, as people talked before there were grammar and rhetoric. Practical needs had taught men to mix and analyze materials and to apply the powers of nature to human purposes, before chemistry and physics had methodically investigated nature and expressed its laws in scientific form.

Recollections also belong to humanity's deepest nature and needs. However narrow or wide the circles which they may embrace, they are never in any wise wanting to men. In the highest degree personal as they at first appear, they yet form a bond between the souls which meet in them. No human community is without them. Each possesses in its previous life and history the image of its being, a common possession of all participants, which makes their relationships so much the firmer and more intimate.

We can believe that the memories of highly gifted peoples are embellished in their sagas, and become types for the expression of the ideals to which the spirit of the people is directed. We can suppose also that their faith gets for them its basis in the form of sacred stories, which present the contents of it to the eye as actual occurrences, and that such myths grow along with the sagas. But when this restlessly living fusion, finally satiated, comes to an end in the form of great epics, myths will no longer belong to the naive faith alone. . . .

Only after the natural sciences, sure and conscious of their way, had established their method and thereby made a new beginning in scientific thought, did the notion emerge of finding a methodical side even for the "methodless matter" of History. To the time of Galileo and Bacon belongs Jean Bodin; to that of Huygens and Newton, Pufendorff and also

Leibnitz, the thinker who broke paths in all directions at once. Then the English Enlightenment, if it is permitted thus to name the period of the so-called deists, took up this question. To its representations was due the first effort to divide our science according to its problems or departments. They spoke of the History of the World, the History of Humanity, Universal History, the History of States, of peoples, and so on. Voltaire, the pupil and continuator of this English tendency, contributed to it the unclear designation *"philosophie de l'histoire."* The Göttingen historical school developed a kind of system among the newly created sciences and associate sciences in their field, and began to infuse its spirit even into branches but remotely connected with History. More than one of the great poets and thinkers of our nation went deep into the theoretical question of historical certitude; and there developed in historical labor and investigation itself a habit of sharp and certain criticism, which produced entirely new and surprising results in every realm of History where it was applied. In this historical criticism the German nation has ever since Niebuhr outstripped all others, and the style or technique of investigation maintained in the splendid labors of German *savants* seemed to need only expression in general and theoretical propositions in order to constitute the historical method.

To be sure, the great public was not at once served by this application of our historical toil. It wished to read, not to study, and complained that we set before it the process of preparing food instead of the food itself. It called the German method in history pedantic, exclusive, unenjoyable. How much more agreeable to read were Macaulay's Essays than these learned and tiresome investigations! How the accounts of the French Revolution in Thiers's splendid delineation caught on! In this way it came to pass that not only German historical taste but German historical judgment, and consequently in no slight degree also German political judgment, being all formed and guided for three or four centuries by the foreign style of making History, were dominated by the rhetorical superiority of other nations.

This is not all. While such rhetorical art takes weighty and tremendous events, with the difficult entanglements in which they are usually wrought out or at least prepared for, and sadly metamorphoses them, as it depicts the horror of men's unchained passions and fanatic persecutions, the false representation, though discordant enough artistically, yet has a thrilling and dramatic effect when read. Composition is cer-

tain to be so much the more comprehensible and persuasive
for being of that kind. It is able to make even the less intelligent reader acquainted with things which in their actual
course demanded from the contemporary who wished to understand them in never so moderate a degree, a thousand
points of previous knowledge, besides much experience and a
calm and collected judgment. Historical art knows how in the
most felicitous manner to avoid all this, so that the attentive
reader, when he has perused his Thiers or Macaulay to the
end, is permitted to believe himself the richer by the great experiences of the revolutions, party-wars, and constitutional
developments of which they treat. "Experiences," forsooth!
when they lack the best of what makes experiences fruitful,
the earnestness of actual men hard at work, responsibility for
irrevocable decisions, the sacrifice which even victory demands, the failure which treads under foot the most righteous
cause! The art of the historian lifts the reader above thought
of any such side issues. It fills his fancy with representations
and views which embrace but the splendidly illuminated tips
of the broad, hard, tediously slow reality. It persuades him that
these sum up all the particular events and constitute the truth
of the realities not dwelt upon. It helps in its way the limitless influence of public opinion, leading people to measure
the reality according to their ideas and to call upon reality to
form or transform itself accordingly. Readers demand this the
more impatiently the easier custom has made it for them to
think of such a reversal of things. We Germans, too, already
boast an historical literature answering the popular need.
Among us as elsewhere the insight is attained or the confession made that "History is at once art and science." At the
same time the question of method, which is what we are concerned with here, is falling into obscurity anew.

What then, in works of an historical kind, is the mutual relation between art and science? For instance, is the fact that
History is marked by "criticism and learning" enough to give
it a scientific character? Is that incumbent on art which the
historian ought in any event to do? Should the historian's
studies actually have no other aim than that he may write a
few books? Should they have no application but to entertain
by instructing and to instruct by entertaining?

History is the only science enjoying the ambiguous fortune
of being required to be at the same time an art, a fortune
which, in spite of Platonic dialogues, not even philosophy
shares with it. It would not be without interest to inquire the
reason for this peculiarity of History.

We, however, pass to another side of the question. In artistic labors, according to an old manner of expression, technique and Muses' work go hand in hand. It belongs to the nature of art that its productions make you forget the defects which inhere in its means of expression. Art can do this in proportion as the idea which it wishes to bring out in given forms, upon such and such materials, and with this technique, vivifies and illumines all these. What is created in such a manner is a totality, a world in itself. Muses' work has the power to make the observer or hearer fully and exclusively receive and feel in a given expression what that work was meant to express.

It is different with the sciences. Particularly the empirical ones have no more imperative duty than to make clear the gaps which are based in the objects of their search; to control the errors which arise out of their technique; to inquire the scope of their methods, recognizing that they can give right results only within the limits essentially pertaining to them.

Perhaps the greatest service of the critical school in History, at least the one most important in respect to method, is to have given rise to the insight that the groundwork of our studies is the examination of the "sources" from which we draw. In this way the relation of History to past events is placed at the point which yields a scientific rule. This critical view that past events lie before us no longer directly, but only in a mediate manner, that we can not restore them "objectively," but can only frame out of the "sources" a more or less subjective apprehension, view, or copy of them, that the apprehensions and views thus attainable and won are all that it is possible for us to know of the past, that thus "History" exists not outwardly and as a reality, but only as thus mediated, studied out, and known,—this, so it seems, must be our point of departure if we will cease to "naturalize" in history.

What is before us for investigation is not past events as such, but partly remnants of them, partly ideas of them. The remnants are such only for historical consideration. They stand as wholes and on their own account in the midst of this present, many of them, fragmentary and widowed as they are, instantly reminding us that they were once different, more alive and important than now; others transformed and still in living and practical application; others changed almost beyond recognition and fused in the being and life of the present. The present itself is nothing else but the sum of all the remnants and products of the past. Furthermore, views of what was and happened are not always from contemporaries, those acquainted with the facts, or impartial witnesses, but often views of views, at third or fourth hand. And even when contemporaries tell what happened in their time, how much did they personally see and hear of what they relate? One's own eye-sight and hearing embrace after all but a part, a side, a tendency of the occurrences. And so on.

In point of method the character of these two kinds of materials is so extraordinarily different that one does well to keep them separate even in technical nomenclature; and it behooves such as wish their writings to be sources to name their sources even when in most respects they are like the other remnants, being literary remains of the time in which they arose.

The now usual method or technique of historical investigation was developed from the study of times which have transmitted, at least for political history, nothing or little but the sort of views above characterized, from more or less contemporary narrators. Much for which we should like to seek and inquire, these accounts do not touch at all. To the question how our emperors when they crossed the Alps on their journeys to Rome cared for thousands of men and horses, to the question in what form the commerce of the Mediterranean was carried on after the revolution which Alexander the Great effected over all Asia, the sources give us no information.

How superficial, how unreliable our knowledge of earlier times is, how necessarily fragmentary and limited to particular points the view which we can now gather therefrom, we become conscious even when we study times from which the archives offer us something more than the "original documents" of closed public law cases; giving us diplomatic reports, reports of administrative authorities and state papers of all kinds. And further, how vividly prominent in such study is the difference between the "views" of the foreign ambassadors or of the domestic authorities, and the remains that survive of the actual course of diplomacy, the deliberations back and forth, the protocols of the negotiations, and so on. Certainly these state documents do not as a rule, like those narrations, lay before us an already formed idea of the case, a preliminary historical picture of what had just happened. They are remnants of that which happened; they are pieces of the transaction and of the course it pursued, which still lie directly before our eyes. And if I may give the expression so wide an application, it is as a "transaction," in the broad maze of the present, conditioned and conditioning in a thousand ways, that those events come to pass which we afterwards apprehend successively as History. We thus look at them in a quite different way from that in which they occurred, and which they had in the wishes and deeds of those who enacted them. So it is not a paradox to ask how History (*Geschichte*) comes out of transactions (*Geschäften*), and what it is which with this transfer into another medium, as it were, is added or lost.

I may be permitted to offer a single remark in conclusion. I have in another place sought to refute the contention made against our science by those who view the method of natural science as the only scientific one, and who think that History must be raised to the rank of a science through the application of that method. Just as if in the realm of the historical, that is, of the moral life, only analogy were worthy of regard and not also anomaly, the individual, free-will, responsibility, genius. As if it were not a scientific task to seek ways of investigation, of verification, of understanding for the movements and effects of human freedom and of personal peculiarities, however high or low the estimate which may be placed upon them.

We certainly possess immediately and in subjective certainty, an understanding of human things, of every expression and impression of man's creation or behavior which is perceptible to us, so far as it is perceptible. What we have to do is to find methods, in order to secure objective rules and control for this immediate and subjective grasp of events, especially as we now have before us, to represent the past, only the views of others or fragments of that which once existed. We need to ground, sound and justify our subjective knowledge. Only this seems able to assert itself as the sense of the historical objectivity so often named.

We are to discover methods. There is need of different ones for different problems, and often a combination of several is required for the solution of one problem. So long as History was believed to be essentially political history, and the task of the historian was just to recount in new presentation and connection what had been transmitted about revolutions, wars, state events, etc., it might suffice to take for us from the best sources, which had perhaps been critically authenticated as the best, the material to be wrought into a book, a lecture, or the like. But since the insight has been awakened that also the arts, jural formations, everything of human creation, all the formations characterizing the moral world, can and must be investigated in order to deduce that which is from that which was, demands of a very different kind are made upon our science. It has to investigate formations according to their historical connection, formations of which perhaps only individual remnants are preserved, to open fields hitherto not considered or treated as historical, least of all by those who lived in the midst of them. Thus questions are pressing upon History from all sides, questions touching things for the most part incomparably weightier than the often very superficial and accidental accounts which have hitherto passed for History. Is investigation to lay down its arms here?

When we enter a collection of Egyptian antiquities, we have at once the subjective view of their wonderful ancientness, and the accompanying strange impression; but at least in certain directions we can by investigation come to more positive results. Here are these colors, these woven fabrics. What tools, what metals were required to work such hard stone? What mechanical contrivances were needed to raise such masses out of the quarry and put them aboard ship? How were these colors prepared chemically? Out of what materials are these fabrics made and whence did they come? In the way of such technological interpretation of remains, facts are made out which in numerous and important directions fill up our meagre tradition concerning ancient Egypt; and these facts possess a certainty so much the greater for the indirectness of the manner in which they were deduced.

Many think it the part of criticism, touching, for instance, the constitution of ancient Rome or Athens before the Persian wars, to allow only that to pass as good history which is explicitly transmitted and attested. The reader's fancy will not fail to combine these scanty notices and thus to fill them out into a picture; only, this filling out is commonly a play of the fancy, and the picture more or less artificial. Is it not possible to find methods which will regulate the process of such filling out, and give it a foundation? In the pragmatic nature exhibited by things of this kind—and writers should leave off misapprehending Polybius's expression "pragmatic"—lie elements, conditions, necessities, traces of which, provided we look more sharply, may perhaps be re-recognized in what still lies before us. The hypothetical line which enabled us to trace that pragmatic nature of things then confirms itself, since this or that fragment exactly fits into it.

When it was necessary to work out the history of art during the times of Raphael and Dürer, not much advance could be made with the "sources" and the criticism of sources, although in Vasari and others, at least for the Italian masters, was found just the external information that was desired. In their works and those of their German contemporaries, however, was found something entirely different, exactly the material for investigation, though confessedly of a nature which required in the investigator who was to derive exact results from it, an outfit of an especial kind. He was obliged to know the technique of painting, in order to distinguish that of the different artists, the tint of each one's tone, his chiaroscuro, his brushstroke. He was obliged to be sure how Albrecht Dürer's eye envisaged the human form, else he could not show whether a given crucifix was from his hand. In order finally to decide whether this or that important portrait head was by Leonardo da Vinci or Holbein, he had to bring to his work, so to speak, a learned apparatus of etchings, hand sketches, etc. He must be familiar with the mode of looking at things in that age, the range of its general knowledge, its common convictions, ecclesiastical and profane, its local and daily history, that he might be able rightly to interpret what was presented in the works of art or in things related thereto. He was called upon not only aesthetically to feel but persuasively to point out the artist's deeper or more superficial view or intention.

The same in all other departments. Only the deep and manysided technical and special knowledge, according as it is art, law, commerce, agriculture, or the State and politics that is to be historically investigated, will put the investigator in condition to ascertain the methods demanded for the given case, and to work with them. Just so new methods are continually found out in the natural sciences to unlock dumb nature's mysteries.

All such methods which come into play in the realm of historical studies move within the same periphery and have the same determining center. To unite them in their common thought, to develop their system and their theory, and so to establish, not the laws of objective History but the laws of historical investigation and knowledge,—this is the task of *Historik*.

§86 FROM *The Principles of History*

History is Humanity's knowledge of itself, its certainty about itself. It is not "the light and the truth," but a search therefor, a sermon thereupon, a consecration thereto. It is like John the Baptist, "not that Light but sent to bear witness of that Light."

9

HISTORICAL MATERIALISM:
Marx and Engels; Jaurès

[Karl Marx (1813-1883) and Friedrich Engels (1820-1895)
are not usually remembered as historians—the standard works
on historiography barely mention them—and yet they were
not only practicing historians but their dialectical materialistic
conception of history was the core of their system and had a
profound impact on subsequent historical thought and writing.
For Marx himself the formulation of historical materialism in
the mid-1840's represented the link between his earlier philosophical interest and his later concern with the economic
structure and the political development of capitalistic society.
The German Ideology (written by Marx and Engels in 1846,
published in its entirety only in 1932), from which the following selection is taken, contained the first exposition of historical materialism: "Life is not determined by consciousness,
but consciousness by life." The modes of production and the
social relations to which they give rise determine the consciousness of men, the ideological superstructure of society.
Both in short historical studies of the 1848 Revolution—
Marx's *The Class Struggles in France* (1850) and Engels'
Germany: Revolution and Counter-Revolution (1852)—and
in several studies on remoter periods—Engels' *The Peasant
War in Germany* (1850)—Marx and Engels sought to analyze
particular historical events in light of their historical system.
That they became increasingly concerned about the rigidity
of a literal application of historical materialism was demon-

strated in a letter of Engels in 1893 in which he stressed that the "ideological spheres" can react on the material causes which give rise to them.

While Marx had not been the first to emphasize the material basis of history, there can be no doubt that it was his system which most sharply, though not immediately, challenged prevailing historiography and directly influenced the development of social and economic history and of sociology. Historical materialism influenced Marxists and non-Marxists alike, and it can be argued that the latter derived greater benefit from it than the former. Max Weber and C. A. Beard, to cite only two examples, acknowledged their debt to Marx, although completely rejecting rigid Marxian theory. The best example of the advantages and limitations of Marx's historical approach can be found in the great Socialist historian, Jean Jaurès (1859-1914) whose historical work gained from his avowedly Marxian orientation yet who, as a practicing historian, disavowed a narrow deterministic system. Trained in philosophy, a graduate of the École Normale and a professor of philosophy at Toulouse, Jaurès turned to politics in the 1880's, becoming first a moderate republican deputy and later, in his most prominent phase, a leading Socialist. He had two passionate loyalties, France and the proletariat, and he celebrated both in his history of the French Revolution. In 1903 he asked the Government to establish a commission to collect and publish the scattered sources for the economic and social history of the Revolution, and a few months later he was himself appointed chairman of such a commission, with Aulard, Lavisse, Seignobos and other leading historians as members. The commission did in fact publish many such sources, in particular the invaluable *cahiers* of 1789. Convinced that the real basis of the Revolution had not yet been explored, Jaurès set out to write a *Histoire Socialiste de la Révolution Française* (originally published as vol. i-iv of *Histoire Socialiste*, in 13 vols. 1901-1909), covering the years from 1789 to Thermidor. Though written for peasants and workers and richly illustrated with authentic reproductions from the Revolution, Jaurès' *History* had high scholarly merit and a remarkably dispassionate tone; it was widely hailed as a major contribution to the history of the Revolution. The following selections from Jaurès' Preface and Introduction were translated for this volume by Dora Weiner.]

MARX AND ENGELS: FROM *The German Ideology*

. . . The premises from which we begin are not arbitrary ones, not dogmas, but real premises from which abstraction can only be made in the imagination. They are the real individuals, their activity and the material conditions under which they live, both those which they find already existing and those produced by their activity. These premises can thus be verified in a purely empirical way.

The first premise of all human history is, of course, the existence of living human individuals. Thus the first fact to be established is the physical organization of these individuals and their consequent relation to the rest of nature. Of course, we cannot here go either into the actual physical nature of man, or into the natural conditions in which man finds himself —geological, orohydrographical, climatic and so on. The writing of history must always set out from these natural bases and their modification in the course of history through the action of man.

Men can be distinguished from animals by consciousness, by religion or anything else you like. They themselves begin to distinguish themselves from animals as soon as they begin to *produce* their means of subsistence, a step which is conditioned by their physical organization. By producing their means of subsistence men are indirectly producing their actual material life.

The way in which men produce their means of subsistence depends first of all on the nature of the actual means they find in existence and have to reproduce. This mode of production must not be considered simply as being the reproduction of the physical existence of the individuals. Rather it is a definite form of activity of these individuals, a definite form of expressing their life, a definite *mode of life* on their part. As individuals express their life, so they are. What they are, therefore, coincides with their production, both with *what* they produce and with *how* they produce. The nature of individuals thus depends on the material conditions determining their production.

This production only makes its appearance with the increase of population. In its turn this presupposes the intercourse of individuals with one another. The form of this intercourse is again determined by production.

The relations of different nations among themselves depend upon the extent to which each has developed its productive forces, the division of labour and internal intercourse. This statement is generally recognized. But not only the relation of one nation to others, but also the whole internal structure of the nation itself depends on the stage of development reached by its production and its internal and external intercourse. How far the productive forces of a nation are developed is shown most manifestly by the degree to which the division of labour has been carried. Each new productive force, in so far as it is not merely a quantitative extension of productive forces already known, (for instance the bringing into cultivation of fresh land), brings about a further development of the division of labour.

The division of labour inside a nation leads at first to the separation of industrial and commercial from agricultural labour, and hence to the separation of town and country and a clash of interests between them. Its further development leads to the separation of commercial from industrial labour. At the same time through the division of labour there develop further, inside these various branches, various divisions among the individuals co-operating in definite kinds of labour. The relative position of these individual groups is determined by the methods employed in agriculture, industry and commerce (partriarchalism, slavery, estates, classes). These same conditions are to be seen (given a more developed intercourse) in the relations of different nations to one another.

The various stages of development in the division of labour are just so many different forms of ownership; i.e. the existing stage in the division of labour determines also the relations of individuals to one another with reference to the material, instrument, and product of the labour. . . .

The fact is, therefore, that definite individuals who are productively active in a definite way enter into these definite social and political relations. Empirical observation must in each separate instance bring out empirically, and without any mystification and speculation, the connection of the social and political structure with production. The social structure and the State are continually evolving out of the life-process of definite individuals, but of individuals, not as they may appear in their own or other people's imagination, but as they really are; i.e. as they are effective, produce materially, and are active under definite material limits, presuppositions and conditions independent of their will.

The production of ideas, of conceptions, of consciousness,

is at first directly interwoven with the material activity and the material intercourse of men, the language of real life. Conceiving, thinking, the mental intercourse of men, appear at this stage as the direct efflux of their material behaviour. The same applies to mental production as expressed in the language of the politics, laws, morality, religion, metaphysics of a people. Men are producers of their conceptions, ideas, etc.— real, active men, as they are conditioned by a definite development of their productive forces and of the intercourse corresponding to these, up to its furthest forms. Consciousness can never be anything else than conscious existence, and the existence of men is their actual life-process. If in all ideology men and their circumstances appear upside down as in a *camera obscura*, this phenomenon arises just as much from their historical life-process as the inversion of objects on the retina does from their physical life-process.

In direct contrast to German philosophy which descends from heaven to earth, here we ascend from earth to heaven. That is to say, we do not set out from what men say, imagine, conceive, nor from men as narrated, thought of, imagined, conceived, in order to arrive at men in the flesh. We set out from real, active men, and on the basis of their real life-process we demonstrate the development of the ideological reflexes and echoes of this life-process. The phantoms formed in the human brain are also, necessarily, sublimates of their material life-process, which is empirically verifiable and bound to material premises. Morality, religion, metaphysics, all the rest of ideology and their corresponding forms of consciousness, thus no longer retain the semblance of independence. They have no history, no development; but men, developing their material production and their material intercourse, alter, along with this their real existence, their thinking and the products of their thinking. Life is not determined by consciousness, but consciousness by life. In the first method of approach the starting-point is consciousness taken as the living individual; in the second it is the real living individuals themselves, as they are in actual life, and consciousness is considered solely as *their* consciousness.

This method of approach is not devoid of premises. It starts out from the real premises and does not abandon them for a moment. Its premises are men, not in any fantastic isolation or abstract definition, but in their actual, empirically perceptible process of development under definite conditions. As soon as this active life-process is described, history ceases to be a collection of dead facts as it is with the empiricists (themselves still abstract), or an imagined activity of imagined subjects, as with the idealists.

Where speculation ends—in real life—there real, positive science begins; the representation of the practical activity, of the practical process of development of men. Empty talk about consciousness ceases, and real knowledge has to take its place. When reality is depicted, philosophy as an independent branch of activity loses its medium of existence. At the best its place can only be taken by a summing-up of the most general results, abstractions which arise from the observation of the historical development of men. Viewed apart from real history, these abstractions have in themselves no value whatsoever. They can only serve to facilitate the arrangement of historical material, to indicate the sequence of its separate strata. But they by no means afford a recipe or schema, as does philosophy, for neatly trimming the epochs of history. On the contrary, our difficulties begin only when we set about the observation and the arrangement—the real depiction—of our historical material, whether of a past epoch or of the present. The removal of these difficulties is governed by premises which it is quite impossible to state here, but which only the study of the actual life-process and the activity of the individuals of each epoch will make evident. We shall select here some of these abstractions, which we use to refute the ideologists, and shall illustrate them by historical examples.

Since we are dealing with the Germans, who do not postulate anything, we must begin by stating the first premise of all human existence, and therefore of all history, the premise namely that men must be in a position to live in order to be able to "make history." But life involves before everything else eating and drinking, a habitation, clothing and many other things. The first historical act is thus the production of the means to satisfy these needs, the production of material life itself. And indeed this is an historical act, a fundamental condition of all history, which to-day, as thousands of years ago, must daily and hourly be fulfilled merely in order to sustain human life. Even when the sensuous world is reduced to a minimum, to a stick as with Saint Bruno [Bruno Bauer], it presupposes the action of producing the stick. The first necessity therefore in any theory of history is to observe this fundamental fact in all its significance and all its implications and to accord it its due importance. This, as is notorious, the Germans have never done, and they have never therefore had an earthly basis for history and consequently never a historian. The French and the English, even if they have conceived the relation of this fact with so-called history only in an extremely one-sided fashion, particularly as long as they remained in the toils of political ideology, have nevertheless made the first attempts to give the writing of history a materialistic basis by being the first to write histories of civil society, of commerce and industry.

The second fundamental point is that as soon as a need is satisfied, (which implies the action of satisfying, and the acquisition of an instrument), new needs are made; and this production of new needs is the first historical act. Here we recognize immediately the spiritual ancestry of the great historical wisdom of the Germans who, when they run out of positive material and when they can serve up neither theological nor political nor literary rubbish, do not write history at all, but invent the "prehistoric era." They do not, however, enlighten us as to how we proceed from this nonsensical "prehistory" to history proper; although, on the other hand, in their historical speculation they seize upon this "prehistory" with especial eagerness because they imagine themselves safe there from interference on the part of "crude facts," and, at the same time, because there they can give full rein to their speculative impulse and set up and knock down hypotheses by the thousand.

The third circumstance which, from the very first, enters into historical development, is that men, who daily remake their own life, begin to make other men, to propagate their kind: the relation between man and wife, parents and children, the *Family*. The family which to begin with is the only social relationship, becomes later, when increased needs create new social relations and the increased population new needs, a subordinate one (except in Germany), and must then be treated and analysed according to the existing empirical data, not according to "the concept of the family," as is the custom in Germany. These three aspects of social activity are not of course to be taken as three different stages, but just, as I have said, as three aspects or, to make it clear to the Germans, three "moments," which have existed simultaneously since the dawn of history and the first men, and still assert themselves in history to-day.

The production of life, both of one's own in labour and of fresh life in procreation, now appears as a double relationship: on the one hand as a natural, on the other as a social relationship. By social we understand the co-operation of several individuals, no matter under what conditions, in what manner and to what end. It follows from this that a certain mode of production, or industrial stage, is always combined with a certain mode of co-operation, or social stage, and this mode of co-operation is itself a "productive force." Further, that the multitude of productive forces accessible to men determines the nature of society, hence that the "history of humanity" must always be studied and treated in relation to the history of industry and exchange. But it is also clear how in Germany it is impossible to write this sort of history, because the Germans lack not only the necessary power of comprehension and the material but also the "evidence of their senses," for across the Rhine you cannot have any experience of these things since history has stopped happening. Thus it is quite obvious from the start that there exists a materialistic connection of men with one another, which is determined by their needs and their mode of production, and which is as old as men themselves. This connection is ever taking on new forms, and thus presents a "history" independently of the existence of any political or religious nonsense which would hold men together on its own.

Only now, after having considered four moments, four aspects of the fundamental historical relationships, do we find that man also possesses "consciousness"; but even so, not inherent, not "pure" consciousness. From the start the "spirit" is afflicted with the curse of being "burdened" with matter, which here makes its appearance in the form of agitated layers of air, sounds, in short of language. Language is as old as consciousness, language is practical consciousness, as it exists for other men, and for that reason is really beginning to exist for me personally as well; for language, like consciousness, only arises from the need, the necessity, of intercourse with other men. Where there exists a relationship, it exists for me: the animal has no "relations" with anything, cannot have any. For the animal, its relation to others does not exist as a relation. Consciousness is therefore from the very beginning a social product, and remains so as long as men exist at all. Consciousness is at first, of course, merely consciousness concerning the immediate sensuous environment and consciousness of the limited connection with other persons and things outside the individual who is growing self-conscious. At the same time it is consciousness of nature, which first appears to men as a completely alien, all-powerful and unassailable force, with which men's relations are purely animal and by which they are overawed like beasts; it is thus a purely animal consciousness of nature (natural religion).

We see here immediately: this natural religion or animal behaviour towards nature is determined by the form of society and *vice versa*. Here, as everywhere, the identity of nature and man appears in such a way that the restricted relation of men to nature determines their restricted relation to one another, and their restricted relation to one another determines men's restricted relation to nature, just because nature is as yet hardly modified historically; and, on the other hand, man's consciousness of the necessity of associating with the individuals around him is the beginning of the consciousness that he is living in society at all. This beginning is as animal as social life itself at this stage. It is mere herd-consciousness, and at this point man is only distinguished from sheep by the fact that with him consciousness takes the place of instinct or that his instinct is a conscious one.

This sheep-like or tribal consciousness receives its further development and extension through increased productivity, the increase of needs, and, what is fundamental to both of these, the increase of population. With these there develops the division of labour, which was originally nothing but the division of labour in the sexual act, then that division of labour which develops spontaneously or "naturally" by virtue of natural predisposition (e.g. physical strength), needs, accidents, etc., etc. Division of labour only becomes truly such from the moment when a division of material and mental labour appears. From this moment onwards consciousness *can* really flatter itself that it is something other than consciousness of existing practice, that it is *really* conceiving something without conceiving something *real;* from now on consciousness is in a position to emancipate itself from the world and to proceed to the formation of "pure" theory, theology, philosophy, ethics, etc. But even if this theory, theology, philosophy, ethics, etc. comes into contradiction with the existing relations, this can only occur as a result of the fact that existing social relations have come into contradiction with existing forces of production; this, moreover, can also occur in a particular national sphere of relations through the appearance of the contradiction, not within the national orbit, but between this national consciousness and the practice of other nations, i.e. between the national and the general consciousness of a nation.

Moreover, it is quite immaterial what consciousness starts to do on its own: out of all such muck we get only the one inference that these three moments, the forces of production, the state of society, and consciousness, can and must come into contradiction with one another, because the division of labour implies the possibility, nay the fact that intellectual and material activity—enjoyment and labour, production and consumption—devolve on different individuals, and that the only possibility of their not coming into contradiction lies in the negation in its turn of the division of labour. It is self-evident, moreover, that "spectres," "bonds," "the higher being," "concept," "scruple," are merely the idealistic, spiritual expression, the conception apparently of the isolated individual, the image of very empirical fetters and limitations, within which the mode of production of life, and the form of intercourse coupled with it, move.

With the division of labour, in which all these contradictions are implicit, and which in its turn is based on the natural division of labour in the family and the separation of society into individual families opposed to one another, is given simultaneously the distribution, and indeed the unequal distribution, (both quantitative and qualitative), of labour and its products, hence property: the nucleus, the first form, of which lies in the family, where wife and children are the slaves of the husband. This latent slavery in the family, though still very crude, is the first property, but even at this early stage it corresponds perfectly to the definition of modern economists who call it the power of disposing of the labour-power of others. Division of labour and private property are, moreover, identical expressions: in the one the same thing is affirmed with reference to activity as is affirmed in the other with reference to the product of the activity.

Further, the division of labour implies the contradiction between the interest of the separate individual or the individual family and the communal interest of all individuals, who have intercourse with one another. And indeed, this communal interest does not exist merely in the imagination, as "the general good," but first of all in reality, as the mutual interdependence of the individuals among whom the labour is divided. And finally, the division of labour offers us the first example of how, as long as man remains in natural society, that is as long as a cleavage exists between the particular and the common interest, as long therefore as activity is not voluntarily, but naturally, divided, man's own deed becomes an alien power opposed to him, which enslaves him instead of being controlled by him. For as soon as labour is distributed, each man has a particular, exclusive sphere of activity, which is forced upon him and from which he cannot escape. He is a hunter, a fisherman, a shepherd, or a critical critic, and must remain so if he does not want to lose his means of livelihood; while in communist society, where nobody has one exclusive sphere of activity but each can become accomplished in any branch he wishes, society regulates the general production and thus makes it possible for me to do one thing to-day and another to-morrow, to hunt in the morning, fish in the afternoon, rear cattle in the evening, criticize after dinner, just as I have a mind, without ever becoming hunter, fisherman, shepherd or critic.

This crystallization of social activity, this consolidation of what we ourselves produce into an objective power above us, growing out of our control, thwarting our expectations, bringing to naught our calculations, is one of the chief factors in historical development up till now. And out of this very contradiction between the interest of the individual and that of the community the latter takes an independent form as the *State,* divorced from the real interests of individual and community, and at the same time as an illusory communal life, always based, however, on the real ties existing in every family and tribal conglomeration (such as flesh and blood, language, division of labour on a larger scale, and other interests) and especially, as we shall enlarge upon later, on the classes, already determined by the division of labour, which in every such mass of men separate out, and of which one dominates all the others. It follows from this that all struggles within the State, the struggle between democracy, aristocracy and monarchy, the struggle for the franchise, etc., etc., are merely the illusory forms in which the real struggles of the different classes are fought out among one another (of this the German theoreticians have not the faintest inkling, although they have received a sufficient introduction to the subject in *The German-French Annals* and *The Holy Family*).[1]

Further, it follows that every class which is struggling for mastery, even when its domination, as is the case with the proletariat, postulates the abolition of the old form of society in its entirety and of mastery itself, must first conquer for itself political power in order to represent its interest in turn as the general interest, a step to which in the first moment it is forced. Just because individuals seek *only* their particular interest, i.e. that not coinciding with their communal interest (for the "general good" is the illusory form of communal life), the latter will be imposed on them as an interest "alien" to them, and "independent" of them, as in its turn a particular, peculiar "general interest"; or they must meet face to face in this antagonism, as in democracy.[2] On the other hand too, the *practical* struggle of these particular interests, which constantly *really* run counter to the communal and illusory communal interests, make *practical* intervention and control necessary through the illusory "general-interest" in the form of the State. The social power, i.e. the multiplied productive force, which arises through the co-operation of different individuals as it is determined within the division of labour, appears to these individuals, since their co-operation is not voluntary but natural, not as their own united power but as an alien force existing outside them, of the origin and end of which they are ignorant, which they thus cannot control, which on the contrary passes through a peculiar series of phases and stages independent of the will and the action of man, nay even being the prime governor of these. . . .

Our conception of history depends on our ability to expound the real process of production, starting out from the simple material production of life, and to comprehend the form of intercourse connected with this and created by this (i.e. civil society in its various stages), as the basis of all history; further, to show it in its action as State; and so, from this starting-point, to explain the whole mass of different theoretical products and forms of consciousness, religion, philosophy, ethics, etc., etc., and trace their origins and growth, by which means, of course, the whole thing can be shown in its totality (and therefore, too, the reciprocal action of these various sides on one another). It has not, like the idealistic view of history, in every period to look for a category, but remains constantly on the real ground of history; it does not explain practice from the idea but explains the formation of ideas from material practice; and accordingly it comes to the conclusion that all forms and products of consciousness cannot be dissolved by mental criticism, by resolution into "self-consciousness" or transformation into "apparitions," "spectres," "fancies," etc., but only by the practical overthrow of the actual social relations which gave rise to this idealistic humbug; that not criticism but revolution is the driving force of history, also of religion, of philosophy and all other types of theory. It shows that history does not end by being resolved into "self-consciousness" as "spirit of the spirit," but that in it at each stage there is found a material result: a sum of productive forces, a historically created relation of individuals to nature and to one another, which is handed down to each generation from its predecessor; a mass of productive forces, different forms of capital, and conditions, which, indeed, is modified by the new generation on the one hand, but also on the other prescribes for it its conditions of life and gives it a definite development, a special character. It shows that circumstances make men just as much as men make circumstances.

This sum of productive forces, forms of capital and social forms of intercourse, which every individual and generation finds in existence as something given, is the real basis of what the philosophers have conceived as "substance" and "essence of man," and what they have deified and attacked: a real basis which is not in the least disturbed, in its effect and influence on the development of men, by the fact that these philosophers revolt against it as "self-consciousness" and "the unique." These conditions of life, which different generations find in existence, decide also whether or not the periodically recurring revolutionary convulsion will be strong enough to overthrow the basis of all existing forms. And if these material elements of a complete revolution are not present (namely, on the one hand the existence of productive forces, on the other the formation of a revolutionary mass, which revolts not only against separate conditions of society up till then, but against the very "production of life" till then, the "total activity" on which it was based), then, as far as practical development is concerned, it is absolutely immaterial whether the "idea" of this revolution has been expressed a hundred times already; as the history of communism proves.

In the whole conception of history up to the present this real basis of history has either been totally neglected or else considered as a minor matter quite irrelevant to the course of history. History must therefore always be written according to an extraneous standard; the real production of life seems to be beyond history, while the truly historical appears to be separated from ordinary life, something extra-superterrestrial. With this the relation of man to nature is excluded from history and hence the antithesis of nature and history is created. The exponents of this conception of history have consequently only been able to see in history the political actions of princes and States, religious and all sorts of theoretical struggles, and in particular in each historical epoch have had to share the *illusion of that epoch.* For instance, if an epoch imagines itself to be actuated by purely "political" or "religious" motives, although "religion" and "politics" are only forms of its true motives, the historian accepts this opinion. The "idea," the "conception" of these conditioned men about their real practice, is transformed into the sole determining, active force, which controls and determines their practice. When the crude form in which the division of labour appears with the Indians and Egyptians calls forth the caste-system in their State and religion, the historian believes that the caste-system is the power which has produced this crude social form. While the French and the English at least hold by the political illusion, which is moderately close to reality, the Germans move in the realm of the "pure spirit," and make religious illusion the driving force of history. . . .

JAURÈS: CRITICAL INTRODUCTION TO
The Socialist History of the French Revolution

I have refrained from indicating my references in every instance for fear of overburdening this work; furthermore, I think it unnecessary to reprint here the general bibliography of the history of the Revolution. I have tried to read all the essential material. It will be obvious as this account proceeds that I have always consulted the original texts and sources. I have often used the *Parliamentary Archives* which M. Aulard [3] seems to judge with excessive harshness. True, they are full of misprints and the documentation is sometimes vague. But they constitute an invaluable reference work, for they contain the texts of laws and decrees, and excerpts from the *Moniteur* and from the Portiez de l'Oise collection.

Need I say that I have continually used M. Aulard's great collection of documents? Also, I have diligently studied the major newspapers of the Revolution. I have not skimmed over them nor have I consulted them in the manner of many previous historians; rather, I have perused them with the most scrupulous care. I mean the newspapers published by Marat, Hébert, Brissot, Condorcet, Prud'homme, and Carra. I found that, thanks to this painstaking reading, I was able to make more than one valuable discovery.

I have been criticized for the title "The Socialist History." I have been told that history is history. Of course one must aim at an exact record of men and events—at "objectivity." But the historian also observes happenings from the point of view of his general conception of life and society. Why should not the socialists, when they study the political and social developments since 1789, declare in the title of their work that they find the meaning of this whole historical movement in its ultimate goal?

I do not think that I can be accused of having yielded to the socialist obsession of having arbitrarily magnified the role which the proletariat played in the French Revolution. I have indicated, on the contrary, how humble and weak a part it had at the beginning. But I have also shown how, by ceaseless action and by a daring use of revolutionary idealism in tackling economic and social problems, its influence rapidly grew.

M. Hauser recently contributed to the *Revue historique* a brief analysis of a book by M. Germain Martin in which the reviewer commits a strange error with regard to my ideas. He pretends that, in the first volume of *The Socialist History*, already published in installments, I wrote that the workers had not taken an active part in the great revolutionary "days." What the reader will find on p. 169 is that I did not refer to the workers but to the beggars and tramps, the "proletariat in rags" (*Lumpenproletariat,* as the Germans call it) which according to M. Taine dominated Paris.[4] I have tried to show, on the contrary, how the stature of the proletariat grew with the Revolution and how it took shape in the heat of events. This will stand out most clearly in the three volumes of *The Socialist History* devoted to the Revolution, unless I have completely failed in my design.

Engels wrote that, in 1793, the dictatorship of the proletariat was exercised through the democratic Republic. In what sense and to what degree is this true? And how, in a Revolution essentially bourgeois in its conception of property, did the creation of a proletarian dictatorship come about? What complex and innumerable interactions between political and economic phenomena prepared the ground for this dictatorship? That is what I have tried to set down in a day-by-day account, just as the physicist records the changes in color and consistency of a metal while it is heated. And the more thoroughly I have studied the revolutionary movement, the more convinced have I become that democratic principles imply socialism, that democracy favors and stimulates the growth of the working class. . . .

As the proletariat came to intervene more and more actively in the progress of the bourgeois revolution, it gained consciousness of its own interests; an admirable demand for wage increases paralleled popular political action. Thus the affirmation of the right to life assumed an entirely new and deeper interpretation. The political action of the proletarians gradually infused the very Declaration of the Rights of Man with a bold meaning which paved the way for the communism of Babeuf. It is thus impossible, in that great movement which is the Revolution, to separate economic from political changes.

The danger of those books, however useful or interesting they may be, in which M. Lichtenberger[5] has studied the social ideas of the Revolution is that the meaning of many theories, formulas, and words is lost when they are judged apart from the complex political events which provoked or determined them.

I am neither foolish nor unjust enough to take issue with M. Aulard over the general plan of his informative, masterly, and enlightening book, *The Political History of the French Revolution.* The historian has the right to isolate one important aspect of events. But he must never forget that he then deals with a mere abstraction. How can he fully understand the change that occurred during the Revolution from a bourgeois oligarchy to a democracy without conceiving of the social and political upheavals as intimately linked?

I have tried to encompass this complex and total reality. But I must here discuss a preliminary difficulty which M. Aulard puts in my path and which would tend to discredit my whole undertaking: "I hope," he writes in the Foreword to his *Political History,* "that my references will inspire a confidence implicit in the very nature of my subject. A lifetime is quite long enough to read all the essential documents. Other topics are different. The economic and social history of the Revolution, for example, is dispersed among so many sources that it is at present impossible, in the span of a human life, to find them all or even the chief among them. The man who would write this whole history unaided could only make a thorough study of some part; he would achieve but a superficial sketch based on secondary references or worse."

Surely no one is more aware than I of the enormous lacunae which remain in the economic history of the Revolution or of the shortcomings of my own attempt to fill them. And I would respectfully beg M. Aulard to support my efforts to get the economic documents pertaining to the Revolution published by the national government, by the ministries, by the Society for the History of the French Revolution, and by the city of Paris.

So far, it is mainly political documents that have been published: the records of the Constituent and Legislative Assemblies and of the Convention, the minutes of the Paris Commune, of the Jacobin Club and of the Committee of Public Safety, the correspondence of the commissaries of the Convention, and the proceedings of the Committee on Public Instruction. From these excellent and essential publications the alert reader can easily pick out many elements of economic and social life. However, these aspects of the Revolution have not been brought to light in full, and the wonderful documents in the archives of Paris and of the departments are beyond the reach of most researchers.

It would be urgent, first of all, to gather and publish whatever can be discovered of the parochial Lists of Grievances [*Cahiers*] of 1789. They express the true thought of the peasants. They depict their real life. The urban bourgeoisie, in drawing up its Lists, dropped the most vital demands, presumably in order to be brief and clear. The peasants were less concerned with the political than with the economic organization of society. They often said: "We leave the task of planning a Constitution to wiser men; these are the conditions under which we live, these are the wrongs we suffer."

The liveliest and most varied picture of rural France could be drawn if one could obtain the regional Lists of Grievances for all French provinces, for the wine regions and the grain regions, for the coastal lands and the great central plains; these Lists are expressive, descriptive, sometimes no doubt bitter and poignant, as for example the Lists of the Autun region, published by M. de Charmasse, or those of the Eure-et-Loir department which I have already quoted from a provincial yearbook.

Then one should publish all the documents relating to the sale of "national property," the property of the Church and that of the Order of Malta and of the émigrés. . . .

The Society for the History of the French Revolution should guide and stimulate local researchers to inquire into the fate, immediately after sale, of the rural or urban real estate acquired by the bourgeois or the peasant, and to ascertain what transformations it underwent and to what uses it was put. I have occasionally been able to discover, from contemporary newspapers, how certain Paris monasteries fared immediately after purchase. If one could ascertain accurately into what kinds of stores and shops many abbeys, refectories or chapels were transformed, one could discover the details of an extraordinary economic effervescence caused by the Revolution.

Finally, apart from the Lists drawn up by the peasants, apart from the registers of sales of national property, it would be of the greatest importance to publish all the documents pertaining to the cost of living, the whole correspondence of the Committee on Subsistence, all the decrees, all the tables, all the letters and petitions relating to the establishment and to the functioning of the Maximum. They represent a dazzling mine of information. The man who would explore it at length and at leisure might extract from it the most decisive facts about the state of the industries, about the prices of all kinds of goods, of manufactured articles and of raw materials, about salaries and the relationship of the fixed and the variable capital in each branch of industry, about the lively or sluggish activity of the factories, about the demands of the workers and the economic and social ideas of the Revolution. M. Biollay,[6] despite his conscientiousness, overlooks innumerable elements. But how can one use all these riches so long as they have not been scientifically catalogued, collected and published? I have carefully studied the documents of this kind which are to be found in the archives of the Tarn department; several of them, which I had photostated, will be published in my volume on the Convention; they show the Maximum in action in the smallest rural communities.

I have tried to extract from the archives of the city of Paris as much information as possible. But it is in fact difficult for a researcher to use these rich sources to the best advantage. Not only because, as M. Aulard says, a human life would not suffice to study them in their present state of dispersion, but also because one would need to compare price tables from one region and one town to another in order to understand all the diversities of production and all the variations of manual labor. In practice it is impossible to transcribe and compare all these tables.

The combined efforts of many patient research workers would be required to assemble and analyze all the existing economic and social data which should be published in one huge work. The Labor Bureau which is accustomed to salary and price statistics, to industrial investigations and professional surveys, should be provided with sufficient funds to undertake, in conjunction with the Society for the History of the Revolution, the large and necessary project which would at last allow us to depict an extraordinary social movement vividly and factually. In this area everything needs to be done, since M. Taine only busied himself searching in the archives to count the number of windows broken during the Revolution by the rioting populace.

It is true that writers like myself, who try to encompass not only the economics of the Revolution but its total political and economic life, still lack some necessary working tools and some indispensable means of gathering data. Nevertheless M. Aulard's words must not create the impression that the historian is completely resourceless.

To begin with, even if he cannot exhaust the archives, he can at least orient himself and obtain some general and clear perspectives. Furthermore, many known and long since published texts, such as the speeches of the Assemblies, the reports of the Commissions and ministers, the printed opinions of the deputies, or the newspapers take on an entirely new meaning and reveal hitherto unsuspected facts if one reads them from the point of view of economics. The lacunae and the incredibly naïve interpretations which abound in the works of the greatest historians of the Revolution today leave one surprised and shocked. One could undertake a rather curious study of the historians of the Revolution from that point of view; but it would not be appropriate to do so here. What even the greatest among them have lacked is not the documents but rather a concern with and insight into economic evolution as well as into the depth and movement of social life. We can now read and see better, since such an understanding has been awakened in the most modest among us by the vistas that Marx opened, by the progress of socialism, and by the work of the French and Russian Historical Schools. Do the results justify my efforts? The reader will be able to judge as my work unfolds.

I shall add only three very brief remarks:

1. It may seem that I have sometimes used quotations too freely or that I have not been content to quote the most apposite and characteristic sentence. But I have often found that one twists the meaning of quotations by curtailing them too much and I have wanted, even at the risk of excessive length, to put the reader in direct touch with the uncut original.

2. Although I have generally been careful to note the birth of an idea and to record its vicissitudes, I have sometimes refrained from discussing certain arguments and questions, such as the debates of the Constituent on the right of succession, until the time when the idea had been translated into a law, that is to say, into action. The reader should therefore not be surprised if he cannot find, in this first volume, a record of the background and growth of all these ideas.

3. All the pictures included in the text are reproductions of contemporary prints or caricatures. I hope they will be found to have serious documentary value. Naturally, I do not

necessarily share the feelings they convey. Some of them are revolutionary, some are counter-revolutionary. Some are delicate and charming, some are vulgar and these I like less; but such is the variegated expression of a vast movement.

I acknowledge with great pleasure the help of the gracious M. Georges Cain and of his collaborators at [the Musée] Carnavalet in gathering these living pictures, these rustling and stirring leaves, still full of the warm and colored sap of the Revolution. And I also take pleasure in throwing them again to the wind of life.

GENERAL INTRODUCTION TO *The Socialist History of the French Revolution*

I want to present to the people—to the workers and peasants —a socialist interpretation of history as it unfolded from 1789 to the end of the nineteenth century. I consider the French Revolution an immense event of wonderful richness. It is not, to my mind, a finite fact: there is no end to its consequences. The French Revolution indirectly prepared the ground for the advent of the proletariat because it brought about the two essential prerequisites of socialism: democracy and capitalism. But the fundamental significance of the Revolution lay in the rise to political power of the bourgeois class.

We are now witnessing a new social crisis whose causes include economic and political progress, the emergence of large industries, the rise of the working class with its increased numbers and heightened ambitions, the unrest of the peasantry crushed by competition and exploited by the barons of industry and trade, the moral malaise of the intellectual middle class whose sensitivities are shocked by the brutal business world around them. The proletariat will seize power in this new and more profound Revolution and will transform both property and morality. I intend to paint in broad strokes the development and interplay of the social classes since 1789. It is always somewhat arbitrary to delimit or to circumscribe the uninterrupted and everchanging flow of life. Yet, in the past century, three periods in the history of the middle class and of the proletariat can be quite clearly distinguished.

First, from 1789 to 1848, the revolutionary bourgeoisie triumphed and took possession. It used the strength of the proletariat in its fight against royal absolutism and against the nobility. But the proletariat remained a subordinate and minor force despite its prodigious activity and despite the decisive part it played on certain days. At times, it terrified the propertied classes while actually still working for them. The proletariat had no radically different conception of society: the communism of Babeuf and of his few disciples was but the dying gasp, the supreme spasm of the revolutionary crisis before the calm of the Consulate and of the First Empire. Even in 1793 and 1794 the proletarians were but a part of the Third Estate: they had neither a clear class consciousness nor the desire or image of a different form of property. They barely went beyond the sterile thought of Robespierre: a democracy, politically sovereign but economically immobile, made up of petty peasant landowners and petty bourgeois artisans. The marvellous sap of socialism, creator of riches, beauty and joy, was not in them: on terrible days they burnt but with a dry flame, a flame of anger and envy. They did not know the attraction, the potent sweetness of a new ideal. . . .

How has the proletariat grown, through what crises has it passed, whose efforts and what events have prepared it for the decisive role it is destined to play tomorrow? That is what all of us, militant socialists, propose to tell. We know that economic conditions, the form of production and the type of property, are the foundation of history. Usually a man's profession constitutes the essence of his life; and this profession—man's economic activity—commonly determines his habits, thoughts, pains, joys, even his dreams. In the same way the economic structure of society in each era determines the political regime, the social mores, even the general trend of thought. I shall therefore be at pains to seek out the economic basis of human life for each epoch of this narrative. I shall try to follow the shifts in property and the evolution of industrial and agricultural techniques. And, as is proper for a summary picture, I shall outline the influence of economic conditions on governments, literature, and social systems.

But I will not forget, just as Marx himself never forgot—notwithstanding narrow-minded interpretations by uninspired critics—that economic forces act on men. Men have a prodigious variety of passions and ideas; the almost infinite complexity of human life cannot be brutally and mechanically reduced to an economic formula. Moreover, though man is essentially human, though he is ever subject to the continuous and enveloping influence of his social environment, he also partakes through his senses and his mind of a vaster milieu which is the universe itself.

Even the light of the most distant star, most foreign to man's world, evokes dreams in the imagination of the poet which are in harmony with the general sensibilities of his time and with the innermost secrets of his culture; so do the moon's rays mingle with the hidden moistures of the earth to create a thin haze which floats over the meadow. In this sense the social system and the economic forces which determine it are influenced and modified even by the light of the stars, however distant and indifferent they may seem. Goethe once visited a factory and was appalled by the amount of machinery required to make his clothes. And yet, without this first industrial effort of the German middle-class, the sleepy and fragmented old German world could never have felt nor understood the magnificent intolerance of restrictions which rent the soul of Faust.

Whatever the relationship of man's most daring or most subtle dreams to the economic and social system, his soul transcends the human environment and partakes of the immense universe around him. The infinite stirs up deep and mysterious forces in man's soul, forces of eternal life which preceded the creation of human societies and will outlast them. It would be futile and incorrect to deny that thinking, and even dreaming, depend on the economic system or on the existing forms of production but, at the same time, the explanation that changes in human thought are determined by economic conditions alone is summary, crude and naïve. The human mind often transcends and resists the society from which it sprang; thus the relationship of the individual to his culture is one of simultaneous solidarity and opposition. Men like Kepler and Galileo could pursue their science in freedom under modern national monarchies, half emancipated from the Church. But once in possession of the truth, the mind was no longer subject to prince, society, or even mankind. One might say that Truth, with its own order and logic, then became the immediate climate of the mind; although Kepler and Galileo had started with the basic tenets of the modern state, they perfected their own observations and their astronomical work and then became independent and free of all bonds once their experiments and calculations had been concluded. The social world from which they had derived their support and impetus set them free, and their thought no longer knew any laws but those of astral infinity.

I shall always uphold the exalted dignity of the free mind that transcends the half-mechanical growth of economic and social systems and is delivered from mankind itself by the eternal universe. Not even the most uncompromising Marxist could hold this against me. In an admirable passage Marx declared that in the past human societies have been governed by mere chance, by the blind movement of economic forces. Institutions and ideas have not been the conscious work of free men but the products of man's perception of an inchoate social system. According to Marx, we still live in pre-history. Human history will truly begin only when man, escaping at last from the bondage of irrational forces, will govern production itself by reason and by will. His mind will then no longer be subject to the tyranny of economic institutions; instead he will create and control them and contemplate the universe with a free and fearless look. Marx thus envisages a period of complete intellectual freedom when human thought, no longer distorted by economic servitude, will not pervert the world. But certainly Marx does not deny that, even in the darkness of the irrational ages, some great minds had already attained freedom; they presaged and prepared the truly human era. Our task is to gather these first manifestations of consciousness; they allow us to anticipate the full, ardent, and free life of communist humanity which, liberated from all servitude, will conquer the universe through science, action, and imagination. We are witnessing the first breeze which stirs only a few leaves in the human forest but portends strong gusts and mighty blasts.

My interpretation of history will therefore be marked by both the materialism of Marx and the mysticism of Michelet. Economics are the basis and mainspring of human history but, throughout the ages, thinking man has aspired beyond economics to the full intellectual life, to the ardent communion of his restless and searching mind with the mysterious universe. The great mystic of Alexandria said: "The big waves of the sea have hoisted my boat and I have seen the sun as it was rising from the waters." Similarly, the swelling tide of the economic revolution will raise man's bark till he, poor fisherman exhausted by long nocturnal work, can greet from on high the first rays of that transcendent spirit which will reign over us.

Despite the economic interpretation that I have placed on human events, I shall not overlook the moral worth of history. I know that in the past century, under the guise of "liberty" and "humanity," men have been exploited and oppressed. The French Revolution proclaimed the rights of man which the propertied classes have interpreted to mean the rights of the bourgeoisie and of capital.

The bourgeoisie proclaimed the freedom of mankind at a time when the rich had no other means of subjugating the poor than through the medium of property: but property is the sovereign power on which all others depend. Bourgeois society is thus based on a monstrous form of class egotism compounded by hypocrisy. There were, however, repeated moments during the infancy of the Revolution when it would have been impossible to separate the aspirations of the revolutionary bourgeoisie from those of all mankind, when men's hearts were filled with a universal fervor. In the many conflicts unleashed by bourgeois anarchy, in the battles between parties and classes, moments of daring, valor and courage abounded. I shall always venerate every idealistic hero regardless of partisan loyalty; I shall revere both the republican bourgeois outlawed in 1851 by the successful coup d'état and the glorious proletarian fighters who fell in June 1848.

But no one can chide me for being most mindful of the militant virtues of these oppressed proletarians who, for a century, have so often paid with their lives for an ideal dimly perceived. The success of the Social Revolution depends not only on a gradual historical evolution but on the actions of men, on conscious and purposeful striving. History will always need individual valor and nobility. And the moral tone of the future communist society will be set by the highmindedness of the leaders who will emerge from the present militant class. It is thus in honor of the coming Revolution that I shall hail all those heroic fighters who, in the past century, combined passionate idealism with a sublime scorn for death. I do not smile at the revolutionaries who read Plutarch's *Lives*. No doubt, the admirable bursts of enthusiasm which they thus engendered within themselves had little influence on history. But at least they remained steadfast in the tempest, their faces were not contorted by fear during the lightning of great storms. And if the passion for glory filled them with a thirst for freedom and a fighting spirit—who will dare hold this against them?

In this socialist history which spans the period from the bourgeois Revolution to the beginnings of the proletarian Revolution I shall thus endeavor to touch on all aspects of human life. I shall try to encompass and reveal the fundamental economic forces which govern societies, the ardent aspirations of the mind toward ultimate truth, and the noble passions of the individual conscience defying pain, tyranny and death. The proletariat will attain freedom and universal brotherhood by hastening economic progress toward its inevitable conclusion. The proletariat must therefore become conscious of the role of economics and human greatness in history. At the risk of startling my readers, I would invoke Marx, Michelet and Plutarch as the three great men who inspired this modest history. I shall render the exact thought of all my militant collaborators, knowing that they shared my own basic doctrine, and my belief.

10

HISTORY AS AN ACADEMIC DISCIPLINE: *Prospectuses of Historische Zeitschrift, Revue Historique, English Historical Review*

[By the mid-nineteenth century history had ceased to be a branch of literature and had become an academic discipline. Impressed by the example of the natural sciences, historians, especially in Germany, asserted that their craft too had become a science, and established an elaborate machinery of scholarship. Professional journals were founded in a format that has remained essentially unchanged to the present day, and the study of history in the Universities, a rarity at the end of the eighteenth century, became commonplace. At the same time the link between history and contemporary politics remained close, and it is no accident that the German and French historical reviews were begun at moments of great national stirrings.

Despite the fact that various historical journals had appeared sporadically · before, the *Historische Zeitschrift,* founded in 1859 by Heinrich von Sybel (1817-1895), may be considered as the first, and for a long time, the foremost historical periodical. Although Sybel had become estranged from his teacher Ranke over the latter's deliberate aloofness from politics, the *Historische Zeitschrift,* established in a year of great patriotic agitation, did not become a partisan journal. Sybel's Preface to the first issue, reprinted below, was translated by M. M. Meeker, with two paragraphs omitted.

Political events had an even clearer influence on the founding in 1876 of the *Revue historique* by Gabriel Monod (1844-1912). Before 1876, only a catholic and royalist periodical, *Revue des Questions historiques,* had existed; the defeat of 1870 and the creation of the Third Republic provided the stimulus for the creation of a new, scholarly journal which should be liberal in tone and tendency. Monod was entirely conscious of this political motive, but he also acknowledged his debt to the spirit and techniques of the German historical scholarship that he admired. For the first six years Monod and Gustave Fagniez (1842-1927) were co-editors. Their Preface to the first issue of the *Revue historique* appears below, translated by Nora Beeson.

It may have been the absence of any external pressure that delayed the appearance of an English historical journal. After twenty years of planning, the *English Historical Review* was finally started in 1886, with the Rev. Mandell Creighton (1843-1901), later Bishop of London, as its first editor. Below is the Prefatory Note of the first issue.

The *American Historical Review* was started in 1895, with J. Franklin Jameson as its managing editor. The first issue did not carry a programmatic statement.]

PREFACE: *Historische Zeitschrift*

In order to describe to our readers more closely the point of view and the direction which the enterprise started herewith wishes to adhere to, we quote the following passages from the prospectus which we submitted to our collaborators:

"This periodical should, above all, be a scientific one. Its first task should, therefore, be to represent the true method of historical research and to point out the deviations therefrom.

"On this basis we plan a historical periodical, not an antiquarian or a political one. On the one hand, it is not our aim to discuss unresolved questions of current politics, nor to commit ourselves to one particular political party. It is not contradictory, however, if we indicate certain general principles, which will guide the political judgment of this periodical. Viewed historically, the life of every people, governed by the laws of morality, appears as a natural and individual evolution, which—out of intrinsic necessity—produces the forms of state and culture, an evolution which must not arbitrarily be obstructed or accelerated, nor made subject to extrinsic rules. This point of view precludes feudalism, which imposes lifeless elements on the progressive life; radicalism, which substitutes subjective arbitrariness for organic development; ultramontanism, which subjects the national and spiritual evolution to the authority of an extraneous Church.

"On the other hand, we do not want to establish an antiquarian journal. We, therefore, wish to deal preferably with such material and such relationships in the material, which still have a vital link with present-day life. If the recognition of the lawfulness and unity of all life and processes is the foremost task of historical contemplation, then there is no clearer way to express that recognition than by proving that the past is still contemporaneous, and has a determining influence in us. It is not only the attraction of the piquant, it is an intellectually justified urge that the public should, with decided preference, reach for material of the above description, and that books on such subjects should everywhere have the most important influence. We think it only appropriate that this periodical should in its book review section as well prefer to examine such works in great detail. It is relevant to add here that discussions, which clearly and sharply illuminate the characteristic differences between German and foreign ways of writing history in our days, will be most welcome. For our science has fortunately attained such significance during the present that its existence and progress have become part of our national life. From the foregoing the following general rules emerge for the editors:

"They should generally devote more space to modern history than to the earlier periods, and more to German than to foreign history.

"This periodical will examine equally all the various fields of historical study. Contributions in legal, constitutional, literary and church history—if in keeping with the general principles of our organ—will be presented just as much as works dealing with political history proper."

For general information each issue of the journal will include a bibliographical review of all historical works newly published in Europe, accompanied—as far as possible—by brief comments as to the contents, method and point of view of the major works.

Munich, February 1859

PREFACE: *Revue historique*

The study of history in our times is becoming increasingly important, and it is more and more difficult, even for the professional scholar, to keep up to date with all the discoveries and with all the new research which is being produced every day in this vast field. Also, we believe that we are fulfilling the desires of a great part of the literary public by creating a periodical entitled *Revue historique* which has as its purpose the publishing of original research on the various aspects of history, and providing exact and complete information on historical research in foreign countries as well as in France.

Along with the specialized Reviews, such as the *Revue Archéologique* or the *Bibliothèque de l'Ecole des Chartes,* which seek to clarify the particular aspects of ancient or medieval history, we should like to create a Review of general history which is intended for a larger public, but which applies to these more varied questions the same severity of methodology and of criticism, and the same impartiality. We should like to present a common field for work to all those who, whatever their special tendencies, cherish history for its own sake, and who do not use history as a weapon in defense of their religious or political ideas. While we leave to our collaborators freedom and the responsibility of their personal opinions, we ask them to avoid contemporary controversies, to treat the subjects they are working on with the methodological rigidity and absence of partisanship which science demands, and not to seek arguments for or against doctrines which are only indirectly involved.

We will create, therefore, neither a work of polemics nor a work of vulgarization, nor will our Review be a collection of pure erudition. The Review will accept only original contributions, based on original sources, which will enrich science either with their basic research or with the results of their conclusions; but while we demand from our contributors strictly scientific methods of exposition, with each assertion accompanied by proof, by source references and quotations, while we severely exclude vague generalities and rhetoric, we shall preserve in the *Revue historique* that literary quality which scholars as well as French readers justly value so highly.

Our framework will not exclude any phase of history, although our Review will chiefly be devoted to European history from the death of Theodosius (395) to the fall of Napoleon I (1815). It is particularly in that period that our archives and libraries preserve so many unexplored treasures; and we want as much as possible to remain apart from all contemporary polemics. . . .

We hope that the *Revue historique* will be accorded a

sympathetic reception not only by those who make a special study of history, but also by all those who are interested in intellectual affairs. France has always honored historical research; if today she no longer claims the incontestable superiority which she formerly had in this branch of human knowledge, it appears all the more necessary to favor a project intended to aid and encourage serious scholars. Moreover, the study of France's past, which shall be our principal task, is today of national importance. We can give to our country the unity and moral strength she needs by revealing her historical traditions and, at the same time, the transformations these traditions have undergone.

PREFATORY NOTE: *The English Historical Review*

It has long been a matter of observation and regret that in England, alone among the great countries of Europe, there does not exist any periodical organ dedicated to the study of history. Although the number of persons engaged in this study is large and constantly increasing; although the work done is as thorough in quality as that even of the Germans, and probably larger in quantity than that of the French or Italians; although historical schools of much promise have lately been developed at our universities, English historians have not yet, like those of other countries, associated themselves in the establishment of any academy or other organisation, nor founded any journal to promote their common object. Besides the thirty-five millions of the United Kingdom, there is in America and the British colonies and dependencies an English-speaking population of nearly seventy millions, who form, for the purpose of literature, learning, and science, virtually one people with the inhabitants of the old country. Among these outlying English also (though America has periodicals treating of her own history) there is no organ which concerns itself with history in general, or appeals to an audience of the whole race. The need of some such journal is therefore evident; and there is a corresponding prospect of usefulness and success for one which shall bring to a focus the light now scattered through many minor publications, none of them devoted to this special purpose, which shall present a full and critical record of what is being accomplished in the field of history, and become the organ through which those who desire to make known the progress of their researches will address their fellow-labourers.

The principles by which the promoters of the *Historical Review* are guided, and the methods whereby they seek to apply those principles, will best appear from the contents of the first few issues. But there are several questions likely to be asked by the readers of the present number, to which an answer may properly be given at the outset.

One of these questions relates to the conception which the promoters form of history. Is the Review intended to deal with political history only, or also with the development of various branches of civilisation—with the history, for example, of religion and the church, of language, literature, and art, of metaphysics and the sciences of nature?

Two views prevail concerning the scope of history. One regards it, to use the expression of an eminent living writer, as being concerned solely with states, so that (in the words of another distinguished contemporary) "history is past politics, and politics is present history." [1] The other, which has found illustrious exponents from Herodotus downwards, conceives it to be a picture of the whole past, including everything that man has either thought or wrought. Of these views the former appears to us narrow, and therefore misleading; the latter so wide as to become vague, fixing no definite limit to the province of history as bordering on other fields of learning. It seems better to regard history as the record of human action, and of thought only in its direct influence upon action. States and politics will therefore be the chief part of its subject, because the acts of nations and of the individuals who have played a great part in the affairs of nations have usually been more important than the acts of private citizens. But when history finds a private citizen who, like Socrates or St. Paul or Erasmus or Charles Darwin, profoundly influences other men from his purely private station, she is concerned with him as the source of such influence no less than with a legislator or general. History therefore occupies herself with theology or metaphysics or natural science not as independent branches of inquiry, but only in their bearing on the acts of men. She deals with language as an evidence of the relations of races to one another, or as a force in uniting or disjoining them. She finds in literature and art illustrations of the productive power and the taste of a nation, and notes the effect they exercise in developing national life. An historical review ought therefore, it is submitted, by no means to limit itself to mere political history, but to receive from the students of each special department such light as they can throw upon the whole life of man in the past. Nor is it difficult in practice to draw the line between what belongs to general history, thus conceived, and what is proper for a specialist journal. For instance, a minute account of the diggings at Troy or Tiryns would be fitter for an archaeological magazine than for these pages, but we should be prompt to notice any discovery which bore upon the worth of Homer's evidence regarding prehistoric Greece. A discussion of the meaning of a passage in Cicero about the constitution of Rome would fall within our province if the point involved were of importance to a knowledge of that constitution, but not if it merely brought out some peculiarity in Latin syntax or in the use of Latin words. An article setting forth the views of Aquinas or Occam on the relations of the civil to the ecclesiastical power might be accepted, while one dealing with the metaphysics or theology of those thinkers would be deemed unsuitable. It need scarcely be added that we should draw no distinction between ancient and modern history, nor (subject to the above limitation as to theology) between civil and ecclesiastical.

How will the *Historical Review* avoid the suspicion of partisanship in such political or ecclesiastical questions as are still burning questions, because they touch issues presently contested?

It will avoid this danger by refusing contributions which argue such questions with reference to present controversy. The object of history is to discover and set forth facts, and he who confines himself to this object, forbearing acrimonious language, can usually escape the risk of giving offence. Some topics it will be safer to eschew altogether. In others fairness may be shown by allowing both sides an equal hearing. But our main reliance will be on the scientific spirit which we shall expect from contributors likely to address us. An article on the character and career of Sir Robert Peel will be welcome, so long as it does not advocate or deprecate the policy of protective tariffs; and President Andrew Jackson may properly be praised or blamed if the writer's purpose be neither to assail nor to recommend, with President Cleveland in his eye, the system of party appointments to office. Recognizing the value of the light which history may shed on practical problems, we shall not hesitate to let that light be reflected from our pages, whenever we can be sure that it is dry light, free from any tinge of partisanship.

Will the *Historical Review* address itself to professed and, so to speak, professional students of history, or to the person called the 'general reader'?

It will address itself to both, though its chief care will be for the former. It will, we hope and intend, contain no article which does not, in the Editor's judgment, add something to knowledge, i.e. which has not a value for the trained historian. No allurements of style will secure insertion for a popular *réchauffé* of facts already known or ideas already suggested. On the other hand, an effort will be made to provide in every number some articles, whether articles on a question, an epoch, or a personage, or reviews of books, which an educated man, not specially conversant with history, may read with pleasure and profit. We shall seek to accomplish this not so much by choosing topics certain to attract as by endeavouring to have even difficult topics treated with freshness and point. So far from holding that true history is dull, we believe that dull history is usually bad history, and shall value those contributors most highly who can present their researches in a lucid and effective form. More than in any other countries there is a public in England and America which, without possessing an exact knowledge of history, heartily enjoys it and desires to be set in the way of understanding its critical processes. We believe that history, in an even greater degree than its votaries have as yet generally recognized, is the central study among human studies, capable of illuminating and enriching all the rest. And this is one of the reasons why we desire, while pursuing it for its own sake in a calm and scientific spirit, to make this Review so far as possible a means of interesting thinking men in historical study, of accustoming them to its methods of inquiry, and of showing them how to appropriate its large results.

The *Historical Review* belongs to and represents no particular school of opinion or set of men. It has received promises of aid from nearly all the most zealous and famous labourers in the field it has chosen. It invites the cooperation of all who love historic truth and are striving to find it. Although Englishmen and Americans are chiefly occupied with the history of their own countries, yet the annals of the Mediterranean nations of antiquity, of the nearer and farther East, of the whole foreign world, mediaeval and modern, will be duly cared for; and the help of eminent historians in Germany, France, Italy, and the Scandinavian countries will be welcomed to complete the universal record which the *Historical Review* will endeavour to lay before its readers.

11

THE ETHOS OF A SCIENTIFIC HISTORIAN: *Fustel de Coulanges*

[Insisting that "Patriotism is a virtue and history a science, and the two should not be confounded," N. D. Fustel de Coulanges (1830-1889) broke with the earlier traditions of French historiography and sought to foster the scientific study of history in France. In his teaching, first at Strasbourg and, after the defeat of 1870, in Paris, he called for a proper historical method, which would emphasize the scrupulous study of original texts and cultivate a historical sense which would see the past in its uniqueness and not as a backward projection of the present. His best known work, *The Ancient City* (1864) reinterpreted the life of Greek and Roman cities by analyzing the relations of religious beliefs to political and economic institutions. In his monumental *Histoire des institutions politiques de l'ancienne France* (6 vols., 1875-1892) he described the historic origins of medieval France without becoming a partisan in the old controversy concerning the relative importance and merit of Latin versus Germanic influences on the development of France.

Fustel's Inaugural Lecture, delivered at Strasbourg in 1862, and the Introduction to the first volume of the History of Political Institutions in Ancient France appear below, translated by the Editor.]

AN INAUGURAL LECTURE

According to the regulation which governs our faculties a professor of history must change each year the subject of his lectures. He must lecture successively on ancient, medieval and modern times. Whatever his own inclinations, or even those of his listeners, may be, he is not allowed to linger for several years at a time with any one of these historical periods. Without a break he must recommence the cycle. Thus, as I have talked to you of modern history last year, I must offer you ancient history this year.

I am not complaining. I should add that the regulation even strikes me as utterly sensible, since it provides that the teaching of history shall not be confined to a single period but shall survey successively all epochs and all ages of mankind.

History, I think, fulfills its task only when it covers a long series of centuries. If one restricts one's study to a limited period, one can tell a story full of anecdotes and details which will satisfy the curiosity and occasionally amuse; this would be a pretty picture, a charming tale, but I find it difficult to convince myself that it would be true history.

I want it clearly understood, gentlemen, that history is something more than a pastime, that it is not pursued merely in order to entertain our curiosity or to fill the pigeonholes of our memory.

History is and should be a science. Its object, surely one of the most sublime that could be suggested for the study of man, is man himself—man, who to be wholly known, requires several sciences for himself. The physiologist studies his body, the psychologist and the historian share the study of his soul. The psychologist determines what is immutable in him—his nature, his faculties, his intellectual power, his conscience; the historian observes what changes, what is variable in man's soul—his beliefs, the trends and changes of his ideas—along with the things that are transformed with these ideas—i.e., laws, institutions, art, and science.

In man all these things are in flux. Other beings obey laws which leave them no freedom and permit them no change. But by his native faculties, by the prerequisites of his existence, by the deeds and the progress he has accomplished, man stands alone, distinct from the rest of creation. He alone can act spontaneously, can will, can command himself; the peculiar power to mould oneself and to exercise mastery over oneself has been given to man alone.

He also is the only creature that works. God does not work, for we cannot suppose that he had to exert himself to create the earth, to maintain and govern it. Nor does nature work. The plant which produces its fruit does not work at producing it; the animal digests its food and assimilates it: that is no work, since it is not an act of will or intelligence. But man exerts himself at every moment of his existence. Merely to live amidst the other creatures he must accomplish prodigious feats of dexterity and energy; and self-defense, which for other beings is an instinctual act, is for him an art. If he wants to improve his living conditions and satisfy his unbounded urge for happiness, he must wrestle with all the elements; weak though he is, he must subdue fierce animals and press all nature in his service—he who is so small and frail beside her. Of every obstacle he had to make a tool; of every enemy, a servant.

He wants to live in society, and so he must incessantly struggle against his own personal interest, submit either to force or law, silence his natural hatred of discipline, and make constant sacrifices to the welfare of all. He is born selfish and must somehow forget himself; he is born with powerful desires and with evil passions, and he must repress these desires and turn his passions to good. Nor is that all. When his existence is secure, happy, peaceful, well-governed, he is still dissatisfied, and he embarks on new efforts to seek knowledge; he questions everything; he puts himself face to face with nature, with himself, with his creator, and he attains each particle of knowledge by patient inquiry and by efforts of which he keeps no accounting. Thus he alone knows the law of work, that is to say, the struggle against external obstacles and against his own propensities.

With such remarkable gifts and such energy man cannot remain immutable. In the course of centuries everything changes in him—his form of life, his social condition, the conception of his intelligence, his ideas on law and his morality. The science which studies man cannot therefore apply the same operations as does botany or physiology. The botanist takes a plant, and when he has carefully observed it he is sure to see it as it always has been; its leaves have the same shape today as they had five thousand years ago; its sap runs with the same force; its fruit ripens at the same time of year. But man is not today what he was three thousand years ago;

he does not think what he thought then, he does not live as he then lived. Therefore, to know fully that variable and perfectible being one must study it in all the stages of its existence; other beings can be studied by simple observations; man can be known only through history.

But history thus conceived cannot be content to examine a single period in minute detail, to recount a brilliant biography, to select, in short, those events whose recital will delight or move us the most. One must go back to antiquity, one must understand the institutions of peoples that have ceased to exist, one has to breathe life into the ancient generations that are no longer even dust. Where history has no written records, it must force dead languages to yield their secrets; in their grammatical forms and in their very words it divines the thoughts of the men who spoke them. It must probe the fables and myths, the dreams induced by man's imagination, all the old falsehoods beneath which it must discover something very real—the beliefs of man. Wherever man has lived, wherever he has left some feeble imprint of his life and his intelligence, there is history. History should encompass all centuries, since it is the traditional book in which the human soul inscribes its variations and its progress.

This, gentlemen, is why the regulation which I spoke of before compels me to lecture to you on antiquity. This regulation, beneath its laconic and imperious form, teaches us a great and very profound truth: that history is not entertainment but science, and that its aim is not to have us make a pleasant acquaintance with such and such a period of our choice but to have us know man completely in all the phases of his existence.

Thus antiquity will be our field for this year. I must tell you from the outset of our meetings that among the ancient peoples I shall focus particularly on the Greeks and Romans. The reason for my preference is that these two peoples have exerted a more powerful influence on the destiny of mankind than any other, be it as originators, be it as propagators of truths. Still, the very nature of my subject will often compel me to cast a glance at other nations: I shall have to talk sometimes of the Italian peoples, the Etruscans, occasionally even of the Celts or the Thracians. I shall even have to call your attention to the Orient, and above all to India, where we shall find men who belonged to the same race as the Greeks and Romans. Many of the institutions of Greece and Rome can be explained to you only by the institutions of the

ancient Hindus; actually the similarities, and even the differences which we will encounter will throw a sharp light on
our study.

Among the lofty subjects which Rome and Greece suggest
for our study and for your contemplation I have chosen the
family and the state in particular—that is to say, the domestic
institutions, civil and political, and the different parts of the
law which are related to them. This will be the subject of our
talks, at least on Saturdays.

One does not have to be very familiar with these ancient
peoples to know that their institutions were very different
from ours. All of you have heard talk of cities and republics,
of liberty, of the senate and of popular assemblies, of consuls
or of archons, occasionally of kings, sometimes of tyrants, of
aristocracy and democracy; all matters, gentlemen, in which
it is extremely important to obtain the right idea and in
which there is a great danger of making mistakes; for in each
of these words there is material for several errors.

From childhood we have been raised on Greece and Rome.
These were almost the first words we heard in school, and
they were the most frequently repeated. As Montaigne said,
we know the Capitol before we know the Louvre, and the
Tiber before the Seine. And yet, gentlemen, it does not take
much serious thought to understand that this history presents
us with innumerable problems and difficulties. I do not speak
only of the uncertainty of primitive times; that is, as far as I
am concerned, only a secondary point; I am referring to institutions, and I feel that even the most fully authenticated and
best documented institutions, as soon as they are scrutinized
closely, seem obscure and incomprehensible. Open any work
on Roman history or, still more, on Greek history, and you
will stumble over contradictions and difficulties on every
page; and it is almost inevitable that at each of the terms
that I listed a moment ago—consul, senate, assembly, republic,
liberty, democracy—you will find yourselves surprised and bewildered and will ask yourselves, can this really be the truth,
and do we understand it properly?

On this point, permit me to talk of my own experience;
you might perhaps derive some benefit from my confessions.
It was not so very long ago that I, then as young as the
youngest among you, upon leaving the schools filled with the
rather light staples one gets there, though full of the discipline they train into us, began reflecting on ancient history.
At each step I was hampered by facts which struck me as

odd, which upset my ideas, and which I could not make clear to myself.

Thus I had often heard the liberty of ancient cities talked of, and I saw that the Athenian citizen, for instance, was neither master of his fortune which he had to be ready to sacrifice unconditionally as soon as the lot had designated him to supply a ship by himself or support a choir in the theatre, nor of his body, since he owed military service to the state for thirty-three years; nor of his speech or beliefs, since he could at any moment be arraigned in court on the charge of disloyalty to the state; nor of his conscience, for he had to believe in and worship the deities of the state and he was not allowed to think that there was only one God. And I began to wonder where was that liberty I had heard spoken of so often.

As far as Rome was concerned I had read countless times that the Tarquins had been ousted and liberty put in their place. I had believed it: imagine my surprise when the first Roman historian I happened to pick up taught me that three months after their expulsion the large majority of the Romans lamented them and the liberty that they had lost with them. Why did they oust them, I asked myself, and what was the real intention of those who then changed the form of government?

I had been told of the patricians and the plebeians as if one fine day all the men having duly assembled, nine-tenths of them had taken their places on the right and the remaining tenth, staying on the left had said to the rest: "Let us agree that from this day on we shall be the patricians and you the plebeians, that we shall have all the political rights and you shall have none, that we shall live under civil laws and that these laws shall not exist for you, that we shall hold the offices of state and religion and that you shall be neither magistrates nor priests. You shall not be our slaves exactly, but you will be our clients." And these distinctions, whose origin and nature I could not account for, struck me as very odd. I was still more puzzled when I found these same distinctions outside Rome, in nearly every one of the ancient cities. Everywhere I found popular assemblies as well, and these assemblies were pictured, depending on the personal views of several historians, sometimes as the ideal of good government, sometimes as the most advanced type of political disorder; but neither the one side nor the other thought of explaining how they functioned.

Everybody used to talk to me of democracy as something always good or always bad, and it did not take very much penetration for me to realize that the democracy of one period did not resemble that of another and to draw the inference that two very different parties or classes might be concealed from me under the identical tag.

I had read, both in historians and jurists, that Rome had invented the Civil Law—that that law, which until that time had been unknown to the world, was conceived by the genius of the Romans. Nevertheless it occurred to me that, if the Romans had needed such laws for living in society, the other cities of Italy and of Greece could hardly have done without them, and that since they were older than Rome, there was reason to suppose that they had had a civil law before Rome. Even within the body of Roman Law there were laws—for example, those dealing with inheritance—which puzzled me in the extreme, and I was much surprised to find these same laws, which appeared so odd, with other peoples, particularly with the Athenians. Nor could I explain why the Romans drew such a sharp distinction between possession and property, and I understood nothing of their agrarian laws.

I was not any better off with the history of Sparta. For according to what I had been taught, Sparta had never changed, her laws had been immutable, her institutions had remained the same. For Sparta, in short, time had stood still. And although my experience with human affairs and their ceaseless mobility was still quite limited it seemed to me very unlikely that a people could remain static for such a long time. I could easily believe that their internal revolutions had remained hidden from us; that, having been effected peacefully, they had not captured the imagination like those which break out suddenly in a tremendous upheaval and compel men to remember them for a long time; but that there had been no revolution at all, this I thought impossible.

However, what troubled me the most and inclined me to skepticism was that the majority of those who talked to me about the Romans and the Greeks seemed to be talking of the French or the English of their own time. They nearly always imagined these people as living in the same social conditions as we do and as thinking like us on nearly all issues. Having thus pictured them as similar to us, they told me abruptly, "This is how they governed themselves." So that my first thought naturally was, "Why aren't we governed like them?" In fact, they did not explain to me how these forms of government had developed, to what social needs they had responded, under what conditions they had been able to exist —in short, what ideas or what customs had given them authority over the minds of men and had made it possible for these institutions to exercise mastery over individual wills and to make men happy.

Gentlemen, I shall not enumerate all the difficulties I thus encountered. It was a whole series of insoluble problems. Even as far as the most authenticated facts are concerned, this history seemed to me incomprehensible, and yet the mystery aroused my curiosity.

I then resolved to have no other teachers on Greece than Greeks, nor on Rome than Romans, and I boldly resolved to read the ancient authors. I say boldly: there was courage only in the resolve, and I assure you none was required for the execution. For this was sustained by a greater pleasure than I had imagined; it was easy, and it did not cause me a single moment of distaste or boredom. I encountered these writers in their magnificent diversity and their ever refreshing charm; historians took turns with orators, orators with poets; sometimes the tribune and sometimes the stage. I discovered that I had condemned myself to the most delightful reading of the world. And for three years I enjoyed the greatest pleasure that can be afforded a man: to read great works and to discover truth.

Little by little I got better acquainted with the ancients; I saw their customs, their beliefs, their needs, their laws. Minor points, seemingly insignificant and unnoticed, illuminated their institutions for me. It did not take me long to see that if these institutions are often misunderstood by us, this happens because we study them by themselves as abstractions without reckoning with the exigencies of the environment in which they originated, and above all without giving thought to the state of mind and to the beliefs of the men for whom these institutions were made. Convinced that the external and visible laws which appear among men are only the signs and symptoms of moral facts which originate in our souls, I applied myself to the study of the beliefs of Greeks and Romans, and before long I thought I could see that between beliefs and institutions there is such a close bond that the one explains the other.

From then on the facts became clearer to me. Going back to the first stages of that race, [the Greeks and the Romans] I was struck by the remarkable conception which man at that time had formed of himself, of his nature, of his soul, and of some kind of life after death. I thought it obvious that the opinion that man forms of human nature must in every society have a great influence on the manner in which he lives and governs himself. If man looks on himself simply as a material being, living his short life on earth with nothing beyond it, it is probable that his institutions are merely the result of force or, at best, of enlightened self-interest. But if, in a particular period and by a particular race, man is conceived of as an immortal being, who after this existence would not in truth go to live in another world but always stay in this one, invisible but present and powerful, a shadow, a spirit, a divine guardian watching over his descendants, I should think that the domestic institutions would have had to be the fruit of this belief or at least would have had to be closely connected with it. Indeed, I discovered that this general conception of man, having become a real religion in Greece and in Italy, as it had with the ancient Hindus, was the basis of the Greek and Roman family, had set up the marriage customs, had determined the bonds of kinship in a manner somewhat different from ours, had founded the right of property, and had finally consecrated the right of inheritance in accordance with the very order of succession which had appeared to me so strange at first and since then very logical. I saw afterwards that that same cluster of beliefs, having broadened and extended the family, founded a larger association, the city. Family and city had in fact the same constitution, the same laws, the same customs; and that is why in this study I have brought the two together as being inseparable. Then I caught a glimpse of the constitution, at once political and religious, of these cities: the state was the object of religious worship; customs were sacred rituals; feasts were holy ceremonies; priests were magistrates; and there was an aristocracy of warrior-priests—in short a religion was so completely mingled with government that it was no longer possible to distinguish between them. As you can see, all this led me far away from the ways and thoughts we moderns are accustomed to, but it explained the institutions and the customs of the ancients. Besides, once this basic structure is understood, the subsequent series of revolutions are seen to unfold in a natural order. The cities gradually became transformed according to an almost uniform pattern and for readily perceivable causes. As the beliefs of which I have just spoken to you underwent changes in time, the political institutions, the civil laws, and even private law changed with them, and social change regularly followed the changing mentality.

Please note, gentlemen, that it is not altogether unimportant whether one has the right or the wrong conception of antiquity; the problem is not as immaterial as one would think. The destinies of modern peoples have at times depended on the way in which they understood antiquity, and great misfortunes have been the consequence of a historical error. The generation which lived in France eighty years ago had studied antiquity with an abiding prejudice of admiration; it talked endlessly of the forum and the senate, of consuls and tribunes. It sang the praises of the ancient virtues and put back into circulation the term citizen. To that generation Rome, Athens, Sparta appeared as the most perfect models by which to be guided. From admiration to imitation it is a short step indeed. When the old institutions of France fell by themselves and from natural causes which I need not discuss here, when France found itself almost without institutions, our ancestors, instead of looking for those institutions that would serve us best, dreamt of giving us those of the Romans and the Greeks, which they thoroughly misunderstood. Above all, they did not ask themselves whether these institutions were consonant with the material or moral conditions of modern man. They disinterred them without thinking that they belonged to another epoch, that while they had lived in one epoch, they had no chance to live in ours. From this derived the most exasperating contradictions and the most regrettable errors. In the name of liberty the old charge of disloyalty was reintroduced. In the name of liberty the state was made omnipotent and a dictatorship was established; and because the ancients put to death anyone who was deemed an enemy of the state, one believed that it was a matter of duty and virtue to kill one's political enemies. The inept imitation of antiquity led to the Reign of Terror. Indeed, if antiquity had been better studied one would have discovered so many of the great differences between antiquity and ourselves, between their ideas and ours, between their social structure and ours, that one would not have been tempted to borrow their thoughts, their language, or their forms of government. Especially the democrats, i.e., those who were the most fervent admirers of antiquity, would have been much surprised, I suppose, if an impartial view of the facts had shown them in Rome and Sparta, in other words in the very objects of their naïve enthusiasm, the most imperious, the most tenacious, the most oppressive aristocracy that ever existed. No doubt their admiration would have diminished. Certainly it would have been very desirable if antiquity had been studied without prejudice or partisanship—not in order to revive it in our midst but simply from a historical and philosophical point of view, to know what these ancients thought of matters of government and civil law, and thus to understand one of the strangest ages of mankind.

This is certainly a study that should be undertaken and one which could be profitable in many respects. Whoever is concerned with political questions would see that, whatever his opinions, he ought not to support them by appealing to antiquity. Anyone who specializes in the study of law and consults history as a legist would become convinced of the close tie that necessarily exists between our laws and the state of our soul, and he would see how much the one changes with the other. Finally, he who observes the historical facts philosophically and simply in order to understand man, would learn from such a study how man shapes his own beliefs, how from his beliefs he derives his institutions, what path his thought and his laws have followed, how much the historians of the ancient world differed from ours, and what road mankind has traversed in thirty centuries.

I certainly do not presume to know the answers to all these vast questions. I shall only put them before you and I shall present to you the facts which could help you to resolve them, and I shall submit these problems to your contemplation.

INTRODUCTION TO THE *History of the Political Institutions of Ancient France*

In writing this book I have thought neither to praise nor to disparage the ancient institutions of France. I intend solely to describe them and to indicate their development.

They are so much the opposite of those we see around us that at first it takes some effort to judge them with complete impartiality. It is difficult for a man of our own time to penetrate the mainstream of ideas and of conditions which brought them forth. The only hope of success lies in the patient study of the literature and documents which each century has left behind. There is no other way which allows our mind to free itself sufficiently from our immediate concerns and from every kind of partisanship so that it can depict with some exactitude the life of men of times gone by.

At first glance these old institutions appear singular, abnormal, and above all, violent and tyrannical. Since they lie outside our customs and ways of thought, we are at first left to believe that they lay outside all law and reason, outside the regular path which it would seem people should have followed, outside, so to speak, the usual laws of humanity. One also would believe quite readily that only brute force could have established them, and that a great upheaval had been necessary to bring them forth.

The study of the documents of each period has gradually led me to another impression. It seemed to me that these institutions originated in a slow, gradual, and regular manner and were not at all the product of a fortuitous accident or of a sudden act of force. Moreover, it seemed to me that, despite all appearances, these institutions were not at odds with human nature; for they were in harmony with the customs, the civil laws, the material interests, the forms of thought, and the frame of mind of the generations which they governed. These very factors gave birth to the institutions, and violence contributed but little to establish them.

Political institutions are never the creation of one man's will; even the will of an entire people would not suffice to create them. The human elements which bring them about are not of the kind which the caprice of one generation can change. Peoples are governed not by what they fancy but by what the totality of their interests and the essence of their beliefs prescribe. That is undoubtedly the reason why it takes many generations to establish a political regime and many other generations to tear it down.

Hence, also, the necessity for the historian to extend his investigations to a wide span of time. If he would limit his study to a single period, he would leave himself open to very serious errors, even in regard to that one period. The age in which an institution appears at its height, glittering, powerful, dominating, is hardly ever the time when it was established or when it gathered strength. The causes of its birth, the circumstances from which it drew strength and vigor often belong to a far earlier age. This is particularly true of feudalism, which of all political regimes is perhaps the one most deeply rooted in human nature.

Our point of departure for this study shall be the Roman conquest of Gaul. That event was the first of those which, from generation to generation, have transformed our country and shaped the course of its destiny. We shall then study each of the periods of our history by scrutinizing all the various facets of public life. To understand how each generation was governed we shall have to observe its social conditions, its needs, its manners, and its genius. All these things we shall relate to the public authorities which governed it, the kind of justice rendered, the burden it shouldered in the form of taxes or military service. In surveying the ages in this manner we shall have to show the continuity and the change that existed in their relationship at one and the same time—continuity, because institutions endure whether we like them or not; change, because they are imperceptibly modified by each new development which occurs in the material or moral sphere.

History is not an easy science; its subject is infinitely complex; human society is like a body whose harmony and unity can be grasped only by examining successively and closely each of the organs which compose it and which are its life. Long and careful study of the particular is therefore the only way that can lead to some general outlook. One day of synthesis requires years of analysis. In a quest which demands so much patience and so much effort, so much prudence and so much boldness, the chances for error are countless and none can hope to escape them. If we have not been discouraged by the deep awareness of the difficulties of our task, it is because we believe that the honest search for truth is always rewarding. If we accomplish nothing else but to throw some light on hitherto neglected points or to call attention to some obscure problems, we shall not have labored in vain, and we should moreover feel justified in saying that we have contributed our share to the progress of historical science and to the knowledge of human nature.

12

ON THE TRAINING OF
HISTORIANS: *Mommsen*

[Theodor Mommsen (1817-1903), jurist, epigrapher, and historian, made incomparable contributions to the study of Roman history. Universally acclaimed for his *History of Rome* (3 vols., 1854-1856 plus a fifth volume on the *Roman Provinces from Augustus to Diocletian*, 1885)[1] his more specialized work included a history of Roman coinage (1860) and a monumental treatise on Roman Public Law (*Römisches Staatsrecht*, 3 vols., 1871-1876). He originated, supervised, and contributed to the *Corpus inscriptionum Latinorum*, a collection of all the known Roman inscriptions. The bibliography of his own works listed 1,500 items. Mommsen's *History* exceeded in scope and scholarship anything that had been done before: using a variety of sources, including inscriptions, laws, and coins, he reconstructed the history of the Roman Republic from its origins to the reign of Caesar. Mommsen's *History* was a literary masterpiece as well, and in 1902 he received the Nobel Prize. His frequent allusions in this work to the contemporary scene—to Junkers, journalists, and proletariat, for example—and his undisguised admiration of Caesar whom he depicted as a democratic leader, attested his intense involvement in German politics, his hope for a liberal Germany. The qualities which Mommsen thought indispensable for the historian—a knowledge of law, linguistics, and literature and an immediate perception, an inborn genius which sees meaning and connections in the complex-

ity of history—he himself possessed, and to an extent unsur-
passed by any other modern historian.

The following selection is the second half of his Rectorial
Address, delivered at the University of Berlin in 1874, and
translated by the Editor.]

RECTORIAL ADDRESS

History is one of those academic subjects which cannot be directly acquired through precept and learning. For that, history
is in some measure too easy and in some measure too difficult.

The elements of the historical discipline cannot be learned
for every man is already endowed with them. History, after
all, is nothing but the distinct knowledge of actual happenings, consisting on the one hand of the discovery and examination of the available testimony, and on the other of the
weaving of this testimony into a narrative in accordance with
one's understanding of the men who shaped the events and
the conditions that prevailed. The former we call the critical
study of historical sources and the latter, the pragmatic writing of history. But we historians are not the only ones to pursue this kind of activity: for everyone of you gentlemen,
every thinking man generally, is a searcher after sources and a
pragmatic historian. You must be both in order to understand
any event that takes place before your eyes; every businessman who handles a complicated transaction, every lawyer who
considers a case, is a searcher after sources and a pragmatic
historian. The elements of historical discipline are, I think,
still simpler and more self-evident than those of philology
and mathematics, and that is why they are neither teachable
nor instructive.

In some ways, of course, it is possible to say of every discipline or science that it proceeds from the self-evident. But
history distinguishes itself from its sister disciplines by its inability to bring its elements into a proper theoretical exposition. Where the intellectual ability on which history rests—
the immediate perspicacity for it, as it is aptly called—exists
at all, it can without question be substantially enhanced by
further education, not indeed through theoretical precepts, but
only through practical exercises. The correct evaluation of the
available testimony, the correct connection of the seemingly
unrelated and contradictory material to establish the actual
order of events exhibits in every case such an infinite

simplicity of principles and such an infinite diversity of application that every theory turns out to be either trivial or transcendental. That hearsay evidence possesses only as much validity as the authority from which it derives is just about the only precept which the critical method can boast of. The intuitive certainty of judgment, which marks the outstanding historian, is nine times out of ten nothing more than the unconscious application of this precept to a complicated problem. The stroke which forges a thousand links, the insight into the uniqueness of men and peoples, evinces such high genius as defies all teaching and all learning. The historian has perhaps greater affinity with the artist than with the scholar.

That is why it is a mistake to assign to the study of history, to critical pragmatic research, any but a secondary place in the University. The future historian unquestionably derives real benefit from early, well-directed practice in his field; though practice alone does not make the master, no one has yet become a master without long and arduous practice. But in the brief period spent at the University a student does not have time for this kind of training. It is moreover a dangerous and harmful illusion for the professor of history to believe that historians can be trained at the University in the same way as philologists or mathematicians most assuredly can be. One can say with more justification of the historian than of the mathematician or the philologist that he is not trained but born, not educated but self-educated.

If this were merely a question of the greater or smaller value attributed to historical study at the University, then in the last analysis a dispute about it would be fairly insignificant. But the inflated value which is put upon direct historical study leads to very practical, detrimental consequences since, because of it, the really necessary preparation for history is often overlooked. In this way a certain, very definite kind of historical pseudo-preparation is engendered which corrodes true history like a cancerous growth.

There is, of course, a preliminary training indispensable for the historian; only it is not the direct training in history itself, but an indirect one: the study of the language and of the law of a particular period. It may seem foolish to make a special point of this, but alas, it is not superfluous. Among scholars, too, there are some historical fanatics who believe they can get along with the so-called systematic treatment of sources, even if one's mastery of the language of these sources is poor or non-existent. The theory is sometimes advanced that the exact understanding of the sources is a specifically philological task and that for the historian it suffices if he can follow their general drift: and the practice of indolence welcomes this theory all too readily. The final result of this tendency is those monstrous histories of the Jews or the Assyrians that are written by men who confess without the least inhibition that they do not understand the pertinent languages. That there are countless historians who do not really understand Greek, Latin or German, is only too well known to the initiate. The greatest evil which comes from this is not the individual misunderstandings which result, but the lack of intellectual penetration of the subject. A people's language is always its greatest, most enduring and most multifarious monument. Take Rome: anyone who is unable to empathize with Ennius and Horace, with Petronius and Papinian will forever talk of Roman life as a blind man of color, however accurate his pragmatic inquiry into the source may be.

A similar situation exists in the study of law; by which I do not mean primarily jurisprudence itself, but the knowledge of public law, of the constitution of a given state which is, of course, in turn entirely inseparable from the knowledge of the civil law of that people. There can be no question but that history is itself precisely this constitution with its changes, and that of course no historian can properly ignore it. But there are two essentially different ways of pursuing this study: you can study either the constitution as a whole as a more or less enduring system, or a particular detail as it concretely affects actual events. The first is the correct way though the second is generally followed. How many of those who discourse about archons and generals, about consuls and praetors, have ever seriously considered these magistracies in the totality of their constitutional positions? How many of those who deal extensively with bishops and electors have the Roman-canonical and the German imperial law for these institutions clearly in mind? Yet the writing of pragmatic history may only be undertaken by someone who has a clear conception of these, its most important elements. The same superficiality which in philology characterizes pseudo-history appears in the field of constitutional law. Here also people talk too often of what they do not understand, or still worse, of what they only half-understand, superficially repeating vague tradition.

Let me confess, gentlemen, that when I see on your records the notation "student of history," I become disturbed. It can of course mean that the young man seeks to acquire the necessary introductory knowledge of the language and political institutions needed particularly for a certain field of historical study, and I know that this is what it signifies for quite a few of you. But it can also signify the belief that one can pretty much do without these things, that one can find in history a refuge from the hardships of rigorous philology, that one can manage with systematic source study and systematic historical pragmatism. When the latter is meant, nemesis will follow swiftly. The critical study of sources becomes that mechanical dissection of the material, which at most requires patience and not the inspired patience of the scholar who divines the distant goal, but the workaday patience of the laborer. The study of historical fact then becomes either pedantry or fraud. Retribution always follows the lack of genuine training, since the false training becomes either pedestrian or fanciful, or both. In either case the historical sense vanishes.

I recommend to you, my young fellow historians, the example set by jurisprudence. The task of practicing lawyers is essentially similar to the historian's, but it has never occurred to anyone to suggest that the great art of the practising lawyer could be acquired primarily from university study. The University can prepare a student for the correct understanding of the individual law case, but it cannot give him that understanding by direct instruction. Likewise the historian should use his university years to prepare himself indirectly and not directly for his future work. Anyone who leaves the University with a thorough knowledge of Greek, Latin and German, and of the political institutions of these peoples, is prepared to become a historian. Anyone lacking this knowledge is not so prepared. After you have striven for this necessary preparation, the critical method and the pragmatic presentation of history will come to you by themselves, just as surely as the heavy cloud is bound to send down rain. And if you do not acquire this preparation, you are gathering fruit that has rotted before it is picked. Through sham accomplishments you will only increase that already excessively long line of men who thought they could learn history as a craft and discovered later, to their horror, that it is an art.

I could proceed with censure and complaint. But it ill fits this occasion to specify and describe the black clouds which hang over the future of the German Universities. They shall not and they will not spoil either our share of the general rejoicing at what has already been attained nor the high spirits with which we face the future. Our German youth will not abandon its traditions; when the time comes, it will carry on if need be under more exacting conditions, the work which we hand down, and will prepare itself even now for this responsibility. For this, you possess what you need above all else: the full freedom of learning. No formal rule prescribes how you should spend your academic years; no interim examination tries to find out what use, if any, you have made of these years. No other nation in the world puts the same faith in its youth as does ours; and our academic youth has so far justified this faith. Continue to go your way and if the path should sometimes lead into the wilderness and you should think it a wrong path—remember that more often than we could dare hope, we have seen that different ways can lead to the same desired goal. Every man of strong individual bent does his best when he follows his own path and for each of you that path is open.

And now, gentlemen, let us begin our common work of teaching and learning, in full awareness of the difficulties of the task and with the full and wholehearted determination to master it. For the presence of danger is a challenge to honor. There are easier ways of entering life than the one that leads through our lecture halls; that is why the best follow the academic path. For the German student, his matriculation is still a patent of nobility by which he joins the ranks of the volunteer fighters for right and truth, and for the freedom of the human spirit. But it is an obligation of indebtedness as well; whoever assumes it, pledges himself to hold his own in this struggle and not to succumb to the evil enemies of all spiritual growth—indolence, officiousness and sham learning. You gentlemen have received, or are about to receive, this patent of nobility. You have assumed or are about to assume this obligation. Show yourselves worthy of it, each in his place, for the honor and welfare of our country.

13

AN AMERICAN DEFINITION
OF HISTORY: *Turner*

[The work of Frederick Jackson Turner (1861-1932) opened
a new era in American historiography. Familiar with European and ancient history, and influenced by the German
historians, especially A. H. L. Heeren, Turner nevertheless demanded that American history must be studied as an outgrowth of the distinct American experience, moulded more
by the frontier of the West than the continuing link with the
Old World. Having become dissatisfied with the traditional
political historiography, he sought in his writings and his influential teaching to grasp the significance, to find the inner
springs of this American experience. He taught first at the
University of Wisconsin and in 1910 accepted a chair at Harvard. His essay on "The Significance of the Frontier in American History" appeared in 1893, and the *Rise of the New West*
in 1906.

"The Significance of History," first published in 1891, reveals in an early form the themes of his later thought and his
anticipation of the "New Historians" whose demand was for a
comprehensive history, serving the needs of the "living present," and promoting civic virtue. That essay is here reprinted, with some passages and one footnote omitted.]

THE SIGNIFICANCE OF HISTORY

The conceptions of history have been almost as numerous as the men who have written history. To Augustine Birrell history is a pageant; it is for the purpose of satisfying our curiosity.[1] Under the touch of a literary artist the past is to become living again. Like another Prospero the historian waves his wand, and the deserted streets of Palmyra sound to the tread of artisan and officer, warrior gives battle to warrior, ruined towers rise by magic, and the whole busy life of generations that have long ago gone down to dust comes to life again in the pages of a book. The artistic prose narration of past events—this is the ideal of those who view history as literature. To this class belong romantic literary artists who strive to give to history the coloring and dramatic action of fiction, who do not hesitate to paint a character blacker or whiter than he really was, in order that the interest of the page may be increased, who force dull facts into vivacity, who create impressive situations, who, in short, strive to realize as an ideal the success of Walter Scott. It is of the historian Froude that Freeman says: "The most winning style, the choicest metaphors, the neatest phrases from foreign tongues would all be thrown away if they were devoted to proving that any two sides of a triangle are not always greater than the third side. When they are devoted to proving that a man cut off his wife's head one day and married her maid the next morning out of sheer love for his country, they win believers for the paradox." It is of the reader of this kind of history that Seeley[2] writes: "To him, by some magic, parliamentary debates shall be always lively, officials always men of strongly marked, interesting character. There shall be nothing to remind him of the bluebook or the law book, nothing common or prosaic; but he shall sit as in a theater and gaze at splendid scenery and costume. He shall never be called upon to study or to judge, but only to imagine and enjoy. His reflections, as he reads, shall be precisely those of the novel reader; he shall ask: Is this character well drawn? is it really amusing? is the interest of the story well sustained, and does it rise properly toward the close?"

But after all these criticisms we may gladly admit that in itself an interesting style, even a picturesque manner of presentation, is not to be condemned, provided that truthfulness of substance rather than vivacity of style be the end sought. But granting that a man may be the possessor of a good style which he does not allow to run away with him, either in the interest of the artistic impulse or in the cause of party, still there remain differences as to the aim and method of history. To a whole school of writers, among whom we find some of the great historians of our time, history is the study of politics, that is, politics in the high signification given the word by Aristotle, as meaning all that concerns the activity of the state itself. "History is past politics and politics present history," says the great author of the *Norman Conquest*. Maurenbrecher of Leipzig[3] speaks in no less certain tones: "The bloom of historical studies is the history of politics"; and Lorenz of Jena asserts: "The proper field of historical investigation, in the closer sense of the word, is politics." Says Seeley: "The modern historian works at the same task as Aristotle in his Politics." "To study history is to study not merely a narrative but at the same time certain theoretical studies." "To study history is to study problems." And thus a great circle of profound investigators, with true scientific method, have expounded the evolution of political institutions, studying their growth as the biologist might study seed, bud, blossom, and fruit. The results of these labors may be seen in such monumental works as those of Waitz on German institutions, Stubbs on English constitutional history, and Maine on early institutions.

There is another and an increasing class of historians to whom history is the study of the economic growth of the people, who aim to show that property, the distribution of wealth, the social conditions of the people, are the underlying and determining factors to be studied. This school, whose advance guard was led by Roscher,[4] having already transformed orthodox political economy by its historical method, is now going on to rewrite history from the economic point of view. Perhaps the best English expression of the ideas of the school is to be found in Thorold Rogers' *Economic Interpretation of History*. He asserts truly that "very often the cause of great political events and great social movements is economical and has hitherto been undetected. . . .

Viewed from this position, the past is filled with new meaning. The focal point of modern interest is the fourth estate, the great mass of the people. History has been a romance and a tragedy. In it we read the brilliant annals of the few. The intrigues of courts, knightly valor, palaces and pyramids, the loves of ladies, the songs of minstrels, and the chants from cathedrals pass like a pageant, or linger like a strain of music as we turn the pages. But history has its tragedy as well, which tells of the degraded tillers of the soil, toiling that others might dream, the slavery that rendered possible the "glory that was Greece," the serfdom into which decayed the "grandeur that was Rome"—these as well demand their annals. Far oftener than has yet been shown have these underlying economic facts affecting the breadwinners of the nation been the secret of the nation's rise or fall, by the side of which much that has passed as history is the merest frippery. . . .

Today the questions that are uppermost, and that will become increasingly important, are not so much political as economic questions. The age of machinery, of the factory system, is also the age of socialistic inquiry.

It is not strange that the predominant historical study is coming to be the study of past social conditions, inquiry as to landholding, distribution of wealth, and the economic basis of society in general. Our conclusion, therefore, is that there is much truth in all these conceptions of history: history is past literature, it is past politics, it is past religion, it is past economics.

Each age tries to form its own conception of the past. *Each age writes the history of the past anew with reference to the conditions uppermost in its own time.* Historians have accepted the doctrine of Herder. Society grows. They have accepted the doctrine of Comte. Society is an organism. History is the biography of society in all its departments. There is objective history and subjective history. Objective history applies to the events themselves; subjective history is man's conception of these events. "The whole mode and manner of looking at things alters with every age," but this does not mean that the real events of a given age change; it means that our comprehension of these facts changes.

History, both objective and subjective, is ever *becoming,* never completed. The centuries unfold to us more and more the meaning of past times. Today we understand Roman history better than did Livy or Tacitus, not only because we know how to use the sources better but also because the significance of events develops with time, because today is so much a product of yesterday that yesterday can only be understood as it is explained by today. The aim of history, then, is to know the elements of the present by understanding what came into the present from the past. For the present is simply the developing past, the past the undeveloped present. As well try to understand the egg without a knowledge of its developed form, the chick, as to try to understand the past without bringing to it the explanation of the present; and equally well try to understand an animal without study of its embryology as to try to understand one time without study of the events that went before. The antiquarian strives to bring back the past for the sake of the past; the historian strives to show the present to itself by revealing its origin from the past. The goal of the antiquarian is the dead past; the goal of the historian is the living present. Droysen has put this true conception into the statement, "History is the 'Know Thyself' of humanity—the self-consciousness of mankind."

If, now, you accept with me the statement of this great master of historical science, the rest of our way is clear. If history be, in truth, the self-consciousness of humanity, the "self-consciousness of the living age, acquired by understanding its development from the past," all the rest follows.

First we recognize why all the spheres of man's activity must be considered. Not only is this the only way in which we can get a complete view of the society, but no one department of social life can be understood in isolation from the others. The economic life and the political life touch, modify, and condition one another. Even the religious life needs to be studied in conjunction with the political and economic life, and vice versa. Therefore, all kinds of history are essential—history as politics, history as art, history as economics, history as religion—all are truly parts of society's endeavor to understand itself by understanding its past.

Next we see that history is not shut up in a book—not in many books. The first lesson the student of history has to learn is to discard his conception that there are standard ultimate histories. In the nature of the case this is impossible. *History is all the remains that have come down to us from the past, studied with all the critical and interpretative power that the present can bring to the task.* From time to time great masters bring their investigations to fruit in books. To us these serve as the latest words, the best results of the most recent efforts of society to understand itself—but they are not the final words. To the historian the materials for his work are found in all that remains from the ages gone by—in papers, roads, mounds, customs, languages; in monuments, coins, medals, names, titles, inscriptions, charters; in contemporary annals and chronicles; and, finally, in the secondary sources, or histories in the common acceptance of the term. Wherever there remains a chipped flint, a spearhead, a piece of pottery, a pyramid, a picture, a poem, a coliseum, or a coin, there is history.

Says Taine: "What is your first remark on turning over the great stiff leaves of a folio, the yellow sheets of a manuscript, a poem, a code of laws, a declaration of faith? This, you say, was not created alone. It is but a mold, like a fossil shell, an imprint like one of those shapes embossed in stone by an animal which lived and perished. Under the shell there was an animal, and behind the document there was a man. Why do you study the shell except to represent to yourself the animal? So do you study the document only in order to know the man. The shell and the document are lifeless wrecks, valuable only as a clue to the entire and living existence. We must reach back to this existence, endeavor to recreate it."

But observe that when a man writes a narration of the past he writes with all his limitations as regards ability to test the real value of his sources, and ability rightly to interpret them. Does he make use of a chronicle? First he must determine whether it is genuine; then whether it was contemporary, or at what period it was written; then what opportunities its author had to know the truth; then what were his personal traits; was he likely to see clearly, to relate impartially? If not, what was his bias, what his limitations? Next comes the harder task—to interpret the significance of events; causes must be understood, results seen. Local affairs must be described in relation to affairs of the world—all must be told with just selection, emphasis, perspective; with that historical imagination and sympathy that does not judge the past by the canons of the present, nor read into it the ideas of the present. Above all the historian must have a passion for truth above that for any party or idea. Such are some of the difficulties that lie in the way of our science. When, moreover, we consider that each man is conditioned by the age in which he lives and must perforce write with limitations and prepossessions, I think we shall all agree that no historian can say the ultimate word.

Another thought that follows as a corollary from our definition is that in history there is a unity and a continuity. Strictly speaking, there is no gap between ancient, medieval, and modern history. Strictly speaking, there are no such divisions. Baron Bunsen dates modern history from the migration of Abraham.[5] Bluntschli makes it begin with Frederick the Great.[6] The truth is, as Freeman has shown, that the age of Pericles or the age of Augustus has more in common with modern times than has the age of Alfred or of Charlemagne. There is another test than that of chronology; namely, stages of growth. In the past of the European world peoples have grown from families into states, from peasantry into the complexity of great city life, from animism into monotheism, from mythology into philosophy; and have yielded place again to primitive peoples who in turn have passed through stages like these and yielded to new nations. Each nation has bequeathed something to its successor; no age has suffered the highest content of the past to be lost entirely. By unconscious inheritance, and by conscious striving after the past as part of the present, history has acquired continuity. Freeman's statement that into Rome flowed all the ancient world and out of Rome came the modern world is as true as it is impressive. In a strict sense imperial Rome never died. You may find the eternal city still living in the Kaiser and the Czar, in the language of the Romance peoples, in the codes of European states, in the eagles of their coats of arms, in every college where the classics are read, in a thousand political institutions.

Even here in young America old Rome still lives. When the inaugural procession passes toward the Senate chamber, and the president's address outlines the policy he proposes to pursue, there is Rome! You may find her in the code of Louisiana, in the French and Spanish portions of our history, in the idea of checks and balances in our constitution. Clearest of all, Rome may be seen in the titles, government, and ceremonials of the Roman Catholic church; for when the Caesar passed away, his scepter fell to that new Pontifex Maximus, the Pope, and that new Augustus, the Holy Roman Emperor of the Middle Ages, an empire which in name at least continued till those heroic times when a new Imperator recalled the days of the great Julius, and sent the eagles of France to proclaim that Napoleon was king over kings.

So it is true in fact, as we should presume a priori, that in history there are only artificial divisions. Society is an organism, ever growing. History is the self-consciousness of this organism. "The roots of the present lie deep in the past." There is no break. But not only is it true that no country can be understood without taking account of all the past; it is also true that we cannot select a stretch of land and say we will limit our study to this land; for local history can only be understood in the light of the history of the world. There is unity as well as continuity. To know the history of contemporary Italy we must know the history of contemporary France, of contemporary Germany. Each acts on each. Ideas, commodities even, refuse the bounds of a nation. All are inextricably connected, so that each is needed to explain the others. This is true especially of our modern world with its complex commerce and means of intellectual connection. In history, then, there is unity and continuity. Each age must be studied in the light of all the past; local history must be viewed in the light of world history.

Now, I think, we are in a position to consider the utility of historical studies. I will not dwell on the dignity of history considered as the self-consciousness of humanity; nor on the mental growth that comes from such a discipline; nor on the vastness of the field; all these occur to you, and their importance will impress you increasingly as you consider history from this point of view. To enable us to behold our own time and place as a part of the stupendous progress of the ages; to see primitive man; to recognize in our midst the undying ideas of Greece; to find Rome's majesty and power alive in present law and institution, still living in our superstitions and our folklore; to enable us to realize the richness of our inheritance, the possibility of our lives, the grandeur of the present—these are some of the priceless services of history.

But I must conclude my remarks with a few words upon the utility of history as affording a training for good citizenship. Doubtless good citizenship is the end for which the public schools exist. Were it otherwise there might be difficulty in justifying the support of them at public expense. The direct and important utility of the study of history in the achievement of this end hardly needs argument.

In the union of public service and historical study Germany has been pre-eminent. For certain governmental positions in that country a university training in historical studies is essential. Ex-President Andrew D. White affirms that a main cause of the efficiency of German administration is the training that officials get from the university study of history and politics. In Paris there is the famous School of Political Sciences which fits men for the public service of France. . . .

Nor does England fail to recognize the value of the union of history and politics, as is exemplified by such men as Macaulay, Dilke, Morley, and Bryce, all of whom have been eminent members of Parliament as well as distinguished historical writers. From France and Italy such illustrations could easily be multiplied.

When we turn to America and ask what marriages have occurred between history and statesmanship, we are filled with astonishment at the contrast. It is true that our country has tried to reward literary men: Motley, Irving, Bancroft, Lowell held official positions, but these positions were in the diplomatic service. The "literary fellow" was good enough for Europe. The state gave these men aid rather than called their services to its aid. To this statement I know of but one important exception—George Bancroft.[7] In America statesmanship has been considered something of spontaneous generation, a miraculous birth from our republican institutions. To demand of the statesmen who debate such topics as the tariff, European and South American relations, immigration, labor and railroad problems, a scientific acquaintance with historical politics or economics would be to expose one's self to ridicule in the eyes of the public. I have said that the tribal stage of society demands tribal history and tribal politics. When a society is isolated it looks with contempt upon the history and institutions of the rest of the world. We shall not be altogether wrong if we say that such tribal ideas concerning our institutions and society have prevailed for many years in this country. Lately historians have turned to the comparative and historical study of our political institutions. The actual working of our constitution as contrasted with the literary theory of it has engaged the attention of able young men. Foreigners like Von Holst and Bryce[8] have shown us a mirror of our political life in the light of the political life of other peoples. Little of this influence has yet attracted the attention of our public men. Count the roll in Senate and House, cabinet and diplomatic service—to say nothing of the state governments— and where are the names famous in history and politics? It is shallow to express satisfaction with this condition and to sneer at "literary fellows." To me it seems that we are approaching a pivotal point in our country's history. . . .

Again, consider the problems of socialism brought to our shores by European immigrants. We shall never deal rightly with such problems until we understand the historical conditions under which they grew. Thus we meet Europe not only outside our borders but in our very midst. The problem of immigration furnishes many examples of the need of historical study. Consider how our vast Western domain has been settled. Louis XIV devastates the Palatinate, and soon hundreds of its inhabitants are hewing down the forests of Pennsylvania. The Bishop of Salzburg persecutes his Protestant subjects, and the woods of Georgia sound to the crack of Teutonic rifles. Presbyterians are oppressed in Ireland, and soon in Tennessee and Kentucky the fires of pioneers gleam. These were but advance guards of the mighty army that has poured into our midst ever since. Every economic change, every political change, every military conscription, every socialistic agitation in Europe, has sent us groups of colonists who have passed out onto our prairies to form new self-governing communities, or who have entered the life of our great cities. These men have come to us historical products, they have brought to us not merely so much bone and sinew, not merely so much money, not merely so much manual skill, they have brought with them deeply inrooted customs and ideas. They are important factors in the political and economic life of the nation. Our destiny is interwoven with theirs; how shall we understand American history without understanding European history? The story of the peopling of America has not yet been written. We do not understand ourselves.

One of the most fruitful fields of study in our country has been the process of growth of our own institutions, local and national. The town and the county, the germs of our political institutions, have been traced back to old Teutonic roots. Gladstone's remark that "the American constitution is the most wonderful work ever struck off at a given time by the brain and purpose of man," has been shown to be misleading, for the constitution was, with all the constructive powers of the fathers, still a growth; and our history is only to be understood as a growth from European history under the new conditions of the New World.

Says Dr. H. B. Adams: "American local history should be studied as a contribution to national history. This country will yet be viewed and reviewed as an organism of historic growth, developing from minute germs, from the very protoplasm of state-life. And some day this country will be studied in its international relations, as an organic part of a larger organism now vaguely called the World-State, but as surely developing through the operation of economic, legal, social, and scientific forces as the American Union, the German and British empires are evolving into higher forms. . . . The local consciousness must be expanded into a fuller sense of its historic worth and dignity. We must understand the cosmopolitan relations of modern local life, and its own wholesome conservative power in these days of growing centralization."

If any added argument were needed to show that good citizenship demands the careful study of history, it is in the examples and lessons that the history of other peoples has for us. It is profoundly true that each people makes its own history in accordance with its past. It is true that a purely artificial piece of legislation, unrelated to present and past conditions, is the most short-lived of things. Yet it is to be remembered that it was history that taught us this truth, and that there is, within the limits of the constructive action possible to a state, large scope for the use of this experience of foreign peoples.

I have aimed to offer, then, these considerations: History, I have said, is to be taken in no narrow sense. It is more than past literature, more than past politics, more than past economics. It is the self-consciousness of humanity—humanity's effort to understand itself through the study of its past. Therefore it is not confined to books; the *subject* is to be studied, not books simply. History has a unity and a continuity; the present needs the past to explain it; and local history must be read as a part of world history. The study has a utility as a mental discipline, and as expanding our ideas regarding the dignity of the present. But perhaps its most practical utility to us, as public school teachers, is its service in fostering good citizenship.

The ideals presented may at first be discouraging. Even to him who devotes his life to the study of history the ideal conception is impossible of attainment. He must select some field and till that thoroughly, be absolute master of it; for the rest he must seek the aid of others whose lives have been given in the true scientific spirit to the study of special fields. The public school teacher must do the best with the libraries at his disposal. We teachers must use all the resources we can obtain and not pin our faith to a single book; we must make history living instead of allowing it to seem mere literature, a mere narration of events that might have occurred on the moon. We must teach the history of a few countries thoroughly, rather than that of many countries superficially. The popularizing of scientific knowledge is one of the best achievements of this age of book-making. It is typical of that social impulse which has led university men to bring the fruits of their study home to the people. In England the social impulse has led to what is known as the university extension movement. University men have left their traditional cloister and gone to live among the working classes, in order to bring to them a new intellectual life. Chautauqua, in our own country, has begun to pass beyond the period of superficial work to a real union of the scientific and the popular. In their summer school they offer courses in American history. Our own state university carries on extensive work in various lines. I believe that this movement in the direction of popularizing historical and scientific knowledge will work a real revolution in our towns and villages as well as in our great cities.

The schoolteacher is called to do a work above and beyond the instruction in his school. He is called upon to be the apostle of the higher culture to the community in which he is placed. Given a good school or town library—such a one is now within the reach of every hamlet that is properly stimulated to the acquisition of one—and given an energetic, devoted teacher to direct and foster the study of history and politics and economics, we would have an intellectual regeneration of the state. Historical study has for its end to let the community see itself in the light of the past, to give it new thoughts and feelings, new aspirations and energies. Thoughts and feelings flow into deeds. Here is the motive power that lies behind institutions. This is therefore one of the ways to create good politics; here we can touch the very "age and body of the time, its form and pressure." Have you a thought of better things, a reform to accomplish? "Put it in the air," says the great teacher. Ideas have ruled, will rule. We must make university extension into state life felt in this country as did Germany. Of one thing beware. Avoid as the very unpardonable sin any one-sidedness, any partisan, any partial treatment of history. Do not misinterpret the past for the sake of the present. The man who enters the temple of history must respond devoutly to that invocation of the church, *Sursum corda,* lift up your hearts. No looking at history as an idle tale, a compend of anecdotes; no servile devotion to a textbook; no carelessness of truth about the dead that can no longer speak must be permitted in its sanctuary. "History," says Droysen, "is not the truth and the light; but a striving for it, a sermon on it. a consecration to it."

HISTORY AS A SCIENCE: *Bury*

[John Bagnell Bury (1861-1927) was a classical philologist before he became a historian, and his works on the late Roman period and the Byzantine Empire were characterized by high competence in both fields. At the age of 28 he wrote *A History of the Later Roman Empire from Arcadius to Irene 395 A.D. to 800 A.D.* (2 vols. 1889), which was generally regarded as a remarkably mature contribution to the literature. Given his own interests and inclinations, Bury was ideally fitted to undertake the definitive edition of Gibbon's *Decline and Fall of the Roman Empire* (7 vols. 1896-1900). He also served as editor of the *Cambridge Ancient History*. In his early years he was concerned with philosophy, especially with Hegel, and he developed a lasting interest in the philosophical problems of historical study; in 1902, when he succeeded Lord Acton as the Regius Professor of Modern History at Cambridge, he delivered an Inaugural Lecture on "The Science of History," reprinted below, which epitomized the historicist tradition in England. Bury's strong rationalistic beliefs, akin in some ways to Gibbon's, inspired his two short works on *The History of Freedom of Thought* (1913) and *The Idea of Progress* (1920). During and after the First World War he grew skeptical about the possibility of establishing historical causality and in his last writings stressed the role of contingency, of mere chance, in history.]

THE SCIENCE OF HISTORY

In saying that I come before you to-day with no little trepidation, I am not uttering a mere conventional profession of diffidence. There are very real reasons for misgiving. My predecessor told you how formidable he found this chair, illuminated as it is by the lustre of the distinguished historian whom he succeeded. But if it was formidable then, how much more formidable is it to-day! The terrors which it possessed for Lord Acton have been enhanced for his successor.

In a home of historical studies where so much thought is spent on their advancement, one can hardly hope to say any new thing touching those general aspects of history which most naturally invite attention in an inaugural lecture. It may be appropriate and useful now and again to pay a sort of solemn tribute to the dignity and authority of a great discipline or science, by reciting some of her claims and her laws, or by reviewing the measures of her dominion; and on this occasion, in this place, it might perhaps seem to be enough to honour the science of history in this formal way, sprinkling, as it were, with dutiful hands some grains of incense on her altar.

Yet even such a tribute might possess more than a formal significance, if we remember how recently it is—within three generations, three short generations—that history began to forsake her old irresponsible ways and prepared to enter into her kingdom. In the story of the nineteenth century, which has witnessed such far-reaching changes in the geography of thought and in the apparatus of research, no small nor isolated place belongs to the transformation and expansion of history. That transformation, however, is not yet complete. Its principle is not yet universally or unreservedly acknowledged. It is rejected in many places, or ignored, or unrealised. Old envelopes still hang tenaciously round the renovated figure, and students of history are confused, embarrassed, and diverted by her old traditions and associations. It has not yet become superfluous to insist that history is a science, no less and no more; and some who admit it theoretically hesitate to enforce the consequences which it involves. It is therefore, I think, almost incumbent on a professor to define, at the very outset, his attitude to the transformation of the idea of history which is being gradually accomplished; and an inaugural address offers an opportunity which, if he feels strongly the importance of the question, he will not care to lose.

And moreover I venture to think that it may be useful and stimulating for those who are beginning historical studies to realise vividly and clearly that the transformation which those studies are undergoing is itself a great event in the history of the world—that we are ourselves in the very middle of it, that we are witnessing and may share in the accomplishment of a change which will have a vast influence on future cycles of the world. I wish that I had been enabled to realise this when I first began to study history. I think it is important for all historical students alike—not only for those who may be drawn to make history the special work of their lives, but also for those who study it as part of a liberal education—to be fully alive and awake to the revolution which is slowly and silently progressing. It seems especially desirable that those who are sensible of the importance of the change and sympathise with it should declare and emphasise it; just because it is less patent to the vision and is more perplexed by ancient theories and traditions, than those kindred revolutions which have been effected simultaneously in other branches of knowledge. History has really been enthroned and ensphered among the sciences; but the particular nature of her influence, her time-honoured association with literature, and other circumstances, have acted as a sort of vague cloud, half concealing from men's eyes her new position in the heavens.

The proposition that before the beginning of the last century the study of history was not scientific may be sustained in spite of a few exceptions. The works of permanent value, such as those of Muratori, Ducange, Tillemont,[1] were achieved by dint of most laborious and conscientious industry, which commands our highest admiration and warmest gratitude; but it must be admitted that their criticism was sporadic and capricious. It was the criticism of sheer learning. A few stand on a higher level in so far as they were really alive to the need of bringing reason and critical doubt to bear on the material, but the systematised method which distinguishes a science was beyond the vision of all, except a few like Mabillon.[2] Erudition has now been supplemented by scientific method, and we owe the change to Germany. Among those who brought it about, the names of Niebuhr and Ranke are pre-eminent. But there is another name which historical students should be slow to forget, the name of one who, though not a historian but a philologist, nevertheless gave a powerful stimulus to the introduction of critical methods which are now universally applied. Six years before the eighteenth century closed a modest book appeared at Halle, of which it is perhaps hardly a grave exaggeration to say that it is one of half-a-dozen which in the last three hundred years have exercised most effective influence upon thought. The work I mean is Wolf's *Prolegomena to Homer*. It launched upon the world a new engine—*donum exitiale Minervae*—which was soon to menace the walls of many a secure citadel. It gave historians the idea of a systematic and minute method of analysing their sources, which soon developed into the microscopic criticism, now recognised as indispensable.

All truths (to modify a saying of Plato) require the most exact methods; and closely connected with the introduction of a new method was the elevation of the standard of truth. The idea of a scrupulously exact conformity to facts was fixed, re-fined, and canonised; and the critical method was one of the means to secure it. There was indeed no historian since the beginning of things who did not profess that his sole aim was to present to his readers untainted and unpainted truth. But the axiom was loosely understood and interpreted, and the notion of truth was elastic. It might be difficult to assign to Puritanism and Rationalism and other causes their respective parts in crystallising that strict discrimination of the true and the false which is now so familiar to us that we can hardly un-derstand insensibility to the distinction. It would be a most fruitful investigation to trace from the earliest ages the his-tory of public opinion in regard to the meaning of falsehood and the obligation of veracity. About twenty years ago a German made a contribution to the subject by examining the evidence for the twelfth, thirteenth, and fourteenth centuries, and he showed how different were the views which men held then as to truth-telling and lying from those which are held to-day. Moreover, so long as history was regarded as an art, the sanctions of truth and accuracy could not be severe. The historians of ancient Rome display what historiography can become when it is associated with rhetoric. Though we may point to individual writers who had a high ideal of accuracy at various ages, it was not till the scientific period began that laxity in representing facts came to be branded as criminal. Nowhere perhaps can we see the new spirit so self-conscious as in some of the letters of Niebuhr.

But a stricter standard of truth and new methods for the purpose of ascertaining truth were not enough to detach his-tory from her old moorings. A new transfiguring conception of her scope and limits was needed, if she was to become an independent science. Such a conception was waiting to inter-vene, but I may lead up to it by calling to your recollection how history was affected by the political changes in Europe.

It was a strange and fortunate coincidence that the scientific movement in Germany should have begun simultaneously with another movement which gave a strong impetus to historical studies throughout Europe and enlisted men's emotions in their favour. The saying that the name of hope is remembrance[3] was vividly illustrated, on a vast scale, by the spirit of resurgent nationality which you know has governed, as one of the most puissant forces, the political course of the last century, and is still unexhausted. When the peoples, inspired by the national idea, were stirred to mould their destinies anew, and, looking back with longing to the more distant past, based upon it their claims for independence or for unity, history was one of the most effective weapons in their armouries; and consequently a powerful motive was supplied for historical investigation. The inevitable result was the production of some crude uncritical histories, written with national prejudice and political purpose, redeemed by the genuine pulse of national aspiration. But in Germany the two movements met. Scientific method controlled, while the national spirit quickened, the work of historical research. One of the grave dangers was the temptation to fix the eyes exclusively on the inspiring and golden periods of the past, and it is significant to find Dahlmann,[4] as early as 1812, warning against such a tendency, and laying down that the statesman who studies national history should study the whole story of his forefathers, the whole development of his people, and not merely chosen parts.

But the point which concerns us now is that the national movements of Europe not only raised history into prominence and gave a great impulse to its study, but also partially disclosed where the true practical importance of history lies. When men sought the key of their national development not in the immediate but in the remoter past, they had implicitly recognised in some measure the principles of unity and continuity. That recognition was a step towards the higher, more comprehensive, and scientific estimation of history's practical significance, which is only now beginning to be understood.

Just let me remind you what used to be thought in old days as to the utility of history. The two greatest of the ancient historians, Thucydides and Polybius, held that it might be a guide for conduct, as containing examples and warnings for statesmen; and it was generally regarded in Greece and at Rome as a storehouse of concrete instances to illustrate political and ethical maxims. Cicero called history in this sense *magistra vitae,* and Dionysius designated it "Philosophy by examples." And this view, which ascribed to it at best the function of teaching statesmen by analogy, at worst the duty of moral edification, prevailed generally till the last century. Of course it contained a truth which we should now express in a different form by saying that history supplies the material for political and social science. This is a very important function; but, if it were the only function, if the practical import of history lay merely in furnishing examples of causes and effects, then history, in respect of practical utility, would be no more than the handmaid of social science.

And here I may interpolate a parenthesis, which even at this hour may not be quite superfluous. I may remind you that history is not a branch of literature. The facts of history, like the facts of geology or astronomy, can supply material for literary art; for manifest reasons they lend themselves to artistic representation far more readily than those of the natural sciences; but to clothe the story of human society in a literary dress is no more the part of a historian as a historian, than it is the part of an astronomer as an astronomer to present in an artistic shape the story of the stars. Take, for example, the greatest living historian. The reputation of Mommsen as a man of letters depends on his Roman History; but his greatness as a historian is to be sought far less in that dazzling work than in the *Corpus* and the *Staatsrecht* and the *Chronicles.*

This, by way of parenthesis; and now to resume. A right notion of the bearing of history on affairs, both for the statesman and for the citizen, could not be formed or formulated until men had grasped the idea of human development. This is the great transforming conception, which enables history to define her scope. The idea was first started by Leibnitz, but, though it had some exponents in the interval, it did not rise to be a governing force in human thought till the nineteenth century, when it appears as the true solvent of the antihistorical doctrines which French thinkers and the French Revolution had arrayed against the compulsion of the past. At the same time, it has brought history into line with other sciences, and, potentially at least, has delivered her from the political and ethical encumbrances which continued to impede her after the introduction of scientific methods. For notwithstanding those new engines of research, she remained much less, and much more, than a science in Germany, as is illustrated by the very existence of all those bewildering currents and cross-currents, tendencies and counter-tendencies, those various schools of doctrine, in which Lord Acton was so deeply skilled. The famous saying of Ranke—"Ich will nur sagen wie es eigentlich gewesen ist" [5]—was widely applauded, but it was little accepted in the sense of a warning against transgressing the province of facts; it is a text which must still be preached, and when it has been fully taken to heart, though there be many schools of political philosophy, there will no longer be divers schools of history.

The world is not yet alive to the full importance of the transformation of history (as part of a wider transformation) which is being brought about by the doctrine of development. It is always difficult for those who are in immediate proximity to realise the decisive steps in intellectual or spiritual progress when those steps are slow and gradual; but we need not hesitate to say that the last century is not only as important an era as the fifth century B.C. in the annals of historical study, but marks, like it, a stage in the growth of man's self-consciousness. There is no passage, perhaps, in the works of the Greek tragedians so instructive for the historical student as that song in the *Antigone* of Sophocles, in which we seem to surprise the first amazed meditation of man when it was borne in upon him by a sudden startling illumination, how strange it is that he should be what he is and should have wrought all that he has wrought—should have wrought out, among other things, the city-state. He had suddenly, as it were, waked up to realise that he himself was the wonder of the world. "None is more wonderful than man." [6] That intense expression of a new detached wondering interest in man, as an object of curiosity, gives us the clue to the inspiration of Herodotus and the birth of history. More than two thousand years later human self-consciousness has taken another step, and the "sons of flesh" have grasped the notion of their upward development through immense cycles of time. This idea has recreated history. Girded with new strength she has definitely come out from among her old associates, moral philosophy and rhetoric; she has come out into a place of liberty; and has begun to enter into closer relations with the sciences which deal objectively with the facts of the universe.

The older view, which we may call the politico-ethical theory, naturally led to eclecticism. Certain periods and episodes, which seemed especially rich in moral and political lessons, were picked out as pre-eminently and exclusively important, and everything else was regarded as more or less the province of antiquarianism. This eclectic and exclusive view is not extinct, and can appeal to recent authority. It is remarkable that one of the most eminent English historians of the latter half of the last century, whose own scientific work was a model for all students, should have measured out the domain of history with the compasses of political or ethical wisdom, and should have protested as lately as 1877 against the principle of unity and continuity. That inconsistency is an illustration of the tenacity with which men cling to predilections that are incongruous with the whole meaning of their own life-work.[7] But it is another great Oxford historian to whom perhaps more than to any other teacher we owe it that the Unity of History is now a commonplace in Britain. It must indeed be carried beyond the limits within which he enforced it, but to have affirmed and illustrated that principle was not the least useful of Mr. Freeman's valuable services to the story of Europe. In no field, I may add, have the recognition of continuity and the repudiation of eclecticism been more notable or more fruitful than in a field in which I happen to be specially interested, the history of the Eastern Roman empire, the foster-mother of Russia.

The principle of continuity and the higher principle of development lead to the practical consequence that it is of vital importance for citizens to have a true knowledge of the past and to see it in a dry light, in order that their influence on the present and future may be exerted in right directions. For, as a matter of fact, the attitude of men to the past has at all times been a factor in forming their political opinions and determining the course of events. It would be an instructive task to isolate this influence and trace it from its most rudimentary form in primitive times, when the actions of tribes were stimulated by historical memories, through later ages in which policies were dictated or confirmed by historical judgments and conceptions. But the clear realisation of the fact that our conception of the past is itself a distinct factor in guiding and moulding our evolution, and must become a factor of greater and increasing potency, marks a new stage in the growth of the human mind. And it supplies us with the true theory of the practical importance of history.

It seems inevitable that, as this truth is more fully and widely though slowly realised, the place which history occupies in national education will grow larger and larger. It is therefore of supreme moment that the history which is taught should be true; and that can be attained only through the discovery, collection, classification, and interpretation of facts—

through scientific research. The furtherance of research, which is the highest duty of Universities, requires ways and means. Public money is spent on the printing and calendaring of our own national records; but we ought not to be satisfied with that. Every little people in Europe devotes sums it can far less well afford to the investigation of its particular history. We want a much larger recognition of the necessity of historical research; a recognition that it is a matter of public concern to promote the scientific study of any branch of history that any student is anxious to pursue. Some statesmen would acknowledge this; but in a democratic state they are hampered by the views of unenlightened taxpayers. The wealthy private benefactors who have come forward to help Universities, especially in America, are deplorably short-sighted; they think too much of direct results and immediate returns; they are unable to realise that research and the accumulated work of specialists may move the world. In the meantime, the Universities themselves have much to do; they have to recognise more fully and clearly and practically and preach more loudly and assiduously that the advancement of research in history, as in other sciences, is not a luxury, subsidiary though desirable, but is a pressing need, a matter of inestimable concern to the nation and the world.

It must also be remembered that a science cannot safely be controlled or guided by a subjective interest. This brings me to the question of perspective in ecumenical history. From the subjective point of view, for our own contemporary needs, it may be held that certain centuries of human development are of a unique and predominant importance, and possess, for purposes of present utility, a direct value which cannot be claimed for remoter ages. But we should not forget that this point of view if legitimate and necessary, in one sense, is subjective, and unscientific. It involves a false perspective. The reason is not merely the brevity of the modern age in comparison with the antecedent history of man; it is a larger consideration than that.

In his inaugural lecture at Oxford sixty years ago,[8] Arnold propounded as his conviction the view that what we call the modern age coincides with "the last step" in the story of man. "It appears," he said, "to bear marks of the fulness of time, as if there would be no future history beyond it." He based this view on the ground that one race had followed another in the torch-bearing progress of civilisation, and that after the Teuton and the Slav, who are already on the scene, there exists on earth no new race fitted to come forward and succeed to the inheritance of the ages. This argument rests on unproven assumptions as to the vital powers and capacities of races, and as to the importance of the ethnical factor in man's development. The truth is that at all times men have found a difficulty in picturing how the world could march onward ages and ages after their own extinction. And this difficulty has prejudiced their views. We may guess that if it had been put to a king of Egypt or Babylonia 6000 years ago, he would have said that his own age represented the fulness of days. The data to which Arnold appealed are insufficient even to establish a presumption. The only data which deserve to be considered are the data furnished by cosmic science. And science tells us that—apart from the incalculable chances of catastrophes—man has still myriads and myriads of years to live on this planet under physical conditions which need not hinder his development or impair his energies. That is a period of which his whole recorded history of six or seven thousand years is a small fraction.

The dark imminence of this unknown future in front of us, like a vague wall of mist, every instant receding, with all its indiscernible contents of world-wide change, soundless revolutions, silent reformations, undreamed ideas, new religions, must not be neglected, if we would grasp the unity of history in its highest sense. For though we are unable to divine what things indefinite time may evolve, though we cannot look forward with the eyes of

> "the prophetic soul
> Of the wide world brooding on things to come,"

yet the unapparent future has a claim to make itself felt as an idea controlling our perspective. It commands us not to regard the series of what *we* call ancient and medieval history as leading up to the modern age and the twentieth century; it bids us consider the whole sequence up to the present moment as probably no more than the beginning of a social and psychical development, whereof the end is withdrawn from our view by countless millenniums to come. All the epochs of the past are only a few of the front carriages, and probably the least wonderful, in the van of an interminable procession.

This, I submit, is a controlling idea for determining objectively our historical perspective. We must see our petty periods *sub specie perennitatis*. Under this aspect the modern age falls into line with its predecessors and loses its obtrusive prominence. Do not say that this view sets us on too dizzy a height. On the contrary, it is a supreme confession of the limitations of our knowledge. It is simply a limiting and controlling conception; but it makes all the difference in the adjustment of our mental balance for the appreciation of values —like the symbol of an unknown quantity in the denominator of a fraction. It teaches us that history ceases to be scientific, and passes from the objective to the subjective point of view, if she does not distribute her attention, so far as the sources allow, to all periods of history. It cannot perhaps be too often reiterated that a University, in the exercise and administration of learning, has always to consider that more comprehensive and general utility which consists in the training of men to contemplate life and the world from the highest, that is the scientifically truest point of view, in the justest perspective that can be attained. If one were asked to define in a word the end of higher education, I do not know whether one could find a much better definition than this: the training of the mind to look at experience objectively, without immediate relation to one's own time and place. And so, if we recognise the relative importance of the modern period for our own contemporary needs, we must hold that the best preparation for interpreting it truly, for investigating its movements, for deducing its practical lessons, is to be brought up in a school where its place is estimated in scales in which the weight of contemporary interest is not thrown.

Beyond its value as a limiting controlling conception, the idea of the future development of man has also a positive importance. It furnishes in fact the justification of much of the laborious historical work that has been done and is being done to-day. The gathering of materials bearing upon minute local events, the collation of MSS. and the registry of their small variations, the patient drudgery in archives of states and municipalities, all the microscopic research that is carried on by armies of toiling students—it may seem like the bearing of mortar and bricks to the site of a building which has hardly been begun, of whose plan the labourers know but little. This work, the hewing of wood and the drawing of water, has to be done in faith—in the faith that a complete assemblage of the smallest facts of human history will tell in the end. The labour is performed for posterity—for remote posterity; and when, with intelligible scepticism, someone asks the use of the accumulation of statistics, the publication of trivial records, the labour expended on minute criticism, the true answer is: "That is not so much our business as the business of future generations. We are heaping up material and arranging it, according to the best methods we know; if we draw what conclusions we can for the satisfaction of our own generation, we never forget that our work is to be used by future ages. It is intended for those who follow us rather than for ourselves, and much less for our grandchildren than for generations very remote." For a long time to come one of the chief services that research can perform is to help to build, firm and solid, some of the countless stairs by which men of distant ages may mount to a height unattainable by us and have a vision of history which we cannot win, standing on our lower slope.

But if we have to regard the historical labours of man, for many a century to come, as the ministrations of a novitiate, it does not follow that we should confine ourselves to the collection and classification of materials, the technical criticism of them, and the examination of special problems; it does not follow that the constructive works of history which each age produces and will continue to produce according to its lights may not have a permanent value. It may be said that like the serpents of the Egyptian enchanters they are perpetually swallowed up by those of the more potent magicians of the next generation; but—apart from the fact that they contribute themselves to the power of the enchantment which overcomes them—it is also true that though they may lose their relative value, they abide as milestones of human progress; they belong to the documents which mirror the form and feature of their age, and may be part of the most valuable material at the disposal of posterity. If we possessed all the sources which Tacitus used for his sketch of the early imperial period, his *Annals* would lose its value in one sense, but it would remain to the furthest verge of time a monument of the highest significance, in its treatment, its method and its outlook, for the history of the age in which he lived. When the ultimate history of Germany in the nineteenth century comes to be written, it will differ widely from Treitschke's work, but that brilliant book can never cease to be a characteristic document of its epoch.

The remarks which I have ventured to offer are simply deductions from the great principle of development in time, which has given a deep and intense meaning to the famous aphorism of Hippocrates, that Science is long, a maxim so cold and so inspiring. The humblest student of history may feel assured that he is not working only for his own time; he may feel that he has an interest to consult and a cause to advance beyond the interest and cause of his own age. And this does not apply only to those who are engaged in research. It applies also to those who are studying history without any intention of adding to knowledge. Every individual who is deeply impressed with the fact that man's grasp of his past development helps to determine his future development, and who studies history as a science not as a branch of literature, will contribute to form a national conscience that true history is of supreme importance, that the only way to true history lies through scientific research, and that in promoting and prosecuting such research we are not indulging in a luxury but doing a thoroughly practical work and performing a great duty to posterity.

One of the features of the renovation of the study of history has been the growth of a larger view of its dominion. Hitherto I have been dwelling upon its longitudinal aspect as a sequence in time, but a word may be said about its latitude. The exclusive idea of political history, *Staatengeschichte,* to which Ranke held so firmly, has been gradually yielding to a more comprehensive definition which embraces as its material all records, whatever their nature may be, of the material and spiritual development, of the culture and the works, of man in society, from the stone age onwards. It may be said that the wider view descends from Herodotus, the narrower from Thucydides. The growth of the larger conception was favoured by the national movements which vindicated the idea of the people as distinct from the idea of the state; but its final victory is assured by the application of the principle of development and the "historical method" to all the manifestations of human activity—social institutions, law, trade, the industrial and the fine arts, religion, philosophy, folklore, literature. Thus history has acquired a much ampler and more comprehensive meaning, along with a deeper insight into the constant interaction and reciprocity among all the various manifestations of human brain power and human emotion. Of course in actual practice labour is divided; political history and the histories of the various parts of civilisation can and must be separately treated; but it makes a vital difference that we should be alive to the interconnexion, that no department should be isolated, that we should maintain an intimate association among the historical sciences, that we should frame an ideal—an ideal not the less useful because it is impracticable —of a true history of a nation or a true history of the world in which every form of social life and every manifestation of intellectual development should be set forth in its relation to the rest, in its significance for growth or decline.

Cambridge has officially recognised this wider view of history by the name and constitution of the body which administers historical studies—the "Board of Historical and Archaeological Studies." If that branch of historical research which we call archaeology bears a distinct name and occupies its distinct place, it is simply because the investigation of the historical records with which it deals requires a special training of faculties of observation not called into play in the study of written documents. But it must not be forgotten that the special historian whom we call an archaeologist needs a general training in history and a grasp of historical perspective as much as any other historical specialist. It must be borne in mind that this, as well as his special scientific training, is needed to differentiate the archaeologist from the antiquarian of the prescientific Oldbuck type, who in the first place has no wide outlook on history, and secondly cannot distinguish between legitimate profitable hypotheses and guesses which are quite from the purpose. Such antiquarians have not yet disappeared. It is significant that two brilliant historians, to both of whom the study of history in this country is deeply indebted, built perilous superstructures in regard to the English Conquest upon speculations which were only superior specimens of the prescientific type. It is earnestly to be wished that the history schools of the Universities may turn out a new kind of critical antiquarians in Britain who instead of molesting their local monuments with batteries of irrelevant erudition and fanciful speculation, with volleys of crude etymologies, will help to further our knowledge of British history, coming with a suitable equipment to the arduous, important and attractive task of fixing, grouping, and interpreting the endless fragments of historical wreckage which lie scattered in these islands. I venture to insist with some emphasis on this, because there are few fields where more work is to be done or where labourers are more needed than the Celtic civilisations of Western Europe. In tracing from its origins the course of western history in the Middle Ages, we are pulled up on the threshold by the uncertainties and obscurities which brood over the Celtic world. And for the purpose of prosecuting that most difficult of all inquiries, the ethnical problem, the part played by race in the development of peoples and the effects of race blendings, it must be remembered that the Celtic world commands one of the chief portals of ingress into that mysterious prae-Aryan foreworld, from which it may well be that we modern Europeans have inherited far more than we dream. For pursuing these studies it is manifest that scholars in the British islands are in a particularly favourable position.

Most beginners set to work at the study which attracts them, and follow the lines that have been constructed for them, without any clear apprehension or conviction of the greater issues involved. That apprehension only comes to them afterwards, if indeed it ever comes. It has seemed to me that it might not be amiss if historical students, instead of merely taking the justification of their subject for granted, were brought at the outset to consider its significance and position from the highest point of view—if they were stimulated to apprehend vividly that the study of history and the method of studying it are facts of ecumenical importance. In attempting to illustrate this—very inadequately in the small compass of an introductory address—I have sought to indicate the close interconnexion between the elevation of history to the position of a science and the recognition of the true nature of its practical significance as being itself a factor in evolution.

I may conclude by repeating that, just as he will have the best prospect of being a successful investigator of any group of nature's secrets who has had his mental attitude determined by a large grasp of cosmic problems, even so the historical student should learn to realise the human story *sub specie perennitatis;* and that, if, year by year, history is to become a more and more powerful force for stripping the bandages of error from the eyes of men, for shaping public opinion and advancing the cause of intellectual and political liberty, she will best prepare her disciples for the performance of that task, not by considering the immediate utility of next week or next year or next century, not by accommodating her ideal or limiting her range, but by remembering always that, though she may supply material for literary art or philosophical speculation, she is herself simply a science, no less and no more.

PART II

CLIO REDISCOVERED: *Trevelyan*

[George Macaulay Trevelyan (b. 1876), the grand-nephew
of Macaulay, has done more than any other living English
writer to restore history to its earlier station as a literary art
which instructs and entertains the general public and profes-
sionals alike. As a student at Trinity College in Cambridge,
Trevelyan was told by the then Regius Professor of Modern
History, Sir John Seeley, that Macaulay and Carlyle were
charlatans, and this awakened in him an abiding suspicion of
"scientific" historians. A prolific writer, his works—from his
dissertation on *England in the Age of Wycliffe* (1899) to
his *History of England* (1926) and his several works on
Garibaldi—are mostly literary, narrative histories with a
marked bent for social history. He supplemented his research
by direct observation, traversing on foot a good part of England and Italy, and retracing in this way Garibaldi's campaign
of 1860. The following essay was originally written as a polemical answer to J. B. Bury's *The Science of History*
(see
preceding selection) and published in December, 1903, in the
Independent Review. After Bury's death, Trevelyan reprinted
it, omitting all mention of Bury, as the leading essay in the
volume *Clio, A Muse* (1913), from which the following,
somewhat shortened, selection has been taken.]

CLIO, A MUSE

The last fifty years have witnessed great changes in the management of Clio's temple. Her inspired prophets and bards

have passed away and been succeeded by the priests of an established church; the vulgar have been excluded from the Court of the Gentiles; doctrine has been defined; heretics have been excommunicated; and the tombs of the aforesaid prophets have been duly blackened by the new hierarchy. While these changes were in process the statue of the Muse was seen to wink an eye. Was it in approval, or in derision?

Two generations back, history was a part of our national literature, written by persons moving at large in the world of letters or politics. Among them were a few writers of genius, and many of remarkable talent, who did much to mould the thought and inspire the feeling of the day. Of recent years the popular influence of history has greatly diminished. The thought and feeling of the rising generation is but little affected by historians. History was, by her own friends, proclaimed a "science" for specialists, not "literature" for the common reader of books. And the common reader of books has accepted his discharge.

That is one half of the revolution. But fortunately that is not all. Whereas fifty years ago history had no standing in higher education, and even twenty years ago but little, to-day Clio is driving the classical Athene out of the field, as the popular Arts course in our Universities. The good results attained by University historical teaching, when brought to bear on the raw product of our public schools, is a great fact in modern education. But it means very hard work for the History Dons, who, in the time they can spare from these heavy educational tasks, must write the modern history books. Fifty years ago there were no such people; to-day they are a most important but sadly overworked class of men.

Such is the double aspect of the change in the status of history. The gain in the deeper, academic life of the nation must be set off against the loss in its wider, literary life. To ignore either is to be most partial. But must we always submit to the loss in order to secure the gain? Already during the last decade there are signs in the highest quarters of a reconciling process, of a synthesis of the scientific to the literary view of history. Streaks of whitewash have been observed on the tombs of those bards and prophets whose bones Professor Seeley burned twenty years ago. When no less an authority than Professor Firth[1] thinks it worth while to edit Macaulay; when Mr. Gooch[2] in his History of Historians can give an admirable appreciation of Carlyle, times are evidently changing a little in those high places whence ideas gradually filter down through educational England. Isis and Camus, reverend sires, foot it slow—but sure. It is then in no cantankerous spirit against the present generation of academic historians, but in all gratitude, admiration and personal friendship towards them, that I launch this "delicate investigation" into the character of history. What did the Muse mean when she winked?

These new History Schools, still at the formative period of their growth, are to the world of older learning what Western Canada is to England to-day. Settlers pour into the historical land of promise who, a generation back, would have striven for a livelihood in the older "schools" and "triposes." The danger to new countries with a population rapidly increasing is lest life there grow up hastily into a raw materialism, a dead level of uniform ambition all directed to the mere acquisition of dollars. In the historical world the analogue of the almighty dollar is the crude document. If a student digs up a new document, he is happy, he has succeeded; if not, he is unhappy, he has failed. There is some danger that the overwhelming rush of immigrants into the new History Schools may cause us to lose some of the old culture and the great memories. But I hope that we shall not be forgetful of the Mother Country.

And who is the Mother Country to Anglo-Saxon historians? Some reply "Germany," but others of us prefer to answer "England." The methods and limitations of German learning presumably suit the Germans, but are certain to prove a strait waistcoat to English limbs and faculties. We ought to look to the free, popular, literary traditions of history in our own land. Until quite recent times, from the days of Clarendon down through Gibbon, Carlyle and Macaulay to Green and Lecky, historical writing was not merely the mutual conversation of scholars with one another, but was the means of spreading far and wide throughout all the reading classes a love and knowledge of history, an elevated and critical patriotism and certain qualities of mind and heart. But all that has been stopped, and an attempt has been made to drill us into so many Potsdam Guards of learning.

We cannot, however, decide this question on a mere point of patriotism. It is necessary to ask *a priori* whether the modern German or the old English ideal was the right one. It is necesary to ask, "What is history and what is its use?" We must "gang o'er the fundamentals," as the old Scotch lady with the ear trumpet said so alarmingly to the new minister when he entered her room on his introductory visit. So I now ask, what is the object of the life of man *quâ* historian? Is it to know the past and enjoy it forever? Or is it to do one's duty to one's neighbour and cause him also to know the past? The answer to these theoretic questions must have practical effects on the teaching and learning, the writing and reading of history.

The root questions can be put in these terms:—"Ought history be merely the Accumulation of facts about the past? Or ought it also to be the Interpretation of facts about the past? Or, one step further, ought it to be not merely the Accumulation and Interpretation of facts, but also the Exposition of these facts and opinions *in their full emotional and intellectual value* to a wide public by the difficult art of literature?"

The words in italics raise another question, which can be put thus:—

"Ought emotion to be excluded from history on the ground that history deals only with the science of cause and effect in human affairs?"

It will be well to begin the discussion by considering the alleged "science of cause and effect in human affairs." This alleged "science" does not exist, and cannot ever exist in any degree of accuracy remotely deserving to be described by the word "science."

The idea that the facts of history are of value as part of an exact science confined to specialists is due to a misapplication of the analogy of physical science. Physical science would still be of immense, though doubtless diminished value, even if the general public had no smattering thereof, even if Sir Robert Ball had never lectured, and Huxley had never slaughtered bishops for a Roman holiday.[3]

The functions of physical science are mainly two. Direct utility in practical fields; and in more intellectual fields the deduction of laws of "cause and effect." Now history can perform neither of these functions.

In the first place it has no practical utility like physical science. No one can by a knowledge of history, however profound, invent the steam-engine, or light a town, or cure cancer, or make wheat grow near the arctic circle. For this reason there is not in the case of history, as there is in the case of physical science, any utilitarian value at all in the accumulation of knowledge by a small number of students, repositories of secrets unknown to the vulgar.

In the second place history cannot, like physical science, deduce causal laws of general application. All attempts have failed to discover laws of "cause and effect" which are certain to repeat themselves in the institutions and affairs of men.

The law of gravitation may be scientifically proved because it is universal and simple. But the historical law that starvation brings on revolt is not proved; indeed the opposite statement, that starvation leads to abject submission, is equally true in the light of past events. You cannot so completely isolate any historical event from its circumstances as to be able to deduce from it a law of general application. Only politicians adorning their speeches with historical arguments have this power; and even they never agree. An historical event cannot be isolated from its circumstances, any more than the onion from its skins, because an event is itself nothing but a set of circumstances, none of which will ever recur.

To bring the matter to the test, what are the "laws" which historical "science" has discovered in the last forty years, since it cleared the laboratory of those wretched "literary historians"? Medea has successfully put the old man into the pot, but I fail to see the fine youth whom she promised us.

Not only can no causal laws of universal application be discovered in so complex a subject, but the interpretation of the cause and effect of any one particular event cannot rightly be called "scientific." The collection of facts, the weighing of evidence as to what events happened, are in some sense scientific; but not so the discovery of the causes and effects of those events. In dealing even with an affair of which the facts are so comparatively well known as those of the French Revolution, it is impossible accurately to examine the psychology of twenty-five million different persons, of whom—except a few hundreds or thousands—the lives and motives are buried in the black night of the utterly forgotten. No one, therefore, can ever give a complete or wholly true account of the causes of the French Revolution. But several imperfect readings of history are better than none at all; and he will give the best interpretation who, having discovered and weighed all the important evidence obtainable, has the largest grasp of intellect, the warmest human sympathy, the highest imaginative powers. Carlyle, at least in his greatest work, fulfilled the last two conditions, and therefore his psychology of the mob in the days of mob rule, his flame-picture of what was in very fact a conflagration, his portraits of individual characters—Louis, Sieyès, Danton, Marat, Robespierre—are in the most important sense more true than the cold analysis of the same events and the conventional summings up of the same persons by scientific historians who, with more knowledge of facts, have less understanding of Man. It was not till later in his life that Carlyle went mad with Hero-worship and ceased to understand his fellow-men with that all-embracing tolerance and sympathy which is the spiritual hall-mark of his *French Revolution.* . . .

But the fatal weakness even of that great book is that its author knew nothing in detail about the *ancien régime* and the "old French Form of Life." He described the course of the fire but he knew nothing of the combustibles or of the match.

How indeed could history be a "science"? You can dissect the body of a man, and argue thence the general structure of the bodies of other men. But you cannot dissect a mind; and if you could, you could not argue thence about other minds. You can know nothing scientifically of the twenty million minds of a nation. The few facts we know may or may not be typical of the rest. Therefore, in the most important part of its business, history is not a scientific deduction, but an imaginative guess at the most likely generalisations.

History is only in part a matter of "fact." Collect the "facts" of the French Revolution! You must go down to Hell and up to Heaven to fetch them. The pride of the physical scientist is attacked, and often justly. But what is his pride compared with the pride of the historian who thinks that his collection of "facts" will suffice for a scientific study of cause and effect in human affairs? "The economist," said Professor Marshall, "needs imagination above all to put him on the track of those causes of events which are remote or lie below the surface." Now if, as Professor Marshall tells us, imagination is necessary for the economist, by how much more is it necessary for the historian, if he wishes to discover the causes of man's action, not merely as a bread-winning individual, but in all his myriad capacities of passion and of thought. The man who is himself devoid of emotion or enthusiasm can seldom credit, and can never understand, the emotions of others, which have none the less played a principal part in cause and effect. Therefore, even if history were a science of cause and effect, that would be a reason not for excluding but for including emotion as part of the historian's method.

It was no unemotional historian, but the author of *Sartor Resartus,* who found out that Cromwell was not a hypocrite. Carlyle did not arrive at this result by a strictly deductive process, but it was none the less true, and, unlike many historical discoveries, it was of great value. Carlyle, indeed, sometimes neglected the accumulation of facts and the proper sifting of evidence. He is not to be imitated as a model historian, but he should be read and considered by all historical students, because of his imaginative and narrative qualities. While he lacks what modern historical method has acquired, he possesses in the fullest degree what it has lost.

Carlyle uses constantly an historical method which Gibbon and Maitland use sometimes, and other historians scarcely at all—humour. The "dignity of history," whether literary or scientific, is too often afraid of contact with the comic spirit. Yet there are historical situations, just as there are domestic and social situations, which can only be treated usefully or even truthfully by seeing the fun of them. . . .

I conclude, therefore, that the analogy of physical science has misled many historians during the last thirty years right away from the truth about their profession. There is no utilitarian value in knowledge of the past, and there is no way of scientifically deducing causal laws about the action of human beings in the mass. In short, the value of history is not scientific. Its true value is educational. It can educate the minds of men by causing them to reflect on the past.

Even if cause and effect could be discovered with accuracy, they still would not be the most interesting part of human affairs. It is not man's evolution but his attainment that is the great lesson of the past and the highest theme of history. The deeds themselves are more interesting than their causes and effects, and are fortunately ascertainable with much greater precision. "Scientific" treatment of the evidence (there only can we speak to some extent of "science") can establish with reasonable certainty that such and such events occurred, that one man did this and another said that. And the story of great events is itself of the highest value when it is properly treated by the intellect and the imagination of the historian. The feelings, speculations and actions of the soldiers of Cromwell's army are interesting in themselves, not merely as part of a process of "cause and effect." Doubtless, through the long succeeding centuries the deeds of these men had their effect, as one amid the thousand confused waves that give the impulse to the world's ebb and flow. But how great or small their effect was, must be a matter of wide speculation; and their ultimate success or failure, whatever that may have been, was largely ruled by incalculable chance. It is the business of the historian to generalise and to guess as to cause and effect, but he should do it modestly and not call it "science," and he should not regard it as his first duty, which is to tell the story. For, irrespective of "cause and effect," we want to know the thoughts and deeds of Cromwell's soldiers, as one of the

higher products and achievements of the human race, a thing
never to be repeated, that once took shape and was. And so,
too, with Charles and his Cavaliers, we want to know what
they were like and what they did, for neither will they ever
come again. On the whole, we have been faithfully served in
this matter by Carlyle, Gardiner and Professor Firth.

It is the tale of the thing done, even more than its causes
and effects, which trains the political judgment by widening
the range of sympathy and deepening the approval and disapproval of conscience; that stimulates by example youth to
aspire and age to endure; that enables us by the light of what
men once have been, to see the thing we are, and dimly to
descry the form of what we should be. "Is not Man's history
and Men's history a perpetual evangel?"

It is because the historians of to-day were trained by the
Germanising hierarchy to regard history not as an "evangel"
or even as a "story," but as a "science," that they have so much
neglected what is after all the principal craft of the historian
—the art of narrative. It is in narrative that modern historical
writing is weakest, and to my thinking it is a very serious
weakness—spinal in fact. Some writers would seem never to
have studied the art of telling a story. There is no "flow" in
their events, which stand like ponds instead of running like
streams. Yet history is, in its unchangeable essence, "a tale."
Round the story, as flesh and blood round the bone, should be
gathered many different things—character drawing, study of
social and intellectual movements, speculations as to probable
causes and effects, and whatever else the historian can bring to
illuminate the past. But the art of history remains always the
art of narrative. That is the bed rock. . . .

One day, as I was walking along the side of Great Gable,
thinking of history and forgetting the mountains which I
trod, I chanced to look up and see the top of a long green
ridge outlined on the blue horizon. For half a minute I stood
in thoughtless enjoyment of this new range, noting upon it
forms of beauty and qualities of romance, until suddenly I remembered that I was looking at the top of Helvellyn! Instantly, as by magic, its shape seemed to change under my
eyes, and the qualities with which I had endowed the unknown mountain to fall away, because I now knew what like
were its hidden base and its averted side, what names and
memories clung round it. The change taking place in its aspect seemed physical, but I suppose it was only a trick of my
own mind. Even so, if we could forget for a while all that had

happened since the Battle of Waterloo, we should see it, not as we see it now, with all its time-honoured associations and its conventionalised place in history, but as our ancestors saw it first, when they did not know whether the "Hundred Days," as we now call them, would not stretch out for a Hundred Years. Every true history must, by its human and vital presentation of events, force us to remember that the past was once real as the present and uncertain as the future.

Even in our personal experience, we have probably noticed the uncanny difference between events when they first appear red hot, and the same events calmly reviewed, cold and dead, in the perspective of subsequent happenings. . . .

To recover some of our ancestors' real thoughts and feelings is the hardest, subtlest and most educative function that the historian can perform. It is much more difficult than to spin guesswork generalisations, the reflex of passing phases of thought or opinion in our own day. To give a true picture of any country, or man or group of men in the past requires industry and knowledge, for only the documents can tell us the truth, but it requires also insight, sympathy and imagination of the finest, and last but not least the art of making our ancestors live again in modern narrative. Carlyle, at his rare best, could do it. . . .

But since history has no properly scientific value, its only purpose is educative. And if historians neglect to educate the public, if they fail to interest it intelligently in the past, then all their historical learning is valueless except in so far as it educates themselves.

What, then, are the various ways in which history can educate the mind?

The first, or at least the most generally acknowledged educational effect of history, is to train the mind of the citizen into a state in which he is capable of taking a just view of political problems. But, even in this capacity, history cannot prophesy the future; it cannot supply a set of invariably applicable laws for the guidance of politicians; it cannot show, by the deductions of historical analogy, which side is in the right in any quarrel of our own day. It can do a thing less, and yet greater than all these. It can mould the mind itself into the capability of understanding great affairs and sympathising with other men. The information given by history is valueless in itself, unless it produce a new state of mind. The

value of Lecky's Irish history did not consist in the fact that
he recorded in a book the details of numerous massacres and
murders, but that he produced sympathy and shame, and
caused a better understanding among us all of how the sins of
the fathers are often visited upon the children, unto the third
and fourth generations of them that hate each other. He does
not prove that Home Rule is right or wrong, but he trains
the mind of Unionists and Home Rulers to think sensibly
about that and other problems. . . .

But history should not only remove prejudice, it should
breed enthusiasm. To many it is an important source of the
ideas that inspire their lives. With the exception of a few
creative minds, men are too weak to fly by their own unaided
imagination beyond the circle of ideas that govern the world
in which they are placed. And since the ideals of no one
epoch can in themselves be sufficient as an interpretation of
life, it is fortunate that the student of the past can draw upon
the purest springs of ancient thought and feeling. Men will
join in associations to propagate the old-new idea, and to re-
cast society again in the ancient mould, as when the study of
Plutarch and the ancient historians rekindled the breath of
liberty and of civic virtue in modern Europe; as when in our
own day men attempt to revive mediaeval ideals of religious
or of corporate life, or to rise to the Greek standard of the individual. We may like or dislike such revivals, but at least
they bear witness to the potency of history as something quite
other than a science. And outside the circle of these larger influences, history supplies us each with private ideals, only too
varied and too numerous for complete realisation. One may
aspire to the best characteristics of a man of Athens or a citizen of Rome; a Churchman of the twelfth century, or a Re-
former of the sixteenth; a Cavalier of the old school, or a
Puritan of the Independent party; a Radical of the time of
Castlereagh, or a public servant of the time of Peel. Still more
are individual great men the model and inspiration of the
smaller. It is difficult to appropriate the essential qualities of
these old people under new conditions; but whatever we
study with strong loving conception, and admire as a thing
good in itself and not merely good for its purpose or its age,
we do in some measure absorb.

This presentation of ideals and heroes from other ages is
perhaps the most important among the educative functions of
history. For this purpose, even more than for the purpose of
teaching political wisdom, it is requisite that the events

should be both written and read with intellectual passion. Truth itself will be the gainer, for those by whom history was enacted were in their day passionate.

Another educative function of history is to enable the reader to comprehend the historical aspect of literature proper. Literature can no doubt be enjoyed in its highest aspects even if the reader is ignorant of history. But on those terms it cannot be enjoyed completely, and much of it cannot be enjoyed at all. For much of literature is allusion, either definite or implied. And the allusions, even of the Victorian age, are by this time historical. For example, the last half dozen stanzas of Browning's *Old Pictures in Florence,* the fifth stanza of his *Lovers' Quarrel,* and half his wife's best poems are already meaningless unless we know something of the continental history of that day. Political authors like Burke, Sydney Smith,[4] and Courier,[5] the prose of Milton, one-half of Swift, the best of Dryden, and the best of Byron (his satires and letters) are enjoyed *ceteris paribus,* in exact proportion to the amount we know of the history of their times. And since allusions to classical history and mythology, and even to the Bible, are no longer, as they used to be, familiar ground for all educated readers, there is all the more reason, in the interest of literature, why allusions to modern history should be generally understood. History and literature cannot be fully comprehended, still less fully enjoyed, except in connection with one another. I confess I have little love either for "Histories of Literature," or for chapters on "the literature of the period," hanging at the end of history books like the tail from a cow. I mean, rather, that those who write or read the history of a period should be soaked in its literature, and that those who read or expound literature should be soaked in history. The "scientific" view of history that discouraged such interchange and desired the strictest specialisation by political historians, has done much harm to our latter-day culture. The mid-Victorians at any rate knew better than that. . . .

The value and pleasure of travel, whether at home or abroad, is doubled by a knowledge of history. For places, like books, have an interest or a beauty of association, as well as an absolute or aesthetic beauty. The garden front of St. John's, Oxford, is beautiful to every one; but, for the lover of history, its outward charm is blent with the intimate feelings of his own mind, with images of that same College as it was during the Great Civil War. Given over to the use of a Court whose days of royalty were numbered, its walks and quadran-

gles were filled, as the end came near, with men and women
learning to accept sorrow as their lot through life, the ambitious abandoning hope of power, the wealthy hardening
themselves to embrace poverty, those who loved England
preparing to sail for foreign shores, and lovers to be parted
forever. . . .

St. John's College is not mere stone and mortar, tastefully
compiled, but an appropriate and mournful witness between
those who see it now and those by whom it once was seen.
And so it is, for the reader of history, with every ruined castle
and ancient church throughout the wide, mysterious lands of
Europe.

Battlefield hunting, a sport of which my dear master, Edward Bowen,[6] was the most strenuous and successful patron, is
one of the joys that history can afford to every walker and
cyclist, and even to the man in the motor, if he can stir himself to get out to see the country through which he is whirled.
The charm of an historic battlefield is its fortuitous character.
Chance selected this field out of so many, that low wall, this
gentle slope of grass, a windmill, a farm or straggling hedge,
to turn the tide of war and decide the fate of nations and of
creeds. Look on this scene, restored to its rustic sleep that was
so rudely interrupted on that one day in all the ages; and
looking, laugh at the "science of history." But for some honest soldier's pluck or luck in the decisive onslaught round
yonder village spire, the lost cause would now be hailed as
"the tide of inevitable tendency" that nothing could have
turned aside! How charmingly remote and casual are such
places as Rosbach and Valmy, Senlac and Marston Moor. Or
take the case of Morat.[7] There, over that green hill beneath
the lowland firwood, the mountaineers from alp and glacier-
foot swept on with thundering feet and bellowing war horns,
and at sight of their levelled pikes the Burgundian chivalry,
arrayed in all the gorgeous trappings of the Renaissance
armourers, fled headlong into Morat lake down there. From
that day forward, Swiss democracy, thrusting aside the Duke
of Savoy, planted itself on the Genevan shore, and Europe,
therefore, in the fulness of time, got Calvin and Rousseau. A
fine chain of cause and effect, which I lay humbly at the feet
of "science"!

The skilled game of identifying positions on a battlefield
innocent of guides, where one must make out everything for
oneself—best of all if one has ever done it properly before
—is almost the greatest of out-door intellectual pleasures. But

the solution of the military problem is not all. If the unsentimental tourist thinks of the men who fought there merely as pawns in a game of chess, if the moral issues of the war are unknown to him or indifferent, he loses half that he might have had. . . .

In this vexed question whether history is an art or a science, let us call it both or call it neither. For it has an element of both. It is not in guessing at historical "cause and effect" that science comes in; but in collecting and weighing evidence as to facts, something of the scientific spirit is required for an historian, just as it is for a detective or a politician.

To my mind, there are three distinct functions of history, that we may call the *scientific,* the *imaginative* or *speculative,* and the *literary.* First comes what we may call the *scientific,* if we confine the word to this narrow but vital function, the day-labour that every historian must well and truly perform if he is to be a serious member of his profession—the accumulation of facts and the sifting of evidence. "Every great historian has been his own Dry-as-dust," said Stubbs, and quoted Carlyle as the example. Then comes the *imaginative* or *speculative,* when he plays with the facts that he has gathered, selects and classifies them, and makes his guesses and generalisations. And last but not least comes the *literary* function, the exposition of the results of science and imagination in a form that will attract and educate our fellow-countrymen. For this last process I use the word literature, because I wish to lay greater stress than modern historians are willing to do, both on the difficulty and also on the importance of planning and writing a powerful narrative of historical events. Arrangement, composition and style are not as easily acquired as the art of type-writing. Literature never helps any man at his task until, to obtain her services, he is willing to be her faithful apprentice. Writing is not, therefore, a secondary but one of the primary tasks of the historian.

Another reason why I prefer to use the word "literature" for the expository side of the historian's work, is that literature itself is in our day impoverished by these attempts to cut it off from scholarship and serious thought. It would be disastrous if the reading public came to think of literature not as a grave matron, but as a mere *fille de joie.* Until near the end of the nineteenth century, literature was held to mean not only plays, novels and *belles lettres,* but all writing that rose above a certain standard of excellence. Novels, if they are bad enough, are not literature. Pamphlets, if they are good enough, are literature—for example, the pamphlets of Milton, Swift and Burke. Huxley's essays and Maine's treatises are literature. Even Maitland's expositions of mediaeval law are literature. Maitland, indeed, wrote well rather by force of genius, by natural brilliancy, than by any great attention paid to composition, form and style. But for us little people it is just that conscious attention to book-planning, composition and style that I would advocate.

All students who may some day write history, and in any case will be judges of what is written, should be encouraged to make a critical study of past masters of English historical literature. Yet there were many places a little time ago where it was tacitly accepted as passable and even praiseworthy in an historical student to know nothing of the great English historians prior to Stubbs. And, for all I know, there are such places sti...

In France historical writing is on a higher level than in England, because the Frenchman is taught to write his own language as part of his school curriculum. The French *savant* is bred, if not born, a prose writer. Consequently when he arrives at manhood he already writes well by habit. The recent union effected in France of German standards of research with this native power of composition and style, has produced a French historical school that turns out yearly a supply of history books at once scholarly and delightful. . . .

The idea that histories which are delightful to read must be the work of superficial temperaments, and that a crabbed style betokens a deep thinker or conscientious worker, is the reverse of the truth. What is easy to read has been difficult to write. The labour of writing and rewriting, correcting and re-correcting, is the due exacted by every good book from its author, even if he knows from the beginning exactly what he wants to say. A limpid style is invariably the result of hard labour, and the easily flowing connection of sentence with sentence and paragraph with paragraph has always been won by the sweat of the brow.

Now in the case of history, all this artistic work is superimposed on the labours of scholarship, themselves enough to fill a lifetime. The historical architect must quarry his own stones and build with his own hands. Division of labour is only possible in a limited degree. No wonder then that there have been so few historians really on a level with the opportunities of their great themes, and that, except Gibbon, every one of them is imperfect either in science or in art. The double task, hard as it is, we little people must shoulder as best we may, in the temporary absence of giants. And if the finest intellects of the rising generation can be made to realise how hard is the task of history, more of them will become historians.

Writing history well is no child's-play. The rounding of every sentence and of every paragraph has to be made consistent with a score of facts, some of them known only to the author, some of them perhaps discovered or remembered by him at the last moment to the entire destruction of some carefully erected artistic structure. In such cases there is an undoubted temptation to the artist to neglect such small, inconvenient pieces of truth. That, I think, is the one strong point in the scholar's outcry against "literary history"; but if we wish to swim we must go into the water, and there is little use in cloistered virtue, nor much more in cloistered scholarship. In history, as it is now written, art is sacrificed to science ten times for every time that science is sacrificed to art. . . .

Gibbon was scarcely in the grave when a genius arose in Scotland who once and probably for ever transformed mankind's conception of itself from the classical to the romantic, from the uniform to the variegated. Gibbon's cold, classical light was replaced by the rich mediaeval hues of Walter Scott's stained glass. To Scott each age, each profession, each country, each province had its own manners, its own dress, its own way of thinking, talking and fighting. To Scott a man is not so much a human being as a type produced by special environment whether it be a border-farmer, a mediaeval abbot, a cavalier, a covenanter, a Swiss pikeman, or an Elizabethan statesman. No doubt Scott exaggerated his theme as all innovators are wont to do. But he did more than any professional historian to make mankind advance towards a true conception of history, for it was he who first perceived that the history of mankind is not simple but complex, that history never repeats itself but ever creates new forms differing according to time and place. The great antiquarian and novelist showed historians that history must be living, many-coloured and romantic if it is to be a true mirror of the past. Macaulay, who was a boy while Scott's poems and novels were coming out, and who knew much of them by heart, was not slow to learn this lesson.

Then followed the Victorian age, the period when history

in England reached the height of its popularity and of its influence on the national mind. In the eighteenth century the educated class had been numerically very small, though it had been a most powerful and discriminating patron of letters and learning, above all of history. No country house of any pretension was without its Clarendon, Robertson, Hume, and Gibbon, as can be seen in many an old neglected private library to-day, where now the inhabitants, in the intervals of golf and motoring, wear off the edge of their intellects on magazines and bad novels. . . .

Indeed, in the period immediately following on Macaulay's death, history seemed to be coming to her own. His works and Carlyle's continued to be read, and those of Motley, Froude, Lecky, Green, Symonds, Spencer Walpole, Leslie Stephen, John Morley and others carried on the tradition that history was related to literature. The foundations of a broad, national culture, based upon knowledge of our history and pride in England's past, seemed to be securely laid. The coming generation of historians had only to build upon the great foundation of popularity laid for them by their predecessors, erecting whatever new structures of political or other opinion they wished, but preserving the basis of literary history, of history as the educator of the people. But they preferred to destroy the foundations, to sever the tie between history and the reading public. They gave it out that Carlyle and Macaulay were "literary historians" and therefore ought not to be read. The public, hearing thus on authority that they had been "exposed" and were "unsound," ceased to read them—or anybody else. Hearing that history was a science, they left it to scientists. The craving for lighter literature which characterised the new generation combined with the academic dead-set against literary history to break the public of its old habit of reading history books.

At the present moment the state of affairs seems to me both better and worse than it was twenty years ago when I came to Cambridge as an undergraduate, and was solemnly instructed by the author of *Ecce Homo*[8] that Macaulay and Carlyle did not know what they were writing about and that "literary history" was a thing of nought. The present generation of historians at Oxford and Cambridge have ceased, so far as I am aware, to preach this fanatical crusade; they recognise that history has more than one function and are ready to welcome various kinds of historians. There is therefore much hope for the future, because ideas on such matters in the end spread down from the Universities to the schools and the country, and gradually permeate opinion far away.

But for the present things in the country at large are scarcely better than they were twenty years ago. We are still suffering the consequence of the anti-literary campaign carried on by the historical chiefs of the recent past. . . . I have more than once come across the case of schoolboys being positively forbidden to read Macaulay, who, whether he be a guide for grown-ups or not, is certainly an admirable stimulus to the sluggish youthful mind, none too apt to develop enthusiasm either for history or for literature. And I have known a history book condemned by a reviewer on the ground that it would read aloud well! Often, when recommending some readable and stimulating history, I have been answered: "Oh! but has not his view been proved incorrect?" Or "Is he not out of date? I am told one ought not to read him now." And so, the "literary historians" being ruled out by authority, the would-be student declines on some wretched textbook, or else reads nothing at all.

This attitude of mind is not only disastrous in its consequences to the intellectual life of the country, but radically unsound in its premises. For it assumes that history—"scientific history"—has "proved" certain views to be true and others to be false. Now history can prove the truth or falsehood of facts but not of opinions. When a man begins with the pompous formula—"The verdict of history is—" suspect him at once, for he is merely dressing up his own opinions in big words. Fifty years ago the "verdict of history" was mainly Whig and Protestant: twenty years ago mainly Tory and Anglo-Catholic; to-day it is, fortunately, much more variegated. Each juror now brings in his own verdict—generally with a recommendation of everyone to mercy. There is even some danger that history may encourage the idea that all sides in the quarrels of the past were equally right and equally wrong.

There is no "verdict of history," other than the private opinion of the individual. And no one historian can possibly see more than a fraction of the truth; if he sees all sides, he will probably not see very deeply into any one of them. The only way in which a reader can arrive at a valuable judgment on some historical period is to read several good histories, whether contemporary or modern, written from several different points of view, and to think about them for himself. But too often the reading of good books and the exercise of individual judgment are shirked, while some vacuous text-book is favoured on the ground that it is "impartial" and "up-to-date." But no book, least of all a text-book, affords a short cut to the historical truth. The truth is not grey, it is black and white in patches. And there is nothing black or white but thinking makes it so.

The dispassionateness of the historian is a quality which it is easy to value too highly, and it should not be confused with the really indispensable qualities of accuracy and good faith. We cannot be at too great pains to see that our passion burns pure, but we must not extinguish the flame. Dispassionateness—*nil admirari*—may betray the most gifted historian into missing some vital truth in his subject. In Creighton's treatment of Luther, all that he says is both fair and accurate, yet from Creighton alone you would not guess that Luther was a great man or the German Reformation a stirring and remarkable movement.[9] The few pages on Luther in Carlyle's *Heroes* are the proper complement to this excessively dispassionate history. The two should be read together. . . .

The public has ceased to watch with any interest the appearance of historical works, good or bad. *The Cambridge Modern History* is indeed bought by the yard to decorate bookshelves, but it is regarded like the *Encyclopaedia Britannica* as a work of reference; its mere presence in the library is enough. Publishers, meanwhile, palm off on the public books manufactured for them in Grub Street,—"publisher's books," which are neither literature nor first-hand scholarship. This is the type generically known as "Criminal Queens of History," spicy memoirs of dead courts and pseudo-biographical chatter about Napoleon and his family, how many eggs he ate and how many miles he drove a day. And Lady Hamilton is a great stand-by. The public understands that this kind of prurient journalism is history lightly served up for the general appetite, whereas serious history is a sacred thing pinnacled afar on frozen heights of science, not to be approached save after a long novitiate.

By itself, this picture of our present discontents would be exaggerated and one-sided. There is much truth in it, I fear, but on the other hand there is much good in the present and more hope in the future. For a new public has arisen, a vast democracy of all classes from "public" school and "council" school alike, taught to read but not knowing what to read; men and women of this new democracy of intellect, from millionaire to mechanic, refuse to be bored in a world where the means of amusement have been brought to every door; but subject to that condition, the best of them, the natural leaders of the rest, are athirst for thought and knowledge if only it be presented to them in an interesting form. . . .

If, as we have so often been told with such glee, the days of "literary history" have gone never to return, the world is left the poorer. Self-congratulation on this head is but the mood of the shorn fox in the fable. History as literature has a function of its own, and we suffer to-day from its atrophy. Fine English prose, when devoted to the serious exposition of fact and argument, has a glory of its own, and the civilisation that boasts only of creative fiction on one side and science on the other may be great but is not complete. Prose is seldom equal to poetry either in the fine manipulation of words or in emotional content, yet it can have great value in both those kinds, and when to these it adds the intellectual exactness of argument or narrative that poetry does not seek to rival, then is it sovereign in its own realm. To read sustained and magnificent historical narrative educates the mind and the character; some even, whose natures, craving the definite, seldom respond to poetry, find in such writing the highest pleasure that they know. Unfortunately, historians of literary genius have never been plentiful, and we are told that there will never be any more. Certainly we shall have to wait for them, but let us also wish for them and work for them. If we confess that we lack something, and cease to make a merit of our chief defect, if we encourage the rising generation to work at the art of construction and narrative as a part of the historian's task, we may at once get a better level of historical writing, and our children may live to enjoy modern Gibbons, judicious Carlyles and skeptical Macaulays.

SPECIALIZATION AND HISTORICAL SYNTHESIS: *Lord Acton and Berr*

[By the end of the last century historians were swamped by the monographic output of their colleagues and by the work of scholars in related fields—sociology, anthropology, psychology, and economics. The individual historian no longer had the command of all of history, or even of that substantial part which his forbears had possessed as a matter of course. The historian, like other specialists too, was in danger of knowing more and more about less and less. To combat these dangers efforts were made to find new syntheses, both by bringing together several specialists in one collaborative effort and by combining several disciplines to arrive at a broader view of the whole.

Collaborative efforts of the first kind are at least as old as the *Magdeburg Centuries* (1559-1574), a Protestant attempt to compile the history of the early Church. At the end of the nineteenth century similar collaborative works were planned and carried out in the United States, France, and Germany, and in England where *The Cambridge Modern History* (12 vols. 1902-1910), planned by Lord Acton, set a high standard for such works. Lord Acton (1834-1902), one of the most erudite of modern historians, brought to the task not only his enormous knowledge—F. W. Maitland said of him that he could write unaided all twelve volumes of the Cambridge History—but his informed concern with historiography. His letter to the prospective contributors, reprinted below, reveals his acceptance of some of the basic tenets of the historicist position, although in his Inaugural Lecture of 1895 he had said: "But the weight of opinion is against me when I exhort you never to debase the moral currency or to lower the standard of rectitude, but to try others by the final maxim that governs your own lives, and to suffer no man and no cause to escape the undying penalty which history has the power to inflict on wrong."

In France, alongside the splendid productivity of traditional historians, there grew up a school of historians seeking a new scientific synthesis for history. Its founder was Henri Berr (1863-1954), its physical home the International Center for Synthesis in Paris, its organ the *Revue de synthèse historique,* founded in 1900, of which the programmatic statement is reprinted below, translated for this volume by Deborah H. Roberts. Berr was also the originator and editor of a singularly ambitious series of historical monographs, each written by a specialist, all embodying Berr's vision of a scientific history that encompasses sociology and psychology, called *L'Evolution de L'Humanité* (in 100 vols.; 65 vols. 1920-1954). This work was intended to cover the history of civilization from prehistoric times to the present.]

LORD ACTON: LETTER TO THE CONTRIBUTORS TO THE *Cambridge Modern History*

1. Our purpose is to obtain the best history of modern times that the published or unpublished sources of information admit.

The production of material has so far exceeded the use of it in literature that very much more is known to students than can be found in historians, and no compilation at second hand from the best works would meet the scientific demand for completeness and certainty.

In our own time, within the last few years, most of the official collections in Europe have been made public, and nearly all the evidence that will ever appear is accessible now.

As archives are meant to be explored, and are not meant to be printed, we approach the final stage in the conditions of historical learning.

The long conspiracy against the knowledge of truth has been practically abandoned, and competing scholars all over the civilised world are taking advantage of the change.

By dividing our matter among more than one hundred writers we hope to make the enlarged opportunities of research avail for the main range of modern history.

Froude spoke of 100,000 papers consulted by him in manuscript, abroad and at home; and that is still the price to be paid for mastery, beyond the narrow area of effective occupation.

We will endeavour to procure transcripts of any specified documents which contributors require from places out of reach.

2. It is intended that the narrative shall be such as will serve all readers, that it shall be without notes, and without quotations in foreign languages.

In order to authenticate the text and to assist further research, it is proposed that a selected list of original and auxiliary authorities shall be supplied in each volume, for every chapter or group of chapters dealing with one subject.

Such a bibliography of modern history might be of the utmost utility to students, and would serve as a substitute for the excluded references.

We shall be glad if each contributor will send us, as early as he finds it convenient, a preliminary catalogue of the works on which he would rely; and we enclose a specimen, to explain our plan, and to show how we conceive that books and documents might be classified.

3. Our scheme requires that nothing shall reveal the country, the religion, or the party to which the writers belong.

It is essential not only on the ground that impartiality is the character of legitimate history, but because the work is carried on by men acting together for no other object than the increase of accurate knowledge.

The disclosure of personal views would lead to such confusion that all unity of design would disappear.

4. Some extracts from the editor's Report to the Syndics will show the principles on which the Cambridge History has been undertaken.

"The entire bulk of new matter which the last forty years have supplied amounts to many thousands of volumes. The honest student finds himself continually deserted, retarded, misled by the classics of historical literature, and has to hew his own way through multitudinous transactions, periodicals, and official publications, where it is difficult to sweep the horizon or to keep abreast. By the judicious division of labour we should be able to do it, and to bring home to every man the last document, and the ripest conclusions of international research . . .

"All this does not apply to our own time, and the last

volumes will be concerned with secrets that cannot be learned from books, but from men . . .

"The recent Past contains the key to the present time. All forms of thought that influence it come before us in their turn, and we have to describe the ruling currents, to interpret the sovereign forces, that still govern and divide the world . . .

"By Universal History I understand that which is distinct from the combined history of all countries, which is not a rope of sand, but a continuous development, and is not a burden on the memory, but an illumination of the soul. It moves in a succession to which the nations are subsidiary. Their story will be told, not for their own sake, but in reference and subordination to a higher series, according to the time and the degree in which they contribute to the common fortunes of mankind . . .

"If we treat History as a progressive science, and lean specially on that side of it, the question will arise, how we justify our departure from ancient ways, and how we satisfy the world that there is reason and method in our innovations . . .

"To meet this difficulty we must provide a copious, accurate, and well-digested catalogue of authorities . . .

"Our principle would be to supply help to students, not material to historians. But in critical places we must indicate minutely the sources we follow, and must refer not only to the important books, but to articles in periodical works, and even to original documents, and to transcripts in libraries. The result would amount to an ordinary volume, presenting a conspectus of historical literature, and enumerating all the better books, the newly acquired sources, and the last discoveries. It would exhibit in the clearest light the vast difference between history, original and authentic, and history, antiquated and lower than high-water mark of present learning . . .

"We shall avoid the needless utterance of opinion, and the service of a cause.

"Contributors will understand that we are established, not under the Meridian of Greenwich, but in Long. 30° W.; that our Waterloo must be one that satisfies French and English, Germans and Dutch alike; that nobody can tell, without examining the list of authors, where the Bishop of Oxford laid down the pen, and whether Fairbairn or Gasquet, Liebermann or Harrison took it up." [1]

BERR: ABOUT OUR PROGRAM

Our project is very broad, some will say excessively so. It has seemed desirable to give some indication of what a journal of historical synthesis might be expected to include. Among living seeds only a small number ever develop. Among ideas, in like wise, an inevitable process of selection takes place; and a program must be too rich in order to be sufficiently so. It is through the development of the *Revue* that we shall see what is fated to prosper and what has no future. Nothing rigid here, but rather the flexibility of life itself: it is possible that at some point the interest of a given section of the program may be exhausted, and that one kind of article may make way for another, previously neglected.

Studies in theory will perhaps abound to begin with: but unless we repeat ourselves, this is a vein that will not be slow to exhaust itself. Furthermore the word "theory" should not give alarm: it does not presuppose, it absolutely does not presuppose, vague, excessively general speculations put forth by thinkers who have never been working historians. We should particularly like to have, and expect to obtain, a series of articles on the method of the various historical sciences. To set forth what political history, economic history, history of religion, and what histories of philosophy, science, and art have in common and what distinguishes each from the other: to collect in one place the results of work done, the reflections of the great minds that have applied themselves successfully to this or that portion of historical study: to induce philosophers to define more precisely one important section of the logic of science which has remained unclear and incomplete even in the best writings on the subject, is perhaps not without its usefulness. It does not appear that a science enjoys better conditions in being abandoned to routine and empiricism. And if, generally speaking, theory only sanctions practice, a concern to arrive at a theory can, on the other hand, lead to advances in practice.

More than the section on theory, the part of the program devoted to historical psychology seems destined to be gradually enriched. Articles in this field will attract others. To come via history to psychology—here is a process absolutely necessary but infinitely delicate. This *Revue,* in calling for works of this nature, is not attempting to conceal the difficulties involved: it is not anxious to encourage fantasies unrelated to science. It would like to submit to synthesis the results of sound scholarly research, not merely by comparing them but also by giving them depth and unity; it hopes, in short, to obtain writings in historical psychology—but specific, and therefore methodical and controlled.

But this historical synthesis, this psychology to which the new *Revue* aspires, how is it related to sociology? This is the question on which we must make our position clear if we are to satisfy the truly critical. It is a matter of defining the scientific position of the *Revue*. The indications given below will be designedly slight. We must not appear to be providing answers from the very first, when we propose above all to uncover problems in order that all may here strive to solve them gradually and systematically.

A short historical aside will not, as we shall see, be amiss at this point.

A period in the evolution of historical studies in France began around 1870—it would not be entirely accurate to say after the events of 1870-71. The founding of the *Ecole des Hautes Etudes* under the Duruy ministry, the creation of the *Revue Critique* (1866) show that the need for radically altering our higher education, for restoring our science, had become apparent before our disaster. The conviction, prevalent after the war, that Germany's victory was in fact the triumph of German science, served only to widen the scope of the reform already undertaken.

Information on the state of history in France during this period is to be found in the important introduction written by M. Monod in 1876 for the *Revue Historique:* "We have," said he, "understood the danger of premature generalizations, of great *a priori* systems that claim to cover everything and explain everything. We have sensed that history should be the object of a slow methodical process of investigation in which one moves gradually from the particular to the general, from details to the whole; where all obscure points are successively illuminated in order to have the whole picture and to be able to base general ideas, susceptible to proof and verification, upon groups of established facts."

Now if we consider the nature of historical work in this last third of the century, this cautious and intentionally limited effort, this preoccupation with a "good method" to be applied rather than sweeping results to be arrived at, we are better able to understand the rapid advances of sociology and the popularity that it enjoys. There are doubtless many reasons for this success: by far the most important is the soundness of the idea that there is something social in history, that society is a factor in the interpretation of history: such an idea, furthermore, was too closely related to practical concerns of the moment not to find favor as soon as it was brought to light. But it appears that for many people sociology had above all the virtue of satisfying an abiding taste for general concepts: it served to bring philosophy back into history—more particularly so since the earliest sociologists were theoreticians renewing in their own way the vague and contradictory efforts of German or French philosophers of the end of the 18th and beginning of the 19th century. They derived arbitrary or fanciful consequences from a sound and fertile concept just as others earlier had done with the concept of race or the concept of environment—both of them useful and fertile too. Moreover, they were absorbing all of history into sociology.

But, without wishing to deny the interest inherent in certain considerations and speculations of social philosophy, we believe that sociology, to establish itself as a discipline, must be primarily a study of what is social in history; we believe that its point of departure must be the concrete data of history. It seems to us, that among French sociologists, the great merit of M. Durkheim and his group—a merit that is not to be denied even by those who dispute this or that general concept of the founder of the *Année Sociologique*—is to have applied a precise, experimental, comparative method to historical facts . . .

For all the importance and legitimacy of sociology, is it the whole of history? We do not think so. But whatever our personal convictions, it must be acknowledged that there is a real problem here. Sociology is the study of what is social in history: but is everything social? The role of individual men, the role of the great historical figures, with whom comparative sociology need not concern itself, is it, slight though it may be, worthy of no attention at all?

There is a first stage of historical studies, crude scholarship, wherein facts are critically examined. Proven facts, the raw material of history, can subsequently be handled in one of two ways: either grouped as they relate to certain units—great men, peoples, eras, institutions—in separate categories, so to speak; or compared in order to know what is universal in history, to discover the general in the sequence of particular events, in the diversity of individuals and of peoples. It is necessary—and it may seem more scientific—that the historian study what, being in the highest degree social, is invariable and universal, that he look for stages, if there are any, which recur invariably and universally in the evolution of societies. But it is no less necessary, perhaps, that the historian give some attention to the individual peculiarities that make for the variations in history and that explain even the most general transformations of societies. And the more we study the most highly developed forms of societies, the more, perhaps—at least up to a certain level of development—does the "individual" importance of what is distinctive grow, by very reason of the advancement of the societies. It is interesting to note that whereas the sociology of religion is already contending with undeniable difficulties, no one has heretofore attempted to establish a sociology of philosophy. It is not, in truth, that the development of philosophy is unaffected by any social action, but rather that the history of ideas depends in large part upon individual men, and has also, perhaps, some special characteristics that render it not readily accessible to the straight sociologist.

It appears thus that the study of history may be approached in various ways. It is doing a real service to the sociologist— and to the anthropologist and the ethnographer as well—to invite him to be more specific, to limit his efforts, instead of allowing him to grapple with anything and to solve all historical problems, both great and small, from his own point of view. Historical synthesis is not intended to confuse what was beginning to be clear, but to induce the various teams, together, each to perform its particular function and to be of greater mutual assistance through a clearer conception of the common task.

And it seems also that these various undertakings, amalgamated through historical synthesis, must lead ultimately to psychology. The comparative study of societies must lead to social psychology and to a knowledge of the basic needs to which institutions and their changing manifestations are the response.

The study of historical categories must lead to the psychology of great men of thought and action, of ethnic groups and of historical crises. And it is an important and delicate psychological problem to arrive at a clear picture of the role of the intellectual element in history.

Upon the aggregate of these studies, and upon the further development of historical psychology depends not only our understanding of the past but also our control of the future. It is rightly said that the biologist neglects the particular characteristics of each individual organism. The same could not be said of the doctor. He must be acquainted with both the general and the particular—or even better, with the individual. This is true also of the ideal statesman: and the ideal statesman is the perfect historian.

Some of what has been sketched in these pages needs either proof or qualification. Let us say once more, the foregoing is not laid down as a fundamental principle, but rather put forth for the purpose of discussion. Friends of this *Revue* will in time show us the truth in its pages. It will, moreover, have irreconcilable adversaries only among those who are frightened or angered by the mere word synthesis. There are minds of undeniable merit who cannot think of science except in terms of detailed researches, and who, since detail is infinite, push forward this research of theirs only to see the goal retreat before them. They pity the rash souls who wish to move outside the limits of what they themselves have studied and aspire to a comprehensive view, albeit of a field that remains limited. They feel that the human mind is periodically seized with a terrible craving for synthesis, to the detriment of patient analytical work. Every thirty or forty years, they say, thinking humanity gives way to a temporary insanity that it mistakes for a normal activity.

If this need does manifest itself at regular intervals, it undoubtedly does so because it is deep-seated. Myriad facts are nothing. There is no science, as the old adage has it, but general science. Searching pages in this *Revue* will be evidence that analysis and synthesis are logically inseparable. In fact one or the other prevails. Premature generalization engenders a return to analysis. Over-emphasis on analysis engenders a return to synthesis. These returns to synthesis serve to remind the scientist of his role. If science were only the satisfying of a curiosity for retrospective reporting, it would be singularly futile. The collector of facts is no more admirable than the collector of stamps or shells. Synthesis is useful, even morally, in giving us a conception of the dignity of science.

And perhaps each time there is a new attempt at synthesis, conditions are more favorable; it is both more legitimate and more cautious. Instead of compensating for the deficiencies of analysis, it completes it. Here the organization of the historical journals and the names of the authors they represent would suffice to demonstrate the firmness of the foundation upon which the loftier structure of synthesis will henceforth rest. To establish how far the work has progressed, what has been done, but above all what is yet to be done, is not prematurely to conclude research, but rather to organize it, to obtain a better distribution of effort. If one's hope is that the spirit of synthesis should penetrate progressively deeper into analysis in order to make it more effective, more aware, more joyous, one can likewise wish that the precision, the rigor of analytical work should carry over into the experiments in synthesis.

Let no one fear a return of the philosophy of history, by which is meant—for the word itself is not intrinsically bad —*a priori*, metaphysics, clouds in theory and, consequently, utopias in practice. It would be unfortunate to confuse generalizations born of fantasy or ratiocination with those based on acquired knowledge. It is science that we wish to practice here, true science, science in its entirety. None may enter here who does not bring with him a sound method.

Moreover, we must not promise too much. There will be in this undertaking, as in all human endeavor, unevenness and failure. In the beginning, especially, we shall perhaps witness some groping. Whoever approves the plan will be tolerant of its attempted execution. It depends, moreover, upon whosoever believes in the project to help it succeed by bringing to it his good will, his suggestions and his objections from which we may profit. We shall have here a science laboratory, where, if mistakes are made, we shall work together to correct them. This *Revue* is open to all who are interested in its objective. And the idea from which it proceeds is a good one to unify efforts: namely that in the human sciences there is an urgent and a good task to be performed —one that, over and beyond the men of science, will serve mankind.

A "NEW HISTORY" IN AMERICA:
Robinson and Beard

[James Harvey Robinson (1863-1936) spent his lifetime battling against the conventional history taught in American schools, and sought to replace it with "The New History." Trained both in this country and in Germany in the exacting methods of nineteenth century historiography, Robinson became dissatisfied with its exclusively political, constitutional, and military emphasis. After writing an orthodox doctoral dissertation on the German *Bundesrath,* he edited and translated a series of original sources in European history. A highly effective teacher at Pennsylvania and Columbia Universities, he introduced a novel course on the History of the Intellectual Class of Europe and inspired some of his graduate students—among them Lynn Thorndike, C. J. H. Hayes, Preserved Smith, and James T. Shotwell—to embark on a study of intellectual history. But his greatest influence came through his many, widely-used textbooks, beginning with *An Introduction to the History of Western Europe* (2 vols. 1902-1903). These high school and college texts stressed the intellectual and social trends of a particular age, and were designed to be more popular in their appeal than the older political chronicles. Attuned to the progressive, pragmatic mood of the early twentieth century, Robinson pleaded for a history that would be immediately useful. As he wrote in *The New History* (1912): "The present has hitherto been the willing victim of the past; the time has now come when it should turn on the past and exploit it in the interests

of advance." The following selection is taken, with some
omissions, from the leading essay in *The New History*.

In his crusade for a new history Robinson recruited allies
among contemporary historians. C. A. Beard (cf. ch. XXII)
collaborated with him on a text, *The Development of Modern Europe* (2 vols. 1907-1908) of which the Preface is reprinted below.]

ROBINSON AND BEARD: PREFACE TO
The Development of Modern Europe

It has been a common defect of our historical manuals that,
however satisfactorily they have dealt with more or less remote periods, they have ordinarily failed to connect the past
with the present. And teachers still pay a mysterious respect
to the memory of Datis and Artaphernes which they deny to
gentlemen in frock coats, like Gladstone and Gambetta. The
gloomy incidents of the capture of Numantia are scrupulously impressed upon the minds of children who have little
chance of ever hearing of the siege of Metz. The organization
of the Achaean League is given preference to that of the
present German Empire.

There are some teachers, perhaps, who would seek to justify
the current disregard of recent history, but many others would
agree with one of the guild who, when criticised for giving
more attention in her instruction to Charlemagne than to
Bismarck, complained with truth, "But we know so much
more about Charlemagne than about Bismarck." The great
majority of those interested in history would no doubt gladly
readjust their perspective if they had the means of doing so;
and, indeed, there has been a marked improvement in this
respect in the newer books which are giving more and more
space to recent events.

In preparing the volume in hand, the writers have consistently subordinated the past to the present. It has been
their ever-conscious aim to enable the reader to catch up with
his own times; to read intelligently the foreign news in the
morning paper; to know what was the attitude of Leo XIII
toward the social democrats even if he has forgotten that of
Innocent III toward the Albigenses.

Yet, in permitting the present to dominate the past, they
do not feel that they have dealt less fairly with the general
outline of European history during the last two centuries than
they would have done had they merely narrated the events

with no ulterior object. There has been no distortion of the facts in order to bring them into relation to any particular conception of the present or its tendencies. Even if certain occurrences of merely temporary prominence have been omitted as irrelevant to the purpose of the work, this cannot mean any serious loss.

The way in which the narrative emerges into the living present is, then, one of the claims of this new manual to be regarded as an adventurer in the educational world. A second trait of novelty is the happy reunion of the eighteenth and nineteenth centuries, which should never have been put asunder by the date 1789. The nineteenth century was often too arrogant to recognize its dependence upon the eighteenth, from which it derived most of its inspirations as well as its aversions. It was the eighteenth century which set the problems of progress and suggested their solutions, leaving to its successor the comparatively simple task of working them out in detail and making fuller application of them.

Lastly, the writers have ventured to devote much less space to purely political and military events than has commonly been assigned to them in histories of the nineteenth century. On the other hand, the more fundamental economic matters have been generously treated,—the Industrial Revolution, commerce and the colonies, the internal reforms of the European states, even the general advance of science, have all, so far as possible, been given their just due. . . .

ROBINSON: THE NEW HISTORY

In its amplest meaning History includes every trace and vestige of everything that man has done or thought since first he appeared on the earth. It may aspire to follow the fate of nations or it may depict the habits and emotions of the most obscure individual. Its sources of information extend from the rude flint hatchets of Chelles to this morning's newspaper. It is the vague and comprehensive science of past human affairs. We are within its bounds whether we decipher a mortgage on an Assyrian tile, estimate the value of the Diamond Necklace, or describe the over-short pastry to which Charles V was addicted to his undoing. The tragic reflections of Eli's daughter-in-law, when she learned of the discomfiture of her people at Ebenezer, are history; so are the provisions of Magna Charta, the origin of the doctrine of trans-substantiation, the fall of Santiago, the difference between a black friar and a white friar, and the certified circulation of the *New York World* upon February 1 of the current year. Each fact has its interest and importance; all have been carefully recorded.

Now, when a writer opens and begins to peruse the thick, closely written volume of human experience, with a view of making an abstract of it for those who have no time to study the original work, he is immediately forced to ask himself what he shall select to present to his readers' attention. He finds that the great book from which he gains his information is grotesquely out of perspective, for it was compiled by many different hands, and by those widely separated in time and in sentiment—by Herodotus, Machiavelli, Eusebius, St. Simon, Otto of Freising, Pepys, St. Luke, the Duchess of Abrantés, Sallust, Cotton Mather. The portentously serious alternates with the lightest gossip. A dissipated courtier may be allotted a chapter and the destruction of a race be left unrecorded. It is clear that in treating history for the general reader the question of selection and proportion is momentous. Yet when we turn to our more popular treatises on the subject, the obvious and pressing need of picking and choosing, of selecting, reselecting, and selecting again, would seem to have escaped most writers. They appear to be the victims of tradition in dealing with the past. They exhibit but little appreciation of the vast resources upon which they might draw, and unconsciously follow, for the most part, an established routine in their selection of facts. When we consider the vast range of human interests, our histories furnish us with a sadly inadequate and misleading review of the past, and it might almost seem as if historians had joined in a conspiracy to foster a narrow and relatively unedifying conception of the true scope and intent of historical study. This is apparent if we examine any of the older standard outlines or handbooks from which a great part of the public has derived its notions of the past, either in school or later in life.

The following is an extract from a compendium much used until recently in schools and colleges: "Robert the Wise (of Anjou) (1309-1343), the successor of Charles II of Naples, and the champion of the Guelphs, could not extend his power over Sicily where Frederick II (1296-1337), the son of Peter of Aragon, reigned. Robert's granddaughter, Joan I, after a career of crime and misfortune, was strangled in prison by Charles Durazzo, the last male descendant of the house of Anjou in Lower Italy (1382), who seized on the government. Joan II, the last heir of Durazzo (1414-1435), first adopted Alfonso V, of Aragon, and then Louis III, of Anjou, and his brother, René. Alfonso, who inherited the crown of Sicily, united both kingdoms (1435), after a war with René and the Visconti of Milan."

This is not, as we might be tempted to suspect, a mere collection of data for contingent reference, no more intended to be read than a table of logarithms. It is a characteristic passage from the six pages which a distinguished scholar devotes to the Italy of Dante, Petrarch, and Lorenzo the Magnificent. In preparing a guide for more advanced pupils and the general reader, the author's purpose was, he tells us, "that it should present the essential facts of history in due order, . . . that it should point out clearly the connection of events and of successive eras with one another; that through the interest awakened by the natural, unforced view gained of this unity of history and by such illustrative incidents as the brevity of the narrative would allow to be wrought into it, the dryness of a mere summary should be so far as possible relieved." Now, in treating the Italian Renaissance, this writer has chosen barely to mention the name of Francesco Petrarca, but devotes a twelfth of the available space to the interminable dynastic squabbles of southern Italy. We may assume that this illustrates his conception of "the essential facts of history presented in due order," for the extracts quoted above can hardly be an example of "illustrative incidents" wrought in to relieve the dryness of a mere summary. . . .

Hitherto writers have been prone to deal with events for their own sake; a deeper insight will surely lead us, as time goes on, to reject the anomalous and seemingly accidental occurrences and dwell rather upon those which illustrate some profound historical truth. And there is a very simple principle by which the relevant and useful may be determined and the irrelevant rejected. Is the fact or occurrence one which will aid the reader to grasp the meaning of any great period of human development or the true nature of any momentous institution? It should then be cherished as a precious means to an end, and the more engaging it is, the better; its inherent interest will only facilitate our work, not embarrass it. On the other hand, is an event seemingly fortuitous, isolated, and anomalous,—like the story of Rienzi, the September massacres, or the murder of Marat? We should then hesitate to include it on its own merits,—at least in a brief historical manual—for, interesting as it may be as an heroic or terrible incident, it may mislead the reader and divert his attention from the prevailing interests, preoccupations and permanent achievements of the past.

If we have not been unfair in our review of the more striking peculiarities of popular historiography, we find them to be as follows:

1. A careless inclusion of mere names, which can scarcely have any meaning for the reader and which, instead of stimulating thought and interest, merely weigh down his spirit.

2. A penchant more or less irresistible to recite political events to the exclusion of other matters often of far greater moment.

3. The old habit of narrating extraordinary episodes, not because they illustrate the general trend of affairs or the prevailing conditions of a particular time, but simply because they are conspicuous in the annals of the past. This results in a ludicrous disregard of perspective which assigns more importance to a demented journalist like Marat than to so influential a writer as Erasmus.

II

The essay which immediately follows this will be devoted to a sketch of the history of history, and will explain more fully the development of the older ideals of historical composition. It will make clear that these ideals have changed so much from time to time that it is quite possible that an essentially new one may in time prevail. History is doubtless

> An orchard bearing several trees
> And fruits of different tastes.

It may please our fancy, gratify our serious or idle curiosity, test our memories, and, as Bolingbroke says, contribute to "a creditable kind of ignorance." But the one thing that it ought to do, and has not yet effectively done, is to help us to understand ourselves and our fellows and the problems and prospects of mankind. It is this most significant form of history's usefulness that has been most commonly neglected.

It is true that it has long been held that certain lessons could be derived from the past,—precedents for the statesman and the warrior, moral guidance and consoling instances of providential interference for the commonalty. But there is a growing suspicion, which has reached conviction in the minds of most modern historians, that this type of usefulness is purely illusory. The present writer is anxious to avoid any risk of being regarded as an advocate of these supposed advantages of historical study. Their value rests on the assumption that conditions remain sufficiently uniform to give precedents a perpetual value, while, as a matter of fact, conditions, at least in our own time, are so rapidly altering that for the most part it would be dangerous indeed to attempt to apply past experience to the solution of current problems. Moreover, we rarely have sufficient reliable information in regard to the supposed analogous situation in the past to enable us to apply it to present needs. Most of the appeals of inexpensive oratory to "what history teaches" belong to this class of assumed analogies which will not bear close scrutiny. When I speak of history enabling us to understand ourselves and the problems and prospects of mankind, I have something quite different in mind, which I will try to make plain by calling the reader's attention to the use that he makes of his own personal history.

We are almost entirely dependent upon our memory of our past thoughts and experiences for an understanding of the situation in which we find ourselves at any given moment. To take the nearest example, the reader will have to consult his own history to understand why his eyes are fixed upon this particular page. If he should fall into a sound sleep and be suddenly awakened, his memory might for the moment be paralyzed, and he would gaze in astonishment about the room, with no realization of his whereabouts. The fact that all the familiar objects about him presented themselves plainly to his view would not be sufficient to make him feel at home until his memory had come to his aid and enabled him to recall a certain portion of the past. The momentary suspension of memory's functions as one recovers from a fainting fit or emerges from the effects of an anaesthetic is sometimes so distressing as to amount to a sort of intellectual agony. In its normal state the mind selects automatically, from the almost infinite mass of memories, just those things in our past which make us feel at home in the present. It works so easily and efficiently that we are unconscious of what it is doing for us and of how dependent we are upon it. It supplies so promptly and so precisely what we need from the past in order to make the present intelligible that we are beguiled into the mistaken notion that the present is self-explanatory and quite able to take care of itself, and that the past is largely dead and irrelevant, except when we have to make a conscious effort to recall some elusive fact.

What we call history is not so different from our more intimate personal memories as at first sight it seems to be; for very many of the useful and essential elements in our recollections are not personal experiences at all, but include a multitude of things which we have been told or have read; and these play a very important part in our life. Should the reader of this page stop to reflect, he would perceive a long succession of historical antecedents leading up to his presence in a particular room, his ability to read the English language, his momentary freedom from pressing cares, and his inclination to center his attention upon a discussion of the nature and value of historical study. Were he not vaguely conscious of these historical antecedents, he would be in the bewildered condition spoken of above. Some of the memories necessary to save him from his bewilderment are parts of his own past experience, but many of them belong to the realm of history, namely, to what he has been told or what he has read of the past.

I could have no hope that this line of argument would make the slightest impression upon the reader, were he confined either to the immediate impressions of the moment, or to his personal experiences. It gives one something of a shock, indeed, to consider what a very small part of our guiding convictions are in any way connected with our personal experience. The date of our own birth is quite as strictly historical a fact as that of Artaphernes or of Innocent III; we are forced to a helpless reliance upon the evidence of others for both events.

So it comes about that our personal recollections insensibly merge into history in the ordinary sense of the word. History, from this point of view, may be regarded as an artificial extension and broadening of our memories and may be used to overcome the natural bewilderment of all unfamiliar situations. Could we suddenly be endowed with a Godlike and exhaustive knowledge of the whole history of mankind, far more complete than the combined knowledge of all the histories ever written, we should gain forthwith a Godlike appreciation of the world in which we live, and a Godlike insight into the evils which mankind now suffers, as well as into the most promising methods for alleviating them, *not because the past would furnish precedents of conduct, but because our conduct would be based upon a perfect comprehension of existing conditions founded upon a perfect knowledge of the past.* As yet we are not in a position to interrogate the past with a view to gaining light on great social, political, economic, religious, and educational questions in the manner in which we settle the personal problems which face us—for example, whether we should make such and such a visit or investment, or read such and such a book,—by unconsciously judging the situation in the light of our recollections. Historians have not as yet set themselves to furnish us with what lies behind our great contemporaneous task of human betterment. They have hitherto had other notions of their functions, and were they asked to furnish answers to the questions that a person *au courant* with the problems of the day would most naturally put to them, they would with one accord begin to make excuses. One would say that it had long been recognized that it was the historian's business to deal with kings, parliaments, constitutions, wars, treaties, and territorial changes; another would declare that recent history cannot be adequately written and that, therefore, we can never hope to bring the past into relation with the present, but must always leave a fitting interval between ourselves and the nearest point to which the historian should venture to extend his researches; a third will urge that to have a purpose in historical study is to endanger those principles of objectivity upon which all sound and scientific research must be based. So it comes about that our books are like very bad memories which insist upon recalling facts that have no assignable relation to our needs, and this is the reason why the practical value of history has so long been obscured.

In order to make still clearer our dependence upon history in dealing with the present, let the reader remember that we owe most of our institutions to a rather remote past, which alone can explain their origin. The conditions which produced the Holy Roman Apostolic Church, trial by jury, the Privy Council, the degree of LL.D., the Book of Common Prayer, "the liberal arts," were very different from those that exist today. Contemporaneous religious, educational, and legal ideals are not the immediate product of existing circumstances, but were developed in great part during periods when man knew far less than he now does. Curiously enough our habits of thought change much more slowly than our environment and are usually far in arrears. Our respect for a given institution or social convention may be purely traditional and have little relation to its value, as judged by existing conditions. We are, therefore, in constant danger of viewing present problems with obsolete emotions and of attempting to settle them by obsolete reasoning. This is one of the chief reasons why we are never by any means perfectly adjusted to our environment.

Our notions of a church and its proper function in society, of a capitalist, of a liberal education, of paying taxes, of Sunday observance, of poverty, of war, are determined only to a slight extent by what is happening today. The belief on which I was reared, that God ordained the observance of Sunday from the clouds of Sinai, is an anachronism which could not spontaneously have developed in the United States in the nineteenth century; nevertheless, it still continues to influence the conduct of many persons. We pay our taxes as grudgingly as if they were still the extortions of feudal barons or absolute monarchs for their personal gratification, although they are now a contribution to our common expenses fixed by our own representatives. Few have outgrown the emotions connected with war at a time when personal prowess played a much greater part than the Steel Trust. Conservative college presidents still feel obliged to defend the "liberal arts" and the "humanities" without any very clear understanding of how the task came to be imposed upon them. To do justice to the anachronisms in conservative economic and legal reasoning would require a whole volume.

Society is today engaged in a tremendous and unprecedented effort to better itself in manifold ways. Never has our knowledge of the world and of man been so great as it now is; never before has there been so much general good will and so much intelligent social activity as now prevails. The part that each of us can play in forwarding some phase of this reform will depend upon our understanding of existing conditions and opinion, and these can only be explained, as has been shown, by following more or less carefully the processes that produced them. We must develop historical-mindedness upon a far more generous scale than hitherto, for this will add a still deficient element in our intellectual equipment and will promote rational progress as nothing else can do. The present has hitherto been the willing victim of the past; the time has now come when it should turn on the past and exploit it in the interests of advance.

The "New History" is escaping from the limitations formerly imposed upon the study of the past. It will come in time consciously to meet our daily needs; it will avail itself of all those discoveries that are being made about mankind by anthropologists, economists, psychologists, and sociologists—discoveries which during the past fifty years have served to revolutionize our ideas of the origin, progress, and prospects of our race. There is no branch of organic or inorganic science which has not undergone the most remarkable changes during the last half century, and many new branches of social science, even the names of which would have been unknown to historians in the middle of the nineteenth century, have been added to the long list. It is inevitable that history should be involved in this revolutionary process, but since it must be confessed that this necessity has escaped many contemporaneous writers, it is no wonder that the intelligent public continues to accept somewhat archaic ideas of the scope and character of history.

The title of this little volume has been chosen with the view of emphasizing the fact that history should not be regarded as a stationary subject which can only progress by refining its methods and accumulating, criticizing, and assimilating new material, but that it is bound to alter its ideals and aims with the general progress of society and of the social sciences, and that it should ultimately play an infinitely more important rôle in our intellectual life than it has hitherto done.

HISTORICISM AND ITS
PROBLEMS: *Meinecke*

[Throughout his long life Friedrich Meinecke (1862-1954), the best-known German historian of the twentieth century, tried to deepen and strengthen the Ranke tradition, even as the crises of his country and his discipline threatened that tradition. A student in Droysen's course in historical method and an early admirer of Dilthey, Meinecke sought to broaden historicism by bringing it closer to the philosophical revival of the late nineteenth century. After several years as an archivist, Meinecke became co-editor of the *Historische Zeitschrift* in 1894, and in 1902 received his first full-time academic appointment at the University of Strasbourg. In his most important historical works *Weltbürgertum und Nationalstaat* (1908) and *Die Idee der Staatsräson in der neueren Geschichte* (1924), he broke with the prevailing genre of political and institutional history and, by analyzing the historically most important ideas of the leading statesmen and political thinkers, reinterpreted several epochs of modern history. This *Ideengeschichte* has in turn been criticized for being narrowly intellectualistic and neglectful of the general historic conditions of society. Meinecke dealt extensively with the philosophical and moral problems of contemporary historiography; *Die Entstehung des Historismus* (2 vols. 1936) analyzed the origins of that historical consciousness which found its fullest expression in Ranke, though the work itself ends with a study of the historical thought of Goethe. The following essay, first published in 1928 and translated for this volume by Julian H. Franklin, is a characteristic statement of his views on history. In his 85th year Meinecke wrote *The German Catastrophe* (1946), in which he attempted a historical explanation of Germany's collapse and counselled his compatriots to return to the humanistic, cosmopolitan ideals of Goethe and his age.]

VALUES AND CAUSALITIES IN HISTORY

At the present stage in the development of the historical sciences[1] we can distinguish two great tendencies which do not, however, act in isolation since each contains elements of the other in greater or less degree. Neither of these tendencies can be pursued one-sidedly; each needs the other to achieve its goal. What appears to be a goal for one is a path or signpost for the other. The search for causalities is one of these tendencies; the comprehension and exposition of values is the other. The search for causalities in history is impossible without reference to values; the comprehension of values is impossible without investigation of their causal origins.

What are causalities? What are values?

From the standpoint of direct historical observation, we can distinguish three modes of causality—the mechanistic, the biological, and the spiritual-moral. The mechanistic involves the complete equality of cause and effect (*causa aequat effectum*). The biological seemingly permits the effect to grow beyond its cause through the full unfolding of a life in embryo to a life developed—with its own structure, purpose, and lawfulness. The spiritual-moral breaks through the purely mechanistic causal complex even more. Spontaneous and purposive impulses of personality—to be explained neither mechanistically nor biologically—affect the activities of men and thereby interrupt a mechanistic complex which otherwise appears to our thought as all-prevailing and continuous, excluding any interruption.

Miracle on miracle! Each of the three causalities remains at bottom an enigma. Our thought is thus beset by contradictions which it cannot solve or can solve only in appearance and deceptively. Each of the three causalities irresistibly imposes itself upon the open-minded scholar as a real force in the life of history. And he is constantly forced to deal with all of them. If he seeks the reasons for the poverty and wealth of nations, their victories and defeats in battle, he will come up against a set of causes that are purely mechanistic in their operation and are to be mechanistically conceived—and these will have to be investigated. His interest will mount when a process of crystallization is seen to be working in events, when distinct forms and shapes of the human community appear before his eyes, unfold, develop, and flourish of themselves, and then decline. At last it seems to him that every phenomenon of history, indeed human existence as a whole, is determined morphologically. And yet not morphologically alone. For beyond the contingent operation of mechanistic causalities the spontaneous acts of men may now intervene to interrupt, divert, intensify, or weaken the morphology of events and so impart to history that complexity and singularity which makes a mockery of all attempts to explain it by invariable laws.

Three different seals are thus stamped upon the face of history and the signature, the image, left by any one of them is overlaid by the imprint of the others. Only the dilettante would think himself capable of distinguishing these signs and images sharply and unexceptionably. Simplest and clearest, and least contestable, is the imprint of the first seal, that of mechanistic causalities. But in distinguishing the second or the third it is only too easy to make the mistake of tending to read only one of them and ignoring both the others.

The older historiography up through the enlightenment saw history primarily as the effect of individual-personal decisions and actions and then, as "pragmatic" historiography, sought to order the welter of these actions according to the rationality or irrationality of their motives. Modern historiography, on the other hand, expanded its horizon to include supra-individual causalities and processes. But here again there was a tendency, especially among the rash or dilettantish, to underrate the independent influence of the individual and to consider him merely as the organ of greater collective forms and forces. These forces, in turn, could be represented as more or less endowed with life, as primarily mechanistic or primarily organic in their source and operation. Positivism inclined to a more, although never exclusively, mechanistic conception of collective forces; the most modern tendency, oriented more to the organic and culminating in Spengler, presumes to explain all individual historical phenomena through the various biological laws of formation underlying each great culture.

Against all this, the scientific approach to history which stems from Ranke eschewed any unequivocal and general causal explanation. It therefore left itself open to the charge that it lacked the essential attributes of science. But for this very reason it saw the interaction and interpenetration of mechanistic, biological, and individual-personal causality all the more vividly and immediately. It too could not evade the attempt to distinguish the three elements and to establish now the one, now the other, as the greater influence. But it bore a kind of inborn aversion lest any one of these causes be overpowered and extinguished by the others. In explaining individual phenomena and assembling them in larger sequences and structures it preferred to be guided more by indefinable finesse than by an explicit and principled position. It regarded artistic intuition and the artistic-intuitive shaping of events not only as a beautiful, but more or less superfluous, embellishment of an historical substance discovered purely causally, but as an essential and indispensable technique in view of the only partially, never completely, decipherable manner in which the three imprints interpenetrate.

Science here reaches out to the instruments of art. It seeks to supplement knowledge through means that lie outside the field of knowledge proper. In other words it does not remain pure science, which seeks only causal explanation, but passes over into something else. In the formal sense, therefore, the charge "unscientific," which positivism raises against historiography in Ranke's sense, is not entirely wrong. But the latter can reply in justification that the very nature of things, the complicated sources of history in its larger aspects, requires such procedures. The attempt to master historical materials exclusively with causal means, when it is carried out with radical imprudence, does violence to the stuff of history, leads to the extinction of one causal imprint by the others—and when it is undertaken with tactful prudence must soon stand helpless before the stuff of reality. Only a path no longer purely scientific, that is, no longer purely causal, can lead us a step further into the depths of reality. And although it, too, can never fully reveal these depths, it can give us an intuitive understanding of them, can give us a sympathetic sense of them through unmediated seeing. Where science fails it is wiser for history to use these supra-scientific means than to apply scientific means where their application must lead inevitably to false results.

But the right to use supra-scientific means in history has an even deeper basis than the impossibility of mastering the interpenetration of the three causal imprints in any other way. For if history should wish to remain a purely causal science it would be obliged to accept the totality of human events as its domain and in principle at least to master all of them. This history obviously does not do. From the huge and unencompassed mass it selects only the tiniest segment, that, namely, which is held to be essential, and rightly regards occupation with unessential human happenings as idle microscopic curiosity. But what is the meaning of essential? Only causally essential? Only what has affected the fate of men and peoples in an especially pervasive and decisive way? Sometimes this is what is meant, and it is argued that only what has been "influential" to an unusual degree merits the historian's attention. But as Rickert has correctly put it, "Degree of influence alone can never provide the criterion for that which is historically essential." Considered purely causally the crude physical conditions and necessities of life, the soil and the sun, hunger and love, are the "most influential" factors in human events. But the historian, the non-materialist historian at least, usually takes all these for granted as causal presuppositions for those events which interest him, and pays attention to such factors only when they come into play in some special way and unusual degree.

Furthermore, along with these basic factors of human life the great decisions arising from the power struggles of nations and states are also highly "influential" causally and have always commanded the historian's attention even in the most primitive historical writing. So also the whole range of institutions of state and society which rightly interests all schools of modern history in common—positivist and idealist, political as well as cultural.

But in this practice of singling out the "influential" as "essential" and therefore pushing aside other masses of human events as unessential, two different uses of the word "influential" are usually combined. Sometimes it means anything which has exerted a causal influence on human life and thus refers only to the realm of pure causality. But it may also mean something of enduring influence which still operates on us who are alive today. And this kind of influence has both causal and supra-causal meaning.[2] Causal meaning, in that mighty events of the past, the founding of the Roman empire for example, causally determines our present existence through a thousand after-effects. Supra-causal meaning, in that the chain of causality is not only of purely scientific interest, since we wish to derive profit from it for our lives. Whether this gain be practical in character, thereby enabling us to act more effectively in life, or whether it subsist in the pure realm of contemplation free of all immediate and practical concerns, it is values, life-values, that we win from history in either case. In either case—and later we must discuss this more precisely—history gives us the content, wisdom, and signposts of our lives. And it is the need for this, along with and beyond the pure will to causal knowledge, which at bottom has drawn men to history in every age, and in modern times especially.

Now only do we fully understand why causal inquiry, in seeking to unravel the interpenetration of the three imprints, is at bottom led by the most personal of motives to reach beyond the arsenal of purely causal means of gaining knowledge and like the artist to seek closer contact with historical phenomena through intuition and through living form. It is history's value for ourselves and for our lives that we wish to conquer in this way.

The theoretical need for causal knowledge and the need for values in our life are thus closely, indeed indissolubly, bound together in our interest in history. Is not the theoretical need as such simultaneously a need for value, the value of truth? Every science, to be sure, should serve the search for truth, the search for true causalities, consistently and rigorously, undisturbed by practical distractions. But for us who are servants of science, life could not be full were it not filled with this pure aspiration towards the truth. We deepen life and heighten it through this, and our theory, in this, is transformed into a culture and a way of life. But the practical tendency must not intrude too soon and prematurely influence investigation of causalities. The road of causality must first be travelled to its utmost limits. Then only one may, nay must, call on supra-causal means to satisfy the need for values arising from one's depths.

That the "essential" in history involves not only causalities but values may be illustrated by a hypothetical example. Suppose the work of an unknown author of the past has been discovered, that it is of great depth and spiritual power, but that it was completely unknown to its contemporaries and was thus entirely devoid of influence in its own times. Would we, for this reason, declare such a work historically unessential and uninfluential? It could affect us very strongly, and thus begin to operate causally through us, but only because it presents us with a value. The value, then, is central to our interest and realizes itself in us in the only way it can, through causality. But what counts here for our historical interest is not the analysis of this causality but the comprehension and resurrection of a great spiritual value of the past. This attempt at comprehension must naturally rely on causal means and must seek to ascertain the causal origins of such a work—but here again the causal inquiry is only the means to the end of a complete restoration of a spiritual value.

A fanatic for causality might object that indeed one may and must investigate a work without causal influence in its own times, but that it merits investigation only because it is a product of causalities, only because it brings to light hitherto unknown energies of the period which could produce such a work. The answer, however, is that these causalities would not interest us at all were we not in the presence of a major value which is prepossessing in and of itself and offers enrichment to our lives.

No, behind the search for causalities there always lies, directly or indirectly, the search for values, the search for what is called culture in the highest sense, i.e. break-throughs and revelations of the spiritual within the causal complex of the natural. It is the third of the three causal imprints that produces these values. And our choice of what is worth investigating among the huge mass of events depends, as Rickert has shown, on the relationship of these events to the major cultural values. The historian, he tells us, investigates only value-related facts and the historian's task, he adds, is merely to inquire and exposit, and to make no evaluations of his own if he would remain within the boundaries of his discipline. The first thesis is correct, and merely corroborates a point which historians have always more or less consciously accepted. The second thesis arises from a concern to preserve the scientific character of history, to prevent the intrusion of subjective tendencies. But can this second condition be fulfilled? It cannot be.[3] Even the mere selection of value-related facts is impossible without an evaluation. It would only be possible if the values to which the facts related subsisted, as Rickert thinks, solely in general categories like religion, state, law, etc. But the historian selects his material not only according to general categories like these but also according to his living interest in the concrete content of material. He lays hold of it as something having more or less of value, and in this he is evaluating it. The presentation and exposition of culturally important facts is utterly impossible without a lively sensitivity for the values they reveal. Although the historian may, in form, abstain from value-judgments of his own, they are there between the lines and act as such upon the reader. The effect then, as in Ranke for example, is often more profound and more moving than if the evaluation were to appear directly in the guise of moralizing, and therefore it is even to be recommended as an artifice. The historian's implicit value-judgment arouses the reader's own evaluating activity more strongly than one which is explicit. In that, seemingly, causalities alone are offered, the element of value, the revelation of a spiritual power in the midst of a network of causality, comes through more immediately and more productively.

But even direct evaluation is often not to be avoided, if the value of events is to be fully clarified. It is to be found in certain forms of religious service where holy silence and the words of the priest alternate in praise of the divine. History, too, is divine service in the broadest sense. One wishes to see the spiritual goals one feels to be one's own confirmed by revelation in the world. One seeks to become conscious of the strength and continuity of the stream of spiritual life which wells up within the individual self, to find the path by which man came and to anticipate the path that he will take. One wishes to revere the powers that have brought our existence from a state of servitude to nature to the freedom of the spirit. However one conceives divinity, he will look for it in history.

Even those researchers, who admit only a causal complex emptied of divinity and will therefore look for nothing but causalities within it, are, as we have shown, driven by the need for a supreme inclusive value, be it only the value of truth as such. The natural scientist, too, of course, is motivated by the value of truth, and it may still be possible for him to carry on his work without regard to any other values. But of the three functions of "distinguishing, choosing, and judging," which constitute humanity specifically, only distinguishing is used in his domain. The scientist of culture has to use all three because the events that he investigates stem from the whole range of human nature, come into existence through "distinguishing, choosing, and judging," and are understandable only in these terms. Whereas the natural scientist can work apart from values, the scientist of culture, even when he would deal with history through the methods of natural science alone, is bound to values by his work. Even the mere compiler of material is rarely able to escape this.

It is now clear that there can be two main tendencies in writing history: one of them attracted by causalities, yet never able to escape from values and hardly ever from its own intrinsic value; the other attracted by values without being able to dispense with causalities. Both are thus bipolar.

Nuances and shadings, varying admixtures, of one tendency are always possible and present in the other.

Greater clarity in the distinction between these tendencies could only come when history began to be more strictly scientific, and the question of the essence of history and the task of the historian was posed in deeper terms. Ancient political historiography, in its epic recital of events, confused naïvely felt values with causalities. Enlightenment history wished to show that the cultural values of the developing enlightenment were the only worthwhile subjects for historical writing. But the mass of political events, which could not simply be ignored, resisted permeation by these values, so that the two elements were only related inorganically by placing one beside the other. History with a political bias has a special interest in demonstrating values, namely, those of its political ideals. But, from our point of view, this must be completely rejected because the concept of historical value in our sense embraces not only one's own ideals, political or otherwise, but every significant revelation of authentically spiritual existence and therefore the ideals of one's opponents as well.

Wilhelm von Humboldt was perhaps the first to call for history in our sense—a history oriented to all of mankind's spiritual values (for this is what is meant by his *Ideas*) and founded on the investigation of all knowable causalities. The fulfillment came with Ranke who, in ideal fashion, organically connected the exposition of value to causal inquiry, and in the last analysis, therefore, sought God in history. Hence he may be claimed, for that tendency which gravitates to values as the final and decisive basis.

The positivism of the later 19th century brought a countermovement in the demand for a value-neutral, purely causal history. Although it was able to penetrate the practice of scientific history in full measure only at isolated points, it strengthened a tendency to put causal investigation in the forefront. The result was a tremendously specialized, detailed investigation, which still goes on today. In the process hitherto unknown values of the past came to light everywhere among the facts that were causally investigated. But due to the division of labor inherent in the enterprise, the research was so mechanistic and the number of discoveries so great that these values have not yet been assimilated and appreciated spiritually.

Hence there developed a reaction, still in progress, towards a stronger and more impassioned sensitivity to values, a tendency to refine and to condense, to repress the lower values and to heighten and even exaggerate the higher cultural ones. In all of this, of course, the need for a solid foundation in causal investigation is accepted in principle, but here and there in the practice of the younger men there is already a disturbing tendency to neglect this on occasion. With the catchword "synthesis" they seek to rise above the trivia of causal inquiry to the majestic values of life and of the past. Subjectivist and mystical impressions are aroused, and drive towards immediate unification with the spirit of the past without traveling the wearisome detours of detailed inquiry. The aim, as they prefer to put it, is to extract the "eternal" and the "timeless" from the past, allowing its historical conditioning in time to fade from view. One constructs the past, more or less without induction, from a few striking hints in the tradition and with an excessive addition of one's own ideals. The result is that one ends by embracing a self-created phantasy. This aspiration towards the highest cultural values finds its most peculiar expression in the so-called Georgite school, the followers of Stefan George. Due to the rigid standards they set for themselves their best works are free from the errors of slovenly procedures and are often of a high degree of formal perfection. But there is a tendency to over-refine and rarefy the spiritual atmosphere, allowing the rude, earthy causalities to be dissolved.

The work of the profession proper is still relatively unaffected by these tendencies, but anyone who knows the feelings of the younger generation is aware that among them these tendencies are often immoderately strong. These tendencies have been produced by the whole spiritual constellation of our times. They are a reaction of the soul, as one may call it, against the threat of a mechanistic civilization and against the monstrous mass forces which broke loose in the world war and the Collapse of 1918. Therefore they are presumably a rising current and will undoubtedly become an important factor in the future of historical science. And since my own efforts also move in this direction, I speak from my most intimate experience in saying that I feel the great inner necessity of this tendency as well as its dangers.

Ossified academicism, subjectivism run riot—these are the rocks on which our discipline could founder in the coming generation. The safeguard will always be the same: no causalities without values, no values without causalities. Without a strong desire for values, causal inquiry becomes a lifeless task —no matter how much technical virtuosity is lavished on it. Without immediate delight in concrete reality and its gross and subtle complexes of causality the exposition of ideal values loses contact with the soil in which it is nourished and becomes vacuous and arbitrary. Balance in these tendencies will no longer be achieved, as matters stand today, with the same perfection that was possible for Ranke, for modern problems and modern ways of thinking have destroyed the harmonies which he experienced inwardly and outwardly. It seems as if only a certain one-sidedness can protect contemporary men of thought from the overwhelming pressure and disarray of their environment. But the aspiration towards harmony must continue as an impulse, and could only die out if our culture were completely to decay or to collapse.

II

When Rickert published his pioneering work on cultural values and made this concept central to the craft of history, Alfred Dove spoke suspiciously and skeptically of its "eely slipperiness." A man who had studied directly under Ranke, who habitually placed intuition above conceptual understanding, and who therefore had always lived and breathed cultural values, needed no name for something which was second nature. And yet conceptual thinking follows closely on intuitive thinking, and will not be dissuaded from its attempt to delimit more sharply what has only been intuited. If now, as in the case before us, it must be said that the more intuitive way of thinking does not really reach its goal, brings more obscurity than clarity to the problem now at issue, it may well excuse itself in terms of the poverty of language which compels the use of an ambiguous term; and yet perhaps it must still attempt to remedy the indistinctness of this new concept by more precise and specific definition.

This is what we wish to try. How often has it not turned out that an originally glittering catchphrase, born of experience, develops unsuspected fruitfulness in that it promotes the unification of scattered individual phenomena into larger complexes. Clarification and delimitation, insofar as these are possible, can in such cases only follow gradually. Humanity, humanism, nationality, nationalism, historism, individualism, etc.—originally ambiguous and slippery concepts and catchphrases—are nonetheless indispensable and fruitful. And they have gradually, if never perfectly, been deepened and clarified through usage.

Determination of the essence of values is the chief concern

of modern philosophy. The historian may seek to learn from this discussion, but he need not and cannot refrain from forming an idea of the essence of values based upon his own experience. From the standpoint of the philosopher, this idea will appear to be all too sketchy, ambiguous, and therefore insufficient. But because it is drawn from the practice of historical inquiry, it will possess more instinctive certainty, perhaps, than one which arises from more logical-abstract procedures.

Along with Troeltsch we distinguish the lower, purely animal values, which the historian can only deal with as causalities, from the higher spiritual or cultural values[4] which constitute the historian's authentic field of interest and whose comprehension is his highest goal. By spirit we do not mean the psychic generally but, as in the older meaning, the more highly developed psychic life, namely that which produces culture by "distinguishing, choosing, and judging." Culture is thus the revelation and the breakthrough of a spiritual element within the general complex of causality.

Between cultural and natural existence lies a middle realm which participates in both. Using a term which is becoming increasingly current, we call this the sphere of civilization, and distinguish it from higher, fully spiritual culture. There is however a less precise, but very widespread, usage which treats these two concepts interchangeably.[5]

Civilization lifts itself above pure nature; the latter is reshaped by the intellect which is driven by the will to live and focused on the useful. The whole range of technical invention belongs primarily to this domain. As inventions, as achievements of a spiritually productive and original brain, they are also contributions to culture. But one can also explain them biologically in terms of what is called "adaptation." The act of inventing thus has a biological and a cultural aspect. And once accomplished, applied, and popularized, it threatens to sink back to the level of mere nature unless sustained by an independent spiritual existence. For applied technology is also found among the animals.

In my work on *raison d'état*, I have attempted to present an example of this utilitarian middle region. The historian will have to deal with it continually, not only because by far the greatest number of causalities which he investigates belong here, but because occurrences in this domain can become cultural achievements through an often imperceptible process of enhancement. The soul itself is swept along—there is no other way to put it—when the merely useful becomes something beautiful or good. Otherwise the technical remains but a soulless, spiritless product of the intellect, civilization merely and not culture.

Culture enters only when man takes up the struggle against nature with all his inner powers, not only with his will and intellect; only when his acts have value in the higher sense, i.e. when he creates or seeks something good or beautiful for its own sake or for its own sake seeks the truth.[6] All evaluating action in this sense is valuable to the historian as well.[7] It assures him of the continuity and fertility of the spiritual element in history and shows him the course of its unfolding up to his own day. But to understand it fully he must, as we have said, also investigate the root domains of causal processes which have nothing to do with culture for the most part. Therefore, in an historical account which has been conscientiously performed, as in life itself, the valued and the valuable will glitter only here and there like a rare blossom among ordinary growths.

But rare as they may be in comparison to the general mass of human events, these cultural achievements and values are immeasurably numerous in history. For every human soul is capable of creating cultural values, be it only the simple performance of duty for the sake of doing good. By what principles, then, is a selection to be made by the historian? One, certainly, is causal influence. All cultural achievements which have strongly and continuously influenced the preservation and further development of culture are worthy of research and exposition. The borderline between the important and the unimportant is fluid, therefore, and will vary with the finesse and the perspective of the historian. It varies with his perspective, in that he will sift the factual material differently as he focuses on a more limited or on a more encompassing historical formation. Thus, in writing the history of a city, for example, facts will be studied as important which, on a higher plane, as in the history of a nation, must be accounted insignificant. Equally fluid and dependent on finesse is the application of the second criterion for selecting cultural achievements which we have already mentioned in another connection: the inner and authentically cultural value of historical phenomena. Great cultural achievements and revelations of the spiritual element may never under any circumstances be assessed solely by their degree of causal influence on the course of culture. They also stand upon their own, quite independently of whether they have influenced their time or not, and they are worth research, exposition, and reverence solely for their own sake. What the poet said of the antique lamp, which was no longer useful but enchanted him, would also apply to them: "Whatever is beautiful seems to be blessed in itself." This is a point which has not yet penetrated the ordinary notions of the historian as to what is worth investigation. Troeltsch and I have often talked about the "overestimation of causalities" which still predominates in the selection of material.[8]

Causalities are overestimated, namely, when the individual moment in the genesis of cultural values is not properly recognized, and thus those causalities are neglected which stem from the spontaneity of spiritual-moral, personal activity and are therefore not so easily ordered in the causal complex as are causalities of a mechanistic or biological nature. Cultural values arise only from the breakthrough of a unique spiritual power into the mechanistically or biologically determined causal series. Everything spiritual, each cultural value, is unique, individual, irreplaceable. To savor its individuality is also to have a feeling for its value, and therefore to esteem it not only as an important link within the causal chain, but also for its own sake. There is also indifferent and value-neutral individuality—every object has something of this. Historical individualities, however, include only those phenomena which exhibit some tendency towards the good, the beautiful, or true, and thereby become meaningful and valuable to us. And they are all the more valuable, the more strongly this tendency joins with the more self-affirming and survival tendency of human structures and ennobles them.

The deeper understanding of individuality, both in the single personality and in trans-personal human structures, is the great advance which came in Germany through idealism and romanticism and which created modern historism. This understanding brought with it a correct estimate of evolutionary thinking, which is often incorrectly taken as the key criterion of modern historism, but which is much too ambiguous and versatile for this.[9] The evolution of the human foetus is a biological, not an historical evolution. The latter type occurs only when the spontaneous factor of human action for the sake of values intervenes, and thereby produces something unique and individual. With this an historical individuality "evolves," and all things that evolve historically are always individualities and through evolution alone are they revealed.[10] Even world-history—understood about in Ranke's sense—for with a few corrections and reservations we may still accept his viewpoint—is but a single great individuality filled with countless other individualities great and small. All the cultural values of this history are likewise historical individualities encased in various higher individualities up to the highest of them all which is world-history. Hence each of them is fully understandable only in terms of its connections to world-history.

Everything that lives strives towards form and structure and is driven by the laws of formation and of structure. This morphological insight, represented most extremely and one-sidedly in history by Spengler, increasingly predominates in modern thought. Of value to history, however, are only those forms and structures of human life which serve not only the necessities of life, but an ideal of some sort and spiritual-moral values. As soon as something spiritual and individual becomes apparent in a form, it awakens the historian's interest in values. Where this is lacking, the form remains in the biological realm of mere survival and can be taken into account by the historian only as a causal element in explaining other values, not as a value in itself.

But for human eyes at least the sphere of the biological and the sphere of spiritual-moral values are not clearly and unambiguously divided, but often merge with each other imperceptibly. We showed how this occurs—and I again refer to the exposition in my book on *raison d'état*—in the intermediate realm of the utilitarian. It is really this fact, the absence of any sharp boundaries between the two spheres, which has evoked all the differences of opinion in the modern sciences of culture (*Geisteswissenschaften*). For these boundaries may be differently interpreted and drawn, may be recognized or not recognized at all.

This is the most agonizing question imposed on the historian. Only too often must he wrestle with uncertainty as to whether this or that fact which he is studying is to be explained by the mere necessities of life and nature or by spiritual-moral and valuative factors. Moreover, the necessities of life and nature, biological causalities, flow through every vein of even the human agent committed to values and threaten to impair the purity of values, to mirror illusory values in the place of true ones. Most staggering of all is the fact that both spheres are linked by a very close causal bond, the fact that great and blessed cultural values often have a commonplace and impure origin and have struggled upwards from depths of darkness, so that it sometimes seems as though God needed the devil to realize Himself. Then, when one is again attuned to believe in the unity of the divine nature in Goethe's sense, these relationships appear in a more comforting light. Where the processes natural to human life do not contradict the commands of ethics, do not become sinful, therefore, they may appear as an indispensable, congenial, and nourishing subsoil for the genesis of noble fruits. Did not Goethe himself allow his sensuality to work freely in his great art—the question whether there was sin in this or not retreating completely in the background?

It is peculiar that in this question even that type of historical investigation which is usually more oriented to causalities, slights causalities for values. That is, confronted with great cultural achievements, it ignores or veils their often frightful and repulsive origins. Very few historians possess the acute perception Burckhardt had when he revealed the political and social bases of Renaissance culture in all their frightfulness and showed how it was even inwardly affected by its connection to daemonic forces. The great results of power politics, which have reshaped culture and revitalized its life, are more than ever recorded with a certain equanimity, and their Machiavellian basis and by-effects treated merely as *conditio sine qua non*. They are this, too, of course—but to treat them thus is to lose all feeling for the tragedy of history.

Culture based on spontaneity, on a causality generative of spiritual-moral values, and yet bound to causalities of a biological and mechanistic type—this is the enigma that the historian can never solve. Culture and nature, we might say God and nature, are undoubtedly a unity, but a unity divided in itself. God struggles loose from nature in agony and pain, laden with sin, and in danger, therefore, of sinking back at any moment. For the ruthless and honest observer, this is the final word—and yet it cannot be accepted as the final word. Only a faith which, however, has become ever more universal in its content and must struggle endlessly with doubt, holds out the solace of a transcendental solution to the problem, insoluble for us, of life and culture. But we have lost our faith that any philosopher has given, or can ever give us, this transcendental solution.

Thus the value of philosophic systems and ideologies as truth is dubious—while their cultural value is undoubted. The thought constructions of the great thinkers are all but the highest towerings of spirit amid the nature which sustains it, all but the highest achievements of a poor, truth-thirsting, ever-erring mankind. Only the work of great religious figures and the perfected work of art rank higher still.

Two types of cultural values now emerge from all that has been said. One set is deliberately created through effort previously directed to that goal—religious and philosophical, political and social, thought constructions, the work of art, science. The others grow immediately and without premeditation from the necessities of concrete, practical existence. In the former man seeks the most direct and most precipitous ascent from nature up to culture. In the latter he remains upon the plane of nature but with glance lifted upward to the guiding peaks of value. In satisfying life's necessities he seeks a way of satisfaction which will allow the values of the true or the good or the beautiful to be realized simultaneously. In this Aristotle's saying about the state applies—it arose to make life possible but it exists to make life beautiful. And it is in the state, above all, that nature becomes culture in this manner, that is, by a rotation of the axis.

In all cases, whether the work of building culture be direct or indirect, spiritual entities arise, historical individualities, whose causal genesis and impact and whose value the historian investigates together. The subjectivism, which in fact is always bound up with evaluation, is repressed, at least in part, by the fact that priority is given to the value which the phenomenon possesses in itself, as a unique and irreplaceable manifestation of spiritual existence.[11] This means to enter into the very souls of those who acted, to consider their works and cultural contributions in terms of their own premises and, in the last analysis, through artistic intuition to give new life to life gone by—which cannot be done without a transfusion of one's own life blood. Thus only a tolerant and loving sensitivity to all humanity will achieve that degree of objectivity which is possible. At this point Troeltsch's doctrine o value-relativity is relevant.[12] "Value-relativity is not relativism, anarchy, accident, arbitrariness. It signifies rather a fusion of the factual and normative, which is ever moving and newly created and cannot, therefore, be determined universally and timelessly." Value-relativity, in other words, is nothing other than individuality in the historical sense. It is the unique and intrinsically valuable imprint of an unknown absolute—for this kind of absolute will be acknowledged by faith as the creative ground of all values—upon that which is relative and bound to time and nature.

From the inherent value of historical individualities we can logically distinguish their value for us and for our lives. In the determination of this element of value the subjective need will naturally be of greater influence. The desire to derive lessons, examples, or admonitions from history belongs among the ineradicable basic motives which have always led to historical writing. From this come the greatest dangers to its scientific character—tendentious distortion, idealization, or misrepresentation. A purified historical sense, which would do justice both to the scientific and supra-scientific character of historical writing, will concede that we indeed wish to learn something for our own lives from history. The very study of causalities in history yields practical lessons in abundance. Whatever has occurred in history due to general, typical, and recurring causes can also recur in the present and can be handled in the light of the experience of bygone times.[13] On the other hand, the individual, inimitable, and irreplaceable in history offers no such practical utility. But it can become a spiritual content, an ideal model, for those who possess a related and receptive individuality, and it can help to deepen and enrich their culture. Whole ages and generations can draw nourishment from the cultural values of a particular period in the past which is specifically related to them. Late cultures, as a rule, normally require props like this. But there is always the danger of epigonal dependency, of succumbing inwardly to the spirits of the past. Conversely, a strong spirit like Max Weber could motivate his unrealistic project of value-neutral historical research with the most value-laden goals: "I wish to see how much I can endure."

The finest and highest instruction that history can give, however, is surely that which springs unsought from the pure appreciation of historical individualities as such, in the way we have described above.[14] It is then history's own value which becomes valuable to us. It consists in nothing else than the corroboration of the infinitely creative power of the spirit, which although it does not guarantee us rectilinear progress, yet promises an eternally new birth of valuable historical individualities within the bounds of nature. And since all these are causally connected and together form the great overall individuality of world history, the specific historical individuality—the nation, state, society, church, etc., in which we presently live and which we help to influence—becomes conscious of being rooted in the total process. And precisely this consciousness can then develop ethical forces of the greatest strength. The tradition which, unaided and unconsciously, like a natural process one might say, operated as the link of generations and the guardian of acquired cultural values, now becomes truly spiritualized, becomes a cultural value in the fullest sense.

> *And so the living substance wins*
> *New strength from stage to stage.*

It follows from all that has been said that history is nothing but the history of culture, culture signifying the production of unique spiritual values, of historical individualities. The dispute between the partisans of political history and cultural history could only arise because neither side was clear as to the relationship of values and causalities in history. Political historiography saw the state as the central factor in historical life—which is perfectly correct in causal terms since the strongest causal influences even on cultural life have always emanated from the state. And since the investigation of cultural values needs the most extensive causal basis, there is yet another reason why the state must always remain at the center of historical inquiry. But is the state also the highest possible cultural value? Since Hegel there has been a certain inclination to raise it to this height, although this was always limited by the healthy sentiment, that religion is superior in value. The state cannot be the highest value because it is more strongly bound than almost any other historical individuality to natural, biological necessities and is thereby prevented from becoming fully spiritual and moral. Religion in its purest form, and art in its highest expressions—these are the highest cultural values. And the next rank may be claimed by philosophy and science.

But, it will be asked, is not the active and productive life of man thus depreciated in favor of purely contemplative and spiritual activities? Shall flight from life, which is surely bound up with the latter in some degree, rank higher than attempts to shape life?

The answer is not a simple yes or no. The intertwining of values is most characteristically revealed here. If one asks for the realms in which man can raise himself highest over nature, these are undoubtedly the realms of religion, of art, of philosophy and science. Productive life binds man to nature more closely. The cultural values which he creates in this domain contain more of earthly stuff, are muddier and less pure than those of the more contemplative and world-escaping realms. But the task of producing them is not only more burdensome; it is also more urgent and insistent than that which brings forth the cultural values of the purely spiritual realms. Even the task of producing the cultural value of religion attains its full urgency and insistency only when religion does not remain the mystic enjoyment of divinity but penetrates productive life and becomes a ferment in it. It is the same with the other contemplatively created cultural values of art, philosophy, and science. Of them, too, it may be justly demanded that they fructify productive life, not directly, to be sure, but indirectly, for all the highest cultural values are duty-bound to serve this life. Productive life itself, we may now formulate it, does not, to be sure, create the highest cultural values, but the first and most urgent of tasks is to create cultural values in it and upon it. Contemplative life forms only images of life, not life itself. For this reason it produces more perfectly, more spiritually than does productive life. These images can and should serve as guiding lights to productive life in its struggle for cultural values. The attention of the historian must thus always be directed most intensely to the question how far and in what degree that aspect of life which is bound to the necessities of nature has been reshaped and transformed into culture.

These considerations, we think, establish the central place of political history in the historical sciences more profoundly than any of the arguments hitherto adduced. Political history deals with less perfect values than the history of religion, art, etc. It does not begrudge them their good fortune in moving among the heights of humanity. But in studying the state, the causally most influential factor of historical life, and in probing at the same time for the values the state is able to produce, it takes account of both the depths and heights of life, and in order to do this, must reflectively place itself at the center of life.

Of all historical sciences, political history is closest to life. Whether economic or social history are even closer can be argued differently according to the concept of historical life which one holds. We understand this concept as the interpenetration of nature and culture. The more intense, the more heated the war between these two, the greater the measure of historical existence. And most intensively we see this dualism working in the state. The state does not achieve the highest victories of culture, but it does provide the most impressive and striking spectacle of culture wrestling with nature. Next to the elevation of one's own personality spiritually and morally, the attempt to spiritualize and moralize the state in which one lives, even when one knows that this cannot be attained completely, is the highest demand that can be laid upon ethical activity. For the state will always constitute the most influential and extensive community of life, and the man who aspires to perfection can breathe freely only in a state which aspires to perfection. And it is precisely the problematic, the uncertain, and the precarious in the cultural values of the state which, with magnetic power, has attracted the political historian, unconsciously for the most part, to the great statesmen of world-history in whom this struggle of nature with culture becomes grandiose.

There still remains a middle realm between political history, which exhibits the struggle for cultural values in political life, and the history of cultural values produced in contemplation. This is the realm of political ideas. Here the *vita activa* merges with *vita contemplativa.* From the very needs of active political life there arises the impulse to form images of this life in which reality and ideal are interwoven. In the hopes of their creator they are designed to react on life directly—and not only indirectly as with the images formed by art and science. When this is their result, they become the preludes to real historical processes, and for this reason alone are already worth investigation as significant causalities. With what zeal have men traced the beginnings of the idea of popular sovereignty and of the socialist ideal! But the authentic cultural value of these ideas lies in an attempt, as direct and as precipitous as for the men of the *vita contemplativa,* to rise above the purely nature-bound and to spiritualize the state at least in phantasy. Hence they too are to be considered for their own sake, for the sake of their own individual value, and not only for the sake of their causal influence; they too are to be relived and represented with all the life blood that one can pour back into them.

And although others may be more affected by other characteristics of historical life, as for me I do not hesitate to say that the vista of individual ideas, awakened in the clashes of the rude earthly powers of political life and striving for deliverance from their oppressive weight, has always moved me most deeply. They, too, are more earth-bound, more commingled with realities, than the spiritual products of the pure *vita contemplativa.* Therefore they are to be all the more vividly appreciated as the nourishing subsoil in natural reality without which no spiritual creation, not even the highest, would be possible.

Political ideas combine the smell of earth with the scent of the spirit. States themselves may also do this if, as Ranke has taught us, they reach the level of real spiritual entities. Where, then, shall the greater source of cultural value be located—in the state itself or in the ideas of the minds that soar above it; in the Greek city-state, for example, or in the Platonic ideal which grew out of it? To decide this in each instance would be pedantic. Sometimes it is unquestionably the state, at other times the political idea arising from the state to affirm it or deny it, which represents the higher spiritual achievement. And in many other instances, like the one invoked above, evaluation ought to be withheld. The ranking of cultural values must in general be done summarily. This is demanded by their individual character which makes a mockery of any single universal standard. In taking cultural values as individualities, one summarily senses their relative spiritual potency or bondage to nature without being able to calculate degrees precisely. The very impenetrability of the intermediate zone between nature and culture already bars the way to complete precision.

Individuum est ineffabile. On this very fact depends the infinite fascination of the historical world, which secretly, yet openly, is constantly creating new spiritual entities and yet does not arrange them in a progression of ascending rank. For every epoch, said Ranke, is immediate to God.

We close with the words that followed on this sentence for, taken precisely, they state all that we have sought to establish in our battle against an opinion widespread in our profession. "Its value lies not at all in what comes forth from it, but **in its** own existence, in its authentic self."

HISTORICAL CONCEPTUALIZATION:
Huizinga

[J. Huizinga (1872-1945) belonged to that remarkable group of Dutch, Belgian, and Swiss historians—Jakob Burckhardt, Henri Pirenne, Pieter Geyl, and Werner Kaegi—who have contributed so much to the development of history, especially cultural history. By his own account a highly unconventional historian—he had studied linguistics and was known first as a student of Sanskrit—Huizinga had been attracted to history by his aesthetic pleasure in viewing the past, by his exceptional empathy for it. He was appointed professor of history at Gröningen in 1905, and called to the University of Leyden ten years later. Like Burckhardt, he was able to capture a moment's impression in masterly pencil sketches and wrote history in a similarly precise, yet impressionistic manner. In his greatest work, *The Waning of the Middle Ages* (1919), Huizinga, with an intuitive grasp of the spirit of late medieval art and popular culture, portrays that period not as the seedtime of the Renaissance but as a period of decay and decline. In his *Erasmus* (1923) he attained an equally sure sense of the inner life of the great humanist and compatriot.

Although Huizinga frequently disclaimed competence in philosophy and historical theory, he did in fact write extensively on the nature of history and his essays belong to the best that has been written on the subject in our century. The following essay, which first appeared in 1934, was translated

289

for this book by Rosalie Colie, and appears without Huizinga's footnotes.]

THE IDEA OF HISTORY

The foregoing remarks on the nature of historical knowledge seemed to lead to the discovery of a train of weaknesses necessarily accompanying the process of acquiring that historical knowledge. These ideas were discussed in order: that history is pre-eminently an inexact science, that its concept of causality is extremely defective, that it resists the formulation of laws, that the concept of historical evolution can be considered valid only with great reservations and can be applied only so far as one accepts the organic analogy.

A closer examination reveals that at the root of all these problems lies the age-old antinomy of a realistic versus a nominalistic world-view. To what extent may one isolate from the eternal flux of disparate units, specific, consistent groups as entity, as phenomena, and subject them to the intellect? In other words, in the historical world, where the simplest thing is always endlessly complex, what are the units, the self-contained wholes (to give the German *Ganzheiten* an English equivalent)?

Are they individual men? But an individual man is himself a phenomenon of infinite complexity; moreover, man as such, in his individuality, is never an historical phenomenon, an historical object. He is a unit, biologically and intellectually, but in neither the first nor the second respect is he an object of history. He becomes an historical unit only by his involvement in life, by his relation to his environment and his time, by his dealings with his fellow-men, by the resolution of his fate. And his environment is limitless and indeterminable.

Our intelligence, however, requires that that inevitable nominalism—which makes us continually split and dissolve every image, every idea, even down to the atom, into its components—be supplemented by an equally inevitable realism. We must conceive of eternal variety in terms of self-contained wholes; from the welter of perceptible things we must mark off certain composite units to which we give names and assign forms—in short, which are ideas. We are forced to make abstractions.

This once accepted, in the limitation of such wholes there is no reason to stop at the biologically separate individual or at the single fact defined in space and time. It is well-known that where the lower forms of life are concerned, the biologist cannot draw the line between the individual and the colony. On the intellectual level the same applies to the historian. The group, the institution, the state live their historical lives as units, and it is as units that the science of history must consider and analyze them.

The justification in the study of history of the doctrine of ideas is indispensable and inevitable, just as it is in daily, personal, and social life. Man cannot live by a consistent nominalism, at least not spiritually. The need to give form to the particulars of existence, either in the present or in the past, entails certain further consequences.

The historical observer never confronts a bare and simple fact unrelated to a broader general context. Even the smallest fact has significance for him only because it fits into a system of ideas he has already formed, to which in some way or other it corresponds. An historical fact is particular only insofar as it can be included in a more general frame. As Othmar Spann,[1] who has so clearly set forth these matters, correctly says, "History is unthinkable without theory." And thereby history simply proves anew its close connection with the forms of thought of ordinary human life, which also would be impossible without general categories into which intelligence organizes phenomena.

What bearing has this fundamental reflection on historical method? We began by doubting whether the science of history can approach its objective, the past, with the tools of concept, of formula, and of analysis. We have denied to history even the capacity precisely to delineate and determine its object; though afterwards we had to accept the fact that history is nevertheless constantly required to consider its materials within ideal limitations. Does this mean that we have once more subjected history to the demands of a normative discipline? Does it mean that history is sentenced to reduce and to limit its material to mere schemes and formulas after all?

No. The particular quality of history that gives it its real worth, that places it more than any other discipline at the center of life, shall always lie in just this fact: that history conceives of and treats its material as events, not as organisms. The sociologist and the psychologist are concerned mainly that the facts of a case conform to a system of ideas; for the historian this conformity has little or no importance— indeed, the term "case" does not belong in history at all.

It is the facts in psychology, jurisprudence, sociology, that are conceived of as "cases"; for the historian the facts will always be "a series of events that happened at a given time."

And, it must be added, that could have happened differently. Here perhaps the root of the difference in point of view becomes even clearer. The sociologist, etc., deals with his material as if the outcome were given in the known facts: he simply searches for the way in which the result was already determined in the facts. The historian, on the other hand, must always maintain towards his subject an indeterminist point of view. He must constantly put himself at a point in the past at which the known factors still seem to permit different outcomes. If he speaks of Salamis, then it must be as if the Persians might still win; if he speaks of the *coup d'état* of Brumaire, then it must remain to be seen if Bonaparte will be ignominiously repulsed. Only by continually recognizing that possibilities are unlimited can the historian do justice to the fulness of life.

With this we gradually approach a certain insight into the task of historical scholarship. The historian tries to discover some sense in the remains of a certain period in human society. To express this "sense" he must organize historical phenomena according to the categories with which his *Weltanschauung,* his intellect, his culture provide him. I want to stress at this point (and shall revert to it later) that I do not mean to preach a relativism allowing all interpretations of history an equal truth so long as they simply correspond to the conviction from which they arise. I state only that an historical narrative is always dependent on the culture in which and from which it springs.

The historian thus recognizes in the phenomena of the past certain ideal forms that he tries to describe. He does not define them, for definition is the task of the sociologist. He exhibits them in the definite context of a unique historical course of events. What he sees are forms of society, economy, religion, justice and law, of thought, of artistic and literary expression, of political and civil life—in a word, of culture. And he always sees these forms in action. Each of them is a form of life, and therefore each form has a function. Once more, the historian does not try to reduce to formulas these functions of life or culture, or to organize them systematically, but to show them in their visible operation in time, place and context. The way in which they manifest themselves is almost always that of conflict: clash of arms and clash of opinions are the constant themes of history. Fundamentally history is always epic or dramatic, however weak at times these aspects may be.

It goes almost without saying that in this approach the boundaries between the historical and sociological points of view are often crossed. To make his picture intelligible, the historian must make repeated use of the terms and methods of the systematic social sciences, particularly in dealing with special aspects of culture, such as the history of religion, art, or law, where the dividing line between the descriptive and the formulative is hazy.

The following remains to be said of the ideal units or the wholes of historical knowledge. They always concern a change taking place in complex phenomena at a certain time. We have come to accept a terminology designating form as organism and function as evolution. The ideas of organism and evolution imply the recognition of a goal or a destiny. The historical context we posited, the creation of our mind, has sense only insofar as we grant it a goal, or rather a course toward a specific outcome, whether that outcome be glorious perfection or decay and ruin, whether that goal be thought of as set by human will, by blind necessity, or by God's providence and continual act of creation.

Therefore historical thinking is always teleological. Though the past supplies our material and compels our attention, though the mind realizes that not one minute of the future can be predicted, none the less it is the eternal future that moves our mind. The widespread and persistent opinion that history should deal with our understanding of the present rests on a misconception: a "present" is as little known to historical thought as it is to philosophical thought. For history the question is always "Whither?" History must be granted to be the teleologically-oriented discipline *par excellence*.

A dramatic interpretation based on a morphology of human society would probably in the final analysis provide the most balanced definition for expressing the nature of history, as long as it places special emphasis upon its unsystematic, descriptive character and upon the necessity of seeing its object in action. As soon as history loses sight of these two considerations, it overshoots its mark. We shall try to illustrate the necessity for utmost care by calling attention to several dangers obstructing the acquisition of sound historical knowledge. I call these dangers inflation of terms, use of stereotypes, and anthropomorphism. The last is the most important and the most basic, and should be dealt with first.

We began with a recognition of the intellectual necessity for a certain "realism" in ideas: which is to say, that in order to express our thoughts about the world and about life, we must attribute unity and existence to phenomena that our nominalistic understanding tends to analyze into an infinity of atoms and functions of atoms. This "realism," in the scholastic sense, inevitably implies a certain slight degree of anthropomorphism—i.e., the attribution of human qualities to ideas which in the strict sense do not allow it. When I say, "Society refuses," or "Honesty demands," I express myself anthropomorphically—strictly speaking, I do so when I say, "The spring uncoils." All this is part of the unavoidable and plain anthropomorphism without which our capacity to express ourselves would cease to exist.

It is clear that whenever I warn against the danger of historical anthropomorphism, I take the suffix "-ism" in its common sense of the excessive use of certain devices in themselves correct or useful. I should have asked the critic who once reproached me for my committing the very fault against which I issued this warning if he would also accuse me of alcoholism because I sometimes enjoy a glass of wine.

By historical anthropomorphism, then, I understand the tendency to attribute to an abstract notion behavior and attitudes implying human consciousness. As I have said, language inevitably entails such metaphorical expressions. The danger lies in the fact that a metaphor can, as it were, become the basis for further constructions and that the slightly humanized figure of speech thus can turn into a phantom, allowing a mythological conception to steal into the place of a scientific one. This happens continually wherever an historical presentation is fraught with passion, whether political, social, religious, or some other kind. An abstract concept like "Capitalism" is seen as a diabolical being full of cruelty and cunning; "Revolution" may be seen first as an idea, but it soon becomes an almost living being.

Only one step separates anthropomorphism from rhetorical and allegorical personification. In many cases rhetoric renders anthropomorphism harmless: a strong rhetoric functions like the skull-and-crossbones on a poison-bottle. When "the Throne" casts a shadow or "Revolution" is given a torch and, with mouth open, crosses the barricades, it is a warning that metaphors are at work.

Anthropomorphism is dangerous when beneath the metaphors the claim somehow remains that the figure of speech is still to be taken philosophically or scientifically. That is nowhere clearer than in Oswald Spengler's *Decline of the West*. The genius of his correlation, the depth of his observation, the brilliant perspectives that he revealed cannot make up for the basic flaw of that great book. Spengler forced world history into a scheme in which everything that did not suit his fancy (for example, Christianity, America, the Latin peoples) was either neglected or planed down. Nor is this all: while he tyrannically assigned his cultures to their places, he gave them human form, attributed to them a biological life-cycle, and in this way did violence to history.

But has not the sound historical sense of the civilized world actually triumphed in this matter? Spengler's great mind has had its effect, certainly, but who now, before even twenty years have passed, speaks of his series of cultures; outside Germany where has anyone accepted the "Faustian man" as a useful historical term?

The danger is even greater where from historical material purely political aims form ideal conceptions then offered up as "new myth"—i.e., as a sacred system of thought forced upon the common man. Our vision is deliberately obscured here by a horrible and totally hypocritical confusion of religion, mythology and science. The historical conscience of our time must beware lest in the name of history bloodthirsty idols be raised that devour culture.

But let us return to the serene field of historical scholarship. I spoke of a danger that I called inflation of terms. I shall illustrate my meaning at once by its most striking example. In the first half of the nineteenth century the term "Renaissance" took its place in historical thought as a reference to a clearly-circumscribed intellectual movement, marking a definite period. Later it was discovered, first, that the nature, range and time of this movement could by no means be precisely marked off; second, that similar movements had occurred at other times and in other places. The use of the word Renaissance was broadened in an unprecedented way. One allowed the Renaissance to begin as early as the thirteenth century and to last until the seventeenth; one began to hear of a Carolingian Renaissance and of renaissances in general. With this, though, the word had imperceptibly lost its pith, its flavor, its value. For an historical term preserves its value only so long as it smacks of a very definite historical past that can be evoked in characteristic images. When I say "Italian Renaissance,"

I want to see everything between Donatello and Titian, but nothing more.

The concept of the Renaissance had become inflated. The same thing happened later to the terms Gothic and Baroque. Both originally referred to a style of architecture, including sculpture. Then it was discovered that certain characteristics of these styles were common to the intellectual production of the whole period. Then the term came to designate the entire culture of the period, and was finally elevated to an abstract concept of style in general. To some extent this can be justified, but meanwhile for the historian the word has lost its savor. It has become a surgical instrument instead of a blooming branch.

I called the third danger the stereotype, to which, just because of its unsystematic and inexact character, history is highly vulnerable. It is forced to work with general terms by which it can encompass a great deal. At the same time, history is prevented from actually testing the strict validity of those general terms by the very heterogeneity, selective nature, incomparableness and limitlessness of all its particular ideas. There is a great temptation to apply as a stereotype a concept once found useful to data that really require a re-thinking and a new specific qualification. I am thinking now of the all-too ready application of almost all the general terms produced by the study of social and political phenomena and institutions: terms like capitalism, feudalism, reaction, bourgeoisie, democracy, and countless others. History can do without none of them, but the historian who is serious about presenting a living and accurate reflection of the past must be wary of using those terms, loaded as they are with feeling and ill-feeling.

This is perhaps the place to say a word about the merits of the great schematic division that makes us speak of Antiquity, the Middle Ages, and the Modern Period.

Grafted upon the trunk of classical civilization, Christianity saw the course of history as a pattern of successive empires, of which the Roman Empire was to be the last. The humanists first provided a new conception of the sequence periods that was ultimately to become the general basis of the periodization of history. They saw Antiquity in a great splendor; they thought that they had recaptured its perfection. A great new period had dawned for them, and they called the period of barbarism and darkness that separated them from ancient glory *media aetas* or *medium aevum*, that is, the middle period, the period between, an entirely negative term. Only much later, about 1700, the triad Antiquity-Middle Ages-Modern Period was accepted as an academic classification in the study of history. An emotional content, however, soon began to be attached to each of these terms, in themselves purely chronological. "Antiquity" maintained the original glory attributed to it from the beginning. The "Middle Ages" became the term for cultural decay, ignorance and terror. The "Modern Period" implied the conquest of the New World, printing, a renovation in art and religion, the rise of science and much more. Finally Romanticism gave the Middle Ages too, a lustre of beauty and nostalgia, so that each of the three terms acquired the value of a cultural idea with positive content.

As soon as these chronological divisions gained such a lively perspective, their chronological inadequacy had to be reckoned with. The so-called end of the Roman Empire in the West in 476 was as little a cultural frontier as was the discovery of America and the conquest of Granada in 1492. And now the need for these once-useful terms, with their positive cultural implications, became stronger than the realization of their lack of chronological motivation. There have been and are still occasional conflicts over the question of whether or not to set the end of the Middle Ages at 1600. Nor is this all: the term "Middle Ages" as an idea of a period has been applied to totally different cultures, such as the Greek, the Indian, and the Japanese.

The recognition of the inadequacy of this general division cannot prevent the historian from using the terms. He knows that they are simply aids to understanding. But the most important fact remains: history so needs to characterize a general complex by a specific term, however vague, that a phrase like the "Middle Ages," in itself meaningless, could assume so specific a flavor, could conjure up a picture as full of life as history is able to confer.

We constantly return to that series of polarities between which historical thought must operate. Does history strive after knowledge of the particular or of the general, of the concrete or of the abstract, of the unique or of the repetitive? Does historical knowledge consist in graphic presentation or in concepts? Is the aim of historical method analysis or synthesis, its subject the individual or the mass, particular actions or collective?

And, in the end, by reason of its natural bent historical sense always inclines toward the particular, the graphic, the concrete, the unique, the individual. The historian's gaze must always be directed at various events themselves in their changing course. Knowledge that has lost sight of actual men and actual events may be worthwhile, but it is no longer history.

On the other hand, we have already seen that for historical understanding, indeed, for an understanding of life itself, the particular must always relate to something more general, that it is always general compared with the still more particular. The unique event is comprehensible only in its general context. For a person with no knowledge of history the murders of Floris V and the De Witts are entirely equivalent miscellaneous items. The concrete can be distinguished only be means of the abstract. Presentation and idea are not diametrically opposed.

Once this polarity of historical knowledge is thoroughly understood, it is easy to answer a number of questions that have given rise to lively disputes and heated arguments. To all these apparently contradictory questions,—which is right, this or that?—the answer is clear. Both, the one contained within the other.

Is the aim of history knowledge of particular facts or of large phenomena and contexts? Of both. In particular facts great contexts are recognized; without knowledge of the particular, that of general phenomena becomes dry and lifeless. At just one point in time, in the Roman Empire shortly before the dawn of Christianity, Caesar lived. But Caesar is comprehensible to me only because I can compare him with Alexander and Napoleon. Was I looking for a comparison, the Emperor-general as such? If that were so, I might lay aside Caesar, Alexander, and Napoleon at the end of my research just as the biologist throws away the remains of his experiment. I was looking for the figure of *Caesar* in its uniqueness, in its difference from countless other figures, in its likeness to a few.

The recognition that the presentation of a proper development hardly holds good in history implies also the necessity of knowing the particular facts. For at no point can the incalculable fate of the individual, who may divert or cause the destruction or the birth of a world, be lost sight of in the process of acquiring historical knowledge.

Loud and long the cry has been heard—of which I spoke earlier—"Stop giving us heroes and tyrants, stop describing mortal lives from the cradle to the grave, stop searching for what motivated the individual. Give us the life of the masses, their toil and suffering, their hopes and their delusions, their passion and their violent deeds!" Good, but you will never understand all that, understand it historically, without seeing the picture of the individuals who first formed ideas, who found the courage to perform deeds, who risked and won or who witnessed and suffered where the masses despaired.

The spirit of the modern period, with its new respect for collectivism, with its hatred of all individualism, has cried out with great conviction: "It is not heroes, the few, who make history; it is groups, classes, peoples, races." Certainly, and that would be all there was to say about it, if the components of these groups or peoples were the simple and identical quantities of the bushel of grain about which Heraclitus asked this question: "Which single grain causes the roar of their fall, the first or the thousandth?"

Observe: Heraclitus did not draw the conclusion that the single grains caused it all together, and that's an end to it. With this question he pointed out the logical fault of every generalization in those cases where each unit in the event is a microcosm. The question of whether the individual or the group makes history is logically unanswerable and is irrelevant for the historian.

But the purely methodological question remains. Is it the historian's task to analyze or to synthesize? Here again the answer (the same one, by the way, for every discipline) is, to do both.

Doubtless history, perhaps more than any other discipline, has sinned and continues sinning daily by an excess of analytical work, in which all too often any sense of the larger context of events, any realization that beyond a certain point details lose their interest, seems to be missing.

But there is a threefold excuse, even justification, for the historian. The first is this: by the nature of its materials history is a discipline in which its practitioners are constrained to work independently and to meet with each other only rarely. The material—and I repeat at this point—is endlessly varied and endlessly complicated. A living knowledge can be acquired only by penetration into the particular, and this is not always necessarily followed by a reduction to general principles.

In the second place, as I have already remarked, it must not be forgotten that no knowledge of the particular is possible without its being understood within a general frame. This does not mean that each researcher into local history must always keep world history in mind, but that his modest work must certainly be directed toward a totality of knowledge, within his limited range toward synthesis. By assiduously entering into detail, he lets us see a city, a village, a guild, a monastery, a family—alive in its past. And if we carry this over to the larger complexes—an area, a people, a state, a continent—where is the borderline between the unimportant and the merely interesting? There is none. Every historical fact opens immediately into eternity. If it is important to perceive a state in its past, then it is as important for a village and so on. It is not the size of the subject that determines the importance of a study: the student of a world-shaking conflict can produce the most short-sighted analysis. The important thing is the spirit in which the work is undertaken. It may sound paradoxical, but in history synthesis occurs to a certain extent in the act of analysis itself, since historical knowledge is primarily a view of something—much as people passing through a landscape absorb its beauty as they go.

Meanwhile our argument of the local historian has raised a point that till now we have not touched upon: that is, the fact that history is not the same thing for everybody, that the very choice of a particular field is determined by attraction, attachment, congeniality. I know that in every discipline one specializes in one's preference, but in historical interests, preference for a particular period of the past is bound up with a variety of feelings far exceeding purely scholarly aspirations. Imagination plays a large part, temperament a still larger one. Interest in history is a love of the past, a desire to see dead things revived and warm with life.

This is the justification for all those small historical undertakings that countless people in all countries are daily devoting to a limited subject of their choice. Nietzsche was entirely wrong in his scornful judgment of this impulse toward the small things of the past as mere antiquarian interest. It is a respectable form of the lust for knowledge.

And it is also the proper sphere for the historical amateur, where he is indispensable. In no area is he so useful and welcome as in history, free as it is for everyone.

These considerations lead us back to one more antithesis that we have earlier met, but which has assumed threatening proportions now: that of the subjective and objective elements of the practice of history. In describing the nature of historical activity and knowledge, have we not attributed so much space to the subjective that the degree of certainty of historical knowledge has become quite dubious?

This degree of certainty must be thoroughly considered as the conclusion to this chapter.

Let us sum up what has already been said about the subjective element of all historical knowledge. It is always present, at work even in the posing of questions. Depending on the question, one thinks of different facts, makes different connections, different interpretations. Whenever connections are seen, they are based on a value attributed to things by the person thinking about them. Historical knowledge is dead and worthless that has not as its sounding-board and its measuring-rod the historian's personal intellectual and spiritual life.

The point is this: how far does personal evaluation control judgment and permit criticism? The more cherished one's personal view of life, the more passionately professed one's own ideas, the more historical judgment is likely to be led astray. A gentle slope leads from an unavoidably subjective approach to problems down to crass prejudice and partisanship.

Given these facts, how do we defend ourselves against a far-reaching scepticism that calls the whole pageant of history a "fable convenue," a shaky and worthless knowledge? Perhaps we can take comfort from history itself.

Historical scepticism, not to be equated with general philosophical scepticism, is an old disease. It is by no means a product of modern learning or of the critical method, neither did it spring from ancient Pyrrhonism. It seems to arise whenever a powerful new trend of thought forces a period to redefine its point of view with regard to history. Humanism brings with it such an access of scepticism, of which Vives and Agrippa of Nettesheim[2] are examples; the seventeenth century met it in Pierre Bayle and Fontenelle. Scepticism appears both in a more refined and a coarser form; the latter denies outright the authenticity of sources. Thus about 1700 the French Jesuit Jean Hardouin[3] pronounced the whole classical tradition, together with that of the early Middle Ages, deliberately falsified so as to injure Christianity. The more refined form of scepticism does not *a priori* deny the authenticity of sources, but denies the possibility that factual evidence, even that of contemporaries and eye-witnesses, can be correct. This is the substance of the story told of Sir Walter Raleigh, who watched a tumult in the courtyard of his prison and afterwards heard the affair described by the jailer who brought him food, and who then, troubled by the discrepancies between his own observation and that of another eye-witness, is said to have flung his newly-finished *History of the World* into the fire.

There is sufficient reason for doubt of this kind. We know

that psychology, especially in the service of the courts, amazingly confirms Raleigh's experience every day. If one stages a disturbance, planned in advance, in a lecture-hall and asks the eye-witnesses, each quite unaware that it is planned, to write down their versions of the affair, it turns out that their observations are hopelessly divergent. The conclusion is obvious: if the untrustworthiness of every witness' evidence can so easily be demonstrated in simple cases of everyday life, how far can we trust the indirect, often partisan, often embroidered accounts of the past?—The man who permits himself to be misled by this basic historical scepticism usually forgets the following: first, that modern critical historical scholarship does not by preference draw its information from deliberately biassed narrative sources but rather from direct survivals of the past, material or literary; and moreover, that its method has taught it to examine historical sources critically. Furthermore, the laboratory of the courtroom that demonstrated the limited value of each witness at the same time offers the counterproof. When the contradictory evidence was placed in the hands of an experienced judge, he was usually able to reconstruct the actual event, as previously recorded, from the faulty materials.

The following, too, must be noted. It is just the hypercritical historical scholar, the sceptic *par excellence,* who is usually forced into fantastic constructions for his own aberrant presentation of the facts; and who having started from critical doubt, thus ends up by falling into the profoundest credulity.

The strongest argument against historical scepticism, however, is this: the man who doubts the possibility of correct historical evidence and tradition cannot then accept his own evidence, judgment, combination and interpretation. He cannot limit his doubt to his historical criticism, but is required to let it operate on his own life. He discovers at once that he not only lacks conclusive evidence in all sorts of aspects of his own life that he had quite taken for granted, but also that there is no evidence whatever. In short, he finds himself forced to accept a general philosophical scepticism along with his historical scepticism. And general philosophical scepticism is a nice intellectual game, but one cannot live by it.

Here again history shows its relation to life itself. We live, we form opinions, we continually act on the basis of evidence —i.e., of clear appearances sufficient to convince. For history, too, evidence is the degree of certainty at its disposal. In accepting evidence, history is stricter than ordinary life, for its method permits taking very little on faith.

Reliance upon authentic documents, the comparative method, systematic criticism, have all decreased the danger of sceptical despondency. Careful observation, able to reject the false and unreliable on the basis of experience and comparison, raises the value and certainty of things proved true and correct. The trained historian feels sure enough in his use of criteria; only the untrained are inclined now to accept flagrantly false versions, now to reject the most authenticated. The critical historical faculty makes three demands: common sense, practice, and above all an historical sense, a high form of that discrimination by which a connoisseur knows a true work of art from a false one, knows one style from another.

In our time every educated person shares a certain historical discrimination. Everyone has some sense of the difference between periods, styles, cultures, can project himself at will into the atmosphere of Antiquity, of the Middle Ages, of the Renaissance, of the eighteenth century. To a high degree our spirit and our culture accommodate history. Historical thinking has entered our very blood.

6

ECONOMIC HISTORY:
Unwin and Clapham

[Although there had been occasional historians, A. H. L. Heeren, for example, or P. E. Levasseur or Thorold Rogers, who had dealt with the economic factors in history, the separate discipline of economic history did not gain institutional recognition until the end of the nineteenth century. It was not till 1892 that Harvard University appointed the English scholar, William James Ashley, to a chair in economic history, the first to have been established anywhere. After the turn of the century, with the growing availability of economic and demographic statistics and with the increasing awareness of the decisive influence of economic developments upon society, the study of economic history developed rapidly, particularly in France, England, and the United States.

George Unwin (1870-1925), the son of an English tradesman, studied philosophy and theology at Oxford, turning to economic history only after having completed his formal education. A moralist and a philosopher, he had a deep-rooted affection for England's common people, considering them and their autonomous organizations and spontaneous economic life the real agents of economic change. In this he broke with his continental colleagues who saw in the state the main source of economic development. After his *Industrial Organization in the Sixteenth and Seventeenth Centuries* (1904) appeared, he was appointed a lecturer on economic history at Edinburgh, and moved to the University of Manchester in

1910. The following selection, first published in 1924, suggests how much Unwin was concerned with teaching, which afforded him his greatest satisfaction.

Under the influence of Lord Acton and the economist Alfred Marshall, Sir John Clapham (1873-1946) began his study of the economic history of modern Europe. His reputation was established with the publication of *The Economic Development of France and Germany, 1815-1914* (1921) and his masterly *An Economic History of Modern Britain,* (3 vols. 1926-1938). In 1928 Cambridge University appointed him its first professor of economic history. With Eileen Power he planned the *Cambridge Economic History of Europe,* and after her death, became its editor.

The following selection first appeared in the *Encyclopedia of the Social Sciences* (1932).]

UNWIN: THE TEACHING OF ECONOMIC HISTORY IN UNIVERSITY TUTORIAL CLASSES

History is an account of the things that mattered most in the past, and it derives its chief interest from the assumption that those things were largely the causes of what matters to us now. And, if the things that matter most are the same now as then, the assumption seems natural. To Seeley, the British Empire is what matters most now—the central result of history. Looking back over the eighteenth century, he finds that "the great events are all foreign wars." These at first seem a chaotic imbroglio. But, if we steadily ignore much that seems to lead nowhere and much that leads in the opposite direction, we soon perceive a chain of historic causation leading to one great result, and thus History becomes a science and Imperialism a religion.

But, if what matters most to us now is not Empire, but class conflicts and the interests of Labour, we are driven to re-explore history, and to dig for these aspects of the past beneath the political surface, where we shall certainly find them. The stimulus of discovery and the discipline of a higher criticism combine to give "Industrial History" a high educational value, and they account for some of its popularity, but not for all. The deeper reason is to be found in the belief that, behind what seemed to matter most to the historians, we are getting at what really mattered most to most people in the past, and that these things are causally connected with what matters most to most people of today.

The economic interpretation of history thus claims to be at once scientific and religious.

I am glad to find that other tutors agree with me in rejecting this economic interpretation as inadequate, but the search for some scientific, religious or philosophic interpretation is what gives the strongest interest to our subject, and, even if we cannot fully direct it, we need not disown it. I find it best to meet this explicit attitude of faith with a *confessio fidei* of my own. I believe in the spiritual interpretation of history. I hold, that is to say, that the central and ultimate subject of history lies in the development of the inward possessions and experiences of men, through religion, art, literature, science, music, philosophy, but, above all, through the deepening and widening of ordinary social communications.

Social history in this full sense, though concerned with prime realities, is itself an ideal. Political history, as actually written, is concerned largely with illusions. Our task as scholars and teachers lies between the two. We have to build up the New Jerusalem with one hand and repair the old Jericho with the other. But where does economic history come in? I answer that it provides a foothold in actualities, and an approach on the right hand and on the left to the Jerusalem and Jericho of social and political history.

Social history should be concerned with Life, Truth and Beauty—with the energizing souls of men in community; and these are ends in themselves. Political history and economic history are concerned with means to social ends, and with the enormous abuse of those means perverted to such ends as power and wealth. They are largely a story of destruction and waste, disguised as constructive achievements till they end in unmistakable catastrophe, and counteracted by vitalizing social forces of which history as yet takes little or no account. The deeper causes of this ever-recurrent collapse of civilization are moral and social, but the immediate symptoms and clues to the pathological process are economic. "Great is bankruptcy," cries Carlyle, as he contemplates the end of the *ancien régime*. Professor Firth, in his account of Cromwell's finance, lays a more scientific finger on the same place. But a *post-mortem* autopsy is not enough; we need diagnosis of the patient at an earlier stage, and this the professed economic historian should supply. The story of taxation, direct and indirect, of the anticipation of revenue, of war debts and of the rise of a *rentier* class provides the main clue to the reactions of State policy upon western societies from the early days of the Italian republics till now. The best starting-point is given in Professor Sieveking's *Genueser Finanzwesen*.

The reactions of this fiscal pressure afford again the main clue to the development of the "mercantilist" policy, which the national monarchies borrowed from the Italian republics and the republics from the Byzantine emperors, and they in turn from the Ptolemies. The same causes stopped the growth of town industry all through western Europe, and explain the restrictive and static aspects of Tudor and Stuart social legislation and policy.

This is not "the economic interpretation of history." It is concerned almost wholly with negative and restrictive factors. But, in view of the obscurantist influences that have prevailed in the popular histories, this Higher Criticism may serve as a liberating and constructive force in tutorial class teaching.

So much for the critical approach which economic history furnishes to political history. The approach to social history is of a more directly constructive kind. Class conflict, which is a very real factor in history—Marx is more scientific than Seeley—and the class interests which account for most social legislation, are not constructive forces; but they are evidences of a creative evolution in communities, which is, I think, the central positive aspect of history. The economic historian finds what is, perhaps, his main task in the study of communities of life and kinship, of work and vocation, of property and enterprise, *on the side of their economic results*. Adequately to account for, or at any rate to formulate, the emergence of new forms of community, new social species, implied in the growing complexity and fluidity of class relations, is the chief task of social history, as of social science and of social philosophy. To those who distrust the *a priori* approach to these subjects, the discipline which we call economic history provides an *a posteriori* approach along the solid causeway of objective fact. Most economic historians are consciously or unconsciously social philosophers in the making, and a large proportion of the students in the classes of the Workers' Educational Association belong to the same category. To acknowledge the goal of a high calling, whilst insisting on respect for the facts, is the highest form of teaching, and one to which the University Tutorial Class is admirably adapted.

CLAPHAM: ECONOMIC HISTORY AS A DISCIPLINE

Economic history is a branch of general institutional history, a study of the economic aspects of the social institutions of the past. Its methodological distinctiveness hinges primarily upon its marked quantitative interests; for this reason it is or should be the most exact branch of history. But it is often difficult or even impossible to introduce quantitative treatment into the institutional study of the subject. Thus for all but the most modern period the absence of statistical material may make only very rough and uncertain quantitative treatment possible. Even such simple questions as the membership of guilds or early trade unions, the sizes of villages and towns and the ratio of wage earners to non-wage earners in industry at different dates often defy accurate answer.

It would not be difficult to give some simple aspects of institutional history a more quantitative and graphic treatment than they have generally received. Maps of England in 1300, 1400 and 1500, marking the principal towns at each date and indicating those which are known either to have had well developed craft guilds or not to have had them and those about which information is lacking, might prove most instructive. So might maps based on *Domesday* and the Hundred Rolls of Edward I, indicating those villages which appear to have coincided with the manor and those which do not. Such elementary quantitative statements, which could be made more easily for mediaeval England than for most countries because of the relative perfection of the English records, can, however, only touch the externals of institutions and illustrate the frequency of institutional types. In the study of institutional organization and function quantitative methods are usually inapplicable and the method of economic history differs in no way from that of history in general.

Should the records happen to be abundant, quantitative treatment of the economic aspect may become possible and very fruitful. *Domesday Book,* a tax book with some of the features of a census, is primarily an economic and only incidentally a legal and institutional record. From the "valets" of *Domesday* an almost exact "business" statement has been worked out (see Corbett, in *Cambridge Medieval History,* vol. V, ch. XV) of how William of Normandy assigned the shares of England, taken over as a going concern. It was to the abundant business records of English landowners (bailiffs' accounts, etc.) that the quantitative method in mediaeval history was first applied on a large scale by Thorold Rogers; it provided series of price, wage, crop yield and other statistics over long periods. The quantitative method is still being applied and the records have still much to furnish. For some countries, e.g. Spain, the comprehensive study of price records has only recently begun.

For handling the records of the economic history of the ancient, mediaeval and early modern world the necessary training is mainly that of the general historian—the linguistic, epigraphic and palaeographic knowledge appropriate to the age and country studied. For the ancient world epigraphic knowledge is particularly important because the literary sources contain little precise economic information. It is only to the study of the most recent history, that of the last century and a quarter and particularly of the last half century— the age of census and other official statistics—that methods requiring any but the most simple statistical knowledge can profitably be applied. But the study of price history for any period for which records are reasonably abundant, i.e., for any period since the twelfth century, requires familiarity with contemporary methods of price inquiry and with the elementary principles of index numbers. For the most recent period a fairly complete statistical equipment is necessary, because the abundance and variety of the statistical material permit the application of some of the more refined statistical methods. This work tends therefore to fall into the hands of the inductive economist, who is only secondarily a historian.

Every economic historian should, however, have acquired what might be called the statistical sense, the habit of asking in relation to any institution, policy, group or movement the questions: how large? how long? how often? how representative? The requirement seems obvious; but a good deal of the older politico-institutional economic history was less useful than it might have been through neglect of it. The latifundia were not so representative of Roman economic life in the early part of the first century B.C. as historians once supposed. Many theories of urban origins which have found support among continental scholars break on the question "how representative." The manorial map of England might put the manor village in its proper place. The political importance that has sometimes been assigned to the English trading companies of the sixteenth century has been greater than is warranted by their economic importance as understood at present. American scholarship has reduced the economic hardships inflicted by the old colonial system to their proper and rather limited size. Many accounts of the industrial revolution in Great Britain would hardly suggest that in 1830 only one person in eighty worked in a cotton mill: they omit to state clearly "how many."

Neglect of the question "how representative?" vitiates most of the schemes, made particularly by German scholars, for scheduling states in economic development. Such schemes besides concealing the variety of history may confuse logical with temporal succession. The most general of them was that of Bruno Hildebrand, which postulated the sequence of natural economy, money economy and credit economy (*"Natural-, Geld- und Kreditwirtschaft"* in *Jahrbücher für Nationalökonomie und Statistik,* vol. II, 1864, pp. 1-24). Its drawback when applied to history has been that the labeling of an age as one of natural economy may easily lead to neglect of evidence for the coexistence of other types of economy. Thus prolonged research and controversy have been required to establish the fact that the early Middle Ages in northern Europe were not ages of pure natural economy. Moreover, the term natural economy may cover both exceedingly simple and very complex economic systems. Exchange in ancient Egypt was predominantly that of goods for goods; but Egyptian civilization had little in common with that of primitive Germany or of primitive modern societies in which money is unknown. And since, except in prehistoric and in the earliest historic times, money using and non-money using societies have always existed side by side, since remnants of natural economy have long survived and still survive in money using communities, and since credit in some form appears at a very early stage in most civilizations and never completely dominates any, the assignment of a particular age or even of a particular society in that age to one or other of the stages becomes a delicate problem of fact and of degree scarcely worth attempting.

Similar but more destructive criticism applies to the stage scheme of Karl Bücher (*Die Entstehung der Volkswirtschaft,* 1893), based on that of Schönberg of 1867 (*"Zur wirtschaftlichen Bedeutung des deutschen Zunftwesens im Mittelalter"* in *Jahrbücher für Nationalökonomie und Statistik,* vol. IX, pp. 1-72, 97-169), with its succession of self-sufficient domestic economy, in which there is no exchange but every household meets all its own needs; town economy, in which the goods pass directly from producer to consumer and from countryman to townsman; and national economy, in which intermediaries between producer and consumer appear.

Bücher claimed that the whole course of economic development, at least for the peoples of central and western Europe, could be brought under this scheme. But it most certainly cannot. It is impossible to distinguish such stages with precision in the history of those peoples; and the first two are arbitrary conceptions not corresponding to any known group of historical facts, although it is easy to find places and periods in which most households have been comparatively self-sufficing or in which the simple intercourse between small towns and the surrounding country has been dominant. Although stage schemes have furnished convenient categories for the classification of economic phenomena and have provided scholars with Max Weber's "ideal types" with which the varied reality may be contrasted, they have done more harm than good to the study of economic history. They may be specially harmful when history is being summarized for the use of students.

The inevitable breaking up of economic history into periods for convenience of study and teaching has some of the dangers of the stage schemes, if period and stage are unduly identified or if the period specialist loses perspective through relative ignorance of what went before and came after the age of his choice and so is unable to select for special attention those of its features which are of the greatest general significance. These are the ordinary dangers of historical periodization and specialism. The tendency of economic history to take over ready made the conventional divisions of general history has at times produced unfortunate results but need not do so. Clear dividing lines purely economic in character do not exist or at least have not yet been generally agreed upon. If periods are recognized as simply slices of time, within which some particular economic phenomenon—slavery, economic feudalism, early capitalism, corporate capitalism—may be of special importance but not necessarily to the exclusion of phenomena of other types, their study has no serious drawback. It is, however, probably even more important in economic than in other branches of history that period study should be associated with adequate study of the contemporary world, the *terminus ad quem.*

Stage schemes in economic history were devised mostly by members of the German historical school of economists, who attempted to substitute, as it were, historical generalization for economic theory. Most scholars are now agreed that such an attempt failed even in the hands of Schmoller. The central problems of economic theory, although they may be stated in terms of some particular historic phase, are in essence independent of history. In theoretical discussion it is necessary to isolate forces and factors in a way which history does not permit. Even more important than this independence and the necessity for abstraction is the fact that the absence from all history, except that of the latest statistical age, of enough trustworthy sequences of ascertained facts makes impossible the exact treatment at which theoretical inductive economics aims. Even the statistical age has not yet supplied nearly enough tested sequences of facts for the economist's needs, and the necessarily defective historical record will scarcely satisfy him. For example, there can be no exact discussion of English unemployment before 1886, when certain trade union statistics were first issued. There are countries in which such exact discussion is hardly possible even yet. Generalizations about the unemployment complained of in Shakespeare's *Henry VIII* (act i, scene 2) or even about that in Lancashire at the time of the American Civil War will give the contemporary economist little help. The historian recognizes that except in price history and other quantitative sections of his work his results will be on a lower plane of truth than that to which the fully equipped inductive economist may conceivably attain. It remains true, however, that some parts of economic theory, such as the succession of industrial types, the evolution of money and the problem of population, are or purport to be generalizations from history.

The relation of economic history to social history is much closer. It is true that with certain aspects of social history the economist as such is not concerned, unless he is in a position to trace the play of economic forces upon them. For example, his interest in costumes, manners, recreation and non-economic ideals may be limited only to such aspects as the clothing of India in Lancashire cotton, the aping of the millionaire, the professionalizing of games and the commercializing of ideals. But as the main concerns of society are and always have been economic, by far the greater part of social history, it may be argued, is simply economic history. As a critic of particular social histories the economist's main question will tend to be "is this representative?" The social historian may with fairness reply to such criticism that he deliberately studies society at leisure with more care than society at work, because in the spiritual history of mankind the important matter is the use made of time saved from the plow or the machine. To this there is no conclusive rejoinder; but plow and machine remain important and representative. The economic historian, on his side, can hardly afford to be ignorant either of non-economic social history or of general history. If he is, he will almost certainly mistake the importance of the economic factor in any group of historical factors. It is unfortunate that the progress of specialization tends to increase rather than reduce this risk.

The links between economic history and human geography as now studied are similarly close. Although in the strict statistical or institutional treatment of economico-historical problems, geographical considerations may be irrelevant, they obviously are relevant to the wider economic history which would trace the evolution of societies getting their living in particular environments and altering those environments in the process. How far and in how much detail geographical description should be introduced into economic histories depends on the scale of the work and the amount of knowledge which may reasonably be expected of the typical reader. The geographer must describe; the historian may often assume. But it should be said that economic history as hitherto written has much more often suffered from neglect not merely of geographical description but even of essential geographical considerations than it has erred by incorporating too much geography. It would be easy to cite agrarian histories which almost ignore climate and soil. The modern school of anthropogeographers, on the other hand, makes full use of the conclusions of economic history and sometimes even writes it, although with a geographical bias (e.g. Brunhes and Deffontaines' *Géographie humaine de la France*, 2 vols., 1920-26). It is much to be desired that there should be a closer union between the two studies. The inevitable overlap at this or any other margin is not dangerous: it is at the overlapping margins of disciplines and sciences that the most important discoveries are usually made.

7

HISTORICAL RELATIVISM:
Beard

[Versatile, prolific, and creatively unconventional, Charles A. Beard (1874-1948) had a great influence on the American historiography of this century. In his early years a student of European history—his first book *The Industrial Revolution* appeared in England in 1901—he maintained his interest in European thought after he shifted to American history. There he became a pioneer in the analysis of the economic roots of political behavior—and his works *An Economic Interpretation of the Constitution of the United States* (1913) and *Economic Origins of Jeffersonian Democracy* (1915) created a great, and on the whole salutary, stir among historians and laymen alike. Deeply concerned with the problems of the present, and devotedly democratic, Beard saw in history a means of democratic education, and his massive, highly successful survey, *The Rise of American Civilization* (2 vols. 1927, written with Mary R. Beard) opens with the characteristic sentence: "The history of a civilization, if intelligently conceived, may be an instrument of civilization." Many of his forty-seven books enjoyed great popularity and it has been estimated that eleven million copies of them have been sold in various countries. Throughout his life, Beard dealt with the general questions of historiography and particularly with the relation of history to the social sciences; in the 1930's he became more particularly concerned with the philosophic foundations of historical knowledge, and under the influence of Croce, Mannheim, and Heussi, formulated a relativistic position which was most fully stated in the essay "That Noble Dream" (1935), reprinted below, without Beard's footnotes. Beard's thought came to be accepted by a great many American historians of the last twenty years.]

THAT NOBLE DREAM

In a thought-provoking paper read at the last meeting of the American Historical Association Mr. Theodore Clarke Smith [1] laid his colleagues under a deep obligation. His essay is not only significant for its intrinsic merits; it indicates an interest in problems of historiography that have been long neglected. If it had been merely expository, it might well be accepted without further analysis as opening the way for an extension of thought along the same lines. But it is in spirit and declaration challenging as well as descriptive, monitory as well as narrative. Mr. Smith makes a division between scholars affiliated with the Association. He insists that they must be, broadly speaking, grouped under two banners and that there is a gulf between them which cannot be bridged. One group, with which he ranges himself, had "a noble dream," and produced sound, creditable, and in many cases masterly works on American history. Although he does not say that the opposition is ignoble, unsound, discreditable, and weak, that implication lurks in the dichotomy which he makes.

The issues presented by Mr. Smith transcend personalities and call for the most thoughtful consideration that the intelligence of the Association can bring to bear upon them. Is there in fact a deep-seated division in the Association? Has a battle line been drawn in such a fashion that members must align themselves on the one side or the other? Is it impossible to find a synthesis that will reconcile apparent contradictions or suggest a suspension of judgment, at least for the time being? Are the facts employed by Mr. Smith to illustrate his thesis so precisely accurate in every case as to be beyond amendment in a quest for "objective truth"? Surely these questions are of more than passing importance. They concern the young members of the Association and the fate of the society. They invite us to stop for a moment to review the assumptions on which historical work is to be done in the future; and perhaps answers to them may reveal some overarching hypothesis or suggest a healing diffidence, at least.

The division which Mr. Smith makes in the Association seems to be positive and sharp. On the one side are the scholars who have made "the impressive output of sound, creditable, and in many cases masterly, works on American history during the period under review" [1884-1934]. The works of this class of scholars "are dominated, from monograph to many-volumed work, by one clear-cut ideal—that presented to the world first in Germany and later accepted everywhere, the ideal of the effort for objective truth." Theirs was "a noble dream," now threatened with extinction, and the hope is expressed that members of this school may go down, if necessary, "with our flags flying." "In that case, it will be time for the American Historical Association to disband, for the intellectual assumptions on which it is founded will have been taken away from beneath it." Here then is a clear-cut ideal, a noble dream, and the American Historical Association was "founded" on it. And who are the men who threaten this ideal, dream, and Association? They are writers who do not "consider it necessary to be impartial or even fair." They are partial and doctrinaire. Especially doctrinaire are those who resort to an economic interpretation of history. Among the menaces to the old and true faith, mentioned by Mr. Smith, is James Harvey Robinson who once flatly declared that what is called "objective history" is simply history without an object, and proposed that historical knowledge be used to throw light on "the quandaries of our life today"—to facilitate "readjustment and reform." Here are the contending parties of light and darkness.

The dichotomy so presented seems to involve ideal, method, and belief in the possibility of achievement. Scholars of the Old Guard desired above all things to search for "objective truth." Were the men whom Mr. Smith puts on the other side of the fence opposed to the ideal of the search for truth? Is the scholar who seeks knowledge useful to contemporaries wrestling with "the quandaries of our life today" unconcerned about the truth of that knowledge? His end may be different but surely he does not seek falsehood or believe that false history can be serviceable to the cause posited. Nor can it be said that the student who tries to penetrate the pageant of politics to the economic interest behind the scenes is necessarily hostile to the ideal of the search for truth. Conceivably he might be as much interested in truth as the scholar who ignores or neglects the economic aspects of history. As far as method goes, those scholars who are placed in opposition to the noble dream may be as patient in their inquiries and as rigorous in their criticism and use of documentation as the old masters of light and leading. In intentions and methods, therefore, no necessary antagonism appears to arise.

Now we come to achievement—to the possibility of finding and stating the objective truth of history. Here we encounter something more difficult to fathom than intentions or methods. We encounter questions which run deeply into the nature of the human mind, the substance of history as actuality, and the power of scholarship to grasp history objectively. Beyond doubt, scholars of competence can agree on many particular truths and on large bodies of established facts. But is it possible for men to divest themselves of all race, sex, class, political, social, and regional predilections and tell the truth of history as it actually was? Can Mr. Smith's noble dream, his splendid hope, be realized in fact? That is the fundamental issue at stake.

This theory that history as it actually was can be disclosed by critical study, can be known as objective truth, and can be stated as such, contains certain elements and assumptions. The first is that history (general or of any period) has existed as an object or series of objects outside the mind of the historian (a *Gegenüber* separated from him and changing in time). The second is that the historian can face and know this object or series of objects and can describe it as it objectively existed. The third is that the historian can, at least for the purposes of research and writings, divest himself of all taint of religious, political, philosophical, social, sex, economic, moral, and aesthetic interests, and view this *Gegenüber* with strict impartiality, somewhat as the mirror reflects any object to which it is held up. The fourth is that the multitudinous events of history as actuality had some structural organization through inner (perhaps causal) relations, which the impartial historian can grasp by inquiry and observation and accurately reproduce or describe in written history. The fifth is that the substances of this history can be grasped in themselves by purely rational or intellectual efforts, and that they are not permeated by or accompanied by anything transcendent— God, spirit, or materialism. To be sure the theory of objective history is not often so fully stated, but such are the nature and implications of it.

This theory of history and of human powers is one of the most sweeping dogmas in the recorded history of theories. It condemns philosophy and throws it out of doors. As practiced, it ignores problems of mind with which philosophers and theologians have wrestled for centuries and have not yet set-

tled to everybody's satisfaction. As developed into Historicism (it may be well to Anglicize *Historismus*), it takes on
all the implications of empiricism, positivism, and, if not materialism, at least that rationalism which limits history to its
purely experiential aspects. If sound and appealing, it is
nonetheless an all-embracing philosophy of historiography,
even though it denies philosophy.

Although Ranke contributed powerfully to the growth of
this historical theory, and claimed to be writing history as it
actually had been, he did not in fact follow the logic of his
procedure to its empirical conclusion. He opposed the philosophic method of Hegel—that powerful thinker who boldly
attempted to grasp the scheme entire—and at the same time
Ranke conceived history as, in some strange manner, "a revelation of God." But he did not openly employ this belief in
selecting and arranging "objectively" the facts of history as it
actually had been. He did not think that man could know
God as history, but he imagined that man could see "God's
finger" in human affairs and dimly grasp God's handiwork in
history. In history, as Ranke conceived it, God stood there,
"wie eine heilige Hieroglyphe, an seinem Aeussersten aufge-
fasst und bewahrt." [2] History was "der Gang Gottes in der
Welt." [3] In the true spirit of Lutheran piety, Ranke flung
himself down before the impenetrable mystery of things:
"Allgewaltiger, Einer und Dreifaltiger, du hast mich aus dem
Nichts gerufen. Hier liege ich vor deines Thrones Stufen." [4]
Yet he fain would write history, so enclosed in mystery, as it
actually had been, impartially, from the critical study of written documents. He rejected philosophy, proclaimed positive
history, and still was controlled by a kind of *Pantheismus.*

Ranke could write history, certainly, with a majestic air of
impartiality and say that he had written as it actually had
been. For example, he could write of popes in a manner pleas-
ing to both Catholics and Protestants of the upper classes. He
doubtless believed that he was telling this history of the
popes as it actually had been. Did he realize his claim? There
is stark validity in the Jesuit objection that Ranke avoided
the chief actuality of the story: Was the papacy actually what
it affirmed itself to be, "an institution of the Son of God made
man," or was it a combination of false claims, craft, and man-
made power? How could Ranke avoid that question and yet
even claim to be writing history as it actually was?

I make no pretensions to knowing Ranke as he actually was
or his motives in writing the kind of history he chose to write.
But records are available to establish the fact that he did not

abstain entirely from those hot political controversies which are supposed to warp the pure thought of the empirical historian. In directing the *Historisch-Politische Zeitschrift* he chose a way between French constitutionalism and that extreme Prussian conservatism which would yield not a point to democratic aspirations. After the July Revolution Ranke favored a confederate law against the political press and political literature—a proposition that must have pleased Metternich and Gentz, who opened their archives to him. After the March upheaval of 1848 Ranke came vigorously to the support of Frederick William IV in resistance to popular demands for a constitution based on democratic principles. On this occasion the "impartial" historian proved to be a bulwark for Prussian authoritarianism—against which so many "impartial" historians in the United States wrote vigorously in 1917-1918. Ranke also rejoiced in the events of 1870-1871 "as the victory of conservative Europe over the Revolution," showing that he could not completely separate his political from his historical conceptions. Persistently neglecting social and economic interests in history, successfully avoiding any historical writing that offended the most conservative interests in the Europe of his own time, Ranke may be correctly characterized as one of the most "partial" historians produced by the nineteenth century.

Whether Ranke was fully conscious of what he was doing himself, he was able to see that other historians were writing from some angle of vision. He once said to George Bancroft: "I tell my hearers, that your history is the best book ever written from the democratic point of view. You are thoroughly consistent; adhere strictly to your method, carry it out in many directions but in all with fidelity, and are always true to it." In making his statement, Ranke expressed the hope that it would not make Bancroft angry. Bancroft was not certain that this was "high praise." Shortly afterward he declared: "I deny the charge; if there is democracy in history it is not subjective, but objective as they say here, and so has necessarily its place in history and gives its colour as it should. . . ." Is it possible that Ranke, who was quick to discover subjective ideas in Bancroft's writings, was totally unaware of the fact that he might be writing from the point of view of the conservative reaction in Europe? If he never applied the criterion to himself, then he was doubly "partial" and utterly devoid of any sense for reality and humor.

If, as Mr. Smith says, the "objective" method of Ranke and his school was "accepted everywhere," it is due to history as it was to record that the conception was subjected all along to a running fire of criticism by German historians, even by those "von Fach." Leaving aside the penetrating skepticism of Schopenhauer (who certainly was no mean thinker) and the critique of Eugen Dühring, we find searching examinations of the theory and logic of Historicism by German scholars in the early issues of the *Historische Zeitschrift,* and in the writings of Droysen, Ottokar Lorenz,[5] Bernheim,[6] and Lamprecht,[7] for instance. There were not wanting at that time historians "die in naiver, selbstgewisser Technik ihre Historie trieben, ohne zu ahnen, an welchen theoretischen Abgründen sie sich bewegten," [8] but many German scholars early went behind Ranke's formula and challenged its validity. They did this long before a host of critical thinkers fell upon it during the opening years of the twentieth century.

And if the Ranke formula or theory of history was accepted in the United States by members of the American Historical Association, as Mr. Smith states, it is not quite in line with the facts in the case to say that it was "everywhere" accepted. Was it in reality adopted as the official creed of the Association in the good old days before ignoble, doctrinaire, and partial students appeared upon the scene? Surely the creed was never drawn up and signed by all faithful members. Whether the majority were acquainted with the philosophical discussion that had long raged around it and threw themselves positively on the Ranke side seems to be a statistical problem not yet solved. Hence judgment should be suspended.

Pending the determination of this historical fact by research, one item in the story may be cited—the presidential address delivered at the opening session of the American Historical Association in 1884 by Andrew D. White. Ranke was yet living. Did Mr. White commit himself or the Association to Historicism or the Ranke formula? Emphatically, he did not, as any member can discover by reading again that noteworthy address. In fact Mr. White, with mature wisdom, recognized both sides of the problem of historiography: the special, the detailed, the verified, the documented—and the philosophical. He said categorically: "While acknowledging the great value of special investigations . . . to historical knowledge in individual nations, it is not too much to say that the highest effort and the noblest result toward which these special historical investigations lead is the philosophical synthesis of all special results in a large, truth-loving, justice-loving spirit."

"Bearing on this point, Buckle, in a passage well worthy of

meditation, has placed *observation* at the foot of the ladder, *discovery* next above it, and *philosophical method* at the summit." In this spirit Mr. White declared that at the annual meetings of the Association there ought to be a session or sessions dealing with special studies, and also a session or sessions "devoted to general history, the history of civilization, and the philosophy of history." He recognized the dangers of the latter—"looseness and vagueness"—but thought that the consideration of both aspects of history would contribute to a sounder development of each. "These difficulties," Mr. White warned us, "the Association must meet as they arise."

Nor did the first President, Andrew D. White, see in the use of history as an instrument of "social control" the perils to scholarship lamented by Mr. Smith. On the contrary, Mr. White closed with an exordium in line with the thought later expressed by James Harvey Robinson, whose ideal Mr. Smith puts on the other side of the fence from "a noble dream." Mr. White proposed no neutral, value-free history. "Certainly," he said near the close of his address, "a confederation like this— of historical scholars . . . ought to elicit most valuable work in both fields [special and philosophical], and to contribute powerfully to the healthful development on the one hand of man as man, and on the other to the opening up of a better political and social future for the nation at large." This is asking historians to do what James Harvey Robinson suggested: bring historical knowledge to bear "on the quandaries of our life today."

Henry Adams was also once President of the American Historical Association. He cannot be placed among those who have recently invaded the circle of the pure faith and threatened to destroy the Association by "the final extinction of a noble dream," driving Mr. Smith and his adherents to consider the frightful alternative of going down "with our flags flying." Did Henry Adams limit the function and thought of the historian to Historicism, the Ranke formula, or neutrality in the face of life's exigent forces? Members who care to know before they take sides in a discussion of the theory of history must read the letter which Henry Adams, as President of the Association, wrote to his colleagues as long ago as 1894. There he invited the members to consider what a science of history would look like and the devastating challenge which it would make to the church, state, property, or labor. Mr. Adams, with amazing foresight, predicted a crisis in Western economy and thought, and warned his colleagues that they "may at any time in the next five years be compelled to find an answer, 'Yes' or 'No,' under the pressure of the most powerful organizations the world has ever known for the suppression of influences hostile to its safety."

One more colleague may be mentioned. Mr. Smith has referred to H. L. Osgood [9] as holding to the "high ideals" of the school which now seems to be threatened by doctrinaire writers. Mr. Osgood was, as Mr. Smith says, expository, analytical, and for the most part impersonal. Did Mr. Osgood imagine himself to be writing history as it actually was? His ambition was more limited. He sought to tell the truth, as best he could, about certain aspects of history. Did he imagine himself to stand outside the *Zeitgeist?* Not for a moment. Mr. Osgood had been one of my masters, and shortly after I presented him with a copy of my *Economic Interpretation of the Constitution* I asked him whether it offended him or appeared to be *ultra vires?* His response was positive. He said in effect: "Men of my generation grew up in the midst of great constitutional and institutional debates and our interest turned to institutional history. Profound economic questions have now arisen and students of the younger generation, true to their age, will occupy themselves with economic aspects of history." Far from deeming this interest reprehensible, Mr. Osgood regarded it as "natural" and proper. Near the end of his life he spoke to me of the heavy hand of time that lies upon all our work, dating us, revealing our limitations.

How many other members of the older generation did in fact think their way through the assumptions and convictions enclosed in Mr. Smith's "noble dream" and accept it whole heartedly? The data for answering that question are not at hand. How many watched carefully the development of the critical attitude toward Historicism in Europe at the turn of the century, and especially after 1914? Materials for answering that query are not available either. Judging by the files of the *American Historical Review* and the programs of annual meetings such philosophical issues have received scant consideration, little exploration and examination. Judging by the writings of American historians slight attention has been given to the intellectual problems involved in the choice of subjects, the selection of facts, and the construction of monographs and many-volumed works. If there has been any real searching of historical minds and hearts in the United States, any fearless and wide-reaching inquiry into preliminary assumptions, tacit or deliberate, any procedure save on the level of ingenuous convictions, historical literature bears only a few evidences of its fruits. If engines of skepticism and verification have been mercilessly applied to what passes for constructive thought, as distinguished from eclecticism and documentation, news of the fact has not spread far and wide enough in the American Historical Association to make a profound impression upon its proceedings. Some countervailing evidence may be cited, no doubt, but the exceptions would seem merely to prove the rule. It may be that the major portion of American scholars in the good old days imagined that they could discover and know the objective truth of history as it actually was, but there is good reason for thinking that a large number of them did not labor under that impression respecting their activities and powers.

Having indicated some grounds for holding that Historicism is not and never has been "accepted everywhere" as the official creed of the American Historical Association, it is now appropriate to inquire whether the Ranke formula is valid in itself. Can the human mind discover and state the "objective truth" of history as it actually was? Space does not admit even a brief summation of the voluminous literature dealing with this conception and demonstrating, if not its delusive character, its rejection by scholars and thinkers of high competence in Europe. Those American students who care to examine the history and nature of the European revolt against Historicism may find guidance in Croce, *History: its Theory and Practice*, in Heussi, *Die Krisis des Historismus*, and in the numerous works cited by Heussi as supporting evidence. In these volumes is presented the development of historical thought which culminated in the rejection of the Ranke theory and its formulation as Historicism.

At this point only a bare outline of the argument is possible, but it may be given, very inadequately, in the following propositions:

1. The idea that history took place in the past as actuality outside the mind of the contemporary historian is accepted as the commonsense view.

2. The historian is not an observer of the past that lies beyond his own time. He cannot see it *objectively* as the chemist sees his test tubes and compounds. The historian must "see" the actuality of history through the medium of documentation. That is his sole recourse.

3. The documentation (including monuments and other relics) with which the historian must work covers only a part of the events and personalities that make up the actuality of history. In other words multitudinous events and personalities escape the recording of documentation. To realize the signifi-

cance of this, as Heussi says, it is only necessary to consider an effort to describe the battle of Leipzig alone, to say nothing of the Napoleonic wars or the history of the Roman Empire.

4. Not only is the documentation partial. In very few cases can the historian be reasonably sure that he has assembled all the documents of a given period, region, or segment. In most cases he makes a partial selection or a partial reading of the partial record of the multitudinous events and personalities involved in the actuality with which he is dealing.

5. Since the history of any period embraces all the actualities involved, and since both documentation and research are partial, it follows that the total actuality is not factually knowable to any historian, however laborious, judicial, or faithful he may be in his procedures. History as it actually was, as distinguished, of course from particular facts of history, is not known or knowable, no matter how zealously is pursued "the ideal of the effort for objective truth."

6. The idea that there was a complete and actual structurization of events in the past, to be discovered through a partial examination of the partial documentation, is pure hypothesis, as Th. Lessing shows in his *Geschichte als Sinngebung des Sinnlosen.*

7. The events and personalities of history in their very nature involve ethical and aesthetic considerations. They are not mere events in physics and chemistry inviting neutrality on the part of the "observer."

8. Any overarching hypothesis or conception employed to give coherence and structure to past events in written history is an interpretation of some kind, something transcendent. And as Croce says, "transcendency is always transcendency, whether it be thought of as that of a God or of reason, of nature, or of matter."

9. The historian seeking to know the past, or about it, does not bring to the partial documentation with which he works a perfect and polished neutral mind in which the past streaming through the medium of documentation is mirrored as it actually was. Whatever acts of purification the historian may perform he yet remains human, a creature of time, place, circumstance, interests, predilections, culture. No amount of renunciation could have made Andrew D. White into a Frederick Jackson Turner or either of them into a neutral mirror.

10. Into the selection of topics, the choice and arrangement of materials, the specific historian's "me" will enter. It may enter with a conscious clarification of philosophy and

purpose or, as Croce says, surreptitiously, without confession or acknowledgment.

11. The validity of the Ranke formula and its elaboration as Historicism is destroyed by internal contradictions and rejected by contemporary thought. The historian's powers are limited. He may search for, but he cannot find, the "objective truth" of history, or write it, "as it actually was."

Now we come to the validity of an antithesis of the Ranke formula—the economic interpretation of history. Is it partial, in the sense that it does not cover all the events of history? It certainly is. Surely none will contend that it could be otherwise than partial in its scope. Is it "the correct" interpretation of history? If the word interpretation is taken to mean "explanation," then neither it nor any other historical hypothesis can be regarded as valid and final, on the ground that in the nature of things—documentation and the human mind—the past as it actually was cannot be known. If the word be taken, however, in a manner equally admissible under linguistic usage, to mean simply the writer's version, construction, or conception of his subjects, then an economic interpretation is merely what it professes to be—a version, not the absolute truth, of history.

Seekers after truth in particular and general have less reason to fear it than they have to fear any history that comes under the guise of the Ranke formula or Historicism. It bears its own warning. A book entitled *An Economic Interpretation of the Constitution*, like every other book on history, is a selection and an organization of facts; but it serves advance notice on the reader, telling him what to expect. A book entitled *The Formation of the Constitution* or *The Making of the Constitution* is also a selection and organization of facts, hence an interpretation or conception of some kind, but it does not advise the reader at the outset concerning the upshot to be expected.

Does an economic interpretation, open and avowed, violate the "ideal of the effort for objective truth"? Not necessarily. The historian who searches out and orders economic aspects of life, events, and interests may possibly be as zealous in his search for truth as any other historian searching out and ordering facts in his way. Is the student who seeks an economic interpretation more partial, in the sense of partisanship, or more doctrinaire than the historian, who assumes that he can know the past as it actually has been? Not necessarily. He may conceivably view the structure of classes, their ideologies, formulas, projects, and conflicts as coldly and impartially as any disciple of Ranke that the American Historical Association has furnished.

Did the economic interpretation of history, as Mr. Smith alleges, have "its origin, of course, in the Marxian theories"? I cannot speak for others, but so far as I am concerned, my conception of the economic interpretation of history rests upon documentation older than Karl Marx—Number X of the *Federalist,* the writings of the Fathers of the Republic, the works of Daniel Webster, the treatises of Locke, Hobbes, and Machiavelli, and the *Politics* of Aristotle—as well as the writings of Marx himself.

Yet I freely pay tribute to the amazing range of Marx's scholarship and the penetrating character of his thought. It may be appropriate to remind those who may be inclined to treat Marx as a mere revolutionary or hot partisan that he was more than that. He was a doctor of philosophy from a German university, possessing the hallmark of the scholar. He was a student of Greek and Latin learning. He read, besides German, his native tongue, Greek, Latin, French, English, Italian, and Russian. He was widely read in contemporary history and economic thought. Hence, however much one may dislike Marx's personal views, one cannot deny to him wide and deep knowledge—and a fearless and sacrificial life. He not only interpreted history, as everyone does who writes any history, but he helped to make history. Possibly he may have known something. At least the contemporary student, trying to look coldly and impartially on thought and thinkers in the field of historiography, may learn a little bit, at least from Karl Marx.

But that does not mean that any economic interpretation of history must be used for the purposes which Marx set before himself. It may well be used for opposite purposes. It has been. It may be again. Or it may be employed as the basis for impartiality and inaction on the ground that a conflict of mere material interests cannot be a matter of concern to virtue itself. In other words there is nothing in the nature of an economic interpretation of history that compels the interpreter to take any partisan or doctrinaire view of the struggle of interests. In fact such an interpretation of the Constitution is less liable to invite a surge of feeling than Mr. Smith's interpretation that the formation and adoption of the Constitution was "a contest between sections ending in the victory of straight-thinking national-minded men over narrower and more local opponents." An economic interpretation does not inquire whether men were straight-thinking or crooked-thinking. It inquires not into their powers of mind or virtues, but into the nature and effects of their substantial possessions. Nor is it necessarily in conflict with Mr. Smith's conclusions. It pushes the inquiry one step further than he does. It asks how it happened that some men were national-minded and others were local-minded, and perhaps throws some light upon the subject.

What conclusions, then, may be drawn from this excursion, hurried and cursory, into historiography, for members of the American Historical Association? In my opinion, they are as follows: The formula of Ranke and its extension as Historicism do not and have never formed an official creed for the Association. From Andrew D. White down to the present moment there have been members who have believed that the wider and deeper philosophic questions involved in the interpretation of history should be considered as having an importance equal to, if not greater than, the consideration of documentation, special studies, and writings done on the assumption that history "wie es eigentlich gewesen ist" can be known and expounded by historians. The Ranke formula and Historicism are not the official creed of the Association and ought not to be, for they now lie amid the ruins of their own defeat. Nor are the other creeds placed in antithesis to the "noble dream" by Mr. Smith deemed official. They should not be. No school that makes pretensions to exclusive omniscience or exclusive virtue, that claims to know history as it actually was can long escape the corroding skepticism that search and thought bring to it. It is undesirable to invite the Association to split over two absolutes. It is not necessary for any member, fraction, or group, however large or small, to feel that a war to the hilt is on and that the one or the other must go down with, or without, "flying colors."

The task before the American Historical Association seems to be something other than that of deepening a division artificially made. The collection, preservation, and publication of archives must be carried on with ever increasing zeal. All the engines of criticism, authentication, and verification, so vigorously used by the German school, must be employed with all the powers of intelligence available. Monographic studies must be promoted. But this is not enough.

The philosophic side of historiography, as Andrew D. White warned the Association, must also receive the consideration required for all constructive work in historical writing. The effort to grasp at the totality of history must and will be continued, even though the dream of bringing it to earth must be abandoned. This means a widening of the range of search beyond politics to include interests hitherto neglected—economic, racial, sex, and cultural in the most general sense of the term. Certainly by this broadening process the scholar will come nearer to the actuality of history as it has been. The distinction between particular facts that may be established by the scientific method and the "objective" truth of history must be maintained, if illusions are to be dispelled.

Still more pressing, because so generally neglected, is the task of exploring the assumptions upon which the selection and organization of historical facts proceed. In the nature of things they proceed upon some assumptions concerning the substance of history as actuality. We do not acquire the colorless, neutral mind by declaring our intention to do so. Rather do we clarify the mind by admitting its cultural interests and patterns—interests and patterns that will control, or intrude upon, the selection and organization of historical materials. Under what formulas is it possible to conceive history? What types of controlling patterns are to be found in the declarations of historical writers, in the diverse opinions of the world at large, and in the works of historians already before us? Instead of waging a war, followed by victory or defeat, we need to provide for the Association's annual meetings a section or sections dealing with the assumptions and procedures of historiography. What do we think we are doing when we are writing history? What kinds of philosophies or interpretations are open to us? Which interpretations are actually chosen and practiced? And why? By what methods or processes can we hope to bring the multitudinous and bewildering facts of history into any coherent and meaningful whole? Through the discussion of such questions the noble dream of the search for truth may be brought nearer to realization, not extinguished; but in the end the members of the American Historical Association will be human beings, not immortal gods.

8

HISTORY UNDER MODERN DICTATORSHIPS:
Pokrovsky, Frank, and Von Müller

[Both the Soviet and the German totalitarian regimes destroyed the freedom of historical inquiry by imposing political restrictions upon research and prescribing in minute detail a politically acceptable version of the past. History became a political weapon, the historian a warrior at "the historical front." In the Soviet Union this inherent feature of totalitarianism became entangled with the Marxian legacy and its claims to have discovered the objective laws of historical development.

M. N. Pokrovsky (1868-1932) whose *Russian History From the Earliest Times* (5 vols. 1910-1912) is a substantial work of scholarship despite its avowed materialistic basis, was the undisputed leader of Soviet historians in the first fifteen years of the regime. A Bolshevik since 1905 and a close follower of Lenin, he filled important government posts after the 1917 Revolution and organized the entire field of historical scholarship, founding exclusively Bolshevik professional journals and societies. The following selections, taken from two of his major speeches and translated for this volume by Rufus Mathewson, reveal his twin concerns with the political loyalty of the historian and with correct Marxist historical theory.

In 1934, Pokrovsky was posthumously purged by the Stalin regime, which charged that he had failed to understand "the active role of the superstructure, the creative role of the masses and of individuals" and which ordered instead a new, patriotic glorification of Russian history. As this book goes to press, in the spring of 1956, Stalin is in his turn being condemned for self-glorification, "the cult of the personality," against which Pokrovsky had so strongly inveighed, and the first favorable references to Pokrovsky have appeared in Soviet historical journals.

In Nazi Germany, history was similarly controlled and distorted, both by the purging of historians and the imposition of party ideology, especially on modern history. The tone of Nazi scholarship, the contempt for objectivity and scholarly detachment, emerges from an address by the leading Nazi historian, Walter Frank (b. 1902) given in 1935 at the opening of his Institute for Modern History. Excerpts appear below. While Nazi nationalism and racism had little bearing on the scholarship of remoter periods, the organs of historical scholarship, and especially the venerable *Historische Zeitschrift,* had to be in politically reliable hands. Consequently, in 1936, Friedrich Meinecke, who had grudgingly acquiesced in the new regime but who clung to the older tradition of scholarship, resigned the editorship and his place was filled by Karl Alexander von Müller, whose first editorial pronouncement is reprinted below. The translations from the German are by Paul Seabury.]

POKROVSKY: THE TASKS OF THE
SOCIETY OF MARXIST HISTORIANS

(*A speech delivered at the opening of the Society during the session of June 1, 1925*)

For a long time, now, we have felt the need to unite the scientific endeavors of the already numerous contingents of Communist comrades who are teaching history in our institutions of higher education, and the ever-increasing cadres of bourgeois historians who are close to us, who "accept" Marxism. When they were in school this need was met by the history seminars of the Institute of Red Professors, but as soon as their instruction came to an end, scientific ties were broken; yesterday's participants in collective work became solitary individuals, that is to say, they deteriorated in the most evident and obvious way. The bourgeois historians close to us have been deprived of the opportunity to become associated with any kind of collective work.[1]

The idea of organizing a society composed of Marxist historians arose simultaneously in Moscow and in Leningrad, among the Communist historians who were sent there to work. But there were too few of them; they were an inconspicuous island in a bourgeois-historical ocean. Local centers sensed the danger that the waves of this ocean might engulf the island, and the "dangerous experiment" was not carried through. Now, here in Moscow, we are supported by a far larger circle of Party youth; here, the "older generation" is also in evidence. Before us now there is every prospect, at least every formal prospect, of success.

It does not follow from this that our task is an easy one, or that our road is a smooth one. The historical materialism of our day is much more subtle and complex than the historical materialism of 1917, not to mention 1897. . . .

Not until the beginning of the new century did genuine revolutionary Marxism manage to find its way into the open. Such important works as Lenin's *The Development of Capitalism in Russia* and a series of works by Plekhanov[2] appeared in large-scale legal [3] editions, and, in comparison with the previous decade, there were many more translated works.

But was this in any sense a "final" achievement? The dialectic of history does not recognize anything as final; and it required no more than a strong wind to begin to strip the gingerbread from the new edifice, the edifice of revolutionary Marxism. Our first revolution, as I have felt compelled to say more than once, was the great instructor of Russian historians.

After the revolution, many people who had had no connection with historical materialism, even those who had quarrelled with it bitterly in the nineties, became Marxists. This "post-1905 Marxism" did not prove very stable. But as compared with the nineties it was responsible for a vast dissemination of ideas about history which were more or less close to genuine Marxism. The department of police had good reason to become anxious at the end of this period and to start talking about "legal Social-Democratic propaganda" and even about legal Bolshevik propaganda. In a word, then, at the beginning of the second decade of the twentieth century, the quantitative dissemination of historical materialism was a fact which could not be disputed even by those who, in the face of the enormous popularity enjoyed by historical materialism, were forced to abandon their earlier tactics of ridicule and derision, and to resort to tactics of silence which they carried to such lengths that several Marxist historical works were not even listed in [important] bibliographical surveys. It took a noisy trial, which developed around one of these works, and which was brought on by the anxiety of the department of police to win this honor for it.

But if quantity was unmistakably on our side, the same cannot be said of quality. Foremost among those with the opportunity to publish on a large scale were the Mensheviks,[4] whose role as bourgeois agents among the proletariat had become perfectly clear by 1907. They had men of letters and they had publishers; the Bolsheviks were notably lacking in both. Moreover, what was permitted to the Cadets[5] and the Mensheviks was strictly forbidden to the Bolsheviks. For the history of the first Russian revolution there were only Menshevist manuals, in which the formula "the dictatorship of the proletariat and peasantry," so brilliantly validated in 1917, was declared utter, non-Marxist, foolishness. The censors went so far in their discrimination that a Cadet could cite documents freely, whereas, both the author, if he was a Social Democrat, and his publisher, would be brought to trial for citing excerpts from the same documents.

Meanwhile the demands which the post-revolutionary period made on the historian differed from those made before 1905. For example, anyone who continued to support the brand of "revolutionary" Marxism which he had supported before the revolution was left far behind, and usually moved quickly toward the political right, going over to the Mensheviks. Those who remained true to the "irreducible slogans" were forced to conduct a rigorous inspection of their own historical baggage. The meeting will forgive me an example of a very personal nature (no other comes to mind at the moment). Having received a commission from the Mir press[6] to prepare an extensive course in Russian history, I had hoped simply to publish my lectures, after reworking them somewhat from the purely academic viewpoint. The result was a completely new pamphlet which raised many new questions that would never have crossed my mind before 1905. The principal thing bequeathed to us by this memorable year was the transformation of the dialectic of the historical process from an abstract literary term into a living, tangible, concrete fact, a fact which we had not only observed with our own eyes but had actually *lived through*. We—and here I have in mind those who remained true to the "irreducible slogans"—were simply unable to look at the past through the eyes of a man who had *not* lived through the revolution. This represented a new stage in the development of historical materialism in Russia which corresponded exactly to the new historical stage which our country had entered upon.

Did this represent a final form of our historical world-view? To reiterate, history's dialectic recognizes nothing as final. We lacked two things which would have made it possible for our historical materialism not only to be imbued with the spirit of the revolution but to rise to the high level of the demands the revolution made upon it. In the first place, the creative role of the masses continued to be evaluated in the old way. The pre-revolutionary Russian historian was accustomed to look upon the masses as the object of actions from above, never as the *subject* . . . The revolution of 1905, unfortunately, was unable to destroy [this illusion]. In the first place, the activity of the masses was unsuccessful and in the second place the details of this activity remained unknown to us, particularly as it concerned the villages. The data on the agrarian movement of 1905-6 which the Free Economic Society collected from its correspondents gave a patently distorted picture. What we needed was the publication of the reports of the gendarmerie—the gendarmes were practical men and didn't occupy themselves with tendentious journalism in their secret correspondence—in order to get a true picture of the Russian rural revolution and to convince ourselves that it was far more conscious and far more political, and not nearly so far removed from the workers' revolution, as we had thought. It is a primary task of the coming generation of Marxist historians to correct this sin of the old Russian historiography. Our worker and our peasant must finally have a book in their hands which would represent the past not as the business of landowners and officials but as their own business, the peasants' and workers' business.

It is more difficult to straighten out another historical kink, since it was a professional deformity which was very useful to us at a certain stage of the development of our craft. I am talking about *economic materialism*. In order to provide an economic basis for the explanation of political changes, in order to knock out once and for all the saccharine legends of "subjective sociology," which divided all historical figures into the good and the bad, the sympathetic and the antipathetic, in order to pave the way for even an elementary scientific understanding of history, we had to collect an enormous amount of economic, or, more particularly, of historical statistical material. We were proud of it; it made our argument extraordinarily graphic and mathematically incontrovertible. And even now, in passing from an idealist to a materialist understanding of history one must inevitably pass through this gate. Historical statistics in themselves are necessary, even vital, but it is completely improper to substitute them for history. We must never forget the words of Marx and Engels to this effect —both repeatedly insisted on this point—that, although history is made in a definite economic setting, on a definite economic base, without an understanding of which history itself would be incomprehensible to us, history nevertheless is made by living human beings who need not be directly motivated by economic factors. The analysis of these motives, even of those that are completely individual (Marx deliberately stresses this) does not in the least lead us away from the ground of the historical materialist method, and does not change us into "psychologists."

This defect of ours—these remnants of "economic materialism"—showed itself with complete clarity after the imperialist war and the October Revolution. No statistical analysis, no columns of figures in explanation of these events will take us beyond an understanding of the sociological base on which the events occurred. And we must understand the events themselves, and understand them as a Marxist would, from the standpoint of historical materialism, and of the dialectic. In the nineties it might possibly have seemed a revelation of genius to explain the beginnings of the 1914 war by fluctuations in the price of wheat, but now that we know in the most minute detail about such things as the Russo-French military and the Anglo-Russian naval conventions; now that we know with complete exactness about the complicated machinations behind the assassination of Francis Ferdinand, we realize that wheat prices are beside the point. The politics of the imperialist war were based on the workings of the imperialist economic system, without which, to put it simply, there would have been no political policies; but, once born out of the womb of finance capitalism, this governmental policy, like every newborn infant which has become separated from the maternal organism, began to live its own life, and one may not regard the entire future life of the child from the vantage of the foetal period of its existence.

It is to be feared that the correction of this anomaly will suffer primarily from the "law of inertia"; Engels noted that there were substantial practical conveniences in the economic-materialistic explanation of history, but he warned against over-enthusiasm for these conveniences. I must buttress my remarks, therefore, with an important authority, and I think that it will not be hard for me to find him. Who was it who approached our October Revolution from the point of view of economic materialism? Primarily, of course, our good friends, the Mensheviks. According to "the level of the development of productive forces," Russia in 1917 was totally unsuited for the beginning of the socialist revolution; here statistics were decisively against us—the figures refused with finality "to go along." Just take a look at the productivity of labor at that time in Russia and abroad, at the relations between large and small economic enterprises, and so on. Therefore, the Mensheviks argued, an attempt to overthrow the power of the bourgeoisie was condemned in advance to failure. The bourgeoisie would return immediately (the lapse of time was originally set at three weeks, as you know), and nothing would come of the whole undertaking but the discrediting of socialism. Not three weeks have passed, but a little more, nearly six years, and Lenin wrote about these soothsayers: "They all call themselves Marxists, but they understand Marxism in an impossibly pedantic way. They have completely failed to understand the decisive thing about Marxism, its revolutionary dialectic." And he finished his article with these words: "Needless to say, a Kautskian textbook was a very useful thing in its day. But it is time to reject the idea that this textbook foresaw all the forms of development that subsequent periods of world history would assume. It is high time to declare that people who think this way are simply fools."

This is harshly said but it is said in Lenin's way—right straight in the eye. And since society, undoubtedly, will go the way Lenin indicated—else there would be no purpose in society's having come into existence [sic]—so, undoubtedly, it will have to outgrow, among other things, the "economic materialism" of the nineties, still firmly rooted in many of us. The harsh Leninist formula will urge us more quickly along this course, and this will help us become not only Marxist historians but Leninist historians. Permit me to conclude my introductory remarks with this wish.

THE TASKS OF MARXIST HISTORICAL SCIENCE
IN THE RECONSTRUCTION PERIOD (1931)

The Society of Marxist Historians began its work in 1925, toward the end of, and at the very height of the reconstruction period. The utilization of bourgeois specialists was one of the fundamental problems of this period. We were forced to build communism with the hands of non-communists, and determining whether or not these hands were clean or capable was one of the conditions for the success of this construction work. Hence the first task the Society had to undertake in order to link theory with practice, was the ideological verification of its own specialists, the historical specialists we inherited from bourgeois Russia. At the very moment the reconstruction period came to an end, these specialists produced a whole series of works, which amounted to declarations. . . . These declarations made it possible to establish what kind of people they were, as judged by their world-view, and how useful they were to us as comrades in the building of communism. In the Society a number of reports were read about the work of these bourgeois specialists, and the reports made it clear that it was quite impossible to build communism with their hands.

Here the Society fulfilled its elementary Party duty, and, I repeat, acted completely in the spirit of the directive on the linking of theory and practice, because at that time both the scientific-research work and, to a significant degree, the teaching in our universities, were in the hands of the specialists who underwent critical examination in our Society. The taking of a large part of the research work from their hands was one of the consequences of this examination. Unfortunately, we did not succeed then in reaching the higher citadel of the old historiography, the second department of the All-Union Academy of Sciences, and these dyed-in-the-wool reactionary historians were removed from their posts in a quite different connection and much later. We succeeded only in averting the spread of this harmful growth in the body of Soviet historiography, by blocking the establishment of a new historical institute within the walls of the Academy of Sciences.

This first fulfillment by the Society of Marxist Historians of its Party duty has already called forth the manifest disapproval of several groups who, at that time, still seemed to be completely on the Party's side (now some of the representatives of these circles are formally outside the Party, others have been formally condemned by the Party, and have been kept only on the condition that they reform). The unmasking of the bourgeois historians in the way in which it was done in our discussion and in the pages of "The Marxist Historian," appeared to these circles as "revolutionary infantilism," and one of the pioneers in unmasking the anti-communist ideology of our old professors, Comrade Friedland, was immediately punished for it by a supremely insolent review in a publication edited at that time by Slepkov.

In connection with the unmasking of Petrushevsky,[7] Tarle,[8] and Co., the Society of Marxist Historians had to come to grips for the first time with its fundamental enemy in the period ahead—the deviationists. Since then we have had to concern ourselves very little with native bourgeois historians, because the important ones among them have already been unmasked by us, and the others were taken care of by the appropriate institutions, and the frank confessions they have made relieved us of any obligation whatever to unmask them. There is absolutely no need to expose as a monarchist a man who announces that he wants to put one of the former grand dukes on "the all-Russian throne," just as there is no need to prove that a horse is a horse, not a chicken.

In the new phase we were obliged to unmask not bourgeois specialists (except for the Western ones—here our unmasking work was much delayed; for example, our critique of Dopsch's theory was completed only this year)—but their friends and followers among the Party deviationists—both right and "left." This was an incomparably more difficult and more vital struggle than the earlier one. At a time when the bourgeois historians, as honest reactionaries, were formulating their views more or less clearly, the opportunists, from the Party deviations, did their best to avoid this, justifying Lenin's famous description of opportunism: "When it is a question of the struggle with opportunism, the characteristic traits of all contemporary opportunism in any and all fields must not be forgotten: its vagueness, its diffuseness, and its elusiveness. The opportunist, by his very nature, avoids a definite and irrevocable statement of the question, looks for the 'resultant,' wriggles like a grass snake between mutually exclusive points of view, trying 'to be in accord' with each, developing his disagreements into corrections, into doubts, into innocent, well-intentioned desires etc., etc."

Our contemporary opportunists are especially fond of hiding behind Lenin, concocting out of quotations from Lenin the kind of dish that no Menshevik would have refused at an earlier time. The words are genuinely Leninist, but not a drop of Leninist content is left in them because the words are torn out of context, and because other words which would explain the quotations in a quite different sense are carefully hidden from the reader. For inexperienced people, particularly for inexperienced young people, this volley of quotations undoubtedly makes a definite impression. It must be remembered that Bernstein's famous book—the gospel of opportunism—is sprinkled with quotations from Marx and Engels, despite the fact that its primary aim is the overthrow of revolutionary Marxism.

Self-criticism is another camouflage of the opportunists. When you catch an opportunist saying anti-Party things, when you catch him falsifying Lenin and actually fighting against Leninism, a violent shriek goes up about the suppression of self-criticism.

It is perfectly obvious that there can be no Leninist study of any subject whatever without the link between theory and practice, that there is no such thing as an a-political science that can be detached from the current class struggle going on at the time. But what is the link between theory and practice on the historical front?

Here there are two conceptions of the matter, one of which is undoubtedly a narrow-minded approach to the question, completely un-Leninist. Only the second is correct. The first formula proposed to us maintains that historians must take an active part in ordering and reorganizing our archives. This is perfectly correct as far as it goes. Historians must undertake this work. But it would be extremely short-sighted to understand in this way the link between theory and practice in the realm of history. It would mean an unbelievable humiliation for that science which Marx and Engels were prepared to consider the "only" science, about which they were prepared to say that "nearly all ideology results either in a distorted understanding of this history (the history of people), or in rendering it completely abstract. Ideology itself is only one aspect of this history."

To lock up "all ideology" in the archives means to stop being a Marxist.[9] It is the essence of history, as has been said repeatedly, that it is the *most political* of all sciences, and the link between theory and practice in history rests on the fact that history must interpret directly and tirelessly the current class struggle for the masses, must uncover the roots, sometimes deeply concealed, of class contradictions; in a word, it must reveal and submit to a merciless Marxist-Leninist analysis all those political conflicts which are going on before our eyes—an impossibility without an historical approach to these conflicts.

I have already had occasion to point out that the roots of the right and of the "left" deviation, are not to be found only in the first years of the NEP when some comrades managed to recall, of all the things Lenin had to say about the New Economic Policy, only that "the New Economic Policy signifies a transition to the restoration of capitalism to a considerable degree," and did not remember that in the same speech Lenin said that "the dictatorship of the proletariat is the most furious and bitter struggle, in which the proletariat must fight against the whole world," but that the NEP is simply another solution to the problem that arose in the very earliest years. "If we had tried to solve this problem head on, by a frontal attack, so to speak, we would have failed. If the frontal attack does not succeed, let us adopt a roundabout approach, let us operate by means of sieges and sapping operations."

This Leninist course was entirely forgotten by certain comrades ten years ago, and when the means of reaching socialism changed sharply, these comrades were left in old positions, positions which were condemned by Lenin ten years ago. As I had occasion to remark elsewhere these are not the deepest roots of present-day opportunist tendencies. Without going into the general source of all opportunism, the petty bourgeoisie—the "sociological" root, so to speak, of opportunism—it is not difficult to uncover its concrete historical roots, if not for centuries, at least for decades. At this point we come upon a very curious fact. We find the present tangle of right and leftist deviations duplicated in the seventies in the tangled situation of the Narodniks,[10] who maintained with a single voice that the Russian government at that time was a non-class organization and that the peasant was the hero and creator of all Russian history. The deification of the individual peasant at that early date resembles the special historical form the struggle against collectivization and against the liquidation of the kulaks as a class has taken in our day. It is completely in harmony with Trotsky's thesis that capitalism "was imposed" on us by a non-class organization, that is, by the autocracy, and "was imposed" on an extremely primitive economic base, which is why only "people whose heads have been put together in a peculiar way" can talk about socialism in Russia.

All of these things are interrelated and they can be brought to light only by *historical* analysis. In this historical analysis of the contemporary political situation, without which the political situation cannot be understood, there is to be found the specific form for the union of theory and practice which is peculiar to history.

All the historical works of Marx and Engels and all of Lenin's historical works and analyses were devoted to this question and answered this need. Not one of our great teachers was concerned with history for history's sake. The study of history for history's sake, as we now understand the phrase, was always undertaken by untalented minor historians, or by intelligent people who wished to hide their own political faces under a pile of quotations, and to adhere to views which corresponded to the political interests of one or another class. In particular, bourgeois democracy with its system of fooling the masses, has worked out the formula of "objective" history, a formula which, unfortunately, still clouds the gaze of many of our comrades. It is not that they fail to acknowledge theoretically that service in the proletariat's political struggle against the world bourgeoisie both inside and outside the USSR constitutes their primary task. They understand this, theoretically, that is, bookishly, cut off from reality, but this theoretical understanding itself is not worth a broken kopeck for it is in itself a stigma, the mark of Cain, standing for the rupture of theory and practice. Only he who fights in history for the interests of the proletariat, who, in this connection, chooses his subjects, chooses his opponent, chooses his weapons for the fight with his opponent, is a genuine Leninist historian.

We must brace ourselves now on this front and the sooner the better. Perhaps, the historians of the USSR may need to exert themselves less here, although it must be said that the writing of the history of the peoples of the USSR is still a matter of the future, and there is a whole vast area which we have only begun to develop—the area of the nationality question and of everything that is connected with it: the fight against great-power chauvinism as the major danger, and against local nationalisms, as a secondary danger, the repulse of which is no less urgent. So the historians of the USSR have nothing particular to boast about.

But the position on the Western historical front most urgently requires reinforcement. The leaders on this front must have noticed that the coordination of theory and practice in their area has begun spontaneously, among the rank and file: actually, students of Western history in the Institute of Red Professors are all connected with sections of the Comintern, and it was appropriate that one of the leaders of the Comintern was invited to open a discussion on Western history. But where are the actual leaders in Western history? They are sitting somewhere amidst the debris of the French Revolution or of the history of German social-democracy in the old days, or in other remote places, which, both by their remoteness, and by the manner in which they are being investigated, represent a break between theory and practice. Here chronology is not the question at issue. Engels studied the history of primitive societies and was very much interested in the history of ancient Egypt: he needed both in order to formulate his conception of historical materialism, a perfectly proper concern in the days when Marxism was being founded. Now the question of social formations, that is, the question of feudalism, of the natural economy, even the question of tribal customs as it relates to the study of the peoples of the USSR, is very urgent even though all these things are now dealt with in the first pages of our history textbooks. The question is not one of chronology, but of approach, whether we study history as such, falling into the traps of crafty bourgeois researchers, who actually are pursuing definite class aims, or whether we take history as a weapon in the class struggle, as a means of exposing each and every "ideology" of our bourgeois enemies, and of the opportunists who are closer to us, who sometimes conceal themselves under Party slogans. It is in the struggle with bourgeois historiography, and with opportunism, and in the merciless unmasking of both, that the fundamental union of theory and practice is taking place on the historical front. To this is joined a large number of specific tasks having to do with the history of the class struggle which is currently under way in various countries, and with the task of assisting both on the Western and on the Eastern fronts, those organizations, the Comintern in the first instance, which cannot get along without historians.

Unless we resolve these many concrete questions, which we do not have to enumerate here, our historical work can easily degenerate into polemics that are quite superficial, requiring no historical knowledge. If such degeneration be allowed, one fine day we may hear this question: why do we have historians here at all—the all-Party press handles this kind of thing magnificently.

We must not forget this. History is the concrete investigation of concrete social questions. In this investigation we must beat our enemy, and we must so define this research that it answers our problems. Most importantly we must unite the historical work we are carrying out with the proletariat's fight against wage slavery. Where this union is not achieved, there is no genuine Leninist history.

FRANK: GUILD AND NATION

We stood, at that time, at a great cross-road of history: the collapse of the old Imperial Germany under the impact of the western democracies, of the monied powers, and of the masses; we stood at the beginnings of a new nationalism which had been summoned to offer a new and creative solution to the problem of the masses; we stood at the homecoming of the great, never-before-defeated, yet now defeated, army; we stood at the birth of a new army still in the stage of becoming.

And so it came about that the battle broke in upon our consciousness and upon our condition.

This is not to mean that we were therefore transformed from scholars into men of political deeds, nor that we had ceased to be men of quiet contemplation.

But it now was the case that at every hour of the day, through our quiet, year-long research and study there broke upon us the drum-roll of endless war. And it was now the case that, at every hour, as we worked amongst thousands and thousands of yellowed volumes of documents, papers, and books, the march-step of our folk resounded in our ears—the march out of the Great War through the black valley of defeat to new heights of national greatness.

And it could not have been otherwise: we were a part of this column which marched into the future—a small part, but a part which had its job to do. And in that we were the soldiers of a revived science, we were at the same time the soldiers of a new Reich, which was then not visible, but which lived inwardly in the glowing visions of men.

And then the rebuking fingers of those academicians were waggled at us. And their rebuke was: Commitment is the arch-enemy of knowledge.

And since we had been in deadly earnest about knowledge, we struggled against this rebuke.

And we came to know [one] thing:

We came to see how those academicians had become trapped in a grotesque self-deception about their own origins. They believed that they lived outside of history, and they blamed us because we, as men of flesh and blood, had thrown ourselves into the maelstrom of our times. But in reality they were themselves chained to a quite specific historical context from which they did not escape. It was the epigonic post-

Bismarckian age of the years between 1890 and 1914. And what they called their scientific objectivity was nothing but a product of that secure bourgeois era in which they had grown up as time-bound prisoners. . . .

As we express our thanks [to the National-Socialists] we would not have them construed as the thanks of a science servile to political power, of which we originally spoke; nor in the sense of loyalty of minions, who submissively court the good-will of authority. This kind of loyalty we leave to fawning philistines. What we vow is not loyalty. Our vow is this: We are blood of blood and flesh of flesh of your Revolution and your Reich.

We, and with us our work, have become great in the turbulence of your Revolution.

And, in our work and being, even if we wished otherwise, we could never be anything other than a spiritual expression of your Revolution and your Order, an expression of the great Age of Adolf Hitler.

And with the same innermost conviction with which we say this, we turn to the other side of this gathering—to the side of the sciences. With the same unshakeable determination we bear witness to the eternally-great virtues of German learning.

Being German, to us, means seriousness.

Being German, to us, means thoroughness.

Being German, to us, means having a conscience.

Being German, to us, means going to the depths of things, even if this means our death.

For ten years you may bury yourselves in the quiet of your studies. And yet even in such quietude you can serve as officers of your fatherland, by being the weapon-makers and engineers of science. And with these weapons, after ten years you can have won a battle for your fatherland, which History will rank as possessing importance equal to a political or military battle.

Recently a member of this Institute wrote me how, as he watched the embarking Italian battalions in the harbor of Naples, an agonizing melancholy had overcome him as he realized that the writer of history could not also be the maker of history. To him I would say:

My comrade! If it is both the honor and the curse of the man of inner contemplation that he is not able also to do what he, as artist, observes and portrays—still at no time has a history-making role been denied to really noble and vital creations.

If we possess the strength to write history in such a way that history-makers will carry it in their knapsacks, then we, too, will have made history.

VON MÜLLER: EDITOR'S NOTE TO THE *Historische Zeitschrift* [1936]

At this turning-point in world history, our own German folk —fully awake to its historical role—now has been summoned and inspired by a great, creative Leader to construct out of its new inner community a new Reich; summoned to move out of its age-old fragmentation into unity; summoned out of its brimming and often shapeless multiplicity to close its ranks into compact form. For us, the movement of our time is doubly strong, every task doubly rich in responsibilities. But our will likewise has been given wings of great and guiding purpose.

German historiography would have to perish if this earth-shaking revolution now being experienced by our folk did not also shake it to its very roots. The harsh clatter of tramping soldiers and the masses has not only seeped into every scholar's study: our work itself, in its innermost being, has swung into march-step with the times. The lot of our generation is that of tension and unrest; the task given us is to dare. Whether it approves or not, no science will be exempted from this general law of our time—least of all the study of history, which so closely impinges on the field of politics. More than others it is obligated today to bring the new spirit of the times into the trenches of scientific battle, and to work with that spirit in remoulding the countenance of Germandom for the years ahead. . . .

The evolution [of the *Historische Zeitschrift*] in the past seventy-five years characteristically and often accurately mirrors the inner course of our nation's growth, as well as its spiritual life: The improbable fortune of a swift, overwhelming, though superficial growth; the all-too-premature inner satiety; the absence of a new goal for the future, perceived by the whole folk. We all know of the great internal crisis which our—as well as almost every other—intellectual discipline encountered at the turn of the century: the feeling of oppression from the masses of ever-growing factual knowledge which piled up around us, lacking the support of a strong *Weltanschauung* to order them and make them meaningful; the progressive fragmentation and alienation amongst the various branches of knowledge; the inner relativism which, in the last analysis, threatened everything with dissolution; the sterile plant of formalism which, so to speak, nourished itself from roots in the air, having no vital connection with the soil of primitive folkish strength, bereft of even elementary life-hunger, and for that reason no longer capable of satisfying the real cravings for life.

This above all we understand, as the winds of the new times breathe upon us: the profound realization of being an inseparable and co-equal part of the folk as a whole: bound to the folk in both life and death; partaking of the terrible will and the mountain-moving faith which, as the old order of things collapsed, arose out of the depths of our Leader: the faith which comes from once more standing within the camp of a struggling people. The scientific method, for which the *Historische Zeitschrift* in its early days had to struggle, has long since been achieved; the contemporary crisis of our discipline in no way is a crisis of methodology. The conscious Pan-German *Anschauung,* which we now represent, as against the little-Germany [*klein-deutsch*] conceptions of Sybel and Treitschke, has been transformed since the first days of our journal; our eyes are turned toward a united German folk, in which we are all embodied. The spiritual environment in which we live is no longer that of an elevated middle class, but rather that of a fundamentally restratified folk struggling for a new, all-encompassing community as well as for a new mode of leadership. . . .

Today the storm-clouds of a great historical epoch surround us as they have surrounded few generations. For us, as for few generations, are revealed the primitive, daemonic forces which such furious eras carry with them—both magnificent and terrible. For us, as for few generations, comes the consciousness that we have something to say in the decisions of the present, and in determining the future of our whole folk. Out of that which is becoming, we will search for and illumine that which has been, and revivify its bones with our blood; out of the real past we will recognize and strengthen the forces of a living present. The writing of history has always been given wings by deeds, and like its closest sister, the art of poetry, it is capable once again of making deeds.

From the fullest participation in the life of our times, we hope, our science will also win new life; out of our science, we hope, will once again stream new springs of courage and strength for our folk. . . .

9

HISTORY AND THE SOCIAL SCIENCES: *Cochran and Hofstadter*

[Some years ago when the University of Chicago set up separate divisions of the social sciences and the humanities, the historians, puzzled about their allegiance, decided to split, some going to one division, some to the other. While this kind of Solomon's judgment is required of few historians, the uncertainty about the place of history among the social sciences is characteristic of the contemporary American scene. In the following selections two American historians deal with the problem in markedly different fashion.

Thomas C. Cochran (b. 1902), a leading economic historian, has written extensively on American economic development, including *The Age of Enterprise* (1942, with William Miller) and *The Railroad Leaders 1845-1890* (1953), and on the general problems of historical method. His essay on "The Social Sciences and the Problem of Historical Synthesis" appeared in the Social Science Research Council Bulletin 64, *The Social Sciences in Historical Study*, and is here reprinted with some of the footnotes omitted.

As his essay suggests, Richard Hofstadter (b. 1916) has been largely concerned with the analysis of American political culture, with the relation of men and ideas to politics. In his best-known works *The American Political Tradition* (1948) and *The Age of Reform* (1955) he advanced new hypotheses, based in part on his humanistic insights into problems raised by the social sciences. The following essay appears here for the first time.]

THE SOCIAL SCIENCES AND THE PROBLEM
OF HISTORICAL SYNTHESIS [1]

In the field of American history, selected as the one with which most readers of this report will be familiar, the past fifty years of rapid progress in the development of social science methods and hypotheses have had surprisingly little effect on historical interests, content, or forms of synthesis. This statement applies to American history either as taught in universities and colleges, as presented in textbooks, or as reflected in general literature. The main props of a synthetic structure, erected more or less unconsciously by such gifted pioneers as Channing, Hart, McMaster, and Turner, are still securely in place.

THE NARRATIVE SYNTHESIS

The synthesis in terms of great men and a sequence of important or unique events still appears in historical thinking. This leads to a narrative organization in which the nation's presidents and its wars play major parts in both substance and periodization. It is not so much that the matters with which the social scientist commonly deals are altogether unnoticed; it is rather that they are treated as incidental to a narrative of men and events. For example, how different from the historian's usual definition of his task is that of economic historian Alexander Gerschenkron: "Historical research consists essentially in application to empirical material of various sets of empirically derived hypothetical generalizations and in testing the closeness of the resulting fit, in the hope that in this way certain uniformities, certain typical situations, and certain typical relationships among individual factors in these situations can be ascertained." [2] Yet it seems probable that most social scientists would readily subscribe to the Gerschenkron definition.

Objections to the prevailing synthesis of American history might be lodged by thoughtful scholars of many different points of view. Judged by the complex of values and standards that may generically be referred to as humanistic, a synthesis built around great men and events falls short of the mark. It satisfies a follower of Toynbee, for example, but little better than it does a disciple of Kroeber. But in this chapter we shall discuss only its inadequacy in dealing with the types of problems in modern society that most interest social scientists, or what may be termed from their point of view the historians' lack of a satisfactory method of analysis.

To members of the disciplines that have to study the problems of industrial society, the events or trends with which the historian has traditionally dealt often appear to be surface manifestations that are not of the highest importance; and the studies themselves seem to many social scientists correspondingly limited. These social scientists would like historians to give more attention to such topics as the causes and conditions of economic growth or stagnation; the effect on enterprise of community approbation, competition, monopoly, and regulation; the social adjustments demanded by growing urban centers, new types of employment, and changing levels of opportunity; the psychological frustrations developing from urban impersonality, badly selected social goals, and altered family relationships; the origins and persistence of social manners, attitudes, and beliefs; and the nature of political action, leadership, and motivation. The rapid rise of such group problems has characterized history-as-reality in the last century and a half but, needless to say, they are not the central features of existing historical syntheses. Moreover, study of general European history writing indicates that this weakness is not confined to the history of the United States.

LIMITATIONS OF THE NARRATIVE SYNTHESIS

How has this situation arisen? What has caused this relative lack of communication between history and the social sciences?

An obvious part of the answer lies in the fact that the writing of history is a time-honored and traditional occupation long antedating the modern emphasis on empirical method in the social sciences or present-day problems or source materials. The historical record prior to 1800 here or abroad is relatively scanty. The historian has to use the materials he can find rather than those that might best answer his questions. To begin with, for many ages these materials are largely governmental, and the fact that the modern syntheses were developed in a period of growing nationalism led to a still greater preoccupation with political sources. Historians, accustomed to confining themselves to these old and easily available records for the earlier periods, failed to make use of the new types of material which became available in the later nineteenth century. The habits of the older historian, educated to a scarcity of records, were perpetuated amidst a later-day abundance. Statistical data, specialized periodicals, new types of correspondence, recorded interviews, and the records of many organizations, profit making or otherwise, were all relatively neglected, while the traditional sources were reinterpreted again and again.

This tendency has been noted or implied in various ways from the time of Buckle and Green in England and of the graduate seminars of the 1880's in America. Yet, in spite of an increasing recognition of the importance and complexity of the elements in modern society that are but faintly reflected in important events, no mature "social science" synthesis of American history has been produced to challenge the traditional formula.[3]

The explanation of such a striking intellectual anachronism is bound to be subtle and complex, for if the conventional structure rested on one or two easily recognized errors it could not have withstood the pressures of new generations of historians. A long list of causes must therefore be investigated, the absolute importance of any one of which is hard to evaluate, but all of which together seem largely responsible for the general failure of historians to think or write as social scientists.

The written record itself, particularly when buttressed with systematic documentation, exercises a tyranny that has been commented on frequently by students of the nature of language but often overlooked by scholars in other fields. The mere fact that a previous writer has organized his material and phraseology in a certain way creates a predisposition in its favor. The later writer can no longer respond quite freshly to the original data; he may agree with or object to what has been said, but in either case his orbit of thought is likely to center around the existing interpretation. A. M. Schlesinger, Jr. and Joseph Dorfman, for example, may argue about the interpretation of "Jacksonian Democracy," but they both accept the traditional concept as central to the synthesis of the period. Charles A. Beard introduced new economic factors, but employed them within what was essentially the existing political synthesis. With its great quantities of traditional literature, and its lack of accepted conceptual tools for new theoretical analysis, history probably suffers more than any other discipline from the tyranny of persuasive rhetoric.

In still another way, the inner compulsions of writing have ruled the historian. The traditional basis of history has been effective narrative. The "great" histories of the past such as Gibbon's *Decline and Fall,* Macaulay's *England,* or Motley's *Dutch Republic* have been exciting "stories." Furthermore, since historians like to have their books published and are not averse to sales, the popular dramatic frame of reference has been used whenever possible. This general approach is often valid when applied to the actions of a single individual, but neither narrative nor popular drama is usually suited to the analysis of mass phenomena. While drama will still be found in the conflict and resolution of forces or in group challenge and response, this is likely to be drama on a nonpopular abstract level. The historian has, of course, been aware of this dilemma but, faced with the choice of retaining a misleading emphasis on colorful individuals and exciting events or of giving up the narrative style, he has clung as long as possible to storytelling and treasured most those source materials that permitted narration.[4]

By taking the written record that was easiest to use and most stirring from a sentimental or romantic standpoint, that is, the record of the federal government, the American historian prepared the way for one of the major misconceptions in American synthesis: the primary role of the central government in our historical development. While political scientists carefully pointed out that up to World War I, at least, most of the normal governmental contacts of the citizen were with his state, and historians dwelt on the importance of sectionalism and state rights and joined with business leaders in emphasizing the laissez-faire doctrines that for a large part of the nineteenth century circumscribed the role of the federal government, the same men, influenced perhaps by nineteenth century European training, persisted in writing a national history revolving around presidential administrations and passing controversies over constitutional law. In the early stages of the economic development of each region, government and politics were in truth of great importance; but government was that of the state, and politics revolved around such material questions as loans or subsidies to banking and transportation, practices of incorporation, the degree of government ownership thought desirable, and how to secure honest administration. In a later stage of economic growth the states led the way in regulating business and economic activity in the public interest. In neither stage, prior to 1900, was the federal government of major importance except for the initial disposal of public land, adjustment of the tariff, and widely separate changes in banking policy. The sporadic transference of ultimate power from state to federal government by decisions of the Supreme Court and acts of Congress from the 1880's on at first freed certain citizens from state controls without imposing effective federal ones. Not until the first decades of the twentieth century was the theoretical shift in power implemented by much effective federal action.

The realistic history of nineteenth and even early twentieth century politics, therefore, whether viewed from the standpoint of political parties or of the community, should be built around the states. This, of course, imposes an enormous burden on the historian. The situations in from 13 to 48 states cannot be adequately described in a unified narrative; to have meaning they need to be seen in an analytical structure. Furthermore, the older state histories are inadequate as a basis for such synthesis. Scholars must first produce new monographs on business and government in the states, and new cultural interpretations of state politics.[5] Indeed, at present, a general American history has to be more a series of suggestions of what ought to be known than a comprehensive synthesis.

A somewhat similar obstacle in the path of the historian who approaches the problem of systematic analysis and the building of some empirically based hypotheses is the extent to which our knowledge of the past depends on the writings of a small group of cultural leaders. He will tend to see events not only through the eyes of men of more than average vigor, property, education, and intelligence but also in the light of the metaphors of those who wrote the most enduring and readable prose. The circle of possible deception is completed when the statements of such abnormal citizens are read back as typical of their class, section, or society as a whole, and the resulting analysis is used to explain still other situations. The brilliant John Taylor of Caroline was not the typical Southern planter, Susan B. Anthony's problems were not those of the average woman, nor was Herbert Croly a good representative of many phases of the progressive movement.

A major reason for this reliance on leaders is that historical data on average people and everyday situations are hard to find. What was the typical rural community of 1840 from the statistical standpoint? What were normal ideas among its average citizens? Until there are answers to such questions, generalizations regarding the role of ideas in social change must rest on tenuous deductions. Both quantitative and typifying studies are sadly lacking. Some of these data can be obtained through better use of published and manuscript census reports; others will have to be obtained by sampling methods, governed by proper statistical controls. The normal ideas of the average citizen in any time and place will have to be assembled from many indirect sources, such as the speeches of astute local politicians who, knowing what their constituents wanted to hear, mirrored public prejudices; the blurbs of discerning advertisers who sought in local papers to cater to public taste; and the letters of businessmen discussing public reactions that vitally concerned the future of their trade. Such materials are relatively hard to find and to use, but there are many indications of their widespread existence.

Research using such sources immediately brings the scholar to a level of social relations deeper than that of conventional historic events, and exposes another major reason for the persistence of the narrative synthesis. As long as history consists of a series of important unique acts, thought to symbolize or cause change in society, a narrative account based on national happenings has a certain logic. But once the historian penetrates to the level of the social conditioning factors that produce persons capable of such acts and tries to find the probability of the occurrence of any type of event, the acts themselves become a surface manifestation of more fundamental forces. While events are an indispensable part of the data of history, and even chance events, granting there are such, may have strong repercussions on their environment, the use of social science approaches focuses attention on the aspects of the event that reveal the major dynamics of the culture, the uniformities rather than those features that appear to be most colorful or unique. The latter elements, by definition not being representative of the general culture pattern, will presumably have only a limited effect or significance. Southern secession, for example, had its roots in cultural factors underlying such events as the tariffs, the acts of abolitionists, or territorial laws that seemed to produce the friction. These events are chiefly useful as clues to the nature of the basic differences between the sections. Similarly the American people in the early 1930's, facing a new cultural situation, displayed qualities of resignation not easily explicable on the basis of either the traditional or immediate events of their past.

Historical change on this level of basic social conditioning is, to be sure, a difficult and—in the present stage of social science knowledge—a highly speculative study. Furthermore, the large quantities of material to be examined and the various types of special knowledge required often make group, rather than individual, research essential. The generally individualistic work habits of the historian, therefore, suggest another reason for the lack of historical scholarship in this area. But the topography of this field has been charted sufficiently to allow even individual historians to make rewarding sorties into its intricate terrain.[6]

RESEARCH REQUIREMENTS FOR A SYNTHESIS IN TERMS OF A SCIENCE OF SOCIETY

In the space of a single chapter one can suggest only a few of the many types of research that will help build a synthesis in social science terms. As a beginning, it should be possible with patience and ingenuity to assemble the large number of career lines of different types of social leaders, essential for a picture of who succeeded in the society and how. Beside the pattern of how men succeeded in fact, there should be further study, based on qualitative sources such as private correspondence, of the alternative goals that influenced men's expectations. How did their "level of expectations" from material or intellectual standpoints vary? What was the true "American dream"? Such considerations would lead not only to a higher level of generalization in social history but to possible scientific comparisons between American and other cultures.

A more difficult excursion into the field of basic historical factors is the tracing of the changing character of family relations, including both the relationships within the family circle and the aims and aspirations of the members of the family in their real and imaginary contacts with the outside world. Whether one uses a striking term like Kardiner and Linton's "basic personality" [7] or some time-honored word like "background" to cover the effects of familial conditioning, few scholars will deny the fundamental importance of this factor in shaping the course of civilization. But the investigation of the precise reaction to change is difficult, calling for psychological and sociological knowledge seldom possessed by the historian, and hence the family seldom appears as a factor on the level of historical events.

An additional deterrent to historical analysis is that there are many "American families" at any given period. The variation in conditioning between the family of a back-country mountaineer and a rural professional man, or a city slum dweller and a Park Avenue millionaire, may easily be greater than the variation between the Maori family and the Maricopa. As in recent studies in cultural anthropology, such as *Plainville, U.S.A.* or the "Yankee City Series," half a dozen different types of families based on income and occupational levels must be studied. The upper-class groups offer data in the form of memoirs, letters, and contemporary comments;[8] the poorer groups, particularly before 1890, offer only a challenge to the investigator. But the scholar striving to check theories and hypotheses regarding the family against historical data (and no one not so motivated should essay the task) will doubtless find many clues that have been concealed from the eyes of the conventional historian. Perhaps some day it will be possible to guess wisely at the degree to which group aggressions, political radicalism, or instability in mass reactions were due to the stresses and strains of a family conditioning that became unsuited in varying degrees to the changes in surrounding society.

Looking at the situation more broadly, the new social-psychological problems of Western civilization by 1900 can be seen as the result of contrary types of conditioning: in youth, family and school conditioning, based either here or abroad on mores and folkways largely inherited from a pre-industrial society; in maturity, conditioning in urban offices and factories, based on new mores and folkways that were evolving from the needs of business; and almost from birth to death, conditioning by pulpit, press, or other media of communication, based on a heterogeneous mixture of traditional and pragmatic doctrines.

Shifting attention on this fundamental level to the rise of urban industrialism, the chief external pressure that upset existing family patterns, one enters a field where historians have done considerably more work but have in general subordinated their findings to the events of the narrative synthesis, and have failed, because of their disinterest in theory, to deal with many of the problems basic to urban sociology. Even A. M. Schlesinger, Sr. who did much to start study of urbanism by historians and whose general synthesis in the latter half of *Land of the Free* is one of the best, keeps the city in a relatively subordinate position. Special areas of sociology of first importance, such as urban demography and its social consequences, are not properly considered in our general histories. The whole argument might be summed up by saying that we have many "social" accounts of American historical data but few sociological interpretations.

In all this confusing historic picture of shifting ideas, folkways, and mores, of new family relationships and of growing urban problems, the massive physical force producing change has been industrialism. Yet, judging from the narrative synthesis, the obvious fact that it was industrialism that moved us from the world of George Washington to that of the present day apparently needs still more emphasis. The spearhead of the multiple pressures of industrialization has been business, and businessmen have been of necessity the human agents who transmitted to society most of the physical changes born of science and industrial technology. The institutions of business, therefore, became the central mechanisms in shaping a new society and imposing industrial customs upon it. Before mid-century, the sensitive New England intellectuals were well aware of the change. Emerson complained in 1844:

In America, out-of-doors all seems a market; .... I speak of those organs which can be presumed to speak a popular sense. They recommend conventional virtues, whatever will earn and preserve property; always the capitalist; the college, the church, the hospital, the theatre, the hotel, the road, the ship of the capitalist,—whatever goes to secure, adorn, enlarge these is good; what jeopardizes any of these is damnable.[9]

From 1840 to 1860 the new impact of business and its urbanism upon American culture was perhaps greater relatively than in any other equal period, yet such forces appear only in the form of a few isolated phenomena in the usual treatment of the pre-Civil War era.

In the post-Civil War years the continuing cultural pressures of business, on which the War itself had relatively little effect, are better recognized by general historians. But a new difficulty now appears. Just as in the case of public opinion, the family, or urbanism, the spectacular and exotic rather than the normal have tended to find their way into the traditional synthesis. Our textbooks, for example, tell much of the resistance of certain farm groups to elevator and railroad practices but little of the growing force of business folkways and mores in the rural community.

In this case the approach to a more comprehensive and meaningful synthesis will be much easier than in those previously discussed. Business records of all types are becoming available in increasing quantities.[10] Monographic reports are steadily accumulating. The general historian surveying this field, however, will find that while existing studies in economics and in history give much of the internal picture of the workings of business, the connections between business and society are not elaborated. The business leader or entrepreneur, for example, was the arbiter not only of change within his company but also, to a large extent, of change in his community. Since his money, and hence his approbation, was generally necessary for community welfare and improvement, he sat on the boards of the educational, charitable, political, and business institutions that dominated social customs and set social goals. And necessarily, he carried into these other fields the patterns of behavior formed by the needs of survival in business. He strove to make education, charity, politics, and social life "businesslike." Generations of historians have analyzed the thought of Clay, Webster, and Calhoun to extract every last vestige of social meaning, while Nathan Appleton, John Murray Forbes, and a host of other important business figures of the same period, awaiting their first full-length social interpreter, do not appear in the traditional narrative.

The modern corporation, a new social instrumentality developed primarily by business leaders, must also be given a much larger place in this more meaningful synthesis. Here the problem is a very difficult one, challenging the scholar not so much from the standpoint of data or materials for research as from that of theory. The role of the corporation in modern society has never been adequately analyzed by legal, social, or economic theorists. Noncorporeal, but quite real, the corporation of both the profit and nonprofit variety has established substates and subcommunities within our political and geographical divisions. It has created both highly responsible and highly irresponsible entities with which all citizens are forced to deal, and under the influence of which most citizens spend a large part of their lives. Ownership as represented by stock in large corporations has become a functional relationship. Control of the property has passed into the hands of professional, and frequently nonowning, administrators. The resultant problems of historical interpretation are too complex to discuss here, and have been in fact too complex for the wisdom of modern society, but complexity and difficulty are not valid excuses for historical neglect.

In summary, at the center of any comprehensive and meaningful synthesis, determining its topical and chronological divisions, should be the material and psychological changes that have most affected, or threatened most to affect, such human conditioning factors as family life, physical living conditions, choice of occupations, sources of prestige, and fundamental beliefs. While the historical analysis itself, in the present stage of psychological knowledge, must be concerned with concrete physical, political, or social changes or events, these should be assigned place and importance on the basis of their estimated relation to underlying social forces. The precise social effects of the rapid rise of the corporation from 1850 to 1873, for example, have not been examined, but the social scientist is reasonably sure that they are of more importance than the details of presidential campaigns.

For the period since the middle of the nineteenth century, there is available source material for an amplified synthesis based on changes in major social forces. While present knowledge leads us to believe that business and economic changes should be recognized as the most dynamic elements in this particular place and period, further investigation may reveal alterations in family life or in social beliefs not stemming directly from business sources as more powerfully operative. But as long as the historian will equip himself with the knowledge necessary to probe these deeper levels, and approach the problems in the spirit of scientific analysis, social scientists will applaud the results as steps in the direction of historical realism.

Such a backbone of synthesis would not only place the narrative structure of events in proper perspective but would alter the look of most of the other familiar landmarks as well. War studied as a social institution would preserve its importance, but war as an arbitrary milestone for historical periodization would probably disappear. The Civil War, for example, that great divide of American historiography, shrinks in magnitude when viewed in the light of these long-run social criteria. Even in the deep South, the dramatic change in race and property relations brought on by the war will lose some of its importance when measured against the full background of the gradual social changes coming from the increase in middle-class farmers and industrial workers.[11] In any case, for nations as a whole, basic social change seems to come less cataclysmically than is indicated by wars or revolutions. Periodization should be recognized as wholly arbitrary and dependent on the central focus of the synthesis employed. From the business and economic standpoints, for example, 1850 and 1885 are available points for periodization, the one symbolically marking the beginning of the rapid opening of a national industrial market, the latter roughly coinciding with the rise of a number of large semimonopolistic business units and the beginning of federal regulation; but if the family or urbanism is made the central phenomenon other dates might be selected.

For those historians who will mourn the passing of the

historiographic sway of Jeffersonian and Jacksonian Democracy, the Era of Good Feeling, the Irrepressible Conflict, the Tragic Era, the Square Deal, the New Freedom, and the New Deal, there is the poor consolation that time must doom the ancient subdivisions. When the United States is even two hundred years old instead of a hundred and seventy, it will no longer be possible to discuss all the traditional men and events. Broader and less detailed syntheses will be demanded by the exigencies of space and time, and it will be up to the historian to choose whether he will attempt an intuitive resynthesis of the type presented by Spengler or Toynbee, or avail himself of the aid offered by the social sciences.

HOFSTADTER: HISTORY AND THE SOCIAL SCIENCES

The professional academic historian suffers in these times from a persistent uncertainty about precisely what he is. Two traditions govern his training and his work. On one side there is the familiar historical narrative, a form of literature for which there is always much demand. On the other is the historical monograph, ideally supposed to approximate a scientific inquiry, which the historian is professionally trained to write. Authors of narrative histories rarely hesitate to retell a story that is already substantially known, adding perhaps some new information but seldom in a systematic fashion or with a clear analytical purpose. Authors of monographs, on the other hand, take it upon themselves to add new information to the fund of knowledge, or to analyze in a new way the meaning of a given sequence of historical events. Many historians, especially the great ones, have combined in single works both sides of this dual tradition, but in the profession as a whole the double function of the historian has been an important cause of the uncertain value of much historical writing. Many a historian feels that it is unsatisfactory merely to repeat with minor modifications what we already know of the past; but many a monograph, though intended to overcome this limitation, leaves its readers, and perhaps even its author, with misgivings as to whether that part of it which is new is truly significant.

This duality is reinforced by the demands made upon the historian. Society and special interests in society call upon him to provide them with memory. The kind of memory that is too often desired is not very different from what we all provide for ourselves—that is, memory that knows how to forget, memory that will rearrange, distort, and omit so much as is needed to make our historical self-images agreeable. In a liberal society the historian is free to try to dissociate myths from reality, but that same impulse to myth-making that moves his fellow men is also at work in him. Society has another, more instrumental task for the historian: to analyze its experience in such a way as to put into its hands workable tools for the performance of certain tasks. In this spirit the military services ask historians to compile the records of previous wars in the hope that such information will be useful in future wars. In the same spirit the Japanese government called upon Charles A. Beard to help with the problems arising out of the Tokyo earthquake of 1923, and wired him: "Bring your knowledge of disaster."

Both advantages and disadvantages arise from this duality of tradition and of function. They bring certain confusions to the historian's role: understandably he may wonder whether he is a writer or a technician, a scientist or a prophet. But there are compensations. The same ambiguities that present him with his problems of method and even of identity give him an opportunity to have valuable interchanges with many kinds of intellectual and practical activity, with politics and public affairs, with journalism and mass media, with literature and criticism, with science, philosophy, and art, and with the social sciences.

I speak of the historian as having contacts with the social sciences rather than as being a social scientist for reasons which I hope to make clear. Although each of the disciplines that study human culture has characteristics that in one way or another set it off from the rest, history is in a still further degree set off from the others by its special constellation of problems, methods, limitations, and possibilities. But the historian's contact with the social sciences is clearly of more importance to the present generation of historians than it has been at any time in the past. Perhaps this closer relationship is in some part attributable to a more receptive frame of mind among historians to inter-disciplinary work; it is more largely due to the fact that in the past quarter century the achievements of the social sciences have been impressive. My interest here is not in the ultimate nature of history or the social sciences or the relations between them, but in the progress of inter-disciplinary work, which I should like to illustrate by reference to some of my own intellectual experiences. What I hope to do, then, is not to deal with philosophical issues but in some measure to clarify an attitude which is becoming fairly widespread among contemporary historians.

Despite what is surely no more than a fragmentary and random acquaintance with the literature of the social sciences, I have found that my interest and gratification in my own discipline have been enormously intensified by what I have been able to take for it from the other disciplines. That I am unable to systematize or formalize what it is that I owe, as a historian, to the social sciences I find puzzling. But I feel sure that in a general way what the social sciences have helped to do is to suggest a new resolution—not a solution, for such problems are never solved—to the problems created by the duality of the historian's role. In brief what they offer him is a host of new insights and new creative possibilities.

When I was first attracted to history as a vocation, it was by a two-fold interest: I was attracted both by what might be called orthodox political history and also by the history of ideas. At first these two seemed parallel rather than converging. Not only did I not have a very clear idea of how the two might be put together, but I had little interest in doing so. As time went on I realized that what I most wanted to write about were things marginal to both political historians and to practitioners of the history of ideas who stem, say, from the severe tradition in which Arthur O. Lovejoy has done such impressive work. My interests lay between the two fields, at the intersection of their perimeters.

I belong to the generation that came of age during the middle thirties. This was a period, of course, of tremendous conflict on a world scale and of intense and lively controversy in American domestic politics. A battle of ideologies roughly similar to that which took place in a world-wide theatre of action could be seen at home as well. For many of us an interest in studying the formation and development of ideologies was a natural intellectual response to the conflict raging around us.[12] But to a detached observer these ideologies were far more interesting for their extraordinary appeal to various types of individuals than they were for their rational or philosophic content. I found myself, therefore, becoming interested in individual and social character types, in social mythologies and styles of thought as they reveal and affect character, and in politics as a sphere of behavior into which personal and private motives are projected.

Such phrases as "styles of thought" and "projective behavior" suggest fundamental influences stemming from Mannheim and from Freud. For me Mannheim provided the link I had been seeking between ideas and social situations. In this respect too his work has, for the historian, a significance similar to that of the cultural anthropologist: for the anthropologist's feeling for cultural styles and for styles of life is similar to Mannheim's feeling for styles of thought. All these ideas—of cultural configuration, of styles of life and thought, and of political style—are filled with significance for the historian, and he has only begun to sound their potentialities. The influence of Freud upon the historian, though even more far-reaching, must of necessity be more indirect than that of a thinker like Mannheim. Historians may hate to admit it, but they do work with certain general psychological presuppositions. The intellectual revolution that we associate with Freud is beginning to have some effect, however subtle and unformalized, upon the way they see their materials. Understandably they look with caution upon a mechanical or self-confident application of Freudianism, especially of orthodox Freudianism, to their data. At first the historian has to read Freud more or less passively; but when he sees the use that such men as Harold Lasswell or John Dollard make of Freudian concepts in a political context, or observes, say, how David Riesman employs concepts of character-type in a historical setting, or finds that social psychologists can shed light on contemporary political movements, he begins to get an inkling of the possibilities of psychology for history.

It is here that the social sciences may become particularly valuable to any historian who shares these concerns. The monograph has been unsatisfactory, most commonly as literature but often even in the very analytical functions it was designed to perform. The narrative, while it is sometimes good literature, has too often disappointed our desire for new understanding. What his use of the social sciences promises to the historian is a special kind of opportunity to join these two parts of his tradition in a more effective way. That the social sciences, with their striking methodological self-consciousness. should have something to contribute to the analytical dimension of the historian's work will not surprise us. But our attention may well be arrested by the likelihood that the literary possibilities of his work will also be enhanced, that the monograph, without in the least losing its analytical quality, may take on more of the literary significance that was previously preeminent in the historical narrative. The monograph, in short, may yet cease to be a poor imitation of science and may flourish as a kind of exploratory essay which will be a fuller consummation of the mind and spirit of the historian. We may well ask how this could be possible; how the social sciences, whose characteristic practitioners have not usually aspired to distinguish themselves through literary expression, should be able to help to quicken history as a literary art. The answer, I believe, lies largely in this: that it is the achievement of those forms of literature that are most like history that they deal significantly with the problems of human character. History too aspires to deal understandingly with character, and the means for the formal understanding of character have grown enormously in the past half century. Perhaps the most important function which the social sciences can perform for the historian is that they provide means, in some cases indispensable means, by which he can be brought into working relationship with certain aspects of the modern intellectual climate. They bring to him a fresh store of ideas with which to disturb the excessively settled routines of his thought; but they also serve a catalytic function for him: they show him how he may adapt for his own purposes certain modern insights into human behavior and character which he cannot, on his own, immediately and directly appropriate.

The next generation may see the development of a somewhat new historical genre, which will be a mixture of traditional history and the social sciences. It will differ from the narrative history of the past in that its primary purpose will be analytical. It will differ from the typical historical monograph of the past in that it will be more consciously designed as a literary form and will focus on types of problems that the monograph has all too often failed to raise. It will be informed by the insights of the social sciences and at some points will make use of methods they have originated. Without pretending to be scientific, it may well command more reciprocal interest and provide more stimulation for social scientists than a great deal of the history that is now being written. In this genre the work of the historian can best be described as a sort of literary anthropology. His aim will be a kind of portraiture[13] of the life of nations and individuals, classes and groups of men; his approach to every system of culture and sub-culture will be that sympathetic and yet somewhat alien and detached appreciation of basic emotional commitments that anthropologists bring to simpler peoples.

Most discussions of inter-disciplinary work with which I am familiar begin with the assumption that its value rests chiefly upon the exchange or cross-fertilization of methods. For the historian this means that he can acquire new methods with which to tackle his old problems. There are indubitable advantages for the historian in such techniques as panel studies, career-line analysis, content analysis, the comparative method, more sophisticated sampling, an increased use, where it is possible and appropriate, of measurement—all of them methods in which the social sciences have gone far ahead of him.

But to me it is not the formal methods of the social sciences, useful as they may be, that are of central significance, but rather their substantive findings, their intellectual concerns, and their professional perspectives. Taken in this way, their value paradoxically rests not in their ability to bring new methods to bear upon old problems but in their ability to open new problems which the historian has usually ignored. Prompted by the social sciences, the historian begins to realize that matters of central concern to other disciplines force him to enlarge his conception of his task. Questions associated with social status, social mobility, differences and conflicts between generations, child-rearing in its relation to culture, the sociology of knowledge and of the professions, are questions which he might properly take upon himself, and which are interwoven with his traditional concerns. It seems inevitable, too, that some of the discoveries made by modern social research about current mass political behavior and political influence will revise some of the historian's assumptions about political behavior in the past. In short, the other disciplines ask questions about society which the historian has not commonly asked, and collect data which have a bearing, at least by inference and analogy, upon his problems. Even though the historian cannot always answer these questions with the evidence available to him they remain significant for his work.

But it is not necessarily a scientific use that the historian makes of his conceptual borrowings. I have never thought, when approaching a historical problem from a perspective which I imagine to be rather like that of a sociologist or of an anthropologist, that I would therefore be able to answer my questions with greater definiteness and rigor. For me the fundamental value of these perspectives is in their addition to the speculative richness of history. The more the historian learns from the social sciences, the more variables he is likely to take account of, the more complex his task becomes. The result may be that his conclusions become more tenuous and tentative, but this is a result to be welcomed. The closer the historian comes, with whatever aids, to the full texture of historical reality, the more deeply is he engulfed in a complex web of relationships which he can hope to understand only in a limited and partial way.[14] While he may acquire some usable methods from the social sciences, I doubt that the new techniques that he may acquire will outweigh the new problems that he will take on. His task has not been simplified; it has been enlarged. His work has not greater certainty, but greater range and depth.

Thus far I have spoken only about the value of the social sciences for the historian. While I should prefer to hear a sociologist speak on the other side of this relationship, I would not be fair to my own discipline if I did not say that history has much to offer in return. It is one of the characteristics of our present-minded and journalistically-minded culture that our sense of history is very thin. Oddly enough, while our age pays considerable deference to historians, our capacity to use history to enlarge our understanding is not impressive. Contemporary discussion of mass culture, for instance, is often carried on as though no previous age had ever presented problems to specialized intelligence and cultivated sensibility; because the media of mass communications are new, it is assumed that the past can teach us nothing about the relationship of artists and intellectuals to the public. Historians themselves are by no means immune to the general failing of which this is an example; the failing is also widespread among social scientists, not least among social psychologists and sociologists who need history very much.

While it is the primary business of these disciplines to analyze the relations among special abstracted factors in cultural situations, it is the distinctive business of the historian to define the actual situations in which these factors come into play, and to set the problems of social inquiry in their temporal relations and as nearly in their totality as it is given to the human mind to be able to do. However impartial and imperfect the achievement of these objects, it is history's primary gift to the other cultural disciplines. The historian tries to remind his fellow inquirers that, in the words of Michelet, "He who would confine his thoughts to present time will not understand present reality."

Most inquiries in sociology or social psychology are of necessity planned in a flat time-dimension. The character of a social-psychological experiment, or of most of the fruitful empirical work that has recently been done in mass communications, political behavior, and market research, demands that this be so. But in the long run and when it deals with the large questions, inquiry into human affairs must be historical in character, for the real development of human affairs cannot be sliced out of time in order to appease our curiosity. The trans-historical generalizations that are made by other disciplines that seek for a general theory of action—that is, generalizations about human behavior of such applicability that they cover more than one historical situation or one culture—have an operational meaning that is different from historical generalizations, in the sense that the non-historical generalizations are not intended to shed light upon any historical events, but rather to answer questions about certain abstracted factors of behavior. Social scientists, concerned as they are with the dynamics of behavior, are like the engineers who can tell us about the dynamics of flight. Historians are concerned with such questions as why a particular scheduled flight has ended in a crash.

It is difficult to show in the abstract how history and the social sciences complement each other. But when we get away from abstract discussions of the character and methods of the disciplines to focus our attentions upon actual problems of common concern, their mutual interaction and their value to each other emerge unmistakably. Not long ago a small group of social scientists and historians met to discuss the resurgence over the past five or six years of extreme right-wing politics in this country. We began by talking about the movement in terms set by the study of *The Authoritarian Personality* by T. W. Adorno and his co-workers; but as we got deeper into the problem, one of the most interesting aspects of the discussion was the way in which we found ourselves moving quite spontaneously back and forth between social-psychological categories and historical events, because neither approach was for long entirely adequate. There was no need for the historians to take the initiative in pushing the line of argument into the historical frame of reference; for since we were analyzing a problem that had been posed, so to speak, by historical events themselves and were not trying to work out a general theory of behavior, the relevance and mutual helpfulness of both the historical and the social-psychological approaches were immediately apparent to everyone.

There are important and increasingly numerous links between history and the social sciences, but the two are also held apart by real differences. Some of these differences arise out of problems of communication or out of institutional arrangements. Others have intellectual substance and among these probably none is so important as a difference over the scientific ideal, by which I mean the belief that the closer social science gets to the methods of the natural sciences, the more perfect it becomes. The prominence of this commitment to science is expressed in our terminology, for when we grow dissatisfied with "social sciences" we speak of "policy sciences" or "behavioral sciences"—retaining the noun as clear testimony to an enduring ideal.

For many historians the scientific ideal has been a moving faith, since the days when Buckle asserted that he hoped to follow the example of natural science in his *History of Civilization in England*. But in our own time the scientific ideal no longer has quite the same plausibility for historians as it did for their predecessors in the Darwinian age, or as it now has for their colleagues in the social sciences.[15] Most historians continue to feel that they deal with events which, though in some sense comparable, are essentially unique; and that this differentiates history from most branches of natural science, as well as from those branches of social science in which statistical generalization prevails and even some statistical prediction is possible. Formidable criticisms have been written of the familiar distinction between the nomothetic sciences (which can make general laws about repeatable events) and the ideographic sciences (which seek to understand unique and nonrecurrent events). I am here more concerned with the prevalent state of mind among historians than with the substance of this philosophic issue;[16] and such criticisms, however impressive as forays in logical analysis, do not succeed in spreading among historians the conviction that what historians do is in any very satisfactory sense of the term scientific; and, perhaps what is still more important, do not affect profoundly the way they go about their tasks.

Unlike the philosopher of history or the philosopher of science, the working historian is not nearly so much interested in whether history can, after all, be logically classed with the natural sciences as he is in how far his mode of procedure is in fact a scientific one or could be changed to resemble it. Certainly, in the broad sense that he operates from a basis in fact, aspires to make warrantable assertions, and works in a self-critical discipline, the historian can see that he has something in common with science. But if the term science has any special meaning, he sees equally important differences. Since in his work quantification plays so limited a role, and since he cannot conduct experiments, or, strictly speaking, make predictions, he naturally feels that the difference between his methods and results and those prevailing in most branches of the natural sciences are of central importance. I do not forget that there are branches of natural science which are themselves historical. Perhaps the most notable of these is evolutionary biology; and yet the experience of some nineteenth-century historians in modelling their conceptions upon this type of scientific work is not such as to inspire historians today to follow their example. If history falls short of science, it may help to classify history as a *Wissenschaft*—no word in English quite conveys this distinction—that is, as a learned discipline with a firm cognitive element, based upon verifiable facts and yielding valid knowledge.

We may say, then, that few historians but many social scientists are attracted by the scientific ideal. If we were in a position to inquire into the reasons for this difference, we might find that somewhat different types of persons are recruited into the two professions. Aside from this there are institutional reasons. History is an old and established discipline with strong traditions that weigh heavily against drastic innovation. Since its traditions have been pre-eminently those of a literary art, it has in the literary ideal a powerful alternative or competitor to the scientific ideal. The social sciences, by contrast, are relatively new, and have had to wage a hard struggle within universities to establish their legitimacy—a struggle which in some parts of the university world, as in Britain, is still going on. Having more rapport than history has with some of the pragmatic demands of a scientific and technological age, they have naturally tended to put themselves on a scientific basis as a means of establishing their case. They have, moreover, found themselves in rapport with the practical world not so much for their broader humanistic interests as for their practical results in social and clinical work, in market research, in poll-taking. Of course the differences are not, with this, entirely explained. Historical data are different from social science data, and the terms upon which the inquirer gains access to them are not at all alike. Important branches of the social sciences can conduct interviews, take projective tests, submit the reactions of large numbers of persons to elaborate analysis, cross-tabulate many kinds of relationships, set up a complicated and sophisticated apparatus for the verification of hypotheses, and emerge with a statistical summation of the evidence. Historians do not have direct access to their subjects. The only questions they can ask with the expectation of getting answers are those questions which happen to be dealt with in surviving documents. While they have an abundance of material in history, they do not have such masses of material focussed upon a given subject as is available to modern sociology. Frequently they are driven to reconstruct partially hypothetical accounts from fragmentary evidence. Rarely if ever do they have enough material to warrant setting up such an elaborate method of processing it as the sociologist frequently does. Working under such limitations, the historian is quickly driven to a kind of agnostic modesty about his own achievement. He may not disparage science, but he despairs of it.

One problem history shares with the social sciences even here. History seems most objective, most definite, most uncontroversial—most "scientific" if you must—in those monographs in which historians exhaustively explore an extremely narrow segment of reality. Similarly social science seems to have the greatest precision where it is focussed on small questions susceptible of careful examination, and is often characterized by great caution in its choice of problems.[17] The answers to small questions sometimes shed bright but narrow beams of light on the larger problems of human behavior and the social process, and it is not unthinkable that they may have some important cumulative result. But there is no reason to think that the answers to all such questions will add up to a comprehensive view of society or of historical processes. The historian stands in somewhat the same relation to his pile of monographs. Monographs are useful, but when put together they do not yield comprehensive answers to the comprehensive questions. No synthesis—at least no "scientific" and commonly acceptable synthesis—can be reached through sheer addition.

At this point the social scientist has, in the scientific ideal, a challenge, but also a refuge and a comfort that is not available to the historian. The history of natural science itself has been the history of cumulative progress, much of it made by very small forward steps. One may therefore get a sense of craftsmanlike satisfaction, if by soundly executing a minute inquiry one feels one is taking a part, however small, in a similar cumulative progression of knowledge. But the historian has before him a discipline which, however industriously it accumulates knowledge, experiences again and again through the generations somewhat the same kind of arguments and disagreements about its matters of central concern. The historian who hopes to achieve important work is unable to rest content with the completion of a small but sound unit of craftsmanship, because the tradition of his profession is not so much to look for the perfection of microscopic units of research as it is to try to cope with certain insistent macroscopic questions. Eventually the historian must deal in such categories as the Reformation, the Renaissance, the Industrial Revolution, with wars and social upheavals, with the great turning points in human experience, still tantalizingly unexplained or half-explained, still controversial.

No historian can do great or lasting work without addressing himself, at least at the margins, to one or another of these major problems. And yet the historian does not approach them with the expectation that he will "solve" them, that the cumulation of knowledge will put him in a position to do what the entire fraternity of historians has not yet been able to do, or even that there is any operational way to define the "solution" of such problems. To appreciate this is to understand the kind of enterprise the historian must feel himself to be engaged in: it is to understand that he must see in his own task—so big in its implications, so hopelessly complex, so triumphant over his professional forebears, and yet so formidably challenging that he must again take it on—nothing more nor less than a microcosmic representation of the human situation itself. As soon as the historian's span of attention becomes sufficiently enlarged to take in more than a tiny segment of the historic past, he confronts the precariousness of human effort, sees the passing not only of great states and powerful institutions but of militant faiths and, most pertinent for him, of the very historical perspectives that were identified with them. At this point he is persuaded to accept the imaginative as well as the cognitive side of his own work, to think of history as being not only the analysis but the expression of human experience; he sees his search as a search for clues not simply as to how life may be controlled but as to how it may be felt, and he realizes more fully than before how much history is indeed akin to literature.

10

HISTORY AND POLITICAL
CULTURE: *Namier*

[Every page of Sir Lewis Namier's (b. 1888) work bears the distinct imprint of his bold, analytical mind, his slightly sardonic judgment, and his illuminating wit. While the style is immediately recognizable, the argument is never predictable, and Sir Lewis, born in the old Austro-Hungarian Empire, and recently knighted in England where he has lived and taught for many decades, has been a somewhat unconventional critic of past historians and contemporary politics. Concerned with the relation of politics to culture, of men to ideas and institutions, his study of the members of George III's first Parliament, *The Structure of Politics at the Accession of George III* (1929), fundamentally revised the traditional picture of eighteenth century English politics and by his use of hitherto neglected biographical details of minor political figures introduced a new way of analyzing political history. His shorter works on European diplomacy are also characterized by his meticulous attention to detail as well as by his exceptional grasp of the character of men and epochs. He is now one of the editors of the projected *History of Parliament*.

The essay on "History" appeared in *Avenues of History* (1952) and the one on "Human Nature and Politics" in *Personalities and Powers* (1955).]

HISTORY

The subject matter of history is human affairs, men in action, things which have happened and how they happened; concrete events fixed in time and space, and their grounding in the thoughts and feelings of men—not things universal and generalized; events as complex and diversified as the men who wrought them, those rational beings whose knowledge is seldom sufficient, whose ideas are but distantly related to reality, and who are never moved by reason alone. Yet in all intelligent historical quest there is, underneath, a discreet, tentative search for the typical and recurrent in the psyche and actions of man (even in his unreason), and a search for a morphology of human affairs, curbed though that search be by the recognition that absent from the life of communities is the integration peculiar to living organisms: "fifty men do not make a centipede." On the practical side history should help man to master the past immanent both in his person and in his social setting, and induce in him a fuller understanding of the present through a heightened awareness of what is, or is not, peculiar to his own age. Knowledge and understanding are required before any reasonable endeavour can be made to direct and control; and man, despite a thousand dismal failures and though more and more oppressed by his own creations, can never abandon the attempt to navigate the seas of destiny, and resign himself to drifting in them: he therefore tries to gain a better comprehension of the circumstances in which he is set and of his own ways of acting. History further provides a mental discipline and, as "case history," supplies materials for training in specific professions. And last but not least, it is written and read for its own sake: it answers a need in human nature and a curiosity; it pleases and inspires; and as all the works of man are historically conditioned, knowledge of history is required for the full enjoyment of man's cultural heritage in literature, in painting and sculpture, architecture, or music.

Even animals have inherited habits and preconceived ideas which may, or may not, answer the exigencies of reality. Man is born into a world which swaddles him in the material and spiritual inheritance of society. Primitive man is probably even more the captive of custom and tradition, and is certainly less capable of conceiving and contriving change. But has constant and rapid change, now the law of our lives, set man free? Man-generated, it is seldom man-controlled; it has acquired a momentum of its own, while the vastly extended and infinitely complex social setting adds enormously to the mass of human actions determined neither by vital instinct nor by reason, but by a routine inherent in that setting. Thus the past is on top of us and with us all the time; and there is only one way of mastering it even remotely in any one sector: by knowing how these things have come to be, which helps to understand their nature, character, and their correlation, or lack of correlation, to the present realities of life.

Maladjustment in human affairs is a concomitant of change. Forms, procedure, and ideas outlive the conditions which gave them rise: disbodied they continue an independent existence. Thus the "separation of powers" once supplied a rough delimitation and working compromise between separate centres of power—the Crown and Parliament, or the British Government and Colonial Assemblies; but next, enshrined in a doctrine or in systems based on that doctrine, the separation was continued even in undivided sovereignty; it has weighed on the constitutional development of France and shaped that of the United States. Or again, nations fight ghosts: for about two generations after 1815 the new France passionately defended herself against the return of an *ancien régime* which nothing could have resurrected, while conservative France, old and new, dreaded the repetition of a political revolution which had run its course and was extinct—a semblance of flames that could neither warm nor scorch. In this country the fear of Spain survived deep into the seventeenth, and of France deep into the nineteenth century, after either had ceased to be a danger to Britain: and each time those out-dated fears favoured the rise of the nation which, in turn, was to become a menace. The *cri de cœur* of a member of the Long Parliament, "You will shout, 'Fire, fire,' be it in Noah's flood," describes one aspect of the ever-recurring divergence between fixed ideas and a changing reality. From such examples some people will readily draw the lesson that a similar situation has now arisen with regard to Germany and Russia: which may, or may not, be the case, but must not be adjudged on the force of historical analogy.

While ideas outlive reality, names and words outlast both. The nature and meaning of what they serve to denote or express, change often by wellnigh imperceptible deflection: a gentle, reassuring process which in practice preserves continuity and fosters an illusion of stability; but which is apt to give rise to wrong inferences. Take two examples: there were bishops in the fourth century, and party names were in use in eighteenth-century England; yet conclusions must not be drawn from either fact without a thorough understanding of what those terms then covered. On the other hand there are permanent elements in the lives of communities which, refracted through the prism of ages, reappear in different colours. In the sixteenth century religion was the primary conscious bond of communities, in the nineteenth it was supplanted as such by nationality: the emphasis has changed and the terms in which certain things are expressed or disputed; much less the underlying reality—there always was a strong national element in religion, and there is a religious element in nationality. Caught in the perennial tangle of names, ideas, and reality, man plays with them, and they play with him.

At times, when the burden of the past becomes unbearable, men stand forth determined to brush "the clouds away of precedent and custom," and to live by "the great beacon light God set in all"; the Puritans called it conscience, the French of 1789 called it reason. But even conscience and reason move in the grooves of inherited, historically conditioned ideas and words; and when man has wiped the slate clean and tries to write his own message, the past which lives in him and has moulded him will bring back the very things he has tried to obliterate. The French Revolution, on its ideological side, set out with Rousseau's dictum: "Man is born free, yet everywhere he is in chains"—a historical statement equally incorrect with regard to the individual as to mankind; but though the men of 1789 thought themselves omnipotent by force of reason, in order to feel assured that liberty was possible they had to believe that once it had been: they appealed to history while consciously trying to break with the past. And when under pressure of war an efficient government had to be found, "in the chaos of pure reason," writes Albert Sorel, "men brutally fell back on past practice: instinct made them revert to habits, routine, and precedents: and of these there were none to favour liberty, but plenty for despotism."

The way of life of a nation, *les mœurs,* cannot be transformed by an act of will or an edict; attempts to do so, expressive of intellectual *hubris* (*eritis sicut Deus* . . .), invariably lead to confusion. Planned change can envisage only a narrow sector of life, while the wider repercussions can seldom be forecast. Hence the admitted superiority of "organic change": of empiric practice advancing by slow, tentative steps. Yet human society is not an organism capable of unconscious growth: at every stage thought and theory intervene, more often impeding than promoting readjustments imposed by circumstances and achieved in practice. No one ever planned the role of the British Prime Minister or of the Cabinet: theory and sentiment alike were averse to them in the early, formative stages; and as for political parties, no sooner had they appeared than men started praying for their extinction.

A dilettante is one who takes himself more seriously than his work; and doctrinaires enamoured of their theories or ingenious ideas are dilettanti in public affairs. On the contrary, the historical approach is intellectually humble; the aim is to comprehend situations, to study trends, to discover how things work: and the crowning attainment of historical study is a historical sense—an intuitive understanding of how things do not happen (how they did happen is a matter of specific knowledge). Yet study unsupported by practical experience will seldom produce a historian: hence the poverty of a great deal of history written by cloistered generations. We have been brought up on the tale that the King "left the Cabinet" because George I did not know English (an occurrence and explanation unknown to contemporaries, or to eighteenth-century authors); what did happen was that business gradually passed from the large and dignified Cabinet presided over by the King to a much smaller body of working Ministers: a characteristically English process. Or again, the German historian, Professor Dahlmann, probably the most eminent intellectual in the Frankfurt Parliament, having in April 1848 completed his first draft of a constitution for Germany—the product of a week's intensive labours—hoped thus "with a few incisive paragraphs to heal the ills of a thousand years." Would anyone now think that possible? Even the scepticism of the masses with regard to election promises derives probably from a greater maturity; though often consciously turned against the "politicians," it expresses subconscious doubts concerning the feasibility of vast programmatic action.

A neurotic, according to Freud, is a man dominated by unconscious memories, fixated on the past, and incapable of overcoming it: the regular condition of human communities. Yet the dead festering past cannot be eliminated by violent action any more than an obsession can be cured by beating the patient. History has therein a "psycho-analytic" function; and it further resembles psycho-analysis in being better able to diagnose than to cure: the beneficial therapeutic effects of history have so far been small; and it is in the nature of things that it should be so. Science can construct apparatus which the user need not understand: a child can switch on the electric

light. Nor does surgery depend for its success on being understood by the patient. But psycho-analysis works, if at all,
through the emotions and the psyche of the individual; and
history, to be effective, would have to work through those of
the masses. It would have to educate them. But how can it?
what can it give them? The study of history—of human affairs
—has to go deep and remain uncontaminated to be of value;
and then the value is not in its factual contents—"education
is that which remains after one has forgotten all one has
learnt." Wisdom does not spring from remembered events, and
the mind is cluttered up by an excess of recollections. "One
is apt to perish in politics from too much memory," wrote
Tocqueville. But ways of thinking—"an intellectual climate"
—can apparently be transmitted without traversing the experiences which went to shape them.

Popularized history is mostly dull and valueless; "popular"
history, that which grips and sways the masses, is mostly a
figment. To popularize usually means to oversimplify: fine
shades and distinctions disappear, the tree is stripped of its
foliage and branches, there remains a dead stump. On the
other hand, to affect the masses history has to work on their
passions and emotions, projecting them through a distorted,
mythical past into a coveted future: it is then the product of
imagination and fervour, and not of accurate perception and
critical understanding. Such pseudo-history, in which the Germans excel but which is known also in other countries, has
been supplied in profusion during the last 150 years: *la
trahison des clercs* Jules Benda has called it; and Paul Valéry
indicts all history as "the most dangerous product distilled
in the laboratory of the human mind." But articulate speech
and articulate thought do endow man with a cognizance and
a conscious memory of things not of his own experience,
which is history; and this will inevitably influence his conscious actions: he will talk and think in terms of historical
experience however small and uncertain his factual knowledge.
The choice therefore lies between an attempt at critical inquiry and thought, and the mere babble of blurred reminiscences and fanciful interpretations. The foremost task of
honest history is to discredit and drive out its futile or dishonest varieties.

"Does history repeat itself?" No two events or chains of
events are identical any more than two individuals or their
lives. Yet the lives of all men can be summed up, as in
Anatole France's story, in eight words: "They were born,

they suffered, and they died." The elimination of individual variants, which tend to cancel out each other where large numbers are involved, is likely to disclose certain basic regularities. There may be cycles in history and a rhythm: but if there are, the range of our experience and knowledge is insufficient to establish them; and if there are not, the turn of our minds will still incline us to assume their existence and to invent them. "Is there a thing whereof men say, See, this is new? it hath been already, in the ages which were before us."

Man is a repetitive, aping animal; and to basic regularities and individual variations he adds the element of imitation and of expected repetition. The memory of the sudden German collapse in 1918, after a long series of conquests, helped to sustain our morale in 1940, and was the skeleton at the German feast of victories. A German soldier who had been in Warsaw in 1918, and returned there with the conquering German armies in 1939, said to a friend: "Last time a washerwoman disarmed me. I wonder who will this time." When the Russian revolution broke out in March 1917, there were people who expected that the Russian armies would now fight with a new *élan,* forgetting that in 1792 war broke out in the third year of revolution, while in 1917 revolution broke out in the third year of war; the French peasant-soldier—to mention but one factor—went to the front to retain the land he had seized, while the Russian peasant-soldier went home to seize it. One of the aims of sound historical education must be to wean men from expecting automatic repetition and from juggling with uncorrelated precedents and analogies; they must be trained to fit things into long-range historical processes, and not to think in isolated word-concepts working in a void: for it is possible to believe anything so long as the question is not asked how it could come to be, or how it could work. When in 1938 Chamberlain and Halifax signified their readiness to admit territorial changes in Central Europe provided these were effected "by reasonable agreements and not by force," they were using a-historical concepts; had ever a European continental nation ceded territory except under extreme duress, or if possessed of crushing superiority used it with moderation? There was escapism in that sham-expectation but also a lack of historical thinking. Or again, in the 1,250 large pages of British pre-Munich diplomatic documents, Czechoslovakia is treated throughout as an untenable creation but the question is never asked what the political and strategic configuration of Europe would be after Czecho-

slovakia had been obliterated: an escapist reticence favoured
by man's innate reluctance to think out the long-range consequences of his actions.

In certain disciplines, such as diplomacy, military art, politics, or finance, individual experience is obviously and necessarily inadequate: men have to draw on history, which is
vicarious experience, less vivid and formative but much wider.
Can men learn from it? That depends on the quality and
accuracy of the historian's perceptions and conclusions, and on
the critical faculties of the reader—on the "argument," and on
the "intellects" to comprehend it. When erudition exceeds intelligence, past results are rigidly applied to radically changed
situations and preparations are completed for fighting the
previous war. Conclusions drawn primarily from experience in
the narrow theatre of the Crimean War gave rise to Frossard's
doctrine of systematic defence; next, the German victories of
1870 made military opinion swing back in favour of relentless
attack; the price paid for it in the trench-warfare of 1914-18
produced in turn the Maginot mentality among the French
public and politicians, though much less among the soldiers
who continued to plan offensive action: but in the slow-mo-
tion style of 1918. The Germans in 1914 neglected Clause-
witz's injunction, if there is one enemy to go for his capital,
but if two, for their line of communication. In 1940 they
correctly went first for the Channel ports, and only next for
Paris; but in 1941 they perhaps unduly neglected a new
factor in warfare: had their main initial offensive been
directed against the Caucasus, they might have cut off Russia's
oil supply and immobilized her armies. The time lag in
disciplined military thought is aggravated on the victorious
side by the glory which attaches to past successes and by the
prestige of their ageing artificers. Yet in all spheres alike,
even in the freest, false analogies, the product of superficial
knowledge and reasoning, are the pitfall of history as *magistra
vitae*.

Human affairs being the subject matter of history, all human pursuits and disciplines in their social aspects enter into
it. But as no human mind can master more than a fraction of
what would be required for a wide and balanced understanding of human affairs, limitation and selection are essential in
the historian's craft. Analytic insight into the tangle of human
affairs coupled with a consciousness of his own limitations is
the mark of the real historian, and maturity is attained perhaps
later in his work than in any other discipline.

As history deals with concrete events fixed in time and

space, narrative is its basic medium—but guided by analytic selection of what to narrate. The function of the historian is akin to that of the painter and not of the photographic camera: to discover and set forth, to single out and stress that which is of the nature of the thing, and not to reproduce indiscriminately all that meets the eye. To distinguish a tree you look at its shape, its bark and leaf; counting and measuring its branches would get you nowhere. Similarly what matters in history is the great outline and the significant detail; what must be avoided is the deadly morass of irrelevant narrative.

History is therefore necessarily subjective and individual, conditioned by the interest and vision of the historian. His interest if intense and sincere is contagious, and the test of his originality is whether it is convincing; once stated, his discoveries should appear obvious. The discussion whether history is an art or a science seems futile: it is like medical diagnosis; a great deal of previous experience and knowledge, and the scientific approach of the trained mind, are required, yet the final conclusions (to be re-examined in the light of evidence) are intuitive: an art. The great historian is like the great artist or doctor: after he has done his work, others should not be able to practise within its sphere in the terms of the preceding era. Yet the great mass of the work even of the masters of the craft is devoted to studies of a preparatory character and primarily for the use of the profession. One must plough and sow before one can reap; and it is in such studies that the historian receives his training and keeps up his proficiency. The hackneyed witticism about "dry-as-dust" historians who "know more and more about less and less" comes mostly from people who write and read history without real thought or intellectual purpose—as a senseless ritual.

Biographies have become the ritualist form of English historiography; they predominate as much as portraits do in English oil-painting: both answer a custom and a demand, and pay homage to the importance ascribed to individuals; but they may also be due to fear of unbounded fields or to a lack of creative imagination. A biography has a beginning and an end, and a track to follow between the two points; and even great historians sometimes use its framework for studies of wider transactions and problems. But the typical political biography mixes up three different functions, and in that mixture finds an excuse for doing each badly. It uses the papers and correspondence of the biographee; an editor would have to annotate them carefully, collate them with other material, explain obscure transactions, and deal with problems on their own ground; the biographer can select whatever he chooses—"the human being" is his subject. But to deal with the human being would require knowledge of ancillary disciplines, foremost of psychology, both normal and pathological, and insight into the human mind and character; while most biographers if asked for their qualifications could only answer more or less like the girl who applied for the post of nurse to children: that she herself was once a child. Lastly, the "background" can be compiled from elementary text-books—"after all," the biographer will protest, "I do not claim to write an original history of the time." Even "and his Time" in the title is often treated as a mere excuse for sticking in anything, however irrelevant, found among the papers of the person concerned. True biography is a great and exacting art; but even biographies written on the assumption that this is the easiest form of history, find a much wider public than works of an impersonal character: they seem more human, and are therefore supposed to be "easy reading."

In each period the subject of history is determined by the interest of its authors and readers. When clerics formed the bulk of the reading public, religious history was the dominant subject; in Courts the interest shifted to princes and their reigns, their diplomacy and wars; in the Parliamentary era statesmen and their careers became the standard theme; and with the rise of the middle classes, economic history moved to the foreground, but through a certain inertia long remained a mere history of economic policy, dealing in this country with enclosures, the repeal of the Corn Laws, factory legislation, etc. Even the advent of Everyman has so far failed to add demographic history to the older well-established branches—but how could historians working in isolation successfully tackle the task? No one would expect a contemporary survey of the life and work of the people or of political behaviour to be undertaken otherwise than by teams. Why then for a past period? The low productivity of historical research in this, and even in many another, direction, is due to antiquated concepts and methods—"always scribble, scribble, scribble! eh, Mr. Gibbon?"—but the questions now asked and the materials to be mastered would have baffled even that greatest and most industrious of eighteenth-century historians. Unless there is concerted research, history cannot deal with aggregates otherwise than in vague generalizations: to treat them as entities in which each person retains his individuality requires a new technique.

A beginning in that direction is being made in the new, officially sponsored, History of Parliament based on the biographies of all the Members who sat in the House of Commons up to 1901: a demographic study of the most significant group-formation in the life of this country. Are we then going back to "biographies" after all? Criticism of inept biography does not imply that history can ever deal with anything but "men in action." But it is a new pattern of an aggregate character, and based on materials much richer than were ever tapped in the past, that we are trying to delineate.

HUMAN NATURE IN POLITICS

The title of this essay reproduces that of a famous book published nearly fifty years ago: *Human Nature in Politics,* by Graham Wallas. Its first sentence read: "The study of politics is just now (1908) in a curiously unsatisfactory position." "The thinkers of the past," he wrote, "from Plato to Bentham and Mill, had each his own view of human nature, and they made those views the basis of their speculations on government"; but he complained that his own contemporaries no longer prefaced their treatises on political science by a definition of human nature, and indeed, he found it difficult to discover whether they possessed any conception of it at all.

Not that he commended the naive, dogmatic definitions supplied by earlier writers: for instance, by the Utilitarians who thought they had found the key to man's behaviour in the hedonistic principle of his seeking pleasure and shunning pain, or by the classical economists with their *homo oeconomicus* desirous to obtain additional wealth with the least sacrifice—systems based on the assumption of man's essential rationality. "When we see the actions of a man," wrote Macaulay in 1829, "we know with certainty what he thinks his interest to be." It was thus assumed that man always acts on a valid, reasonable inference of how best to achieve a preconceived end. Graham Wallas's own conclusion about human nature in politics was that "most of the political opinions of most men are the result, not of reasoning tested by experience, but of unconscious or half-conscious inference fixed by habit"; and he exhorted students of politics to fight against the tendency to "exaggerate the intellectuality of mankind."

Graham Wallas's criticism of the *homo sapiens* in politics won an easy victory; the time was ripe for his thrust, and the silence of writers about human nature in politics, of which he complained, may have been a dim, uneasy precognition of his analysis. By now we have travelled a great deal further along Graham Wallas's path. For him atavistic memories and mental habits formed the stock material of man's unconscious thinking. Since then we have learnt about fixations in both individuals and groups, about psychological displacements and projections, and the externalization of unresolved inner conflicts. A man's relation, for instance, to his father or to his nurse may determine the pattern of his later political conduct or of his intellectual preoccupations without his being in the least conscious of the connexion; and self-deception concerning the origin and character of his seemingly intellectual tenets enables him to deceive others: the intensity of his hidden passion sharpens his mental faculties and may even create the appearances of cold, clear-sighted objectivity. I remember how many years ago, when a perfect case in support of a political thesis was presented to a very wise friend of mine, he replied: "I should be convinced by the argument if I did not know the passion which is behind it." He was right to be cautious though he did not apprehend the source of that passion; yet even the recognition of it does not necessarily prove that the thesis was wrong. Or to take a historical example: a sentence in Talleyrand's *Memoirs,* seemingly unrelated to politics, in a flash illumines one aspect of his political conduct. He writes: "I say in order to have said it once, and hoping never to think of it again, that I am perhaps the only man of distinguished birth . . . who has not for a single week of his life known the joy of staying under his parental roof." Here was bitterness which he, writing at the age of over sixty, wished he could overcome. Neglected by his parents and brought up by dependents who extolled to him the greatness of his family, he went through life a very conscious *grand seigneur* who associated by preference with inferiors and, devoid of any feeling for his own class—its primary representatives were to him his parents—contributed with cold indifference to its downfall.

Examples of this kind, positive and negative, to be found in the life of any man, make us less prone to accept at face value interpretations of beliefs, principles, and actions, even if given in all sincerity. Unconscious promptings combine with rational thought, and in every action there are inscrutable components. Undoubtedly one of the most important lines of advance for history, and especially for biography, will be through a knowledge of modern psychology. Still, care is required in applying it. The unqualified practitioner must not be let loose, not even on the dead, and a mere smattering of psychology is likely to result in superficial, hasty judgements framed in a nauseating jargon. But even to the expert, available psychological data yield at best a fragmentary picture. Lastly, there is pragmatic validity in conscious thought unaffected by psychological origins; and action, however prompted, speaks its own language of unmistakable reality. Although we know that man's actions are mostly conditioned by factors other than reason, in practice we have to assume their rational character until the contrary has been specifically established; and when dealing with the mysteries of the human mind, we had best say with the preacher: "And now, brethren, let us boldly face the difficulty, and then pass it over." Yet awareness of the vast depths, unprobed and largely unfathomable, enjoins on us both humility and caution in approaching the problem of human nature in politics.

Even worse than our position with regard to the psychology of individuals, the politicians, is that regarding groups, the masses, the crowd in action. We are as yet merely groping for an approach to mass psychology: some of the positive chapters of Graham Wallas's book now strike one as almost as naive as the beliefs he effectively destroyed. We do not even know some of the means whereby men communicate thoughts or emotions to each other. I remember a remark which in 1911 I heard from Sir Reginald Wingate: he said that after all the years in the Sudan it remained a mystery for him how news travelled among the natives—even heliographs would not have enabled them to transmit it with that speed. *La grande peur,* the panic which seized the French countryside in July 1789 and consolidated the Great Revolution, is the outstanding example of a nation-wide psychological upheaval; but smaller tremors of that kind can be traced in almost every revolution. Besides, there is what in current terminology would be described as the "intellectual climate," dimly communicated and developed by some kind of unconscious telepathy, which seems to affect the great mass of the population.

Very seldom do we come across in history powerful political movements, such as the revolution of 1688, planned and executed with a clear purpose: this was a rising of politically conscious men against the civil and spiritual tyranny of the Stuarts. In most cases the essence of political mass movements is shrouded in darkness. It is hard to believe that on the Paris barricades men died in 1830 in order to preserve the Charter, or in February 1848 in order to obtain an extension of the franchise; more probably behind these two risings were much the same forces as behind that of June 1848, described by Alexis de Tocqueville as the greatest and most singular insurrection in French history. And singular it certainly was, in that 100,000 insurgents fought with remarkable skill and cohesion, though, to quote Tocqueville once more, "without a war-cry, without chiefs, or a standard"; or in simpler terms: without intellectuals having stamped their doctrines or ideas on the rising. George Meredith calls it an ironical habit of mind to believe that the wishes of men are expressed by their utterances; even more ironical, or naive, would it be to judge of the essence of mass movements by the pronouncements or professions of those who manage to filch them. So far we have hardly reached the fringes of the field of mass psychology, the most basic factor in history. All we can do is to try faithfully to state discernible facts, pose problems, but be chary of drawing conclusions.

One inevitable result of heightened psychological awareness is, however, a change of attitude towards so-called political ideas. To treat them as the offspring of pure reason would be to assign to them a parentage about as mythological as that of Pallas Athene. What matters most is the underlying emotions, the music, to which ideas are a mere libretto, often of very inferior quality; and once the emotions have ebbed, the ideas, established high and dry, become doctrine, or at best innocuous *clichés*. Even the principles of the Glorious Revolution, after victory had been irrevocably won and they had changed into an accepted profession of faith, came to sound somewhat hollow. I have been blamed by a very friendly and appreciative critic of my work for taking the mind out of history, for discerning self-interest or ambition in men, but showing insufficient appreciation of political principles and of abstract ideals to which their votaries try to make reality conform. That criticism is so relevant to the subject of this essay that I propose to make it the text of what I have still to say.

To start with taking the mind out of history. It certainly seems impossible to attach to conscious political thought the importance which was ascribed to it a hundred, or even fifty, years ago. History is primarily, and to a growing extent, made by man's mind and nature; but his mind does not work with the rationality that was once deemed its noblest attribute—which does not, however, mean that it necessarily works any worse. Strictly logical conclusions based on insufficient data are a deadly danger, especially when pride is taken in the performance; and our data in politics are necessarily exiguous and fragmentary. Even within that range, the facts we can at any time consciously muster and master in a quasi-scientific manner are a mere fraction of what is present in our subconscious mind. The less, therefore, man clogs the free play of his mind with political doctrine and dogma, the better for his thinking. And the irrational is not necessarily unreasonable: it may only be that we cannot explain it, or that we misinterpret it, in terms of our conscious thought. An absurd proof does not necessarily invalidate a contention: wrong labels are sometimes stuck on produce of unknown provenance.

I came across a striking case of that kind some forty years ago, when working at Yale on the correspondence of Ezra Stiles, an eighteenth-century president of the college. A New England doctor reported to him exciting news: he had discovered that the Red Indians were of Mongol extraction; but being that day in a hurry, he was going to produce his evidence in his next letter. This was indeed exciting—it reminded me of the story of Fermat's famous mathematical theorem; so I went in search of that next letter; but as the papers were not properly arranged and indexed, it took me some time to trace it. When I did, this I found was his evidence: Noah had three sons, Japhet, Shem, and Ham, and wherever we go we find that the descendants of Ham serve those of Japhet; but the Red Indians had no Negro slaves: hence they must be descended from Shem. Funny, isn't it? In time I have come to think differently. The doctor, a trained observer, must unconsciously have based his conclusion on similarly unconscious observations; but being a New England Puritan, he sought and found his evidence in the Old Testament. Every age and every country has a cherished lore and will draw on it in season and out of season; and political principles are often as irrelevant as the argument of the doctor.

As for human motives: tell a story without attributing any, and they will be readily supplied by others from the common stock. The "economic motive" of the Victorians and the "will to power" of the Germans are current coin, and acquisitive instincts or ambition offer plausible explanations of human actions, which can be contrasted with the unselfish pursuit of ideals. But is there such a clear division in the depths of the human mind and nature? Fear, conscious or unconscious, is often the impelling force behind money-making, over-eating, intellectual pursuits, or endeavours to benefit humanity. And even behind money-making there may be a creative urge or thought for the community. On the other hand, is there no ambition, and no *hubris*, in the man who tries to make reality conform to his so-called ideals? To react against cruelty, injustice, or oppression is one thing; to have a nostrum for securing man's freedom or his happiness is a very different matter. And "idealism" or "idealist" are misnomers when bestowed merely because self-interest or ambition is not writ large on the surface.

I remember a story from that admirable book, *The Ladies of Alderley*. In September 1841 Mrs. Stanley, in a letter to her mother-in-law, expressed her dislike for a house because it was "very romantic." "I *don't* understand" wrote back Lady Stanley "why you should wish it not to be *very romantic.*" Mrs. Stanley replied: "When I said romantic I meant damp." Probably it was not merely creepers and thatched roofs which made these terms synonymous for her: the affinity of sound between "romantic" and "rheumatic" may have played its part. So it does in the frequent confusion between an "ideologue" and an "idealist." And what shams and disasters political ideologies are apt to be, we surely have had opportunity to learn. Never have the popular masses been worse enslaved than under what calls itself "the dictatorship of the proletariate," nor has ever worse scum wielded power than under the Nazi régime proclaiming "the rule of the *élite.*" But even far less cruel or fierce political ideologies have played havoc with human welfare. There is a fixity in them that makes them outlive even the few factors to which they were originally correlated; which is the reason why radicals who rely on systems so often produce mere junk—*des vieilleries: ils ne changent pas leur baggage*—they do not repack their ideological baggage. Moreover, almost all ideologies vastly overrate man's capacity to foresee the consequences and repercussions of ideals forced on reality.

Some political philosophers complain of "a tired lull" and the absence at present of argument on general politics in this country: practical solutions are sought for concrete problems, while programmes and ideals are forgotten by both parties. But to me this attitude seems to betoken a greater national maturity, and I can only wish that it may long continue undisturbed by the workings of political philosophy.

11

CULTURAL HISTORY AS A SYNTHESIS: *Barzun*

[As a historian, critic, teacher, Jacques Barzun (b. 1907) has had a marked influence on contemporary academic life, and especially on the teaching of the humanistic disciplines. In his works on European and American culture, past and present, he has come to define a genre of cultural history which comprehends the history of thought and society and yet is distinct from the more exclusive field of intellectual history and the all-embracing efforts of the cultural anthropologists. In his studies of nineteenth century culture, *Race: A Study in Modern Superstition* (1937), *Darwin, Marx, Wagner* (1941), *Romanticism and the Modern Ego* (1943), *Berlioz and the Romantic Century* (2 vols. 1950; Rev. Ed. *Berlioz and His Century,* 1956) and most lately in his *Energies of Art* (1956), he has defined the unity of the Romantic Age and reaffirmed its creative role in Western culture. The following essay appears here for the first time.]

CULTURAL HISTORY: A SYNTHESIS: [1]

I

Every reader today understands the meaning of the term Cultural History and could indicate its bearing. The idea of culture has not only been popularized by History's sister disciplines, Sociology and Anthropology, but men of letters have also made use of the word and the idea to explain the literature and the temper of recent times. "Our culture" is an entity to reckon with.

But thirty years ago, in the mid-twenties, when I began my training in history, cultural history meant little or nothing outside professional circles. And there the phrase, taken as a literal translation of the German *Kulturgeschichte*, carried a taint of fraud. Good men sincerely doubted whether the thing denoted by it could be history at all. With a few exceptions, solid historians feared that a dangerous kind of philosophy lurked behind any professed history of culture. How could it deal with tested and tangible facts? And if it did not, it must dabble in ideas and "forms"; it must talk of the spirit of an age; it must reduce the past to essences and pursue the *Zeitgeist* by means which, strictly considered, would prove incommunicable.

The recognized traditions of historiography in the period I speak of were few. The oldest was the political. It dated from the beginning of the nineteenth century and took its motto from Edward Freeman, who had said in the later "scientific" phase of the tradition that history was "past politics." Buttressing political history was diplomatic and military history. But a second, newer tradition proclaimed the shallowness of these state-ridden histories and regarded its events as being but the surface manifestation of underlying economic forces. The influence of Karl Marx was at work in this departure from "standard" history, but he himself had in fact been jolted out of his Hegelian historical philosophy by the writings of the Saint-Simonians and other socialists, as well as by the histories of Sismondi, Guizot, and Louis Blanc; so that he was not the sole cause of the new departure. It had taken a century for the acknowledged economic element in human affairs to generate a specialized form of research and writing. We can judge of its unfamiliarity to American readers when we remember the hostile reception given Beard's *An Economic Interpretation of the Constitution* in 1913.

The first world war, coming soon afterwards, brought about a great change in public opinion. The war itself was visibly an industrial effort and the postwar generation was led by writers of note to believe that such catastrophes were the work of bankers, cartels, and munition makers. Historians who could not be dismissed as popularizers wrote as if men and nations were "pawns" in a perpetual struggle of "interests." Imperialism, which so regularly brought about wars, was the product of that same capitalist greed to which every other movement in society was but a "cloak." In the Europe of the twenties the historical assumptions roughly summed up here seemed to be verified by the success of socialism and communism, which renewed the vogue of Marx and Engels' writings and prepared the post-depression cult of "Marxist Science."

But although the economic interpretation made earlier histories seem narrow, it did not prevail for long. To be sure, it left a valuable residue of economic studies free from doctrine. But other considerations made the tendentious view seem narrow in its turn, and more than narrow—mechanical and dogmatic in ways alien to the very method of history. In the first place, the war had brought many Americans to Europe, of whom an influential part returned there as soon as they could after demobilization. Amid the pleasures of Paris or Capri they began that elementary cultural criticism which consisted in satirizing their native land through novels and plays; and in doing this they consciously or unconsciously denied the first premise of economic causation: the capitalist systems of Europe and America might be identical in form and purpose, the two cultures *felt* very different.

When the depression came, repatriating the exiles and luring them into Marxist study groups, their awareness of cultural fact was doubtless obscured, but it was replaced by a new concern which is still with us, the preoccupation with ideas that we call ideology. Though Marxist in origin, this concern also worked against the materialist conception of history. For in both immersions, in foreign culture and in ideology, the mind is led away from the tangible elements of society expressible in laws, battles, statistics, and toward the imponderable influence of habits, assumptions, and beliefs.

In the late twenties, the interest in these last was made systematic through the flowering of new disciplines that had been founded or reconceived by great innovators around 1900: the cultural anthropology of Franz Boas, the sociology of Durkheim, and the psychiatry of Freud. The culture pattern, the social group, the unconscious mind were beginning to be talked of as real forces—almost as independent beings —which made election returns and the price of wheat seem futilities by comparison. Indeed, a revulsion of feeling against the practical and business life took place in the United States in the thirties, which quite transcended the resentment against an economic system that had broken down. It was as if the articulate had made over the image of modern industrial man. Hard work and the emblems of success were rejected as civilized goals and replaced by the aims and rewards of the artist—leisure for sensation and the fine arts.

This recurrence of a mood which had swept Western Europe during the nineties was accompanied by ponderings on the fate of civilizations. Spengler's *Decline of the West* appeared in 1918 and inspired critics and imitators, from Egon Friedell to Arnold Toynbee. Thoughtful readers were taken back to earlier prophets of doom or decay—Tocqueville, Gobineau, Nietzsche, Burckhardt, Flinders Petrie—and without abandoning their interest in the local and contemporary, came to feel that mere events, however great or striking, were trivial compared with the rise and fall of whole cultures. As the second world war swept the entire world into another maelstrom, it seemed as if we were witnessing at once the fulfillment of nineteenth-century prophecy and the spectacle of our new historical interest: old cultures sinking in the West and new ones rising in the East.

Today, therefore, anyone who thinks at all is something of a cultural historian. He thinks with the notions of cultural force, cultural crisis, cultural trend perpetually in mind. Newspapers and magazines are one mass of cultural "analysis," and books of every kind, not excepting fiction, make a large place for "the cultural context" as something far more intimate and compelling than the old economic base, the physical environment, or the still older "manners and morals."

These very remarks of mine, though hasty and incomplete, are an act of cultural retrospect testifying to the receptivity which can be assumed in the modern reader: the ground has been prepared and the demand is there. But a general and fragmentary résumé of this sort differs from cultural history in the scholarly or professional sense. In that domain, the difficulties foreseen by the earlier skeptics subsist, and always will, though the skepticism itself has been gradually overcome by a combination of boldness with intelligent trial-and-error. The chief obstacles are: the indefiniteness of "ideas" when considered as historical agents and the apparent remoteness of the arts from the main stream of history. Clearly, if cultural history cannot embrace art and thought, it makes an empty claim; without them, we might as well content ourselves with politico-economic history, seasoned with a dash of "social history" whenever some powerful movement of feeling disturbs familiar customs.

I remember being counseled, when I began in my graduate studies to show a taste for cultural affairs, to keep such things as an avocation. Fortunately, there existed in the Columbia University History Department a tradition that countenanced specializing in the history of thought. James Harvey Robinson, then retired, had made his reputation by a course and a textbook on the intellectual development of modern Europe, and some of his successors—notably David Muzzey and Carlton J. H. Hayes, continued to teach such kindred subjects as the history of ancient thought and culture and the rise of modern nationalism. It was on these foundations that Hayes built to prepare his students for the doctorate, and it was under his guidance and protection that my eccentric determination grew.

My purpose was of course not original or unique but reflected another tendency then expressing itself in the movement that was to be known later as General Education. In the twenties this meant chiefly the possibility of uniting some parts at least of philosophy, history, and the arts in an intelligible account of our past as thinking beings. In this endeavor George Edward Woodberry, Frederick J. E. Woodbridge, and John Erskine had played leading roles, and their success could be measured a decade later, when Hayes in 1932-34 transformed his *Political and Social History of Modern Europe* into a *Political and Cultural History*. Students and teachers across the country were evidently ready for the full sections on art and the numerous, admirably chosen illustrations which proved wordlessly to the eye that culture does change in determinate ways. When about the same time the Harper Series on modern history was being planned under the editorship of William L. Langer, a versatile diplomatic historian, each volume was designed to contain at least one chapter on thought and culture.

These innovations were in fact a return. At the critical period when American universities were being fashioned around or out of the former colleges, that is to say in the 1880's, the proponents of specialized graduate study assumed that undergraduate education would remain untouched. They did not foresee that by their very success in scholarship all subject-matters would split, after which every fragment would enlarge into a specialty, so that in time the unity of knowledge would disappear. We have the words of a representative university builder, John W. Burgess, to show how unsuspecting of future harm that generation was: we may assume, says Burgess in effect, that every young man who comes to our graduate school will have previously acquired the elements of *general literature and universal history*.

Whether the old classical education did in fact impart this knowledge of cultural history is of no moment here. It was an ideal which could no longer be followed when men gave up omnicompetence for specialization and resigned professorial chairs carved out of half a dozen branches of learning in order to become masters of one subbranch or period. For fifty years, as we saw, it seemed both undesirable and impossible to reconstruct the fabric of cultural history. But it was not for want of warnings. Philosophical minds saw the danger of atomized knowledge, however exact, and none expressed it more clearly than William James when he said:

You can give humanistic value to almost anything by teaching it historically. Geology, economics, mechanics, are humanities when taught with reference to the successive achievements of the geniuses to which these sciences owe their being. Not taught thus, literature remains grammar, art a catalogue, and natural science a sheet of formulas and weights and measures.

But for the reasons noted earlier, the sponsorship of philosophy was still suspect. Hegel was a menace and Buckle a solemn caution. History having painfully achieved the status of science must not fall back into the incertitude of ideas, even if it was occasionally forced to take account of such ideas as patriotism, nationalism, and imperialism. These must be reduced to causes that were facts, or history lost its virtue. Thus matters stood, until changes working within history itself, within culture, brought the public and the profession face to face with a desire and a capacity for cultural history.

II

To say that now we all more or less take cultural history for granted does not, of course, mean that we all understand it in the same way. Its wide acceptance is less a common intellectual conclusion than a sign of the self-consciousness which characterizes our times: we love to talk about our culture as we do about our psyches. The genre also records a shift from the last century's individualism to the collective awareness imposed on ours. Everything inclines us to believe that no man and no part of a man exists independently of the rest, and that consequently in history no single element is a prime mover, no single kind of clue an explanation of everything else.

But for the reader of cultural history or criticism—and all the more for the writer—many fundamental questions remain, questions that must be clearly put even if no hope exists of final answers. To begin with, what is "culture"? It is not for the historian what it is for the anthropologist. For him culture is an all-inclusive term covering everything from pots and pans to religion. But the historian writing about his own culture obviously need not describe for his readers what they know from daily use. Indeed he must not, or he will swamp his valuable new thoughts under tedious detail. Yet the historian cannot, either, take culture in its purely honorific sense of "things of the mind." The highbrow's culture is too likely to be a very thin slice of life—all butter and no bread—and as such incapable of standing by itself. It requires what we call background and might better be called underpinning. Given the task of appreciating all that is historically wrapped up in a Cavalier lyric, one must know what a Cavalier was, how he looked, whence he drew his ideas of honor and to what wars he was going when he bade farewell to Lucasta.[2] Immediately, the historian is face to face with King Charles's head, the ritual of knighthood, Puritanism, and the origin of the fashion for men to wear long hair in curls. All this and more is necessary for an *historical* understanding of the unique cultural product from which we quote "I could not love thee, dear, so much . . ." Conversely, the poem preserves an historical moment and can help us reconstruct the cultural, that is to say at once the factual and emotional, past.

The cultural historian, in other words, must steer a middle course between total description (which is possible only to the anthropologist working on a limited tribal culture) and circumscribed narrative (which is the task of the specialist in the institutionalized products of culture: poetry or metaphysics or old silver). No one can say, not even the cultural historian himself, what class of facts he may be called on to bring into his narrative in order to make it intelligible. For example, writing of the 1840's in England or the 1860's in the United States, he would surely have to say a good deal about railroads, for they were diversely new and influential in the culture. In a history of the 1940's or 60's he might neglect railroads altogether. The intelligibility of the whole, the relevance of the part are his sole criteria. This means that the cultural historian selects his material not by fixed rule but by the *esprit de finesse* that Pascal speaks of, the gift, namely, of seeing a quantity of fine points in a given relation without ever being able to demonstrate it. The historian in general can only show, not prove; persuade, not convince; and the cultural historian more than any other occupies that characteristic position.

In his private, shifting definition of culture the historian must moreover have regard to his audience. A cultural history of Japan for Western readers must include much that is useless to the Japanese; and even a cultural history of England written for the English will need supplementing for Americans. This is as much as to say that cultural facts do not unmistakably exist as such—a corollary from our elastic understanding of culture. Unlike a political, diplomatic, or economic fact, a cultural fact is generally not singled out for us by gross visible consequences. The publication of *The Origin of Species* in 1859 may resemble a political fact in the uproar it provoked, but we know that evolutionary theory and the belief in it do not date from 1859. This imposes on the cultural historian the delicate task of telling us how and where Evolution existed as a cultural fact for a century before 1859.

Contrast again the clear-cut overturn of a dynasty or the defeat of a government at the polls with the gradual destruction of a moral order such as Victorianism. When does it take place? It begins in the mind, in many minds, but how do we date and measure its progress? Is it from Samuel Butler's conception of *The Way of All Flesh*, finished in 1885, but not published till 1903? Or earlier, from the time when Dr. Clifford Allbutt began to give private lectures on sexual hygiene and Swinburne shocked all decent people with the sensuality of *Poems and Ballads?* In short how does the moral atmosphere change so that Fitzgerald's *Omar Khayyam*, a complete failure in the 1860's, is everybody's bedside book in 1900, by which time almost all the respectable beards and stovepipe hats have disappeared, decadence is fashionable and woman is emancipated? And to add some material factors, how do the bicycle, the typewriter, and the automobile fit into this great cultural revolution? Has the vogue of outdoor sports anything to do with it? And what of the Boy Scout Movement and the prevalence of appendicitis?

All the questions that might be asked raise the one great problem of assessing connectedness and strength of influence —again a task for the *esprit de finesse* and often a grievance to the student. The beginner is impatient and wants "the facts"; he contrasts unfavorably what he calls "straight history" with the apparently crooked ways of cultural history; and in a certain sense he is right. The ways of cultural history are devious and uncertain to the degree that there can never be a handbook which will list all the valuable facts, and no short cut to arrive at an understanding of relationships. Political and diplomatic history may be intricate in detail but they are emotionally simple—just like war, which they replace and resemble. But cultural life is both intricate and emotionally complex. One must be steeped in the trivia of a period, one must be a virtual intimate of its principal figures, to pass judgment on who knew what, who influenced whom, how far an idea was strange or commonplace, or so fundamental and obvious as to pass unnoticed.

This kind of expertise does not of course exclude the use of statistics when these are available—the numbers of people who attended the Handel Festivals in the 18th century, who welcomed Jenny Lind to the United States in 1850, or who visited the Crystal Palace the following year. But most often counting merely confirms; or else—as in the record of a book's sales—the figures themselves need confirmation. When, for example, we refer quantitatively to the great dissemination of Toynbee's *Study of History* in full and abridged forms, we must look elsewhere to make sure of what we are asserting: is it the acceptance of the author's thesis, and if so is it assent to the whole or to some part? Is it a generalized understanding of his tendency, or do the figures indicate a mere *interest* in the subject, coupled with a vague wish to believe some of the writer's conclusions—conclusions often derived from second-hand reports and preceding the purchase of the book? In a word, what is being counted? Whatever account future historians give of the vogue of Toynbee, the fact of mere interest is what a present historian would assert about the comparable diffusion of, say, Herbert Spencer's works. The verdict would then be that his influence was extensive rather than deep, symptomatic rather than creative. Yet large sales do not always signify the same thing. In the success of Byron's *Childe Harold*, for example, real novelty fell in with a public appetite created by the circumstances of English isolation; and the new work, instead of ending with itself, inspired hundreds of artists for the better part of a century.

That these discriminations are not idle should be apparent. They have to be made in assigning magnitudes within the constellations of those who made the past, and they are the very substance of biography.[3] In making such distinctions it is clear that nothing can supersede insight and judgment, neither the sending of questionnaires to the living nor the measuring of radioactivity from the tombs of the dead. And because this is true the skeptic at this point enters a caveat against cultural history. He deems it the most unreliable of historical genres, the farthest removed from the official, literal documents and figures that other kinds of history are directly based on. "You admit," says the skeptic, "that you cannot measure and demonstrate the influence of ideas, the effect of art forms, the impact of social change, yet you expect us to believe that 'the culture' of France or Germany or the American Colonies two centuries ago was as you describe it. Why, the chances are a thousand to one against there being any connection between your so-called evidence—a pitiful heap of books and letters and music and furniture—and the vast reality you pretend to reconstruct. What culture leaves to the historian is but vestiges of the doings of a very few. The more articulate your sources, the less likely that they are representative. You fill in and sketch out with your imagination and in the light of your present-day concerns. How can you honestly set forth the cultural history of so recent a time and so near a place as eighteenth-century Europe and America?"

This looks like a formidable indictment, but there is a sufficient answer to it. In the first place, culture has continuity; it lives on as other kinds of facts do not. We have to learn what happened in the election of 1888 but we do not have to learn what is meant by progress, patriotism, natural science, or grand opera. The cultural historian therefore deals in large part with the modifications, the combinations, the rearrangements of ideas, feelings and sensations familiar to all who lead a conscious existence. This is what enables him to have insight, much in the manner of the anthropologist, who begins to feel the force of minute events once he has gained familiarity with the culture he has been living in. The cultural historian lives imaginatively in his own culture and also in that he has made his own by study; if at home in both, he is as trustworthy about the one as about the other, no more, no less.

As to the objection that cultural history is restricted to the doings of the highly conscious part of the population, it must be answered that the same objection applies to political and diplomatic history. And if the rejoinder is that the latter activities, led by the few, nevertheless affect the entire people, then the same must be said of cultural affairs. The new ideas of a handful of men in one generation become the fashionable thoughts of the upper class in the next, and the common beliefs of the common man in the third. Everybody now repeats as platitudes what were fresh thoughts in the minds of Jefferson and Franklin; and men of affairs who outside their business seldom give admittance to an idea without a struggle are now convinced that things first said by Adam Smith are self-evident propositions.

Nor is this descent-with-modification limited to opinions. The folk tune is often the art song of an earlier composer, and designs that originate in sophisticated minds and places wind up on wallpaper and chintzes by the yard. In short, regardless of cultural starting points, social groups and classes and nations exist in history through their conscious activities, through the distinctive forms, the characteristic combining of features, by which they strike the observer, contemporary or subsequent. "Exist in history" could be translated "are memorable," for in the definitive words of *1066 and All That,* "history is what you can remember." Just as in biography we take for granted the subject's daily routine of hair-combing and tooth-brushing, so in history we take for granted the great dull uniformities of vegetative behavior.

Hence it is beside the point to argue that millions of our fellow men live and die without bothering their heads about the work of Einstein or Freud or Bernard Shaw. Either the indifferent masses will ultimately feel the impact—the bomb will explode over their heads—or their existence is demonstrably related to mankind's articulate thought through their acting as background, subject matter, or chief obstacle. For the makers of culture do not make it in a vacuum, and whether they are hindered by the conservative third-hand culture of the mass, or draw the inspiration of their work from pondering over the vast stream of unconscious life, they are part of it, shaped by it. The example of a work such as Hegel's *Philosophy of History* shows how unimportant can be the gap between rarefied thought and its raw material—in this instance the philosopher's difficult vision encompassing the dumb travail of Europe's millions during the Napoleonic wars. It is the same miracle which in Goya's drawings of the same period turns the casual disasters of war—pillage, rape, hanging and shooting—into spiritual treasure. The unrecordable comes to exist for history through a cultural product of the most deliberate and elevated kind.

III

It follows from this reciprocal dependence of the articulate and the inarticulate in life that cultural history differs greatly from intellectual history or the history of ideas narrowly defined. Cultural history cannot dwell upon the logic or lack of it in the various conceptions of philosophy, religion, or art without losing its historical character and distorting theirs. The study of these relations has value, but it is historical only in a limited sense, for it rests on exact definitions; and the outstanding characteristic of history as of life is indefiniteness; which is why, again, the *esprit de finesse* is required to grasp it. In communicating his vision the historian does indeed make an apparently hopeless confusion graspable by a certain amount of defining, grouping, and tidying up; but the moment the picture begins to look like a checkerboard, he has overshot the mark; he is no longer on earth but on Mars, where everything is canals.

On earth, for instance, the periods of culture have troublesome historical names—Renaissance, Baroque, Puritan, Classical, Romantic and the like—which cover multitudinous manifestations of spirit. In using these names to denote men or periods, one cannot avoid trying to disentangle appearance from reality and prejudice from fact. But there is danger to truth in wanting things too clear; in wanting to make the names cover absolutely homogeneous ideas or persons. I for one see no use and great harm in those refined distinctions that profess to sort out eighteen kinds of Romanticism, or Humanism, or Pragmatism. I doubt whether the maker of such distinctions could himself respect them in an extended narrative; and supposing that he could, I fail to see what he would accomplish *as a historian*—unless it were to reduce the battle of ideas to a regulated ballet. To put intellectual order in place of the intelligible disorder of history is to apply the geometrical spirit to a subject that calls for the spirit of finesse.

The very point of tracing an idea to its source is that we then see it at work, meeting a problem or paradox, misunderstood, struggling for life like a newborn infant—not as we shall see it later, washed and dressed up for the photographer. The idea's obscurity or strangeness then has a meaning, and we can all the better gauge its force and do justice to the mind that brought it into the world. We are then not bothered by *his* inconsistency, because for the first time we are in a position to discern what he was thinking of and why he set it forth just so: we see him and it *in history,* pragmatically moving toward an unknown future, instead of as an event already classified—a pioneer, or a sad case, or an imperfect product of his times, now assimilated as one more institution in the body of all institutions we call our cultural heritage.

When we scan that heritage and its growth in any given stretch of time, one of the plainest sights afforded the observer is the extraordinary coherence and striking family likeness among the products of the age. This might in fact be made the test of the cultural historian's knowledge—not how much bibliography he can remember but how infallibly he recognizes a sample of prose, music, or painting, or even a particular deed. For acts too carry their dates engraved upon them, regardless of the motives which, abstractly considered, are eternal.

The historian familiar with the forms will therefore keep all the names of periods and schools as they are given him by history and concentrate on the rationale of their successive *styles*—a term by which he means a good deal more than the outward marks of a fashion. For unless he does mean more, he can hardly encompass the diverse tendencies and warring schools of one age which he knows belong together. Some fifteen years ago, in a series of Lowell Lectures on Romanticism later gathered into a book, I offered as an explanation of the internal unity of cultural periods that it came not from the ideas and forms themselves but from the problems to which these ideas and forms offered answers. On that view it becomes obvious how liberals like Byron and Hazlitt can be Romanticists equally with conservatives like Scott and Joseph de Maistre: they radiate from one center, which is to them no matter of choice but of time's compulsion. And this explanation, if true, also helps to mark off the part in cultural effort that is individual and creative from that which is "given," a product or resultant of anonymous forces.

Having seen my notion accepted as a commonplace in professional circles, I am emboldened to amplify it in hopes of making another lucky hit. As it stands, the source of unity I have suggested is abstract. Retracing it helps us to understand the convergence of opposites in science, philosophy, and political thought. It may even be stretched to cover the technical problems of the fine arts. In either realm, it presupposes the intellectual ability to find and state what these problems are. But what is it that gives to the products of an age their common feel and texture—the quality I have called their family likeness, which has nothing to do with intellect, cuts across genres, and unites things strictly not comparable? We feel, for example, that there is a kinship between the early music of Mozart and the prose of Voltaire—a prose that notoriously does not sing—and we wonder why these twins go so well with Louis XVI furniture. Is it an acquired association of ideas or is there some organizing principle at work? In short, is *style* explicable or arbitrary?

Since we cannot believe in a *Zeitgeist* invisibly at work like Ariel on Prospero's Isle, I submit that style, too, is an answer to a common want; but not so much to formulated problems as to felt difficulties of an emotional kind. Style will vary, of course, with the materials that give it body, but forget the stuff of verse or dress or chairs and an attitude remains: style is fundamentally a pose, a stance, at times a self-delusion, by which the people of any period meet the peculiar dilemmas of their day. In bad times the pose is sheer self-defense. At other moments, being creatures of ambition, men want to "be themselves" by repudiating their fathers—and imitating their grandfathers. Energetic and insatiable they want to make the best of both worlds—be gay yet profound, loyal yet canny, heroic yet safe, and so on—resisting choice while strength lasts. In the end they have to adopt the look which affords them the best chance of appearing as they wish to be. They take, as we say, a line; they form a style. Style is the solvent in which incompatibles are meant to merge. If it fits, it catches on and is imitated, to the point of absurdity and paradox— which is why, at least once, every historical style is suddenly seen to be ridiculous. It is then repudiated and a new one devised.

If this genesis of styles is accurate, we can account for a good many curious combinations of human characteristics that are periodic in both senses—time-bound and recurrent; for instance Roman *gravitas* mingled with the satirical spirit, which recurs in England's Augustan age; the boastfulness and gloom of epic heroes from Homer to Beowulf, the elegant frivolity mixed with false tears and real sadness of the late eighteenth century, the demonism and melancholy of the nineteenth, the sentimental toughness and lowbrow pretentions of our own. To ourselves we have no style—we just are—but posterity will smile just the same.

The advantage (and the test) of this hypothesis is that it makes genuine at last the connection between style in cultural products and the oft-invoked "existing conditions." These material elements, forces, states of being, are rightly named: conditions, not sole causes; but they cease to be vague and begin to yield to analysis only when we see them as namable facts arousing the emotions reflected in style.

A further corollary is of even more immediate importance to the practitioner. I refer to the present vogue of Revisionism in the history of ideas. It is no doubt excellent to keep delving back into the past for origins. Men and ideas are all too easily overlooked, and our evolving interests also demand that we revalue what earlier workers neglected. It is moreover useful, as time clears the view, to correct overemphatic distinctions between periods—for example, between the Enlightenment and Romanticism. We should no longer say that the Enlightenment had no sense of history in the face of great researchers like the Benedictines of St. Maur and of great historians such as Voltaire, Gibbon, Hume, and Robertson. In fact, with his *Essay on the Manners and Customs of Nations,* plumb in the middle of the century, Voltaire is the fountainhead of every succeeding movement to create a new and encyclopedic history.

But let us not forget style, and in our zeal to discredit a black-and-white contrast, let us not assume that gray has but one shade. The eighteenth century cultivated history, granted, and Voltaire was a pioneer cultural historian, but there is still a profound difference between the emotion that led him to choose four periods of civilization as alone worthy of record and the emotion behind Ranke's dictum that all periods are immediately before God and equal in His sight. There is an abyss between Gibbon's contempt for the barbarous centuries, his ironic pomp without circumstance, and Michelet's tender, eloquent intimacy with the Middle Ages. They are, we are, all are cultural historians together, but by their styles we may know them apart.[4]

And though by style I explicitly mean more than words, I do not intend to exclude them. They are often the diagnostic signs of "period style" in the sense I have in mind. Depending more on written sources than on any other kind, the modern historian must in all his visions and revisions pay the closest attention to words, making sure that he does not betray them any more than they betray him. This vigilance can save him from the excesses of the root-and-branch revisionists, who would translate all continuity into identity. If he knows, for example, what "genius" meant to Addison, and what it meant to Goethe, he will not fall into the error of supposing that the principles of Romantic literary criticism were already germinating in *The Tatler.* Or if, again, Tocqueville's claim to having introduced the word "individualism" in 1840 arouses the researcher's skepticism, he may properly look for the antecedents of the idea. But it must be *that* idea, in its concreteness and time-born accidents. It will not do to go back to the early Renaissance and exhume Petrarch's introspection as a first fact. That will only challenge others to find in Jacques de Vitry and Robert Sorbon still earlier proofs of soul-searching. Soon we are reading Abelard and mustering heretics—all strong individualists before God. But none—to the candid eye —resemble Tocqueville's model any more than Fenimore Cooper's heroes of free enterprise resemble Mr. Herbert Hoover.

Nor should our concentration on like products within a

cultural cycle blind us to the radically unlike which co-exists with the dominant forms, though submerged by them, or subdued. Every period has its minority interests, which the discerning eye must note even when the minority does not enlarge into the majority of the next generation. The burden of diagnosis is then to say what the dissonant note contributed to the harmony, how it came to be part of it, and what fresh, unsuspected, general problem its resolution would imply. The motions of the whirligig of taste present a multitude of riddles—why did the geometrical Spinoza languish in the century of geometry and flourish in the biological century of Goethe? Why are there so few avowed Pragmatists today, when pragmatic doctrine oozes out of the pores of all our straining existentialists and positivists? These questions, like the rest, will not be evaded by the cultural historian, present or future, who sees his duty clear. But he will be able to answer them only by the application of such finesse as he is gifted with. Intelligibility being his goal, he cannot escape the effort to understand; he cannot ask somebody else to explain nor shut his eyes and count. It is insight, after the count has shown a preponderance of old-fashioned dwellings, that makes him say the dominant architecture of New York is modern. The rest is footnotes.

12

TIME, HISTORY, AND
THE SOCIAL SCIENCES: *Braudel*

[Lucien Fevbre once called Henri Berr's *Revue de synthèse historique* a "Trojan horse" in the camp of traditional historians. In 1929, Fevbre and the great historian Marc Bloch founded the *Annales d'histoire économique et sociale,* in order to continue that challenge to conventional historiography. Around that journal grew up a school which for decades has had an extraordinary influence. Combining a traditional, humanistic view of history with questions and methods adopted from other disciplines and insisting on a broad definition of the historian's proper field, the *Annales* school has inspired meticulous scholarship of an interdisciplinary character as well as continuous, critical reflection on historical methods. "By example and accomplishment," the editors of *Annales* hoped to promote what at the end of his life Bloch called "that broadened and deepened history which some of us—more every day—have begun to conceive."

Fernand Braudel (b. 1902) has been a leading member of that school; his monumental *La Méditerranée et le monde méditerranéen à l'époque de Philippe II* (1949) is the record of an historian gradually extending his field, beginning with the relatively narrow subject of Philip's policy and ending up by placing that subject into a wider context of a regional culture, defined by its physical, human, and material setting. The book stands as the history of a civilization at a particular time and embodies the breadth that the *Annales* school had always sought. That a scientific historian can also bring deep empathy and, indeed, love for his subject Braudel's work exemplifies—and even his well-known essay on method suggests the balanced concern between the historian's need to understand the structure of a society as it evolved over a long time and his pleasure at reconstructing the particular as it occurred at a given moment.

This essay, which first appeared in *Annales* in 1958, is here reprinted, translated by Sian France, with one section shortened.]

HISTORY AND THE SOCIAL SCIENCES: THE LONG TERM

There is a general crisis in the human sciences: they are all overwhelmed by the extent of the progress they have made, if only because of the accumulation of new knowledge and the need for collective research, which has yet to be imaginatively organized. Directly or indirectly, willingly or unwillingly, all are affected by the advances achieved by the most active among them, while on the other hand they still have to contend with an insidious and backward-looking humanism which can no longer provide them with an adequate framework. All, some more consciously than others, are preoccupied with their position in relation to the monstrous body of research, old and new, the co-ordination of which now seems essential.

Will the human sciences find a way out of these difficulties by a further effort at definition or an increased display of bad temper? Perhaps they mistakenly think they have found a way out, since at present they seem to be increasingly preoccupied (at the risk of going back over very old ground or raising false problems) with redefining their aims, methods, and hierarchies. There are endless border disputes over the frontiers which divide them, or fail to divide them, or only inadequately divide them from neighboring disciplines. For each secretly dreams of remaining inside, or returning to, its original territory. A few isolated scholars are working toward closer links: under the impulsion of Claude Lévi-Strauss,[1] "structural" anthropology is moving toward the methods of linguistics, the horizons of "unconscious" history, and the youthful and expansionist empire of "qualitative" mathematics. His aim is to create a "science of communication" which would combine anthropology, political economy, and linguistics. But is anyone else prepared to step over the boundaries and set up interdisciplinary groups? At the slightest provocation, even geography would sever its link with history.

But let us be fair: such disputes and hesitations are not without interest. The desire for self-assertion lies behind all fresh inquiry: denial of another's position is in itself a measure of recognition. What is more, without explicitly seeking to do so, the social sciences do overlap to some extent, each one tending toward a comprehensive view of society in its "totality"; each one, believing itself on home ground, encroaches on its neighbor's territory. Economics discovers common frontiers with sociology; history, perhaps the least structured of the human sciences, is willing to draw the lessons taught by its many neighbors and to spread their influence. Thus in spite of reluctance, opposition, and complacent ignorance, the outline of a future "common market" can be glimpsed; it is an ideal worth pursuing in the coming years, even if at a later stage each discipline would find it profitable for awhile to return to a more narrowly individual path.

But the immediate need is for closer links. In the United States, this cooperation has taken the form of collective research into the cultural groupings of the world today: "area studies" consist primarily of research by teams of social scientists into the political giants of modern times: China, India, Russia, Latin America, the United States. To understand them has become a matter of survival. Even when this pooling of techniques and information has been achieved, there is still the danger that each of the participants might remain buried in his own particular area, as deaf and blind as in the past to what is being said, written, and thought by others. And there is still the danger that not all the social sciences will be drawn into the project, that the older disciplines, for example, might be neglected in favor of the younger, whose promise is so great, even if their achievement is not always on the same level. The place allotted to geography, for example, in these American projects is negligible, and that given to history extremely small. And one might well ask what kind of history.

The other social sciences are very little aware of the crisis through which history has passed in the course of the last twenty or thirty years, and they have tended to neglect not only the work of historians but also that aspect of social reality of which history has always been a faithful servant, if not always a good public relations officer: that is, the dimension of time in society, the many-stranded and contradictory notions of time in the lives of men, which make up not only the substance of the past but the very fabric of social life in the present. There is therefore all the more reason, in the current debate within the social sciences, to stress as forcefully as possible the importance and usefulness of history, or rather of the dialectic of the different notions of time, which repeatedly emerges from the historian's activity; to us there is nothing more important—indeed, central to social reality—than the sharp, intimate, and indefinitely repeated opposition between the single moment and the slow unfolding of time. Whether one is studying the past or the present, a clear awareness of the plurality of social time is indispensable if there is to be any shared methodology of the social sciences.

I shall therefore have much to say about history and historical time: not so much for the benefit of the students of history who are likely to read this article and who are familiar with our work, as for that of our colleagues in neighboring disciplines: economists, ethnographers, ethnologists (or anthropologists), sociologists, psychologists, linguists, demographers, geographers, even social mathematicians or statisticians—all colleagues whose experiments and research we have watched with interest for many years, because it seemed (and still seems) to us that, by following in their footsteps or by making contact with them, history could be made to appear in a new light. Perhaps we in turn have something to offer them. From recent historical research and experiment there has emerged—although the degree to which it has been consciously formulated and accepted may vary—an increasingly precise concept of the multiple nature of time and, in particular, of the value of the long-term view of time. It is this concept, rather than history in general—history in all its diversity—which should interest our colleagues in the social sciences.

1. *History and the Different Notions of Time*

The work of every historian breaks down the chronological reality of past time, more or less consciously choosing and excluding. The dramatic, staccato rhythms of traditional historiography, with its emphasis on the short term, the individual, and the event, have long been familiar to us.

Recent economic and social history places the concept of cyclical change at the center of its research and intends to keep it there. It has been captivated by the mirage—and the reality

—of the cyclical rise and fall of prices. So alongside the narrative (or "dramatic rendering") of traditional history, there is another kind of history, which takes as its subject large periods of time—ten, twenty, or fifty years—in order to discover the background circumstances of events.

Over and above this second type there is a third, this time on an even greater scale, a history which measures in centuries: this is the history of the long, even the very long, term. Whatever its merits, I have found this expression useful for describing the opposite of what François Simiand was one of the first after Paul Lacombe to call "the history of events" *(l'histoire événementielle)*. The expressions are not very important: whatever one chooses to call them, the present discussion will range from one end of the spectrum of time to the other, from the instantaneous to the long term.

Not that one can be absolutely sure about these words: the word "event," for example. I should like to see it confined to a very short period of time: an event is like an explosion "blaring out the news," as they would have said in the 16th century. Contemporary consciousness is blinded by its deceptive smoke, but its flash is brief and cannot be recalled.

Philosophers would no doubt argue that this is to empty the word of a good deal of its meaning. An event, in really determined hands, can be loaded with a whole series of meanings and relationships, respectable or not. It may sometimes bear witness to very deep-seated movements, and through the interaction, whether real or imagined, of the "causes" and "effects" much loved by yesterday's historians, it may acquire a resonance reaching far beyond its own duration. Capable of infinite extension, it may be more or less closely attached to a whole chain of events and underlying realities which thereafter seem impossible to disentangle one from another. By this game of infinite addition, Benedetto Croce could claim that the whole of history and the whole of mankind are contained in embryo in every event, where they can be re-discovered at will. The necessary condition, of course, being that the searcher must add to this fragment something that it did not at first appear to contain and must therefore know what it is admissible—or inadmissible—to add. It is this ingenious and dangerous game which is proposed in recent articles by Jean-Paul Sartre.[2]

So for the sake of clarity, let us speak not of time measured in events but of time in the short term, time as the individual understands it, time in our daily life, our dreams, and our superficial consciousness of the past—time as understood by the diarist and the journalist. Alongside the great, so-called historic events, however, a diary or a newspaper records the trivial incidents of everyday life: a fire, a railway accident, the price of corn, a crime, a theatrical performance, or a flood. It will be clear from this that there is a short term in all forms of life, economic, social, literary, institutional, religious, geographical even (a gale or a thunderstorm), as well as political.

At first glance, the past appears to consist of this mass of details, some spectacular, others unsensational and constantly repeated, the same details which supply the daily raw material of microsociology or sociometry in their study of the present (there is a microhistory too). But this mass is far from constituting the whole of reality, the immense and complex fabric of history which alone can be the object of scientific study. Social science shies away from the event: and not without reason, for the short-term perspective is the most distorting and unpredictable lens through which to view reality.

For this reason, some of us historians are extremely wary of traditional history, the so-called history of events, a label which is sometimes confused with political history, somewhat inaccurately, since political history is neither necessarily nor inevitably confined to events. But it is a fact that apart from the artificial generalizations without any real existence in time with which it used to punctuate its narrative,[3] apart too from the long-term explanations which could not very well be avoided, the history written during the last hundred years, almost invariably political history, focusing on the drama of "great events," worked in and through the short-term perspective. Perhaps this was the price that had to be paid for the progress made during the same period toward the scientific perfection of the tools of research and of a more rigorous methodology. The large-scale discovery of historical documents led historians to believe that the whole truth lay in documentary evidence. Not very long ago, Louis Halphen could still write: "One has only to let oneself be, as it were, carried along by the documents, read in sequence just as they occur, to see the great chain of events reconstruct itself almost automatically before one's eyes."[4] Toward the end of the 19th century, this ideal of "history in the making" led to a new style of narrative, governed by a desire for accuracy at all costs, following, step by step, the history of events as it emerged from diplomatic correspondence and parliamentary debates. The historians of the 18th and early 19th centuries had been very much more concerned with the long-term view of history, which at a later date only the great mind of a Michelet, a Ranke, a Burckhardt, or a Fustel de Coulanges was able to rediscover. If it is accepted that this ability to see beyond the short term has been the most valuable, because the most rare, quality of historical writing during the last hundred years, it will be easy to recognize the outstanding role played by the history of institutions, religions, and civilizations and, thanks to archaeology, which is used to working in great chronological depth, the pioneer role played by studies of classical antiquity. In the recent past, they were the salvation of our profession.

The recent break with the traditional historiography of the 19th century has not meant a complete break away from the short-term view. It operated, as we know, to the advantage of economic and social history, but political history was less well served. It undoubtedly provoked a revolution, a renewal of ideas, inevitably accompanied by methodological change and a shift of centers of interest with the introduction of quantitative history, of which we have certainly not heard the last.

But above all, there has been a change in the traditional concept of historical time. A day or a year were perfectly acceptable units for measuring time as far as the political historian of yesterday was concerned. Time was a sum of days. But a price curve, a population increase, wage movements, variations in interest rates, the study of production (which is still something of a dream), a precise analysis of the circulation of goods—all require much greater units of measurement.

A new type of historical narrative has appeared, which we might call the "recitative" of the total situation, of the cycle or indeed the "intercycle"; it offers us a selection of time scales: the decade, the quarter century or, as its largest unit, the half century of Kondratieff's classic cycle. For instance, apart from some minor superficial fluctuations, prices rose in Europe from 1791 to 1817; they declined from 1817 to 1852: this leisurely twofold movement of rise and fall represents a complete intercycle for Europe and, more or less, for the rest of the world. Of course, these particular chronological periods have no absolute value. If one were measuring something other than prices—economic growth, for instance, national income, or national product—François Perroux[5] would no doubt suggest other, possibly more valid divisions. But this continuing debate is of secondary importance. The historian undoubtedly now has a new time perspective at his disposal, one which attains the status of an explanatory framework into which attempts can be made to fit history, organizing it according to new patterns determined by these cyclical fluctuations.

It is in this spirit that Ernest Labrousse and his pupils, following the presentation of their manifesto at the last historical congress in Rome (1955), have set to work on a vast survey of social history under the banner of quantification. I do not think I am misrepresenting their intention when I say that this inquiry must inevitably lead to the definition of long-term social factors (or even social structures) whose rate of movement cannot automatically be assumed to be the same as that of economic factors. We should not, by the way, let these two imposing figures, economic situation and social situation, cause us to lose sight of other actors whose movements will be difficult, perhaps impossible, to trace for lack of precise methods of measurement. Science, technology, political institutions, intellectual equipment, civilizations (to use that convenient term), all have their own rhythm of life and growth, and the new situational history will only be ready for performance when all the instruments are assembled.

Logically, this new type of historical narrative, because of the tendency of its field of inquiry to expand, should have led toward a long-term perspective on history. But for a variety of reasons, expansion has not been the rule, and we are now seeing a return to the short-term perspective. Perhaps this is because it has seemed more necessary (or more urgent) to forge links between "cyclical" history and traditional short-term history than to go forward into the unknown. In military terms it is what would be called consolidating acquired positions. Ernest Labrousse's first great book, published in 1933,[6] was a study of the general movement of prices in France during the 18th century—a movement, that is, covering a whole century. In 1943, in the most important historical work to be published in France during the last twenty-five years, the same author, succumbing to the need to return to a more manageable time-span, discovered in the depths of the 1774–1791 depression one of the most powerful sources, or "launching pads," of the French Revolution. Even then he was considering half an intercycle, a fairly extensive period of time. His contribution to the International Congress in Paris in 1948, *Comment naissent les révolutions?* ("How Are Revolutions Born?"), attempts to link a dramatic rendering of short-term economic factors (new style) with a dramatic rendering of political factors (very old style)—the revolutionary days. This takes us right back to a short-term view of history. It is, of course, a perfectly legitimate and useful exercise, but how symptomatic it is! Historians are fond of dramatization. How can they resist the theatrical possibilities of the short-term view of history, the best tricks of a very old trade?

Over and above cycles and intercycles, there is what economists, without necessarily having studied it, call the secular trend. As yet it has only tempted a few economists, and their ideas on structural crises, untested by historical verification, are at this stage little more than suggestions and hypotheses which, at most, only penetrate into the recent past, as far back as 1929 or the 1870's at the outside.[7] But they do offer a useful introduction to long-term history. They provide the first key.

A second, much more useful concept is that of *structure*. For good or ill, this word is of the greatest importance in problems arising from the long-term view of history. To students of society, structure means organization, coherence, a set of fairly stable relationships between social reality and the body of society. To historians like ourselves, while structure does, of course, mean an assembly of parts, a framework, it signifies more particularly a reality which survives through long periods of time and is only slowly eroded. Some particularly long-lived structures become the stable elements of generation after generation: they resist the course of history and therefore determine its flow. Other structures disintegrate more quickly. But all structures act both as foundations and obstacles. As obstacles, they may form a sometimes insuperable barrier (an *envelope* in the mathematical sense) to man and his attempts at experiment. How difficult it would be to transform certain geographical and biological realities, restrictions on productivity, or even to break out of intellectual constraints: for mental habits too can be a long-term prison.

The most obvious and accessible example is still that of geographical determinism. Man may remain for centuries a prisoner of the climate, vegetation, animal population, types of crops, and the gradually accumulated equilibrium of his habitat, which he cannot disturb without compromising the entire structure. Take, for example, the importance of the seasonal migration of flocks in the life of mountain populations; the permanent establishment of maritime civilization at certain favored sites on the coast; the enduring location of cities; the survival of certain routes and flows of traffic: the astonishing persistence of the geographical framework of civilizations.

Similar examples of permanence and survival can be found in the immense history of culture. Ernst Robert Curtius's magnificent book,[8] which is at last to appear in French, is the study of a cultural system which, while selectively distorting it, yet prolonged the Latin civilization of the late Empire which was itself crushed under the burden of its own enormous heritage: until the 13th and 14th centuries, until the birth of national literatures, the civilization of the intellectual élite continued to be nourished on the same themes, the same comparisons, the same maxims and commonplaces. Following a similar line of thought, Lucien Febvre's study *Rabelais et le problème de l'incroyance au XVIᵉ siècle* ("Rabelais and the Problem of Unbelief in the 16th Century"),[9] sets out to analyze the intellectual framework of French thought in the age of Rabelais, the body of conceptions which, well before Rabelais and long after him, regulated the expression of life, thought, and belief and imposed strict limits on the spirit of intellectual adventure in even the most emancipated minds. Similarly the subject studied by Alphonse Dupront[10] is one of the best examples of the new research being carried out by the French school of history. The survival of the idea of the crusade in the West after the 14th century, that is, long after the "true" Crusades, is traced by Dupront in the persistence of a lasting attitude constantly reemerging in the most diverse societies, civilizations, and psychological climates and illuminating with its last rays the men of the 19th century. In yet another related field, Pierre Francastel's *Peinture et société* ("Painting and Society")[11] describes the continuance of a "geometric" conception of pictorial space which remained unchanged from the very beginning of the Florentine Renaissance until the coming of cubism and the intellectual painting of the early 20th century. The history of science too has its examples: theories of the universe which for all their inadequacy as explanations were nevertheless regularly accepted for centuries and only discarded after very long service. The Aristotelian system ruled virtually undisputed until Galileo, Descartes, and Newton; it then gave way to a totally geometric theory of the universe which was to crumble in turn, but much later, in the face of the revolutionary theories of Einstein.[12]

By an apparent paradox, the area where the long-term approach encounters the greatest difficulty is that very area where historical research has achieved undoubted success: economic history. Here the concepts of cycles, intercycles, and structural crises may obscure the continuity and permanence of economic systems or, as some would say, economic civilizations[13]—that is, established patterns of thinking and acting, stubborn patterns which have sometimes survived against all logic.

Let me illustrate this with an example, one that is quickly analyzed. Close at hand, in the history of Europe, we have an economic system which can be characterized according to a few lines and fairly clear general rules: it remained in position more or less from the 14th to the 18th century; to be on the safe side, let us say until about 1750. For several centuries, economic activity was dependent on demographically vulnerable populations, as can be seen from the great decline of 1350–1450 and doubtless from that of 1630–1730.[14] For several centuries waterways and shipping dominated the exchange of goods: any land mass was an obstacle, very much a second best. All the centers of trade expansion in Europe, apart from exceptions that prove the rule (the fairs of Champagne, already in decline at the beginning of the period, or the Leipzig fairs at the end, in the 18th century), were situated on the coastal fringes. Other characteristics of this system were the prime importance of the merchant class; the prominent part played by precious metals, gold, silver, and even copper, competition between which did not abate, and even then not completely, until the vital development of credit machinery at the end of the 16th century; the recurrent catastrophes of seasonal agricultural crisis; the instability of the very basis of economic life; and lastly, the disproportionate importance, at first sight, of one or two large foreign trading areas: the Levant from the 12th to the 16th century and the colonies in the 18th century.

I have just defined, or rather listed like others before me, the major features of commercial capitalism in Western Europe, a system which had a long life. In spite of all the obvious changes which affected them, these four or five centuries of economic life did have a *certain* coherence, which lasted until the convulsions of the 18th century and the industrial revolution from which we have not yet emerged. Certain features remained constant throughout this period, while all around, despite continuity in some other areas, disruption and upheaval were changing the face of the world.

Of the possible approaches to the problem of time in history, then, the long-term perspective is one which is somewhat awkward, complicated, and often unprecedented. To make it central to our discipline will be no straightforward matter, no ordinary extension of studies and horizons. Nor will it be a matter of adopting the new perspective to the exclusion of all others. The historian, if he is to accept it, must be prepared for a change in style and attitude, a reorientation of his thought, and a new conception of social reality. It will mean familiarizing himself with a notion of time which moves so slowly as hardly to be moving at all. Only at this stage and at no other—we shall be coming back to this—will he be entitled to detach himself from the inexorable march of historical time, to step outside it and then to return, but this time seeing it through new eyes, with new preoccupations and new questions to ask. It is only in relation to these slow-moving expanses of history that the whole of history can be thought out afresh, as it were, from its infrastructure. All its layers, all the many thousands of layers, all the thousands of splinters of historical time will form a comprehensible pattern only when viewed against these almost motionless depths: they are the center of gravity around which all revolves.

I do not claim to have given in the preceding lines a definition of the historian's task—merely one conception of what that task might be. It would take some confidence—and naiveté—to believe that after the storms of recent years we have found the correct principles, the unchallenged boundaries, or that we are in a position to found a school. In fact, of course, all the branches of the social sciences are in a state of constant transformation caused both by internal change within each subject and the vigorous development of the whole complex. History is no exception. There is no immediate prospect of quiet waters, nor has the time come for founding schools. It is a long way from Charles Victor Langlois and Charles Seignobos to Marc Bloch. But the wheel has continued to turn since Marc Bloch. For me, history is the sum of all possible histories—a collection of specialized tasks and perspectives from the past, the present, and the future.

To my mind, the greatest mistake would be to adopt one kind of history to the exclusion of all others. That would be to repeat the error of the historicists. Of course, it will be no easy task to convince all historians of this, still less the social scientists who seem to be so determined that we should return to the historiography of the past. A great deal of time and effort will be required before all these changes and innovations are accepted under the old label of history. Nevertheless, a new historical "science" has come into being and is still at the stage of questioning and transforming its own nature. It began in France in 1900, with the *Revue de synthèse historique,* and continued after 1929 with the *Annales*. The historian now became anxious to concern himself with *all* the human sciences, and this has led our subject toward unfamiliar frontiers and fields of inquiry. So do not let us imagine that the same barriers still divide the historian from the social scientist as separated them in the past. All the human sciences, including history, are contaminated by each other. They all speak, or are capable of speaking, the same language.

An observer attempting to understand the world, whether in 1558 or in the year of grace 1958, must first define a hierarchy of forces, currents, and individual movements, then stand back to take a comprehensive view. At every step in his research he will have to distinguish between long and continuing movements and short outbreaks of activity, the latter to be analyzed from their origins in the immediate past, the former from their starting point far back in time. The world of 1558, somber as it was for France, was not created at the beginning of that unappealing year, any more than another difficult year for France began on New Year's Day of 1958. All "current affairs" are a compound of movements of varying origin and rhythm: today's time is the result of yesterday, the day before yesterday, and many days before that.

2. *The Case against the Short-term View*

These may seem commonplace truths. The social sciences, however, have shown little inclination to pursue research into time past. Not that they can be formally accused and found guilty of consistently refusing to accept history and time as necessary dimensions of their studies. Indeed, they even appear to welcome them: "diachronic" analysis, which reintroduces history into the argument, is never omitted from their theoretical discussions.

But apart from these concessions, it must be admitted that the social sciences, by inclination, by deeply rooted instinct, and possibly by training, always tend to eliminate historical explanation; they avoid it by two more or less contrasting procedures: either they reduce social studies almost entirely to events, one might even say to current events, by means of an empirical sociology which disdains all history and confines itself to instant material and on-the-spot surveys; or they simply omit the time dimension altogether, seeking from "communication science" the mathematical formulation of structures which are as it were timeless. It is, of course, with this second approach that our chief interest lies. But the event-based school of thought still has enough supporters to make it worthwhile considering both aspects of this question in turn.

I have already expressed my distrust of a history which merely records events. To be fair, however, it must be admitted that history, although frequently singled out, is by no means the only culprit in this respect. All the social sciences are prone to fall into this trap. Economists, demographers, geographers all divide their attention (unevenly) between past and present; they would do well to rectify the balance: this is easy and indeed compulsory for demographers; it goes almost without saying for geographers (especially for French geographers, brought up on Vidal de La Blache); but it is rare indeed among economists, who have become the prisoners of an extremely short perspective, caught between a past which hardly goes further back than 1945, and a present which can be extended by planning and forecasts into an immediate future of a few months, or at very most a few years. I would maintain that the whole of economic thought is inhibited by this temporal restriction. Economists would argue that it is the task of the historian to go back beyond 1945 in search of previous economic systems; but by so doing they are cutting themselves off from a heaven-sent field of observation which they have relinquished of their own free will, while not denying its value. Economists have fallen into the habit of putting themselves at the service of the immediate need and the government of the day.

The position of ethnographers and anthropologists is neither as clear-cut nor as alarming. Some of them, it is true, have firmly insisted on the impossibility (but, then, every intellectual has to face the impossible) as well as the futility of admitting history as an aspect of their subject. But this high-handed rejection of history was not very profitable to Malinowski and his disciples. For how can anthropology fail to concern itself with history? As Lévi-Strauss is fond of saying, anthropologists and historians are both participants in the same intellectual adventure.[15] There is no society, however primitive, on which the "claws of events" have not left their mark, nor is there any society whose history has sunk entirely without trace. It would therefore be quite wrong to complain of neglect from this quarter.

There are, on the other hand, strong arguments for criticizing the short-term perspective taken to its furthest limit in that kind of sociology which relies on instant surveys, surveys on every possible subject, mingling sociology, psychology, and economics. They are as fashionable in France as anywhere else. In their way, they are a constant gamble on the unique value of time present, with its "volcanic" heat and teeming richness. What point can there be in returning to time past? In comparison it is an impoverished, oversimplified wasteland, stripped by silence, a mere reconstruction—and that is the key word, *reconstruction*. But is the past indeed as dead and reconstructed as these arguments would have us believe? No doubt the historian finds it all too easy to extract from a period of the past what he considers to be its essential feature; as Henri Pirenne would say, he has no trouble in selecting the "important events," in other words, "those which have had consequences." The danger inherent in this simplification is plain to see. But what would the observer of the present not give to be able to step back (or rather to step forward to some vantage point in the future) and see contemporary life simplified and stripped of its mask, instead of confused and incomprehensible as it is now under its veil of minor signs and activities? Claude Lévi-Strauss claims that an hour's conversation with a contemporary of Plato would tell him more about the coherence or otherwise of classical Greece than any lectures on Greek history.[16] I dare say it would. But that would be because for years he has been listening to the many Greek voices which have been saved from the silence of oblivion. It is the historian who has equipped him for his journey through time. I doubt very much whether an hour in present-day Greece would tell him a great deal about the coherence or otherwise of contemporary Greek society.

What is more, the investigator of the present can only penetrate to the fine grain of the existing structures by a similar process of *reconstruction,* by advancing hypotheses and explanations, by refusing to accept reality at face value, by either simplifying or adding to it: these are all ways of escaping from one's material the better to understand it, but what they have in common is that they are all reconstructions. I doubt whether the sociological photograph of the present is any more "true" than the historical painting of the past, and the more it tries to avoid reconstruction the less true it will be.

Philippe Ariès[17] has stressed the important part played in historical explanation by surprise, by the sensation of unfamiliarity: when you enter the 16th century you are suddenly aware of being in a strange environment—strange, that is, to you, an observer from the 20th century. Why should it be strange? There is your problem for you. But I would also argue that surprise, unfamiliarity, and distance—which are all paths toward knowledge—are equally necessary for the understanding of the immediate environment which is so familiar that one no longer sees it clearly. If a Frenchman spends a year in London, he will not learn a great deal about England. But by comparison, in the light of his surprise at what he finds there, he will suddenly become aware of some of the most fundamental and individual characteristics of France, which he had never noticed because they had always been there. Compared with the present, the past likewise reveals no familiar landmarks from which bearings can be taken.

Historians and social scientists could no doubt argue indefinitely about lifeless documents and about eye-witness accounts which are too close to life, a past that is too remote and a present that is too close for comfort. I do not think this a fundamental problem. Past and present will always throw mutual light on each other. An observer who studies nothing but the immediate present will continually have his eye caught by anything which moves quickly or glitters (whether gold or not): by sudden changes, loud noises, or ostentatious display. The danger of producing a mere catalogue of events, as exhaustive as any produced by the historical disciplines, is a trap into which any hurried observer may fall—the anthropologist who devotes three months of field study to a Polynesian tribe or the industrial sociologist who parades the snapshots provided by his latest survey or thinks that an ingenious questionnaire and a set of computer cards will enable him to give a complete account of a social mechanism. Social reality is a more elusive prey.

For instance, what can be the possible significance to the social sciences as a whole of the route followed by a young girl as she goes from her home in the 16th *arrondissement* to her music lesson and to *Sciences-Po,* as described in a vast—and not at all bad—survey of the Parisian region?[18] It makes a nice map. But if she had been studying agriculture and practicing water skiing, her triangular journey would have been completely different. I am only too happy to see a map showing the distribution of the homes of employees of a large firm. But if I cannot also have before me a map showing their previous distribution, or if the intervals at which the data has been collected are not long enough to see whether there has been some development, where on earth is the problem, without which the whole operation is a complete waste of time? At best, the value of these surveys for surveying's sake lies in their accumulation of information; they are not at all certain to be useful *ipso facto* even for *future* studies. Let us beware of art for art's sake.

Similarly, I do not see how a sociological survey, such as those we have seen conducted in Auxerre[19] or Vienne in the Dauphiné,[20] can be centered on the study of any single town without being set in a wider historical perspective. Every town, being as it is a society built on tension, with its crises, sudden changes, temporary breakdowns, and its constant need to plan, must be considered in the context of the rural complex which surrounds it and the networks formed by neighboring towns, whose importance Richard Hapke was one of the first to point out. It cannot therefore be studied in isolation from the historical development of this complex, which may often have its roots far back in time. Surely it is not a matter of indifference but, on the contrary, absolutely vital, when one records some particular form of town-country exchange or of industrial or commercial competition, to know whether what one is witnessing is the rise of a new movement, the tail end of an old one, an echo from the very distant past, or a monotonously recurring phenomenon?

To sum up: Lucien Febvre, during the last ten years of his life, was fond of saying, "History, science of the past and science of the future." Indeed, is not history, the dialectic of the different notions of time, in its own way an explanation of social reality in its entirety and therefore of the immediate present as well as the past? The lesson it has to teach us in this context is to be on guard against the event: to beware of thinking exclusively in a short time perspective or of supposing that today's headlines are necessarily the authentic features of our age; there are others who move in silence. As which among us does not know?

3. *Communication and Social Mathematics*

Perhaps it was unnecessary to spend so long at the troubled frontiers of short-term attitudes to time, where the debate continues without producing much of interest or, at any rate, of startling utility. A much more vital debate is that between ourselves and those of our colleagues who have been seduced by the latest experiments in social science, conducted under the twin banner of "communication" and mathematics.

This time it will not be easy to plead my cause; that is, it will be somewhat difficult to relate these new departures to historical time, since at first sight they seem to lie completely outside it. In fact, though, no social study lies beyond the scope of history.

In any case, the reader who wishes to follow this discussion (whether to agree or disagree with what I have to say) would do well to clarify in his own mind, one by one, the terms of a vocabulary which, although by no means entirely new, has been re-adopted and given a new meaning in the course of recent debate. There is clearly no more to be said about "the event" and the "long term," and little about "structures," although the expression—and the reality it expresses—are still to some extent the subject of uncertainty and argument.[21] Nor need we linger long over the words *synchrony* and *diachrony;* they are self-explanatory, although their function in an actual social study is not always as easy to define as it looks. In fact, in historical language (as I understand it), one could hardly speak of perfect synchrony: to halt everything at one moment in time, to suspend as it were all the different concepts of time, is a notion bordering on the absurd or, what comes to the same thing, the extremely artificial. Similarly, a diachronic journey down the slopes of time can only be conceived in the form of many simultaneous journeys down the varied and innumerable streams of time.

With these reservations, a brief mention of these terms will serve for the moment. But we must be more explicit as regards *unconscious history, models,* and *social mathematics.* The necessary comments I am about to make can—and I hope soon will—be regarded as a contribution to the formulation of a set of problems common to all the social sciences.

Unconscious history is, of course, the history of unconscious processes. "Men make their history but they do not know that they are making it."[22] Marx's famous statement illumines but does not explain the problem. In fact we are faced once again, albeit under another name, with the whole problem of long term versus short term, "micro-time" and the significance of events. In the ordinary way, in their own lives, human beings have always felt they understood the passage of time. Can it be that this conscious, straightforward sense of history is misleading, as many historians have for some time been inclined to think? Not long ago students of linguistics thought that the key to everything lay in the study of words. Historians were under the illusion that the key lay in the study of events. Some of our contemporaries would still be willing to believe that everything began with the Yalta or Potsdam agreements, the accidents of Dien Bien Phu or Sidi-Sakhiet-Youssef, or that other, certainly very important event, the launching of the first satellites. Unconscious history flows along far below these surface flashes of light. Let us suppose then that a social unconscious does exist at a certain remove; and suppose furthermore, until we have proof to the contrary, that this unconscious is to be regarded as scientifically richer than the dazzling surface we are accustomed to watching: scientifically richer, that is, simpler and easier to exploit—if not to discover. But the passage from the bright surface to the darkness below—from sound to silence—is a difficult journey full of pitfalls. It should also be added that "unconscious" history, which belongs partly to a situational, but even more to a structural time scale, is often more clearly perceived than is commonly admitted. Each of us senses the existence of a universal history, outside our own lives, although we are more conscious, it is true, of its thrusting force than of the laws which govern it or the direction in which it is moving. Nor is this awareness anything new (in economic history, for instance), although it is felt increasingly strongly today. The revolution—for it has been a revolution of the mind—has lain in the new determination to tackle squarely the half-light of unconscious history and to give it a place of increasing importance, alongside and to the detriment of the history of events.

In the course of prospecting this unexplored region, which is by no means confined to historians (on the contrary, they have merely followed and adapted to their own purposes the initiatives of the new social sciences), new tools of learning and investigation have been developed: amongst them *models,* some of which are more or less perfected, others still at an elementary stage. Models are simply hypotheses, explanatory systems firmly constructed in the form of an equation or a function: A equals B or determines C; X is never found unaccompanied by Y, and close and regular relationships are therefore evident between the two. A carefully constructed model, although in fact based on the observation of one particular social environment, can thus be applied to other social environments of a similar nature occurring at other times and in other places. This gives the model its recurring validity.

Such explanatory systems may be of infinite variety, depending on the temperament, calculation, or intentions of those who use them: they may be simple or complex, qualitative or quantitative, static or dynamic, mechanical or statistical. This last distinction I owe to Lévi-Strauss. A mechanical model adopts the dimensions of the subject under direct observation, which is a small-scale phenomenon affecting small groups of people (and is therefore used by anthropologists studying primitive societies). In advanced societies, where very large numbers are concerned, the calculation of averages becomes necessary and leads to the construction of statistical models. These often debatable distinctions are not, however, central to our discussion.

To my mind the essential task before us, before a common program for the social sciences can be formulated, is to define precisely both the functions and the limitations of the model, whose importance is apt to be exaggerated in some quarters. It is therefore necessary to confront models too with the notion of historical perspective, for to my mind their significance and explanatory value are strictly dependent on the notion of time they contain.

To make this clearer, let us take some examples from historical[23] models, by which I mean models constructed by historians, rather clumsy and rudimentary, seldom developed to the rigorous level of a scientific law and never intended as expressions of a revolutionary mathematical language—models of a kind, nevertheless.

I have already referred to commercial capitalism between the 14th and 18th centuries: this is one of several models which can be taken from the works of Marx. It is fully applicable only to a given group of societies during a given period of time, although it leaves the door open for all kinds of extrapolation.

A somewhat different kind of model is one which I suggested in a book written some time ago,[24] of the cycle of economic development of certain Italian cities between the 16th and the 18th centuries: originally commercial centers, they became "industrialized" and finally specialized in the banking trade; this last activity was the latest to develop and the latest to disappear. This model is both more limited in scope than that of commercial capitalism and at the same time more easy to extend in time and space. It describes a phenomenon (some would call it a dynamic structure, but all historical structures are dynamic at least in an elementary sense) likely to recur in a number of easily discoverable circumstances. Perhaps the same could be said of the model devised by Frank Spooner and myself[25] to explain the history of precious metals before, during, and after the 16th century: gold, silver, copper—and credit, that agile substitute for metal—are all "players" in a game; the "strategy" of any one of them must affect the "strategy" of another. It would not be difficult to transpose this model from the period we chose to observe—the unique and particularly turbulent 16th century. Economists have certainly tried, in the specific case of the underdeveloped countries of the world today, to test the truth of the old quantitative theory of money, itself a kind of model.[26]

But the possibilities of extension in time of all the models mentioned so far are small indeed when compared to those of the model devised by a young American historian and sociologist-historian, Sigmund Diamond,[27] who was struck by the dual language used by the ruling class of great American financiers of the Pierpont Morgan generation: one language being used within the class, the other outside it (the latter being in fact a form of special pleading aimed at public opinion, to which the financier's success was represented as the typical success pattern of the self-made man, and therefore a necessary condition of the nation's fortune). Diamond sees in this dual language the habitual reaction of any ruling class which feels that its prestige is under attack and its privileges threatened; in order to disguise itself, it must appear to be identified with City or Nation, and its own private interests identified with the public interest. Diamond would be prepared to use this model to explain the evolution of the idea of dynasty or empire—English ruling families, say, or the Roman Empire. A model thus constructed is clearly capable of ranging over centuries. It presupposes certain precise social conditions, but history provides plenty of examples of these: consequently it is valid for a far longer time span than any model previously mentioned, but at the same time concerns more precise and strictly limited situations.

Ultimately, as mathematicians would say, this kind of model could be classed with the virtually timeless models popular among mathematical sociologists: virtually timeless—that is to say, moving along the dark and unexplored passages of the very long time perspective.

The foregoing paragraphs are a very incomplete introduction to the science and theory of models. And historians are very far from occupying leading positions on this front. The models we use are little more than bundles of explanations. Our colleagues, who are attempting to combine the theories and languages of information, communication, and qualitative mathematics are far more ambitious and advanced in their research. They have the great merit of accommodating within their field the language of mathematics, a subtle language but one which at the least inadvertence is liable to escape from our control and carry us who knows where! Information, communication, and qualitative mathematics can be grouped together under the comprehensive heading of "social mathematics." Once again I shall do my best to light the way.

4. *Historian's Time and Sociologist's Time*

After an incursion into the timeless world of social mathematics, I have returned to the world of time and the different notions of time. And incorrigible historian that I am, I am amazed yet again that the sociologists should ever have been able to escape from it. The fact is that their notion of time is very different from ours: it is far less demanding, less specific, and never central to their problems and considerations.

The historian by contrast can never extricate himself from a historical conception of time: time clings to his thought like soil to the gardener's spade. Naturally he may dream of escaping from it. Influenced by the anguish of 1940, Gaston Roupnel[28] wrote on this subject in a manner which must pain every sincere historian. Similar sentiments had been expressed earlier by Paul Lacombe, also a historian of repute: "Time is nothing in itself; objectively it is a figment of our imagination."[29] But were these successful attempts to escape? I myself during a rather miserable period of captivity struggled hard to escape the chronicle of those difficult years (1940–1945). Refusing to recognize events and the time during which they occurred was a way of withdrawing to a sheltered vantage point from which one could view them at a distance, judge them more dispassionately, and believe in them a little less. To move from a close-up view to a medium range and then a very distant perspective (the last if it exists must be that of the sages), then having reached that point, to stop, reconsider, and reconstruct the picture one sees, to order the revolving elements—all this is very tempting to the historian.

But these successive attempts to escape are powerless in fact to carry him outside time as it exists, historical time, whose commands cannot be ignored, irreversible time racing on as fast as the earth spins round in space. In fact, all the different concepts of time we can distinguish are bound together. It is not so much the passage of time itself which is a figment of our imagination as the fragments into which we divide it. Yet these fragments come together again when our work is done. The long term, the medium term, and the single event are easily fitted one inside the other since they are all measured on the same scale. So to enter mentally into one perspective is to enter them all. The philosopher, concerned with the subjective, interior aspect of the notion of time, never feels the weight of historical time, of actual, universal time, such as that time of accumulated circumstances which Ernest Labrousse, in the introduction to his book,[30] describes as a traveler who departs from himself as he goes through the world, and who everywhere imposes the same strict order whatever the country, political regime, or social system he lights upon.

For the historian, time is the beginning and the end of everything; a time that is both mathematical and creative—a quaint notion to some perhaps—a time that is a force external to mankind, "exogenous" as economists would say, propelling us forward, controlling us, and carrying away with it our own private time of many colors: this is the time of the world that waits for no man.

Sociologists do not of course accept such a simple concept. They occupy a position more akin to Gaston Bachelard's *Dialectique de la durée*.[31] Social time is merely one dimension of whatever social reality is being observed. Contained within this reality, as it might be contained within an individual, it is one of the symbols—amongst others—with which it is associated, one of the properties which distinguishes it as a separate entity. This accommodating notion of time presents the sociologist with little difficulty: he can cut it off, suspend it, then let it flow again as he pleases. Historical time, however, I repeat, will not lend itself so easily to such juggling with the synchronic and diachronic: it is almost impossible for the historian to imagine that life is a mechanism which can be stopped at any moment and suspended in midair for us to study at our leisure.

This disagreement is more fundamental than it appears: the sociologist's notion of time cannot be ours; the whole structure of our discipline rebels against it. Time for us, as for economists, is a measure. When a sociologist tells us that a structure is continually destroying itself only to build itself up again, we readily accept an explanation which is after all confirmed by historical observation. But in conformity with our usual requirements we should like to know the exact duration of these movements of growth and decline. It is possible to measure economic cycles, the ebb and flow of material goods. It ought to be equally possible to trace a crisis in social structure in time and through time, to situate it both absolutely and, even more, in relation to the movements of concomitant structures. What interests the historian and interests him passionately is the way in which all these movements cut across each other, act upon each other, and reach the point of breakdown; these are things which can only be recorded by using the universal time scale of the historian and not by using the many different time scales of sociology, each of which is appropriate only for one particular phenomenon.

These carping doubts occur to the historian, rightly or wrongly, even when he enters the friendly, almost cognate world of sociology represented by Georges Gurvitch. After all, a philosopher[32] once called him the man "who forced history upon sociology." Yet even in Gurvitch's work the historian looks in vain for his notions of time and historical perspective. The vast social edifice (or should we say model?) constructed by Gurvitch is arranged according to five basic orders of architecture[33]: the *paliers en profondeur* (the hidden levels of social life), patterns of social intercourse, social groups, global societies—and time, the final tier, consisting of different notions of time, the last to be constructed and, as it were, superimposed on the rest.

Gurvitch offers us a wide choice of time perspectives; he distinguishes a whole series of them: long-term or slow-moving time, illusory or startling time, syncopated time, cyclical time, marking time, time running slow, time alternately fast and slow, time running fast, explosive time.[34] What is the historian to make of all this? With all these flashing colors how is he to produce the even white light which is essential to him? Moreover, he soon realizes that this chameleon-like time does no more than provide an extra label, a touch of color, for categories which have already been distinguished. In the architectural edifice built by our friend, time, the latest arrival, is naturally given lodgings along with the other previously installed inhabitants: it must adapt and conform to the living space provided according to the different "levels" *(paliers),* patterns of sociability, groups, or global societies. This is a new, but basically unchanged, formulation of the same equations. Every social reality secretes its own time or time scales, like any ordinary mollusk. But what has this to offer to historians? This huge, ideal architectural edifice stands motionless in time. It lacks history. The world's time, historical time, is there all right, but shut up like the winds in Aeolus's leather bag. It seems that the sociologists' quarrel is not, in the end, with history but, unconsciously, with historical time, the one factor which remains uncontrollable, no matter how we try to rearrange it or split it up into categories. From its iron law the historian can never escape, but the sociologist on the other hand finds little difficulty: he makes his escape either into the ever-present moment, which he imagines as if suspended in time, or into repetitive phenomena belonging to no time in particular. Thus he evades time by two separate mental processes, either confining himself to events in the strictest sense, or to a quasi-eternal vision of time. Is this escape legitimate? That is the real subject of the debate between historians and sociologists and even between historians of different persuasions.

I cannot tell whether such an outspoken article, supported as it is by a historian's excessive use of examples, will meet with the approval of my colleagues in sociology and neighboring disciplines. I rather doubt it. In any case, it will scarcely help if I conclude by stressing once again the *leitmotiv* which has been apparent throughout. While history's natural vocation is to concern itself above all with the dimension of time and all the different perspectives into which it can be divided, it seems to me that of all the possible perspectives the long term is the one most suited to the development of observation and analysis common to all the social sciences. Would it be asking too much of our neighbors to suggest that at some point in their reasoning they should relate their findings or research to this central axis?

As for historians, not all of whom will agree with me, the adoption of this approach will mean a complete about-turn: their instinctive preference goes to the short term. Indeed it is enshrined in the sacrosanct syllabuses of the universities. Jean-Paul Sartre, in some recent articles,[35] lends support to their point of view when, protesting against the over-simple and over-ponderous element in Marxism, he does so in the name of biographical detail and the teeming reality of events. The last word has not been said, he argues, when one has "situated" Flaubert as a bourgeois or Tintoretto as a petit bourgeois. I completely agree. But in every case, the study of a concrete example—Flaubert, Valéry, or the foreign policy of the Girondins—brings Sartre back to the deep structural context. His inquiries lead him from the surface to the depths of history and correspond to my own preoccupations. They would correspond more closely still if the journey was effected in both directions—from the event to the structure, then from the structures and models to the event.

Marxism contains within it a whole range of models. Sartre protests against the rigidity, schematic nature, and inadequacy of the model, in the name of the individual and the particular in life. I would add my voice to his (with only slight differences) in protest not against the model, but against the supposedly legitimate use to which it has been put. The genius of

Marx, the secret of the continuing power of his thought, resides in his having been the first to construct real social models, based on an essentially long-term view of history. These models have been perpetuated in their original simple form by treating them as if they were immutable laws, a priori explanations automatically applicable in all circumstances and to all societies. If they were to be plunged into the changing currents of time, their true texture would become evident, for it is solid and strongly woven; it would constantly reappear but under different lights, sometimes fading into the background, sometimes standing out sharply, under the influence of other structures, themselves subject to definition by other laws and consequently other models. As it is, the creative possibilities of the most powerful social analysis of the last century have been reduced. It can only regain its youthful vigor by a return to the long-term view of history. May I add that contemporary Marxism seems to me to represent very clearly the danger in wait for any social science which is carried away by the model as such, the model for the model's sake?

In conclusion I should like to make it clear that the long-term perspective is only one of the possible common languages which could be envisaged in some future confrontation between the different social sciences. There are several others. I have done my best to describe the experiments in new social mathematics. I find them fascinating, but the traditional mathematics used in the social sciences, and in possibly the most advanced of them—economics—so patently successful, does not deserve the rather disparaging remarks sometimes heard. Many calculations still await our attention in this conventional arena, but we have teams of statisticians and increasingly sophisticated computers to handle them. I am a firm believer in the usefulness of serial statistics and in the need to pursue these calculations and inquiries ever further back into the past. Teams of researchers have already staked out claims all over 18th-century Europe, but some are already at work on the 17th and, even more, the 16th century. Unbelievably long series of statistics have revealed through a universal language the depths of Chinese history.[36] No doubt statistics simplifies in order to facilitate comprehension. But it is the function of all science thus to proceed from the complex to the simple.

Nor should we forget one last language, one last family of models, to be precise: the necessary relation of all social phenomena to the physical space they occupy. We may call it geography or ecology—refusing to be drawn into discussion as to which term is more appropriate. Geography is rather too much inclined to think of itself as a world of its own, which is a pity. What it needs is another Vidal de La Blache to consider, this time, not the relations of time and space but those of space and social reality. The general problems of the social sciences would then be given priority in geographical research. Ecology, on the other hand, as used by the sociologist, is a way of avoiding saying geography, although he may not always admit it, and thereby also evading the problems posed by physical space and, even more, those it reveals to the attentive observer. Maps which offer projections and partial explanations of social realities are in fact spatial models and models which can be used equally well for all time perspectives (in particular the long term) and for all categories of social phenomena. But social science is astonishingly ignorant about them. I have often thought that the geographical school inspired by Vidal de La Blache constituted one of the areas of French superiority in the social sciences; I should hate above all things to see its spirit and lessons betrayed. For their part, the social sciences should make room for an increasingly "geographical conception of humanity,"[37] as Vidal de La Blache was already proposing in 1903.

In practice—for this article has a practical aim—I would urge social scientists to bring to an end, for the time being, their prolonged discussions about their respective frontiers, about what is or is not a social science or what does or does not constitute a structure. I would rather see them concerned in the course of their research, to look both for the guidelines, if such exist, which would point the way to collective research and for the kind of topic which might bring them closer together. I personally see these guidelines as being the increased application of mathematical techniques, the relation of social phenomena to geographical space, and the introduction of a long-term historical perspective. But I would be curious to see what suggestions specialists in other fields would have to offer. For need I say that it is no accident that this article should originally have appeared under the heading "Discussion and Debate."[38] It sets out to ask questions, not to provide answers, in an area where we are all of us, when we venture outside our own field, exposed to obvious risks. These pages are an invitation to discussion.

13

SOCIAL HISTORY: *Perkin*

[Since 1945, there has been a marked revival of interest in social history. In turning from political or diplomatic to social history, historians were responding to new directions in sociology and to new concerns in contemporary society. The achievements of social historians have been diverse and innovative. Their range of interest has been wide, as new work and methods in such fields as local, demographic, and urban history exemplify. Historians have also turned to the study of the family, the child, the sick, and the deviant. The neglected classes of earlier times have received new attention; it is not surprising that some of this history embodies or stimulates a neo-Marxist concern with the impact of changing material conditions on human consciousness and with the emergence of class struggles and revolutionary movements in modern history.

England has been particularly strong in the development of social history, as the works of Asa Briggs, Eric Hobsbawm, E. P. Thompson, and others readily suggest. In 1962, a leading social historian in England, Harold Perkin (b. 1926), addressed himself to the question "What is social history?" and in 1969, in his important *The Origins of Modern English Society 1780–1880,* he has shown that a comprehensive social history could be written, "built around a central organizing theme, the history of society *qua* society, of social structure in all its manifold and constantly changing ramifications."]

SOCIAL HISTORY

Social history as a separate discipline is the Cinderella of English historical studies. Judged by the usual criteria of academic disciplines, it can scarcely be said to exist: there are no chairs and, if we omit local history, no university departments, no learned journals, and few if any textbooks. There seems to be something approaching agreement about its second eldest sister. "There is now a virtual consensus of opinion," wrote Professor J. F. Rees some years ago, "on the scope of economic history. It includes a study of the state of agriculture, industry, commerce, and transport, together with an elucidation of the more technical problems of currency, credit, and taxation." He goes on to say, "These subjects necessarily involve an examination and description of social conditions. In fact the line between the economic and the social cannot be strictly drawn."[1] Sir Maurice Powicke writes in a similar vein: "Political and social history are in my view two aspects of the same process. Social life loses half its interest and political movements lose most of their meaning if they are considered separately."[2]

On social history, then, there seems to be only confusion. Is it, in the words of Professor G. M. Trevelyan, "the history of a people with the politics left out,"[3] or, in those of Dr. A. L. Rowse, how society consumes what it has produced?[4] Is it economic history without the more technical problems of currency, credit, and taxation, or even without the economics? Is it, stripped to the skeleton, simply how men spent their leisure hours? All these definitions seem to me inadequate. Should we, and if so how can we, distinguish it from political or economic history, or even from general history? For, as the late Sir Lewis Namier remarked, "human affairs being the subject-matter of history, all human pursuits and disciplines in their social aspects enter into it."[5] What is the field of the social historian? How can we find a place for him?

I suspect that the social historian, like many others, is here the victim of a metaphor which bedevils even the most casual methodological remark. I mean the agrarian metaphor of "fields of study." According to this the busy cultivators of the academic soil divide it up into allotments on each of which, by a natural division of labor, each cultivator raises the kind of crops (of facts, hypotheses, and generalizations) the ground and green fingers will yield. The ploughland, plotted and pieced, of human knowledge is parceled out like a great open field after enclosure—and woe to the tenant who cannot show a title-deed! The social historian finds his crops still stubbornly growing athwart his neighbors' hedges, and he must trespass, or become a hired laborer serving several masters. Finding a place for him seems an ungrateful task.

But "studies," "subjects," and "disciplines" are not fields, and facts are not crops to be privately harvested and garnered. Facts belong to that category of goods which can be shared without being diminished. All facts are grist to the student's mill, provided his mill will grind them. The outcome of his labors depends on his choice of facts, and this depends on his interests, on the questions he wishes to ask.

Historians know this better than most students, for does not "history" come from a Greek word for an inquiry? All historians start with a question, however frequently they have to change it as they work. What happened? How did it happen? Why? Or at the very least: what will these documents tell me about the past? The social historian differs from other historians only in the questions he asks and the answers he seeks. Finding a place for him does not entail a re-allocation of holdings. It merely involves allowing him access to the evidence.

Social history might be thought to be the historical counterpart of sociology, which "ideally . . . has for its field the whole life of man in society."[6] But all historians ask questions about the life of man in society. What characterizes the questions of the social historian? The word "social" is, *prima facie,* not a help. The Oxford English Dictionary gives thirteen major usages (some of them obsolete). Not one of them covers all that is implied in "social history," or, if it does, covers too much. By virtue of its derivation the word seems at one time or another to have attached itself (in the human sphere alone) to any and every idea or relationship in any way connected with the grouping of men for whatever purpose. For "social" is an omnibus word covering in the first instance all those human activities which display awareness of others. Semantics fails us: we must fall back on common sense.

Professor W. W. Rostow, attempting to "relate economic forces to social and political events," has written: "It is a useful convention to regard society as made up of three levels, each with a life and continuity of its own, but related variously to the others. These three levels are normally designated as economic, social, and political."[7] However useful, it is still, of course, a convention. All three "levels" inhere, if anywhere, in each and every member of society. Society, like the universe, is one and indivisible. It is impossible to isolate, except metaphorically, any one of the "levels," however lively and continuous its existence within the whole. To claim primacy for the impulses from one level is no more than to assert that in each man one kind of interest, appetite, desire, or motivation predominates. The economic interpretation of history asserts the primacy of the economic motive in each man over all others. (Oddly enough, the Marxist view is more a sociological than a purely economic interpretation. "All history is the history of class struggle" is a socio-political rather than an economic maxim. It is true that Marx believed that a man's class and therefore his position in the struggle is determined by his relation to the system of production, but Engels the capitalist goes to prove that men are not invariably motivated by their economic interest alone, while Marx himself goes to prove that men can elect to espouse the cause of a class to which they do not themselves belong.) Put in this way the determinist case becomes an interpretation of the nature of man. It may still hold, but the proofs are metaphysical, and the determinist must meet Professor Ryle's thesis that a man is a single entity, not a bundle of discrete parts and qualities.[8] Men in the past, as we today, lived simultaneously on all three levels, without any division of themselves into abstract "men," either political, economic, or social.

But, like the universe, society cannot be viewed from all sides at once. The spectacular success of the natural sciences since the seventeenth century springs from the device of abstraction, by which the scientist is able to concentrate on a limited number of eminently answerable questions. Abstraction does not change the world, it merely focuses the attention of the observer. In the study of history, of men in past society, it is the difference in focus which justifies the three-fold division of labor. Each specialist has his own focus of attention, his own point of view, his own techniques and tools, his own informing link with an appropriate analytical science (political science, economics, or sociology). It is the labor, we note, not the final product, and in many cases not the raw material, which is divided. Social history is not a part of history. It is, in Professor Arthur Redford's phrase, all history from the social point of view.

But what is the social point of view? "The social level" (as viewed by Rostow) "is very broad indeed. It includes the way people live, the culture and religion which they generate and regard as acceptable, their scientific pursuits, and above all the general political concepts which serve to rationalize their relationship to the community."[9] This last point is surprising, though less so in a later form: "the manner in which general ideas are formed which serve as the basis for a considerable array of political positions on particular issues." G. M. Trevelyan, who takes a similar view of the intermediate rôle of social life between what are usually called the economic basis and the political superstructure, defines the scope of social history as "the daily life of the inhabitants of the land in past ages: this includes the human as well as the economic relation of different classes to one another, the character of family and household life, the conditions of labor and of leisure, the attitude of man to nature, the culture of each age as it arose out of these general conditions of life, and took ever changing forms in religion, literature and music, architecture, learning and thought."[10]

So far, so good: but one feels it is not far enough. Social history, on this pattern, is still auxiliary, peripheral, invertebrate, not, in Professor Arnold Toynbee's terminology, an intelligible field of study, or even an articulation of one. There are some for whom even this is too much, who would confine social history to the kitchen, the wardrobe, the sports field, the ballroom, the garden party, the taproom, and the green circle round the maypole. All these are fascinating places, provided they are seen in significant relation to the wider world of which they form part. What is to be avoided is antiquarianism, the compilation of undigested facts in unpalatable lists without significance or inspiration. Social history of this kind is prone to suffer from the defect remarked by Dr. H. P. R. Finberg in the local historians of the old school: it lacks a central unifying theme.[11]

Local history of the new school, as it has developed in the twentieth century under Sir Frank Stenton, Dr. W. G. Hoskins, and others, gives us the clue. Its central unifying theme seems to be none other than the social history of local communities. I am far from suggesting that social history, like the Department of English Local History at Leicester, should take "the local history of all England for its province," though this would certainly have many advantages: Sir Maurice Powicke long ago acclaimed "the study of local history as the basis of the intimate understanding of social change."[12] What I have in mind is that the social historian should take his society and try to see it whole. That is, in addition to studying the daily life of its members—in the wide sense intended by Trevelyan—he should concern himself with society *qua* society, with social activities and institutions as such, irrespective of their end or purpose. This is the plan adopted by Dr. A. L. Rowse in his excellent study of the structure of society in *The England of Elizabeth*. There he essays to "expose and portray" the whole society, to "extract the juices of the social" from government and economic matters, parliament and the church, law, education, and the cultivation of the land; wherever in short they can be found. "Only so is it possible to write the book and give it a coherent form."[13]

The political and the economic historian are aware of the social framework underpinning the economy and the political system at every point. The shape and structure of society, its growth and decline, the physical distribution of its members by region and district, town, village, and homestead, and their social distribution in the bands of prestige we call classes or the pyramids of connection the eighteenth century called "interests"[14]—all these affect and are affected by events on the levels of politics and economics. The political or economic historian is often driven to ask questions about them, but they are not his primary concern. He is not interested in them for their own sake, but only as they affect the economy or political affairs. Except indirectly, they are not his questions: but they are the social historian's starting point.

The best example of what I mean is the study of population, now a discipline in itself, with its own name, techniques, and journals. Its protagonists point out that demography requires the aid of many different specialisms—statistics, medicine, biology, dietetics, economics, sociology—and its findings must be taken into account by all who study society, from whatever point of view. In the words of one of them, "the significance of population phenomena lies in the meaning for human activity. Population numbers mean markets, military forces, land values. Deaths mean ill-health and disabilities."[15] The political or economic historian can no more ignore population than parliament or prices. An explanation of "bastard feudalism" or the break-up of manorialism without reference to the decline of population in the fourteenth and fifteenth centuries would be *Hamlet* without the prince indeed. Nor is mere reference to an otherwise independent variable enough. If we knew the precise relationship between population growth and the agricultural, industrial, medical, and sanitary improvements during the British Industrial Revolution we should have gone far toward explaining the process of industrialization as a whole. A generation ago we could point to the medical advances of the eighteenth century as evidence that population was more cause than effect in the onset of industrialism.[16] Now the whole question has been re-opened on a subtler basis by a series of analyses designed to show how complex was the interaction between population and economic growth.[17] Cause and effect were so intertwined as to require the most patient demographic research and refined statistical techniques to extricate them.[18] Meanwhile, the most that can be said is that, whatever caused the initial population surge of the mid-eighteenth century, its failure to be met by the usual Malthusian check was not unconnected with the larger supplies of food and opportunities for jobs provided by economic growth—a surprising return after a century and a half to the general, if not the particular, position of Malthus. A necessary adjunct to political and economic history, the study of population is central to the social historian's purpose. Demography as a practical science is a branch of sociology: as a historical study it is a branch of social history.

As for the study of institutions, the House of Lords or the "City" is just as legitimate a topic for the social historian as the kitchen or the wardrobe. Indeed, the social origins of the peerage and the social connections of City-men both cry out for systematic investigation.[19] Every institution, from trial by ordeal to the modern factory, from partible inheritance to political patronage, has its social aspect. Its interest for the social historian is intensified if it throws light on the way in which the society maintains and renews itself, distributes prestige or status, and solves or frets at the recurring problems of adjustment to its environment and its neighbors.

Light may be found in the most improbable place. Sir Maurice Powicke says of the thirteenth-century tournament: "The inducements to violence were too great to allow room for restraint. In the early days, if not later, prisoners might be held to ransom; the booty in valuable horses and equipment might always be large; victory could lead to fortune as well as to fame. The Earl Marshal's prowess in the tournament had laid the foundation of a career which had led to a rich marriage and an earldom; and, although he was certainly an exceptional man, it would be easy to underrate the influence of these martial gatherings on the social fortunes of young men in succeeding generations."[20] There is a clear example of social mobility, all the more important in an age when the opportunities for social advancement were relatively few.

Pilgrimage to the relics of saints might be thought a social activity of some interest, but of not much far-reaching significance. In a book remarkable for its consistently social approach to European history, Professor R. W. Southern writes of the tenth and eleventh centuries: "The deficiencies in human resources were supplied by the power of the saints. They were the great power-houses in the fight against evil; they filled the gaps left in the structure of human justice. The most revealing map of Europe in these centuries would be a map, not of political or commercial capitals, but of the constellation of sanctuaries, the points of material contact with the unseen world."[21] So succinctly is characterized the religious orientation and springs of action of an entire, if small, international society. When he recalls that Rome was the sanctuary of many saints, above all of the two great apostles, a flood of light is thrown on the origins of Papal supremacy.

Social history, then, is nothing more and nothing less than the history of society. If this is an odyssey indeed, it has its wayside hazards. On the one side there is, since nothing human happens outside society, the whirlpool of exhaustiveness, of totality, the desperate, plunging end of those "still climbing after knowledge infinite." On the other side prowls the devouring monster of social science.

First, the history of society is not the history of everything that happens in society. That is total history, ideal history, that complete understanding of mankind's past which every true historian dreams of, works toward, and (since he cannot travel simultaneously by land, sea, and air) forsakes only as a means, not as an end. The social historian must avoid the attempt to be everywhere at once. He must keep firmly in view his immediate goal, the understanding of the life of men in the past, in its setting of society and institutions.

Secondly, social history is not a branch of sociology. It does not seek practical knowledge, descriptive laws, governing principles, predictive generalizations, or what Professor G. C. Homans, emulating Clerk-Maxwell, calls "the nine field-equations" of the science of human relations. It is, first and last, a kind of history. Like all history, it is concerned with "concrete events fixed in time and space,"[22] that is, with particular societies at particular times in particular places. These the social historian studies for their own sake, as an end in themselves, without reference to the practical utility of what he discovers. If an ulterior end is required, it is the hope that "Histories make men wise." Economic history in its early days had to resist the economists' demand that it be "governed by the desire to illustrate economic laws."[23] The social historian differs from the sociologist precisely as the economic historian from the economist. Like the latter, the former pair are colleagues, partners, members of the same team. They cannot afford to neglect each other's insights and *expertise*. If they do, sociology, deprived of the temporal breadth and multiple sensibilities of the historian, becomes historically parochial, restricting itself to such societies and institutions as happen to have survived, without the means of knowing how they came to survive; while social history, deprived of the heuristic depth and theoretical penetration of the sociologist, becomes academically superficial, an antiquarian pursuit of facts-in-themselves, without the means of relating their significance. Yet neither is the master, neither the servant of the other. Both are equals in the study of society, approaching it from different directions and for different purposes. The social historian confronts the same material, may even borrow the sociologist's techniques, but he asks different questions, seeks a different end.

Social history, to justify itself, must ultimately issue in actual social histories. At present it seems to be in, or just emerging from, the situation Cunningham remarked of economic history over forty years ago: "There have been numerous histories of one or another department of economic activity, as for example, merchant shipping, or agriculture, or of particular localities; but comparatively little progress has been made in surveying the growth of economic activities in their interconnection, and the development of the body economic as a whole."[24] Now there is nothing at all to be said against histories of departments of any kind of history, least of all social history. The more there are, the nearer draws the possibility of a comprehensive social history, and the better it will be when it comes. Moreover, there is no need for the specialist historian to consider too closely into what category his interest falls. Let him follow his question, his problem, or his material where it will lead. If he cuts across categories, if like Newton he can unite two hitherto unrelated levels of experience, so much the better. He may be a genius, a man who sets the world thinking in a way which was not possible before. His work in any event will have value for general history, and for some historians in particular. But, to paraphrase Cunningham, there will still be a need to survey the growth of social activities in their interconnection, and the development of the body social as a whole.

Of what ought a comprehensive social history to consist? It

should concern one society, fixed in space and time: Ancient Babylon, Periclean Athens, Imperial Rome, Latin Christendom in the eleventh and twelfth centuries, China under the Great Khan, Elizabethan England, Glossop since the Industrial Revolution. How should the historian approach his society, unfold its themes, write its history, so far as the evidence permits? He should try to see his society as a structured, functioning, evolving, self-regenerating, self-reacting whole, set in its geographical and cosmic environment. He should present the natural history of the body politic, exposing and explaining its ecology, anatomy, physiology, pathology, and, since the body politic may be presumed to exist on more than the physical plane, its psychology too: its awareness of itself, its conscious aims, criteria, and ideals.

This, of course, is a tendentious metaphor which must not be pushed too far. Society is no more a body than it is a machine; it is a *social* entity, an integrated collectivity of human beings, and therefore in important ways both something more and something less than an individual man or woman. Above all, though it has no soul and no putative expectation of eternal life, it has the remarkable property of self-regeneration, that is, of reproducing not some other creature in the same form but *itself* in a great variety of forms. It is a dynamic system which, unlike the body, does not need to organize its members according to a pre-ordained pattern, but can interchange them and evolve new organs according to its requirements. The body metaphor had the tendency in those societies which invented or utilized it of suppressing this potentiality and defending the *status quo ante*—a tendency easily circumvented by those assailants wise enough to appeal to their own version of the *status quo*. Yet the metaphor has the merit of insisting on the essential unity of the thing studied, and, avoiding its obvious traps, we may with its aid usefully explore the implications of the five interrelated aspects of social history.

By the society's ecology is meant its relation to the physical environment, first of all to the geographical background with which it is intimately intermingled, the hard facts of topography, soil, climate, fauna, and vegetation, and the ways in which they have been modified by human action. Adaptation is a two-way process. As society adapts itself to the environment, so it learns to adapt the environment to itself. The well-known English contrast between "woodland" and "champion," between the hamlet-and-homestead settlement of the highland zone and the nucleated-village settlement of the lowlands, is the product of such mutual adaptation—mutual, since open-field villages were by no means unknown in the north and west, and British settlement in the south and east before the English came seems to have been mainly of the highland type. Moreover, East Anglia after the Danes came—if not earlier, after a possibly Jutish immigration—enjoyed down to modern times a highland type of settlement on a lowland topography. This paradox is traceable to the inheritance customs of East Anglican peasants, partible inheritance in an area with abundant land to be reclaimed from waste and fen.[25] The younger son used his inheritance as a base from which to drive back the marsh and reclaim a home, necessarily segregated, for himself. Partible inheritance characterizes socage tenure, and down to this day adjacent fenland parishes bear witness in their differing population densities to their diverse proportions of medieval sokemen and different rates of reclamation.[26] Thus intimately did community and landscape adjust to one another.

At the other extreme from the local is the larger environment of the cosmos. Nothing, it may be thought, changes less from one society or one generation to another than the unchanged and unchanging universe. On the contrary, nothing in human experience can change more and with profounder implications for society than man's view of the universe and his place in it. Quaint, arbitrary, and artificial to the modern scientist, the Aristotelian-Ptolemaic cosmology (responsible for the body metaphor besides much else in our social thinking) was as hard and ineluctable a fact to the medieval European as the stubborn soil or the capricious weather. It had the special virtue of linking human society to everything that existed from the archangel to the lowest worm that crawled, and so endowed it with the same ontological certainty. The prince among his subjects was the natural equivalent of God among the angels, man among the creatures, the lion (or the elephant) among beasts, the eagle (or the phoenix) among birds, the whale (or the dolphin) among fishes. Harmony in the body politic echoed the cosmic harmony of the circumambient spheres; treason and civil strife made discords which heaven rejected and cast out with disgust.[27] When the New Philosophy put all in doubt, shattered the music of the spheres, and overturned the ladder and scale of creatures, European man gained power over nature and, collectively, over his own social organization, at the cost of this old assurance of the continuity of the social, natural, and supernatural worlds. A society's cosmology is from one point of view an aspect of its psychology: from its own it is an integral part of its objective environment.

By way of adaptation a society's ecology leads straight to its anatomy. The structure of society is a great deal more than its class system. In the first place, it embraces the whole of the social "given element" into which the individual is born: the size and shape of society, that is, the population and its distribution by geography and age as well as by occupation and social position; the pattern of institutions, from marriage or inheritance customs to feudal homage, patronage, or contract of employment; and the complex of associations—family, church, gild, chivalrous order, school, hospital, workhouse, club, trade union, professional body, and even factory, political party, or organ of government, in, and only in, their social aspects—in and around which the individual must move and have his being.

Secondly, class is not the only or inevitable division of a hierarchical society. The very concept of class, in the modern sense of broad, mutually hostile, horizontal bands based on conflicting economic interest, is a product of the British Industrial Revolution. Until then the word was used in its neutral, "classifying" sense, and its place supplied by the "ranks," "orders," and "degrees" of a more finely graded hierarchy of great subtlety and discrimination.[28] In that older society the horizontal solidarities and vertical antagonisms of class were usually latent, overlain by the vertical bonds of patronage and dependency and the horizontal antagonisms between different interests, such as the landed, East and West Indian, cloth-manufacturing, and wool-exporting interests. In the small communities—village or tiny town—which made up most of the old society, a man was highly conscious of his exact position in the social hierarchy, not by comparison with his anonymous fellows on his own level elsewhere, but by his face-to-face relationship with his immediate neighbors above and below him. In regard to such a society the concept of class is a bludgeon rather than a scalpel, and crushes what it tries to dissect.

Nor is it much improved by turning it round and calling it status group, at least in the Germanic sense of *Stand*. *Stände* are but classes ancient enough to have acquired a customary title, and to exchange a crudely economic for a quasi-legal criterion. They are appropriate to a schematized feudalism, just as classes are to a schematized capitalism, and in real life schematically correct classes are rare. Modern distinctions, based often enough on a narrow historical experience, fail us, and we must fall back, as in social anthropology, on the terminology used in the society itself. In this case, as explained by a somewhat old-fashioned Irish judge in 1798, "Society consists of noblemen, baronets, esquires, gentlemen, yeomen, tradesmen, and artificers,"[29] though he might have added husbandmen and the "laboring poor."

The structure of society may be a dynamic rather than a static system, even when maintaining itself in substantial equilibrium. The "storm over the gentry" in the century between the English Reformation and the Great Civil War,[30] whatever the outcome of the controversy, has illuminated, if rather fitfully, one of the most important features of English society, not only in that period, but from the fourteenth to the nineteenth century: the continuous recruitment to the landed aristocracy and gentry of "new men" from trade, industry, the professions, and occasionally from agriculture. In the Tudor and early Stuart era of profit inflation, a buyers' land market, and swollen opportunities at Court, the upward flow may have been brisker than at any time before the Industrial Revolution. But it was in principle the same social process which begins with families like the Howards, de la Poles, and Pastons in the fourteenth and fifteenth centuries and is still going strong with the Peels, Strutts, Addingtons, and Scotts (Lords Eldon and Stowell) in the early nineteenth. It is, indeed, a part of the larger mobility of English society, that two-way flow of blood and wealth—an upward flow of rising men from all the lower to all the higher levels, balanced by a downward flow of younger sons from higher to lower, to which must be added an upward flow of heiresses and a downward as well as a sideways flow of dowried daughters—which made England a more open, expansive, and yet a more stable society than any Continental nation. Its dynamic stability created a resourceful landed aristocracy continually replenished from below and in close contact through its own sons with the society it dominated; an active middle layer of business and professional men with powerful incentives to enterprise but none to remain in the towns and form a permanent, frustrated, revolutionary bourgeoisie; and "lower orders" stimulated by social emulation to the twin prerequisites of industrial expansion, proletarian wage-earning, and consumption via the market. In France, by contrast, the segregation from trade and the professions of the privileged old *noblesse,* completed and confirmed by Louis XIV, not only severely impeded French economic development[31] but was perhaps the greatest single cause of political discontent. France had a political, England an industrial revolution; the difference arises from their contrasting social structures.

The third step is to see how the structure works, how the

body politic functions. Its physiology includes how the society gets its living, how it exploits its natural and human resources, how it distributes and consumes what it has produced, what activities other than the means of life it pursues by way of ends in themselves, by what social controls it maintains itself in being and defends itself from unacceptable structural change, and how it regenerates itself and passes on its knowledge and skills, its attitudes and ideals, from one generation to the next. In other words, the historian must "extract the juices of the social" from agriculture, industry, and trade, the distribution of income and capital, government and public order, legislation and public morality, education in all its many forms, religion, intellectual and scientific thought, literature, music, the arts, sports and games, pastimes and amusements. Here we seem very near the whirlpool of totality, if not to have plunged right in.

Yet the problem of keeping a steady course is not so difficult as it at first appears, nor is the pull of the whirlpool peculiar to the social historian. Let us look at what J. R. McCulloch considered the prerequisites of the good economist. "The economist will not arrive at anything like a true knowledge of the laws regulating the production, accumulation, distribution, and the consumption of wealth if he do not draw his materials from a very wide surface. He should study man in every situation; he should have recourse to the history of society, arts, commerce, and civilization, to the works of legislators, philosophers, and travelers, to everything in short that can throw light on the causes which accelerate or retard the progress of nations. . . ."[32] In this breadth of view, McCulloch was joined by John Stuart Mill and, more recently, by Professor Arthur Lewis.[33] Neither he nor they intended the economist to be also a professional social historian, art critic, archaeologist, political scientist, philosopher, or explorer. They simply meant that he should seek his answers wherever they might be found.

Relevance is a matter of questions asked and answers obtained. The political historian cannot refuse to deal with the Black Death, enclosures and engrossing of farms, the Reformation, population growth, inflation, the invention of gunpowder, the General Strike, or the hydrogen bomb, on the grounds that disease, agriculture, religion, demography, currency, technology, industrial relations, and science are not his subjects. They are all his subjects in so far as they affect his central theme, the public issues upon which turned the politics of the age.

The social historian has his own central theme by which to test the relevance of his questions. He will welcome answers to them from any source. He is not concerned with agriculture, industry, and commerce for their intrinsic interest, but he can scarcely give any account of the functioning of society without reference to them. Social structure is by no means the same thing as the distribution of income. "The essence of social class," says Professor T. H. Marshall, "is the way a man is treated by his fellows (and, reciprocally, the way he treats them), not the qualities or the possessions which cause that treatment."[34] But a study of a class system without the economic qualities and possessions of its members would be divorced from reality. Moreover, many of the statistics used by the economic historian, of income and wealth, occupations and unemployment, immigration and emigration, for example, are immediately relevant to the social historian, answering some of his most important questions. The political historian, taking into account the wealth of nations and the sinews of military power, will readily concede the point.

In the same manner, the social historian cannot ignore the social implications of politics, legislation, and administration. Social policy in the days of Burleigh or of Beveridge, the social causes and effects of the war, the social foundations of a ruling aristocracy, the social consequences of taxation and welfare measures, the class connections of political parties, all affect the functioning of society, and are his concern. This point the economic historian, who has since the time of Adam Smith had to take into account the policies and actions of government, will readily concede.

Many of the answers the social historian seeks, or the evidence for them, are already to be found, then, between the covers of books labeled political or economic history. This he can only welcome, as teacher and researcher. If it were not so, the teaching of social history would be next to impossible, since so few satisfactory textbooks yet exist, and undergraduates cannot work entirely from the sources. As for research, history is a co-operative not a competitive endeavor, and we owe a duty to our colleagues and predecessors to use whatever they have discovered of relevance to our interests. Economic and political activities are not the social historian's first interest. He is concerned with them only as they affect social activities and institutions. It is a matter of focus, of priorities, of emphasis. He will follow in the wake of the political or economic historian just long enough to get his questions answered. Though he may for a time fish the same waters, he will use a different net and steer a different course.

There is another approach to the whirlpool of totality, that of the dilettante. Faced with a great multitude of topics, any one of which might become a lifetime's study, the social historian may lose himself in the intellectual dispersion of the jack-of-all-trades. Religion, science, philosophy, literature, music, painting, architecture, gastronomy, costume, furniture, courtship, sport, and entertainment—the list of sirens, each no less seductive than the rest, is endless. Yet the same sense of direction, the same steady navigation, will save him from drowning. He should follow them so far, and only so far, as they lead him in the direction of his central theme.

Let us take, for example, one of the humblest and most antiquarian of these topics, the study of costume. What could be less relevant or more frivolous than how the members of a society were dressed? On the contrary, no single source of evidence can, at a glance almost, tell the historian so much about his society: its comparative prosperity, the distance between rich and poor, the grading of the social hierarchy, its occupational, religious, military, or ceremonial inclinations, its frivolous or serious cast of mind, its attitudes toward women, children, servants, or the poor, something even of its moral standards and its ideal type of man or woman. Sir Walter Raleigh's £600 *ensemble* compared with the Puritan suit of drab testifies as eloquently to courtly society as his "Say to the Court it glows, and shines like rotten wood." Pepys's £20 beaver hat compared with the cottager's fustian is as specific a comment as Gregory King's political arithmetic. Madame Récamier's republican Greek tunic compared with Marie Antoinette's aristocratic panniered gown makes its point as radically as Rousseau's *Contrat Social*.

Probing more deeply, we can see in the familiar fashion cycle, unique to Western civilization from the later Middle Ages till only yesterday, a clue to the expansion of European, and still more of English, society. The fashion cycle requires a special kind of society with a peculiar structure, aristocratic but not exclusive, hierarchical but open to infiltration from below, so that emulation by their social inferiors will force the leaders of society to change their style of dress periodically in order to maintain their visible supremacy. The social emulation and mobility to which the fashion cycle testifies were a source of energy which helped to drive the engine of expansion. England, where the fashion cycle reached furthest down the social scale, affecting according to eighteenth-century observers like Pehr Kalm the very laborers,[35] enjoyed the highest rate of mobility and the most far-reaching industrial and colonial expansion. Used thus to illuminate the structure and functioning of society, the most peripheral of topics is reduced to perspective and becomes of relevance and value to the central theme.

The fourth aspect, the society's pathology, is concerned with social problems and the attempts at remedying them. These are what Cunningham had in mind when he wrote: "We cannot understand the past unless we attempt to realize the precise problems of each age and the success or failure which attended human efforts to grapple with them."[36] The social historian might begin with the five giants of our modern domestic epic, want, disease, ignorance, squalor, and idleness; but there are many others to be found in most societies in most ages—vice and crime, intolerance, civil strife, and the ravages of war. Their remedies take him, without apology, into the sphere of government policy, social administration, police and punishment, as well as individual and organized charity, mutual aid, and simple good-neighborliness.

One of the most ubiquitous of problems is that of social conflict between different groups, orders, classes, or interests within the society's structure. Whether all history is the history of class struggle, whether exploitation and resentment at it, the diminishing size of the exploiting class and the increasing immiseration of the exploited, the final bloody revolution and its classless sequel, are all inevitable concomitants of class society, are questions which can only be answered empirically, and cannot be determined here. One skeptical gloss may be permitted, however. The age which evolved the modern concept of class to describe the massive discontents released by the Industrial Revolution, on the legend of which Marx erected his theory, seems to have been an era not of *class* but of *pre*-class conflict. In a viable class society, such as the mid-Victorian which immediately succeeded it, conflict is institutionalized and rendered acceptable by channeling it through such institutions as industrial negotiation and parliamentary elections. The violence of the age of the Luddites and of the Chartists seems rather to have been the birthpangs of an older society unable to accept or deliver itself painlessly of the new society struggling in its womb. In that older society conflict was not the bargaining of reluctant but inevitable partners forced to adjust their differences by non-violent strike action and negotiation, but the violent disloyalty of insubordinate servants, to be suppressed by legal and military violence.

Paradoxically, even as Marx wrote, the new class society itself was undermining his theory of class struggle: in exact measure as it emerged into the light, and mature class attitudes replaced the outraged paternalism and Oedipean adolescent rebellion of the old society, so the violence subsided and was overtaken by the remarkable and, in Marxist terms, inexplicable pacification of mid-Victorian England. May it not be that non-violent class conflict is the normal relationship between marital partners who cannot live together without bickering, but who apart cannot live at all? And violent revolution the pathological variant, the rending divorce, to which most marriages do not lead?

Social problems are solved or evaded in the light of the fifth and last aspect, the society's psychology, the way it reacts upon itself. It includes the aims which it consciously pursues, the moral criteria by which it judges its success, the public opinion which it applies to its own behavior and concerns, and the ideals which satisfy its aspirations. It has some affinity with social psychology, the study of group behavior, but we must not be misled by the metaphor into thinking it is the same thing or its historical counterpart. It has more affinity with the sociology of knowledge, which sets out to discover the social provenance of ideas and ideologies, and provides the historian with hypotheses which can be tested against the experience of his society.[37] He can, for example, ask whether nineteenth-century Britain, the society in which Marx lived for most of his life, bears out the Marxist view that men's ideas are determined by their relation to the means of production, and if so, what was Marx's own relation to the economic system. He can ask whether Dicey's division of the century into three distinct periods of social-legislative opinion, labeled "Blackstonian optimism," "Benthamism or Individualism," and "Collectivism," can be squared with the empirical facts. Or he can ask why so many reforming minds of the century, including Marx and most of the Benthamites, classical economists, Christian Socialists, Fabians, and Oxford Idealists, belonged to none of the three great classes of landlords, capitalists, and proletarians, but to the "forgotten middle class" of salaried, feed, or dependent brain-workers. The answers to these questions will bring about—are already bringing about—a revolution in nineteenth-century historiography.[38]

Central to this aspect is perhaps the most significant feature of modern developing societies, their increasing self-awareness and control. In our own society self-awareness began even before the great antiquaries of Dr. Rowse's "Elizabethan discovery of England"[39] with the violent xenophobia of the later medieval period. It sought precision through Graunt, Petty, King, and the political arithmetic of the seventeenth century; gained intellectual depth and a sense of growth in the eighteenth with Adam Ferguson, Adam Smith, John Millar, James Steuart of Coltness, and the Scottish historical school of philosophy; made the crucial transition from self-knowledge to social engineering with Edwin Chadwick, Kay-Shuttleworth, Leonard Horner, and the great civil servants of the nineteenth century; and in the twentieth on the social science of Booth, Rowntree, Bowley, and Beveridge founded that great machine tool of social engineering—still underemployed and its potentialities unrealized —the Welfare State. How far this evolution is peculiar to Britain and how far it is a necessary concomitant of industrialization, "development," or "modernization" is a further question for empirical enquiry.

But whether it knows it or not, every society has its ideals: of what constitutes the good life and how society should help which individuals to pursue it, of what society should be and what its relations with its *alter ego,* the state. All such ideals inevitably come back to the ideal of what the individual is, or should in the best of circumstances become. The ideal social type in feudal society was the chivalrous knight, serving God and his lord according to his oath. In the succeeding post-feudal, pre-capitalist society, it was the landed gentleman, the leisured amateur, freed by his unearned income to pursue the ends of life, which by definition were his own pleasures. In Victorian society it was the resourceful entrepreneur, who eschewed idleness and labored in his vocation, providing work for the deserving and the workhouse for the undeserving poor. What does the twentieth century take for its ideal type? Is it not, East and West, in developed and developing societies alike, the professional expert, who alone amongst the non-proletarian classes enjoys ungrudged, unchallenged prestige and security?

Beneath the ideal of what a man should be there lies the deeper ideal of what human life is for. This is the fountainhead of the society's psychology. From it flows the quality and texture of its social thought, and ultimately of society itself. According as it finds the meaning and purpose of life in serving God or the five-year plan, in harrowing the heretic or consoling the brief pilgrimage of fallen man, in bringing light to the Gentile or death to the non-Aryan, in the *recherche du temps perdu* of a supposed golden age or in the *ignis fatuus* of a hypostasized posterity, in negotiating the narrow isthmus between two eternities or in furthering the ever-widening march of progress, in pursuing truth in the interstices of an authoritarian dogma or to the libertarian abyss of existential doubt or universal holocaust, so, consciously or unconsciously, it will create itself in the image of its ideal. Nor does its true belief necessarily cry out in the market place, orate in the forum, or speak in the flat tones of the administrator. It often speaks with the quiet voice of conversation in a private room. It is in the daily talk of ordinary men and women that the real values of a society are felt and heard. And it is at this most intimate of levels that the social historian must seek, if he can, the psychological generating power of his society.

We have now come full circle, from cosmology to the meaning and purpose of life *sub specie aeternitatis*. In the topology of a unitary object every surface is interconnected and every path leads back to where it started. The body politic's ecology, anatomy, physiology, pathology, and psychology overlap and inter-connect because a society is an organic whole in which the functioning of every part affects that of every other. Moreover, just as no man is an island, so no society can live for long in isolation from the great society of mankind. Hence to all the foregoing we must add a further dimension: the mutual relations and influence of diverse societies, the comparative study of their structure and institutions, and ultimately perhaps their involvement in the tortuous evolution which, willy-nilly and for better or worse, has made the modern world one, and all its societies members one of another in the same fateful progress to survival or perdition.

If so capacious a study as social history, thus delimited, sounds a superhuman task, that is because, in relation to any one human being, it is so. No one historian can or should hope to say all there is to say about a society: life is too manifold and too short for that. But a man's reach should exceed his grasp, or what's a subject for? Fortunately for historians, of the making of history there is no end, and much study is a joy to the profession. In practice the teaching of an articulate social history is no more impossible than the teaching of an articulate political or economic history. One of the amenities of history as an educational discipline is that it tailors itself to the capacities of teacher and taught. What can be done at their level in the available time they may do, with pleasure and profit from the very beginning, without having to wait for distant returns.

Two formidable problems still remain, of presentation and of sources. The first is the "rank-and-file dilemma" which Professor Hexter has compared to Heisenberg's indeterminacy principle in quantum physics.[40] The historian cannot simultaneously pursue all the aspects of a complex society *and* show the whole society in motion. He cannot write both narrative and topical history at the same time. But somehow he must try. A great deal may be learnt from local studies, in the handling of small societies over short periods. To larger studies periodization is the key: since the social historian must move forward by periods, he will choose them with an eye to their essential unity as temporal articulations of the whole society. In English social history he will find the old periodization a hindrance, as indeed it is increasingly felt to be by political and economic historians. He will find useful articulations in viable periods by taking the ages between or dominated by great geological shifts in the structure of society: true feudalism, succeeded via the decline of military service, serfdom, and population by 'bastard feudalism'; Tawney's century between the Reformation and the Great Civil War; the Augustan age from the Restoration to the onset of the Industrial Revolution; the Industrial Revolution, so much more than an economic phenomenon; G. M. Young's early Victorian England, succeeded by the different age between it and the First World War; the as yet twilit passage between the World Wars; and the amorphous, unorganized history of post-war England. Any periodization has its difficulties. There is no ideal solution and only one touchstone, that the history, like poetry, should seem to come unforced, like the leaves to a tree.

As for sources, the social historian, like McCulloch's economist, must "draw his materials from a very wide surface." They may be found in whatever has come down to us from the past, in whatever form: in print or manuscript, from love letters to census returns; the myriad artifacts, from clothes to cooking pots, which are the instruments of daily life; the products of past culture, from temples to miniature painting; or the marks of old habitation, from lost villages to landscape architecture, on the face of the country. He must know only how to use them. With documents he should be a skilled researcher; with objects, an amateur archaeologist; with census returns or political arithmetic, a critical statistician; with *objets d'art,* not a connoisseur but at least a dilettante; with works of literature, a literary historian if not a critic. With them all he should have a keen eye for what the mediocre as well as the good of its kind can tell him about the social life of the past. He cannot hope and should not try to do other men's work for them; but what he can do he should do better. He cannot afford, for example, the intolerance of some literary critics toward all but the most perfect products of the creative imagination. Dr. F. R. Leavis believes that to use literary evidence intelligently the student of society needs to be a trained literary critic. "Without the sensitizing familiarity with the subtleties of language, and the insight into the relations between abstract or generalizing thought and the concrete of human experience, that the trained frequentation of literature alone can bring, the thinking that attends social or political studies will not have the edge and force it should."[41] All this is true—but what does it profit a historian of early Victorian England if it teaches him that the *only* work of Dickens worth his serious attention is *Hard Times?*[42]

Moreover, Dr. Leavis is less acutely aware of the need of the student of literature to have studied from non-fictional sources the society of which the literature is the outgrowth. Failure to do this well enough has led some literary critics into a kind of legendary history, geared to what Professor Frank Kermode has called "a myth of catastrophe,"[43] the fall from a primordial state of innocence and grace before the "dissociation of sensibility" and the debasement of popular culture. The mere historian will not question the values upon which the theory of the golden age is erected, but he will question its periodization and its sources. T. E. Hulme found it in the age before the Renaissance and rationalism did their deadly work; W. B. Yeats, before Shakespeare; Dr. Leavis himself, before Milton, since rather unkindly rehabilitated by Mr. Eliot; Mrs. Leavis, before W. H. Smith and the cheap editions on the railway bookstalls; and now Mr. Richard Hoggart, in his childhood, before the working class was corrupted by the popular press. One wonders if they had ever read a broadsheet ballad, a "penny dreadful," or a gallows sheet—the literary sources most relevant to any pronouncement on popular culture.[44]

On his part, the self-respecting social historian will not rely on evidence from one source alone. He will not, for example, expect Moll Flanders to typify the women of Defoe's England —but he may legitimately expect her story to make concrete the human experience behind the "great debate of the poor,"[45] the statistics of London poor relief, the Settlement Acts, the harshness of the penal code, and the chronic fear betrayed in the parish records of the birth of fatherless children.

The multiple sensibility of the historian will connect the most diverse sources. The Cambridge University registers show that the heirs of eighteenth-century landowners did not distinguish themselves academically to the same extent as their fellow students and younger brothers.[46] How this conclusion comes alive when we find a manuscript letter from the anxious widow to her eldest boy at Magdalene! "Your promises aided by my strong affections prove powerful enough to make me give in to what you desire, even to forget past miscarriages if you'll be serious and make the best use of your time you possibly can for the future and study as much as in you lies to retrieve the precious time you have unhappily lost. In order to that you must drop all the Idle part of your acquaintance and they'll not care to trouble you if they find you intent upon a Book. Don't make much of your Self in a bad way. No philosopher in Cambridge will find occasion for more than four-score pound a Year." Perhaps he had justified her earlier fears when Sturbridge Fair was drawing near, "that all the silly Students will lose their time and innocence there," and ignored her advice "to get your Tutor to go along with you. . . ." We are not surprised to learn that there is no record of Jack Egerton's graduation, or that his brothers Samuel and Thomas, who did not go to a university, became successful merchants in Venice and Holland.[47]

Again, the first modern occupational census of 1851 comes to life in Ford Madox Brown's *Work*, painted in the following year.[48] An invaluable document precisely because it is not great art and leaves nothing to the imagination, it offers a microcosm of mid-Victorian society: the equestrian, leisured gentry; the earnest middle-class ladies with crinoline, sunshade, and evangelical tract—*The Hodman's Haven, or Drink for Thirsty Souls;* the thirsty hodman downing a pint; the clean-drawn navvy in all the dignity of labor; the uppish craftsman with buttonhole, watch chain, and *The Times;* the sleeping tramps; the shame-faced, yet pre-Raphaelite, ragged messenger boy; the sandwich-board men and women; the orange girl being moved along by the peeler; the intellectuals leaning on the fence—said to be Carlyle and F. D. Maurice; the merry urchins, the underfed baby with its sad, old-man's face, and of course, the mongrels. On the frame there is the homily, "In the sweat of thy face shalt thou eat bread." Even the work has a mid-Victorian flavor: they appear to be mending a sewer.

The social historian need not be a specialist in every discipline connected with his sources. Professor Butterfield has shown how, without being a scientist, one can offer a more rounded and satisfying history of science than the teleological version which usually passes for it. One does not have to be a scientist to trace the significance of a theory of impetus, which the scientist, impatient to follow only the main line leading to the present, is likely to ignore.[49] Nor does one have to be a musician, a town-planner, a theologian, or a bookmaker to trace the significance of music, urban growth, religion, or gambling in the social life of the past. An educated man, it has been said, is one who can read every page of *The Times* or the *Guardian* with intelligence; but that does not mean that he needs to be an expert in politics, diplomacy, law, finance, technology, court etiquette, fashion design, literary criticism, advertising, midwifery, marriage guidance, and life insurance, as well as the construction of crossword puzzles. The ideal social historian is the ideally educated man.

In spite of its difficulties and demands, the neglect of social history is only apparent. Cinderella has already moved to the center of the stage and is giving cues to the other protagonists. Mr. Charles Wilson recently contrasted with the political and individualist preoccupations of the historians of Acton's generation "the sociologized history of our own day which is less concerned with individuals and more with men as members of social groups."[50] His words are borne out in whatever direction we look: in the biographical approach of Namier, Sir John Neale, and their followers to the history of parliament, "a demographic study of the most significant group-formation in the life of this country;"[51] in the attempts on both sides of the gentry controversy to explain the Great Civil War in terms of the social upheavals of the preceding hundred years; in the interest in the social origins and interconnections of entrepreneurs;[52] in the recognition of the social factors necessary to economic growth;[53] or in the realization that modern international history turns on the competition of rival theories of the organization of society. In all of these the social approach offers insights and understanding not available to Acton's generation. It is a far cry from Seeley's "History is past politics: politics is present history" to Trevor-Roper's "Political history is often a commentary, a corrective and clarifying commentary, on social history, and as such cannot be divorced from it."[54]

Can social history go further than this? Will Cinderella cease to be a handmaiden and become a princess in her own right? There are some signs of a coming transformation. Comprehensive social histories are in progress, or completed: Dr. Rowse's *The Elizabethan Age,* Professor Edward Hughes's *North Country Life in the Eighteenth Century,* the multi-volume *International Social History* under the editorship of Dr. J. H. Plumb. Two front-rank academic publishers are devoting open series to the subject, while a third has widened its economic history text-book series to admit social history.[55] The *International Review of Social History,* published by the *International Instituut voor Sociale Geschiedenis* in Amsterdam, has been revived and by its publication of articles in English partly makes up for the lack of a native journal. Professor Asa Briggs's new appointment in social studies at the University College of Sussex may perhaps by those who know him be regarded as the first chair in social history; at least there is no danger that the subject will be neglected in Brighton.

Perhaps the way forward may be through a new approach to general history, already heralded by the new approaches to political and economic history: the comparative study of what Pareto, Toynbee, and G. D. H. Cole have taught us to call élites.[56] In the interaction of their political power, economic strength, and social roots and connections all three kinds of historian may learn to work together as equal partners in a common enterprise. Professor Habakkuk has already shown the kind of contribution which social history can make to such an approach by his studies of the nobility in eighteenth-century England and of the role of family settlements in the maintenance of their wealth and power.[57]

Such an approach to general history may well reveal the special primacy of the impulses from the social level. I am not putting forward a new species of determinism. Men, we may still believe, choose their ends, although in the light of what seems best for them in the short or the long run. But the ends men have sought—prestige, admiration, culture, fame, knowledge and understanding, family life, philanthropic endeavor, spiritual rebirth, unreflecting enjoyment, or a vicarious eternal life in the seed of their loins—have been as often social as political or economic, while wealth and power under scrutiny often turn out to be means to social ends. Determinism, as we have seen, is at bottom an interpretation of the nature of man. Determinists impute to the majority of men, or at least to a majority of those in key positions, the pathological ends of a few: power or acquisition as ends in themselves. Social ends are so various and manifold that they offer no temptation to oversimplify the multi-centered complexity of human nature. And, since it is only in society that men become human, let alone civilized, there is no better definition of human nature than Aristotle's, translated as he understood it: "Man is a social animal."

Every age has its own interest in the past, its own version of the perennial question of Milton's Adam, "How came I thus, how here?" The interest of our own age can only be described as social. We want to know not only what laws were made and battles fought or even how men got their living, but what it felt like to be alive, how men in history—not merely kings and popes, statesmen and tycoons—lived and worked and thought and behaved toward each other. "Social questions," Beatrice Webb confided to her diary in 1884, "are the vital questions of today: they take the place of religion."[58] In the 1960's they take the place of everything, at least in politics, especially in international politics. And what is politics but the questions we most want to debate in public? At this point Cinderella becomes a princess if not, as the respect and the reluctance of political and economic history to let her go her independent way would seem to suggest, the queen of historical studies.

A NEW ECONOMIC HISTORY: *Fogel*

[One of the fastest growing—and one of the most controversial
—fields of historical inquiry has been the "new economic history." Like new directions in historical demography and social
history, the new economic history has relied very heavily on
quantification, as did the old economic history. But it has also
been very closely linked to economic theory, and thus has
sought to apply or adapt to the study of the past the complicated models of economic behavior that economists have developed for the present. The new economic historians, as well as
other historians who use modern methods of quantification,
have come to use advanced mathematics routinely, as a necessary part of their inquiry. This reliance on quantification has
not gone unchallenged.

One of the most ardent spokesmen for the new economic
history has been Robert William Fogel (b. 1926), currently
professor of history and economics at the University of Chicago. His own work, *Railroads and American Economic
Growth: Essays in Econometric History* (1964), develops the
method of counterfactual analysis, described below. In effect,
Fogel asks what would have happened to the American economy without railroads. It is odd to think that Pascal's celebrated remark about Cleopatra's nose finds a distant echo in
this sophisticated argument and speculation, buttressed by economic theory, designed to illuminate what did happen by a theoretical reconstruction of what did not happen.

It is too early to say how the new economic history will be assimilated into the old stream of historical thought and work. Unlike some other quantifiers and econometricians, who present extravagant claims, Fogel tends to be more circumspect— aware both of the traditional aspects of the new method and of some of its limitations. At the end of his book, he remarks: "Only the scholar who knows what is *unique, special,* and *particular* about a given historical problem can successfully adapt powerful general methods to the study of that problem." His argument for the new economic history, reprinted below and first published in 1966, was presented in a paper delivered at the annual meeting of the Economic History Society in April of that year.]

THE NEW ECONOMIC HISTORY: ITS FINDINGS AND METHODS

The "new economic history," sometimes called econometric history or cliometrics, is not often practiced in Europe. However, it is fair to say that efforts to apply statistical and mathematical models currently occupy the center of the stage in American economic history. The influence of this type of research in the United States is illustrated by the proceedings of the twenty-fifth annual meeting of the Economic History Association, published in the last number of the *Journal of Economic History*.[1] Of the ten major papers included in the issue, three practice the new economic history and a fourth is devoted to a discussion of it. Moreover, if the dissertations presented to the annual meeting are an index of the intellectual direction of the youngest generation of economic historians, then it is worth noting that six of these seven studies are cast in the new mode, and the seventh is a computer analysis (of a large sample of commercial papers) aimed at revealing the motivation for the colonization of the Americas.[2]

Econometric history gained its present eminence with extraordinary rapidity. Perhaps the first definitely formulated expression of the new approach is contained in a pair of essays written by Alfred H. Conrad and John R. Meyer in 1957, less than a decade ago.[3] It was not until three years later that work in cliometrics had gone far enough to warrant a conference devoted to it. In December of 1960 Purdue University sponsored a Seminar on Quantitative Methods in Economic History. Although the organizers of the meeting had difficulty in finding a score of scholars interested enough to attend, the Purdue Seminar did much to stimulate further research in the application of the mathematical and statistical models of economics to the study of history. So successful was the first meeting that the Purdue Seminar has become an annual event. The sixth meeting was held last January. This time the problem was not where to find attendees, but how to choose thirty participants from a list of several times that number of scholars who wanted to attend.

Even more impressive is the fact that many of the principal American centers of post-graduate work in economic history are now devoted to, or encourage, training and research in econometric history. Among the most well-known of these centers are Alexander Gerschenkron's Economic History Workshop at Harvard University, Douglass North's Economic History Seminar at the University of Washington, the graduate program in economic history of Purdue University, the graduate program in economic history at the University of Wisconsin, the interdisciplinary program for economic history at the University of Pennsylvania, the joint Berkeley-Stanford Economic History Colloquium, William Parker's seminar in economic history at Yale, and the Workshop in Economic History at the University of Chicago.

I do not want to give the impression that the new economic history is universally acclaimed in the United States. The growing debate on the methodological implications of the new work reflects the existence of a significant division of opinion. Fritz Redlich is one of the critics. He argues that much of econometric history is based on hypothetical models which can never be verified, and that certain of its methods are "anti-empiricistic" and "anti-positivistic." Hence, Professor Redlich concludes that the new work often produces not history but "quasi-history."[4] Interestingly enough, those features of which Professor Redlich is most critical are, according to George G. S. Murphy, the main virtue of the new approach. Professor Murphy contends that by rigorously developing hypothetico-deductive models the cliometricians are providing economic history with "a really defensible set of techniques" and are "coming close to what a modern empiricist might demand of it."[5]

To say that opinions are divided does not imply that the American wing of our discipline is torn by internecine warfare. While the debate is vigorous, it is also amicable. Moreover, even its severest critics believe that the new economic history has made a positive and lasting contribution to historical research. Despite his strong reservations, Fritz Redlich writes that the new approaches "are here to stay," and predicts an increasing interdependence between the new and the old work.[6]

The Findings

The considerable impact of the new economic history on research in the United States is due primarily to the novelty of its substantive findings. If cliometrics merely reproduced the conclusions of previous scholarship, its methods would be of trivial consequence. However, the studies of the new economic historians have substantially altered some of the most well-established propositions of traditional historiography. They have also yielded knowledge that was hitherto considered unobtainable concerning institutions and processes central to the explanation of American economic development. I cannot within the compass of this paper do justice to the many studies produced by the new economic historians during the past decade. But I will attempt to summarize briefly some typical examples of their work.[7]

The Economics of Southern Slavery

One of the first, and one of the most influential, reinterpretations of the new economic history concerns the effect of slavery on the course of economic development in the South prior to the Civil War. Until recently most history books portrayed the ante-bellum South as an economically backward agricultural region that stagnated under the burden of the plantation system. By the eve of the war, it was held, slavery had become unprofitable and hence the system was moribund. Slavery was kept temporarily in existence by the transitory resolve of a class long accustomed to its peculiar social institutions.[8]

This view was sharply challenged in a paper by Alfred H. Conrad and John R. Meyer.[9] They rejected as inadequate the evidence usually presented to support the proposition that the profits of slaveowners were declining. The contention that slavery was unprofitable rested largely on the fact that the prices of slaves had risen more rapidly than the prices of the commodities that slaves produced. Conrad and Meyer pointed out that this divergency did not necessarily imply declining profits, for the productivity of slaves might have risen by an amount sufficient to maintain the original level of profits. They further argued that, from an economic point of view, slaves were a capital good and hence that one could compute the rate of return on an investment in them by solving the standard equation for the capitalization of an income stream; that is, by finding the rate of return which equated the price of slaves to the discounted value of the stream of annual earnings derived from their employment.

Conrad and Meyer divided the slave economy into two sectors. The first was described by a production function that related the male slaves to the output of such staples as cotton, sugar, and corn. The second was a capital-goods sector in which female slaves were used to produce new slaves. Conrad and Meyer then went on to estimate separate rates of return on slaves of each sex. The computation of the return on male slaves was the simpler case. They first derived the average capital cost per slave, including not only the price of a slave but also the average value of the land, animals, and equipment used by a slave. Estimates of gross annual earnings were then built up from data on the price of cotton and the physical productivity of slaves. The net figure was obtained by subtracting the maintenance and supervisory costs for slaves from gross earnings. The average length of the stream of net earnings was determined from mortality tables. With these estimates Conrad and Meyer computed rates of return on male slaves and found that for the majority of ante-bellum plantations the return varied between 5 and 8 percent, depending on the physical yield per hand and the prevailing farm price of cotton. On the farms in poor upland pine country or in the exhausted lands of the Eastern seaboard the range of rates was merely 2 to 5 percent. However, in the "best lands of the new Southwest, the Mississippi alluvium and the better South Carolina and Alabama plantations" rates ran as high as 10 to 13 percent.[10]

The computation of the rate of return on female slaves was somewhat more complicated. Conrad and Meyer had to take account not only of the productivity of a female in the field, but of such additional matters as the productivity of her offspring between their birth and the time of their sale; maternity, nursery, and rearing costs; and the average number of offspring. Noting that very few females produced less than five or more than ten children that survived to be sold, Conrad and Meyer computed lower and upper limits on the rate of return. These turned out to be 7.1 and 8.1 percent, respectively. Thus, planters in the exhausted lands of the upper South, who earned only 4 or 5 percent on male slaves, still were able to achieve a return on their total operation equal to alternative opportunities. They did so by selling the offspring of females to planters in the West, thus earning rates of 7 to 8 percent on the other half of their slave force. Proof of such a trade was found not only in the descriptions of contemporaries, but also in the age structure of the slave population. The selling states had a significantly larger proportion of persons under 15 and over 50, while the buying states predominated in slaves of the prime working ages.

Of the many studies in the economics of slavery stimulated by the pioneering work of Conrad and Meyer, the most important was the one by Yasukichi Yasuba.[11] Yasuba pointed out that in order to evaluate the viability of the slave system as a whole, rather than merely the viability of slavery in a given region or occupation, one had to equate the stream of net income from slaves not with their market price but with their cost of production—that is, with the net cost of rearing slaves. A discrepancy between the price and the cost of producing capital goods in a given industry ordinarily will not last very long.[12] The existence of an unusually high profit—of economic rent— will induce new capital-producing firms to enter or old firms to expand production until the rent is eliminated, until the market price of the capital good falls to its cost of production.

In the case of slaves, however, the demand curve for them shifted outward more quickly than the supply curve. The lag in supply was due partly to the ban against the importation of slaves after 1808 and partly to the fact that the domestic expansion of supply was limited by biological and cultural factors. As a consequence of these restrictions, the rent on slaves increased over time. Yasuba estimates that, during the quinquennium of 1821–25, the average capitalized rent amounted to $428 out of an average slave price of $736, the balance representing the net cost of rearing the slave to maturity. In other words, during 1821–25 capitalized rent represented 58 percent of the market price of slaves. By 1841–45 the capitalized rent was 72 percent of the price of slaves, and by 1851–55 it was nearly 85 percent.

By showing the existence of a large and rising capitalized rent in the price of slaves over the forty years leading up to the Civil War, Yasuba effectively demonstrated the economic viability of the slave system. Moreover, the fact that Conrad and Meyer computed a return based on the market price rather than on the cost of producing slaves means that they underestimated the return to slavery as a system. Indeed, their computation showed only that slave prices adjusted so that investors who wanted to buy into the slave system could, on average, expect to earn merely the market rate of return.

Although slavery was a viable economic system, it could nevertheless have thwarted economic growth in the South by reducing the saving rate or by stifling entrepreneurship. Historians have long held that, because of slavery, planters acquired extravagant tastes which led them to squander their income on high living. Slavery is also supposed to have bred an irrational attachment to agriculture. As a consequence, it is said, planters shunned opportunities for profit in manufacturing.

The alleged stagnation of the ante-bellum South has been thrown into doubt by recent findings. The work of Conrad, Meyer, Yasuba, and others strongly suggests that the Southern decision to slight manufacturing was not an absurd eccentricity. It now appears to have been a rational response to profits in plantation agriculture that were considerably above alternative opportunities. Moreover, estimates of regional income constructed by Richard Easterlin indicate that per capita income grew as rapidly in the ante-bellum South as in the rest of the nation, averaging about 1.5 percent per annum.[13]

The retarded development of the South during the last third of the nineteenth century and the first half of the twentieth was due not to stagnation during the slave era but to the devastation caused by the Civil War. As Stanley Engerman points out, if ante-bellum growth rates had continued through the war decade, Southern per capita income would have been twice the level that actually prevailed in 1870. So disruptive was the war that it took the South some thirty years to regain the per capita income of 1860 and another sixty years to reach the same relative position in national per capita income that it enjoyed at the close of the ante-bellum era.[14] The case for the abolition of slavery thus appears to turn on issues of morality and equity rather than on the inability of a slave system to yield a high rate of economic growth.

Technology and Productivity

While the issue of slavery looms large in the interpretation of American economic history, it is of limited relevance outside of that context. Of wider interest to European scholars is the new work on technology and productivity. From the time of Arnold Toynbee through that of Paul Mantoux and down to the present day, economic historians have made technological change embodied in specific machines and processes the *sine qua non* of economic advance. As a result of their work, every school-boy has been taught that it was such inventions as the spinning jenny, the power loom, the reverberatory furnace, the rolling mill, the steam engine, and the railroad that brought about the industrial revolutions of England, France, Germany, and the United States. Yet despite a considerable literature which illuminates the history of machines and their employment, we still have much to learn about the precise effects of particular innovations on productivity and about the process by which a given innovation spreads throughout an industry.

It is to the solution of these and related questions that much of the research of the new economic historians has been directed. This work falls into four main categories. The first is the attempt to "explain" observed increases in productivity—that is, to distribute the responsibility for the increase in productivity among various factors. Typical of this approach is William Parker's analysis of wheat production.[15] He finds that between 1840 and 1911 labor productivity in wheat grew by more than threefold. Of this increase he attributes the lion's share, 60 percent, to mechanization; 17 percent to the change in the regional locus of production; 16 percent to the interaction of mechanization and regional relocation; and the remaining 7 percent to other factors. Improvements in machines had their greatest impact on harvesting and post-harvesting operations. Professor Parker estimates that the reaper and thresher alone accounted for 70 percent of the gain from mechanization, or over 40 percent of the increase in overall productivity.

It would be wrong to infer from Parker's study that the new work gives warrant to the preoccupation with technological change embodied in equipment that characterizes so much of the past literature of economic history. Parker's study aims not at extolling machines but at identifying all the important factors that explain productivity advance in agriculture. It so happens that, for the given period and crop, the development of two machines dominates the explanation. Other studies produced quite different results. Thus, new equipment plays virtually no role in Douglass North's explanation of the 50 percent fall in the cost of ocean transportation that he finds for the 250-year period between 1600 and the middle of the nineteenth century. Almost all of the decline is explained by two other factors: the elimination of piracy and the increase in the size of the market. The elimination of piracy substantially reduced manning requirements, since military personnel were no longer needed. The increase in the size of the market lowered shipping costs by encouraging the concentration of surpluses in central markets. This development considerably reduced the amount of time ships spent in port acquiring a cargo.[16]

The second category consists of studies aimed at explaining the growth of particular industries. One of the best examples of this type of work is Robert Brooke Zevin's analysis of the growth of the American cotton textile industry prior to 1860.[17] As Zevin points out, the seventeen years from 1816 to 1833 are the most interesting period in the early history of the industry. During this span the output of cotton cloth expanded from 840,000 to 231,000,000 yards, an increase of over 280 times. Abstracting from cyclical considerations, Zevin puts the average annual rate of growth in production at 17.1 per cent. He finds that one-third of this expansion was due to an increase in demand stimulated mainly by the growth of the urban and Western populations. The remaining two-thirds was due to a downward shift in the supply curve. Zevin explains the change in supply by improvements in textile machinery, the fall in the price of raw cotton, and the growth of skilled technicians. However, the improvement of machinery was the least important of the factors. It accounted for only 17 percent of the expansion of cloth production. The fall in the price of raw cotton accounted for 28 percent, and the growing pool of skilled technicians for the remaining 22 percent.

Zevin's study, taken in conjunction with others, points to the inadequacy of new machinery and other forms of equipment as the sole, or even the primary explanation of growth in the main manufacturing industries of Europe and America during the last two centuries. The preoccupation with machines has led to an underestimation of the role of demand in the promotion of industrial growth. It has also resulted in the slighting of such determinants of supply as the quality of labor, the stock of skills, the efficiency of industrial organization, and economies of scale.[18]

Analyses of the diffusion of technological innovations fall into the third category. The diffusion problem promises to be one of the most popular topics of the new economic history. Peter Temin's explanation of the spread of anthracite and coke blast furnaces has already become well known.[19] A more recent contribution is a paper on reapers by Paul David.[20] Although the reaper was invented in the 1830s, its diffusion proceeded at a very slow pace for two decades. The "first major wave of popular acceptance" of the innovation "was concentrated in the mid-1850s." The literature is ambiguous regarding the cause of this upsurge. Various writers have stressed the rise in wheat prices and the scarcity of farm labor as factors. However, these accounts do not indicate the process by which the rise in wheat prices led to an increased demand for reapers.

David points out that if, on the industry level, the supply curve of labor is less elastic than the supply of reapers, a rise in the price of wheat will raise the price of farm labor relative to the price of reapers. He also notes that reapers had to be purchased rather than rented. Thus, even though the annual cost of a reaper to a farmer was independent of farm size, his average reaper cost, per acre harvested, fell as the number of acres in small grains increased, until the cutting capacity of a single machine was reached. By contrast, the cost per acre of reaping by the old method was constant because, to the farmer, the supply of labor was perfectly elastic and there were no economies of scale in the old method.

The foregoing considerations suggest the existence of a threshold function that relates the farm size at which it just paid to introduce the reaper to the ratio between the price of a reaper and the wage of farm labor. David estimates the parameters of this function and finds that at the beginning of the 1850s, the relationship of reaper and labor prices was such that it became profitable to introduce the reaper only on farms with 46 or more acres in small grains. At the time, however, the average number of acres in such grains per farm was about 25. By the mid-1850s the cost of reapers had fallen relative to the price of labor. The decline reduced the threshold size to just 35 acres. At the same time the average acreage in small grains rose to 30. Thus, within a period of about five years, the gap between the threshold farm size and the average actual farm size was reduced by over 75 percent. It is the precipitous closing of this gap that explains the accelerated diffusion of reapers during the mid-1850s.

The final category of studies on technology and productivity consists of works which attempt to evaluate the net social benefit of particular innovations. My book, *Railroads and American Economic Growth,* belongs to this category.[21] Estimation of the net benefit of railroads involves a comparison between the actual level of national income and the level that would have obtained in the absence of railroads. The amount of national income in the absence of railroads cannot be computed directly. It is necessary to construct a hypothetico-deductive model on the basis of which one can infer, from those conditions that were actually observed, a set of conditions that never occurred.

In my book I attempted to construct such a model for the year 1890. The conceptual foundation of the model is the "social saving" of railroads. The social saving in any given year is defined as the difference between the actual cost of shipping goods in that year and the alternative cost of shipping exactly the same goods between exactly the same points without railroads. This cost differential is in fact larger than the "true" social saving. Forcing the pattern of shipments in a non-rail situation to conform to the pattern that actually existed is equivalent to the imposition of a restraint on society's freedom to adjust to an alternative technological situation. If society had had to ship by water and wagon without the railroad, it could have altered the geographical locus of production in a manner that would have economized on transport services. Further, the sets of primary and secondary markets through which commodities were distributed were surely influenced by conditions peculiar to rail transportation; in the absence of railroads some different cities would have entered these sets, and the relative importance of those remaining would have changed. Adjustments of this sort would have reduced the loss of national income occasioned by the absence of the railroad.

The computation of the social saving required both estimates of the direct payments that would have been made for boat and wagon transportation services and estimates of such indirect costs as cargo losses in transit, the expense resulting from the time lost when using a slow medium of transportation, and the expense of being unable to use waterways during the winter months. Regression analysis was used to derive the cost functions of boats. The water rates that would have obtained in the absence of railroads were computed from these functions. The economic losses caused by slow service and by the vagaries of the weather were quantified by estimating the cost of expanding inventories to a size that would have permitted businesses to maintain their normal temporal pattern of distribution. The expected cargo loss was derived from insurance rates.

Because of the large amounts of data that had to be processed, my study was restricted to the social saving attributable to the transportation of agricultural commodities. The amount of this saving was estimated under three different assumptions regarding the possibility of technological adaptation to the absence of railroads. The first was that society would have relied on only the canals and roads that actually existed in 1890. The second was that at least 5,000 miles of feasible and, in the absence of railroads, highly profitable canals would have been built. The third was that common roads would have been improved. Under the first of these assumptions the agricultural social saving of railroads was $373,000,000, or 3.1 percent of gross national product in 1890. The extension of canals and improvement of roads would have reduced the social saving to 1.8 percent of GNP. It is interesting to note that the two main benefits achieved by the railroad were the reduction in inventories and the reduction in wagon transportation. Together these accounted for about 80 percent of the social saving.

Albert Fishlow's penetrating, many-sided study of railroads during the ante-bellum era contains an estimate of the social saving for 1859.[22] His computation covers not merely agricultural commodities but all other freight and all passenger traffic. Fishlow finds that the social saving of railroads was about $175,000,000, or 4 percent of GNP. Of this total, agricultural commodities account for roughly one-quarter, other freight for another third, and passenger service for the balance. In comparing Fishlow's result with mine, it is important to keep in mind that Fishlow's calculation is for the case in which there would have been no technological adaptation to the absence of railroads. Given that assumption, the correspondence between our findings is extremely close. A computation of the 1859 social saving for the case of limited technological adaptation to the absence of railroads is still to be performed.

I should like to conclude this section of my paper in the way that I began it—by stressing the inadequacy of my survey of the work of the new economic historians. Among the important contributions that I have slighted are studies by Robert Gallman on Southern agriculture, Jeffrey Williamson on the determinants of urbanization before the Civil War, Stanley Lebergott on the role of labor in nineteenth-century economic growth, John Bowman on the agricultural depression of the Gilded Age, and Lance Davis on the evolution of capital markets.

The Methods

The methodological hallmarks of the new economic history are its emphasis on measurement and its recognition of the intimate relationship between measurement and theory. Economic history has always had a quantitative orientation. But much of the past numerical work was limited to the location and simple classification of data contained in business and government records. With the exception of the excellent work on the construction of price indexes, relatively little was done to transform this information in ways that would shed light on "rigorously defined concepts of economic analysis"[23] until the development of national income accounting techniques. The pioneers of the massive statistical reconstructions embodied in national income accounts were not economic historians but empirical economists such as Simon Kuznets in the United States, J. R. N. Stone and Phyllis Deane in Great Britain, and François Perroux and Jean Marczewski in France. While economic historians made considerable use of national income measures, they did not immediately attempt to extend the process of statistical reconstruction to the vast array of issues in their domain. Most discussions of economic historians remained primarily qualitative, with numerical information used largely as illustration.

The new economic historians are trying to end this long-existing void in measurement. They have set out to reconstruct American economic history on a sound quantitative basis. This objective is extremely ambitious, and the obstacles to its fulfillment are numerous. The most frustrating problem is the paucity of data. Information bearing on many vital institutions and processes in the past either was never collected or has been lost. In still other cases the data are extant, but are so numerous or held in such a form that their retrieval without the aid of modern statistical methods would be prohibitively expensive.

As a consequence, statistics and mathematics are widely employed by the new economic historians. Regression analysis is perhaps the most frequently used tool. It is the principal device on which Albert Fishlow relied in his reconstruction of the investment of railroads during the ante-bellum era.[24] Jeffrey Williamson makes heavy use of it in his study of urbanization.[25] And Paul MacAvoy employs a lagged form of the regression model in order to determine the relationship between grain prices and transportation rates.[26] Examples of the usefulness of other mathematical methods include William Whitney's employment of input-output analysis to measure the effect of tariffs on the rise of manufacturing[27] and James K. Kindahl's application of the hypergeometric distribution to estimate, from two incomplete lists, the total number of state banks that were in operation immediately after the close of the Civil War.[28]

Some historians have held that there is no point in applying powerful statistical methods to economic history because the available data are too poor. In actual practice, the correlation often runs the other way. When the data are very good, simple statistical procedures will usually suffice. The poorer the data, the more powerful are the methods which have to be employed. Nevertheless, it is often true that the volume of data available is frequently below the minimum required for standard statistical procedures. In such instances the crucial determinant of success is the ability of the investigator to devise methods that are exceedingly efficient in the utilization of data—that is, to find a method that will permit one to achieve a solution with the limited data that are available.

The way in which economic theory can be employed to circumvent the data problem is illustrated by Paul David's study of mechanical reapers. Utilization of regression analysis to compute a threshold function for reapers would have required county data on the employment of reapers by farm size, on the delivered price of reapers, and on the average wage of labor. Unfortunately, such information was not available for counties. To surmount the problem, David turned to the theory of production. He first noted that a farmer would be indifferent to the choice between mechanized and hand reaping when the cost of cutting grain on a specified acreage was the same by both methods. He also noted the absence of economies and diseconomies of scale in the employment of hand labor. These specifications, together with two linear approximations, yielded a threshold function with only three parameters. The parameters were the rate of depreciation, the rate of interest, and the rate of substitution between reapers and man-days of labor. The data required to estimate these parameters were available.[29]

The union between measurement and theory is most clearly evident when one attempts to establish the net effect of innovations, institutions, or processes on the course of economic development. The net effect of such things on development involves a comparison between what actually happened and what would have happened in the absence of the specified circumstance. However, since the counterfactual condition never occurred, it could not have been observed, and hence is not recorded in historical documents. In order to determine what would have happened in the absence of a given circumstance, the economic historian needs a set of general statements (that is, a set of theories or a model) that will enable him to deduce a counterfactual situation from institutions and relationships that actually existed.

This is precisely the problem when one attempts to evaluate

the frequent claim that railroads extended the area of commercial agriculture in the United States. It is, of course, true that the area of commercial agriculture and the construction of railroads expanded more or less simultaneously. However, it does not follow that railroads were a necessary condition for the commercial exploitation of the new lands. To settle the issue, one must find a method of determining how much of the land actually settled after the advent of railroads would have been settled in their absence.

Without railroads the high cost of wagon transportation would have limited commercial agriculture production to areas of land lying within some unknown distance of navigable waterways. It is possible to use the theory of rent to establish these boundaries of feasible commercial agriculture in a non-rail society. Rent is a measure of the amount by which the return to labor and capital on a given portion of land exceeds the return the same factors could earn if they were employed at the intensive or extensive margins. Therefore, any plot of land capable of commanding a rent will be kept in productive activity. It follows that, even in the face of increased transportation costs, a given area of farmland will remain in use as long as the increased costs incurred during a given time period do not exceed the original rental value of that land.

Given information on the quantity of goods shipped between farms and their markets, the distances from farms to rail and water shipping points, the distance from such shipping points to markets, and the wagon, rail, and water rates, it is possible to compute the additional transportation costs that would have been incurred if farmers attempted to duplicate their actual shipping pattern without railroads. In such a situation shipping costs would have risen not because boat rates exceeded rail rates but because it usually required more wagon transportation to reach a boat than a rail shipping point. In other words, farms immediately adjacent to navigable waterways would have been least affected by the absence of rail service. The further a farm was from a navigable waterway, the greater the amount of wagon transportation it would have required. At some distance from waterways the additional wagon haul would have increased the cost of shipping from a farm by an amount exactly equal to the original rental value of the land. Such a farm would represent a point on the boundary of feasible commercial agriculture. Consequently, the full boundary can be established by finding all those points from which the increased cost of shipping by alternative means the quantities that were actually carried by railroads is equal to the original rental value of the land.

This approach, it should be noted, leads to an overstatement of the land falling beyond the "true" feasible boundary. A computation based on the actual mix of products shipped does not allow for adjustments to a non-rail technology. In the absence of railroads, the mix of agricultural products would have changed in response to the altered structure of transportation rates. Such a response would have lowered shipping costs and hence extended the boundary. The computation also ignores the consequence of a cessation in agricultural production in areas beyond the feasible region on the level of prices. Given the relative inelasticity of the demand for agricultural products, the prices of such commodities would have risen in the absence of railroads. The rise in prices would have led to a more intensive exploitation of agriculture within the feasible region, thus raising land values. The rise in land values would have increased the burden of additional transportation costs that could have been borne and shifted the boundary of feasible commercial agriculture further away from water shipping points.[30]

The method outlined above is the one I used to establish the boundary of feasible commercial agriculture for 1890. It turns out that given only the active waterways of that year, at least 76 percent of the land actually employed in agriculture would have remained employed in the absence of railroads. Moreover, a 5,000-mile extension of the canal system would have increased the land in commercial agriculture to 93 percent of that actually cultivated. The theory of rent also enables one to infer which canals would have been socially profitable. It can be shown that a new canal would have been profitable if the land it brought into the feasible region had an 1890 value which exceeded the canal's construction cost by the present value of any additional wagon transportation that would have been incurred by the absence of railroads.[31]

According to Fritz Redlich, these attempts to answer counterfactual questions by the use of hypothetico-deductive models are the most novel and the most dubious methodological aspect of the new economic history. Professor Redlich argues that counterfactual propositions are fundamentally alien to economic history. He also believes that they are untestable and hence calls essays involving such propositions "quasi-history."[32]

However, if we are to exclude from history those studies which are based on counterfactual propositions, we will have to expurgate not only the new work but much of the old work as well. The difference between the old and the new economic history is not the frequency with which one encounters counterfactual propositions but the extent to which such propositions are made explicit. The old economic history abounds in disguised counterfactual assertions. They are present in discussions which either affirm or deny that tariffs accelerated the growth of manufacturing; in essays which argue that slavery retarded the development of the South; in debates over whether the Homestead Act made the distribution of land more equitable; in the contention that railroads expanded interregional trade; and in virtually every other discussion which makes a legal, social, technological, administrative, or political innovation the cause of a change in economic activity. All of these arguments involve implicit comparisons between the actual state of the nation and the state that would have prevailed in the absence of the specified circumstance.

Indeed, the new economic historians have not been primarily engaged in launching new counterfactual propositions but in making explicit and testing the ones they find in traditional history. One should not underestimate the task involved in demonstrating that comparisons which appear to be between events that actually occurred are in reality counterfactual propositions. Consider, for example, the arithmetic index of productivity popularized by John Kendrick. This measure of total factor productivity, now more than a decade old, is usually described as the ratio of an output index to a weighted index of inputs, where the weights are the shares of the factors in value added. However, a deft proof by Albert Fishlow shows that what appears to be purely a comparison of recorded circumstances is really a disguised comparison between the actual price of the output and the price that would have obtained in the absence of technological change.[33]

Since counterfactual propositions are merely inferences from hypothetico-deductive models, it follows that such propositions can be verified in at least two ways. The first involves the determination of whether the proposition asserted follows logically from its premises. The second requires a determination of whether the assumptions of the model are empirically valid.[34] Most of the revisions of the new economic history follow from a demonstration that one or both of these conditions for valid inferences have been violated. As noted earlier, Conrad and Meyer overthrew Phillips's proposition that slavery was moribund by showing that his conclusion rested on the false assumption that a divergence between the rates of growth of slave and cotton prices implied a decrease in profits. On the other hand, as I attempted to demonstrate in another paper, one cannot rest the case for the indispensability of railroads to the total economy on evidence which shows that railroads had the power to crush particular firms or regions. This argument involves the fallacy of composition and hence gives rise to a non sequitur.[35]

The foregoing suggests that the fundamental methodological feature of the new economic history is its attempt to cast all explanations of past economic development in the form of valid hypothetico-deductive models. This is another way of saying that the new generation seeks to continue an effort that was under way long before it appeared on the scene: namely, the construction of economic history on the basis of scientific methods. If the new economic historians are able to advance that objective, it will be partly because of what they have inherited from their predecessors and partly because they are the beneficiaries of a series of important developments in economic theory, in statistics, and in applied mathematics.

CLIO AND CRISIS: *Woodward*

[In 1961, C. Vann Woodward (b. 1908) wrote "we come of an age that demands a great deal of historians." His own work demonstrates that these demands can be met. Woodward combines the traditional virtues of a historian—extraordinary fidelity to the past and a trained flair for interpretation—with a liberal, self-critical stance. Born in Arkansas, he has made Southern history his central concern. By viewing it from a broad national, indeed, supranational point of view, he has done much to rescue the subject from regionalism. In all his works —from *Tom Watson, Agrarian Rebel* (1938) to *American Counterpoint: Slavery and Racism in the North-South Dialogue* (1971)—he has advanced new interpretations of Southern history and of the racial conflict that in his lifetime has become ever more central to the nation, and has done so with psychological acumen and a cultivated sense of the inherent ironies of human existence. The essay that follows, originally delivered as the presidential address to the Organization of American Historians in 1969, mirrors Woodward's own development and analyzes one of the fundamental problems that historians have had to face in this century: how to respond to the sudden and insistent demands of their own time—demands that may have arisen from a minority struggling to find its historic identity, from a new nation seeking to establish its legitimacy, or from a confused generation seeking its bearings. Few historians have stated the problem as clearly as Woodward, and few have succeeded as he has in making an authentic past speak to present needs.]

CLIO WITH SOUL

All who write or teach American history are aware by now of the demand for more attention to the part that Negro people have played. It may come quietly from a distressed college dean, or it may come peremptorily and noisily from militant student protest. In any case the demand is insistent that we move over and make room. With whatever grace they can muster and whatever resources they command, historians as teachers are responding one way or another. New colleagues are recruited (black if humanly possible), new courses listed ("Black" or "Afro" in the title), new textbooks written, new lectures prepared. Or, in a pinch, old colleagues may have to be pressured and reconditioned and old lectures hastily revised. The adjustment is often awkward and sometimes rather frantic, but American academic institutions are responding, each in its own style and fashion—clumsily, belatedly, heartily, or half-heartedly, as the case may be.

We are concerned here, however, not with the institutional response and its problems, nor even primarily with the social purpose and the overdue ends of justice sought, as important as these things unquestionably are. Rather we are concerned for the moment with the professional problems the movement poses, particularly with the impact, good, bad, or indifferent, it will have—is having, has had—upon the writing and reinterpretation of American history. Will it warp as much as it will correct? Will it substitute a new racism for an old? Will historians be able to absorb and control the outraged moral passions released and bend to the social purposes dictated without losing balance and betraying principle? Or will the historian's moral engagement compromise the integrity of his craft? Granting inevitable losses in detachment, will the gains in moral insight outbalance the losses?

On the positive side, certain corrective influences may be scored up as incremental gain immediately apparent. In the past a certain moral obtuseness and intellectual irresponsibility regarding the Negro people have cropped up again and again in our most respectable historical literature. The tendency appeared very early, but one does not have to go back so far as the romantic school, or even so far as the scientific school and its smugness about Teutonic institutions, for instances. Frederick Jackson Turner could write in his famous paper on "The Significance of the Frontier" that "when American history comes to be rightly viewed it will be seen that the slavery question is an incident."[1] And Charles A. Beard took the view that the results of Negro suffrage and political strivings during Reconstruction "would have been ludicrous if they had not been pitiable."[2] Even historians with abolitionist backgrounds combined their antislavery views with white supremacy and anti-Negro assumptions.[3] One consequence of having Negro critics or colleagues looking over one's shoulder or having more Negro historians is that such embarrassing white-supremacy and ethnocentric gaffes are likely to become much rarer in the pages of respected historians. This is not to say that the profession will thus be purged of moral obtuseness and intellectual irresponsibility. These shortcomings are likely to remain constants in the historical profession as in other parts of the human community. But they are likely to find different forms of expression.

In spite of the warning admonitions of Herbert Butterfield and others about the moral interpretation of history, Negro history seems destined to remain the moral storm center of American historiography. It is hard to see how it could very well be otherwise, at least for some time to come. Slavery was, after all, the basic moral paradox of American history. It was what Dr. Samuel Johnson had in mind when he asked: "How is it that we hear the loudest *yelps* for liberty among the drivers of Negroes?" But the paradox is older and deeper than the temporary embarrassments of 1776, of slaveholders yelping for liberty, writing the Declaration of Independence, and fighting for the natural rights of man. Back of that were the European dreamers of America as an idyllic Arcadia, the New Jerusalem, the Promised Land, the world's new hope of rebirth, fulfillment, and redemption. Before the dreamers came the discoverer of America, who returned from one of his voyages with a cargo of Indian slaves. After him came the explorers and colonizers who competed in the lucrative African slave trade and brought millions of slaves to the New World. It is, in fact, difficult to see how Europeans could have colonized America and exploited its resources otherwise. David B. Davis has phrased the paradox perfectly: "How was one to reconcile the brute fact that slavery was an intrinsic part of the American experience with the image of the New World as uncorrupted nature, as a source of redemption from the burdens of history, as a paradise which promised fulfillment of man's highest aspirations?"[4]

One way of dealing with the problem was that of J. Hector St. John de Crèvecoeur, who wrote the classic statement of the American idyll of democratic fulfillment. "What then is the American, this new man?" was his famous question. And his answer was: "He is either an European, or the descendent of an European. . . ."[5] Crèvecoeur simply defined the Negro out of American identity. It is significant that the tacit exclusion went unnoticed for nearly two centuries.[6] Arthur M. Schlesinger, Sr., took the title and text of his presidential address to the American Historical Association in 1942 from this passage of Crèvecoeur without referring to its racial exclusion.[7] Crèvecoeur's precedent was widely followed in the writing of American history. It might be called the "invisible man" solution.

Another way of dealing with Davis's problem of brute fact and idyllic image was that of Beard and Turner. They recognized the Negro's existence all right, but they either ignored moral conflicts and paradoxes in moral values forced by his existence and status, or they attempted to reduce them to other and morally neutral categories of explanation. Referring to Beard, W. E. B. Du Bois remarked that one has the "comfortable feeling that nothing right or wrong is involved."[8] Beard and Turner are merely two conspicuous examples of the numerous practitioners of what might be called the moral-neutrality approach.

Neither the invisible-man solution nor the moral-neutrality approach is any longer acceptable. Moral engagement ranging upward to total commitment now predominates. This approach divides into overlapping though distinguishable categories. One is embraced in the general class of paternalistic historiography, but divides broadly into Northern and Southern schools. Northern-type paternalism is usually the more self-conscious. One representative of this school assures the Brother in Black that "Negroes are, after all, only white men with black skins, nothing more, nothing less," endowed natively with all the putative white attributes of courage, manhood, rebelliousness, and love of liberty. Another concedes the deplorable reality of the "Sambo personality," but attributes it to potency of the plantation master as white father image and to other misfortunes. Others console the Negro for not producing more Nat Turners and slave rebellions by offering ingenious theories to explain his accommodation to slavery. Still others assure him that he would have been better advised to have chosen men of Iberian and Catholic background rather than those of English and Protestant heritage as masters of the plantation school.

The modern Southern paternalist, falling back on his regional heritage, takes to the role more naturally and with less self-consciousness. He disavows the Phillipsian concept of the benevolent plantation school for Africans, but proceeds as if the school actually worked admirably, with some exceptions, and turned out graduates fully prepared for freedom and equality. Any shortcomings or failings on the part of the blacks are attributed to delinquencies of the "responsible" whites, the paternalists. These assumptions result in a charitable picture of the freedmen during emancipation and Reconstruction and the era following. Instead of a "white man with a black skin," the Negro is elected an honorary Southerner by paternalists below the Potomac.

Moral preoccupations and problems shape the character of much that is written about the Negro and race relations by modern white historians, but they are predominantly the preoccupations and moral problems of the white man. His conscience burdened with guilt over his own people's record of injustice and brutality toward the black man, the white historian often writes in a mood of contrition and remorse as if in expiation of racial guilt or flagellation of the guilty. In this connection it is well to recall Butterfield's observation that "since moral indignation corrupts the agent who possesses it and is not calculated to reform the man who is the object of it, the demand for it—in the politician and in the historian, for example —is really a demand for an illegitimate form of power." It is "a tactical weapon," says Butterfield, valued for its power "to rouse irrational fervor and extraordinary malevolence against some enemy."[9] It is a weapon that is especially useful in polemics—polemics of region against region, party against party, and class against class.

This is not to deny to the historian the role of moral critic or to dismiss what has been written out of deep concern for moral values.[10] The history of the Negro people and race relations has profited more from the insights and challenges of this type of writing in the last two decades than from the scholarship of the preceding and much longer era of moral neutrality and obtuseness. Nor is it to deny the value of what white historians have contributed to the understanding of Negro history. For better or for worse, the great majority of scholars working in this field have been and will continue to be white. Without their contribution, Negro history would be far more impoverished and neglected than it now is.

Granting the value of the part white historians have played in this field, the Negro still has understandable causes for dissatisfaction. For however sympathetic they may be, white historians with few exceptions are primarily concerned with the moral, social, political, and economic problems of white men and their past. They are prone to present to the Negro as *his* history the record of what the white man believed, thought, legislated, did and did not do *about* the Negro. The Negro is a passive element, the man to whom things happen. He is the object rather than the subject of this kind of history. It is filled with the infamies and the philanthropies, the brutalities and the charities, the laws, customs, prejudices, policies, politics, crusades, and wars of whites *about* blacks. "Racial attitudes" or "American attitudes" in a title mean white attitudes. "The Negro Image" means the image in white minds. In this type of history, abolitionists, Radical Republicans, and carpetbaggers are all of the same pale pigmentation. A famous history of the Underground Railroad virtually omitted reference to the blacks, who incurred most of the risks, did most of the work, and suffered nearly all the casualties.[11] The largest and most comprehensive book on the antislavery movement could spare only nine pages for the black abolitionists.[12] Not until the civil rights workers of the 1960s do the prime movers and shakers of Negro history take on a darker hue in the history books, and not in all of them at that.

Negro history in this tradition—and many Negro historians themselves followed the tradition, virtually the only one available in university seminars—was an enclave, a cause or a result, a commentary on or an elaboration of white history. Black history *was* white history. Denied a past of his own, the Negro was given to understand that whatever history and culture he possessed was supplied by his association with the dominant race in the New World and its European background. Thoroughly Europo-centric in outlook, American whites subscribed completely to the myth that European culture, *their* culture, was so overwhelmingly superior that no other could survive under exposure to it. They also shared the European stereotypes, built up by three centuries of slave traders and elaborated by nineteenth- and twentieth-century European imperialists, of an Africa of darkness, savagery, bestiality, and degradation. Not only was the African stripped of this degrading heritage on American shores and left cultureless, a Black Adam in a new garden, but also he was viewed as doubly fortunate in being rescued from naked barbarism and simultaneously clothed with a superior culture. The "myth of the Negro past" was that he had no past.[13]

So compelling was this myth, so lacking any persuasive evidence to the contrary, so universally prevalent the stereotypes of Africans in their American world that until very recently Negroes adopted it unquestioningly themselves. Carter Woodson remarked in 1937 that "Negroes themselves accept as a compliment the theory of a complete break with Africa, for above all things they do not care to be known as resembling in any way these 'terrible Africans.' "[14] And Du Bois wrote that NAACP members had a "fierce repugnance toward anything African. . . . Beyond this they felt themselves Americans, not Africans. They resented and feared any coupling with Africa."[15] White friends of the Negro defended him against any slurs associating him with Africa as if against insults. And Negroes commonly used the words "African" and "black" as epithets of an opprobrious sort. They were *Americans* with nothing to do with Africa or its blackness, nakedness, and savagery. Africa, like slavery, was something to be forgotten, denied, suppressed. With an older American pedigree and a far better claim than first- and second-generation immigrants of other ethnic groups, Negroes could protest the remoteness of their foreign origins and the exclusiveness of their American identity. "Once for all," wrote Du Bois in 1919, "let us realize that we are Americans, that we were brought here with the earliest settlers, and that the very sort of civilization from which we came made the complete adoption of Western modes and customs imperative if we were to survive at all. In brief, there is nothing so indigeneous [*sic*] so completely 'made in America' as we."[16] Until very recently these were the received opinions, the prevailing attitudes of most Negro Americans.

A few years ago a French writer used the word *décolonisation* in the title of a book on the contemporary movement for Negro rights in America.[17] While the analogy that this word suggests is misleading in important respects, it does call attention to the wider environment of the national experience. The dismantling of white supremacy since World War II has been a worldwide phenomenon. The adjustment of European powers to this revolution has appropriately been called decolonization, since this is the political effect it has had on their many possessions in Asia, Africa, and the Caribbean Sea. The outward trappings, the political symbols, the pomp and ceremony of decolonization doubtless contained a considerable amount of collective ego gratification for the ethnic groups concerned. These included the lowering of old flags and the raising of new ones, the drawing of national boundaries, the establishment of new armies, navies, and air forces with new uniforms, foreign embassies, and seats in the United Nations—the full protocol of national sovereignty in the European tradition. The result has been the appearance of thirty-two new black nations, seventeen of them in the year 1960 in Africa alone, and many tiny ones in the Caribbean. But even more gratifying perhaps was the physical as well as symbolic withdrawal of the dominant whites, together with the debasement of their authority and the destruction of the hated paraphernalia of exclusiveness and discrimination. We know from the writings of Frantz Fanon of Martinique and others how much of the colonial syndrome of dependency, inferiority, and self-hatred lingered behind the new facade of national sovereignty and how little the life of the masses was affected.[18] But the gratifications were there, too, and for the ruling-class elites these were no doubt considerable.

The dismantling of white supremacy was simultaneously taking place in the United States, but the process was accompanied by no such pomp and circumstance and no such debasement of white authority and power. What did take place in America was far less dramatic. It came in the form of judicial decisions, legislative acts, and executive orders by duly constituted authority that remained unshaken in the possession of power. It came with "all deliberate speed," a speed so deliberate as to appear glacial or illusory. The outward manifestations were the gradual disappearance of the little signs, "White" and "Colored," and the gradual appearance of token black faces in clubs, schools, universities, and boards of directors. Some of the tokens were more impressive: a cabinet portfolio, a Supreme Court appointment, a seat in the Senate, the office of mayor. By comparison with the immediately preceding era in America, these developments were striking indeed. But by contrast with the rituals and symbols of decolonization in Africa and the Caribbean, they took on a much paler cast. And while the outcome abroad was separation and independence for black people, the outcome for black people at home was desegregation and integration—or rather the renewal of unfulfilled promises of them.[19]

While Africa was being transformed from degraded European colonies to aggressively independent nations with famous heroes of liberation and a conspicuous visibility on the world scene, American Negro attitudes toward the ancestral homeland changed profoundly. The traditional indifference or repugnance for things African, the shame and abhorrence of association with Africa, gave way to fascinated interest, pride, and a sense of identification. The art, folklore, music, dance, even the speech and clothing of Africa have taken on a new glamor and emotional significance for people who have never seen that continent and will never set foot on it. Instead of concealing marks of African identification, many young people increasingly emphasize, invent, or exaggerate them in dress, speech, or hair style.

We are destined to hear a great deal more about Africa from Afro-Americans as time goes on. This will find its way into historical writing, and some manifestations may seem rather bizarre. Before we assume a posture of outrage or ridicule, it might be well to put this phenomenon into historical perspective. We might recall, for example, that the "scientific" school at the end of the last century placed great emphasis on "Teutonic" and "Anglo-Saxon" tribal customs and institutions, and that in doing so it was dipping several centuries deeper into the past for primitive origins than the Afro-Americans are now. The Irish nationalists of the twentieth century in decreeing the use of Gaelic were attempting the revival of a language a good deal less alive than Swahili. While Hebrew has more scholarly uses, its study in America is also dictated by the needs of ethnic identity.

The assimilation of European ethnic groups in America throughout the history of immigration has not only been a story of deculturation and acculturation—the shedding of foreign ways and the adoption of new values. It has also been a story of fierce struggles to assert and maintain ethnic interests and identity.[20] One key element in that struggle has been the group's sense of its past. Each immigrant group of any size established its historical societies and journals in which filiopietism has free rein. According to Marcus Hansen, more than 400 Norwegian journals have been established from time to time in America.[21] Not only the Norwegians but also the Irish and the Jews have contested with Italians the claim to the discovery of America. These assertions of group pride in a common past, mythic or real, have accompanied a strong urge for assimilation and integration in American society. In the opinion of the anthropologist Melville J. Herskovits, "the extent to which the past of a people is regarded as praiseworthy, their own self-esteem will be high and the opinion of others will be favorable."[22]

The priests who taught the children of the Irish slums that St. Brendan, Bishop of Clonfert, discovered America in the sixth century,[23] or the rabbis who taught their charges in the

Jewish slums that the Indians were the lost tribes of Israel,[24] or the Bohemians and Poles and Swedes and Italians who assured the children that it was *their* countrymen who saved the day at Bunker Hill or Bull Run or the Bloody Angle were not advancing the cause of history. But they *were* providing defenses against the WASP myths of the schoolbooks and some sense of group identity and pride and self-esteem to slum dwellers who were, in their turn, regarded by the Best People as the scum of the earth.[25]

Denied a praiseworthy past or, for that matter, a past of any sort that is peculiarly their own, Negro Americans have consequently been denied such defenses and self-esteem as these resources have provided other and less vulnerable American groups. Now that they are seeking to build defenses of their own and a past of their own, they are likely to repeat many of the ventures in mythmaking and filiopietism in which other minorities, including the WASPs, have indulged.

One of their temptations will be to follow the exciting example of their brothers in Africa who are now in search of national identity for brand-new nation-states.[26] Nationalists have always invoked history in their cause and abused it for their purposes. No nations have been so prone to this use of history as new nations. Unable to rely on habituation of custom by which old states claim legitimacy and the loyalty of their citizens, newborn nations (our own, for example) invoke history to justify their revolutions and the legitimacy of new rulers. Like their American kin, the Africans had also been denied a past of their own, for European historians of the imperialist countries held that the continent, at least the sub-Saharan part, had no history before the coming of the white man. Historians of the new African states have not been backward in laying counterclaims and asserting the antiquity of their history and its importance, even its centrality in the human adventure. Inevitably some black patriots have been carried away by their theme. One Ghanian historian, for example, goes so far as to assert that Moses and Buddha were Egyptian Negroes, that Christianity sprang from Sudanic tribes, and that Nietzsche, Bergson, Marx, and the existentialists were all reflections of Bantu philosophy.[27] How much of this overwrought nationalism of the emergent African states will take root in American soil remains to be seen. Already something like it has found expression in cults of black nationalism and is seeking lodgment in the academies.

It seems possible that the new pride in Africa's achievements, identification with its people and their history, and the discovery of ancestral roots in its culture could contribute richly to the self-discovery and positive group identity of a great American minority. What had been suppressed or regarded with shame in this American subculture could now be openly expressed with confidence and pride. The extent of African survivals in Negro-American culture has been debated for a generation by anthropologists.[28] No doubt such survivals have been exaggerated, and admittedly there are fewer in the United States than in Latin America and the West Indies. But the acknowledged or imagined African survivals in religious and marital practices, in motor habits, in speaking, walking, burden carrying, and dancing, however the anthropologists may assess them, have gained new sanction and a swinging momentum.

It seems to me that the reclaimed African heritage could give a third dimension to the tragically two-dimensional man of the Du Bois metaphor. "One ever feels his two-ness," he wrote, "—an American, a Negro; two souls, two thoughts, two unreconciled strivings; two warring ideals in one dark body. . . ." Du Bois thought that, "The history of the American Negro is the history of this strife . . ." and that "this double-consciousness, this sense of always looking at one's self through the eyes of others" was his tragedy.[29] The recovery of an African past and a third dimension of identity might have a healing effect on the schizoid "two-ness," the "two-soul" cleavage of the Negro mind.

There are, unhappily, less desirable consequences conceivable for the preoccupation with Africa as a clue to racial identity. For in the hands of nationalist cults, it can readily become a mystique of skin color and exclusiveness, of alienation and withdrawal. It can foster a new separatism, an inverted segregation, a black apartheid. It can seek group solidarity and identity by the rejection of the White Devil and all his works simply because of white association. This is part of what Erik Erikson meant by "negative identity," the affirmation of identity by what one is not. With reference to that concept, he remarked on "the unpleasant fact that our god-given identities often live off the degradation of others."[30] The most profound insight to be gained from Winthrop D. Jordan's study of American attitudes toward the Negro from English origins to the early nineteenth century is precisely the "negative identity" use that Europeans and white Americans made of Africans. To achieve their own group identity and unity, they systematically debased the Negro to a symbol of the barbarism and licentiousness to which they feared life in the wilderness might reduce Europeans themselves. The Negro thus became, as Jordan says, "a counter-image for the European, a vivid reminder of the dangers facing transplanted Europeans, the living embodiment of what they must never allow themselves to become."[31] American society and identity were thus based on white supremacy. It would be one of the most appalling ironies of American history if the victims of this system of human debasement should in their own quest for identity become its imitators.

One manifestation of black nationalism in academic life is the cry that only blacks are truly qualified to write or to interpret or to teach the black experience. In the special sense that, other things being equal, those who have undergone an experience are best qualified to understand it, there is some truth in this claim. George A. Myers, the Negro friend and faithful correspondent of James Ford Rhodes, pleaded with the historian to do justice to the Negro, but doubted his capacity to do so. "You cannot fully appreciate this," he wrote, "because you have never been discriminated against."[32] Since white historians have written most of American history, including the part assigned the Negroes, it was inevitable that they should have determined the concepts, priorities, values, and interpretations of American historiography and that the values of the white man should have generally prevailed over those of the black man. This situation calls for correction and represents a present challenge to Negro historians.

American history, the white man's version, could profit from an infusion of "soul." It could be an essential corrective in line with the tradition of countervailing forces in American historiography. It was in that tradition that new immigrant historians revised first-family and old-stock history, that Jewish scholars challenged WASP interpretations, that Western challengers confronted New England complacencies, Yankee heretics upset Southern orthodoxies, Southern skeptics attacked Yankee myths, and the younger generation, since the beginning, assaulted the authority of the old. Negro historians have an opportunity and a duty in the same tradition.

An obligation to be a corrective influence is one thing, but a mandate for the exclusive preemption of a subject by reason of racial qualification is quite another. They cannot have it both ways. Either black history is an essential part of American history and must be included by all American historians, or it is unessential and can be segregated and left to black historians.

But Negro history is too important to be left entirely to Negro historians. To disqualify historians from writing Negro history on the grounds of race is to subscribe to an extreme brand of racism. It is to ignore not only the substantial corrective and revisionary contributions to Negro history made by white Americans but also those of foreign white scholars such as Gilberto Freyre of Brazil, Fernando Ortiz of Cuba, Charles Verlinden of Belgium, and Gunnar Myrdal of Sweden. To export this idea of racial qualifications for writing history to Latin America is to expose its narrow parochialism. The United States is unique, so far as I know, in drawing an arbitrary line that classifies everyone as either black or white and calls all people with any apparent African intermixture "Negroes" or "blacks." In Latin America and the Caribbean, the gradations of color, hair, and features—often very fine gradations—are all important. Some Americans who present themselves as qualified by color to write "black" history would mystify many Latin Americans, since by their standards such people are not black at all, and deem themselves so only by unconsciously adopting white racist myths peculiar to the United States.[33]

The fact is that there are few countries left in the New World that are not multiracial in population. In many of them racial intermixture and intermarriage are prevalent. To impose the rule of racial qualification for historians of such multiracial societies as those of Trinidad, Cuba, Jamaica, Brazil, or Hawaii would be to leave them without a history. What passes for racial history is often the history of the relations between races —master and slave, imperialist and colonist, exploiter and exploited, and all the political, economic, sexual, and cultural relations, and their infinitely varied intermixtures. To leave all the history of these relations in the hands of the masters, the imperialists, or the exploiters would result in biased history. But to segregate historical subjects along racial lines and pair them with racially qualified historians would result in fantastically abstract history. This is all the more true since it is the relations, attitudes, and interactions between races that are the most controversial and perhaps the most significant aspects of racial history.

Some would maintain that the essential qualification is not racial but cultural and that membership in the Afro-American subculture is essential to the understanding and interpretation of the subtleties of speech, cuisine, song, dance, folklore, and music composing it. There may be truth in this. I am not about to suggest that the Caucasian is a black man with a white skin, for he is something less and something more than that. I am prepared to maintain, however, that, so far as their culture is concerned, all Americans are part Negro. Some are more so than others, of course, but the essential qualification is not color or race. When I said "all Americans," unlike Crèvecoeur, I included Afro-Americans. They are part Negro, too, but only part. So far as their culture is concerned, they are more American than Afro and far more alien in Africa than they are at home, as virtually all pilgrims to Africa have discovered.[34]

Many old black families of Philadelphia and Boston are less African in culture than many whites of the South. The Southern white "acculturation" began long ago and may be traced in the lamentations of planters that their children talked like Negroes, sang Negro songs, preferred Negro music at their dances, and danced like Negroes. It was observed by travelers like Frederick L. Olmsted, who was "struck with the close co-habitation and association of black and white . . . black and white faces constantly thrust out of doors, to see the train go by."[35] It is still a moot question whether white revivalist behavior— shouts, jerks, "unknown tongues," possession, and the rest—is a reflex of Africanism or vice versa. Even the sophisticated Mary Boykin Chesnut, on attending a Negro church at her plantation, admitted that she "wept bitterly" and added that "I would very much have liked to shout, too."[36] But as Herskovits says, "Whether Negroes borrowed from whites or whites from Negroes, in this or any other aspect of culture, it must always be remembered that the borrowing was never achieved without resultant change in whatever was borrowed."[37] If there was a "black experience" and a "white experience," there was also a "gray experience."

Modern white parents have a complaint that differs from that of the antebellum planters, but resembles it. For where the old planter's children took on their African acculturation unconsciously by a process of osmosis, the contemporary collegiate swinger, protester, and rebel is a deliberate, assiduous, and often egregiously servile imitator. It was Langston Hughes's lament that "You've taken my blues and gone . . . ," and he was probably justified in his complaint in the same poem that ". . . you fixed 'em/So they don't sound like me. . . ." But if so, it was certainly for no lack of effort on the part of the young white imitator, "the White Negro." His is but the latest contribution to the "gray experience."

Whether the revision of Negro history is undertaken by black historians or white historians, or preferably by both, they will be mindful of the need for correcting ancient indignities, ethno-centric slights, and paternalistic patronizing, not to mention cal-culated insults, callous indifference, and blind ignorance. They will want to see full justice done at long last to Negro achieve-ments and contributions, to black leaders and heroes, black slaves and freedmen, black poets and preachers.

As for white historians, I doubt that their contribution to this revision would best be guided by impulses of compensatory exaggeration. The genuine achievements of Negro Americans throughout our history are substantial enough in view of the ter-rible handicaps under which they labored. They should receive the credit that they have been denied. But during the greater part of the struggle for power and place and fame that make up so much of history, black men were kept in chains and illiteracy and subject thereafter to crippling debasement and deprivation. The number of landmarks and monuments they were able to leave on the history of their country was necessarily limited. It is a misguided form of white philanthropy and paternalism that would attempt to compensate by exaggerating or by celebrating ever more obscure and deservedly neglected figures of the past. Equally misguided are impulses of self-flagellation and guilt that encourage the deprecation of all things European or white in our civilization and turn its history into a chorus of *mea cul-pas*. The demagoguery, the cant, and the charlatanry of histori-ans in the service of a fashionable cause can at times rival that of politicians.[38] Also suspect is the standard assumption, sup-ported by a long New England tradition, that this subject can be properly discussed only with an attitude of humorless sol-emnity. Anything so full of tears as the black experience, and anything so full of the absurd as the relations between the races in America, cannot be wholly devoid of existential laughter. I think this is what Ralph Ellison meant by the Negro's "tragi-comic attitude toward the universe."[39] The humor need not come at anyone's expense, but whatever the cost to piety, it should never be entirely excluded from discourse on this sub-ject.

The Negro historian under present circumstances labors under a special set of pressures and temptations. One that will require moral fiber to resist is the temptation to gratify the white liberal's masochistic cravings, his servile yearnings to be punished. This is indeed a tempting market, but historians would do well to leave it to the theater of the absurd. Another temptation, given present license and indulgence, is to give un-inhibited voice to such sentiments as Du Bois expressed in his declaration: "I believe in the Negro race, in the beauty of its genius, the sweetness of its soul. . . ."[40] A sincere sentiment, no doubt. But before releasing such pronouncements for publication, it might be advisable to substitute the word "white" for the word "Negro" and play it back for sound: "I believe in the *white* race, in the beauty of its genius, the sweetness of its soul. . . ." At present, the celebratory impulse runs powerfully through the historiography of this field. Now is the time to praise famous men. Now is a time to do honor to heroes, justice to the obscure, and to demonstrate beyond doubt that the downtrodden seethed constantly with resistance to oppression and hostility to their oppressors. The demand for such history is understandable. But the historian will keep in mind that the stage of history was never peopled exclusively by heroes, villains, and oppressed innocents, that scamps and timeservers and anti-heroes have always played their parts. He might be reminded also that the charlatans and knaves and rakehells of Malcolm X's Harlem were probably as numerous as their white counterparts and represent a neglected field of Negro history.

It is to be hoped that white as well as black historians will reserve some place for irony as well as for humor. If so, they will risk the charge of heresy by pointing out in passing that Haiti, the first Negro republic of modern history, though born of a slave rebellion, promptly established and for a long time maintained an oppressive system of forced labor remarkably similar to state slavery; that Liberia, the second Negro republic, named for liberty, dedicated to freedom, and ruled by former slaves from the United States, established a flourishing African slave trade; and that Kwame Nkrumah, dictator of Ghana, with a misguided instinct for symbolism, selected as his official residence at Accra the Christiansborg Castle, onetime barracoon from which his ancestors had sold their kinsmen into slavery.

These instances are not adduced to alleviate the guilt of the white man, who rightfully bears the greater burden. I would subscribe in general to the admonition of Barrington Moore, Jr., that, "For all students of human society, sympathy with the victims of historical processes and skepticism about the victors' claims provide essential safeguards against being taken in by the dominant mythology."[41] In all the annals of Africa there could scarcely be a more ironic myth of history than that of the New World republic which reconciled human slavery with natural rights and equality, and on the backs of black slaves set up the New Jerusalem, the world's best hope for freedom. The mythic African counterparts look pale beside the American example. They do serve, however, as reminders that the victims as well as the victors of the historical process are caught in the human predicament.

Joseph Conrad once remarked that women, children, and revolutionaries have no taste for irony. These are certainly not the most propitious times for the cultivation of that taste. Not only is it an abomination to revolutionaries, but also equally abhorrent are mixed motives, ambivalence, paradox, and complexity in any department. In times like these the historian will be hard put to it to maintain his creed that the righteousness of a cause is not a license for arrogance, that the passion for justice is not a substitute for reason, that race and color are neither a qualification nor a disqualification for historians, that myths, however therapeutic, are not to be confused with history, and that it is possible to be perfectly serious without being oppressively solemn. To defend this position under the circumstances will require a certain amount of what some call "cool," and others, grace—grace under pressure, which was Hemingway's definition of courage.

NOTES

THE NEW PHILOSOPHICAL HISTORY: *Voltaire*

[1] Here, and throughout the book, I give English titles of foreign
works only if they have been translated; in all other cases the
original title will appear. [Editor]

THE CRITICAL METHOD: *Niebuhr*

[1] Louis de Beaufort (d. 1795), French historian, wrote in 1738
a dissertation on the uncertainty of the first five centuries of
Roman history. [Editor]
[2] Georg Ludwig Spalding (1762-1811), Ludwig Friedrich Heindorf
(1774-1816), and Philipp Karl Buttmann (1764-1829), were German philologists who made important contributions to the study
of Greek and Latin language and literature. Karl von Savigny
(1779-1861), German jurist and founder of the historical school of
jurisprudence. [Editor]
[3] Richard Bentley (1662-1742), English scholar, was one of the first
textual critics. [Editor]
[4] Poet and philologist, Johann Heinrich Voss, (1751-1826),
achieved fame for his translations of Homer, Virgil, and Shakespeare. [Editor]

THE IDEAL OF UNIVERSAL HISTORY: *Ranke*

[1] Lorenz Oken, (1779-1851), German naturalist and *Naturphilos-
oph*, founder of the periodical *Isis*. [Editor]

491

NATIONAL HISTORY AND LIBERALISM: *Thierry*

[1] Among the works that marked the beginning of the reform in writing history, it would be unjust not to list two papers by M. Naudet, of the Académie des Inscriptions et Belles-Lettres, on the social conditions prevailing in Gaul in the centuries following the [Roman?] conquest. These very thorough studies are distinguished from the works of the scholars of the past century by their more solid critical basis, a rare understanding of the era, and the absence of all political bias.

[2] This expression, which unfortunately accurately describes conditions at the time when my generation were entering upon their studies, is no longer applicable to the present teaching in the colleges of Paris. Thanks to the learning and the talent of such professors as MM. Desmichels, Poirson, Caïx, and Michelet, the discoveries and reforms of the new criticism are today making their way into the classroom.

[Translator's note: "Collèges" is synonymous with "lycées," i.e., secondary schools between high-school and college level. The level of instruction is closer to that of American colleges than to that of high schools.]

HISTORY AND LITERATURE: *Macaulay*

[1] The Romance of History. England. By Henry Neele. London 1828.

HISTORY AS A NATIONAL EPIC: *Michelet*

[1] I owed much to the encouragement of my illustrious professors, Messrs. Villemain and Leclerc. I shall always remember how M. Villemain, after the reading of a task that had pleased him, left his chair, and, under an impulse of charming sensibility, came and sat down upon the bench beside me.

[2] I left it with regret in 1837, when the eclectic influence prevailed there. In 1838, the *Institut* and the College of France having equally elected me for their candidate, I obtained the chair I now occupy.

[3] Take the most liberal, a German or an Englishman, at random,—speak to him of liberty; he will answer, "Liberty." And then just try to see what they understand by it. You will then perceive that this word has as many meanings as there are nations; that the German or English democrats are aristocrats at heart; that the barrier of nationalities, which you believe effaced, remains almost entire. All these people, whom you believe so near, are five hundred leagues from you.

HISTORICAL MATERIALISM: *Marx and Engels; Jaurès*
MARX AND ENGELS

[1] Karl Marx and Arnold Ruge edited the *Deutsch-Französische Jahrbücher,* Paris 1844, in which Marx published a critique of Hegelian idealism. Marx and Engels collaborated on *The Holy Family* (1845), an attack on the Young Hegelians, especially Bruno Bauer. [Editor]
[2] The sentence is imperfect in the original.

JAURÈS

[3] Adolphe Aulard (1848-1928), leading Republican historian of the Revolution, whose *French Revolution, a Political History 1789-1804,* appeared in 1901. [Editor]
[4] Hippolyte A. Taine (1828-1892), historian and critic of the arts, vigorous exponent of a positivistic history of civilization, wrote *The Origins of Contemporary France* (6 vols. 1875-1894), a violent attack on the Revolution. [Editor]
[5] The reference is to André Lichtenberger (1870-1914), French novelist and historian, who wrote several treatises on eighteenth-century socialism. [Editor]
[6] Léon Biollay (1830-1920), French historian who wrote several studies on the economic history of the eighteenth century. [Editor]

HISTORY AS AN ACADEMIC DISCIPLINE: PROSPECTUSES OF
Historische Zeitschrift, Revue Historique,
English Historical Review

[1] This is E. A. Freeman's (1823-1892) celebrated definition which, in its day, found widespread acceptance. [Editor]

ON THE TRAINING OF HISTORIANS: *Mommsen*

[1] Mommsen never wrote the fourth volume, which was to have covered the history of the Roman Emperors. It has been argued by a contemporary German critic, Albert Wucher, that Mommsen's failure to complete his work was due to his dismay over the decline of Roman politics after Caesar's death and his hatred of the uncreative absolutism which followed, and perverted, the great Caesar's work. [Editor]

AN AMERICAN DEFINITION OF HISTORY: *Turner*

[1] Augustine Birrell (1850-1933), English author and statesman, whose collection of essays, *Obiter Dicta,* established his literary reputation. [Editor]

[2] Sir John Seeley (1834-1895), Regius Professor of History at Cambridge University, author of *The Expansion of England* (1883), urged that history should have immediate political usefulness, should be a school for statesmen. [Editor]

[3] Wilhelm Maurenbrecher (1838-1902), a student of Ranke and author of several books on modern German history. [Editor]

[4] Wilhelm Roscher (1817-1894), one of the first German economic historians, whose treatises on the system of political economy had a pervasive influence on contemporary scholars. [Editor]

[5] Baron Christian von Bunsen (1791-1860), Prussian diplomat and scholar, secretary to Niebuhr at Rome, and author of several works on the philosophy of universal history. [Editor]

[6] Johann Kaspar Bluntschli (1808-1881), German jurist and political theorist, wrote several treatises on the state which he conceived of as an organism. [Editor]

[7] George Bancroft (1800-1891), American historian, a student of Heeren at Göttingen, wrote a staunchly pro-Jackson *History of the United States* (6 vols. 1834-1882), which depicted the growth of American democracy as the realization of providential design. He was appointed Secretary of the Navy in 1845 and subsequently minister to England and to the German Confederation. [Editor]

[8] Hermann E. von Holst (1841-1904), a German-American scholar, wrote an eight-volume *Constitutional and Political History of the United States*. James Bryce (1838-1922), English historian and statesman wrote *The American Commonwealth* (2 vols. 1888), considered an authoritative account of American institutions. [Editor]

HISTORY AS A SCIENCE: *Bury*

[1] Lodovico Muratori (1672-1751), Italian textual critic and historian, whose superb work on the sources of Italian history had a widespread influence on European scholars. Charles Dufresne, seigneur Du Cange (1610-1688), French philologist and prolific editor of historical texts, compiled monumental glossaries of Medieval Latin and Medieval Greek. Le Nain de Tillemont (1637-1698), a French Jansenist, wrote several works on early Church history and the history of the Roman Empire. [Editor]

[2] Jean Mabillon (1632-1707), a member of the Benedictine Congregation of St. Maur, and the greatest historical scholar of his century. In addition to his critical editions and historical accounts, he wrote the first treatise on the science of diplomatics, the methods of establishing the authenticity of documents, *De Re Diplomatica* (1681). [Editor]

[3] Madame de Staël.

[4] Friedrich Christoph Dahlmann (1785-1860), a member of the 1848 Frankfurt Parliament, belonged to the Prussian school of historians. [Editor]

[5] Bury's citation is inexact; see p. 57 for correct reference. [Editor]

⁶ Sophocles, *Antigone,* lines 331-75.
⁷ The reference is to Stubbs, Lecture of 15 May 1877, printed in *Mediaeval and Modern History,* Oxford, 1886, *v.* esp. pp. 83-7.
⁸ 1841.

CLIO REDISCOVERED: *Trevelyan*

¹ Sir Charles Harding Firth (1857-1936), Regius Professor of Modern History at Oxford and specialist in the history of seventeenth-century England, prepared a new edition of Macaulay's *History* (1913-1915), on which some years later he wrote a commentary as well. [Editor]
² This refers to G. P. Gooch, *History and Historians in the Nineteenth Century* (1913), a standard survey of nineteenth-century historiography. [Editor]
³ Robert Ball (1802-1857), Irish civil servant and amateur naturalist, frequent lecturer on science and for some years director of scientific lectures in Dublin. Trevelyan is referring here to Thomas Henry Huxley's (1825-1895) devastating retort to Samuel Wilberforce, the Bishop of Oxford, during a public discussion of evolution in 1860. Huxley became known as "Darwin's Bulldog" and was an indefatigible popularizer of science. [Editor]
⁴ Sydney Smith (1771-1845), English writer, divine, and tutor, spirited critic of established institutions, proposed the founding of the *Edinburgh Review* (1802), to which he contributed political essays of a vigorous, liberal tone. [Editor]
⁵ Paul Louis Courier (1773-1825), French political pamphleteer, a fearless and persistent critic of the Bourbon Restoration. [Editor]
⁶ Edward Ernest Bowen (1836-1901) was for forty-one years a master at Harrow, famous English school, where he taught history and imparted to his students his intense interest in military tactics. [Editor]
⁷ At the battle of Morat in 1476, the Swiss defeated the Burgundians, who were allied with the Duchess of Savoy, to whose territory the town of Morat had originally belonged. [Editor]
⁸ Sir John Seeley wrote *Ecce Homo: The Life and Work of Jesus Christ* (1866). [Editor]
⁹ This refers to the Bishop Mandell Creighton's *History of the Papacy During the Period of the Reformation* (5 vols. 1882-1894). [Editor]

SPECIALIZATION AND HISTORICAL SYNTHESIS:
Lord Acton and Berr

LORD ACTON

¹ William Stubbs (1825-1901), the foremost English medievalist of his generation, was appointed Bishop of Oxford in 1888. Andrew Martin Fairbairn (1838-1917), Congregational minister and theo-

logian, contributed several chapters to the second volume of *The Cambridge Modern History*. Francis Neil Gasquet (1846-1929), Roman Catholic historian and cardinal, author of *Henry VIII and the English Monasteries* (2 vols. 1888-1889), was appointed prefect of the archives of the Holy See in 1917. Felix Liebermann (1851-1925), German-Jewish historian and legal scholar, wrote extensively on Anglo-Saxon law and English medieval history. Frederic Harrison (1831-1923), leading English positivist, for twenty-five years president of the English Positivist committee, author of several historical studies as well as of essays on the nature of history. [Editor]

HISTORICISM AND ITS PROBLEMS: *Meinecke*

[1] The German term, *Wissenschaft,* is not precisely rendered by "science." The English term tends to connote the natural sciences and their methods whereas *Wissenschaft* is used of any body of disciplined knowledge. In some contexts I have translated it as "discipline."

The German verb *werten,* crucial for this article, contains a concept somewhat alien to English. *Werten* does not discriminate between the subjective and objective elements in "valuing" and applies both to the act of assigning value *to* an object and the act of appreciating or perceiving value *in* an object. The English terms value, evaluate, however, have acquired a subjective connotation.

To provide consistency in terminology I have rendered *werten* as "evaluate" and the noun *Wertung* as "evaluation" wherever possible. But frequently "appreciate," "value" (as a verb), and paraphrases have been used to make the meaning clear. Paraphrases have been especially unavoidable where *Wert* is used as a component in compound nouns and adjectives, e.g. *Lebenswert, wertfrei, wertbezogene.* But in a few places I have introduced, reluctantly, literal jargon equivalents (e.g. "value-neutral" for *wertfrei*) where a unique term was demanded by the context. [Translator]

[2] "By history," says Eduard Meyer (*Geschichte des Altertums*, I, I, 3, 188), "we mean any event of the past the effect of which is not exhausted in its moment of appearance but clearly continues to have an effect upon succeeding periods and to generate new processes in them." In this crucial passage only the causal and not the valuative element in the conceptual determination of "the historical" is mentioned. And yet several pages later the "inner value," i.e. the clear formation of an individual characteristic, reappears as another criterion in the selection of what is historical. This lack of inner harmony is characteristic of the type of thinking current among specialists. It is recognized that both causality and value are related elements in historical interest, but one never really comes to terms with this, so that when it comes to basic

definitions, one succumbs to purely causal thinking. For a critique of Meyer see also Rickert, *Probleme der Geschichtsphilosophie*, 3, 59.

[3] Rickert (*Probleme der Geschichtsphilosophie*, 3, 67) accepts "the psychological inseparability of evaluation and value-relating," but wishes to divorce evaluation from the logical essence of history. Now what is psychologically inseparable from the activity of the historian must be recognized by the logician as being bound up with it in a psychically essential way even when the logician is able to distinguish it through his special methods. Evaluation, furthermore, is not merely a superfluous by-product of the historian's activity. I of course agree with Rickert that "the historian can abstain from value judgment of his object," but history written without such a valuation is either mere amassing of material and preparation for genuine historical writing or, in claiming to be genuine history, is insipid—unless, of course, the temperament of the historian restores life and color through unintentional evaluations as may perhaps be the case with the great historical researches and expositions of Max Weber. Heinrich Maier (*Das geschichtliche Erkennen*, 1914, p. 34), although otherwise in strong disagreement with Rickert, is also of the opinion that "value-judgments are not the business of history." But at the same time he holds it empty pedantry to deny a spirited historian the right to make them. That is, he distinguishes a properly historical approach in which value judgments are excluded, from an ethical-esthetic and therefore evaluative approach which he also holds to be legitimate. And shall the historian try to satisfy both demands within the limits of a single work, although the first, his proper task, is inconsistent with the second? This is impossible and hybrid, a kind of double standard in one's calling which lacerates the inner psychic unity of the historian's activity. A logic of history, to be successful, must take this psychic unity as its starting point, must analyze the concrete and living historian and not a logically constructed one. And the living historian as a rule finds himself making value judgments even when he does not wish to. One who is constantly immersed in the practice of historical writing senses this in a way which the philosopher does not. G. v. Below, (*Die deutsche Geschichtsschreibung von den Befreiungskriegen bis zu unseren Tagen*, 2nd ed., 116) says: "A connection among facts cannot be effected without value judgments." This goes a bit too far perhaps. Certain causal connections of a simple kind can be effected even without a value judgment. But connections of a more complicated kind—for example establishment of the causes of the Reformation, of the French Revolution, and now of the Collapse of 1918—will always be determined in part by value judgments.

[4] I cannot agree with Rickert's distinctions (*Lebenswerte und Kulturwerte*, *Logos* II, 131 ff., and *Die Philosophie des Lebens*, p. 156 ff.) which hold that values in the sense of life-values do not exist in the last analysis and that cultural values are more or less

remote from and opposed to life. This, despite the fact that I am close to Rickert in his conception of the essence of culture. At bottom our differences are more terminological than substantive.

[5] The origin and history of the distinction between culture and civilization must some day be investigated. To my knowledge the first to use it was Kant in the *Idee zu einer allgemeinen Geschichte in weltbürgerlicher Absicht.* In the seventh proposition we read: "The idea of morality still belongs to culture; but the use of this idea, which extends only to the appearance of morality in the love of honor and outward respectability, merely amounts to civilization."

[6] I have relied here on the old threefold division among ideal goods. Although this does not exhaust their scope and content, it may be used as an abbreviation.

[7] Thus I am equating cultural contribution and cultural value. Cultural values do not, as Rickert holds, only "adhere" to historical realities without being realities themselves, but are an integrating factor in historical realities because these can only come about through the cooperation of the spiritual-moral causality, which realizes values, with mechanistic and biological causality. Cf. also Troeltsch's critique (*Historismus,* p. 153) of Rickert's doctrine as to the mere "adhering" of cultural values in real historical phenomena. The question as to the existence of a system of objective values beyond historical reality is a metaphysical problem which the historian must leave to the philosopher.

[8] Alfred Dove was of the same opinion. I refer to his beautiful letter to Rickert of January 27, 1899 (*Ausgewählte Aufsätze und Briefe* 2, 208). The historian, he says, devotes to life gone by "an interest which is completely independent of the extent to which it has paved the way for our life. And why can he do this? Because a relationship to us exists even apart from such causality, as long as the life considered has meaning in itself, and awakens our sympathy as a thing of value from the universal human standpoint. We do not enter into contact with the past through causality alone, but leap across the entire intervening causal space by the force of simple sympathy."

[9] Rickert has been able to distinguish seven different evolutionary concepts! (*Die Grenzen der naturwissenschaftlichen Begriffsbildung,* ch. IV, 5). Dove's letter to Rickert, cited above, also mentions the overestimation of the idea of evolution, but on a basis which I cannot share. "From individual to individual," he says, there can be no evolution." He thus fails to recognize that each individuality is embedded in a higher individuality and that the evolution which takes place within the higher individuality connects the separate and independently evolving concrete individualities through spiritual ties. Thus from Luther as an individual to Kant as an individual, there is, in fact, an evolution; namely, that which takes place in the German Protestant spiritual universe. As to Dove's way of viewing history, see my remarks in *Historische Zeitschrift,* vol. 116, 83.

[10] "Historical evolutions are nothing else than historical individualities understood in their becoming and growth." (Rickert, *Probleme der Geschichtsphilosophie*, 47).

[11] This is also a safeguard against the dangerous tendency of modern "synthesizers" who treat the individual phenomenon as a mere organ and example of universal developments, which means, in practice, as a mere point of intersection for so many abstract "isms." In this they come dangerously close to the positivism they had thought was overcome. In the most recent histories of art and literature there are already disturbing manifestations of this sort.

[12] *Historismus*, p. 211. We do not intend to examine more closely in this context what are called the dangers of historism, i.e. the tendency of historical thinking to make all values relative. We limit ourselves to the remark that only weak souls of little faith could despair and quit under the burden of this relativizing historism. Belief in an unknown absolute cannot be shaken by it. To demand, however, that the unknown absolute unveil itself so that it can be touched and fingered is a survival of anthropomorphic notions of divinity.

[13] Hegel has denied of course, that peoples and governments have learned anything from history, or have ever acted in light of the lessons to be drawn from it. It is probably more correct to say that they have seldom learned the things the observer might wish to see them learn. Yet Bismarck has candidly acknowledged that "For me history is above all something to be learned from. If events themselves do not recur, situations and characters do, and the observation and study of these can stimulate and shape one's mind." (*Gespräch mit Memminger* 1890; Bismarck, *Werke*, IX, 90.)

[14] Relevant here is von Below, (*Deutsche Geschichtsschreibung*, 2nd ed. p. 113, ff.—Thus I do not go along with Troeltsch in regarding "the comprehension of the present as the final goal of all historical study" (*Bedeutung des Protestantismus*, p. 6). It is surely a legitimate and necessary goal, but neither the only nor the highest one. I have often argued this point with Troeltsch, and in his *Historismus*, p. 696, he reproaches me for a "tendency to break loose into objective and pure contemplation."

HISTORICAL CONCEPTUALIZATION: *Huizinga*

[1] Othmar Spann (b. 1878), Austrian economist and leading Catholic theorist of the corporatist state. [Editor]

[2] Juan Luis Vives (1492-1540), Spanish philosopher and publicist, who taught in England and the Low Countries, and attacked the preponderant authority of Aristotle. Agrippa of Nettesheim (1486-1535), German writer, physician and traveller, was appointed archivist and historiographer to Charles V. In several books he ridiculed the pretensions of learned men and attacked the cred-

ibility of the various accretions which had grown up around the simple tenets of early Christianity. [Editor]

³ Jean Hardouin (1646-1729), French classical scholar, contended that most of the ancient classics of Greece and Rome were spurious and had been manufactured by some thirteenth century monks. [Editor]

HISTORICAL RELATIVISM: *Beard*

¹ This refers to Smith's essay "The Writing of American History in America from 1884 to 1934," in the *American Historical Review*, XL, 439-444. [Editor]

² "As a holy hieroglyphic, conceived and preserved in his most external." [Editor]

³ "History: God's march through the world." [Editor]

⁴ "Almighty, One and Three, Thou hast summoned me from nothingness. Here I lie at the steps of Thy throne." [Editor]

⁵ Ottokar Lorenz (1832-1903), German historian, particularly interested in the development of historiography, wrote *Die Geschichtswissenschaft in Hauptrichtungen und Aufgaben* (1886). [Editor]

⁶ Ernst Bernheim (1850-1942), a German medievalist, who wrote the classic *Lehrbuch der Historischen Methode und der Geschichtsphilosophie* (1889), which for some time was considered indispensable for the apprentice to the guild. [Editor]

⁷ Karl Lamprecht (1856-1915), a prolific and polemical German historian who challenged the old political historiography and advocated a new method that would deal with the collective categories of history and would emphasize economic and sociopsychical factors. [Editor]

⁸ "Who wrote their history in naïve, self-confident method, quite unaware of the theoretical abysses all around them." [Editor]

⁹ Herbert Levi Osgood (1855-1918), American historian, whose most important work was a political history of *The American Colonies in the Seventeenth Century* (3 vols. 1904-1907). [Editor]

HISTORY UNDER MODERN DICTATORSHIPS: *Pokrovsky, Frank, and Von Müller*

POKROVSKY

¹ When this speech was delivered, RANION [The Russian Association of Scientific Research Institutes in the Social Sciences] with its Historical Institute and attached seminars, was still only in process of formation. [Translator]

² George V. Plekhanov (1856-1918), a philosopher, literary historian, and one of the principal figures in Russian Marxism before the October Revolution. [Translator]

[3] In the sense that their publication was authorized by the censorship. [Translator]

[4] The Mensheviks were members of the moderate wing of the Russian Social Democratic Labor Party and bitter enemies of their extremist colleagues, the Bolsheviks. [Translator]

[5] The Cadets were members of the liberal Constitutional Democratic Party. [Translator]

[6] "Mir" was the trade name of a large publishing cooperative which was founded in 1906. [Translator]

[7] D. M. Petrushevsky (1863-1942), a medievalist who taught in several Russian universities before the revolution, and continued to work under the Soviet regime until his death, despite attacks like the one mentioned. [Translator]

[8] Eugene V. Tarle (1875-1955), a well-known specialist in Western European history whose academic career began in 1903. He was frequently honored by the Soviet government. [Translator]

[9] Pokrovsky seems to be guilty of a *non sequitur* here. He has apparently misread the meaning intended by Marx and Engels in the quotation in the preceding paragraph, and, in effect, reversed their meaning. [Translator]

[10] Literally, the "Populists," an agrarian revolutionary movement particularly strong in the 1870's. [Translator]

HISTORY AND THE SOCIAL SCIENCES: *Cochran and Hofstadter*
COCHRAN

[1] This discussion in a slightly different form appeared in an article "The 'Presidential Synthesis' in American History," by Thomas C. Cochran, in the *American Historical Review*, LIII, 748-759 (July 1948), and is reprinted here by permission of the Editor.

[2] Alexander Gerschenkron, "Economic Backwardness in Historical Perspective," in Bert F. Hoselitz, ed., *The Progress of Underdeveloped Areas* (Chicago: University of Chicago Press, 1952), pp. 3-4.

[3] Guy Stanton Ford pointed out the need for such a synthesis many years ago in "Some Suggestions to American Historians," *American Historical Review*, XLIII, 267-268 (January 1938). High school textbooks reflect a social scientific approach more than college, but have not attempted any radical resynthesis. Henry B. Parkes, *The American Experience* (New York: Alfred A. Knopf, 1947), while presenting an interpretation based on conflicting social ideologies, rather than the usual narrative, does not in general employ social science concepts or methods. Thomas C. Cochran and William Miller, *The Age of Enterprise* (New York: Macmillan Company, 1942) offers a general synthesis based on the social sciences, but puts specific emphasis on the role of business. See also Caroline F. Ware, ed., *The Cultural Approach to History* (New York: Columbia University Press, 1940), and

Merle E. Curti and others, *An American History* (2 vols.; New York: Harper & Brothers, 1950-51).

⁴ The time and money that have been spent on collecting and publishing even relatively unimportant letters of famous statesmen, compared with that expended in trying to learn something of the norms of the society in which they lived, strikingly indicate the popular trend.

⁵ For studies of government in relation to economic life in the pre-Civil War period, see Oscar and Mary F. Handlin, *Commonwealth: A Study of the Role of Government in the American Economy: Massachusetts, 1776-1861* (New York: New York University Press, 1947), and Louis Hartz, *Economic Policy and Democratic Thought: Pennsylvania, 1776-1860* (Cambridge: Harvard University Press, 1948).

⁶ For a number of suggestive articles, see *Conflicts of Power in Modern Culture,* a symposium edited by Lyman Bryson, Louis Finkelstein, and R. M. MacIver (New York: Harper & Brothers, 1947). Abram Kardiner and others, *The Psychological Frontiers of Society* (New York: Columbia University Press, 1945), and Daniel Lerner, Harold D. Lasswell, and others, eds., *The Policy Sciences* are examples of the type of social-psychological and sociological literature that merits the attention of all historians.

⁷ Kardiner and others, *op. cit.,* p. viii.

⁸ The biographer or historian has used these materials chiefly to enrich and support narrative, but to the cultural anthropologist or psychologist they present clues to social and psychological patterns. Social scientists have made as little use of these historical materials as historians have of the techniques necessary to analyze them.

⁹ Ralph W. Emerson, "The Young American," in *Nature Addresses and Lectures and Letters and Social Aims* (Boston, Houghton Mifflin Company, 1921), p. 388.

¹⁰ A National Records Management Council has been organized and is preserving business records and training business archivists.

¹¹ See, for example, Herbert Weaver, *Mississippi Farmers, 1850-1860* (Nashville: Vanderbilt University Press, 1945).

HOFSTADTER

¹² This no doubt accounts for the surge of interest in the history of ideas that has taken place in the United States during the past twenty years. Not since the era of the French Revolution has America felt itself to be as much involved in the ideological battles of the Western World as it did in the mid-thirties.

¹³ I might almost say caricature rather than portraiture, for most social systems are too complex to be portrayed. Caricature may seem an invidious label, but I do not intend it to be so. Unlike caricature, good history does not attempt to portray through wilful distortion. But caricature has this in common with history,

that its effects must be achieved in broad and exaggerated strokes that cannot render all the features of the subject. And in good caricature the subject is instantly recognizable.

[14] One of the most interesting aspects of this problem has become apparent in connection with what I would call the paradox of quantification. The essence of this paradox is that the recent use of quantitative methods to test historical generalization has resulted in the wholesale destruction of categories that previously held sway in the historian's vocabulary without supplanting them with new generalizations of comparable significance. See, for example, D. Brunton and D. H. Pennington, *Members of the Long Parliament* (London, 1954) and W. O. Aydelotte, "The House of Commons in the 1840's," *History,* n.s., vol. XXXIX (October, 1954), pp. 249-62. Such studies have usually been designed to test the relation between material interest or social status and political behavior. It is, of course, quite conceivable that the uprooted generalizations will be replaced by interpretations having a more social-psychological cast. But in such case it is unlikely that the historian can, with the type of evidence available to him, put these interpretations on any better footing than that of intelligent and partially verified guesses. Should this be true, we might find ourselves in possession of more sophisticated and seemingly more satisfactory explanations which would have to stand largely upon a speculative foundation.

[15] At a recent meeting of representative American historians on the problem of relations with the social sciences, it was the consensus that historians "should not point simply in the direction of becoming 'more scientific,'" and that "historians should not consciously attempt to remake history in the social-science image and should not attempt to restore communication with the social sciences simply by adopting social science methods as their own." The meeting is reported by Richard D. Challener and Maurice Lee, Jr. in "History and the Social Sciences: the Problem of Communications," *American Historical Review,* vol. LXI (January, 1956), pp. 331-38.

[16] Though I am fully aware of the reductionist trap that awaits all efforts to discuss substantive issues only in terms of their psychological backgrounds, I will confess in this case to being far more interested in knowing why some men feel happier when history is classified with the sciences while others feel that they must resist the idea than I am in the question itself. The valuations attached to the use of the word science suggest important differences in intellectual temperament and styles of thought, and shed direct light on the kind of work men choose to do.

[17] To choose at random from some of the social-psychological inquiries cited in the recent volume by Elihu Katz and Paul F. Lazarsfeld, *Personal Influence* (Glencoe, Illinois, 1955), characteristic matters of inquiry were questions like these: Do group leaders know that they are leading? What different uses do well socialized and less socialized children make of their radio listen-

ing? Does an individual tend to accept the outlook of a group more readily if he is attracted to that group? Is an authoritarian atmosphere more likely to restrict conversation in small groups than a democratic or a laissez-faire atmosphere? Does a planted rumor tend to spread outside the ranks of those who are intimately concerned with its content? Do inexperienced soldiers show greater readiness for combat if they are sent into divisions composed of veterans than if they are sent into divisions composed of other :nexperienced soldiers? Do people tend to be more friendly with those who live near them and share their values than with those who live at a distance and have different values? Are children more likely to follow the lead of other children than that of adults in making food choices?

CULTURAL HISTORY AS A SYNTHESIS: *Barzun*

[1] The substance of this essay was delivered before the European History Section of the American Historical Association on December 29, 1954.

[2] Here is how one great political and cultural historian, Walter Bagehot, depicts the cavalier: "A cavalier is always young . . . open to every enjoyment, alive to every passion, eager, impulsive, brave without discipline, noble without principle, prizing luxury, despising danger, capable of high sentiment . . . Over the Cavalier mind this world passes with a thrill of delight. . . . the essense of Toryism is enjoyment."—Essay on Macaulay.

[3] In the instruction sheet sent to consultants by the editors of the *Dictionary of American Biography* the question is raised: "Should an individual's historical importance be judged according to the standards of his own time or those of today? For the purposes of the DAB our answer would be: the individual may qualify by either standard. Users of the dictionary will need information (to take extreme examples) both on the genius unappreciated in his own day and on the former celebrity now forgotten or discredited."

[4] As the merest sample, consider Voltaire's plan for the cultural parts of his *Age of Louis XIV:* "With regard to the arts and sciences, I think all that is needed is to trace the onward march of the human mind in philosophy, oratory, poetry and criticism; to show the progress of painting, sculpture, and music; of jewelry, tapestry making, glassblowing, gold-cloth weaving, and watchmaking. As I do this I want to depict only the geniuses that have excelled in these undertakings." Letter to Abbé Dubos, Oct. 30, 1738.

TIME, HISTORY, AND THE SOCIAL SCIENCES: *Brandel*

[1] *L'Anthropologie structurale,* Paris, Plon, 1958, *passim,* esp. p. 329.

[2] J.-P. Sartre, "Questions de méthode," *Temps modernes* 139, September 1957, pp. 338–417; and 140, October 1957, pp. 658–698.

[3] "Europe in 1500," "The World in 1880," "Germany on the Eve of the Reformation,". . .

[4] L. Halphen, *Introduction à l'histoire,* Paris, Presses Universitaires de France, 1946, p. 50.

[5] Cf. his "Progrès économique," *Cahiers de l'ISEA* 21, July-August 1967; and 22, December 1967.

[6] *Esquisse du mouvement des prix et des revenus en France au* XVIII° *siècle,* Paris, Dalloz, 1933, 2 vols.

[7] For a summary see R. Clémens, *Prolégomènes d'une théorie de la structure économique,* Paris, Domat-Montchrestien, 1952; see also J. Akerman, "Cycle et structure," *Revue économique* 1, 1952, pp. 1–12.

[8] E. R. Curtius, *Europäische Literatur und lateinisches Mittelalter,* Bern, A. Francke, 1948.

[9] Paris, A. Michel, 1943, 2d ed., 1946.

[10] Le Mythe de croisade: Etude de sociologie religieuse," 1957. (Thesis)

[11] P. Francastel, *Peinture et société: Naissance et destruction d'un espace plastique, de la Renaissance au cubisme,* Lyon, Audin, 1951.

[12] One could quote other examples; I would cite in my favor several important articles all tending in the same direction: O. Brunner on European social history, *Historische Zeitschrift* 177 (3), June 1954, pp. 469–494; R. Bultmann, *ibid.,* 176 (1), August 1953, pp. 1–15, on humanism; G. Lefebvre, *Annales historiques de la Révolution* 21, 1949, pp. 97–115; and F. Hartung, *Historische Zeitschrift* 180(1), August 1955, pp. 15–42, on enlightened despotism.

[13] R. Courtin, *La Civilisation économique du Brésil,* Paris, Librairie de Médicis, 1941.

[14] In France. In Spain, the population decline is noticeable from the end of the 16th century.

[15] Lévi-Strauss, *op. cit.,* p. 31.

[16] "Diogène couché," *Temps modernes* 110, 1955, p. 17.

[17] *Le Temps de l'histoire,* Paris, Plon, 1954, in particular p. 298 ff.

[18] P. Chombart de Lauwe, *Paris et l'agglomération parisienne,* Paris, Presses Universitaires de France, 1952, p. 106 (vol. 1).

[19] S. Frère and C. Bettelheim, "Une ville française moyenne: Auxerre en 1950," *Cahiers de la Fondation des Sciences Politiques* 17, 1950.

[20] P. Clément and N. Xydias, "Vienne-sur-le-Rhône: La ville et les habitants; Situation et attitudes; Sociologie d'une cité française," *ibid.,* 71, 1955.

[21] See *Colloque sur les structures,* Ecole Pratique des Hautes Etudes, VIth Section, 1958. (Typed summary.)

[22] Quoted by Lévi-Strauss, *op. cit.,* pp. 30–31.

[23] It would be tempting to mention the "models" of economists which inspired the historians' imitations.

[24] *La Méditerranée et le monde méditerranéen à l'époque de Philippe II,* Paris, A. Colin, 1949, p. 264.

[25] F. Braudel and F. Spooner, *Les Métaux monétaires et l'économie du XVIᵉ siècle: Rapports au Congrès international de Rome,* 1955, vol. IV, pp. 233–264.

[26] A. Chabert, *Structure économique et théorie monétaire,* Paris, A. Colin, Centre d'Etudes Economiques, 1956.

[27] S. Diamond, *The Reputation of the American Businessman,* Cambridge, Mass., Harvard University Press, 1955.

[28] *Histoire et destin,* Paris, B. Grasset, 1943, *passim,* notably p. 169.

[29] *Revue de synthèse historique* 1, July-December 1900, p. 32.

[30] E. Labrousse, *La Crise de l'économie française à la veille de la Révolution française,* Paris, Presses Universitaires de France, 1944, Introduction.

[31] Paris, Presses Universitaires de France, 1950 (2d ed.).

[32] G. Granger, "Evénement et structure dans les sciences de l'homme," *Cahiers de l'ISEA* 1, December 1957, pp. 41–42.

[33] See my no doubt too polemic article "Georges Gurvitch et la discontinuité du social," *Annales* 3, July-September 1953, pp. 347–361.

[34] Cf. G. Gurvitch, *Déterminismes sociaux et liberté humaine,* Paris, Presses Universitaires de France, 1955, pp. 38–40 and *passim.*

[35] J.-P. Sartre, "Fragment d'un livre à paraître sur le Tintoret," *Temps modernes* 141, November 1957, pp. 761–800, and *art. cit.*

[36] O. Berkelbach van der Sprenkel, "Population statistics of Ming China," *BSOAS* 15, 1953, pp. 289–326 (part 2); and M. Rieger, "Zur Finanz- und Agrargeschichte der Ming Dynastie, 1368–1643," *Sinica* 12, 1937, pp. 130–143, 235–252.

[37] P. Vidal de La Blache, in *Revue de synthèse historique* 7, August-December 1903, p. 239.

[38] I.e., when first published in *Annales.* (Translator's note.)

SOCIAL HISTORY: *Perkin*

[1] In A. Redford, *Economic History of England, 1760–1860,* 1931, p. v.

[2] F. M. Powicke, *King Henry III and the Lord Edward,* Oxford, 1947, p. v.

[3] *English Social History,* 1944, p. vii.

[4] *The Use of History,* 1946, p. 69.

[5] "History, Its Subject Matter and Tasks," *History Today,* II, 1952, p. 161.

[6] M. Ginsberg, *Sociology*, 1949, p. 7.

[7] *British Economy of the Nineteenth Century*, Oxford, 1948, p. 134.

[8] G. Ryle, *The Concept of Mind*, 1949, *passim*.

[9] Rostow, *loc. cit.*

[10] Trevelyan, *loc. cit.*

[11] *The Local Historian and His Theme*, Leicester, 1952, p. 17.

[12] *Historical Study in Oxford*, Oxford, 1929, p. 10.

[13] *The Elizabethan Age: I, The England of Elizabeth: The Structure of Society*, 1950, p. viii.

[14] W. J. H. Sprott, *Sociology*, 1949, p. 98; S. H. Beer, "The Representation of Interests in British Government: Historical Background," *American Political Science Review*, LI, 1957, pp. 613–50.

[15] W. F. Ogburn, "On the Social Aspects of Population Change," *British Journal of Sociology*, IV, 1953, p. 26.

[16] M. C. Buer, *Health, Wealth and Population in the Early Days of the Industrial Revolution*, 1926; G. T. Griffith, *Population Problems in the Age of Malthus*, Cambridge, 1926; T. H. Marshall, "The Population of England and Wales from the Industrial Revolution to the World War," *Economic History Review*, V, 1934–35, pp. 65–78.

[17] K. H. Connell, "Some Unsettled Problems in English and Irish Population History, 1750–1845," *Irish Historical Studies*, VII, 1950–51, pp. 225–234; H. J. Habakkuk, "English Population in the Eighteenth Century," *Economic History Review*, 2nd series, VI, 1953, pp. 117–33, and "The Economic History of Modern Britain," *Journal of Economic History*, XVIII, 1958, pp. 486–501; J. T. Krause, "Changes in English Fertility and Mortality, 1781–1850," *Economic History Review*, 2nd series, XI, 1958, pp. 52–70, and "Some Implications of Recent Research in Demographic History," *Comparative Studies in Society and History*, I, 1959, pp. 164–88; T. McKeown and R. G. Brown, "Medical Evidence Related to English Population Changes in the Eighteenth Century," *Population Studies*, IX, 1955, pp. 119–41.

[18] Cf. D. E. C. Eversley, "Population and Economic Growth in England before the 'Take-off'—Some Notes on Methodology and the Objects of Future Research," a paper read at the Economic History Conference, Stockholm, August 1960, and kindly lent to me by the author.

[19] G. E. C. et al., *The Complete Peerage*, 1910–59, gives no systematic information about the origins of newly created peers; on the social connections of City-men a beginning has been made by T. Lupton and C. Shirley Wilson, "The Bank-Rate Tribunal: the Social Background and Connections of 'Top Decision Makers,'" *Manchester School of Economic and Social Studies*, XXVII, 1959, pp. 30–51.

[20] *King Henry III and the Lord Edward*, p. 21.

[21] *The Making of the Middle Ages*, 1953, p. 137.

[22] Namier, *loc. cit.*, p. 157.

[23] W. Cunningham, *The Progress of Capitalism in England*, Cambridge, 1916, p. 6, n. 2.

[24] *Ibid.*, p. 17.

[25] Cf. G. C. Homans, *English Villagers of the Thirteenth Century*, Cambridge, Mass., 1941.

[26] Cf. H. E. Hallam, *The New Lands of Elloe*, Leicester, 1954; and his forthcoming books, *The Lincolnshire Fenland in the Early Middle Ages* (Cambridge University Press) and *Land People: England in the Early Middle Ages* (Routledge and Kegan Paul Ltd.). For the Romano-British landscape see Dr. Sylvia Hallam's forthcoming companion volume, *Land and People: England to the Coming of the English*.

[27] Cf. E. M. W. Tillyard, *The Elizabethan World Picture*, 1950.

[28] Cf. Raymond Williams, *Culture and Society, 1780–1950*, 1958, pp. xiii, xv; Asa Briggs, "The Language of Class in Early Nineteenth-Century England," in A. Briggs and J. Saville (eds.), *Essays in Labour History*, 1960.

[29] G. M. Young, *Victorian England: Portrait of an Age*, 1960, p. 6, n. 1.

[30] For full bibliographies of the controversy between Professors Tawney and Trevor-Roper and their followers, see J. H. Hexter, "Storm over the Gentry," *Encounter*, x, 1958, no. 5, pp. 22–34; and P. Zagorin, "The Social Interpretation of the English Revolution," *Journal of Economic History*, XIX, 1959, pp. 376–401.

[31] Cf. R. B. Grassby, "Social Status and Commercial Enterprise under Louis XIV," *Economic History Review*, 2nd series, XIII, 1960, pp. 19–38.

[32] *Principles of Political Economy*, 4th ed., Edinburgh, 1849, p. 21.

[33] J. S. Mill, *Principles of Political Economy*, 1848; W. A. Lewis, *Theory of Economic Growth*, 1955, esp. pp. 5–6.

[34] *Citizenship and Social Class*, Cambridge, 1950, p. 92.

[35] Pehr Kalm, *Account of His Visit to England on His Way to America in 1748*, trans. J. Lucas, 1892, p. 52; quoted by Dorothy Marshall, *English People in the Eighteenth Century*, 1956, p. 178.

[36] *Op. cit.*, p. 24.

[37] Cf. W. Stark, *The Sociology of Knowledge*, 1958.

[38] On the side of social policy and administration, see J. B. Brebner, "Laissez Faire and State Intervention in Nineteenth-Century Britain," *Journal of Economic History*, Supplement VIII, 1948, pp. 59–73; O. MacDonagh, "The Nineteenth-Century Revolution in Government: A Reappraisal," *Historical Journal*, I, 1958, pp. 52–67; Henry Parris, "The Nineteenth-Century Revolution in Government: A Reappraisal Reappraised," *ibid.*, III, 1960, pp. 17–37.

[39] Rowse, *op. cit.*, chap. ii.

[40] J. H. Hexter, "A New Framework for Social History," *Journal*

of Economic History, xv, 1955, p. 423.

[41] *The Common Pursuit*, 1952, p. 194.

[42] *The Great Tradition*, 1948, pp. 227, 19.

[43] F. Kermode, "A Myth of Catastrophe," *The Listener*, 8 and 15 November 1956; cf. his "The Dissociation of Sensibility," *Kenyon Review*, xix, 1957, pp. 169–94.

[44] See my "Origins of the Popular Press," *History Today*, vii, 1957, pp. 425–35.

[45] Cf. Charles Wilson, "The Other Face of Mercantilism," *Transactions of the Royal Historical Society*, 5th series, ix, 1959, pp. 81–101.

[46] H. Jenkins and D. Caradog Jones, "Social Class of Cambridge University Alumni of the Eighteenth and Nineteenth Centuries," *British Journal of Sociology*, i, 1950, pp. 93–116.

[47] *Egerton Mss.*, kindly placed at the disposal of the History School of the University of Manchester by the late Lord Egerton of Tatton: letter, E. Egerton to John Egerton, postmarked 25 March (1729); *ibid.*, August 1728; W. H. Chaloner, "The Egertons in Italy and the Netherlands, 1729–44," *John Rylands Library Bulletin*, xxxii, 1949–50, pp. 157–70.

[48] In the Manchester City Art Gallery; reproduced in G. M. Young (ed.), *Early Victorian England*, Oxford, 1934, i, opp. p. 4.

[49] Herbert Butterfield, *The Origins of Modern Science*, 1949, chap. I.

[50] *Loc. cit.*, pp. 100–1.

[51] Namier, *loc. cit.*, p. 162; cf. J. E. Neale, "The Biographical Approach to History," *History*, xxxvi, 1951, pp. 193–203.

[52] Cf., e.g., *The Entrepreneur: Papers Presented at the Annual Conference of the Economic History Society at Cambridge, England, April 1957*, Cambridge, Mass., 1957.

[53] Cf. Lewis, *op. cit.*; W. W. Rostow, *The Stages of Economic Growth*, Cambridge, 1960.

[54] H. R. Trevor-Roper, *The Gentry, 1540–1640*, Cambridge, 1953, p. 44.

[55] William Heinemann Ltd., *Kingswood Social History Series*, edited by H. L. Beales and O. R. McGregor; Routledge and Kegan Paul Ltd., *Studies in Social History*, edited by myself; and Longmans, Green & Co. Ltd., *Economic and Social History of England*, edited by Asa Briggs.

[56] A similar suggestion, for the comparative study of the "overmighty subject" at different periods, is made by Professor Hexter, "A New Framework for Social History," *loc. cit.*

[57] H. J. Habakkuk, "England," in A. Goodwin (ed), *The European Nobility in the Eighteenth Century*, 1953, and "Marriage Settlements in the Eighteenth Century," *Transactions of the Royal Historical Society*, 4th series, xxxii, 1950, pp. 15–30.

[58] *My Apprenticeship*, 1926, p. 149.

A NEW ECONOMIC HISTORY: *Fogel*

[1] XXV (Dec. 1965).

[2] *Ibid.*, pp. 680–712.

[3] John R. Meyer and Alfred H. Conrad, "Economic Theory, Statistical Inference and Economic History," *Journal of Economic History*, XVII (Dec. 1957); and Alfred H. Conrad and John R. Meyer, "The Economics of Slavery in the *Ante-Bellum* South," *Journal of Political Economy*, LXVI (Apr. 1958). Both essays are reprinted in Alfred H. Conrad and John R. Meyer, *The Economics of Slavery* (Chicago: Aldine Publishing Co., 1964).

[4] Fritz Redlich, " 'New' and Traditional Approaches to Economic History and Their Interdependence," *Journal of Economic History*, XXV (Dec. 1965), 480–95.

[5] George G. S. Murphy, "The 'New' History," *Explorations in Entrepreneurial History* (2d series), II (Winter 1965), 132–46. Other contributions to the discussion on the methods of the new economic history include: Conrad and Meyer, *The Economics,* chapters 1 and 2; Lance E. Davis, Jonathan R. T. Hughes and Stanley Reiter, "Aspects of Quantitative Research in Economic History," *Journal of Economic History*, XX (Dec. 1960), 539–47; Franklin M. Fisher, "On the Analysis of History and the Interdependence of the Social Sciences," *Philosophy of Science*, XXVII (Apr. 1960); Douglass C. North, "Quantitative Research in American Economic History," *American Economic Review*, LIII (Mar. 1963), 128–30; Robert W. Fogel, "A Provisional View of the 'New Economic History,' " *American Economic Review*, LIV (May 1964), 377–89; Robert W. Fogel, *Railroads and American Economic Growth: Essays in Econometric History* (Baltimore: Johns Hopkins Press, 1964), pp. 237–49; Douglass C. North, "The State of Economic History," *American Economic Review*, LV (May 1965), 86–91; Robert W. Fogel, "The Reunification of Economic History with Economic Theory," *American Economic Review*, LV (May 1965), 92–98; Ralph Andreano, *New Views on American Economic Development* (Cambridge, Mass.: Schenkman Publishing Co., 1965), pp. 3–8, 13–26; Jonathan R. T. Hughes, "Fact and Theory in Economic History," *Explorations in Entrepreneurial History* (2d series), III (Spring/Summer 1966); Douglass C. North, "Economic History" (prepared for inclusion in the *International Encyclopedia of the Social Sciences*).

[6] Redlich, " 'New' and Traditional," pp. 491–95.

[7] For representative selections of essays in the new economic history, see Robert W. Fogel and Stanley L. Engerman (eds.), *The Reinterpretation of American Economic History* (New York: Harper and Row, 1967); and Andreano, *New Views*. For

a more popular, more interpretative survey, see Douglass C. North's *Growth and Welfare in the American Past: A New Economic History* (Englewood Cliffs: Prentice-Hall, 1966).

[8] Cf. Harold D. Woodman, "The Profitability of Slavery: A Historical Perennial," *Journal of Southern History*, XXIX (Aug. 1963), 302–25; and Stanley L. Engerman, "The Effects of Slavery on American Economic Growth," in Fogel and Engerman (eds.), *The Reinterpretation.*

[9] Conrad and Meyer, *The Economics,* chapter 3.

[10] An alternate approach to the estimation of the return on male slaves is contained in Robert Evans, Jr., "The Economics of American Negro Slavery," in H. Gregg Lewis (ed.), *Aspects of Labor Economics,* Conference of Universities—National Bureau Committee for Economic Research (Princeton, N.J.: Princeton University Press, 1962), pp. 185–243. As with other capital goods, there was a market for the rental of slaves. Evans argued that the average annual hire price represented a good estimate of the annual net earnings on the investment in a male slave. He reduced the annual hire price for slaves of a given age by the proportion of the cohort that died during the course of the year. In so doing, Evans avoided the assumption that all slaves lived the average length of life. The result of his computation was a return of over 10 percent during most of the years from 1830 through 1860.

[11] Yasukichi Yasuba, "The Profitability and Viability of Plantation Slavery in the United States," *Economic Studies Quarterly,* XII (Sept. 1961), 60–67; reprinted in Fogel and Engerman (eds.), *The Reinterpretation.* Richard Sutch independently arrived at a position similar to Yasuba's in "The Profitability of *Ante-Bellum* Slavery—Revisited," *Southern Economic Journal,* XXXI (Apr. 1963). See also the discussion by North in *Growth and Welfare,* chapter 7, and Engerman's "The Effects of Slavery."

[12] The cost of production includes the normal rate of profit.

[13] Richard A. Easterlin, "Regional Income Trends, 1840–1950," in Seymour E. Harris (ed.), *American Economic History,* New York: McGraw-Hill, 1961), pp. 525–47. Stanley L. Engerman, "The Economic Effects of the Civil War," *Explorations in Entrepreneurial History* (forthcoming).

[14] Engerman, "The Economic Effects."

[15] William N. Parker, "Productivity Growth in Crop Production," forthcoming in Volume 30 of *Studies in Income and Wealth,* National Bureau of Economic Research.

[16] Douglass C. North, "Determinants of Productivity in Ocean Shipping," in Fogel and Engerman (eds.), *The Reinterpretation.*

[17] Robert Brooke Zevin, "The Growth of Cotton Textile Production after 1815," in Fogel and Engerman (eds.), *The Reinterpretation.*

[18] Cf. North, *Growth and Welfare*, pp. 6–10.

[19] Peter Temin, "A New Look at Hunter's Hypothesis about the Antebellum Iron Industry," *American Economic Review*, LIV (May 1964), 344–51; Peter Temin, *Iron and Steel in Nineteenth-Century America* (Cambridge, Mass.: M.I.T. Press, 1964), chapter 3.

[20] Paul David, "The Mechanization of Reaping in the Ante-Bellum Midwest," in Henry Rosovsky (ed.), *Industrialization in Two Systems: Essays in Honor of Alexander Gerschenkron* (New York: John Wiley and Sons, 1966), pp. 3–39.

[21] Baltimore: Johns Hopkins Press, 1964.

[22] Albert Fishlow, *American Railroads and the Transformation of the Ante-Bellum Economy* (Cambridge, Mass.: Harvard University Press, 1965), chapter 2.

[23] Simon Kuznets, "Summary of Discussion and Postscript," *Journal of Economic History*, XVII (Dec. 1957), 553.

[24] Fishlow, *American Railroads*, chapter 3 and Appendix B.

[25] Jeffrey G. Williamson, "*Ante-bellum* Urbanization in the American Northeast," *Journal of Economic History*, XXV (Dec. 1965), 592–608; Jeffrey G. Williamson and Joseph A. Swanson, "The Growth of Cities in the American Northeast, 1820–1870" (mimeographed).

[26] Paul W. MacAvoy, *The Economic Effects of Regulation: The Trunk-Line Railroad Cartels and the Interstate Commerce Commission before 1900* (Cambridge, Mass.: M.I.T. Press, 1965).

[27] William S. Whitney, "The Structure of the American Economy in the Late Nineteenth Century" (dissertation in progress for Harvard University).

[28] James K. Kindahl, "The Economics of Resumption: The United States, 1865–1879" (unpublished doctoral dissertation, University of Chicago, 1958); published without statistical appendices as "Economic Factors in Specie Resumption: The United States, 1865–79," *Journal of Political Economy*, LXIX (Feb. 1961).

[29] David, "The Mechanization," pp. 28–39.

[30] For a more detailed discussion of the theoretical issues, see Fogel, *Railroads*, chapter 3.

[31] *Ibid.*, pp. 79–84, 92–107.

[32] Fritz Redlich, " 'New' and Traditional," pp. 486–87.

[32] Albert Fishlow, "Productivity and Technological Change in the Railroad Sector, 1840–1910," forthcoming in Volume 30 of *Studies in Income and Wealth*, National Bureau of Economic Research.

[34] A third level of verification, the test of the predictive power of a model, may often be possible in historical analysis. Cf. Fogel, *Railroads*, pp. 176–89.

[35] "Railroads and the Axiom of Indispensability," *New Views*, Andreano, pp. 232–34.

CLIO AND CRISIS: *Woodward*

[1] Frederick Jackson Turner, *The Frontier in American History* (New York, 1920), 24.

[2] Charles A. Beard, *American Government and Politics* (New York, 1911), 86.

[3] For example, see W. E. Burghardt Du Bois, "The Propaganda of History," *Black Reconstruction in America: An Essay Toward a History of the Part Which Black Folk Played in the Attempt to Reconstruct Democracy in America, 1860–1880* (New York, 1935), 711–29; and Benjamin Quarles, "What the Historian Owes the Negro," *Saturday Review*, XLIX (Sept. 3, 1966), 10–13.

[4] David B. Davis, *The Problem of Slavery in Western Culture* (Ithaca, 1966), 10; also Chapter I, "The Historical Problem: Slavery and the Meaning of America," 3–28.

[5] J. Hector St. John de Crèvecoeur, *Letters from an American Farmer* (New York, 1945), 43.

[6] Winthrop D. Jordan, *White Over Black: American Attitudes Toward the Negro, 1550–1810* (Chapel Hill, 1968), 340–41.

[7] Arthur M. Schlesinger, " 'What Then Is the American, This New Man?' " *American Historical Review*, XLVIII (Jan. 1943), 225–44.

[8] Du Bois, *Black Reconstruction*, 714–15.

[9] Herbert Butterfield, *History and Human Relations* (London, 1951), 110.

[10] John Higham, "Beyond Consensus: The Historian as Moral Critic," *American Historical Review*, LXVII (Apr. 1962), 609–25.

[11] Wilbur H. Siebert, *The Underground Railroad from Slavery to Freedom* (New York, 1898). See Larry Gara, *The Liberty Line: The Legend of the Underground Railroad* (Lexington, 1961), for a critique of this and similar works on the subject.

[12] Dwight Lowell Dumond, *Antislavery: The Crusade for Freedom in America* (Ann Arbor, 1961), 326–34.

[13] Melville J. Herskovits, *The Myth of the Negro Past* (New York, 1941), 227, 298–99.

[14] Carter Woodson, review of Melville J. Herskovits, *Life in a Haitian Village*, in *Journal of Negro History*, XXII (July 1937), 367.

[15] W. E. Burghardt Du Bois, *Dusk of Dawn: An Essay Toward an Autobiography of a Race Concept* (New York, 1940), 275.

[16] Quoted in Harold R. Isaacs, *The New World of Negro Americans* (New York, 1963), 222; see also 106–07, 171 on Negro rejection of Africa.

[17] Daniel Guérin, *Décolonisation du Noir Américain* (Paris, 1963).

[18] Frantz Fanon, *Black Skin, White Masks* (New York, 1967), 83–108; O. Mannoni, *Prospero and Caliban: The Psychology of Colonization* (London, 1956).

[19] H. R. Isaacs, *The New World of Negro Americans*, 6–9.

[20] Nathan Glazer and Daniel Patrick Moynihan, *Beyond the Melting Pot: The Negroes, Puerto Ricans, Jews, Italians, and Irish of New York City* (New York, 1963), 13–19.

[21] Marcus Lee Hansen, *The Immigrant in American History* (Cambridge, 1940), 28.

[22] Herskovits, *The Myth of the Negro Past*, 299.

[23] Edward O'Meagher Condon, *The Irish Race in America* (New York, 1887), 3.

[24] Peter Wiernik, *History of Jews in America: From the Period of the Discovery of America to the Present Time* (New York, 1912), 14.

[25] Edward N. Saveth, *American Historians and European Immigrants, 1815–1925* (New York, 1948): Arthur M. Schlesinger, Jr., "Nationalism and History," *Journal of Negro History*, LIV (1969), 19–31.

[26] The stimulus to nationalism was not all one way. For earlier influences of Negro Americans on the rise of nationalism in Africa, see George Shepperson, "Notes on Negro American Influences on the Emergence of African Nationalism," *Journal of African History*, I (1960), 299–312.

[27] Immanuel Wallerstein, "The Search for National Identity in West Africa: The New History," in Werner J. Cahnman and Alfin Boskoff (eds.), *Sociology and History: Theory and Research* (New York, 1964), 303–13.

[28] Herskovits, *The Myth of the Negro Past*; E. Franklin Frazier, *The Negro in the United States* (New York, 1949), 1–21; Isaacs, *The New World of Negro Americans*, 109–13; John A. Davis, "The Influence of Africans on American Culture," *Annals of the American Academy of Political and Social Science*, 354 (July 1964), 75–83.

[29] W. E. Burghardt Du Bois, *The Souls of Black Folk: Essays and Sketches* (Chicago, 1903), 3–4.

[30] Erik Erikson, "The Concept of Identity in Race Relations: Notes and Queries," *Daedalus* (Winter 1966), 154–56.

[31] Jordan, *White Over Black*, 110.

[32] George A. Myers to James Ford Rhodes, Jan. 8, 1918, and Sept. 23, 1915, in John A. Garraty (ed.), *The Barber and the Historian: The Correspondence of George A. Myers and James Ford Rhodes, 1910–1923* (Columbus, 1956), 32–33, 78.

[33] H. Hoetink, *The Two Variants in Caribbean Race Relations: A Contribution to the Sociology of Segmented Societies* (New York, 1961), 31–46.

[34] Harold R. Isaacs, *Emergent Americans: A Report on 'Crossroads Africa'* (New York, 1961), 128–31; Isaacs, *The New World of Negro Americans*, 261–70, 294.

[35] Frederick Law Olmsted, *A Journey in the Seaboard Slave States, With Remarks on Their Economy* (London, 1856), 17.

[36] Mary Boykin Chesnut, *A Diary from Dixie* (Boston, 1949), 149.

[37] Herskovits, *The Myth of the Negro Past*, 225, 231.

[38] Julian P. Boyd, *Between the Spur and Bridle* (New York, 1968), an address to the Association of American University Presses.

[39] Ralph Ellison, *Shadow and Act* (New York, 1964), 131.

[40] W. E. Burghardt Du Bois, *Darkwater* (New York, 1920), 3.

[41] Barrington Moore, Jr., *Social Origins of Dictatorship and Democracy: Lord and Peasant in the Making of the Modern World* (Boston, 1966), 523.

SOURCES AND PERMISSIONS

The page numbers after each work indicate the passages used or excerpted from in the text. The editor wishes to thank the owners of copyright material, whose names appear below, for their permission to reprint.

VOLTAIRE: "Sur l'histoire," from "Conseils à un journaliste," *Oeuvres de Voltaire*, ed. by M. Beuchot, Vol. XXXVII, Paris 1829, pp. 362–367. Translated by Jacques Barzun.

——: "Letter to Abbé Dubos," (30 October 1738), *Voltaire's Correspondence*, ed. by Theodore Besterman, Vol. VII, Geneva 1954, pp. 424–427. Translated by Jacques Barzun.

——: "Introduction," *Siècle de Louis XIV*, ed. by René Groos, Vol. I, Paris 1929, pp. 1–6. Translated by Jacques Barzun.

——: "De l'utilité de l'histoire," from *Dictionnaire Philosophique, Oeuvres de Voltaire*, ed. by M. Beuchot, Vol. XXX, Paris 1829, pp. 207–209. Translated by Jacques Barzun.

NIEBUHR, B. G.: "Vorrede zu der ersten Ausgabe," and "Vorrede zu der zweiten Ausgabe," *Römische Geschichte*, new edition by M. Isler, Berlin 1873, pp. xx–xxxiii. Translated by the Editor.

RANKE, LEOPOLD VON: "Vorrede zur ersten Ausgabe," *Geschichten der romanischen und germanischen Völker von 1494 bis 1514*, 3rd edition, Leipzig 1885, pp. v–viii. Translated by the Editor.

——: *Weltgeschichte*, first to third edition, Part IX, section 2, edited by Alfred Dove, Leipzig 1888, pp. vii–xi and xiii–xvi. Translated by the Editor.

THIERRY, AUGUSTIN: "Avertissement" and "Lettre I," *Lettres sur l'histoire de France, pour servir d'introduction à l'étude de cette histoire*, second, revised edition, Paris 1829, pp. v–xi and 1–8. Translated by J. Christopher Herold.

LORD MACAULAY: "History," *Miscellaneous Works*, edited by Lady Trevelyan, Vol. I, New York 1880, pp. 153–198.

CARLYLE, THOMAS: "On History," *Critical and Miscellaneous Essays,* Vol. II, New York 1900, pp. 83–95.

————: *On Heroes, Hero-Worship, and the Heroic in History,* Lectures I and VI (Everyman's Library: *Sartor Resartus, On Heroes and Hero Worship*), London 1940, pp. 239–240, 249–252, 435–437, 440–441.

MICHELET, JULES: "Introduction," *The People,* translated by C. Cocks, B. L., London 1846, pp. 1–16.

BUCKLE, HENRY THOMAS: *History of Civilization in England,* New York 1866: from the second London edition, pp. 1–6, 23–26, 29–31, 111–113, 166–169, 600–601.

DROYSEN, JOHANN GUSTAV: "On Art and Method," *Outline of the Principles of History,* translated by E. Benjamin Andrews, Boston 1893, pp. 105–118.

————: *Outline of the Principles of History,* p. 49.

MARX, KARL, and ENGELS, FRIEDRICH: *The German Ideology,* edited and translated by R. Pascal, Part I, New York 1939, pp. 6–9, 13–24, 28–30. By permission of International Publishers Inc., New York.

JAURES, JEAN: "Introduction Critique" and "Introduction Générale," *La Constituante, 1789–1791,* Vol. I of Jaurès (ed.) *Histoire socialiste de la révolution française* (revised edition by A. Mathiez), Paris 1922, pp. 9–27. By permission of the Librairie de L'Humanité, Paris. Translated by Dora Weiner.

PROSPECTUSES: "Vorwort," *Historische Zeitschrift,* edited by Heinrich von Sybel, Vol. I, Munich 1859, pp. iii–v. Translated by M. M. Meeker.

————: "Avant-Propos," *Revue Historique* (ed. by G. Monod and G. Fagniez), Paris 1876, pp. 1–4. Translated by Nora Beeson.

————: "Prefatory Note," *The English Historical Review,* edited by the Rev. Mandell Creighton, Vol. I, No. 1, London 1886, pp. 1–6.

FUSTEL DE COULANGES, N. D.: "Leçon d'Ouverture," *Revue de synthèse historique,* Vol. II, Paris 1901, pp. 242–253. Translated by the Editor.

————: "Introduction," *Histoire des institutions politiques de l'ancienne France,* new ed. by Camille Jullian, Paris 1871, pp. xi–xiv. Translated by the Editor.

MOMMSEN, THEODOR: "Rede bei Antritt des Rektorates," *Reden und Aufsätze,* Berlin 1905, pp. 10–16. By permission of Weidmannsche Verlagsbuchhandlung, Berlin. Translated by the Editor.

TURNER, FREDERICK JACKSON: "The Significance of History," *The Early Writings of Frederick Jackson Turner,* Madison 1938, pp. 43–67. By permission of The University of Wisconsin Press, Madison, Wisconsin.

BURY, J. B.: "The Science of History," *Selected Essays of J. B. Bury,* ed. by Harold Temperley, Cambridge 1930, pp. 3–22. By permission of Cambridge University Press.

TREVELYAN, GEORGE MACAULAY: "Clio, A Muse," *Clio, A Muse and Other Essays Literary and Pedestrian,* London 1913, pp. 1–55. By permission of Longmans, Green & Company, Inc.

ACTON, LORD: "Letter to Contributors to the Cambridge Modern History," *Lectures on Modern History,* London 1952, pp. 315–318. By permission of St. Martin's Press.

BERR, HENRI: "Sur notre programme," *Revue de synthèse historique,* Vol. I, Paris 1900, pp. 1–8. Translated by Deborah H. Roberts.

ROBINSON, JAMES HARVEY, and BEARD, CHARLES A.: "Preface," *The Development of Modern Europe,* Vol. I, Boston 1907, pp. iii–iv. By permission of Ginn and Company.

MEINECKE, FRIEDRICH: "Kausalitäten und Werte in der Geschichte," *Staat und Persönlichkeit,* Berlin 1933, pp. 29–53. By permission of R. Oldenbourg, Munich. Translated by Julian H. Franklin.

HUIZINGA, J.: "De Historische Idee," *Verzamelde Werken,* Vol. VII, Haarlem 1950, pp. 134–150. By permission of Robert Harben, representative of the Huizinga Estate. Translated by Rosalie Colie.

UNWIN, GEORGE: "The Teaching of Economic History in University Tutorial Classes," *Studies in Economic History: The Collected Papers of George Unwin,* London 1927, pp. 37–40. By permission of St. Martin's Press, Inc.

CLAPHAM, J. H.: "Economic History as a Discipline," *Encyclopedia of the Social Sciences,* Vol. V, New York 1943, pp. 327–330. By permission of The Macmillan Company.

BEARD, CHARLES A.: "That Noble Dream," *The American Historical Review,* Vol. XLI, No. 1, October 1935, pp. 74–87. By permission of *The American Historical Review.*

POKROVSKY, M. N.: "Zadachi Obshchestva istorikov-marksistov," ("The Tasks of the Society of Marxist Historians"), *Istorik-marksist,* Vol. I, 1926, pp. 3–10. Translated by Rufus Mathewson.

———: "O zadachakh marksistskoi istoricheskoi nauki v rekonstruktivnyi period," ("On the Tasks of Marxist Historical Science in the Reconstruction Period"), *Istorik-marksist,* Vol. XXI, 1931, pp. 4–7. Translated by Rufus Mathewson.

FRANK, WALTER: *Zunft und Nation,* Hamburg 1935, pp. 8–10, 18–19, 33–34. Translated by Paul Seabury.

MUELLER, KARL ALEXANDER VON: "Zum Geleit," *Historische Zeitschrift,* Vol. 153, Berlin 1936, pp. 1–5. Translated by Paul Seabury. By permission of R. Oldenbourg, Munich.

COCHRAN, THOMAS C., "The Social Sciences and the Problem of Historical Synthesis," *The Social Sciences in Historical Study,* Social Science Research Council, New York 1954, pp. 157–171. By permission of *The American Historical Review.*

NAMIER, SIR LEWIS: "History," *Avenues of History,* London 1952, pp. 1–10. By permission of Hamish Hamilton Ltd.

———: "Human Nature in Politics," *Personalities and Powers,* London 1955, pp. 1–7. By permission of Hamish Hamilton Ltd.

BRAUDEL, FERNAND: "History and the Social Sciences. The Long Term," *Social Science Information,* Vol. IX, No. 1, February 1970, pp. 145–174. Translated by Sian France. First appeared as Braudel, Fernand: "Histoire et sciences sociales: la longue durée," *Annales: Economies, sociétés, civilisations,* Vol. 13, No. 4, October–December 1958, pp. 725–753.

PERKIN, H. J.: "Social History," *Approaches to History: A Symposium,* ed. by H. P. R. Finberg, London 1962, pp. 51–83.

FOGEL, R. W.: "The New Economic History," *The Economic History Review,* Second Series, Vol. XIX, No. 3, 1966, pp. 642–656.

WOODWARD, C. VANN: "Clio with Soul," *Journal of American History,* Vol. LVI, No. 1, June 1969, pp. 5–20.

ACKNOWLEDGMENTS

I wish to thank the many friends and colleagues without whose help this volume would have been much more difficult to prepare. First and foremost, I should like to record my gratitude to Jacques Barzun, whose contribution, apparent in the first and last sections, extended in fact to the entire book; his many suggestions, born of his superb familiarity with all aspects of historiography, vastly improved the manuscript, which, with characteristic generosity and precision, he read and criticized as well. I owe much to Henry L. Roberts, to his steady help and criticism, and to the inspiration I derived from his profound historical sense. On countless occasions I discussed this book with Richard Hofstadter, whose kind enthusiasm for this enterprise surpassed and sustained my own. I was also able to consult Hajo Holborn and Leonard Krieger; their perspicacious counsel was of the greatest value. I am grateful to Beatrice Hofstadter, David S. Landes, William E. Leuchtenburg, and R. K. Webb for their criticism of my Introduction.

I regret that it is not possible to list all those colleagues with whom at one time or another I discussed some specific aspect of this work, but I do wish to express my thanks to those who helped in the selection of a particular essay or who went over some part of my translations: Lee Benson, J. Bartlet Brebner, Shepard B. Clough, Arthur C. Danto,

Moses Hadas, J. Christopher Herold, Emery Neff, and Martin Ostwald. I also wish to thank Dwight W. Webb of the Noonday Press, whose cordial interest in the book proved a great help, and Arthur A. Cohen of Meridian Books, whose ready collaboration facilitated the final stages of this work.

The generous counsel of these and other friends and colleagues saved me from all manner of error and omission. For all shortcomings I am, of course, solely responsible.

F. S.

Rochester, Vermont
June 28, 1956

INDEX

A recognized authority on modern Europe, Fritz Stern is Seth Low Professor of History at Columbia University. He was born in Germany in 1926 and he moved to the United States in 1938. Prof. Stern holds three degrees from Columbia, where he has taught for four decades, and served as provost of the University from 1980 to 1983. He has also taught at Cornell, Yale, The Free University of Berlin, and the University of Konstanz in West Germany, and as Élie Halévy Professor at the Fondation Nationale des Sciences Politiques in Paris. He received a D.Litt. degree from Oxford in 1985 and the Leopold-Lucas Prize from the Evangelical-Theological Faculty of the University of Tübingen in 1984. His other books include *Dreams and Delusions: National Socialism in the Drama of the German Past; Gold and Iron: Bismarck, Bleichröder, and the Building of the German Empire*, which was nominated for a National Book Award; *The Politics of Cultural Despair;* and *The Failure of Illiberalism.* He is also co-editor, with Leonard Krieger, of *The Responsibility of Power.* He was a member of the Center for Advanced Study in the Behavioral Sciences at Stanford in 1957–1958, of The Institute for Advanced Study in Princeton in 1969–1970, and of the Netherlands Institute for Advanced Study in 1972–1973. He has been awarded fellowships by the Guggenheim Foundation, the American Council of Learned Societies, and The Ford Foundation. A member of Phi Beta Kappa and the American Philosophical Society, he is on the Editorial Advisory Board of *Foreign Affairs* and of The Collected Papers of Albert Einstein. Fritz Stern is currently at work on a book to be titled *Genius and the Germans: Einstein, Haber, and the Passions of Their Time.*